W9-AXO-732

OXFORD Children's Encyclopedia

Volume 5

OXFORD Children's Encyclopedia

Sea to Zulus

Oxford University Press

Oxford University Press, Walton Street, Oxford OX2 6DP

Oxford New York Toronto
Delhi Bombay Calcutta Madras Karachi
Petaling Jaya Singapore Hong Kong Tokyo
Nairobi Dar es Salaam Cape Town
Melbourne Auckland
and associated companies in
Berlin Ibadan

Reprinted 1991

ISBN 0 19 910139 6 (complete set)

Volume 5: 0 19 910136 1 (not for sale separately)

A CIP catalogue record for this book is available from the British Library

Printed in Great Britain by
William Collins Sons and Company Ltd, Glasgow

Editor Mary Worrall

Design and art direction Richard Morris
Cover design Philip Atkins

Assistant editors Jane Bingham
David Burnie
Tony Drake
Deborah Manley
Sarah Matthews
Pamela Mayo
Stephen Pople
Andrew Solway
Catherine Thompson

Copy preparation Eric Buckley
Richard Jeffery

Proof reader Richard Jeffery

Index Radmila May

Photographic research Catherine Blackie
Libby Howells
Linda Proud
Suzanne Williams

How to use the Oxford Children's Encyclopedia

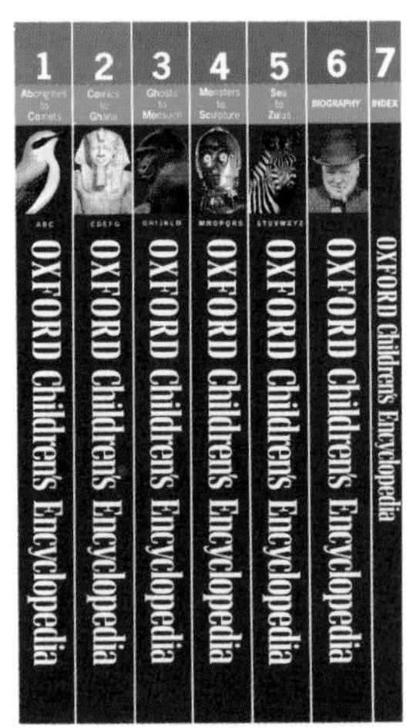

There are three main ways of finding the information you want. You may search for the topics in the headings in the alphabetical sequence. You might think of another word which is close to the topic that interests you and search for that in the headings. Or you could use the index, which is the best method of all.

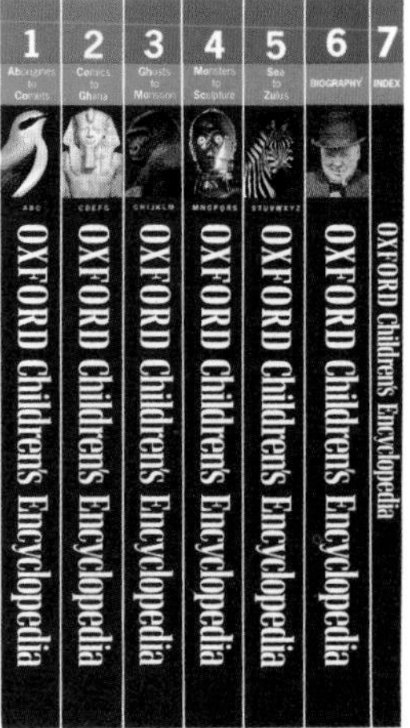

Using the headings

Often the topic you want to look up will be the heading of a whole article. Suppose you wish to read about **space**. This starts with **S** so you find the letter **S** on the spine of Volume 5 (this volume). Once you have found the first letter of the word, search for the second letter which is picked out in bold type at the top of the page like this:
Space exploration.

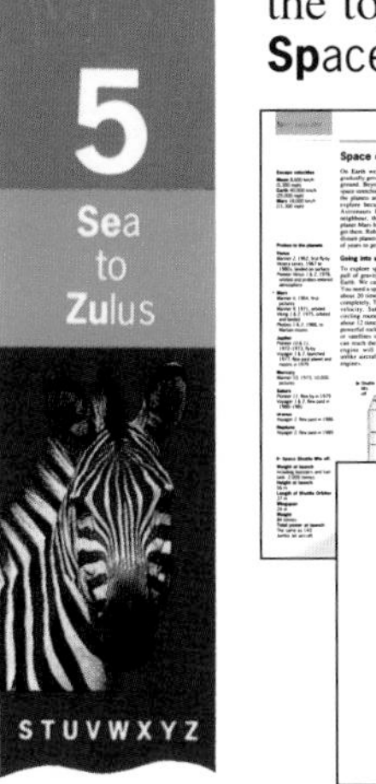

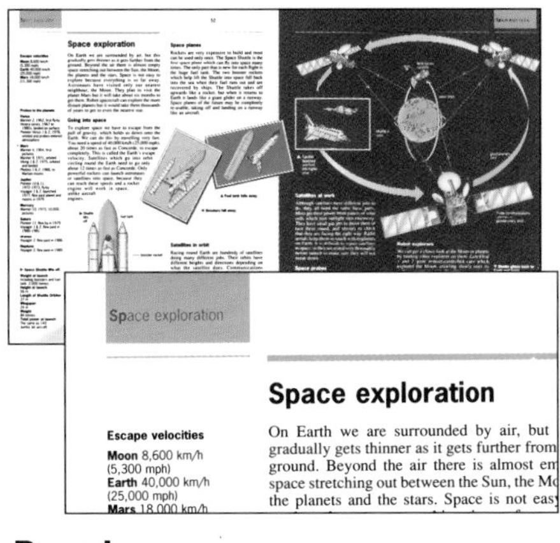

Space exploration

Space exploration

Escape velocities
Moon 8,600 km/h (5,300 mph)
Earth 40,000 km/h (25,000 mph)
Mars 18,000 km/h

On Earth we are surrounded by air, but gradually gets thinner as it gets further from ground. Beyond the air there is almost em space stretching out between the Sun, the Mo the planets and the stars. Space is not eas

People

If you are looking for an article about a person, go straight to Volume 6: the Biography. These articles are in alphabetical order, listed under the surname (family name) as in a telephone directory: **Thatcher,** Margaret.

In ancient times and in the Middle Ages surnames were not common and so you will find many people under their first names: **Tutankhamun**, **Xerxes**.

Spellings of historical characters vary and you may have to search over a few pages.

Think of another word

If you cannot find what you want under the main headings, think of another word or topic that is very close to what you need. Suppose you want to look up **Saturn**. You search in the **S**s and there is no article. But you know that Saturn is one of the planets. So find **Planets**; there is a section on Saturn on the fourth page of that article.

Using the index

The most thorough method is to use the index. You may wish to read about Stonehenge. Stonehenge is listed in the index. Next to it is the reference: **5** 77, which means there is an article in Volume 5 page 77 which describes Stonehenge. So you find Volume 5, page 77 which is the second page of the article on **Stone circles.**

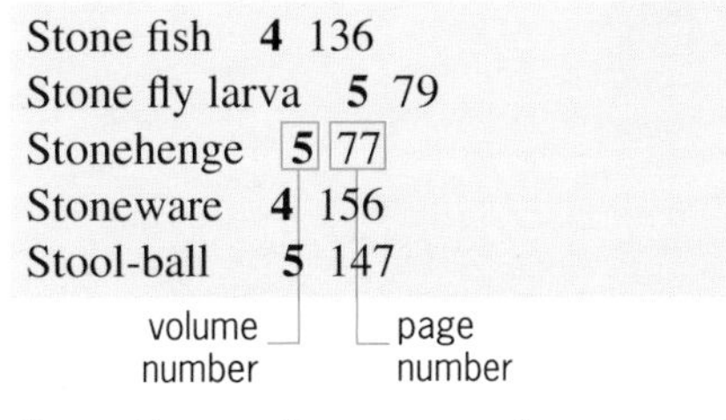

Stone fish **4** 136
Stone fly larva **5** 79
Stonehenge **5** 77
Stoneware **4** 156
Stool-ball **5** 147

Suppose you want to know when Chuck Berry was born. He is not listed in the main part of the biography but the index gives the references **4** *145* **6** 271. The first reference is in *italics*, which means there is only a picture, but the second is for an article on him in the Pop and Rock Special section at the end of the Biography.

Sometimes there may be several articles which have something on the subject you want.

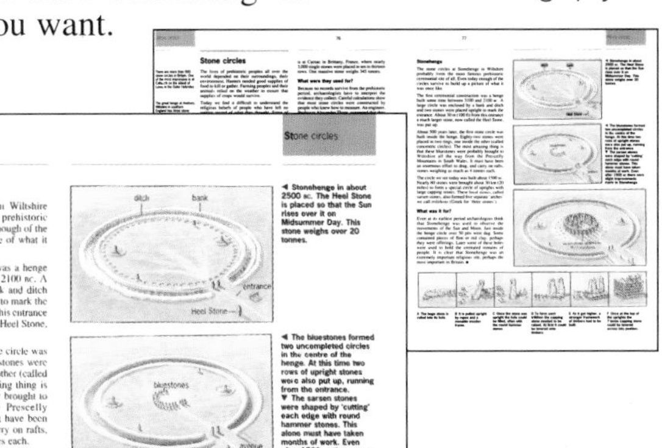

Stone circles

Stonehenge

Cross references

Almost every article leads on to many more. Look for the red **See also** bar in the margin at the end of an article. This lists other articles which have more information related to what you have read.

This list appears at the end of the article on **Space exploration**.

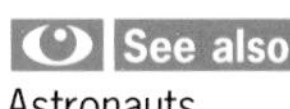

Astronauts
Rockets
Satellites

Biography
Armstrong, Neil
Gagarin
Tereshkova

Contents

Sea

Saltiness of open sea
34–36 parts of salt to 1,000 parts of water
Saltiness of Red Sea
40 parts per 1,000 (because of high evaporation)
Saltiness of Dead Sea
Over 200 parts per 1,000. The Dead Sea is not a true sea, but an inland lake.

Sea water is salty because rivers which run into the sea carry tiny amounts of salt, too small to taste. Some of the water evaporates, sometimes to make rain on land, but the salt remains. Over millions of centuries this has built up to today's level of saltiness.

In the tropics the Sun heats the surface of the sea to over 30°C (86°F), but at depths of a few metres, it is cold. The surface water in polar seas may be below freezing, but it gets slightly warmer with depth, so that most of the ocean is at about the same temperature (4°C/39°F).

The Sun's light is also absorbed by the water. The red part of the light spectrum disappears first, so that below the surface everything looks blue-green. But even in the clearest oceanic waters it is completely dark below about 1,000 m (3,000 ft). At the surface, sea water looks blue because blue light may be reflected back from particles in the water.

The sea is never still. Waves, whipped up by the wind, stir the surface, but do not move the mass of the water. This is done by tides, which shift the water in time with the phases of the moon. There are also great currents, which swirl slowly in a clockwise direction in the northern hemisphere and anticlockwise in the south. ■

See also
Arctic Ocean
Oceans and seas
Salt
Seashore
Waves

Sea anemones

Distribution
Rockpools everywhere
Lifespan
Sea anemones may live for a very long time. One survived in captivity almost 100 years.
Phylum
Cnidaria
Class
Anthozoa
Order
Actinaria
Number of species
Including corals, 6,000

Sea anemones live attached to rocks and breakwaters on the seashore and in shallow water. When the tide is out they seem to be just blobs of jelly, but when they are covered with water they look like flowers. The reason for this is that they have a frill of short tentacles like petals round the top of their jar-like bodies. But in spite of this, and of their name, sea anemones are not plants, but animals. They are flesh eaters, which feed on any small creature which brushes against the tentacles. These are studded with sting cells which paralyse little fishes or shrimps; then their tentacles pull them into the anemone's open mouth. No European sea anemone has sting cells powerful enough to harm a human, though there are some tropical species which can do so.

▼ The mouth is the anemone's only opening, so as well as food being pulled into the mouth, waste products are pumped out through it.

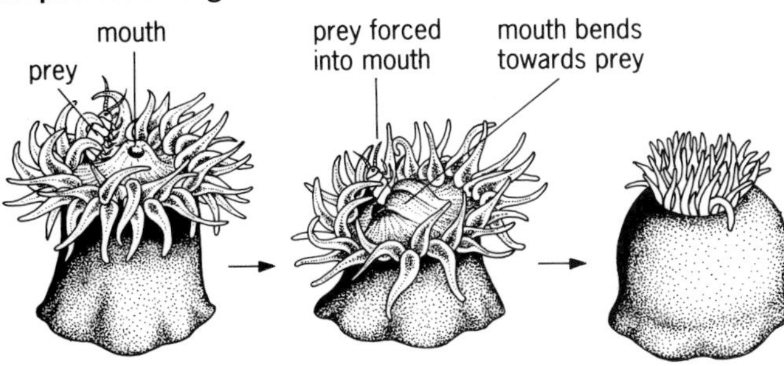

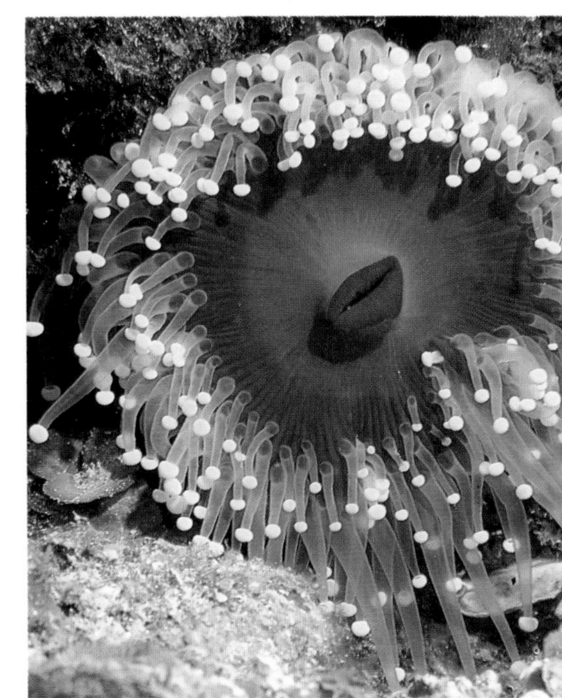

▲ A sea anemone from near Fiji in the South Pacific Ocean.

Sea anemones are entirely soft-bodied, but they have some close relatives that are able to use calcium and other minerals from the water to build a hard skeleton for themselves. These are called corals. Some of them form coral reefs and atolls in the warm seas of the world. ■

See also
Coral
Invertebrates
Jellyfish
Seashore

Sea birds

Subphylum
Vertebrata
Class
Aves
Orders
Charadriiformes (gulls, terns, auks)
Pelecaniformes (pelicans and cormorants)
Procellariiformes (tubenoses)
There are many species.

► Pelicans' huge bills are used to catch fish. When pushed into water the lower bill expands forming a pouch which fills with water and fish. As it lifts its head from the water the pouch contracts, forcing out the water, leaving the fish.

Arctic terns migrate from the Arctic to the Antarctic and back each year. The minimum distance is 12,800 km (8,000 miles) each way.

Almost three-quarters of the Earth's surface is covered by sea. The oceans are as rich in food as the land and it is not surprising that birds take advantage of this food supply. But the open sea can be a harsh place for a bird and there are few safe nesting-sites. To survive and breed, sea birds must be very specially adapted, and that is why only 300 or so of the 9,000 species of birds have come to depend on the sea.

► Atlantic puffins eating sand-eels. They breed from late May, nesting in colonies. The female usually lays one egg only, in an abandoned burrow, or a hole she digs herself with her feet.

All at sea

Ornithologists believe that sea birds belong to several distinct groups (orders). The penguins are all flightless and live south of the Equator. They find their food by diving and hunting fish under water.

Albatrosses and shearwaters are great ocean travellers. The curious shape of their bill gives this group its name, 'the tubenoses'. The tube on the nose may help the bird gauge the strength of the air flow and may help it smell land or food.

A Manx shearwater ringed in Wales was found in Brazil 16 days later. Minimum speed 740 km (460 miles) per day.

Pelicans are related to cormorants, gannets, boobies and frigate birds. Methods of finding food vary from the gannets' plunge-diving to the frigate birds' robbing other birds.

Gulls are a very successful group and many have benefited from people because they eat our rubbish and may even nest on our buildings. Their close relatives the terns feed mainly on fish, and because of this they have not increased in numbers like some of the gulls.

Auks, a group which includes the puffin, belong to the same order as the gulls. They nest in huge colonies on inaccessible sea-cliffs. Even before they are fully grown the young will fly from their cliffs and disappear out to sea for almost a year.

Pirate birds

Skuas normally hunt by following other sea birds and then chasing and harrying them until they drop any fish they have caught.

Other sea birds

Birds such as geese cross the sea on migration, but they are not sea birds. Others, such as mallards, sometimes visit the sea in winter. But there are other ducks, such as eiders, which are generally found around coasts and may be called sea-ducks.

The phalaropes are wading birds, but two of the three species become sea birds when not breeding and live in the open ocean, usually out of sight of land for up to nine months. They find their food on the surface of the sea. ■

See also
Birds
Ducks, geese and swans
Migration
Penguins

Seals

Seals and their relatives the sea lions and walruses are mammals whose four walking limbs are replaced with flippers, which make them slow and clumsy on dry land. But once they have slipped into the water, they are transformed. Their bodies are streamlined, and far more flexible than those of land mammals, so that they can twist and turn with amazing speed and grace as they play or chase after their prey.

Some seals, known as true seals, swim with an up-and-down movement of the rear flippers combined with side-to-side movements of their bodies. The eared seals use their forelimbs and the walruses swim by sculling with their hindlimbs.

Most seals hunt fish, often those not valued by humans. A few kinds feed on krill, and walruses eat shellfish and sea urchins. Seals can hunt in murky or dark water. The huge whiskers round their faces can detect changes in water pressure as something swims past, and so even blind seals are able to feed.

Seals can remain in the water, even in polar regions, for long periods. Beneath their skin they have a thick coat of special fat called blubber which helps to keep them warm. When they dive they are able to close their nostrils and their ears. Some species can stay below the surface for over 30 minutes and can go to depths of over 600 m (2,000 ft). As they dive, they breathe out and hold their breath and at the same time they slow their heart rate to 4–15 beats per minute so that the oxygen carried in their blood is used up more slowly.

Seals have to come to land to produce their young. They haul ashore, sometimes in their thousands, on islands or isolated beaches which are traditional breeding places. Only one well-grown baby is produced by each female. Seal's milk is very rich, being over half fat, so the baby's growth is rapid. The females mate very soon after the birth, and in some cases leave the calf before it is three weeks old. ■

◀ Grey seal cow greeting her pup. The pup still has its creamy-white lanugo (birth coat) which it will shed after 2–3 weeks. Its new coat will resemble that of the adult.

Distribution
Mainly in cold waters of the northern and southern oceans. A few species found in warmer places, and one in Lake Baykal
Largest
Elephant seal: males up to 4·9 m in length; weight up to 2,400 kg. Females much smaller. (A greater difference in size between males and females than in any other mammal.)
Smallest
Ringed seal: length 117 cm, weight up to 45 kg
Number of young 1
Lifespan
Up to 40 years in the wild
Enemies include large sharks, killer whales, leopard seals, polar bears, and most important, humans.

Subphylum Vertebrata
Class Mammalia
Order Pinnipedia
Number of species 33

◀ The walrus uses its huge tusks (up to 1 m long in males) to dislodge clams and other shellfish on the sea-bed. It then gathers them with its mobile, whiskery lips.

See also
Mammals

Seashore

The seashore is where the oceans and seas meet the land. It is the part of the coast between the high tide mark and the low tide mark. In some parts of the world, the tide does not go out very far and the seashore is only a few metres wide. In other places the tides go out up to three kilometres, and the seashore is very wide.

The lower shore is covered in sea water for much of the day, while the upper shore is covered for only a short time. The upper shore dries out between tides and any remaining pools of water become very salty, but after heavy rain they may contain almost fresh water. The temperature may change rapidly, so the animals and plants which live on the shore must be very adaptable.

See also
Crabs
Crustaceans
Fish
Sea anemones
Sea birds
Seaweeds
Wading birds
Zonation

Rocky shores

Rocky shores have many pools, each with its own community of animals. The rocks are often covered with seaweeds. Seaweeds also fringe the rock pools, providing shade from the sun, and a place where small animals can hide from predators such as seagulls. Limpets, periwinkles and barnacles on the upper and middle shore have strong shells to protect them from the waves and the drying effect of wind, and strong muscles to grip the rock. Further down the shore, mussels fix themselves to the rock with tough threads called byssus. Crabs, sea slaters and shrimps survive by hiding in crevices. The lower shore is wetter, and animals such as sea anemones, starfish and sea urchins live among the wet seaweeds in the rock pools, which are also home to small fish such as blennies.

Most of these animals breathe oxygen from the water using gills, and so they come out to feed when the tide is in. Crabs scavenge for seaweed and animal remains. Barnacles and shrimps filter food from the sea water using fine bristles on their legs. Mussels sieve the water with their gills, and limpets and periwinkles graze on the seaweeds.

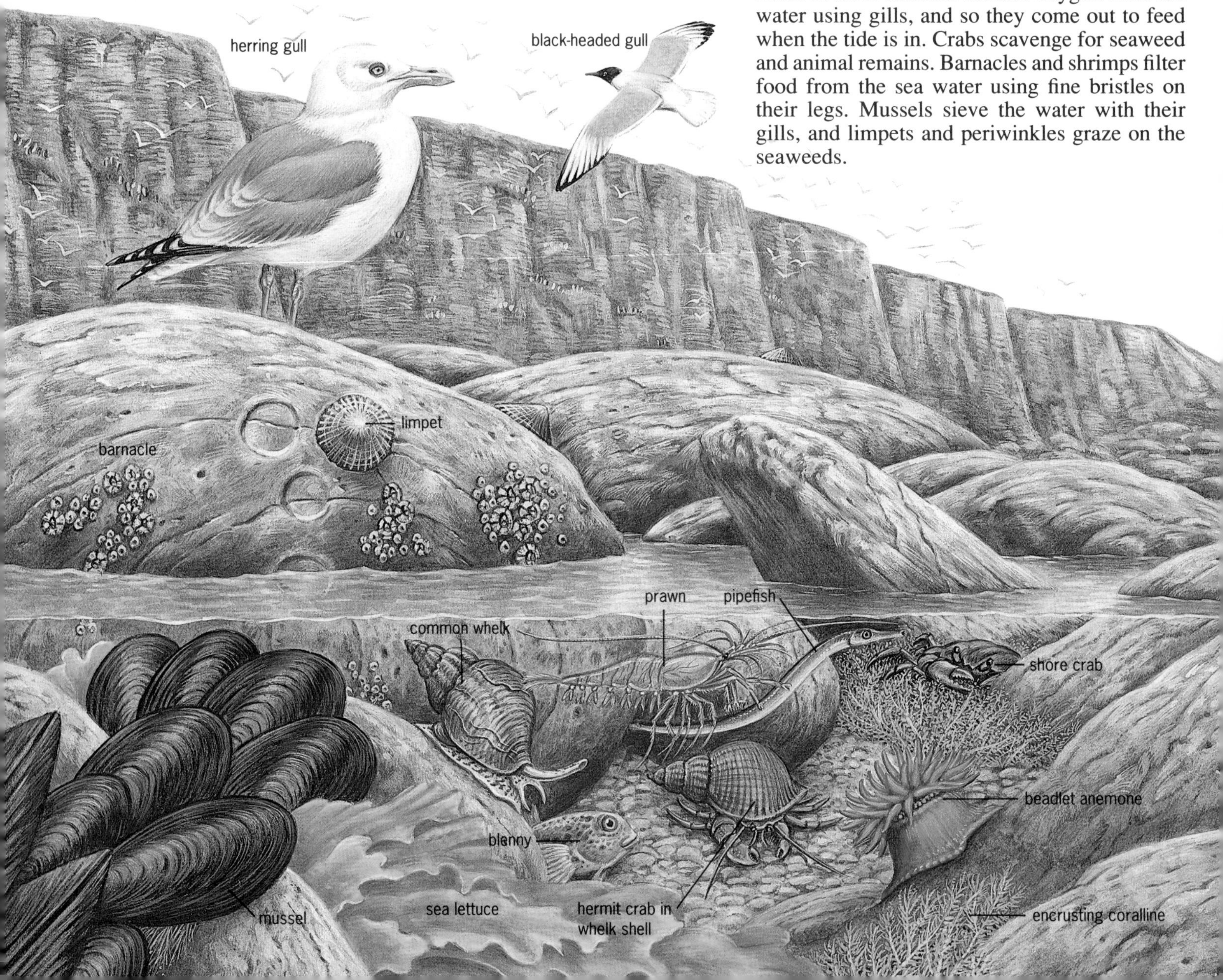

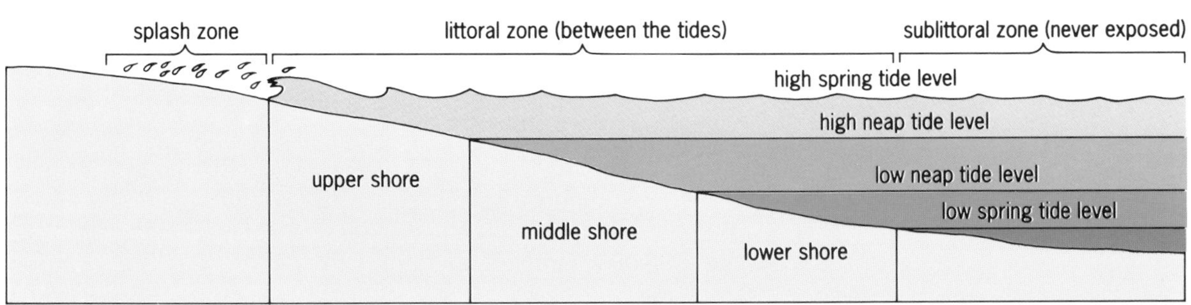

◄ A cross section of the shore showing the zones.

Sandy shores

A sandy shore often appears to have very little life, but there may be as many as 100,000 animals per square metre living in the mud below the sand. They are out of sight of predators and protected from the sun and wind, and emerge to feed only when the tide comes in.

Some live in permanent burrows, drawing in water and sieving out food from it. The lugworm (sandworm) lives in a U-shaped burrow. It takes in water and food at one end, and pushes out a pile of waste to form a squiggly worm cast at the other end. Cockles and razor shells use siphons to sieve the water. Tube worms surround themselves with tubes made of sand and mud. They put out sticky tentacles to trap food from the water. Small shrimps and crabs venture out to feed at high tide, but burrow in the mud before the tide goes out, so they are not swept away.

Muddy shores and estuaries attract large numbers of seagulls and wading birds (shore birds), which come to feed on the seashore animals. ■

The world has 310,500 km (193,000 miles) of seashore.

The different tide levels provide a constantly changing habitat, as parts of the seashore are only under water at certain times of the day.

You may not be able to see much life on sandy beaches, but if you dig down in the wet sand you will probably find a variety of burrowing animals.

Fish egg-cases are sometimes washed up on beaches. The egg-cases, sometimes known as mermaids' purses, are empty as the eggs have already hatched in deeper water. The whelk's egg-cases stick together to form a spongy ball and are a common sight on many beaches.

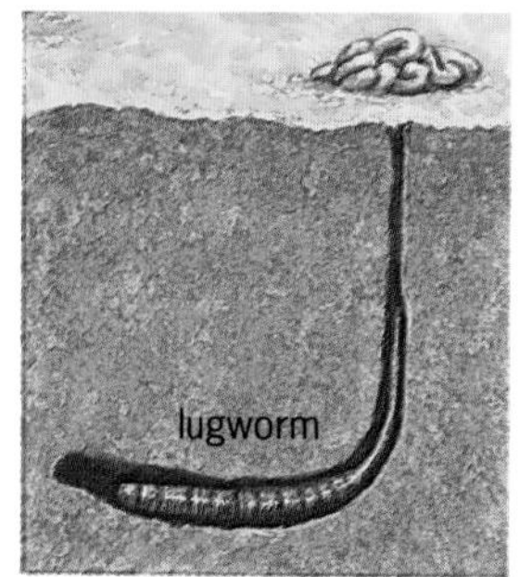

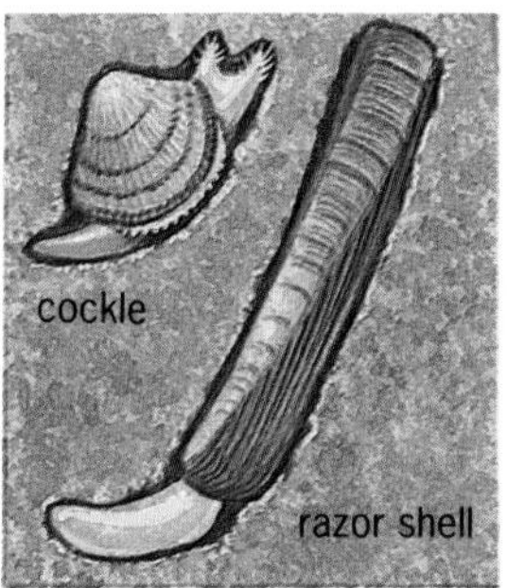

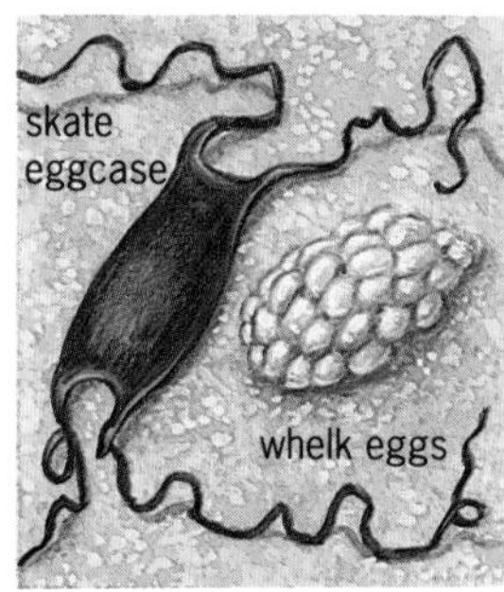

Seasons

As the seasons change through the year, we notice the different things that happen in the world around us. In spring, the days get longer again after the winter and the Sun climbs higher in the sky each day. Because there is more sunshine and warmer weather, plants start to grow and it is a good time for sowing seeds. It is also the season when many animals have their young. Summer is the warmest time of the year. The higher the Sun is, the stronger the warming effect of its rays. Then, in autumn the days shorten again, trees drop their leaves and the weather gets cooler as winter draws nearer.

In the night sky, the constellations you can see also change day by day, so the summer stars are quite different from the ones seen in winter.

The seasonal changes are more extreme the further you are from the Equator. Near the poles, there are enormous differences between the length of winter and summer days, but it never gets really warm because the Sun is not very high in the sky, even in midsummer. Near the Equator, the number of hours of daylight does not change much through the year and the Sun is always high in the sky.

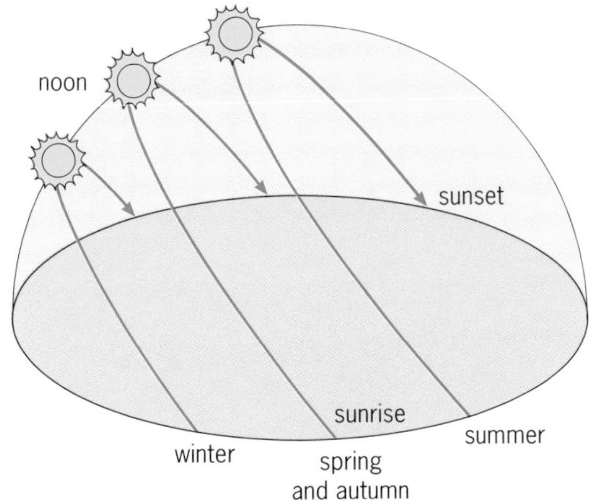

► How the Sun's path through the sky, as seen from somewhere in the northern hemisphere, changes between the seasons. In summer the Sun gets much higher in the sky at midday than it does in winter.

▼ In June, the North Pole is tilted towards the Sun. It is summer in the northern hemisphere. In December, the South Pole is tilted towards the Sun. It is summer in the southern hemisphere.

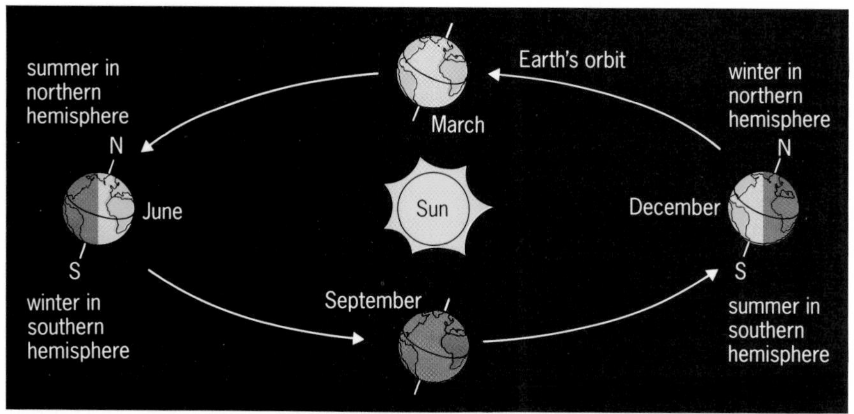

Why we have the seasons

Our planet Earth is spinning around its axis, an imaginary line going through the North and South poles. That is why we get day and night. At the same time, the Earth travels round the Sun once each year. There are seasons because the Earth's axis is tilted to its path round the Sun at an angle of $23\frac{1}{2}°$.

This means that the northern hemisphere is tipped towards the Sun for half the year. During this time, from about 21 March to 21 September, places in the northern hemisphere have spring followed by summer. At the same time, the South Pole is facing away from the Sun and the southern hemisphere is having autumn and winter.

From September through to March, things are the other way round. The North Pole tilts away from the Sun and the northern hemisphere has autumn and winter while the southern hemisphere has spring and summer. The seasons in these hemispheres are always opposite. In July, when it is summer in Europe, it is the middle of the Australian winter. ■

The planet Mars has seasons too. We can see its ice-caps grow in winter and shrink in summer.

See also
Constellations
Day and night
Equator
Equinoxes
Midnight Sun

Seaweeds

Seaweeds belong to a group of plants called algae. Those you find strewn along the tide line of a sandy beach have been detached, by wave action, from rocks out at sea. You have to visit a rocky shore to find seaweed growing. Seaweed is the general name for marine algae, and they grow on rocks, breakwaters, pipes and anything solid which the sea covers at high tides.

Structure

Although some algae are very simple, the seaweeds have parts that look similar to some land plants. Most have spreading fronds which look like leaves. The whole plant is attached to a rock by a branching holdfast which looks like roots. It keeps the plant in place despite the pounding of the strongest waves. Seaweeds are soft and can only stand upright when supported by water.

Reproduction

Some seaweeds spread by losing fragments which break off and grow into new plants. They also reproduce sexually. Male and female sex cells are produced in reproductive organs found in special sacs near the tip of a frond. When ready, the sex cells are squeezed out through pores onto the surface of the seaweed. As the tide comes in they are washed off and mix together. Male and female cells fuse to form a fertilized egg cell. This settles in a suitable place where it can grow into a new seaweed plant.

Zonation

If you look at a rocky shore, sea wall or breakwater at low tide you will notice that different seaweeds occur at different levels. This is called zonation. Those at the top are able to cope with a long period of drying between the tides, whereas those at the bottom will hardly be exposed at all. So there are definite bands of different types of seaweed. This feature is shown particularly by the brown seaweeds, or 'wracks'.

Uses of seaweeds

Seaweeds washed ashore by winter storms are used as organic fertilizers by farmers in many coastal areas. They are a natural source of valuable minerals, especially iodine, and their natural glue is extracted to make agar and other chemicals called alginates. These are used in the food industry as emulsifers, especially in the manufacture of ice-cream. ■

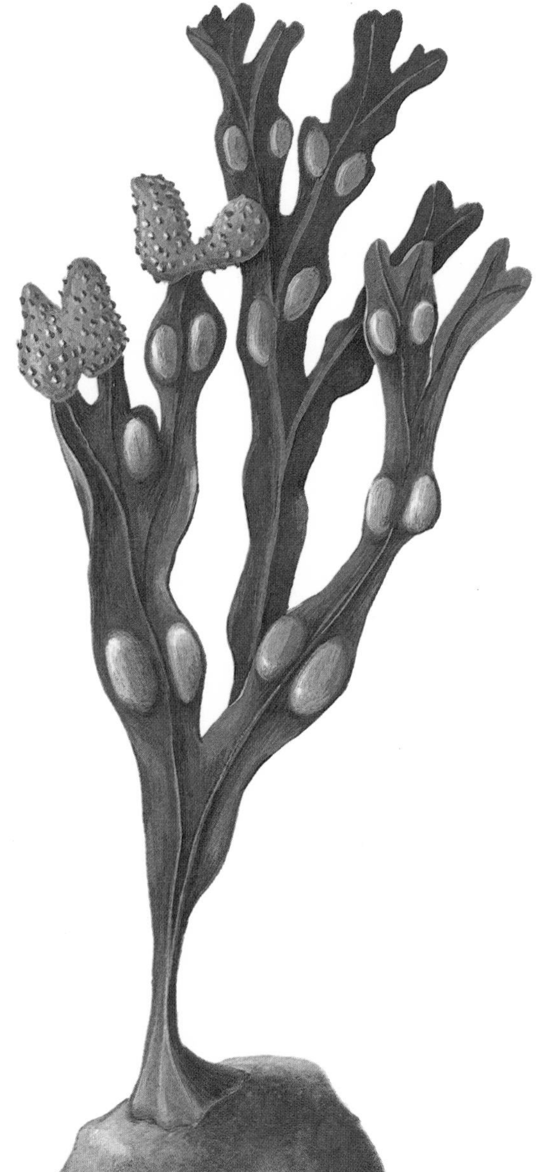

◀ Bladderwrack is a brown seaweed common on rocky seashores exposed at low tide. Air-filled bladders keep it upright and near the light when the tide is in.

In Ireland a seaweed called 'carragheen' is cooked with milk to make a kind of blancmange. Along the south coast of Wales a red seaweed, *Porphyra*, is used to make the great delicacy 'laver-bread'. The Chinese and Japanese also cook with this seaweed.

Something to do

Seaweeds can be preserved by mounting them on strong paper or card. Float the seaweed in a bowl of sea-water and slide the mounting paper under the seaweed. Spread out the fronds in their natural shape. Gently lift the paper with the seaweed on it. Drain, and cover the seaweed with a piece of nylon from a pair of old tights. Sandwich it all between two sheets of blotting paper or newspaper and place under some heavy books. After three days your mounted seaweed will be ready. Seaweed is covered in a natural glue called mucin which sticks it to the paper.

See also

Algae
Seashore
Zonation

Seeds

Seeds are produced by flowering plants and conifers. Each one is able to grow into a new plant given the right conditions. Seeds of flowering plants develop inside fruits while those of conifers develop inside cones.

Structure of a bean

If you soak a bean seed overnight it absorbs water, softens and swells. You can then open it up and see what is inside. Covering the seed is a protective skin called the testa (seed coat). Make a slit around the outer edge of the bean, avoiding the scar where it was attached by the seed stalk to the inside of the pod. Ease off the testa taking care not to damage the radicle (root) which fits into a pocket on one side of the scar. The contents will easily separate into two halves called cotyledons or seed leaves. These contain stored food in the form of starch and protein. Sandwiched between the cotyledons is the tiny plant that would grow into a new bean plant. You will see a radicle (root) and a plumule (shoot) with tiny leaves. Food contained in the cotyledons helps this young plant to grow before it can make its own food. ■

plumule (young shoot)
radicle (young root)
testa (seed coat)
cotyledon (leaf full of stored food)

► **Seeds contain a partly developed plant complete with tiny root, leaves and a supply of food. These are wrapped in a protective seed coat called a testa. Seeds enable plants to survive periods like winter or a dry season when normal growth is impossible.**

See also
Beans
Conifers
Flowering plants
Fruit
Nuts

Something to do

Roll blotting paper into a cylinder and drop it into a glass jar. Put sawdust, loose soil or sand into the centre to hold the blotting paper in place, then slide beans or other seeds in between the paper and the glass. Pour in water to moisten the blotting paper. Watch the seeds sprout roots and leaves. Make drawings of the stages of development.

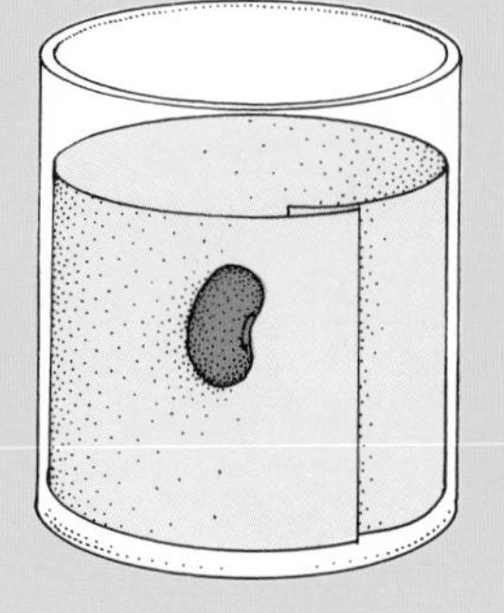

Senegal

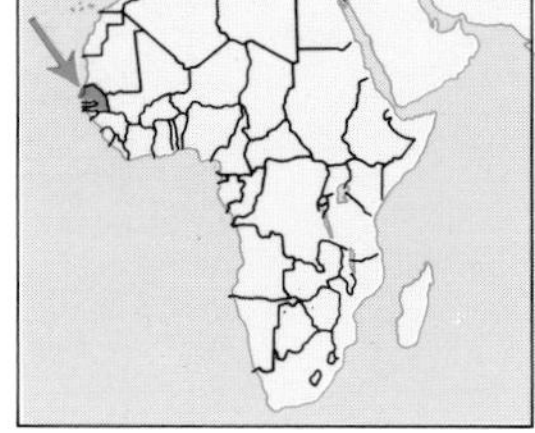

Senegal lies on the Atlantic coast of West Africa. The coastlands are warm and wet. Inland it is hot and drier.

Most people wear colourful cotton robes called *boubous*. They live in villages, growing food crops and groundnuts (peanuts) which are used to make groundnut oil and exported. Peanut sauce, spicy fried fish and chicken stew are all popular dishes. Phosphate rock, which is used to make fertilizers, and fish are also sold abroad. Senegal's capital, Dakar, is one of West Africa's chief industrial cities. It is a major centre of the African film industry.

Flashback

France ruled Senegal as a colony so the country has strong French traditions. It became independent in 1960 under the leadership of Léopold Senghor, a poet as well as a statesman.

In 1982 Senegal made an agreement to work with the Gambia, a country almost enclosed by Senegal. The Senegambia Confederation was set up and cooperated on defence and foreign policy, but in 1989 it collapsed and the two countries became completely independent again. The Gambia is a former British colony and its institutions are based on British ones. ■

Area
196,192 sq km
(75,750 sq miles)
Capital
Dakar
Population
6,540,000
Language
French, Wolof, Tukulor
Religion
Muslim, Christian
Government
Parliamentary republic
Currency
1 African Financial Community (CFA) franc = 100 centimes

See also
Africa
Gambia

Senses

To survive and be successful, an animal needs to know from second to second what is going on in the world around it. Without this information it could not find its food or a mate, stay in the right habitat or avoid being caught by hunting animals. This vital information is provided by its senses.

Vision tells it what things look like and where they are. Hearing tells it the position of something, and helps it to communicate. Smell and taste enable an animal to detect the chemicals in its environment, such as those in its food or those released by rivals or mates. Smell and taste can help the animal choose between safe food and poisonous food. Touch tells an animal what things feel like and when they are near.

Sense organs and the brain

Eyes see, ears hear, tongues taste and noses smell, and the animal's outer surface is its organ of touch. The sense organs pass information along nerves to the animal's brain. The brain merges all the different messages together to produce its 'picture' of the outside world.

Special senses

Animals also need information about their own bodies in order to function well. They need to know where all the parts of the body are in relation to one another in order to move about. They need a sense of balance to stay the same way up, and they need to know when a part of the body is damaged or sick.

This information is provided by special internal sense organs. In people, for instance, there are sense cells in muscles and joints that help control body movement. There are balancing organs connected with the inner ear, and there are sense cells for pain almost everywhere in the body.

▲ **The fleshy tentacles of the star-nosed mole are very sensitive to touch, detecting the movements of prey underground.**

▼ **This chimpanzee's sense organs: its eyes, ears, nose, tongue and skin, are essential for its survival.**

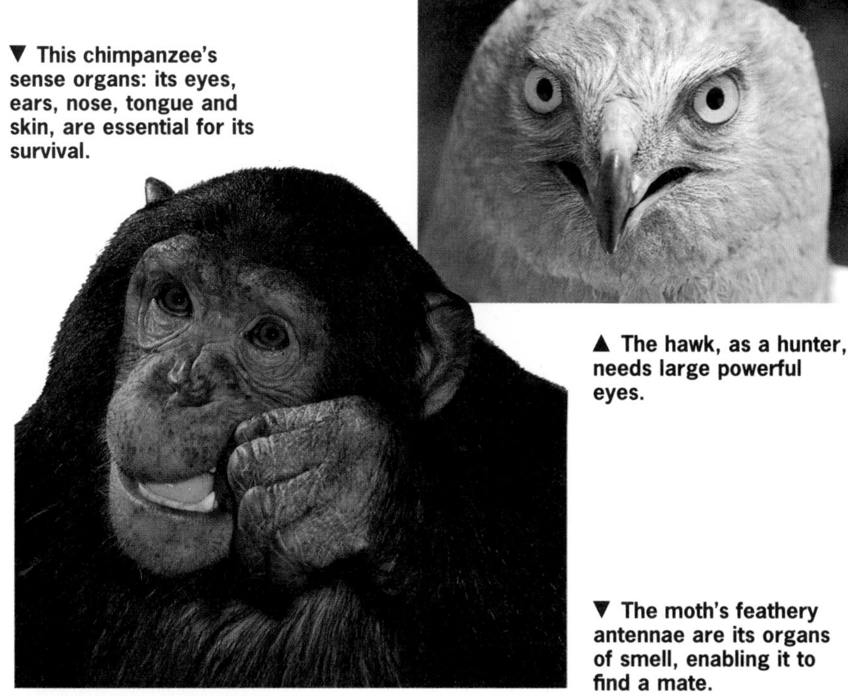

▲ **The hawk, as a hunter, needs large powerful eyes.**

▼ **The moth's feathery antennae are its organs of smell, enabling it to find a mate.**

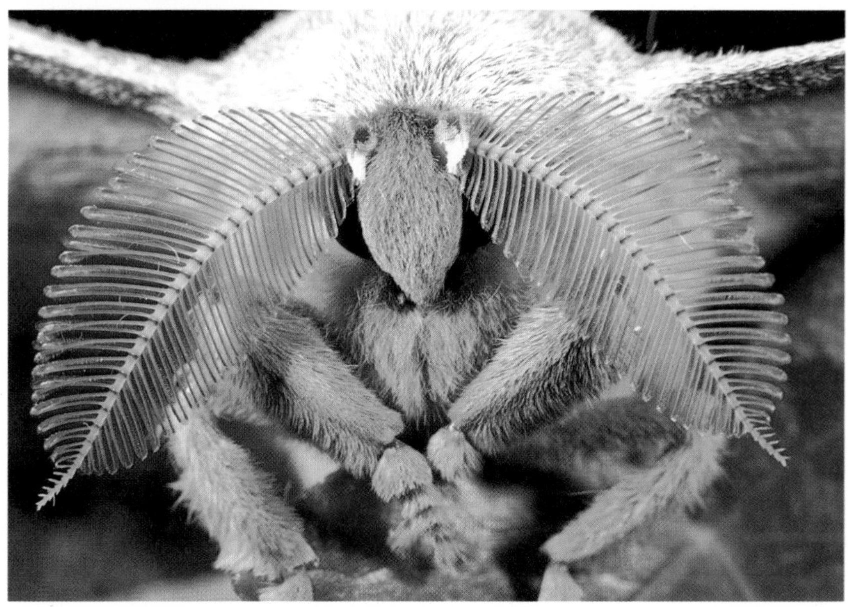

'Super-senses'

In some animals ordinary sense organs may become super-sensitive to fit special ways of life. In other animals completely new senses have evolved. Bats can steer themselves through a dark sky using an ultra-high pitched sound 'radar'. Sharks can hunt for food in the dark by sensing electrical signals given off by prey. A male emperor moth's antennae are so sensitive to the mating smell of the female that it can detect a single molecule from a female up to 11 km (7 miles) away. ■

See also
Bats
Brains
Ears
Eyes
Mouths
Noses
Radar
Skin

Sets

See also
Arithmetic
Mathematics
Numbers

A set is a collection of items which have something in common. For example, you could have a set of four-legged animals or a set of even numbers. {2, 4, 6, 8, 10, . . .} is the set of all the even numbers (the dots show that the set goes on for ever). Each member of the set is called an element. Like every set, it has a clear rule for deciding whether something belongs or not. Here, the rule is that each element must be a multiple of 2. ■

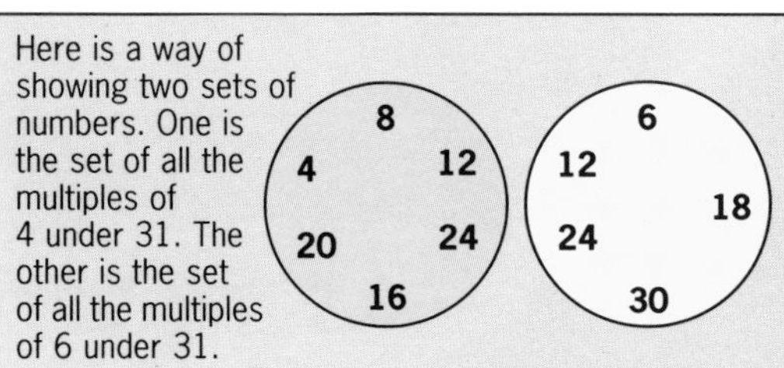

Here is a way of showing two sets of numbers. One is the set of all the multiples of 4 under 31. The other is the set of all the multiples of 6 under 31.

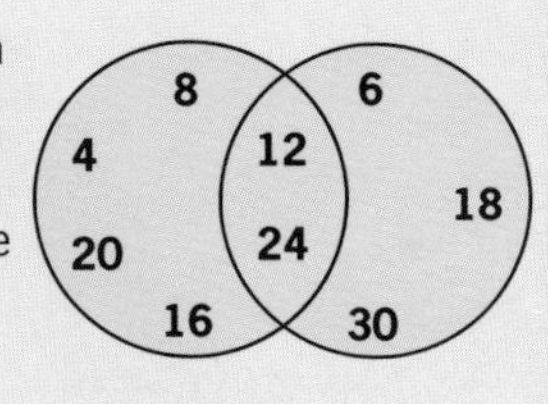

Sets can be combined to make a new set. The **union** of two sets is a new set made up of elements which were in one or the other of the original sets, or both.

The **intersection** of two sets is a new set made up of only those elements which were in both the original sets. Here, the inter-section gives all the multiples of 12 under 31.

Sewage

See also
Pollution
Victorian Britain (photo)
Water supplies

Sewage is waste material from houses and factories. When you flush a toilet, the waste is carried away by drains which empty into sewers. These lead to a sewage works, where the sewage is treated. Sewage has to be treated, because otherwise it can cause pollution and disease.

At the sewage works

When sewage arrives at the sewage works, any large objects like rags or pieces of wood are removed by large metal screens. The sewage then flows slowly through channels where any sand and soil sinks to the bottom.

Next, the sewage flows into large tanks where the sludge (solid matter) settles to the bottom. It is scraped away by electrical machinery. The remaining liquid sewage, called effluent, is often sprayed on circular beds of stone, rock or clinker. Sometimes it may be put in large tanks and have air blown through it. Either way, special bacteria feed on any waste matter in the effluent, turning it into harmless gases and water. The water is then clean enough to be pumped straight into a river or the sea.

Sewage sludge

The sludge is pumped to other tanks containing different kinds of bacteria. These destroy the unpleasant materials in the sludge and change them into the gas methane. This can be burned. Often it is used to make all the electricity and other power needed by the sewage works. The 'digested sludge' is sometimes taken in lorries to be spread on farmland, where it acts as a fertilizer.

Flashback

Sewage has not always been treated. Even today in some places untreated sewage is still poured into the sea. Before this century, sewage flowed down the streets of many villages, towns and cities. It was simply tossed out of the windows of nearby houses. There were a few sewers, but these discharged the sewage straight into the rivers from which drinking water was taken. The sewage polluted the water, and this caused epidemics of diseases such as cholera and typhoid. Gradually, these filthy conditions were overcome. Much work was done to ensure that towns and cities had adequate sewers and sewage was not allowed to spoil drinking water. ■

▼ At a sewage works, sewage is treated to make it clean and safe so that it can be poured into rivers.

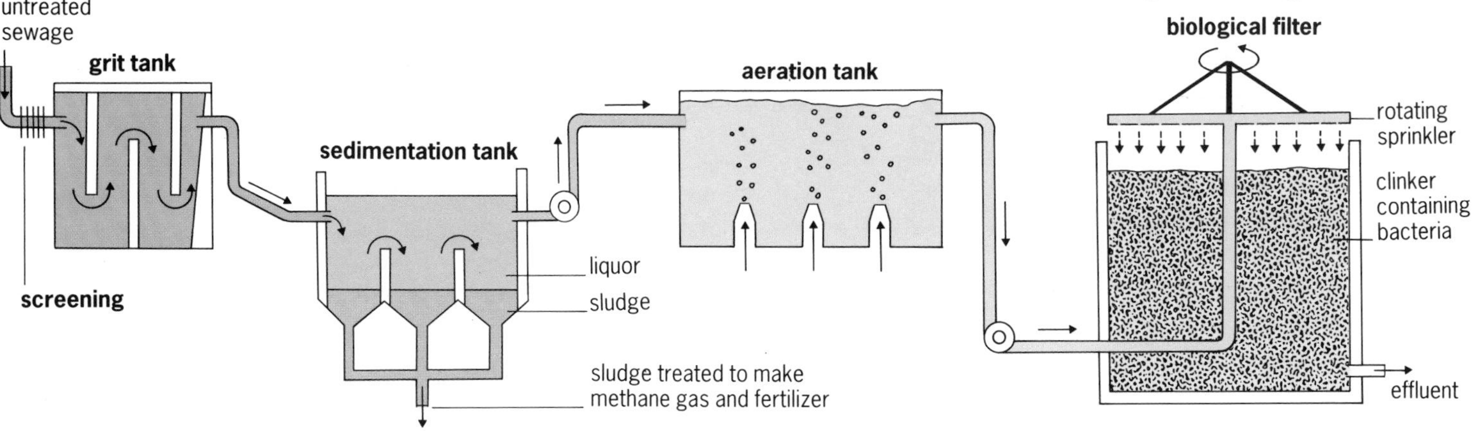

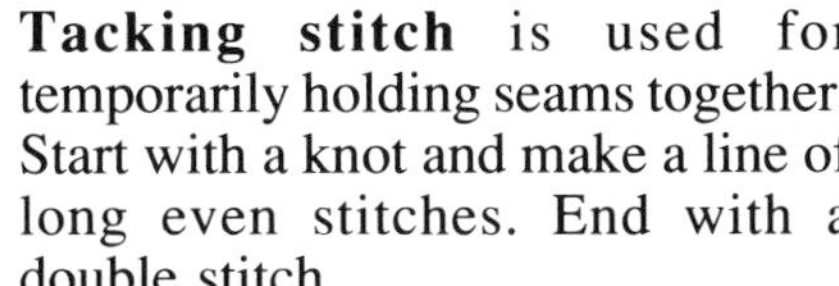

Sewing

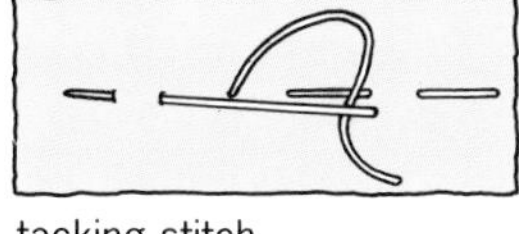

tacking stitch

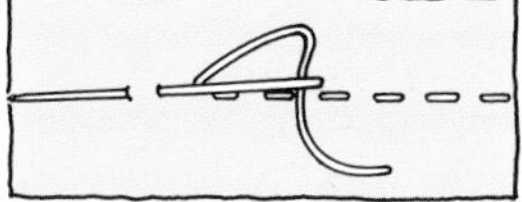

running stitch

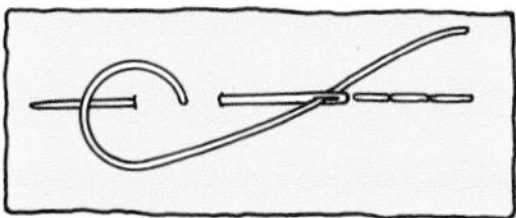

backstitch

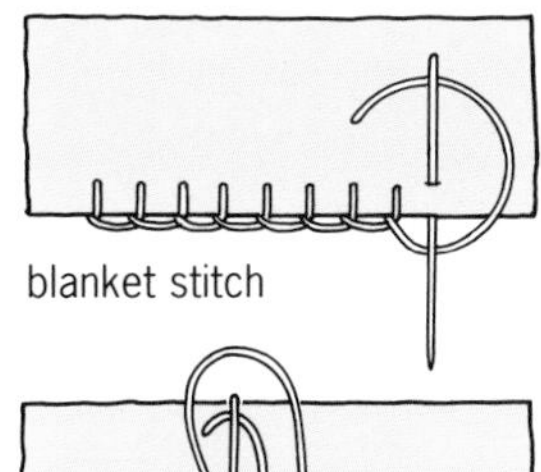

blanket stitch

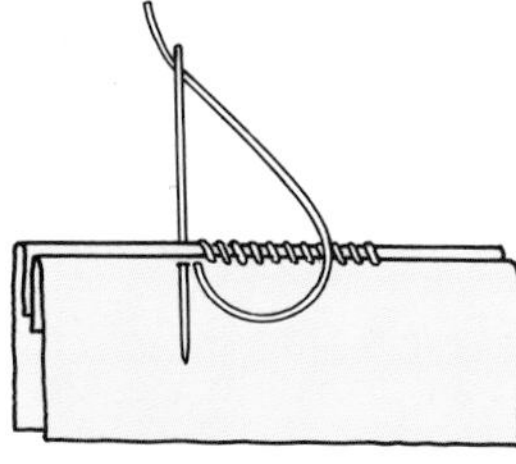

buttonhole stitch

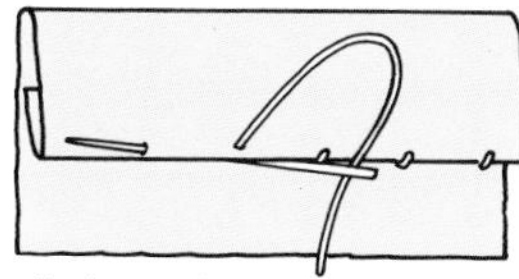

oversewing

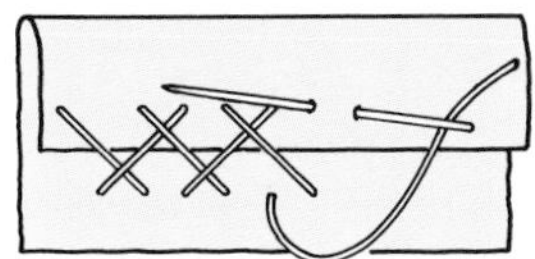

slip hemming

herring bone stitch

Tacking stitch is used for temporarily holding seams together. Start with a knot and make a line of long even stitches. End with a double stitch.

Running stitch is used for gathering fabric. Begin with a knot and make a row of small even stitches. When fastening off use a double stitch.

Backstitch is used to replace machine stitch or fasten off other stitches. Make a stitch backwards and bring the needle up in front of the starting point. Repeat this, starting with a stitch back to meet the beginning of the first stitch.

Blanket stitch is used for neatening edges. Insert the needle a short way from the fabric edge, coming out beneath it. Bring the thread around the needle point and draw the needle through the loop.

Buttonhole stitch is used for strengthening and neatening raw edges. Hold the work in one hand and insert the needle towards you. Wrap the thread around the needle point. Draw the needle through, then away from you, so that a knot forms on the raw edge.

Oversewing is used where two folded edges are sewn together. Insert the needle over and through the fabric close to the edges. Repeat to form a row of small neat oversewn stitches.

Slip hemming is used to hold a folded hem edge down. Make a small hemming stitch to join the fabric and folded edge. The needle then runs inside the folded edge for up to 1 cm (⅜ in) before the next hemming stitch is made.

Herring bone stitch is used to secure a hem in thick fabric. Make a single running stitch on upper line (folded hem) and lower line (fabric) as shown.

Needles

The type of needle that you choose depends on what you want to sew. A thick needle, for example, might leave holes in a fine fabric.

A **sharps needle** has a round eye and a sharp point. It is quite fine and is used for most sewing. A **crewel needle** has a sharp point and a long eye for thicker embroidery thread. Special curved needles are made for repairing chairs, tents, lampshades and sails.

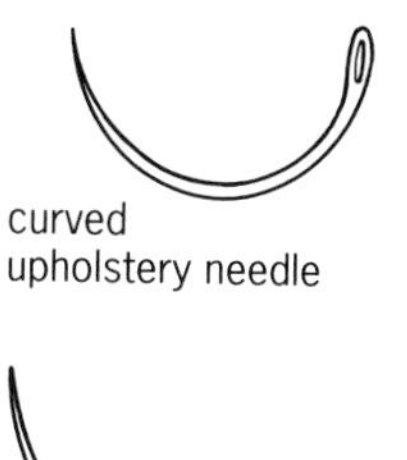

curved upholstery needle

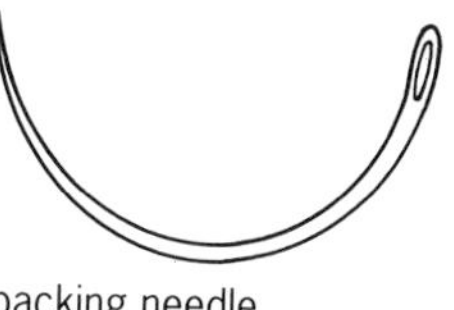

packing needle

Sewing machines

The first sewing machine was invented in 1790 by Thomas Saint in London, and stitched leather not cloth. The leather was pierced by a spike and then a needle looped thread through the holes. A French tailor, Barthélemy Thimonnier, developed a machine in the 1830s that stitched cloth with a needle in one movement. But the garment makers of Paris saw the machines as a threat to their jobs; machines were smashed and Thimonnier's life was threatened.

The first lock-stitch machine was made in the 1840s. It had an eye-pointed needle which stitched on top while a shuttle carried the thread below the fabric. In 1851 Isaac Singer took out a patent in New York for an improved lock-stitch machine with a straight eye-pointed needle made to work up and down. Many poor women worked on these machines to produce fine clothes for rich clients. Treadle machines freed both hands to guide the material through the machine. The swing-needle machine was developed to stitch new synthetic fibres. Its needle moves direction when sewing to produce zigzag and stretch stitches.

▲ A sewing machine made in Lancashire by William Jones during the last half of the 19th century. This machine was made for the tropics and plated against rust.

Modern machines are electrically operated either by foot or knee control. Computerized machines are easy to operate. By touching the keyboard you can programme the number of the stitch you require. ■

See also
Clothes
Embroidery
Fabrics
Mass production (photo)
Textiles

Sex

Men are usually taller, stronger and hairier than women and have larger and heavier skeletons. They have broader shoulders, coarser skin and, when fully grown, a deeper voice than women. For their size they also have more muscle and less fat.

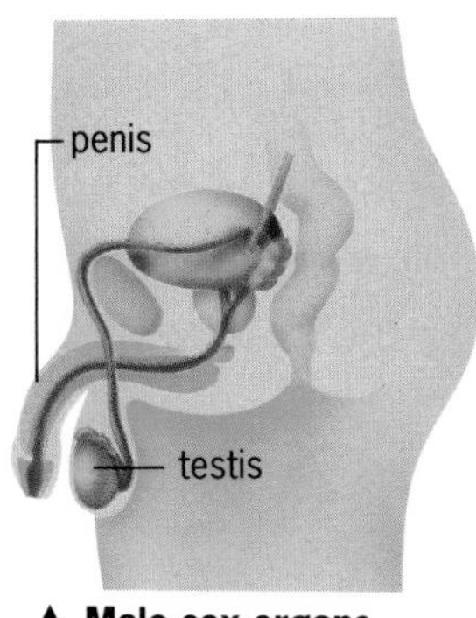

▲ **Male sex organs**

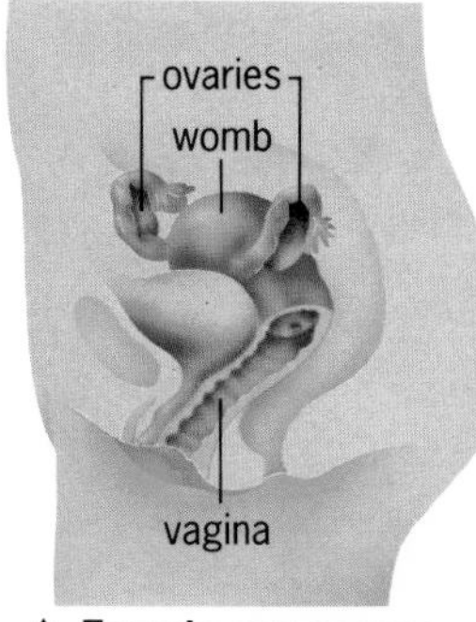

▲ **Female sex organs**

Women have broader hips to allow a baby to pass out of the body at birth. They have breasts which will produce milk when they give birth.

One of the main differences between men and women is their sex organs (genitals). A man has a penis, which is usually quite small and soft, but which becomes larger and harder when he is sexually excited. Below and behind the penis is a bag called the scrotum containing two testes. In an adult, these produce several million sperm each day.

A woman's sex organs are mostly inside her body. The outside opening of these organs is called the vulva and is two thick folds of skin that protect the clitoris, a tiny sensitive area at the front of the vulva. The vulva leads inside the body to the vagina and then the womb (uterus). Two tubes lead from the womb to the ovaries, which produce eggs (ova).

Sexual intercourse

When a man and woman are together and become sexually excited many changes take place in their bodies. Their muscles become tense, and breathing and heartbeats become faster. The man's penis grows larger and harder so it points upwards away from his body. This is called an erection.

Sexual intercourse takes place when the man pushes his penis into the woman's vagina; then one or both partners move their hips so the penis slides in and out. The vagina produces fluid which makes this easier. These movements give both of them pleasurable feelings which eventually reach a peak (an orgasm) and strong muscular contractions occur in the sex organs.

Muscular contractions of tubes inside the man's body squirt semen, a liquid which contains sperm, from his penis into the woman's vagina. This is called an ejaculation.

The sperm swim into the woman's womb and up towards her ovaries. If one of them joins with an egg from the woman (fertilization) the egg and sperm will begin developing into a baby and so the woman will become pregnant.

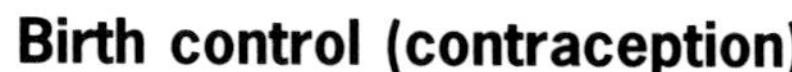

Birth control (contraception)

Birth control includes ways of preventing the woman becoming pregnant. One method is a sheath (condom) which is put onto the man's penis and collects semen as it is ejaculated. A woman can fit a rubber disc called a diaphragm over the opening of her womb, or she can choose to take pills which stop her ovaries releasing eggs. Contraception allows couples to decide when to have children, and how big a family they will have. But no method of contraception yet developed can be completely certain of preventing a baby from developing after intercourse.

The sex of a baby

Whether a baby is a boy or a girl is determined when a sperm joins with an egg at the moment of conception (fertilization). Eggs and sperm each contain 23 chromosomes, and one of this set is called a sex chromosome because it helps decide the sex of the baby. There are two types of sex chromosome, X and Y. All eggs have an X. Half the man's sperm have an X and half have a Y. If a sperm with an X chromosome joins with an egg the baby will be a girl. If a sperm with a Y chromosome joins with an egg the baby will be a boy.

Sexual responsibility

Sexual intercourse is also called 'making love', because it can give not only a lot of pleasure but a feeling of being very special to the other partner. Ideally, sexual intercourse and caring for the other partner should always go together. Sexual feelings can be very strong indeed, but people should give their partners a choice in whether or not they make love. Many people believe that couples should make love only when they are married and committed to staying together all their lives.

Sex roles

In many societies men and women are expected to do different jobs. Men tend to earn money while women look after the home, the children, the old and the sick. What someone is expected to do by society is called their role, like a part in a play. Very often women are not allowed the same rights as men, and may not vote or get equal pay.

This pattern is changing as we realize that people are all different and should be able to develop their talents without restrictions. ■

Sometimes a person is prevented from doing something just because of their sex, by laws or out-of-date ideas about the kind of things men and women can do. We call this **sex discrimination**. In some countries laws have been passed to try to make sure that women and men have equal rights.

See also

Cells
Mating
Parenthood
Pregnancy
Puberty
Reproduction

Shapes

▲ A circle has an edge which is the same distance from the centre all the way round.

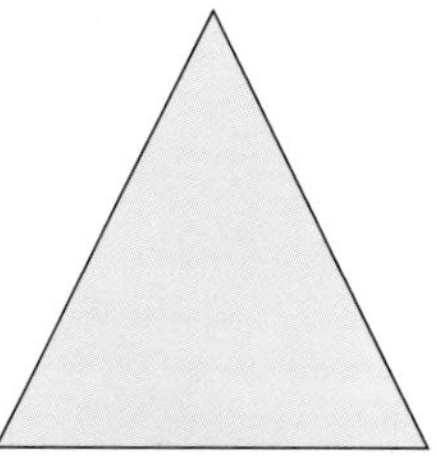

▲ A triangle has three sides.

▲ A square has four sides, all the same length.

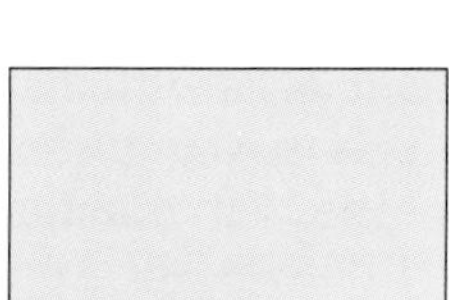

▲ A rectangle has corners like a square, but one pair of sides may be longer than the other.

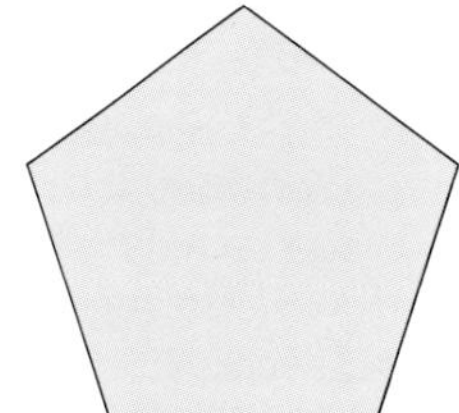

▲ A pentagon has five sides.

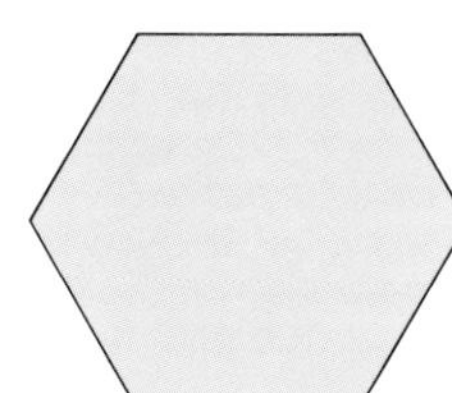

▲ A hexagon has six sides.

Everything you look at has a shape, whether it is a box, a ball, a bottle or a house. If you tried to describe the shape of a house, you might have to use lots of words. However, some shapes are much simpler and have their own special words to describe them.

3D shapes

Shapes like squares and triangles are easy to draw on a piece of paper because they are flat. But some shapes are not flat, they are solid. A cube is a solid shape. It has length, width and height. Mathematicians say that it has three dimensions (3D for short). Spheres, cones and pyramids are all 3D shapes. ■

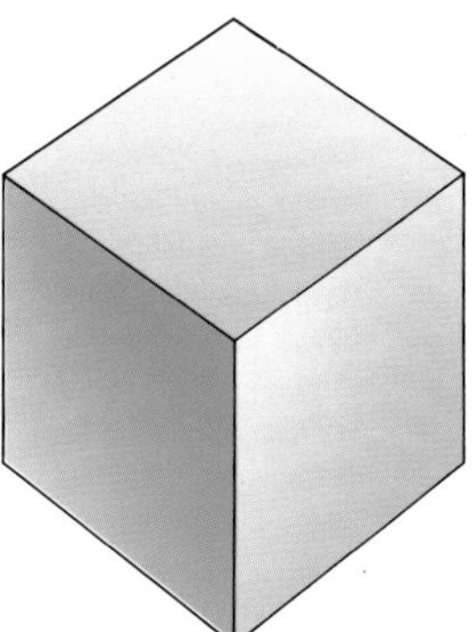

▲ A cube has six faces. Each of these is a square.

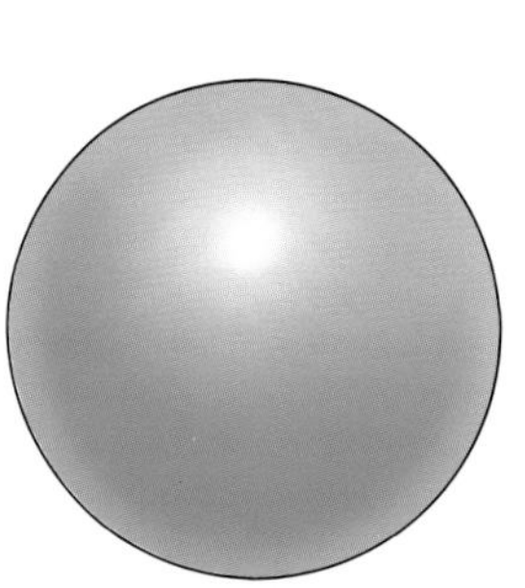

▲ A sphere has the outline of a circle from wherever you look at it.

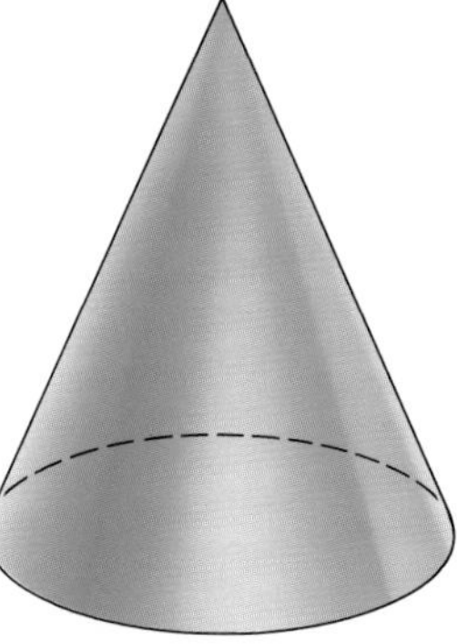

▲ A cone has a point at one end and a circle at the other.

Something to do

A tangram is an old Chinese puzzle. The seven pieces form a square, but you can also fit them together to make other shapes. Copy the pieces and cut them out. Then try fitting them together to make shapes such as triangles, trapeziums and parallelograms. All the pieces must be used and none must overlap.

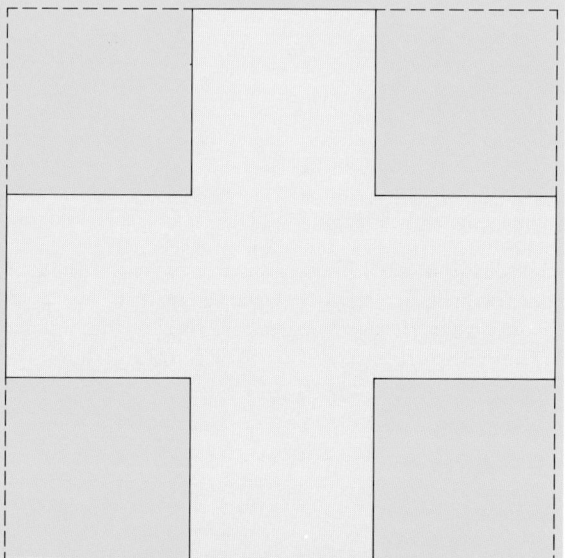

Copy and cut out the shape of the cross in the diagram several times so that you have ten crosses all exactly the same shape. Try fitting them together to form a pattern. There should be no gaps between the shapes and no overlapping. Patterns like this, which use shapes over and over again, are called tessellations.

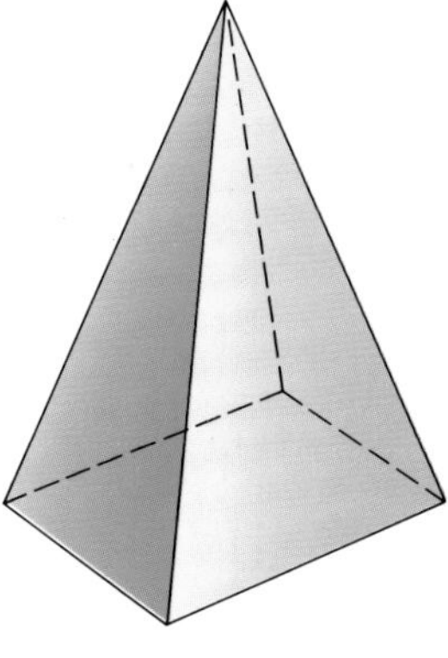

▲ A pyramid may have a square as its base, or a pentagon or any other many-sided figure. Its other faces are all triangles.

See also
Arches
Geometry
Mosaics
Patterns
Symmetry

Sharks

Sharks known to have attacked human beings include: great white shark, hammerhead shark, tiger shark, bull shark, porbeagle, mako shark, grey shark, great blue shark.

There are many different types of shark. Some, like the zebra horn shark, are sluggish bottom-dwellers which feed on shellfish. Others, like the whale shark and basking shark, are filter-feeders and eat plankton. However, the best-known sharks are the fast-swimming predators such as the great hammerhead, the mako and the great white. These sharks feed mainly on fish, though the great white also eats dolphins and seals.

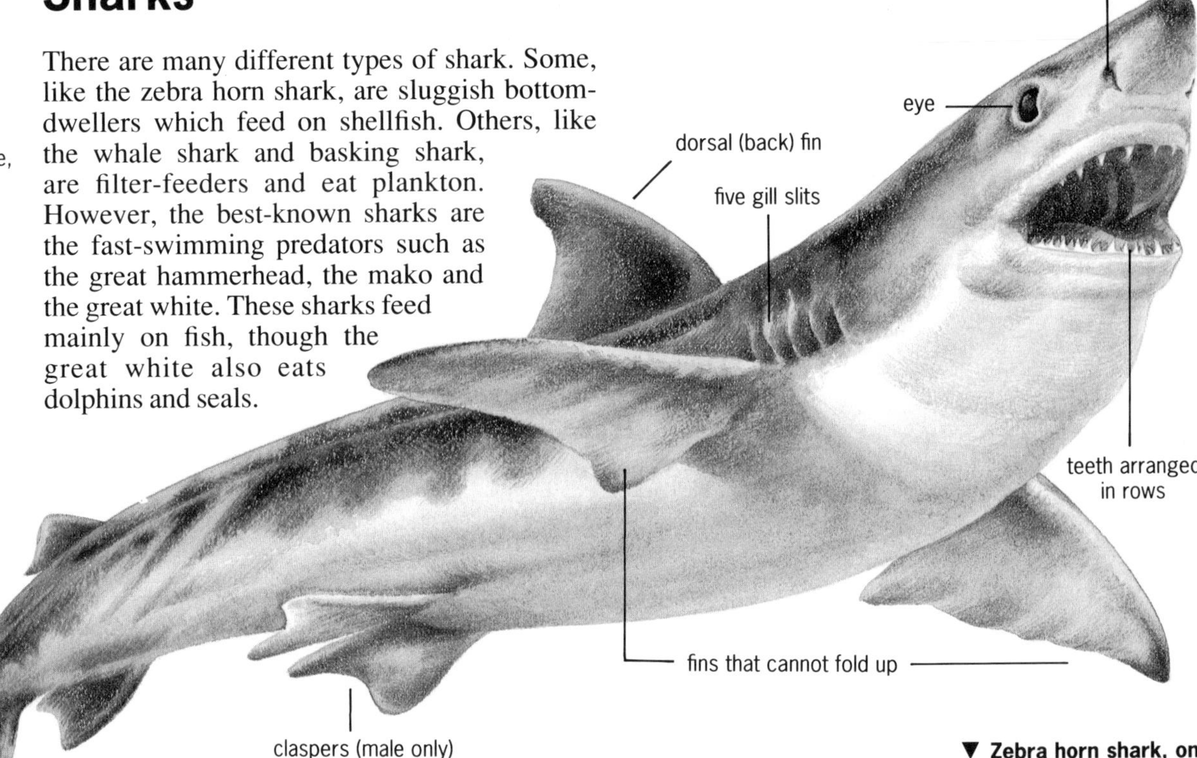

Distribution
In oceans throughout the world but more common in warmer water
Largest
Whale shark, grows to a length of 15 m. (Largest shark in British waters is the basking shark, length 9 m.) Both of these species are plankton feeders.
Largest flesh-eating shark
Great white shark, grows to a length of 6 m
Smallest
Dwarf shark, 15 cm long

Subphylum Vertebrata
Class Chondrichthyes (cartilaginous fishes)
Number of species
370 species of shark

See also
Fish
Teeth
Vertebrates

Sharks, together with rays and skates, are different from other fish. Their skeleton is made entirely of cartilage rather than bone. Their skin is made of thousands of tooth-like structures known as 'placoid scales'. They give shark skin a texture like sandpaper.

The teeth in a shark's jaws are modified placoid scales and grow in rows. When a tooth is damaged it drops out and the next tooth behind moves forward to replace it. At any one time the shark may have up to 3,000 teeth in its mouth. The teeth may be pointed and serrated for sawing flesh or flattened for crushing shellfish.

Sharks produce very few eggs. They are sometimes protected by horny egg cases. The 'mermaid's purse' you may find on the seashore is the egg case of a shark, the dogfish. Other sharks, like the hammerhead, give birth to live young.

Sharks have a keen sense of smell and can detect one part of blood in a million parts of water. They also sense vibrations produced by struggling fish. Shark fishermen in the Pacific islands rattle coconut shells underwater to attract them. All sharks can detect electricity through a series of pits in their snout. This means they can detect the electrical charge produced by the nerves in an animal's body.

▼ Zebra horn shark, one of the smaller shark species.

A completely new species of shark over 4·5 m (15 ft) long was described in 1983. It has been named the megamouth shark because of its huge mouth. It is a filter-feeder like the whale shark and eats shrimps and jellyfish. So far only three specimens have been caught.

There are fewer than 100 shark attacks upon humans every year. However, thousands of sharks are killed for food and liver oil. The 'rock salmon' used in fish and chip shops is a shark, the lesser spotted dogfish. ■

Sheep

◀ The mouflon, smallest of the wild sheep, is the ancestor of today's domestic sheep.

Wild sheep live in mountainous areas. They are good climbers, but are less agile than their cousins the goats, so they are generally found at lower and less rocky levels. Both males and females have horns, which are usually curled into a flat spiral. The horns of the males are larger and are used particularly in fighting for mates. Like goats, wild sheep are wary, tough animals, with dense hairy coats. In the winter-time they grow a thick undercoat (fleece) of fine wool and this helps to keep them warm and dry in even the harshest weather. It is moulted completely in the summer.

A wild ewe about to have her lamb leaves the small group with which she normally lives and finds a safe ledge. The lamb remains there with her for several days after birth. At this time its main enemies are eagles, but later it may have many enemies. Of these, humans are the most dangerous, and largely because of over-hunting most kinds of wild sheep are now very rare.

Domestication

The value of the winter woolly coat for making warm clothing and carpets meant that people kept and bred from sheep which retained their wool into the summer-time. Today, most domestic breeds have lost their hairy coats and have only the woolly fleece. This is not shed, but has to be sheared.

There are now more than 800 breeds and over 680 million domestic sheep. They have been taken by humans to many parts of the world and millions of sheep are reared every year in New Zealand, Australia and North and South America.

The mouflon, a wild sheep from south-west Asia, was domesticated about 9,000 years ago. Today it is an endangered species. A form of mouflon which is found in Europe may be a descendant of the first domestic sheep which were taken to the Mediterranean region by early farmers. Some escaped in remote areas and a few survived in Corsica and Sardinia. They are now strictly protected and their numbers are increasing. Mouflon have even been taken to mountainous parts of Europe, where they thrive on the alpine pastures. ■

Distribution
Mountains of Asia and North America
Size
Up to 180 cm head and body length, 125 cm shoulder height
Weight
Up to 200 kg
Number of young
In the wild 1 lamb, weaned in 4–6 months; domestic sheep often have twins or triplets
Lifespan
Up to 24 years; in the wild, animals in successful breeding herds have a shorter lifespan than those with poor breeding success

Subphylum Vertebrata
Class Mammalia
Order Artiodactyla (cloven-hoofed animals)
Family Bovidae (cattle family)
Number of species 8

◀ Sheep are sheared once a year at the beginning of summer, when the winter coat is attached to the skin by fewer hairs.

See also
Domestication
Goats

Shintoists

Shinto is the name for the folk religion of Japan. It is so old that there is no date for its beginning and no founder figure. Shinto is often translated as 'the *kami* (spirit) way'. The most important kami is Amaterasu, the Sun goddess. Japan is often called the 'land of the rising Sun', and Shinto has been the state religion at certain times in history. There are public Shinto shrines (places of worship) with priests, and also small home shrines. People pray there when they have personal problems, to offer their thanks and to meditate on the harmony there should be between the kami, nature and people. ■

See also
Japan
Japan's history

First modern ship
The *Great Britain*, designed by Isambard Kingdom Brunel and launched in 1845, was built of iron and had a screw propeller.

World's largest ship
The oil tanker *Seawise Giant* (564,000 tonnes) was 458 m long and 69 m wide. She was completed in 1976, but destroyed in a rocket attack in 1988.

Stopping distance
Oil tankers are so massive that it can take them over 10 km (6 miles) to stop even with their engines in full reverse.

Ships

When people talk about ships, they usually mean sea-going vessels with engines driving an underwater propeller. At one time, ships carried sails and relied on the wind, but there are very few large sailing ships in use today.

Most ships have one propeller (also called a screw), but some have two or even three. Usually, the propeller is driven by a diesel engine, but a gas turbine or a steam turbine may be used instead. With a steam turbine, the steam comes from a boiler which uses the heat from burning oil or even from a nuclear reactor.

Cargo ships

At one time, a cargo ship would carry many different cargoes depending on what needed to be transported from port to port. Today, most cargo ships are specially designed to carry one type of goods only. The cargo might be several hundred cars, containers packed with washing machines, or grain pumped aboard through a pipe.

Passenger ships

Nowadays, passenger ships are either ferries, or luxury liners taking people on holiday cruises. However, before air travel became popular, huge passenger liners provided regular services between all the major ports of the world. When people had to travel long distances around the world, they went by sea.

Naval ships

Naval ships are used in time of war to hunt and destroy enemy ships, submarines and aircraft and for launching missiles against targets on land. Aircraft carriers are the largest naval vessels of all; the biggest can carry over 90 aircraft. Frigates and destroyers are used for escorting and protecting other vessels. Minesweepers hunt for explosive mines which might sink other ships. They have plastic or aluminium hulls which do not set off magnetic mines. Most naval vessels are packed with radar and other electronic equipment which can detect and track missiles or torpedoes launched against them.

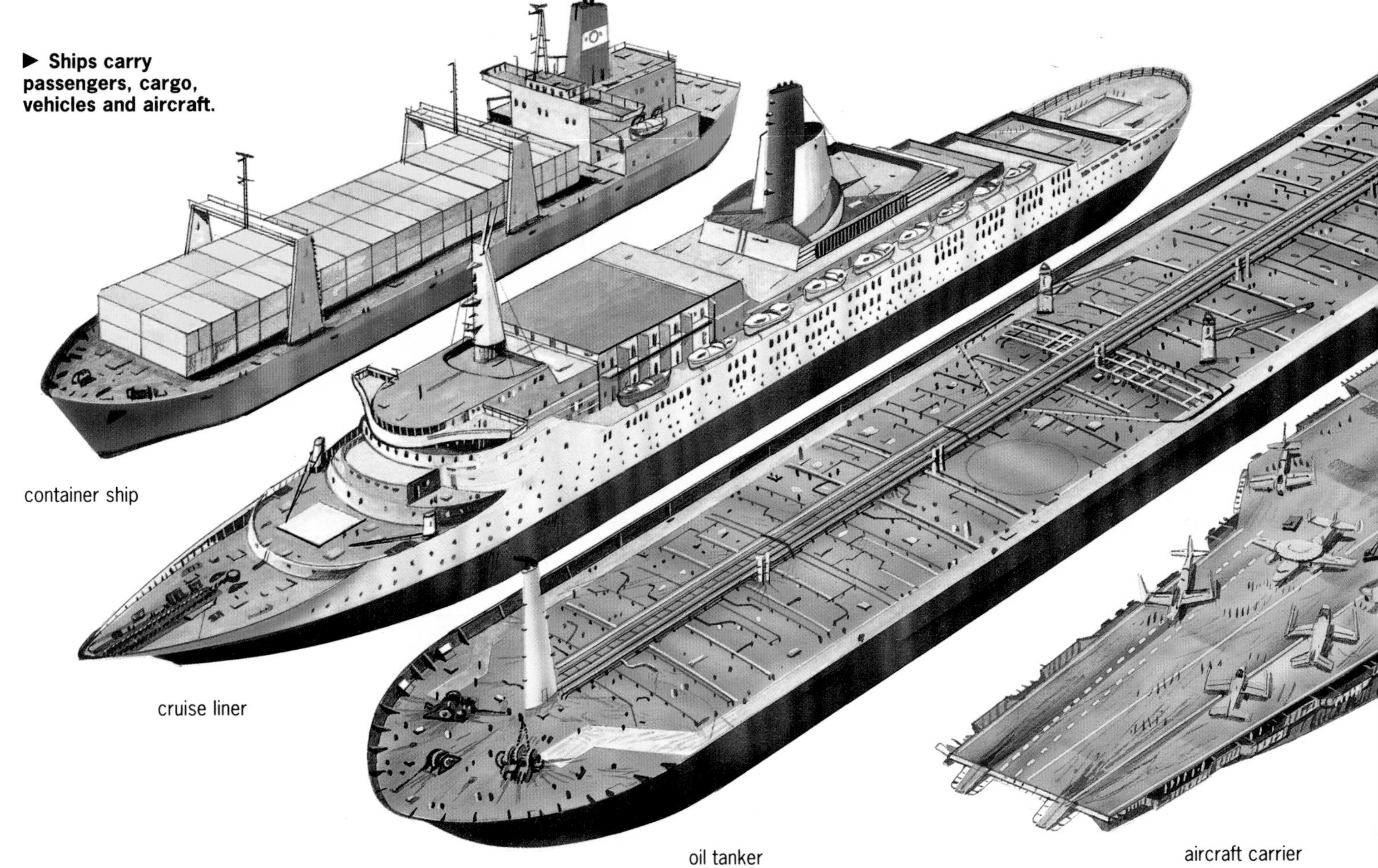

► **Ships carry passengers, cargo, vehicles and aircraft.**

Building a ship

The basic parts of a ship have not changed very much over the years. However, modern ships are built of steel and other metals, and not of wood as the early ships were. Building starts with the keel, followed by the stem, stern and frame. The plates of the hull, deck and inside compartments are then added, together with the engines. The ship is normally built on a gently sloping slipway. When it is ready to be launched, it is allowed to slide slowly down the slipway into the water. It is then floated to a quay where the remaining parts are added. In a modern shipyard, the ship may be built in separate sections which are joined together on the slipway.

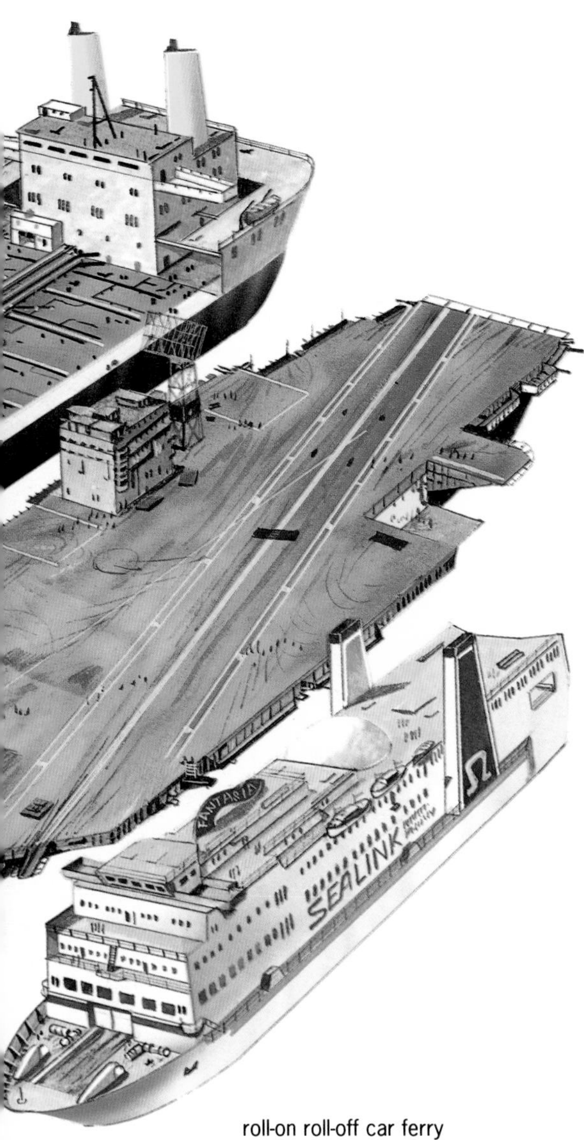

roll-on roll-off car ferry

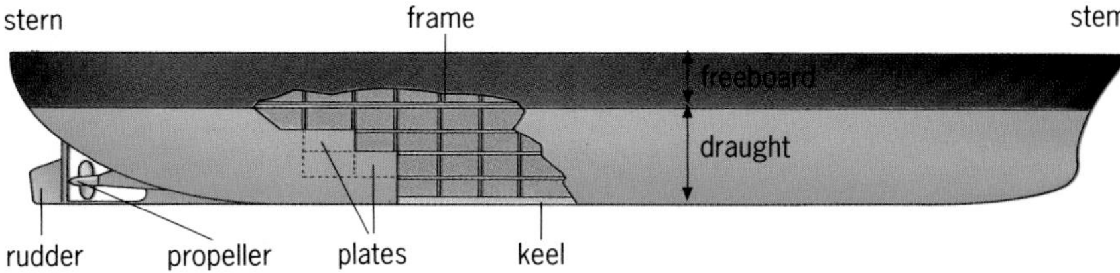

▲ **The hull of a ship.**

Large ships need to be very strong to stop their long hulls bending and cracking in heavy seas. Many are fitted with stabilizers (tiny, movable underwater 'wings') to stop them rolling too much.

See also

Docks
Navies
Nuclear power
Ports and harbours
Sailing ships
Steam-engines
Submarines
Turbines

Biography
Brunel

Flashback

Ships driven by steam-engines started to replace sailing ships at the beginning of the 19th century. At first, steamships were propelled by huge paddle wheels at the sides, but more efficient screw propellers were being used from about 1840 on. Steamships needed huge supplies of coal as fuel, so they became much bigger. Iron rather than wood became the main building material and later steel. By the end of the 19th century, the engine rooms of the biggest liners were almost as large as cathedrals.

From about 1900, steam turbines began to replace steam-engines in the largest ships. Steam turbines are still used in some large ships, but with a nuclear reactor or oil to heat the boiler, rather than coal. Today, most ships are propelled by diesel engines, though some fast naval vessels use gas turbines similar to those in aircraft. ■

1590 galleon

1850 sailing clipper

1858 iron steamship

1907 ocean liner

► **Ships have become larger over the years. The largest ships of all were the giant oil tankers built in the 1970s.**

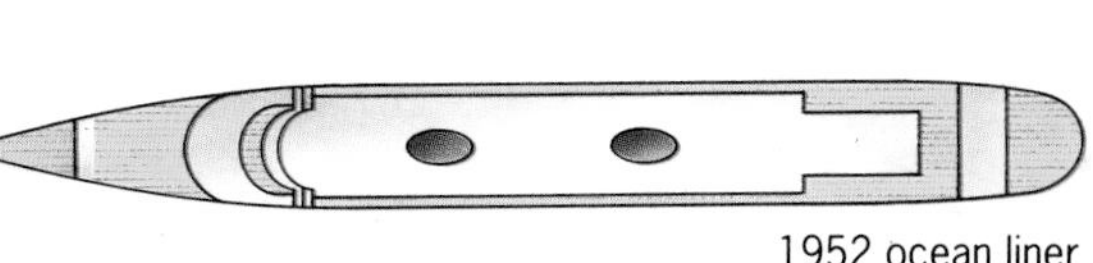

1952 ocean liner

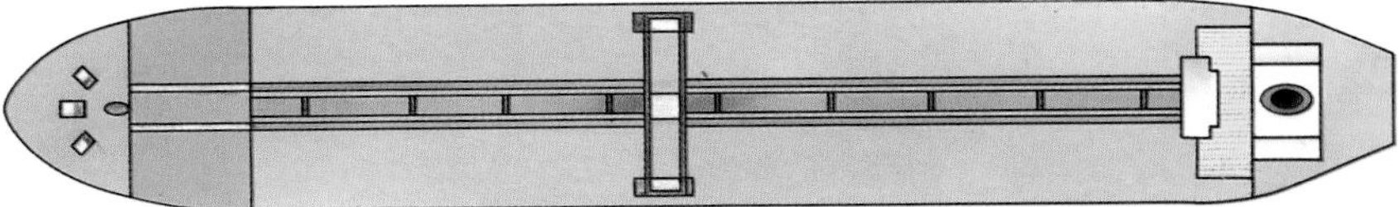

1976 oil tanker

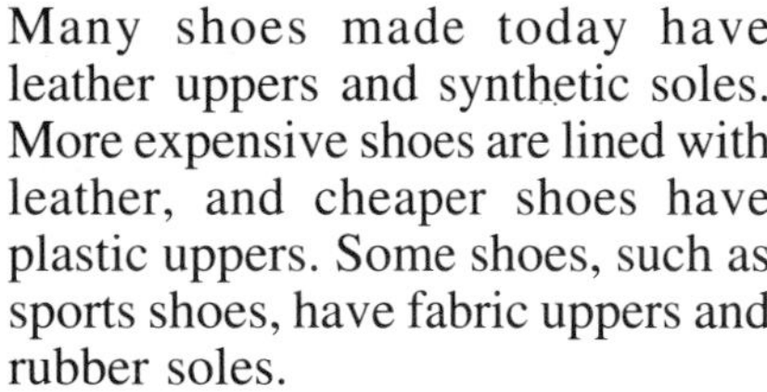

Shoes

Many shoes made today have leather uppers and synthetic soles. More expensive shoes are lined with leather, and cheaper shoes have plastic uppers. Some shoes, such as sports shoes, have fabric uppers and rubber soles.

In a shoe factory the shape of the upper is cut out by a worker known as a 'clicker'. The upper is 'closed' (stitched) and set on a 'last' (mould). It is attached to the sole with adhesive. The sole and heel are usually premoulded in one piece.

1250s

Medieval 1350s

Medieval 1460s

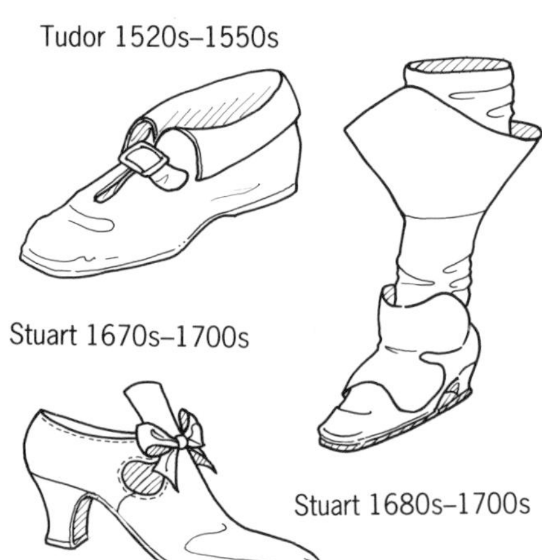

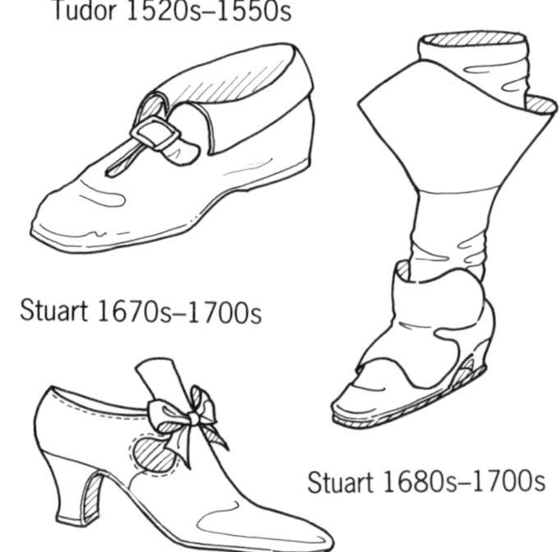

Tudor 1520s–1550s

Stuart 1670s–1700s

Stuart 1680s–1700s

Flashback

Shoes from the Roman and medieval periods have been found near the River Thames in London, because the type of mud there preserves leather well. Shoemaking used to be a highly skilled craft. Cobblers would make stout shoes to last for years as well as fashionable shoes in exaggerated shapes. Pointed toes and high heels have often been fashionable. In the 1470s pointed toes were longer than they have ever been since. Laws were passed to restrict their length. The points were stuffed to keep them firm.

Shoes with silk uppers were popular among fashionable ladies in the Stuart and Georgian periods. They wore shoes with a raised sole which were called pattens or clogs. Very poor people could only afford wooden clogs. ■

Victorian 1870s–1900s

1950s

See also
Costume
Dress
Factories

Shops

Shops are where we go to buy the goods and services we need. Some small shops are run just by one person or by a family. Others are much larger and may be run by companies with branches in different towns and cities. Some large companies have similar shops forming a chain in many different countries of the world.

In North America shops are called stores. *Boutique* is a French word for a small shop which sells clothes or other fashion items.

Different types of shops

Small corner shops sell things that you might want every day. Many sell newspapers and magazines, sweets, tobacco and popular grocery items.

Most shops are in groups called shopping centres. These attract shoppers making more than every-day purchases, and usually include facilities such as banks and parking space which make a shopping trip more efficient.

Smaller shops in a centre generally specialize in one type of goods such as books, shoes, toys or electrical goods. The biggest shops are

▼ In this English grocery shop in the early 1950s some items, like the breakfast cereals, are pre-packaged, but others are not. The owner is slicing bacon for his customers.

See also
Co-operative Societies
Markets

department stores, divided into sections (departments), each of which specializes. To attract shoppers, department stores have special displays, and try to make it easy and convenient for shoppers to find and choose goods. Famous department stores include Harrods in London, GUM in Moscow, Galerie Lafayette in Paris, and Maceys in New York.

In recent years, many groups of shops have been designed and laid out with covered and heated pedestrian areas in centres called arcades or malls.

Large food shops, with self-service facilities for shoppers to pick out their own choice of goods, are called supermarkets. Some of these are in shopping centres; others are in a separate location with their own car park. Extremely large supermarkets, especially those that sell a wide range of non-food products, are known as hypermarkets. Supermarkets and hypermarkets attract shoppers by their huge choice of goods and by lower prices.

Shopping centres, including businesses such as dry cleaners and travel agents that sell services rather than goods, are known as the retail trade. Wholesalers are businesses that store large amounts of goods in a warehouse and supply them to shops. Large retailers have their own wholesale supply, and are able to be more efficient, and sell at lower prices, than smaller shops.

Flashback

Many of the things sold in shops today are sold in packets. The goods have been 'pre-packaged' in the factory. This saves the shop assistant the time taken to wrap things up. Before the 1950s a corner shop would sell you one egg if that was all you wanted. Sugar was weighed out in front of you and wrapped by hand. This still happens in small shops mainly outside Europe and North America, where things are sold separately. ■

Shrews

▲ The European pygmy shrew is one of the smallest of all mammals. Here it is shown about twice life size.

Shrews are easily recognized by their very long noses and tiny eyes. They are the most active of all mammals, hunting for food day and night. Their eyesight is poor, but they use their sense of smell very effectively. Most European shrews need to eat their own weight of insects or grubs every single day of their lives. Some can starve to death if they are forced to go for more than four hours without a meal.

We do not often see a shrew, but you may hear them rustling through dead leaves and squeaking with high-pitched voices that many people take to be the calls of insects. Shrews are defended against larger predators by stink glands, which make them very unattractive food for mammals such as weasels or cats. Birds, which have a poor sense of smell, have no objection to eating shrews, and their remains are often found in the pellets of owls or birds of prey. ■

Distribution
Almost worldwide
Number of young
About 6
Lifespan
Most shrews do not survive much over a year.

Subphylum Vertebrata
Class Mammalia
Order Insectivora
Family Soricidae
Number of species 246

See also
Hedgehogs
Moles

Sierra Leone

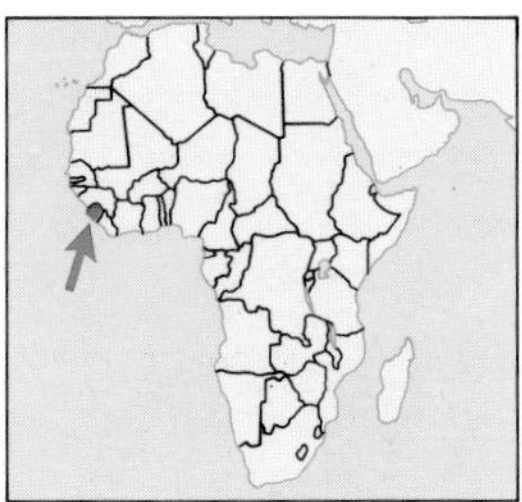

Sierra Leone, which means 'lion mountain', possibly got its name from the shape of a coastal mountain. But it may have been named after the roaring sound of thunder often heard during rainstorms. This hot, wet country has broad, swampy plains, north and south of a rocky, coastal mountain. Inland are plains and uplands.

Rice is the main food crop, and it is grown in the swampy plains. Further inland are small plantations where coffee, cocoa and oil palms are grown for export. But diamonds are by far the country's leading export.

Flashback

In 1787, a British society for freed slaves founded a settlement on the coast of Sierra Leone. They called it Freetown, because it was a home for slaves who had escaped or gained freedom. The descendants of these slaves now form the country's Creole community. About 130,000 Creoles live in and around Freetown and speak Krio, which is a dialect of English. Britain ruled Sierra Leone from 1808 until 1961, when it became independent. ■

Area
71,740 sq km
(27,699 sq miles)
Capital
Freetown
Population
3,700,000
Language
English, Krio, Mende, Temne, others
Religion
Traditional, Muslim, Christian
Government
Parliamentary republic
Currency
1 leone = 100 cents

See also
Africa

Sign language

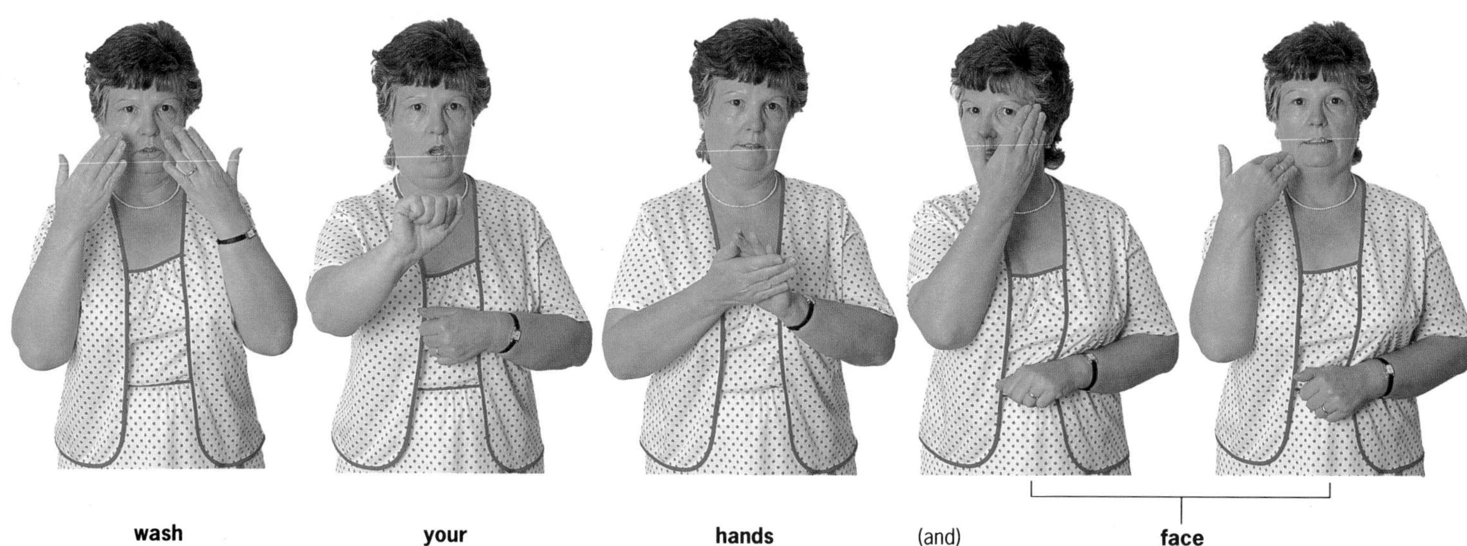

wash your hands (and) face

Sign language is when we use our body instead of our voice to say what we mean. People who are deaf or who cannot speak learn to talk to one another in a language that uses the hands, the face, and the upper part of the body.

The signs they use with their hands do not just mean words on their own: their meaning depends on the person's movements and on the expression on her or his face. So, the difference between saying 'I gave you a hat' and 'Did you give me a hat?' is shown by the hand signs for these words and the direction in which they are made: from me to you or from you to me, raising your eyebrows to show that it is a question. There are as many sign languages in the world as there are spoken ones. ■

▲ These signs are used by deaf people in the Signs Supporting English method. This sequence of signs means 'Wash your hands and face'. The sign for the word 'and' is not used in sentences like this. The meanings of the signs vary with the facial expressions used. Lip patterns are used as well as hand signs.

See also
Deafness

Sikhs

The Sikh religion began in the Punjab in northern India where most Sikhs still live. Sikhs also live in many other countries, particularly North America and Great Britain.

The most important thing for a Sikh is learning about God. The word *sikh* means 'learner' in the Punjabi language and the word *guru* means 'teacher'. God is the True Teacher and is described by Sikhs as the Eternal Being beyond male or female. The title 'Guru' is also given to ten human beings. All the Gurus teach Sikhs three main things.

First, they should remember God frequently by saying or singing his name. One famous prayer is the Mool Mantra.

There is One God, his name is truth eternal.
He is the creator of all things.
Fearless and without hatred, immortal
Beyond birth and death, he is self-existent.
He is known by the Guru's grace.

Secondly, Sikhs should work hard to earn an honest living. They usually marry and have families, feeling that this is the way God wants them to live. All Sikh men and women are equal and can perform any of the religious ceremonies. There are no monks or priests in Sikhism.

Thirdly, Sikhs should share their earnings and serve others, whatever their nationality, religion or social status. If you visit a gurdwara (Sikh temple), you will see boys and girls, as well as adults, helping to prepare and serve food and drink from the *langar*, the Guru's kitchen. Guests are welcome to stay and eat at any time, but especially after a service.

History

The first of the ten Gurus was Nanak, who lived in the Punjab from 1469 to 1539. His background was Hindu, and Sikhs share the Hindu belief in a final liberation from many reincarnations. They also share some of the same festivals, such as Diwali.

In 1604, the fifth Guru, Arjan, collected teachings from earlier Gurus into a book which became the sacred scripture of the Sikhs. It is called the *Guru Granth Sahib* and passages from it are read aloud at all Sikh ceremonies. The first letter from the first hymn of a page opened at random is used to choose the first name of a boy or girl. To this name is added *Singh* for a boy and *Kaur* for a girl. Singh means 'lion' which stands for bravery, and Kaur means 'princess', which shows the dignity of the girl.

The five Ks

In 1699 Guru Gobind Singh introduced five symbols for Sikhs to wear. The *kara* is a steel bangle worn on the wrist. This reminds Sikhs that they are bound to God. *Kesh* is uncut hair, which is placed in a top-knot by boys and men. Men usually wear a turban over the hair and women a long Indian scarf. The hair must be kept tidy with a *kangha*, the comb. The *kachh* are white shorts, now usually worn under clothes. At the time of Guru Gobind Singh, shorts gave more freedom of movement for self-defence than other Indian clothes. The *kirpan* was originally a sword but may now be small enough to be worn on the comb under the turban. It shows a willingness to help the weak and defend the truth. ■

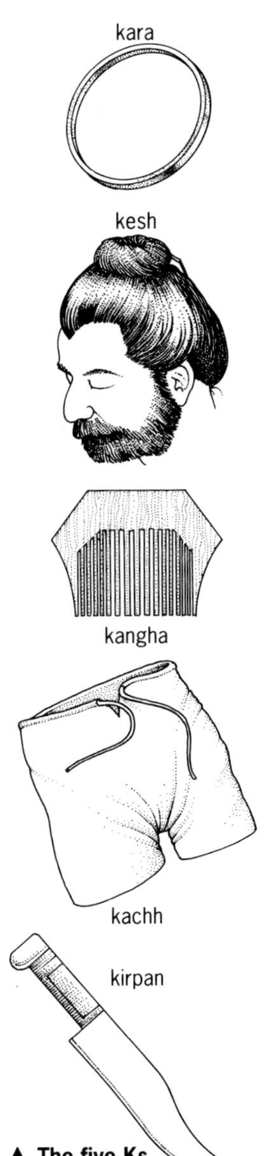

▲ **The five Ks.**

◄ **The Golden Temple is at Amritsar in the Punjab, India. It is built on an island in a lake and its domes, covered in gold foil, are reflected in the waters. Both the lake and the temple are sacred to Sikh people.**

See also
Diwali
Festivals
Gurdwaras
Hindus
Pilgrimages

Biography
Gobind Singh
Nanak

Silicon

See also
Bricks
Computers
Glass
Minerals
Pottery
Rocks

Silicon is everywhere around us. It is found in sand, glass, pottery and bricks. It is one of the most common elements in the Earth's crust, but it is only found joined with other substances as a compound.

These compounds are known as silicates. Most rocks contain silicates, and so do sand and clay. Pure silicon is a hard, shiny, brown-black chemical made up of crystals.

Purified silicon is used in making microprocessors or 'silicon chips'. These tiny wafer-thin slices of silicon contain many complicated electrical circuits. Without 'silicon chips' there would be no computers, pocket calculators or digital watches.

Silicones are chemicals made from silicon. They are widely used as polishes and lubricants. Quartz crystals, which contain silicon, are also used in many watches. ■

Silk

See also
Moths
Pupae
Spinning
Weaving

Silk is a luxurious material which costs a lot of money to buy. This is because the manufacture of silk is a slow process involving a lot of hard work. The thread comes from the cocoon of the silkworm. It is so fine that a very large number of threads are required for every centimetre of woven fabric. However, the end result is very strong and long-lasting. Silk is even used in the nose cone of the supersonic aircraft, Concorde.

Life cycle of silkworms

The silkworms hatch from the 400–500 tiny eggs laid in spring by the moth *Bombyx mori*. This moth feeds exclusively on mulberry leaves and so do the silkworms. The silkworms start off about 2 mm (0·08 in) in length and spend the first four or five weeks of their lives eating. During this time they grow about 8 cm (3 in). They shed their skin about four times as they grow out of it. When they reach their maximum size they start the next stage in their lives and produce cocoons. The silkworm produces threads from two glands in its head. The threads mix with a gummy material which helps to form the cocoon by sticking the threads together. When the cocoon is formed it is about 3 cm (1¼ in) in length. The silkworm then changes, inside the cocoon, first into a pupa and then into a moth. The moth breaks out of the cocoon. It will mate and the female will lay her eggs to begin the cycle over again.

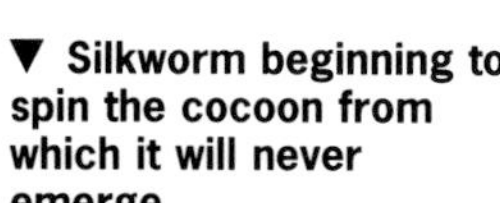

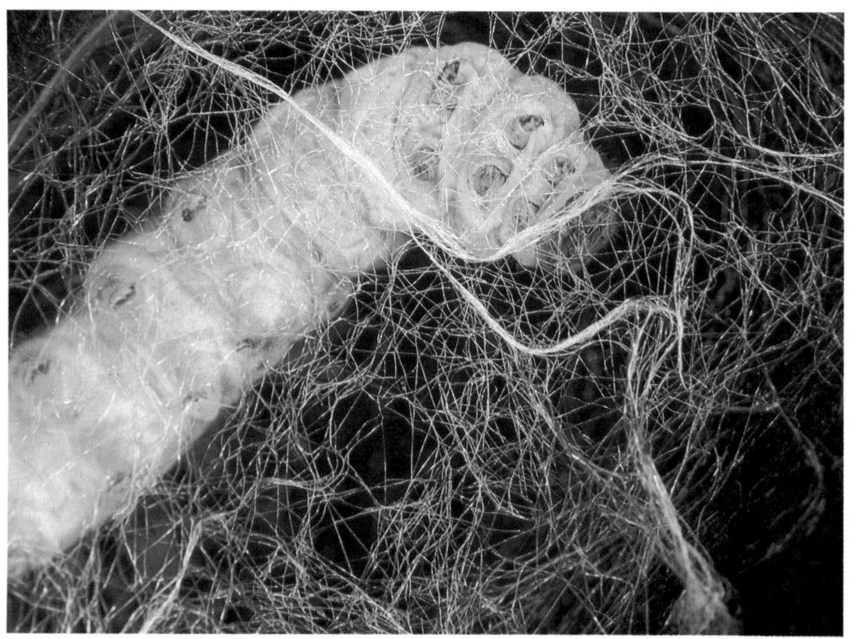

▼ Silkworm beginning to spin the cocoon from which it will never emerge.

Making silk

In order to have complete cocoons from which to unwind the silk threads the pupa must be killed, because if it grew into a moth it would break the cocoon as it emerged, which would ruin it. Hot air or steam is used to do this. The cocoon is put into hot water to soften the sticky gum. It is brushed to find the end of the two threads which form the cocoon. These are joined to the threads of another cocoon to form one complete silk thread. This thread is reeled off and wound into skeins ready to be woven into silk fabric. The thread can be twisted in various ways to make different kinds of materials.

Flashback

Silk was first produced in the Far East over 4,000 years ago. The Chinese empress Xi Ling is said to have discovered that the cocoons on her mulberry bush could be unwound to produce a fine fibre. The way in which silk was produced was kept as a closely guarded secret. Silk was brought to the West by early traders along the 'silk road' from the East to Venice and other busy trading ports. Only the nobles and very rich people could afford silk for their clothes. Elizabeth I of England lists silk clothes among her wardrobe records. Far Eastern countries still supply much of the silk used in the world today. ■

Silver

Some silver is found in the pure state, particularly in Mexico and Argentina. In Australia, parts of South America, the USA, Canada and some other countries, silver is found combined with other substances.

Articles made of silver, gold, or platinum must be tested and hallmarked before sale. From 1300 hallmarking was done at Goldsmith's Hall, London. Now there are four Assay (testing) offices.
The hallmark has:
maker's mark
lion guarantees 92·5% silver
city mark
anchor (Birmingham), leopard (London), castle (Edinburgh), crown (Sheffield)
letter signifying year date

Silver is a brilliant white shining metal. Along with gold and platinum, it is one of our precious metals.

Uses of silver

Silver is widely used to make jewellery, tableware and ornaments. It is also used to coat other cheaper metals in what is called silver-plating. Silver can easily be beaten into shape or be given a highly polished surface. Nothing else reflects light as well as silver. For this reason, it is used to coat mirrors. Silver is also a good conductor of electricity. It is used in the electrical switches in telephones, computers and other electronic equipment. One big drawback of silver, however, is that it quickly tarnishes (turns black) in polluted city air.

Many nations have at various times used silver coins. Nowadays, though, alloys of other metals are often used instead, except for coins to celebrate special events.

Silver in photography

When silver is combined with certain other substances, such as chlorine and iodine, it forms salts which are very sensitive to light. If a light shines on them, they turn black. Because of this, large quantities of silver are used to make the films and special papers used in photography. ■

▲ This bottletop hallmark shows: CM, the maker's mark; an anchor for Birmingham; the lion for quality; d signifying 1802.

See also
Alloys
Gold
Metals

Singapore

Area
618 sq km
(239 sq miles)
Capital
Singapore
Population
2,586,200
Language
Chinese, Malay, Tamil, English
Religion
Buddhist, Christian, Taoist, Hindu, Muslim
Government
Republic
Currency
1 Singapore dollar
= 100 cents

Singapore is one of the smallest countries in the world. But it is densely populated, rich and successful. There is a main island called Singapore where most of the people live, and over 50 smaller islands. The Equator is only 140 km (90 miles) away to the south, so the weather is always hot and humid and rainstorms are common.

Singapore City is a mass of skyscrapers. At the centre are offices, banks, hotels and government buildings. Further out are huge blocks of flats. The government encourages builders to build upwards to save land. But there are still areas of older houses, dwarfed by the skyscrapers.

Outside the city there are a few villages left, and farmland with neat vegetable plots and orchards. But there is not enough land to grow food, and most is imported. Marshy land is being gradually reclaimed to provide more space for homes and industry. The people of Singapore earn their living by working in factories, making clothes, electrical goods, books and other things, and by trade. Singapore has a modern system of roads and motorways and a new underground railway. The island is joined to Malaysia by a road on a causeway. Both the port and airport are among the busiest in the world.

Singapore means 'lion city'.

Flashback

In 1819 a British officer, Sir Stamford Raffles, rented the island from the Sultan of Johore. It became a busy port and an important British naval base. In World War II the Japanese attacked overland and captured the colony in 1942. Singapore became an independent state in 1959. It joined the Federation of Malaysia in 1963, but left in 1965 to become an independent republic. ■

In the years before it became a famous port, Singapore was known as Tumasik, which means 'sea town'.

See also
British empire
Commonwealth
Malaysia

Singing and songs

▲ **To communicate their feelings to the audience, opera singers must express themselves through their gestures as well as their voice.**

Singing is making music with the human voice. A song is a poem set to music which expresses different emotions and different experiences – like love or despair, going to war, having a night out, playing a game or putting a child to sleep. Most songs are accompanied by instruments such as the guitar or piano, but some of the most effective songs stand alone, without accompaniment.

Castrato
This is an adult male soprano who has been castrated in youth so that his voice does not break and remains high. Some of the greatest singers of the 18th century were castrati but nowadays this terrible practice has been abandoned.

Magical songs
Singing has always been associated with religion and magic. Priests and sorcerers have always used singing or chanting to give power to their prayers or spells. Christians sing hymns.

How we sing

The human voice is often compared to a wind instrument. We breathe a column of air up from the lungs. The air passes across the vocal cords, which are tiny folds of muscle in the larynx, so that they vibrate in sound waves similar to those created when a guitar string is plucked. These vibrations are then amplified in the cavities of the throat, the mouth and the sinuses on either side of the nose and above the eyes. Finally the tongue and the lips alter the shape of the sound to produce vowels and consonants which make up words.

The special quality of a voice depends on the size and shape of the larynx and the resonating cavities of the throat, mouth and head, as well as how the sound is produced. Training a person to be a singer can take many years and pop and jazz singers are now realizing the importance of using their voice in the right kind of way for their music.

Breathing

The basis of singing is how we use our breath. This means being able to take in air into all parts of the lungs, and letting it out steadily with the support of the rib muscles and the diaphragm, which is a sheet of muscle beneath the lungs. Most people pick up bad breathing habits very early, and a good voice teacher will spend a lot of time establishing a steady breathing technique.

Pitch

We do not have direct control over the pitch of the sounds we sing. Our minds first imagine the pitch of the note we want, and then the brain sends out a message through the motor nerves to the vocal cords which causes them to shorten or lengthen as they vibrate and so produce a higher or a lower note.

Resonance

Many singing teachers talk about a 'head' or a 'chest' voice. Someone who sings in a head voice will feel vibrations in the mouth and head cavities, while in a chest voice, we seem to feel vibrations in the chest area. For a note like A above middle C, a classical singer will normally use a head voice, which gives a much purer sound than that of a jazz or pop singer, who will use the chest register for a note of exactly the same pitch.

► **Michael Jackson has become well known for his high voice and unique style of singing.**

Type and range of voice

Most children have high voices. As they get older, boys' voices change and gradually become lower from around the ages of 13 to 16. Girls' voices also change very slightly, though they do not break in the same way. Men generally have longer and thicker vocal cords than women and their vocal range is about an octave lower. Some male altos or counter-tenors are also able to sing in an upper register using a falsetto voice. There are a number of sub-groups within the main voices of soprano, mezzo-soprano, contralto, tenor, baritone and bass. For instance a coloratura soprano or a jazz singer who can 'scat', can sing very high notes, while a dramatic soprano is able to give weight and substance to the long, sustained emotional phrases of an aria from an opera.

Styles of singing

As singing is very much to do with expressing emotions, singers combine the techniques they have learnt with the best way of putting over a particular song. Classically trained singers base their interpretation of a song on the notation written by the composer, but all singers bring their personality to performance.

Jazz, rock and pop singers are much more ready and able to use a song as a basis for an individual way of putting over a number. They may swing and syncopate the rhythm, improvise on the chord changes, move into different keys and create their own endings. A 'standard' may be sung up-tempo and with a Latin rhythm by one artist and in a slow blues style by another.

▲ Gospel singing can be highly emotive and is an expression of religious faith.

Cultural differences

Singers in different parts of the world have also developed singing styles which are most suited to their music. Arabic singers, whether in North Africa or the Middle East, have a high nasal quality. Many folk musicians such as country and western singers often use a nasal twang to gain a different effect. Soul singers have voices with a range and resonance that are almost a mixture between blues and opera. ■

◀ A group of Kenyan women singing.

See also
African music
Breathing
Choirs
Country and western music
Folk music
Jazz
Music
Operas
Pop and rock music
Sound
Voice

Skeletons

► **Frogs, like other back-boned animals, have their skeletons inside their bodies. A frog has very large back legs for leaping out of danger and to catch its prey.**

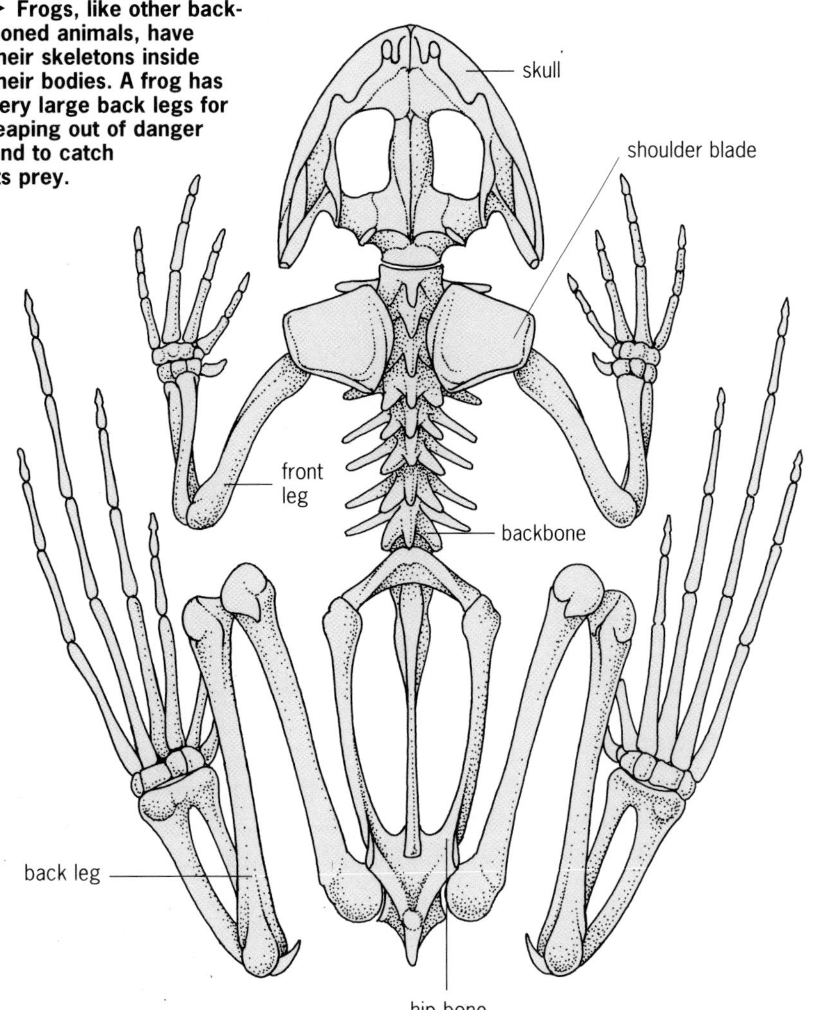

► **Hinge and ball-and-socket joints are the main joints in backboned animals. Hinge joints allow movement in two directions (experiment with your elbow). Ball-and-socket joints allow movement in many directions (experiment with your shoulder). Crayfish, crabs, insects and spiders have an outside skeleton. It is made of a stiff, often hard substance called cuticle. There is thin, flexible cuticle at the joints to allow movement.**

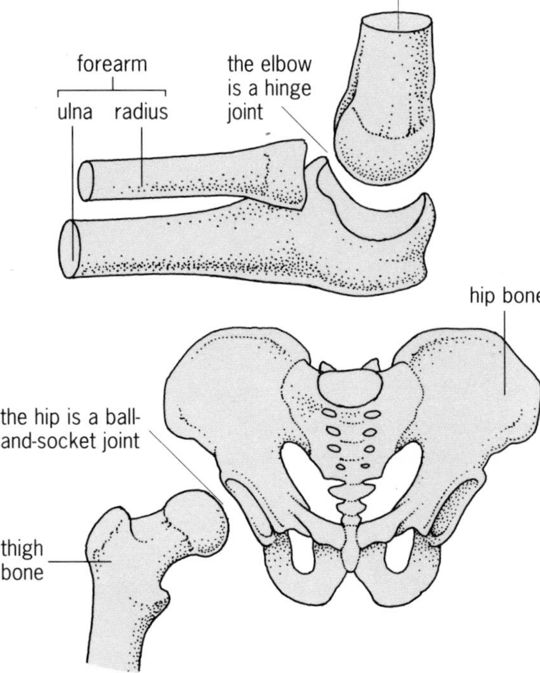

See also
Bones
Fractures
Human body
Invertebrates
Vertebrates

A skeleton is a stiff scaffolding which supports the soft parts of an animal. Without skeletons most animals would be sagging, floppy objects with no distinct shape. Skeletons enable animals to have a wide range of body shapes, with distinct parts to move and carry out separate functions. Without skeletons, swimming, running, picking things up and chewing would be virtually impossible.

Fish, amphibians, reptiles, birds and mammals (the vertebrates) have skeletons of bone and cartilage. All vertebrates have a backbone made up of a chain of vertebrae, and a skull. Most also have four limbs: legs, arms, wings or fins.

The skull and backbone support and protect the central parts of the nervous system, the brain and the spinal cord. In fish, reptiles, birds and mammals the ribs curve round to form the rib cage that protects the heart, guts and lungs. The shoulder and hip are bony connections between the backbone and the limbs. In different land animals the basic five-toed end of the limb has been adapted in many ways. In the horse, for instance, each leg has only a single functional toe, with a hoof (the toe-nail) at its tip.

Joints

Muscles and joints enable bony skeletons to make complicated movements. Joints are the bending and sliding places where bones touch. Muscles are joined to bones by tendons, and where muscles contract they move the bones in relation to each other. Different types of joint allow different sorts of movement. The ends of bones that touch at joints are usually covered in smooth, lubricated cartilage so they move over each other easily.

Other skeletons

Animals without backbones (invertebrates) do not have bony skeletons. Worms, snails and shellfish, for instance, have taut, fluid-filled bags inside their bodies to support them; just as a rubber glove becomes firm when filled with water.

Other invertebrates such as crabs, lobsters, spiders and insects have a surface skeleton. Their soft inner bodies are supported by a stiff, jointed skin (a cuticle) on the outside, which gives them their shape. As the cuticle is hard it does not allow growth. As it grows the animal must shed its cuticle. Underneath is a new soft cuticle which allows growth until it hardens. The animal will have to shed its cuticle a number of times before it is fully grown. ■

Skiing

▲ **In slalom racing skiers have to weave between sets of poles, or 'gates'. As long as both feet pass through the gate the racer is allowed to nudge or even knock over the gate poles. This skier has cut in close to the pole, angling the hips in order to give better control in the turn.**

Skiing is travelling over snow on long, narrow runners which curve up at the front. The most popular form of skiing is Alpine skiing (downhill) in which the skier glides swiftly down steep mountain runs. In slalom the skiers weave skilfully through a series of poles called 'gates'. Nordic skiing includes cross-country skiing (langlauf) and ski-jumping. In freestyle skiing backflips, kicks and other acrobatics are performed. The finest skiers have great strength, quick reactions, and excellent balance.

Ski equipment consists of skis, made of metal and plastic, and ski poles. These have discs a few centimetres from the points to prevent them sinking too deeply into the snow. Stiff plastic boots with a comfortable lining support the feet and ankles. Special clamps called 'bindings' secure the boots to the skis.

The first skiers were the peoples of northern Europe in prehistoric times, who used it as a method of transport. Skiing developed as a sport around 1850 in Norway. ■

The fastest skier
Michael Prufer (Monaco)
224 km/h, 16 April 1988

The major competitions are the World Cup and the Winter Olympics.

Longest ski-jump
Piotr Fijas (Poland) jumped 194 m, 14 March 1987

The oldest ski found in a peat bog in Sweden dates back to 2500 BC.

See also
Biography
Sports special

Skin

Skin is our protective outer surface. It covers all the body and is made up of several layers. The lowest layer is living and makes all the other layers. The skin surface is made up of dead skin cells. It is kept supple by an oily substance made by the skin. The skin also makes hairs and removes sweat from the blood. Some skin cells contain a dark pigment called melanin. People with dark skins have more of these than people with light skins. These dark cells protect us from skin cancer, as they block the dangerous ultraviolet rays in sunlight. ■

Moles and freckles are made up of clusters of cells containing melanin.

See also
Fur
Hair

▼ **A small piece of skin (magnified). The upper dead layer of skin wears away every time you touch anything. But a layer of live dividing cells replaces it as fast as it is removed. It also repairs cuts and other damage.**

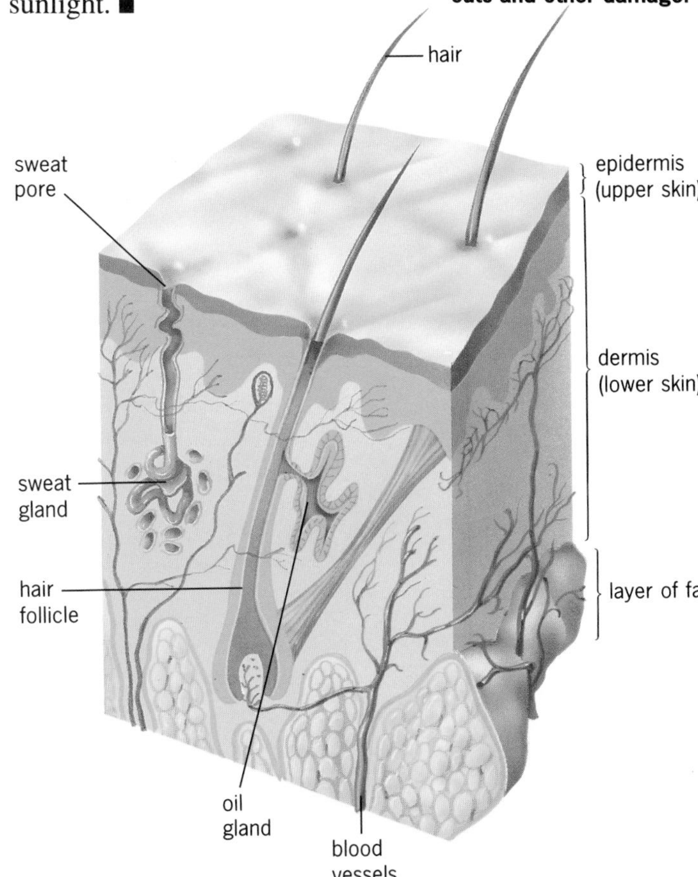

Skunks

Size Length up to 68 cm
Weight Up to 3 kg
Number of young 2–9
Lifespan About 7 years

Subphylum Vertebrata
Class Mammalia
Order Carnivora
Family Mustelidae
Number of species 9

Skunks are members of the weasel family and live in America. Their fur is coloured black with white stripes or spots, and acts as a warning to predators. If a skunk is attacked it defends itself by banging its front feet loudly on the ground and then doing a handstand and squirting a foul-smelling fluid from stink glands just beneath its tail. Most animals leave skunks well alone. ■

See also
Badgers
Fur (photo)
Otters
Weasels

Slaves

Slaves are men and women who are somebody else's property. Their owner can buy and sell them just like any object. There have been slaves in many different parts of the world, and in many different times in history. There are still slaves today in parts of northern Africa.

Slaves in ancient Greece and Rome

The ancient Egyptians used people they had conquered as slaves, just as the Greeks and the Romans did. Slavery continued in Egypt until the late 19th century.

In ancient Greece, slaves often worked in rich people's houses. Women slaves cooked and cleaned, and served the lady of the house. They entertained guests at feasts as flute girls and dancers. Male slaves in Athens sometimes kept order in the streets like policemen. In Sparta the slaves were Helots, the people who had lived in the area before the Spartans arrived and took their land. Helots were forced to do all the hard, heavy work, so that Spartan men could become highly trained fighters.

The Romans too used slaves to run their homes, and to do hard and sometimes dangerous jobs.

► These shackles were found in a silver mine near Athens, so it is fairly certain that slaves worked there.

▼ A Mediterranean galley in the 17th century. Five slaves are working each oar and overseers with sticks are supervising them from a central plank.

Slaves were farm labourers and miners. They trained as gladiators who fought each other, or wild animals, to entertain huge crowds in Roman theatres. Slaves built the aqueduct which supplied Rome with water. Some slaves were well educated. They ran shops, and became secretaries and important government servants.

Slaves won their freedom sometimes, but these 'freedmen' did not have as many rights as people who were born free. There were harsh punishments such as whipping for disobedient slaves. If owners caught escaped slaves they often branded them on the forehead, and the mark stayed for life. For bad crimes like murder, slaves were thrown to wild animals. Spartacus was a slave who led a rebellion in the 1st century BC. When he was defeated, he and over 6,000 other slaves were crucified along the Appian Way, the main road into Rome.

The Middle Ages

When the Roman empire broke up, slaves began gradually to disappear in northern Europe. Instead of keeping slaves in their castles, powerful barons gave the people who worked for them a little land to live on. In return, these 'serfs' had to work for their lord for fixed times, and could not leave their land. They were not bought and sold, but otherwise they were like slaves.

Slavery did not disappear in the Mediterranean. Slaves there were often black Africans or Slavs from the Balkans and further east. The word 'slave' comes from them. Many became human engines in huge warships called galleys which were driven by long rows of heavy oars. A slave was chained to an oar for the whole voyage.

Slavery in Africa

Through the centuries, there have been slaves in the huge continent of Africa. In East Africa, Arab traders sent slaves to Arabia and Asia, probably from the 12th century. In North Africa from the 15th century, Muslims used white European Christians as slaves.

Some of the peoples of West Africa lived in villages; others in well organized towns like Benin. Many were skilled craftsmen and farmers, so prisoners taken in wars between different tribes made useful slaves. In the 15th century European explorers reached West Africa. They discovered they could buy African slaves easily, and sell them across the Atlantic in the Caribbean, Brazil, and North America.

The Caribbean and America

When Europeans discovered the Americas, they soon found they could make a lot of money growing sugar in the West Indies and Brazil. But the wars and diseases they brought with them had killed off most of the native peoples there, so they needed workers. Growing sugar was hard, hot work, and Europeans were not prepared to do it themselves. Slaves from Africa solved their problem. Africans worked long hours cutting tough sugar canes under the blazing sun, and in the hot sugar boiling sheds. From the late 17th century, slaves were also working in tobacco and cotton plantations, in North America.

The owners' comfortable lifestyle depended on the slaves. Slaves worked in their houses, cooking, cleaning, and caring for their children. Slaves looked after their horses and carriages and tended their pleasant gardens. Since slaves were so useful, owners sometimes treated them quite well. But they were harsh and cruel when they feared trouble. Owners were often afraid. There were soon many more slaves than Europeans.

Slaves did not accept their lives easily. Their gospel songs (spirituals) remind us how they longed for Africa, and hated their captivity. Sometimes they rebelled.

In Jamaica many slaves escaped to hidden villages away from the plantations. They were known as Maroons. Often they fought off soldiers who were sent to capture them. In Haiti, an army made up mainly of former slaves defeated the French and British and set up an independent country in 1804.

Slavery was becoming less profitable in the early 19th century and at the same time many white Americans and Europeans were beginning to realize how wrong it was. The British parliament passed a law abolishing slavery throughout the empire in 1833. It came into effect the following year. But some slaves in British colonies were not completely free until 1838.

In the USA there were few slaves in the Northern states by this time, but Americans in the Southern states fought for the right to own slaves. In 1863 during the American Civil War Abraham Lincoln issued a proclamation for the emancipation of slaves. Two years later, after the end of the war, the Congress of the USA abolished slavery throughout the USA. ■

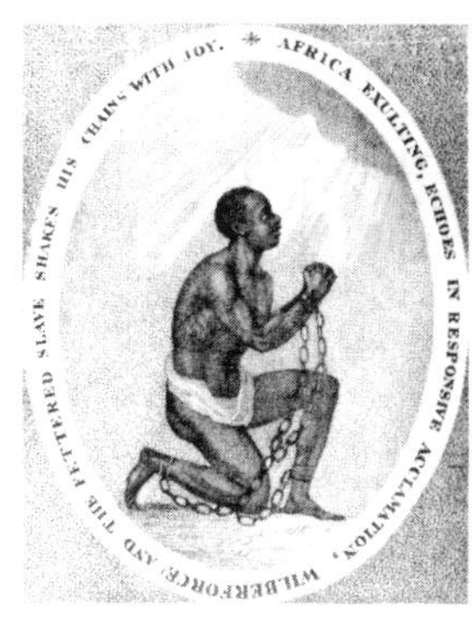

▲ Symbol of the campaign led by Wilberforce to abolish slavery.

Abolition of slavery

French colonies	1848
Puerto Rico	1873
Cuba	1886
Brazil	1888

◀ This photograph of slaves was taken in 1862 on James Hopkinson's estate, South Carolina. They would have been made free by 1865.

See also

African history
American Civil War
American colonial history
Caribbean history
Greek ancient history
Slave trade
USA: history

Biography

Lincoln
Stowe
Toussaint l'Ouverture
Tubman
Wilberforce

Slave trade

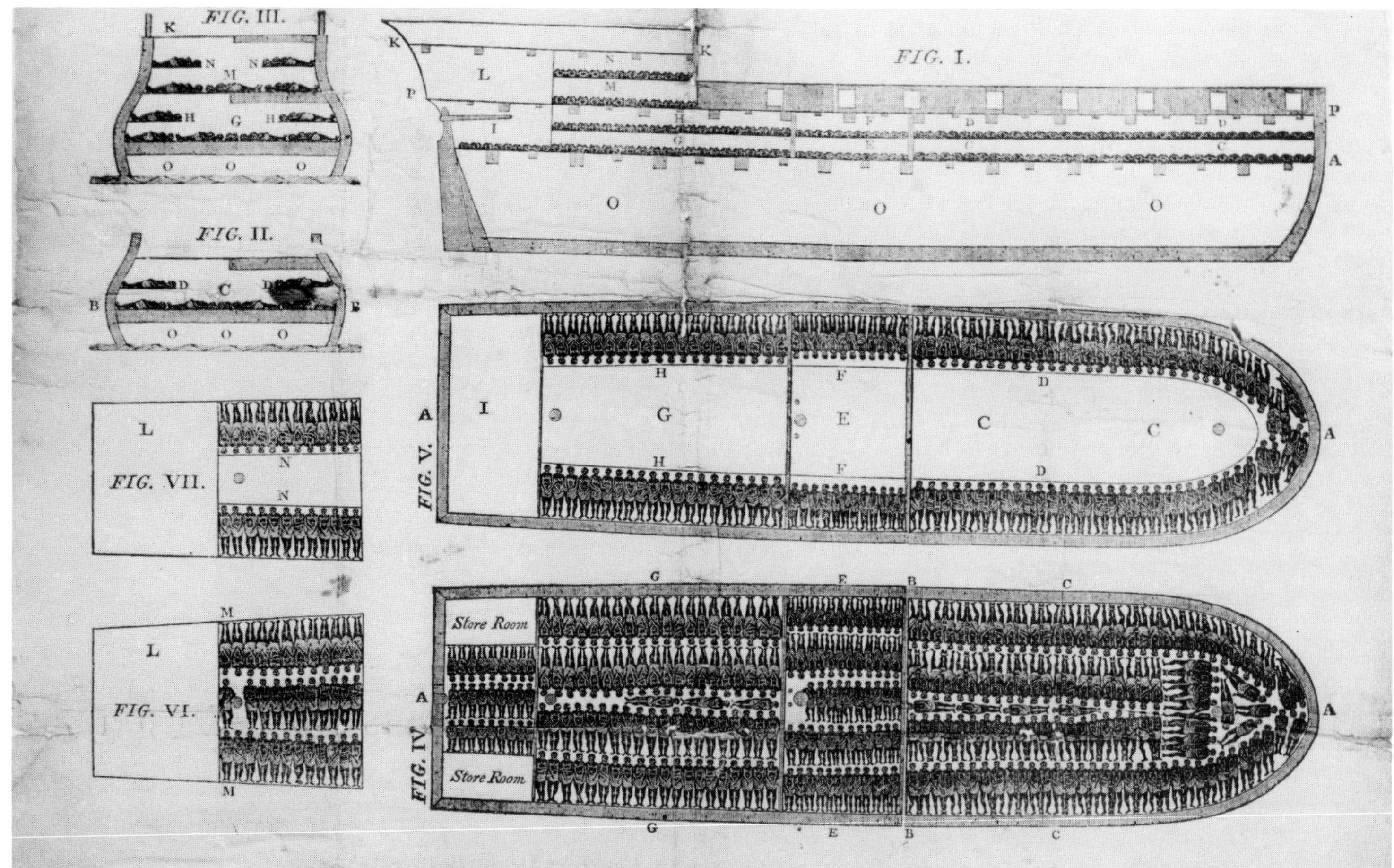

▲ **This is a plan of a slave ship which William Wilberforce showed to the British parliament during his long struggle to kill the slave trade. An observer in 1788 wrote: 'The slaves lie in two rows close to each other like books in a shelf . . . the poor creatures are in irons . . . which makes it difficult for them to turn or move . . . without hurting themselves or each other.'**

In ancient Athens, there was a slave auction in the market-place. Slaves stood on a revolving platform, with placards of information round their necks. Buyers inspected and prodded them; the sellers noisily did all they could to make the buyers compete against each other and pay a high price for the slave they wanted. Rome had a slave market too.

Centuries later, Africans transported across the Atlantic were sold in auctions in Brazil, the Caribbean and North America. Shipowners from several European countries made huge profits out of this cruel trade. By the 18th century the British were making the biggest profits of all.

The route of the British slave trade was like a triangle. On the first stage, ships from Liverpool and Bristol sailed to West Africa, carrying cheap iron goods, beads and guns. The ship captains exchanged these goods for Africans who had been captured by local slave traders.

The second stage was the terrible 'middle passage' across the Atlantic. The ships were packed with slaves. They lay chained together on the dark, stuffy lower decks in horrible conditions, for a journey which could last six weeks. Many died on the way. The slaves who survived were sold by auction.

The empty ships then took on a new cargo for the third side of the triangle: the voyage back to Britain. They carried sugar, tobacco and raw cotton produced on the slave plantations. Slave owners and slave traders did well out of the slave trade. The sufferers were the 20 million or more black Africans transported from their homes to America and the Caribbean.

Abolition

In the end, some people realized the misery the trade caused. It began to make less money too, as the sugar trade became less important. Denmark abolished the trade first. Britain followed with a law passed in 1807 and the USA banned the trade in 1808. Gradually the Atlantic slave trade stopped, but slaves were still bought and sold by American and Caribbean owners until slavery itself was made unlawful. ■

See also
African history
Caribbean history
Slaves

Biography
Wilberforce

Slavs

Russian, Bulgarian and Serbian are written in the Cyrillic alphabet (similar to Greek). The people in these countries were converted to Christianity by missionaries from the Greek Orthodox Church. Polish and Czech are written in the Roman alphabet. Catholic missionaries took Christianity and, with it, the skills of writing to northern and central Europe.

Slavs are people who live mainly in eastern and central Europe. Russians, Bulgarians, Poles, Czechs, Slovaks and Serbs are all Slavonic people. They speak languages which are similar to one another and have developed from the same root language. The first Slavonic tribes moved into eastern Europe from Asia about 4,000 years ago. These tribes were peaceful and hospitable farmers who reared sheep and cattle and worshipped nature gods.

In the 19th century many Slavs wanted to unite together to form one country. This movement was known as Pan-Slavism (meaning all Slavs). But the different Slavonic countries had their own traditions. The movement succeeded only among southern Slavs; in 1918 the country of Yugoslavia was created to include Serbia and five other nationalities. Czechoslovakia was formed at the same time out of Czech and Slovak lands that had been ruled as part of the Austro-Hungarian empire until its defeat in World War I. Between the world wars the Slavonic states were independent; from 1945 to 1989 they were controlled by the USSR and forced to have communist governments. ■

The word slave comes from Slav, because these people were often taken prisoner and enslaved, first by German knights in the early Middle Ages and later by Ottoman Turks.

See also
Bulgaria
Czechoslovakia
Poland
Russia's history
Slaves
USSR
Yugoslavia

Sleep

Newborn babies do not have a night/day sleep pattern. They wake up at regular intervals during night and day. They sleep for about 16 hours in all. Adults need to sleep for between 7 and 8 hours a night.

We do not really understand why we sleep. It may be that the body needs sleep to recover and repair damage.

We all tend to sleep during the night and wake during the day. The night/day pattern of sleep is called the circadian rhythm.

What happens when we fall asleep?

During sleep, heart and breathing rates slow down and muscles relax. Our senses fade. Sight goes first, then hearing and last touch. Our hearing is selective when we are sleeping. A loud noise may not wake someone, but whispering their own name may; parents will often wake at their baby's cry when other people sleep undisturbed. No one yet understands how our brain selects in this way.

Sleep-walking is quite common in children. It usually happens early in the night during deep sleep. About 1 in 7 five- to twelve-year-olds will sleep-walk at least once.

Stages of sleep

Scientists study sleep by measuring the pattern of electrical currents in the brain. They have found that there are four levels of sleep that alternate through the night. We dream during lightest sleep, while making rapid eye movements. ■

See also
Dreams

Sloths

◀ This three-toed sloth and its young will probably move less than 40 m in a day. The young will be carried by its mother for 9 months.

Sloths are upside-down animals, hanging with huge, curved claws from the branches of tropical trees. They can eat, sleep, mate and give birth in this position and very rarely descend to the ground, where they are nearly helpless. There are two groups of sloths; those with two toes on their front feet, and those with three. They look similar, but it is thought that they are not closely related.

Sloths have long coarse hair which is grooved. Tiny plants live in the grooves. They give the sloth a greenish tinge, which acts as a camouflage. Special insects feed on these plants. ■

Distribution
Tropical forests of Central and South America
Size
Head and body length about 70 cm
Weight
Up to 8 kg
Number of young
1
Lifespan
12 years in the wild, but at least 31 in captivity

Subphylum Vertebrata
Class Mammalia
Order Edentata
Number of species 5

See also
Anteaters
Armadillos
Feet and hands

Slugs and snails

To most people, slugs and snails are slow, slimy pests. While it is true that neither slugs nor snails can move very fast, only a few kinds are serious pests.

► **Like snails, slugs are also hermaphrodites (have both male and female sex organs). These mating slugs are exchanging sperm; later both will lay eggs. The breathing hole can be seen clearly on one slug.**

The great difference between snails and slugs is that in times of danger the snail can pull its soft body into a single, usually coiled shell. Sea snails usually have heavy shells, as the shell is supported by the water. An exception is the sea butterflies, which live in the surface waters of the oceans and have shells as fragile as fine glass. Slugs may have a small shell, or an internal shell, but never one in which they can take refuge.

In most other ways snails and slugs are very similar. Both glide along on a large, muscular foot. Slugs and land snails ease their way with slime, which you can see after the animal has passed. Both snails and slugs have simple eyes, which are sometimes on tentacles. They may also have other tentacles which help them to feel and smell. Both slugs and snails have a mouth on the underside of the head. This contains very many tiny teeth. A garden snail may have about 14,000 teeth in its mouth. They are arranged in rows on a ribbon-like tongue, which is called a radula. This works like a file, to rasp away at food.

Garden snails and slugs eat mostly decaying plants. This is why you rarely notice the damage they do in the countryside, or in an untidy garden, where there is plenty of waste. It is only when all the dead and dying material has been cleared away that they eat tender seedlings and young leaves. Some snails and slugs feed on other animals and have fewer, but stronger teeth on their radulae. On the seashore you may sometimes find a mussel or other bivalve shell with a neat hole bored in it. This is the work of the necklace shell or one of its relatives, which rasps through the armour of the bivalve to get at the helpless animal inside. The cone shells, which are tropical sea snails, even feed on fish. These are stilled with a nerve poison injected by a single, hypodermic-like tooth at the end of the radula.

Strangest of all are the sea slugs, which include some of the most brightly coloured of all animals. Though these are soft-bodied, they are far from helpless. Most feed on jellyfish and sea anemones. They are immune to the stings of such creatures, and are even able to transfer these stings to their own skins for protection, though nobody is sure how they do this. ■

Distribution
Most live in the sea, but some live in fresh water and some on land, even in deserts.
Largest sea snail
The baler shell, from the Australian Barrier Reef, 60 cm long
Largest land snail
Giant land snail, *Achatina fulica*, originally from Africa, now found in many parts of the tropics, up to 30 cm long
Some uses of snails and slugs
As food, for mother of pearl from the shells, for dye from the colours which some produce

Phylum
Mollusca
Class
Gastropoda
Number of species
More than 35,000

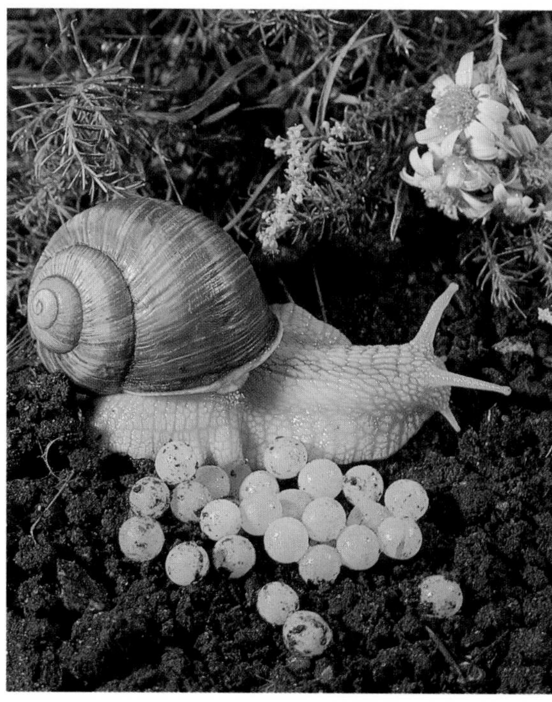

► **Roman snail and its eggs. Land snails are all hermaphrodites (have both male and female sex organs) and so every one produces eggs.**

►► **Baby garden snails hatching. Their shells will grow as they do, so they have the same shell throughout their lives.**

See also
Invertebrates
Jellyfish
Molluscs

Smoking

People smoke tobacco either as cigarettes, cigars or in a pipe, and they smoke for a variety of reasons. But there is now clear proof from studies comparing the health of smokers with that of non-smokers, that smoking causes ill health and early death.

About 100,000 people die each year in Britain as a direct result of smoking. This is seven times as many as die in road accidents.

The total number of cigarettes produced in the world in one year is about 9,900 billion.

Snuff is another tobacco product. It is a brownish coloured preparation of powdered tobacco which is inhaled through the nostrils. It was much more commonly used in the 18th and 19th centuries than it is today.

Tobacco smoke contains tar with chemicals that cause cancers of the lungs, mouth, gullet and bladder. Tar also damages microscopic hairs (cilia) which filter air going into the lungs, and irritates air passages, making them sore and causing bronchitis. It contains nicotine which damages the heart and blood vessels. This causes heart disease and other illnesses. Nicotine is also an addictive drug, which makes it hard for people to give up smoking.

Ninety per cent of lung cancers are caused by smoking, and 95 per cent of people with bronchitis are smokers.

Passive smoking

Tobacco smoke can harm non-smokers. When someone does not smoke themselves but must live or work with people who smoke we say they are passive smokers. Passive smokers suffer higher rates of lung cancer and heart disease than do those non-smokers who live and work with other non-smokers.

Smokers are at least twice as likely to die of heart disease as non-smokers.

Fifty million working days are lost in Britain each year because of poor health caused by smoking.

Flashback

American Indians smoked for pleasure but also for ceremonial reasons and in religious rituals. The Aztec king, Moctezuma, used to smoke a pipe of scented tobacco after feasts. The Spaniards introduced tobacco to Europe in the 16th century. The habit spread rapidly. At the time many people believed smoking was good for them. Others thought it was a vice.

Columbus saw Amerindian people on Cuba using 'smoking reeds'.

Portuguese sailors introduced smoking to Japan and the East Indies.

James I of England imposed heavy duties (taxes) on imported tobacco.

At first people in Britain smoked tobacco in clay pipes. They did not start smoking cigarettes till after the Crimean War in the mid-19th century, having adopted the idea from the Russians. It was not until this century that it became acceptable for women to smoke in public. ■

See also
Addiction
Drugs
Tobacco

Smugglers

Smugglers are criminals who avoid paying taxes when moving goods from one country to another. These taxes are called 'customs duties'. To avoid paying duties, and restrictions on the movement of goods, smugglers use all sorts of tricks. Mostly these involve concealing things in unlikely places. Modern smugglers use cases with false bottoms, cars and lorries with secret compartments, and even the insides of their own bodies. It is forbidden for individuals to bring drugs or guns into most countries, so these are often smuggled. Narcotics (drugs), arms, and currency (money) are the most commonly smuggled goods.

When they travel between countries adults are usually allowed to buy a certain amount of goods at a special 'duty free' shop to take with them. If, however, someone exceeds the 'duty free' limit and does not declare it to the customs officers, they become smugglers themselves. There are severe punishments for such smugglers.

From 1993 the European Community will have no customs barriers between its member states. All citizens of these states will be able to move goods freely from one European Community country to another. This change is intended to encourage trade between the twelve countries of the European Community, but it will also bring an end to smuggling between them.

Flashback

Smuggling was particularly common in the 18th century. At that time tea, spirits, spices and silks carried high duties. More of these were probably taken into England by smugglers than by honest traders. Coffee was smuggled in Europe, and tobacco was smuggled everywhere. In villages close to the English Channel, smuggling was often a major occupation. Violent clashes took place between smugglers and the 'Excise men' sent to catch them.

Excise is any tax but especially one that is charged on goods before they are sold to the public. The Excise men are the people who collect this tax.

Smuggling has caused at least one war. In 1839 when the Chinese tried to stop the smuggling of opium (a drug), this caused the 'Opium War' with the British. When alcohol was banned in the USA (Prohibition, 1920–1933), it was smuggled into that country by land and sea. Crime increased and gangsters flourished. ■

See also
Crimes
Customs and excise
Drugs
European Community
Taxes
Trade

Snakes

▲ **Green python, native to north-east Australia and New Guinea.**

Distribution
In all habitats, including the sea, in warm parts of the world
Largest
Anaconda, may grow up to 10 m in length
Smallest
Thread snake, less than 12 cm in length
Most poisonous
Australian tiger snakes, taipans and kraits
Fastest-moving
The black mamba can travel at 16–19 km/h in short bursts over flat ground.
Lifespan
An Indian python survived for over 34 years in a zoo. Lifespan in the wild is unknown.

Subphylum Vertebrata
Class Reptilia
Order Squamata
Number of species Over 2,000

Most snakes move by throwing their bodies into curves which push against any unevenness of the ground. Snakes which move in this way are helpless on smooth surfaces. Snakes are so long and thin that their bodies are not wide enough for all the internal organs that other vertebrates have, so snakes have only one very long lung, instead of two.

In cool parts of the world snakes hibernate during winter. In spring they look for mates. Males often compete with each other or display to females. After mating, most female snakes lay eggs, although some do give birth to live young.

A snake can track its prey using its long, forked tongue which flickers over the ground, covering a wider area than a single pointed tongue could do. It picks up tiny traces of scent left by animals such as mice. Some snakes, like grass snakes, catch their prey by grabbing and swallowing it. Others, like pythons, loop their body round it and suffocate it by making it impossible for the animal to breathe.

About one-third of all kinds of snakes use poison. This usually affects the nervous system, and paralyses the prey. It also helps to break down the food, so poisonous snakes digest their prey much more quickly than non-poisonous snakes. The poison glands are at the back of the upper jaw, and the poison is always injected into the prey by hollow or grooved teeth called fangs.

In the vipers and their relatives, the fang is like a hypodermic syringe which injects the poison. The fang is on a movable bone, which enables it to be folded away, for it is so large that the snake could not otherwise close its mouth.

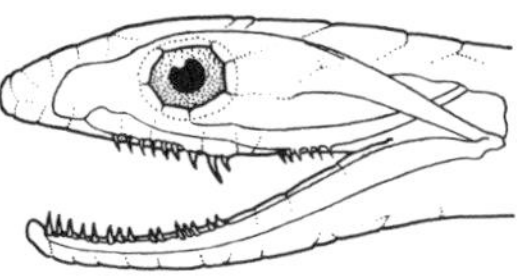

► **Back-fanged snakes, like the boomslang, have large fangs towards the back of the mouth.**

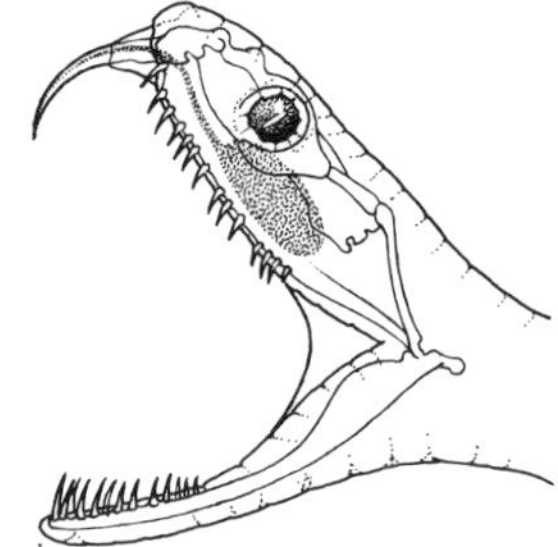

► **Vipers are front-fanged snakes. They have long hollow fangs at the front of the mouth.**

Snakes cannot chew their food, as their teeth are like curved needles. Instead, they swallow it whole. A snake that has just swallowed a large meal will have a distinct bulge in its body. To take such a mouthful they must unhinge their lower jaws, at the centre and the sides. They can move each part of the jaw independently and so 'walk' their prey into their throats.

Snakes also use their poison to defend themselves, and can injure and sometimes kill large animals, including humans. Many people fear and dislike snakes, killing them whenever possible. ■

◄ **Rock python eating a Thomson's gazelle. Snakes cannot chew their food but must swallow it whole. The snake can dislocate its jaws so it can move each part separately and work its prey into its mouth. Its scales stretch apart and its ribs spread as it swallows.**

A snake's scaly skin has an inner and an outer layer. The outer layer is formed of dead cells from the inner layer. When the outer layer becomes worn, the snake sheds it. This is called moulting.

See also
Poisonous animals
Reptiles

Snooker

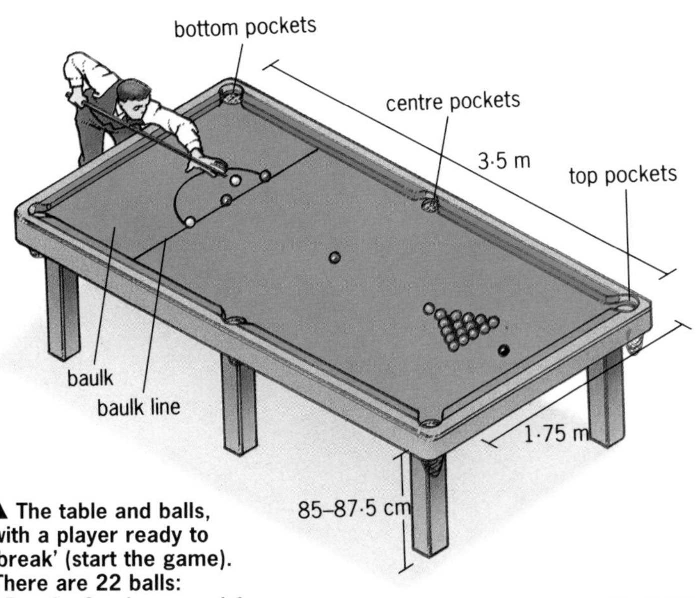

▲ The table and balls, with a player ready to 'break' (start the game). There are 22 balls: 15 reds, 6 colours, and 1 white or cue-ball.

The maximum break is 147. That is 15 reds and 15 blacks followed by all of the colours.

Points scored for each ball	
1 point	5 points
2 points	6 points
3 points	7 points
4 points	

Snooker is a game for two played on a billiards table. A player strikes the white cue-ball and aims to hit one of the fifteen red balls. If he succeeds in 'potting' a red ball into one of the table's pockets he scores one point. He must then choose a 'colour' ball to hit with the cue-ball. If he pots this he scores the value of the colour, which is put back in its place, and returns to playing a red. His turn or 'break' continues until he fails to score or he plays a foul shot. When all the reds have gone, the colours are potted in sequence from yellow to black to the end of the game or 'frame'. The winner of the frame is the player with the most points. The skill is in potting balls and in 'controlling' the cue-ball: leaving it in a good position for the next shot.

The term 'snooker' is used when there is not a clear path from the cue-ball to the target (or 'object') ball. Snooker was invented by British soldiers in India in the 19th century. ■

▼ A player is 'snookered' when the ball he must play is 'hidden' behind a ball he must not play. Here, the red ball is snookered behind the black. The player can try to hit the red either by making the cue-ball swerve round the black, or by bouncing it off the cushions. If he misses the red or hits another ball, points are awarded to his opponent.

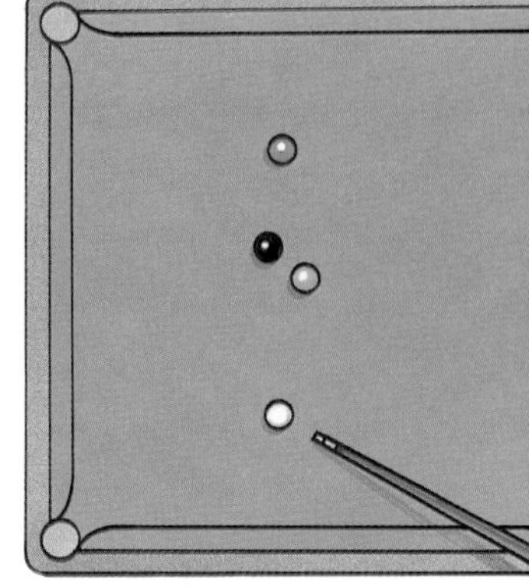

See also
Billiards

Snow

▲ There are thousands of different shapes of snow crystals, but each of them has six spokes.

Sometimes red snow is seen where tiny red plants (called algae) grow in the snow.

If you can, catch a snowflake on a woollen glove and look at it through a magnifying lens. You will see that the flake is made up of tiny ice crystals stuck together. Each crystal has a beautiful six-spoked shape which is usually symmetrical.

Ice is transparent, yet snow looks white. This is because the ice crystals in snow reflect daylight in all directions. Daylight is white, so the snow appears white.

A thick layer of snow does not allow heat to escape from the ground beneath it. It works like a blanket to save plants and animals from the damage caused by freezing temperatures.

Snow is often a very useful source of water supply, especially in hot dry countries. Deep layers of snow on high mountains form a reservoir of water. These snows do not melt until the warmer weather in the spring and summer. Rivers like the Nile in Africa, and the Indus in India, would dry up in hot weather without supplies of melting snow. ■

See also
Cold
Crystals
Frost
Glaciers
Ice
Winter sports

Soap

▲ Soap being squeezed out of a machine called a noodling machine, ready to be made into bars.

Rather surprisingly, water is not very good at wetting things. This is because water often behaves as if it had a skin on it. It runs off a greasy surface or stays there in blobs and droplets. Only when soap or a detergent is added to water can it spread out and clean things by breaking up grease.

How soap is made

All types of washing soap are made by adding plant oil or animal fat to a strong alkali. This is done at high temperatures and pressures. Soap and a substance known as glycerol or glycerine are produced. The glycerine is washed out with a strong salt solution. The molten soap is then poured into mixing machines. There perfumes, preservatives and whiteners or colourings are added to it. The molten soap is cooled and cut or moulded to size.

Soap flakes and soap powder

Soap flakes are made by spreading molten soap over water-cooled drums. This makes ribbons of soap, which are rolled thinner and then broken into flakes. Soap powders are made by adding substances known as silicates and phosphates to soap. The mixture is then heated and sprayed into the top of a tower. As the droplets fall they turn into a powder.

The disadvantages of soaps

Soaps have a number of disadvantages. They do not work in even slightly acid water and, more important, they do not work well in 'hard' water. Hard water contains lots of calcium and magnesium salts that dissolve from rocks in the ground. The soap reacts with the calcium and magnesium salts to form a 'scum'. This leaves rings on baths or a whitish film on glassware. Synthetic detergents have neither of these disadvantages, which is why they have replaced soaps for many cleaning purposes.

Flashback

Soap was probably first made by Egyptians in the Nile Valley. By about 600 BC Phoenician seamen had carried the knowledge of soap-making to the Mediterranean coasts. In the first century AD, the best soap was made from goats' fat and the ashes obtained by burning beech wood.

Soap was made from animal fat and wood ash until the end of the 18th century. At that time it was discovered that caustic soda, an alkali made from common salt, could be used in place of wood ashes. Meanwhile, plant oils such as olive oil, palm oil, coconut oil, sesame oil and soya-bean oil began to replace the animal fats used until then. ■

See also
Alkalis
Detergents
Water

Social studies

Social studies is a term used to describe those subjects that explain how people live as individuals, in groups or larger communities. It includes anthropology, criminology, economics, law, politics and sociology.

Anthropology is the study of how different peoples live; criminology is about crime; economics explains how money and goods and services are used; law and politics are about legal and political systems; sociologists study human society and behaviour. Through social studies people gain a better understanding of the organization and problems of the world.

There are two other main groups of subjects: the natural sciences, such as biology, chemistry, physics and mathematics, and the humanities, which includes the arts, languages, literature, philosophy and religion. ■

Social workers

Social workers are people who are specially trained to help those who for some reason are not coping well with the problems of everyday life. They have come into existence in the 20th century, and in Britain they are an important part of the Welfare State.

Most social workers are employed by local councils. They have a great many duties, but essentially they work with people. For example, some of them work with families who find it difficult to care for their children at home, or offer support to single parents. Others organize services for frail elderly people so that they can continue to live in their own homes. Voluntary workers still play an important part in social work, and the trained social workers can organize the work of volunteers in the community. ■

People who want to become social workers can follow professional courses at polytechnics and colleges. The main British qualification is called the Certificate of Qualification in Social Work (CQSW).

See also
Welfare State

Soil

Soil is formed when rocks are slowly broken down by weathering (the actions of wind, rain and other weather changes). Plants take root among the rock particles. The roots help to bind the particles together, and protect them from rain and wind. When the plants die, they decay and produce a dark sticky substance called humus. The humus sticks the soil particles together and absorbs water.

The soil environment

Soil is made up of a mixture of rock particles of various sizes, with air spaces between them. The particles are coated with humus and a thin film of water. The larger the soil particles, the bigger the air spaces between them and the faster water drains out of the soil.

The air in the soil is important for plants because their roots need oxygen to breathe. The humus supplies minerals to the plants as it decays. In some parts of the world wind-blown dust accumulates to form a soil called loess. In parts of China the loess is 300 m (1,000 ft) thick.

Soil animals

Millions of animals live in the soil. One square metre of fertile soil contains over 1,000 million animals. Many of them are too tiny to see with the naked eye. Fungi and bacteria break down plant and animal remains, releasing minerals which are then absorbed by plant roots. Earthworms tunnel through the soil, letting air in, helping water to drain through, and mixing the different layers. Earthworms can move 10 tonnes of soil per hectare per year. Ants, beetles, centipedes, millipedes and spiders hunt in the soil, and larger animals like foxes, rabbits and mice make their burrows there.

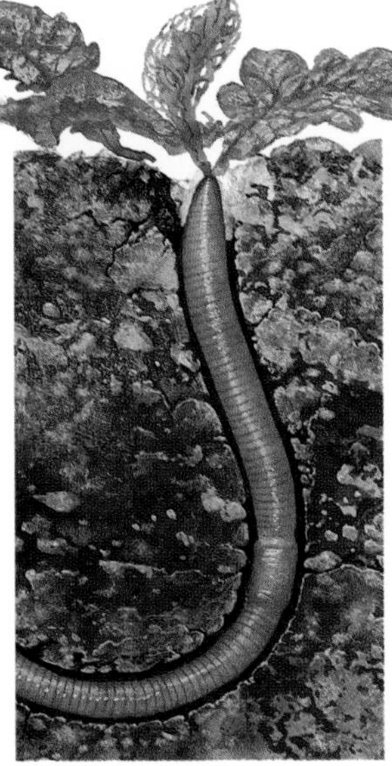

► An earthworm dragging dead leaves down into its burrow. The leaves will decay in the soil providing food for the worm.

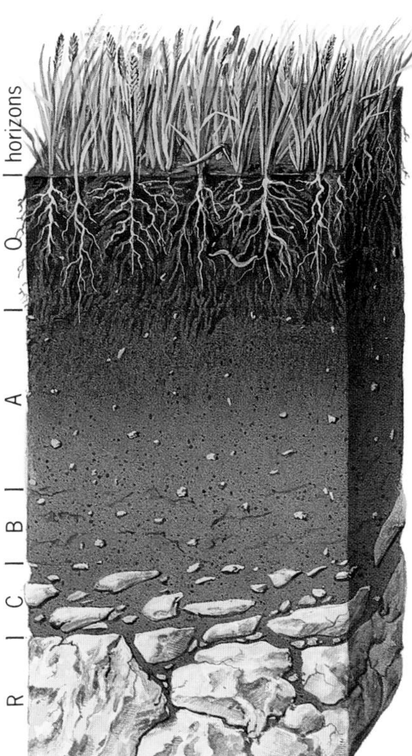

▲ Chernozem or black earth.
Dark mineral-rich soils occurring under grasslands in temperate climates. Humus is spread deep into the soil and there is very little leaching, so there is not much difference between the various layers.

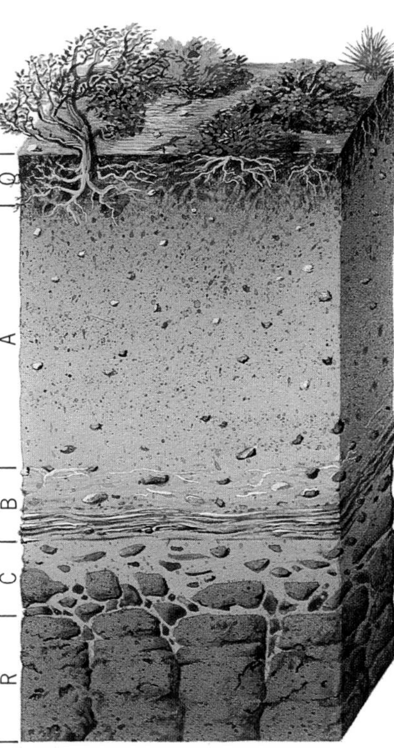

▲ Podzols.
Poor soils occurring in regions of heavy rainfall or acidic rocks, where minerals are rapidly leached from the upper layers. The minerals are often deposited lower down as a hard iron-rich layer called a pan.

Soil profiles

Different kinds of parent (original) rock and different climates produce different kinds of soils. You can see this by looking at soil profiles. A soil profile is a sample taken from the surface down through the soil. Each profile is divided into a series of layers called horizons.

O horizon, the surface layer, contains many plant roots and soil animals. It is rich in dark-coloured humus.

A horizon still has a lot of humus, but is a paler, greyish colour because many of the minerals have been washed out by rain-water, a process called leaching.

B horizon contains much less humus, but some of the minerals washed out of the A horizon are deposited here. If the soil is not too wet, any iron left here will oxidize, producing a yellow or reddish brown colour.

C horizon is where weathering is taking place, and the parent rock is being broken down.

R horizon is the parent rock. ■

See also
Erosion
Grasslands
Worms

Solar power

See also
Electricity
Energy
Heat
Light
Sun

Light and heat from the Sun pour down on the Earth all the time. When we turn this energy into electricity or use it as heat, we call it solar power. On a sunny day, a square patch of Earth facing the Sun with sides 1 m (40 in) long gets up to 1,000 watts of power from the Sun: enough to run one bar of an electric fire. In fact, the Sun could supply all the power we need for the whole world if we could collect it and use it efficiently. The equipment needed to turn the Sun's energy into useful power is expensive but the costs of running and maintaining that equipment are less than those of ordinary power-stations.

▼ A solar panel absorbs heat radiation from the Sun. The heat helps to warm water for the house. There is less for the main heating system to do, so fuel bills are reduced.

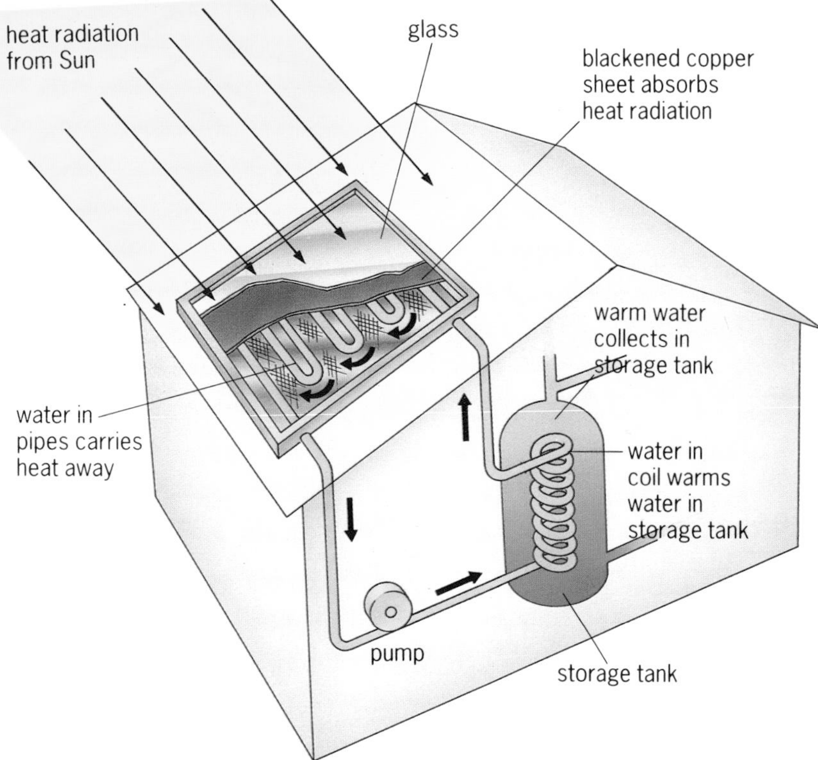

► Solar thermal power-stations have large dish-shaped mirrors. This one is in the Pyrenees. These so-called heliostats reflect the Sun's rays onto a large parabolic reflector, which then reflects all the light it receives onto a special collector. Temperatures of up to 3,000°C can be reached, generating 1 megawatt (1 million watts) of power.

Electricity from sunlight

Electricity is probably the most convenient type of power we use every day, and solar cells can turn sunlight directly into electricity. Solar cells are made from thin slices of pure silicon, a material which can be got from sand. The top of the slice is a slightly different kind of silicon from the bottom, and when light shines on it, an electric current will flow along a wire connecting the top to the bottom. A single solar cell produces only a tiny current, but an array of cells connected together makes a useful amount of power. Solar cells are expensive to make so we use them only where there is no convenient electricity supply. Satellites in space have huge panels of solar cells to supply their electricity. In remote parts of some developing countries, solar cells provide electricity to pump water for drinking and growing crops and to power refrigerators storing medicines.

Using the Sun's heat

If you have ever sat in a car on a hot sunny day you will know that the Sun's energy can be trapped as heat. Solar panels on the roofs of buildings can also trap this heat to give us hot water. In the solar panel, under a sheet of glass, are pipes fixed to a black plate. The Sun heats up a liquid in the pipes and this liquid heats up a tank of water.

Huge solar furnaces use the Sun's heat to make electricity. A field of mirrors collects sunlight and concentrates it onto a furnace where the heat boils water to make steam. This drives a turbine making electricity in the same way as an ordinary power-station. While the Sun is shining, any extra hot water or electricity produced is stored so it can be used at night when the Sun's energy is not available.

Flashback

Energy from the Sun has always been important to people. Over 2,000 years ago the Greeks and Romans were building their houses to face the Sun. In 1714 Antoine Lavoisier, a French scientist, made a solar furnace which could melt metals. The first steam-engine to work on solar power ran a printing press in Paris in 1880. By 1900 many houses in the hotter parts of the USA had solar water-heaters. All these inventions used the heat from the Sun. It was not until 1954 that the first practical solar cells turned sunlight directly into electricity. ■

Solar System

Our Sun has travelling around it a family of planets, some of them with moons, and lots of other smaller objects such as comets and meteor streams. The Sun and all things in orbit around it make up the Solar System, which is over 12,000 million km (7,500 million miles) across.

The largest objects in the Solar System, apart from the Sun, are the nine planets: Mercury, Venus, Earth, Mars, Jupiter, Saturn, Uranus, Neptune and Pluto. All except Mercury and Venus have at least one moon and more than fifty moons are known altogether. There are thousands of minor planets, hundreds of comets and streams of dust and pieces of rock. Astronomers believe that these things are left over from when the Sun formed from a cloud of gas about 5,000 million years ago. The Solar System stays together because of the strong pull of the Sun's gravity.

The paths of the planets

The orbits of the planets round the Sun are not circular but have the squashed oval shape called an ellipse. None of them is tilted very much to the others and so the Solar System has the shape of a flat disc. Pluto is an exception. Its elliptical orbit crosses just inside Neptune's and is tilted at 17°. The way gravity acts means that the further a planet is from the Sun, the longer the period of time it takes to complete an orbit.

The spaces between the planets are huge compared to their sizes. If the Sun were a football, the Earth would be this big ●, and 30 m (98 ft) away! ■

Something to do

The Solar System is bigger than you think! Find out for yourself by making this scale model. First, collect ten lollipop sticks (wide ones). Then find a park or playground with your friends, or a very long garden.

Near the end of one lollipop stick, draw a circle 9 mm across. This is the Sun. Draw a planet on each of the other lollipop sticks. Jupiter is a tiny circle 1 mm across. Saturn is a little smaller. The other planets are dots like this . . . .

Place the stick with the Sun on it upright in the ground. Then place the planets at these distances in metres from the Sun (1 metre is one big step):

Mercury	⅓	Saturn	10
Venus	¾	Uranus	21
Earth	1	Neptune	32
Mars	1½	Pluto	42
Jupiter	5		

The word 'solar' means 'to do with the Sun'. It comes from *sol*, the Latin word for Sun.

See also
Astronomers
Comets
Gravity
Meteors
Moon
Planets
Sun

▼ The major planets in order from the Sun. The planets are drawn to scale, but the distances between them are not to scale.

	Pluto	Neptune	Uranus	Saturn	Jupiter	Mars	Earth	Venus	Mercury
distance from the Sun in million km	5,900	4,497	2,870	1,427	778	228	150	108	58
time to orbit Sun in days	90,502	60,275	30,660	10,767	4,343	687	365	225	88

Somalia

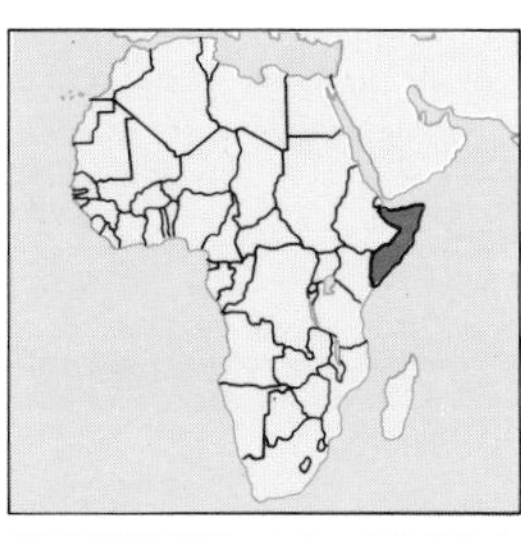

Area
637,657 sq km
(246,200 sq miles)
Capital
Mogadishu
Population
6,111,000
Language
Somali, Arabic, English, Italian
Religion
Muslim
Government
Republic
Currency
1 Somali shilling = 100 centesimi

Somalia is a big country; its area is more than twice as large as the United Kingdom. It dominates what is called the Horn of Africa, the north-eastern tip of the continent. Somalia has coastlines facing both north to Arabia and east to the Indian Ocean. The weather is hot and dry for most of the year and the land is largely desert or semi-desert. Most of the population, who are extremely poor, work on the land, either growing fruit along the coast and in the fertile valleys, or living as nomads, grazing animals further inland.

Over the centuries, trading with Arabian and Indian ports has been part of the way of life. The country's main port is at Mogadishu, with a second one at Berbera.

Towards the end of the 19th century areas of Somalia were controlled by both Britain and Italy. It became independent in 1960 and is a member of the League of Arab States. ■

▲ **Once nomadic, the people in this picture have settled down as farmers. They are threshing the rice which they have managed to grow on this barren land.**

See also
Africa
Arabs
Muslims

Sonatas

Sonatas are pieces of classical music that feature just one instrument. They are often long works, with more than one movement. Keyboard instruments such as piano or organ can accompany themselves with chords and harmonies, so there are many sonatas for them. There are also solo sonatas for guitars, violins, and cellos.

Some instruments, such as the clarinet, can only play one line of music at a time. Sonatas for these instruments often include a part for a piano, to accompany the soloist. ■

See also
Classical music
Musical instruments

Sonic boom

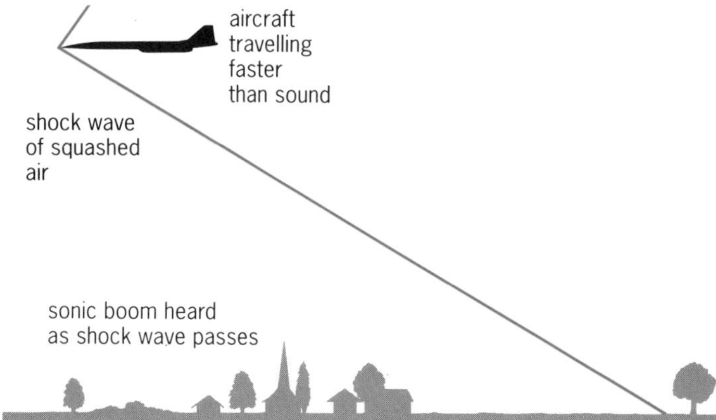

A sonic boom is a loud explosive noise heard when an aircraft flies overhead at a speed greater than the speed of sound. It is caused by a shock wave set off as the plane squashes the air in front of it. At ground level, the speed of sound is about 1,200 km per hour (760 mph). But higher in the atmosphere, where it is colder, the speed is only about 900 km per hour (600 mph). Scientists call the speed of sound Mach 1. Twice the speed of sound is Mach 2, and so on. (Mach is a German name, pronounced 'mark'.) When planes start to travel faster than sound, people sometimes say that they are 'breaking the sound barrier'. ■

The first aircraft to break the sound barrier was the Bell X-1 rocket plane in 1947 in the USA.

The world's fastest jets can travel at Mach 3. At that speed, you would travel the length of eight football pitches in a second.

See also
Aircraft
Sound

Sound

Everything that can be heard is a sound. The sounds that we hear start when something makes the air vibrate (wobble), backwards and forwards quite quickly. Twang a rubber band and you can see it vibrating and hear a sound. Place a finger on the band to stop the vibrations and there is nothing to hear. When the rubber band is plucked, its vibrations make the air next to it vibrate. Then the air next to that is forced backwards and forwards and so the sound moves outwards away from the band. When the vibrating air reaches your ear, it makes the ear-drum move in and out, and you hear a sound.

Making sounds

Anything that vibrates makes a sound. A bee's wing moves backwards and forwards very quickly and we hear a buzz. Put a hand firmly on your throat and sing aaaaah. Sing it low and high. You can feel the vibrations that produce your voice. Speak a few words with the palm of your hand just in front of your mouth and you can feel the air being pushed through your voice-box and out of your mouth. You cannot feel all the tiny vibrations in the air. Only your ear is sensitive enough to detect them.

How sound travels

All that we hear has travelled through the air around us. Remove the air from the room you are in and you would hear nothing. There is no sound out in space where there is no air.

But sound does not travel only through air. Vibrations can travel through water, glass, brick, concrete and other substances. Vibrations move particularly easily and fast through water. Whales and porpoises make sounds which travel over hundreds of kilometres of oceans.

Sound can travel through buildings too. A heavy lorry passing outside your home can make the whole building feel as if it is shaking and produce a low rumbling noise. Vibrations from traffic have damaged some old buildings which are on busy lorry routes.

Loudness of sound

The loudness of a sound is measured in decibels (dB). The closer you are to whatever is producing the sound, the louder it is. If you are close to a very loud sound, like an explosion, your hearing can be damaged. But loud sounds, which may not affect your hearing immediately, can produce serious damage if your ear receives them for a long time. Pop groups and their fans often get hearing damage from standing too close to the loudspeakers. Listening with headphones to loud music can also produce deafness.

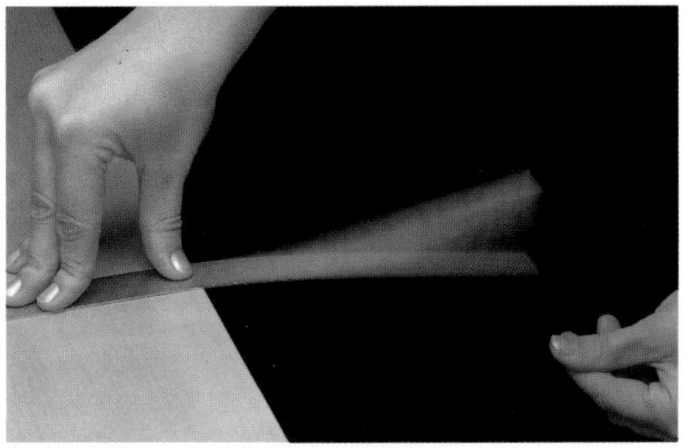

◀ **A twanging ruler. When the ruler moves upwards it pushes against the molecules of air that it hits. These air molecules then bump into the molecules above them, and so on. In this way, air further and further from the ruler is disturbed.**

Speed of sound

In air, sound travels at a speed of about 330 metres every second (740 mph). That is about four times as fast as a racing car but only half the speed of Concorde. Sound travels slightly faster on a hot day than it does on a cold day. Sound travels much faster through solids and through water than it does through air.

High and low sounds

When a sound is made, the number of vibrations every second is called the frequency. Frequency is measured in hertz (Hz): 1 hertz means one vibration every second.

The highest note a human ear can hear has a frequency of about 20,000 vibrations every second (20,000 Hz). This corresponds to a note more than two octaves above the top note on the piano.

The lowest note the ear can hear has a frequency of about 20 vibrations every second (20 Hz). This corresponds to a note even lower than the bottom note of a piano.

Acoustics

Acoustics is the study of the way sound behaves and is important in a room such as a concert hall. The hard, bare walls of any empty room will bounce sound around and make the room echoey. In a small room it helps to prevent this if there are materials on the walls and ceiling which absorb sounds. Heavy curtains and a thick carpet will also help. But in a large room like a concert hall you need smooth, hard surfaces behind the players or singers to help to send out the sound to the audience, and then materials that will absorb the sound at the back of the hall to prevent echoes. ■

Typical sound levels in decibels

See also
Bats
Ears
Echoes
Radiation
Sonic boom
Vibration

South Africa

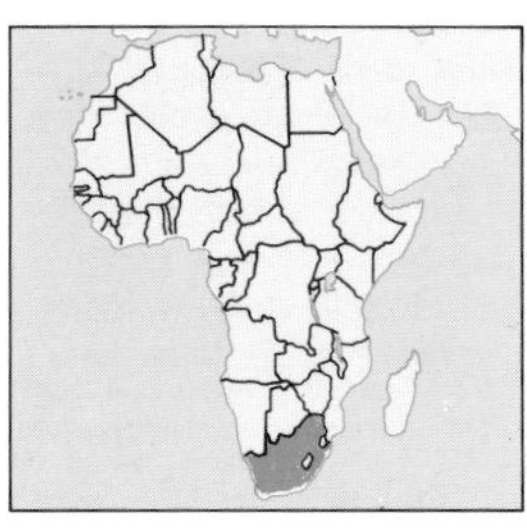

South Africa, as its name describes it, makes up the southern tip of the African continent. The Limpopo and Orange rivers help to form its boundaries. In the heart of South Africa is a huge, grassy plateau called the highveld. In the north-east is the Kruger National Park, one of several areas in South Africa where you can see elephants, lions, zebras and other animals. This park is about the same size as Wales. The western parts of the plateau are dry and the land merges into the Kalahari and Namib deserts. The high-veld is surrounded to the south and east by steep slopes, especially in the south-east where it is bordered by the rugged Drakensberg range. Drakensberg means 'mountain of the dragons'. It may have got its name from legends about fire-eating lizards. Around the plateau are lower mountains and the plains of the Great and Little Karoo. Most of South Africa has a pleasant climate, though the nights can be freezing cold on the highveld in winter. The area in the south-west around Cape Town has a typical Mediterranean climate of hot, dry summers and mild, wet winters.

▼ A group of Xhosa men in the Transkei. Behind are some of their cattle and the rondavels, houses made of branches and mud. The fields are usually cultivated by women.

South Africa has been well known for its policy of apartheid (separate development). Under this policy, black and white people are supposed to lead separate lives in separate areas. Parts of the country, called 'Homelands' or 'Bantustans', have been set aside for black Africans. The ten Homelands cover about 13 per cent of South Africa. The government has said that four Homelands are now separate countries. But the Homelands depend so heavily on South Africa that no other country in the world agrees that they are independent. Instead, they are regarded as parts of South Africa.

The people and how they live

The whites, who make up 18 per cent of the people of South Africa, control the government. They speak Afrikaans (a form of Dutch), or English. About half of the black Africans, who make up 70 per cent of the people, live in Homelands, where most of them are farmers. The rest live in black townships around the cities and have to travel to work in the white areas each day.

Most blacks have lower standards of living than whites and they suffer racial discrimination because of the policy of apartheid. The other main groups in South Africa are the Coloureds (9 per cent), who are of mixed race, and Asians (3 per cent).

South Africa is Africa's richest country. It mines gold, diamonds and many other minerals, produces more food than its people need and it has many large factories in its modern cities. But the whites hold most of the high-paid jobs.

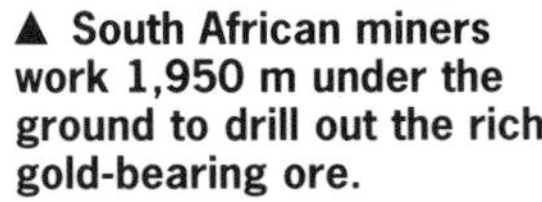

▲ South African miners work 1,950 m under the ground to drill out the rich gold-bearing ore.

◄ Soweto stands for 'South Western Township'. Soweto is a large township, with a population of over 500,000, on the outskirts of Johannesburg.

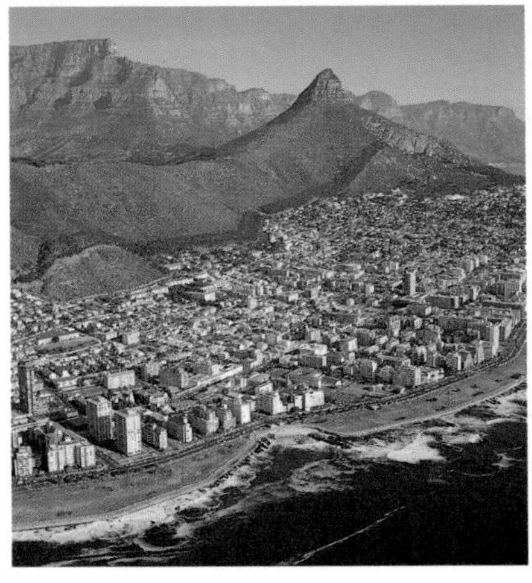

► At the foot of the Table Mountain lies Cape Town, on the peninsula which Sir Francis Drake called 'the fairest cape we saw in the whole circumference of the earth'. The peak in the foreground is Lion's Head.

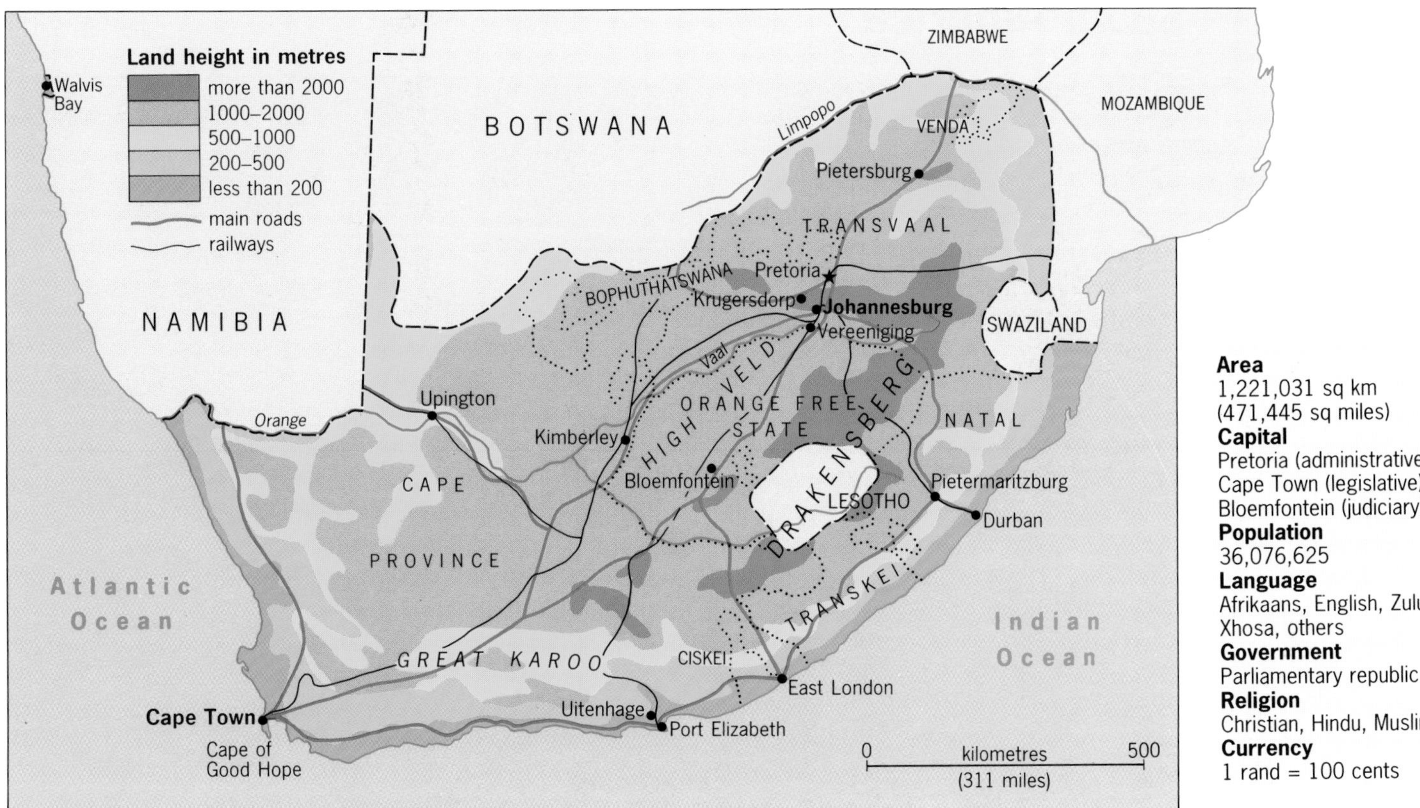

Area
1,221,031 sq km
(471,445 sq miles)
Capital
Pretoria (administrative)
Cape Town (legislative)
Bloemfontein (judiciary)
Population
36,076,625
Language
Afrikaans, English, Zulu, Xhosa, others
Government
Parliamentary republic
Religion
Christian, Hindu, Muslim
Currency
1 rand = 100 cents

Flashback

To understand South Africa's problems today, we must know about its past. The first people in southern Africa were probably Bushmen (San) and Hottentots (Khoikhoi), though very few live in South Africa today. The ancestors of the present black population were moving into the south-eastern part of Africa around 1,600 years ago. These people, who spoke languages belonging to the Bantu family, were mostly farmers.

In 1652 the Dutch established a trading post to provide food and a pleasant half-way stopping place for merchant ships sailing to and from the East Indies. Cape Town was Africa's first European settlement. Dutch settlers soon began to spread inland and the region around Cape Town became known as the Cape Colony. The Dutch brought in slaves from other parts of Africa and later from Asia.

Britain seized the Cape Colony in 1806. In the 1830s, many Boers (Dutch farmers, whose modern descendants are called Afrikaners) moved inland to escape British rule and founded the republics of the Orange Free State and Transvaal. The Dutch settlers clashed with the Zulus and other black Africans, but they found great riches, such as diamonds and gold. These discoveries increased the rivalry between the Boers and the British. In 1880–1881 the Boers beat the British. In the second Boer War in 1899–1902 the British finally defeated the Boers.

South Africa became independent within the British Empire in 1910. It was closely linked with Britain and it later joined the Commonwealth of Nations. Most white people did not regard the blacks as their equals. From 1948, they passed laws making apartheid effective. Protests against apartheid mounted at home and abroad, as did unrest among blacks. In 1961, South Africa became a republic and left the Commonwealth. In the 1980s South Africa changed some of its racial laws and set up a parliament giving a voice to Coloureds and Asians. But black Africans still had no votes outside the Homelands. In 1990 the black ANC leader, Nelson Mandela, was released from prison and talks began between black leaders and the government to try to end the race laws. At the same time there was conflict in the townships among rival black groups. ■

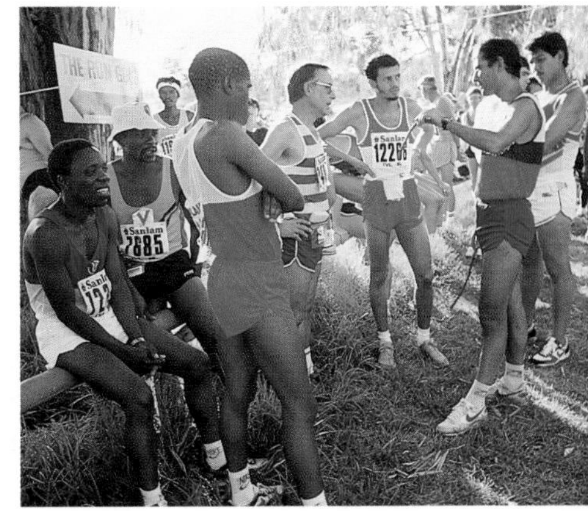

► **Black and white contestants at a Sunday run in Johannesburg.**

See also
Africa
African history
Apartheid
Boer War
British empire
Bushmen
Commonwealth
Zulus

Biography
Kruger
Luthuli
Mandela
Rhodes
Shaka
Smuts
Tutu

South America

Area
17,832,000 sq km
(6,885,000 sq miles)
Highest peak
Aconcagua 6,960 m
Largest lake
Maracaibo (Venezuela)
13,000 sq km
(5,000 sq miles)
Longest rivers
Amazon, Paraná
Largest country (by area)
Brazil 8,511,965 sq km
(3,286,488 sq miles)
Largest country
(by population)
Brazil 135,564,000

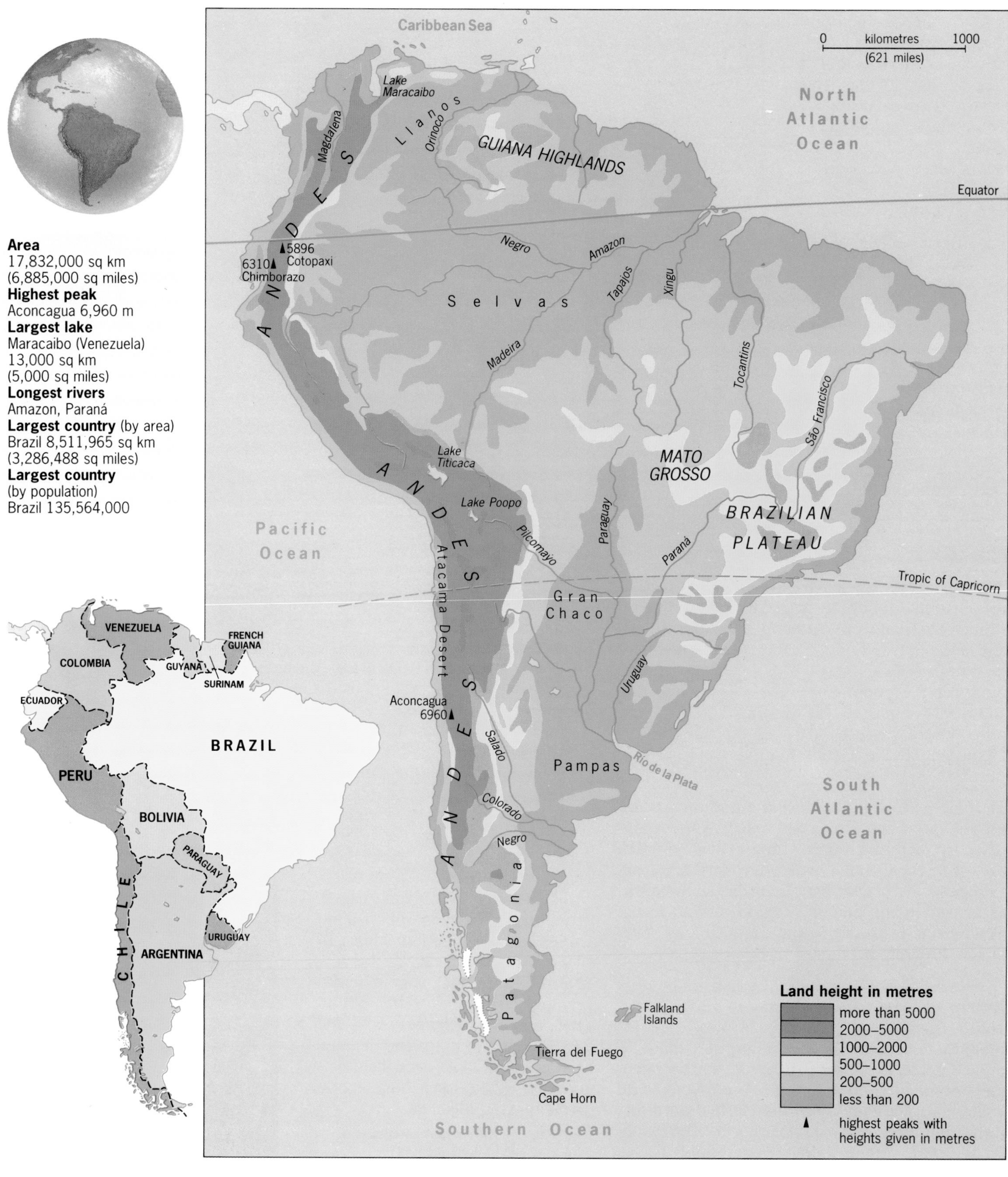

South America includes the land east and south of Panama. Sometimes the phrase Latin America is used, but this includes Central America too (Central America is included in the map of the Caribbean in volume 1, page 186). These are the places which Spanish and Portuguese people explored and settled from the time when Columbus sailed to the Caribbean. It has been called Latin America because the Spanish and Portuguese languages grew out of Latin.

Landscapes

The Andes are the longest mountain range in the world. They extend for over 7,100 km (4,400 miles) along the entire western edge of South America from the Caribbean Sea in the north to Tierra del Fuego in the south. In most areas they are at least 240 km (150 miles) wide. The Andes are the second highest mountain range in the world, after the Himalayas. Snow-capped volcanic cones rise among the mountain peaks. Chimborazo and Cotopaxi are among the highest. Cotopaxi is very active, building up great layers of volcanic ash. Earthquakes are common and have caused much damage in southern Chile.

The western slopes of the Andes are very steep. Between the mountains and the Pacific coast there is an area of barren desert which stretches for 1,600 km (1,000 miles) from southern Ecuador to northern Chile. The eastern slopes are more gentle.

There are three plateau areas in South America. The Guiana Highlands in the north, rising to over 2,500 m (8,000 feet) are rugged, with deep, narrow, forested valleys. These areas are uninhabited. The Brazilian Plateau in the east, in contrast, is where most Brazilians live. This plateau rises to over 2,700 m (9,200 feet) but has no sharp peaks. The western part forms the savanna grasslands of the Mato Grosso. In the extreme south lies the dry plateau of Patagonia. It is mostly over 660 m (2,200 feet) high, but is cut by deep gorges which provide shelter for the sheep farmers of the area.

The lowlands of the Amazon basin are covered with rainforest, dense with a great variety of species of trees, insects, monkeys, and parrots. Away from the Amazon the forest becomes more open, changing to wooded grassland (the Gran Chaco) and more fertile grasslands (the pampas) in the Paraná–Paraguay basin further south, and to the savannah lands (llanos) of the Orinoco basin in the north.

◀ The River Amazon is the second longest river in the world, at approximately 6,440 km (4,000 miles).

Climate

Amazonia and the other equatorial regions are hot all year and very wet. In the Brazilian Highlands the climate is much less extreme. Further south, on the Gran Chaco, there is a distinct wet season and a dry season. From October to April the surface of the land is wet and swampy. From May to September the lakes dry out leaving bare cracked mud. In north-east Brazil frequent drought has created a landscape of low trees, thorny bushes and cacti, known as caatinga.

South America stretches much further south than any other continent and so the far south is cool for most of the year. The tip of the continent is only about 1,000 km (600 miles) from Antarctica.

The Atacama Desert in Chile is the driest place on Earth. Rain has never been recorded in some places.

Countries

Brazil is by far the largest country in South America and contains half the population. Bolivia is the roof of South America. One-third of the republic is over a mile (1·6 km) high. Argentina and Uruguay share the estuary of Río de la Plata, a great trading route to and from the continent. Most South American countries became independent from Spanish or Portuguese rule in the first 30 years of the 19th century.

People

Brazilians speak Portuguese. Most other South Americans speak Spanish. Many American Indian languages can also be heard, especially in the Andes and Amazonia. Indians in the Andes trace their ancestors back to the Incas, a great civilization that existed for centuries before Spanish explorers arrived at the end of the 15th century. The Spanish conquistadores destroyed the Inca empire in their search for wealth. Portuguese people settled in Brazil and in 1494 a treaty was made, dividing the lands of South America between Spain and Portugal.

In the last 100 years other Europeans, including Italians, have settled in South America. Most South Americans live near the coast, especially in the huge cities of Rio de Janeiro, São Paulo, Buenos Aires and Lima. ■

Surinam was ruled by The Netherlands until 1975, when it became independent. French Guiana is a department of France. Guyana became independent from Britain in 1966.

See also
Amazon River
American Indians
Andes
Caribbean
Cities
Conquistadores
Continents
Incas
Spanish colonial history

Space exploration

On Earth we are surrounded by air, but this gradually gets thinner as it gets further from the ground. Beyond the air there is almost empty space stretching out between the Sun, the Moon, the planets and the stars. Space is not easy to explore because everything is so far away. Astronauts have visited only our nearest neighbour, the Moon. They plan to visit the planet Mars but it will take about six months to get there. Robot spacecraft can explore the more distant planets but it would take them thousands of years to get to even the nearest star.

Going into space

To explore space we have to escape from the pull of gravity, which holds us down onto the Earth. We can do this by travelling very fast. You need a speed of 40,000 km/h (25,000 mph), about 20 times as fast as Concorde, to escape completely. This is called the Earth's escape velocity. Satellites which go into orbit circling round the Earth need to go only about 12 times as fast as Concorde. Only powerful rockets can launch astronauts or satellites into space, because they can reach these speeds and a rocket engine will work in space, unlike aircraft engines.

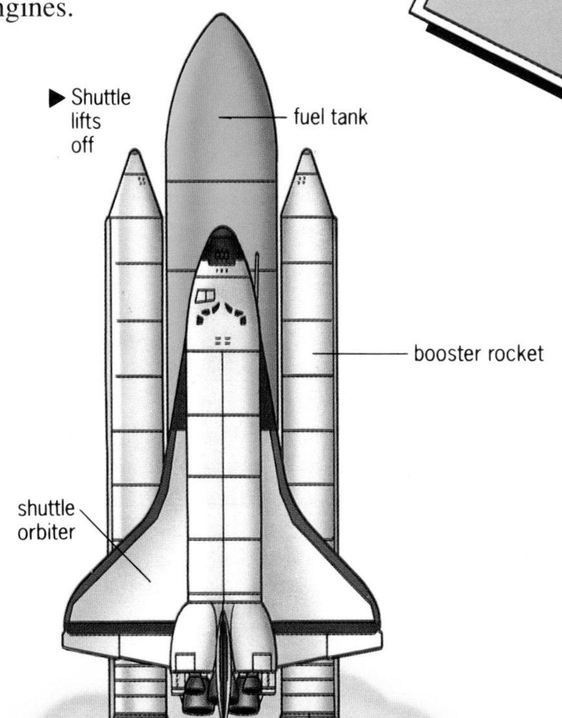

▶ Shuttle lifts off

Escape velocities

Moon 8,600 km/h (5,300 mph)
Earth 40,000 km/h (25,000 mph)
Mars 18,000 km/h (11,300 mph)

Probes to the planets

Venus
Mariner 2, 1962, first fly-by
Venera series, 1967 to 1980s, landed on surface
Pioneer Venus 1 & 2, 1978, orbited and probes entered atmosphere

Mars
Mariner 4, 1964, first pictures
Mariner 9, 1971, orbited
Viking 1 & 2, 1975, orbited and landed
Phobos 1 & 2, 1988, to Martian moons

Jupiter
Pioneer 10 & 11, 1972–1973, fly-by
Voyager 1 & 2, launched 1977; flew past planet and moons in 1979

Mercury
Mariner 10, 1973, 10,000 pictures

Saturn
Pioneer 11, flew by in 1979
Voyager 1 & 2, flew past in 1980–1981

Uranus
Voyager 2, flew past in 1986

Neptune
Voyager 2, flew past in 1989

▶ Space Shuttle lifts off.

Weight at launch
Including boosters and fuel tank: 2,000 tonnes
Height at launch
56 m
Length of Shuttle Orbiter
37 m
Wingspan
24 m
Weight
84 tonnes
Total power at launch
The same as 140 Jumbo Jet aircraft

Space planes

Rockets are very expensive to build and most can be used only once. The Space Shuttle is the first space plane which can fly into space many times. The only part that is new for each flight is the huge fuel tank. The two booster rockets which help lift the Shuttle into space fall back into the sea when their fuel runs out and are recovered by ships. The Shuttle takes off upwards like a rocket, but when it returns to Earth it lands like a giant glider on a runway. Space planes of the future may be completely re-usable, taking off and landing on a runway like an aircraft.

▲ Fuel tank falls away.

◀ Boosters fall away.

Satellites in orbit

Racing round Earth are hundreds of satellites doing many different jobs. Their orbits have different heights and directions depending on what the satellite does. Communications satellites which send TV and telephone signals across the oceans use the high 'geostationary orbit', about 35,000 km (22,000 miles) above the Equator. They seem to hover above the same point on Earth because they circle at the same rate as the Earth spins round. Lower down, other satellites watch the Earth or the weather, circling north and south while the Earth turns beneath them.

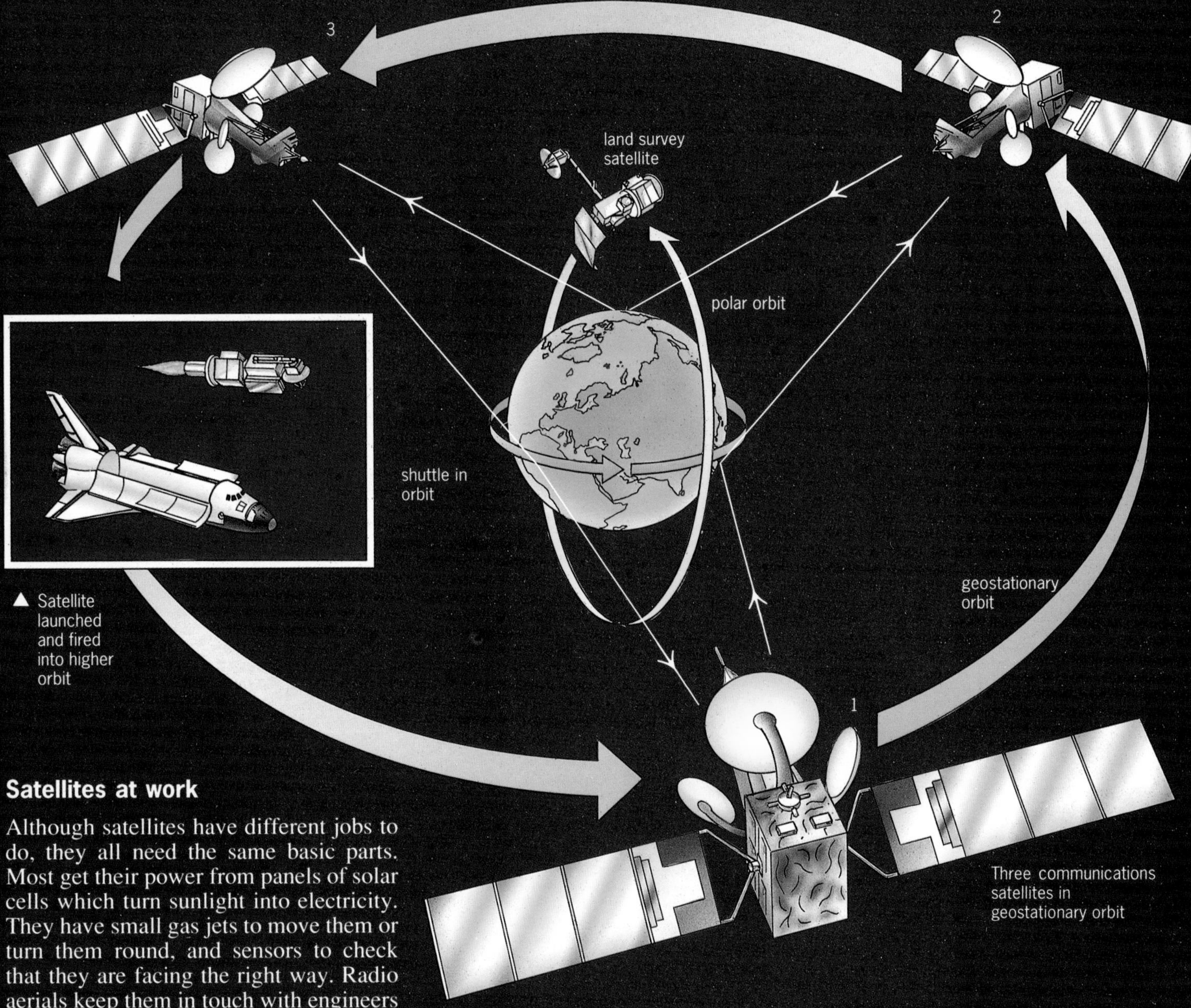

3

2

land survey satellite

polar orbit

shuttle in orbit

▲ Satellite launched and fired into higher orbit

geostationary orbit

1

Three communications satellites in geostationary orbit

Satellites at work

Although satellites have different jobs to do, they all need the same basic parts. Most get their power from panels of solar cells which turn sunlight into electricity. They have small gas jets to move them or turn them round, and sensors to check that they are facing the right way. Radio aerials keep them in touch with engineers on Earth. It is difficult to repair satellites in space, so they are tested very thoroughly before launch to make sure they will not break down.

Space probes

The robot spacecraft sent to explore other planets are called probes. Some fly past the planet, while others circle round it, taking TV pictures and sending information back to Earth. The *Voyager* spacecraft flew past Jupiter, Saturn, Uranus and Neptune, sending us beautiful close-up pictures of the planets and many of their moons. Orbiting probes have photographed almost all the surface of Mars. The ones circling Venus used radar to map the surface hidden by its thick clouds. Pluto is the only planet that has not been visited.

Robot explorers

We can get a closer look at the Moon or planets by landing robot explorers on them. *Lunokhod 1* and *2* were remote-controlled cars which explored the Moon, crawling slowly over its surface testing its soil. Two *Viking* spacecraft landed on Mars to study the soil and weather. They searched for signs of life on Mars, with confusing results. Spacecraft which land on Venus have to be very tough to survive the heat and the atmosphere, which presses down very hard. Some have lasted long enough to send back pictures of the surface.

▼ Shuttle glides back to Earth and lands.

Space stations
Salyut 1, in use 1971
Skylab, in use 1973–1974
Salyut 3, in use 1974
Salyut 4, in use 1975
Salyut 5, in use 1976–1977
Salyut 6, in use between 1977 and 1981
Salyut 7, in use from 1982 to 1986
Mir, launched 1986

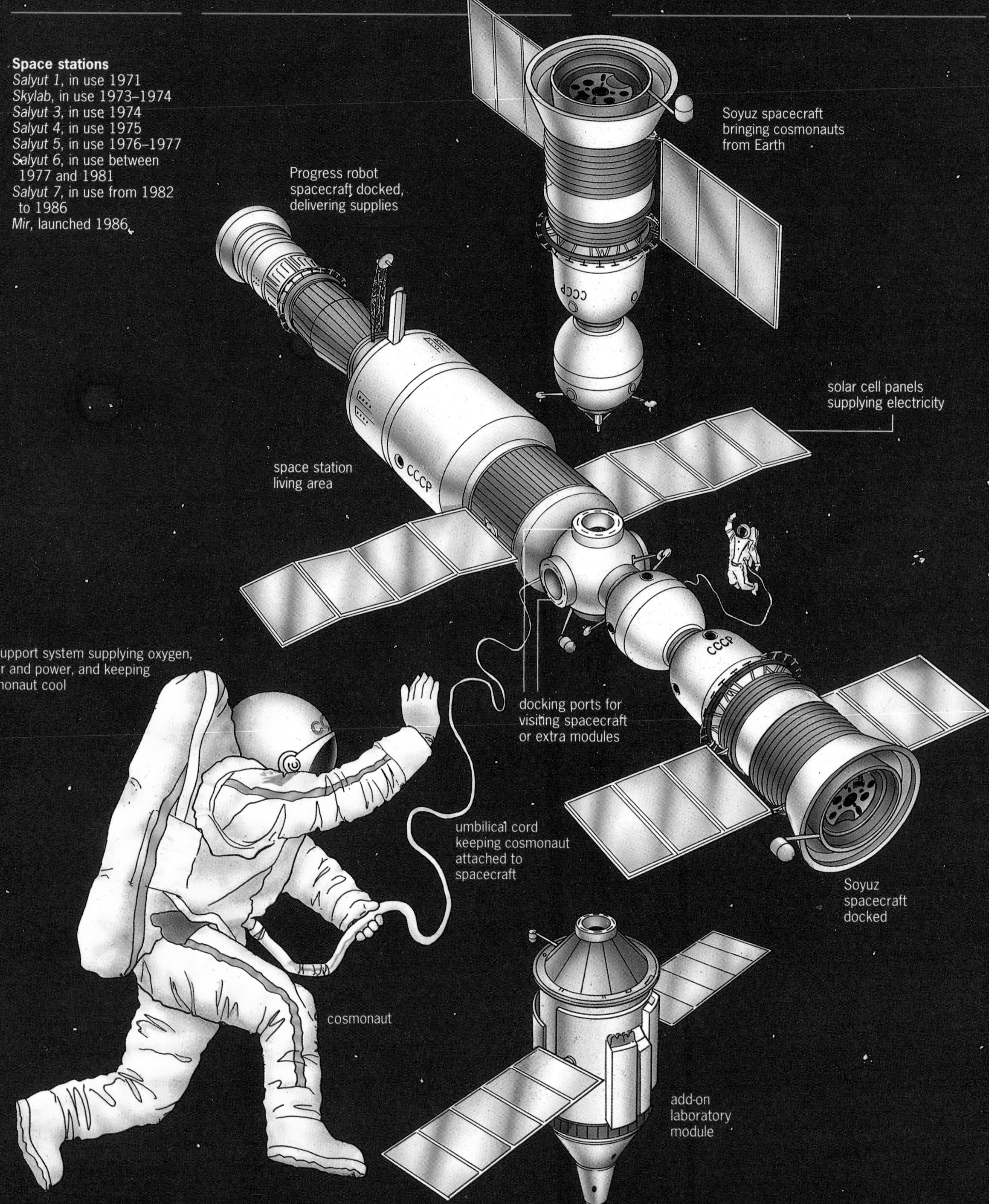

Man on the Moon

In 1969 the giant *Saturn 5* rocket launched three astronauts towards the Moon. They travelled for over three days in a small spacecraft called the Apollo Command Module. Two of the astronauts landed on the Moon in the Lunar Module, leaving the third circling the Moon. After almost a day the Lunar Module took off and met the Command Module, which took them all back to Earth. Five more visits followed, when the astronauts explored the Moon, collecting moonrock, using a moon car called the Lunar Rover on three visits.

Space stations

A space station is a home in space, circling round the Earth, where astronauts can live and work. It contains everything they need, including food, water and air, which must all be brought up from the Earth. It must be strong enough to hold in the air for the astronauts to breathe and to protect them from radiation and the dust speeding through space. Large space stations where people can live for many months are built in space by adding extra sections sent up from Earth.

Living in space

In a space station the main problem is that everything floats, including the astronauts. We call this weightlessness. If astronauts want to stay in one place they have to fix themselves to something. They sleep strapped into a sleeping bag. The food is normal but it is made sticky so it sticks to a spoon, and drinks are in containers with a straw to stop them floating around as a ball of liquid. Astronauts have to use a special toilet. It has a fan which sets up a draught of air so that liquid and solid waste is sucked into the toilet. Weightlessness also affects their bodies so astronauts have to exercise hard while they are in space to keep fit.

Working in space

Astronauts work hard in their space stations, studying the Earth below, the distant stars and galaxies or the space around them. They measure the effects of weightlessness on themselves, on growing plants and on small creatures such as spiders and bees. Some crystals and alloys (mixtures of metals) are very difficult to make on Earth because gravity churns up the melted materials they are made from. In space astronauts can make crystals, alloys and also some medicines for use on Earth.

◀ Astronaut Edwin E. Aldrin Jr, lunar module pilot, descends the steps of the Lunar Module ladder on 20 July 1969. The photograph was taken by Neil Armstrong, the commander of Apollo 11, who had stepped onto the moon first.

Spacesuits

When astronauts leave their spacecraft they must wear a spacesuit, with its helmet and gloves. Its many layers of material protect against radiation and dust. Inside is an inflated layer (a bit like a balloon) which presses against the body. Without this pressure the blood would boil. Next to the skin are tubes with cooling water to take away trapped body heat to a backpack, which also carries a power supply and oxygen gas to breathe.

Returning to Earth

The most dangerous parts of any space flight are the launch and the return to Earth. A returning spacecraft meets the blanket of air surrounding the Earth at very high speed. It rubs against the air, getting so hot that the outside of the spacecraft glows red. This would melt the spacecraft and kill the astronauts if they were not protected. Early spacecraft had a thick outer layer which burned away, but the Space Shuttle has special re-usable heat-proof tiles.

Flashback

Science fiction writers have dreamt of space flight for hundreds of years, but the Space Age began in 1957 when the first satellite, *Sputnik 1*, went into orbit round the Earth. In 1959, *Luna 1* was the first probe to escape from the Earth completely, and in 1961 Yuri Gagarin was the first person to fly in space. Since then astronauts have been to the Moon and lived in space for many months. Almost all the planets circling the Sun have been photographed by robot spacecraft, and some of these are now travelling out towards the distant stars. ■

By January 1988, 200 men and women from eighteen countries had orbited the Earth more than once.

Apollo missions to the Moon

Apollo 11, July 1969, first men on Moon
Apollo 12, November 1969, 32 hours on Moon
Apollo 13, April 1970, no landing because explosion on spacecraft, astronauts returned
Apollo 14, February 1971, visited highlands
Apollo 15, July 1971, first used Lunar Rover
Apollo 16, April 1972, drove 27 km (17 miles) on Moon
Apollo 17, December 1972, last Moon visit

Spacesuit weight (on Earth): 103 kg

Future space stations may be like giant, slowly spinning wheels. The spinning will hold astronauts against the outer wall, just as if gravity were acting.

See also
Astronauts
Rockets
Satellites

Biography
Armstrong, Neil
Gagarin
Tereshkova

Spain

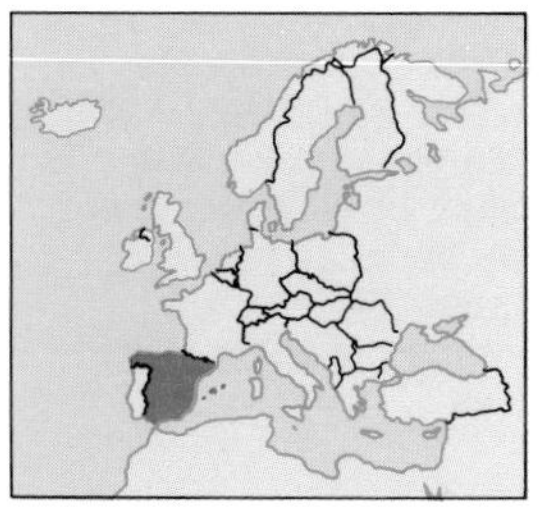

Spain is one of the most mountainous countries in Europe. Madrid, at 646 m (2,119 ft) above sea-level, is Europe's highest capital city. It is near the centre of a high plateau called the Meseta. Rivers such as the Tagus and Duero have cut deep valleys into this plateau. The Meseta is surrounded by high mountains which keep out the winds from the sea. This is 'dry Spain', with little rain, very cold winters and very hot summers. 'Nine months of winter and three months of hell' is an old Castilian saying!

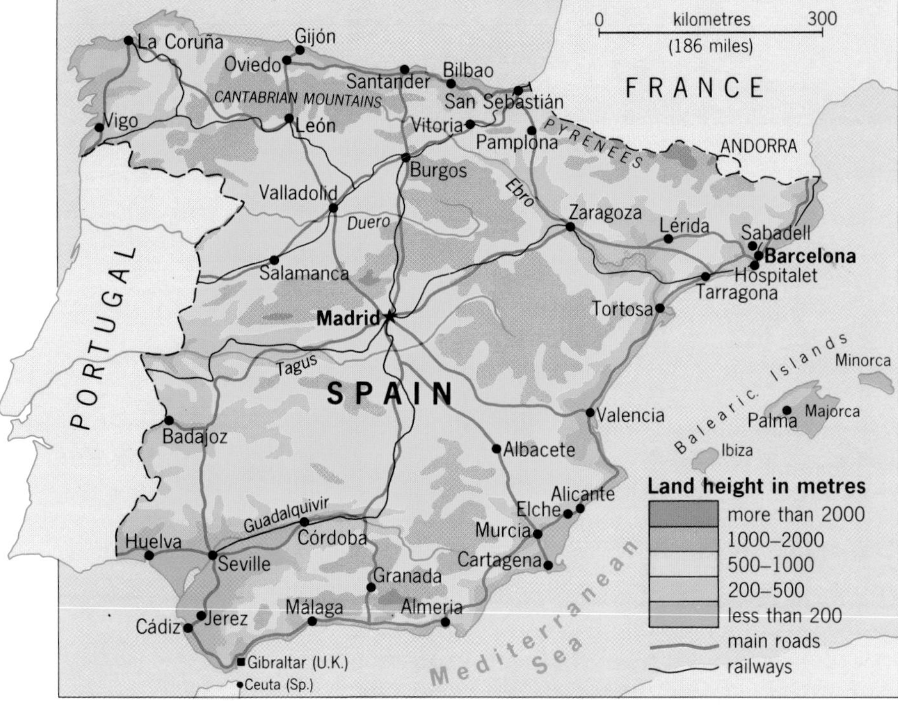

Wet Spain

Mountains called the Pyrenees separate Spain from France. At the western end of the Pyrenees live the Basque people, who have their own language and traditions. Northern Spain is 'wet Spain': a green, lush countryside facing the Atlantic Ocean. It is also an industrial area. Bilbao is Spain's most important industrial town, and Gijón has a steelworks. La Coruña has been a naval port and shipbuilding town since before the days of the Spanish Armada.

Holiday Spain

Spain's south and east coasts face the Mediterranean Sea. This is 'holiday Spain', with skyscraper hotels which accommodate people who come from other parts of Europe to enjoy the hot summers and the warm winters. The Balearic Islands in the Mediterranean and the volcanic Canary Islands in the Atlantic Ocean are also parts of Spain which are popular with tourists.

Towns and villages

Spanish towns and villages are dominated by large churches. Most people are Roman Catholics, and festivals and processions take place on holy days and saints' days. The *plaza mayor* is the central square. The shops around it are often in a cool, covered arcade. Shops are shut from lunch-time to late afternoon for the siesta (time for sleep and rest). But in the cooler evenings, the main streets and plazas come to life as people stroll around and perhaps have a late dinner in an open-air restaurant. ■

Area
504,750 sq km
(194,884 sq miles)
Capital
Madrid
Population
38,820,000
Language
Spanish, Catalan, Basque
Religion
Christian
Government
Parliamentary monarchy
Currency
1 peseta = 100 céntimos

See also
Armada
Basques
Bullfighting
Canary Islands
European history
Spain's history
Spanish colonial history

Football is a popular sport in Spain. Real (Royal) Madrid is just one famous Spanish team. Spain hosted the World Cup in 1982.

Barcelona is the site for the Olympic Games, 1992.

◀ Evening time in Alicante, a town in southern Spain. The blinds on the windows are still down after the afternoon siesta (sleep).

Spain's history

Spain has had an exciting and turbulent history. By the 5th century BC, Phoenicians, Greeks and Celts had established small settlements, but the country was divided among many small, warlike tribes. It is a difficult country to fight over, because of its mountains and its dry central plateau. It was the highly efficient Roman army that finally conquered the whole peninsula and made it part of the Roman empire.

Roman rule lasted for almost 600 years. Then a Germanic tribe, the Visigoths, swept in and took over. They set up a kingdom whose nobles warred among themselves. In AD 711 one of those nobles, Count Julian, called in Berber warriors from Morocco to help him rebel against his king, even though they were Muslims not Christians.

Under their Arab leader, Tarik, the Berbers landed at a rocky point which ever after was called Tarik's Rock; in his language Gebel Tarik (Gibraltar). In seven years the Berbers, aided by a host of fellow Muslims: Arabs, Moors and Syrians, had conquered all but the north of the country. For nearly 500 years most of Spain was an Islamic country, though Muslims were generally tolerant of Christians and Jews. Spain under the Moors became famous for its universities, for medicine and for irrigation, art and architecture. The Alhambra (castle and palace) at Granada is one of the most elegant and finely decorated buildings in Europe.

The years of power

The Muslim rulers quarrelled among themselves and by the 11th century Spain was divided into over 20 small states. The Christian kingdoms of the north, led by Castile, took the opportunity and bit by bit reconquered Spain for Christianity until only the kingdom of Granada in the south remained a Muslim state. The two Christian kingdoms of Castile and Aragon united in 1479, and almost all Spain was under one rule again. In 1492 two very important events occurred: the Muslims were driven out of Granada, and an expedition under Christopher Columbus landed in the Caribbean. Columbus was from Genoa in Italy, but it was Queen Isabella of Spain who provided the funds, and Spaniards who reaped the benefit.

In the next hundred years Spanish adventurers conquered a vast empire in Central and South America, and untold gold and silver were looted and brought back to Europe. In the late 16th century, under King Philip II, Spain became one of the richest and most powerful countries in Europe.

◀ **The Muslim governor of Seville holding a council.**

Spain's 'golden age' did not last. A series of disastrous wars and equally disastrous, feeble kings weakened the country. It declined rapidly in the 18th century, and eventually its American colonies rebelled and became independent.

Civil War 1936–1939

In 1931 the king, Alfonso XIII, was driven into exile and a republic was set up. Five years later a military revolt against an elected left-wing government plunged the country into civil war. Spaniards suffered terribly during the three years of fighting between the Republicans and their allies on the one side and the fascist 'Falange' on the other. In 1939 Spain fell under the rule of a fascist dictator, General Francisco Franco.

Franco held power until his death in 1975. Although he was friendly with the dictators of Germany and Italy, Adolf Hitler and Benito Mussolini, he kept Spain out of World War II. When he died, Alfonso's grandson, Juan Carlos, became king, and free elections were held. ■

◀ **Troops supporting General Franco examining villages and searching for arms. Over 750,000 people were killed in the civil war.**

Ferdinand and Isabella
A wedding led to the unification of Spain in 1479. The couple were cousins, Prince Ferdinand, heir to the throne of Castile, and Princess Isabella, heir to the throne of Aragon. When they succeeded to their thrones, the two kingdoms effectively became one. Isabella and Ferdinand were bigoted Roman Catholics. They introduced the Inquisition to compel all Spain's people to join their religion. At least 2,000 'heretics' were burned at the stake, and the Jews were driven out of Spain.

See also
Armada
Fascists
Gibraltar
Muslims
Spain
Spanish colonial history

Biography
Cervantes
Columbus
El Cid
Franco
Philip II of Spain
Teresa of Avila

Explorers
Balboa
Columbus
Cortés
Pizarro

Artists
El Greco
Goya
Picasso
Velázquez

Spanish colonial history

'Hispanics' is a word used for people of Spanish descent who come from countries in South and Central America.

A band of bold adventurers, known as conquistadores (conquerors), captured an empire for Spain in the early 16th century. Three hundred years later most of the Spanish colonies won their independence. The last colonial territory, in the western Sahara of Africa, was lost in 1975 when it was taken by Morocco and Mauritania.

► **An ancient Aztec drawing shows a Spanish commander, with support from Aztec soldiers as well as Spaniards, attacking the Great Temple.**

Conquering the New World

Spain and Portugal were rivals for the new lands that were opening up for colonization. So in 1493 Pope Alexander VI drew a line on the map called the Line of Demarcation. Spain was to have all the lands to the west of it, Portugal all the lands to the east. By the Treaty of Tordesillas, a year later, the line was moved westward, which gave Portugal the right to Brazil.

Spain lost no time in following up Columbus's exploration of the Caribbean in 1492. Within a few years colonies were set up and by 1501 the first African slaves were working in Santo Domingo. A mainland colony was established on the Isthmus of Panama, and its governor, the conquistador Vasco Núñez de Balboa, saw the Pacific Ocean and claimed it for Spain.

The Aztec empire in Mexico was conquered by an adventurous lawyer and farmer, Hernán Cortés, with an army of only 550 men. Cortés was helped by the fact that his white face and black beard made the Aztecs think he was their god Quetzalcoatl, returned to them. The Inca empire of Peru was conquered by even fewer men, just 180 led by Francisco Pizarro.

The conquistadores were inspired by a greed for gold, of which there was plenty in America, and a desire to bring the benefits of Christianity to the American Indian people. Gold and silver in plenty were looted and shipped to Spain, even though some of the treasure ships were captured by privateers (who were a bit like pirates) such as Sir Francis Drake.

Ruling the empire

At its height in the 16th and 17th centuries Spain's empire included half of South America, all of Central America and the Caribbean, and much of California, Texas, Florida and other parts of North America. The empire was ruled from Madrid, through viceroys.

Many of the conquistadores married local Indian girls. A class structure grew up. Those with all Spanish ancestors owned most of the wealth and had all the power. Those of mixed race often had small farms or were traders. The poorest of all were the Indians and African slaves.

Wars of independence

The unequal wealth of the people led the citizens of Spain's American colonies to rebel. The Wars of Independence began in 1809. At first they failed, but from 1816 onward they were everywhere successful. Mexico and Central America won independence in 1821.

Two men were outstanding among the South American leaders. José de San Martín liberated Argentina, Chile and Peru, helped by the Chilean general Bernardo O'Higgins. In the north Simón Bolívar won freedom for four countries: Bolivia, Colombia, Ecuador and Venezuela, and took over Peru from San Martín.

By 1825 Spain ruled only Cuba and Puerto Rico, plus Guam and the Philippines in the Pacific. Those were lost in 1898, in war with the USA. ■

► **This church in the city of Quito, Ecuador, is typical of the elaborate Baroque style of Spanish colonial architecture.**

See also
Aztecs
Conquistadores
Hispanics
Incas
Spain's history

Biography
Balboa
Bolívar
Columbus
Cortés
Drake
Pizarro

Spastics

People who are spastic have great difficulty in controlling movement in their bodies. This is because the part of their brain that controls movement has been damaged before or at birth or in the early weeks of life. Someone who is spastic suffers from cerebral palsy.

If only one side of the body is affected with cerebral palsy it is called hemiplegia. If both sides of the upper part of the body are affected it is called diplegia. If all four limbs are affected it is called quadriplegia.

People with cerebral palsy often cannot speak easily, because control of the speech muscles is also affected. With special exercises (physiotherapy) people can be helped to make use of the undamaged parts of the brain to gain as much control of movement as possible.

It is important to realize that people with cerebral palsy are often just as clever as other people. ■

See also
Handicaps
Physiotherapists

Species

Number of animal species known
About 1 million
Number of animal species thought to be undiscovered
About 8 million (mostly very small creatures)
Number of plant species
About 380,000

A species is a group of plants or animals that have been classified together because the members of a species differ from all other forms of life in one or more ways. Within a species there are slight individual differences, but these differences are not so marked as those that occur between members of different species.

The members of a species are able to breed together and produce healthy offspring. Even very similar species, such as rabbits and hares, will not breed together. Breeding between different species does not occur in nature, but sometimes, as in the case of horses and donkeys, people interfere. Although horses and donkeys can breed together to produce offspring (the mule), their offspring itself is sterile and unable to breed.

Visit your local park and look at the ducks on the pond. There will probably be several species there, especially in the winter-time. See how the different species look and behave differently. If you look closely at the members of one species, you will be able to see that they are all different too, but the differences are slight. ■

Species of duck include:
goosander
mallard
mandarin
shoveller
teal
tufted duck
wigeon

See also
Animals
Classification
Plants

Spectacles

Marco Polo, the Italian explorer, noted people wearing spectacles in China in 1275.

People wear spectacles so that they can see clearly. Spectacles have glass or plastic lenses which bend the light before it enters the eye. Then the lens in the eye can focus the light and produce a clear picture on the retina at the back of the eye.

Short-sighted people can see objects clearly only if they are close to their eyes; they need concave lenses in their spectacles. Long-sighted people need convex lenses to help them see nearby objects more clearly.

Some people cannot focus on both nearby and distant objects even with spectacles, and may have to change to a different pair for reading, or to use bifocals. Bifocals look quite ordinary but have two types of lenses in one frame: when you look through the top half of the lens you can see things clearly that are far away, and when you want to read you look through the lower part of the lens.

Flashback

We do not know who invented spectacles, but they were first worn in Europe in the 13th century. Their popularity increased with the development of printing in the 15th century, but it is not until this century, with education for all, that they have become truly widespread. ■

See also
Eyes
Lenses
Opticians

Spices

Spices are used in cooking to add flavour and colour to our food. Spices come from a variety of different parts of different plants. They are usually dried to preserve them and should be kept in airtight containers away from light. They may be used whole or ground. The way in which they are used affects their flavour.

Flashback

Spices were known and used by the ancient Chinese, the Egyptians, Greeks and Romans. Everywhere spices were very valuable. They grew in a small number of places such as the Moluccas or Spice Islands of Indonesia, and everyone wanted them. They were used to preserve food, to cover up the taste of food which was going bad, and as medicines.

An important spice trade grew up between East and West. For a long time this was controlled by Venetians and merchants in the Middle East. Then in the 16th century Portuguese sailors discovered the Moluccas and took over the islands and the spice trade. A hundred years later the Dutch East India Company moved in. Their monopoly lasted until the islanders rebelled and the company went bankrupt. Indonesia is still the world's largest producer of cloves and nutmeg. ■

Pepper

Pepper is sometimes called 'The King of the Spices'. It is used all over the world. Peppercorns are the berries of the pepper vine. Black pepper is dried unripe fruit, and white pepper comes from fruit picked when almost ripe, with the dark outer skin removed.

Cloves

Cloves are dried buds of a tropical evergreen tree. They are highly flavoured and only a small quantity needs to be used. They are used to flavour some meat such as ham, and sweet dishes such as apple pie. Cloves are also used in medicine to treat indigestion and toothache.

Nutmeg and mace

These two flavourings come from the fruit of an evergreen tree which originally grew in the Moluccas or Spice Islands. Fresh nutmeg is enclosed in a hard brown shell which is itself enclosed in a crimson mesh called mace. Both are used in savoury stews and sweet food.

Ginger

Ginger is the rhizome (underground stem) of another tropical plant. It is used fresh, dried and ground, or preserved in sugar or syrup. Fresh ginger needs peeling and grating before use. Ginger is used in both sweet and savoury cooking.

Chillis

Chilli is the general name given to a variety of hot South American peppers. They may be green or red and are usually long and tapering and full of seeds. Chillis have a very sharp and fiery flavour. Dried red chillis are ground to make chilli powder.

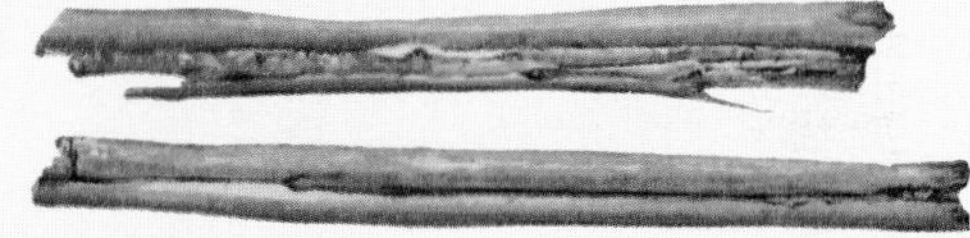

Cinnamon

Cinnamon is the dried and rolled inner bark from the shoots of a small tropical tree. It can be used in this 'stick' form, but more often it is ground. It is mostly used to flavour cakes, biscuits and sweet foods.

Garam masala
This is the Indian name for a mixture of spices. Here is a simple one which is used to add spiciness to an Indian dish towards the end of the cooking time.

2 teaspoons ground cardamom
1 teaspoon each of ground cinnamon, ground cloves, ground black pepper and ground cumin

The word 'curry' in Tamil (a language of southern India) means sauce. Indians, Bangladeshis and Pakistanis use different combinations of spices for each dish.

Whole cumin seeds fried in oil taste different from ground cumin seeds which have been toasted under the grill.

Did you know?
Spices were almost unknown in Britain until the crusaders first tasted them in the Holy Land. When spices did reach the West they were so expensive that they were kept under lock and key in special spice boxes.

See also
Food
Herbs

Spiders

Spiders, like insects, have jointed legs and bodies which are made in sections or segments. But, unlike an insect, a spider's body consists of two, not three parts, and it has eight, not six legs. Also spiders cannot fly, although baby spiders and small adult types may 'parachute' on long silk threads.

All spiders can make silk. It is pushed from special organs called spinnerets which are at the back of the body. Silk is formed as a liquid but hardens instantly on contact with air. Spiders use silk to protect their eggs and to wrap up prey. Some use it to make traps called webs to catch their prey in.

All spiders are carnivores. They feed mainly on the flesh of insects or other tiny creatures, although the largest species may catch animals as big as small birds and mice. When a spider has caught its prey, it uses pointed fangs to inject venom (poison). This paralyses the prey and also contains digestive juices which break down the prey's flesh, making it liquid. The spider then feeds by sucking up this liquid meal.

Some spiders make sticky, circular orb webs, but there are other sorts of trap, including hammock webs, funnel webs and trap-door traps. When an insect blunders into a web, the spider rushes out before it can escape, wraps its victim in silk and then injects it with venom.

Not all spiders build webs. Wolf spiders have larger eyes than web-building types and rely entirely on speed and strength to outrun and overcome their prey.

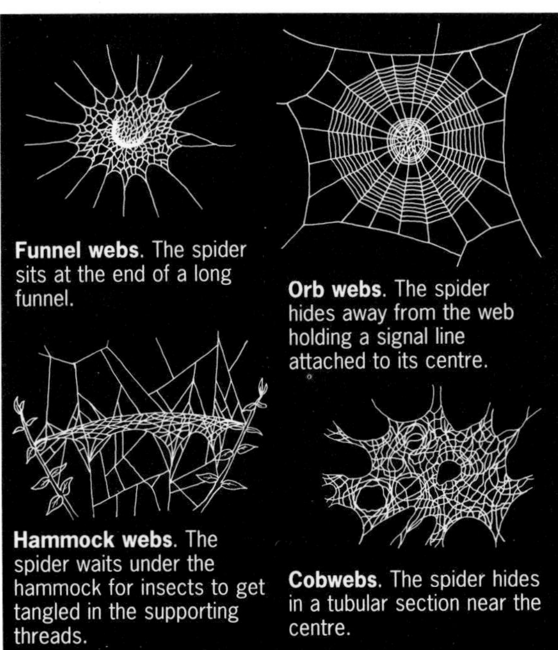

Funnel webs. The spider sits at the end of a long funnel.

Orb webs. The spider hides away from the web holding a signal line attached to its centre.

Hammock webs. The spider waits under the hammock for insects to get tangled in the supporting threads.

Cobwebs. The spider hides in a tubular section near the centre.

◀ Female red-kneed tarantula. Some tarantulas are poisonous, but less dangerous than most people think.

◀ Spiders use their poison to kill strong and active prey. This garden spider has caught a wasp. Many spiders cut free powerful insects such as wasps, which can defend themselves with their stings.

Most spiders have very small eyes and are very short-sighted but jumping spiders have two huge eyes which look forwards and smaller ones looking sideways and backwards. They move like a cat stalking a bird until in jumping range of a fly. Then they leap onto the insect's back and bite it with their fangs.

Spitting spiders get their name from their method of catching insects. They spit a stream of poisonous glue at them. This sticks the insect firmly to the ground so that the spider can eat it at leisure.

A few spiders live entirely under water and even build an underwater web. They swim to the surface regularly and lift themselves quickly out of the water and back again to trap a layer of air under their thick coat of hairs. A water spider's web is dome-shaped and full of air shaken from its body. It lives here while waiting for tiny water creatures to swim by. ■

Largest spider
More than 10 cm long (the leg span may be twice this)
Smallest spider
Less than 1 mm long
Lifespan
Some large spiders have survived for 15 years in captivity. Most probably live for much less than this.
Biggest webs
Some webs spun by orb-weaver spiders have measured 5·7 m around the edge.

Phylum Arthropoda
Class Arachnida
Order Araneae
Number of species
About 20,000

See also
Invertebrates
Poisonous animals
Scorpions

Spinning

Spinning is a way of twisting fibres together to make a stronger thread, also called yarn. Sheep's wool spins easily as it is naturally curly. But hair from other animals, such as the yak, goat, angora rabbit and alpaca, can also be spun. You can spin using just your fingers, but to spin quickly most people use a spindle.

▶ This spinner is pulling some woollen fibres from a bundle of wool kept in a basket. Her foot is on the treadle ready to turn the wheel. She uses wool from different breeds of sheep. The white sheep in the foreground is a Dorset Horn. The black and white is a Jacob's sheep.

▶ Turkish women using hand spindles. People have spun thread in this way for centuries, and in some parts of the world still do.

Spinning with a spindle

A drop spindle is a stick with a small disc at one end. The disc is called a whorl and can be made of wood, clay or stone. It keeps the spindle turning after the spinner has set it going. The thread is tied to the spindle and twists as the spindle turns. The spinner adds more fibres to the thread from a bundle held in the hand or on a stick called a distaff. Every so often she stops and winds the thread she has made onto the spindle. People made thread like this all over the world until the spinning-wheel was invented.

Spinning-wheels

The wheel, which is turned either by hand or by a foot pedal, turns the spindle and twists the wool as it winds it. A string runs over the wheel and over a small pulley to turn the spindle. Spinning-wheels work much faster than hand spindles, but the spinner can still only spin one length of thread at a time.

Flashback

The spinning-wheel was first developed in India. The idea spread and spinning-wheels were used all over Europe by the 14th century, though people continued to use spindles as well.

A machine for spinning a number of threads at once was invented in England in 1764. This was called the 'Spinning Jenny' by its inventor, James Hargreaves. The first machine had eight spindles instead of a single one, so one person could spin eight times as much yarn as could someone using the traditional spinning-wheel. A few years later there were machines using water power to drive the wheels of the spinning machines in cotton mills. Richard Arkwright patented this invention, though he may have got the idea from other engineers. In modern factories each spinning machine has hundreds of spindles and the power to drive them comes from electricity. But however large the machine, it does the same job of twisting fibres together to make thread (yarn). ■

▶ The first Spinning Jenny had eight spindles. Soon there were sixteen and later 120 all worked by one wheel.

See also
Fabrics
Fibres
Industrial Revolution
Sheep
Weaving

Biography
Arkwright

Sponges

▶ **Many tropical sponges, such as this one from Australia's Great Barrier Reef, are brilliantly coloured.**

Although some sponges can creep a little and others react slightly to light or to touch, they are not able to see, hear or move. Until the last century, most people thought that sponges were plants; in fact they are animals.

Sponges may be many different shapes, sizes and colours. Their bodies are covered with a tough skin which is pitted with tiny holes and some larger openings. Inside they have a skeleton made of microscopically small hard parts called spicules. These form a network which supports passages and chambers leading from the small surface holes. The chambers are lined with cells called collar cells, each of which has a whip-like structure. Beating together, they cause water to flow through the passages. The water contains oxygen and tiny fragments of food. Food is caught by the collar cells and passed to amoeba-like wandering cells which carry it to the parts of the body where it is needed. Waste products pass out of the large holes on the surface as the water is pumped out.

No other creatures function in this way, and so it is thought that sponges have evolved differently from all other animals. ■

The skeletons of sponges were used by the Greeks for bathing, scrubbing down tables and as padding for armour.

Distribution
All in water, most in the sea, some in the very deep sea
Largest sponges
About 2 m high, such as the loggerhead sponge, *Spheciospongia vesparia*
Smallest sponges
Several species about 1 mm high
Amount of water filtered by sponges
A sponge 4 cubic cm in volume can filter about 0·5 litres per hour. A sponge 10 litres in volume can filter 360 litres per hour.

Phylum
Porifera
Number of classes
3 (glass sponges, calcareous sponges and horny sponges)
Number of species
About 5,000

See also
Invertebrates

Spores

Spores are minute single cells able to grow into a clone (a new plant identical to the parent). Algae, mosses, ferns, fungi and bacteria all reproduce from spores. Spores usually have a thick, protective outer coat which helps them survive difficult conditions. Some bacterial spores are still able to grow after being boiled for half an hour. Most spores are produced in large quantities to ensure that some will find the right conditions for growth. A giant puffball may contain as many as seven million million spores.

As spores are so small it is easier to look for the sporangia which produce them. Look at the underside of fern leaves in late summer where collections of sporangia form brown velvety patches. The thousands of tiny black dots on mouldy bread are also sporangia. The air is full of millions of different spores ready for growth. ■

See also
Algae
Bacteria
Ferns
Fungi
Mosses
Yeasts

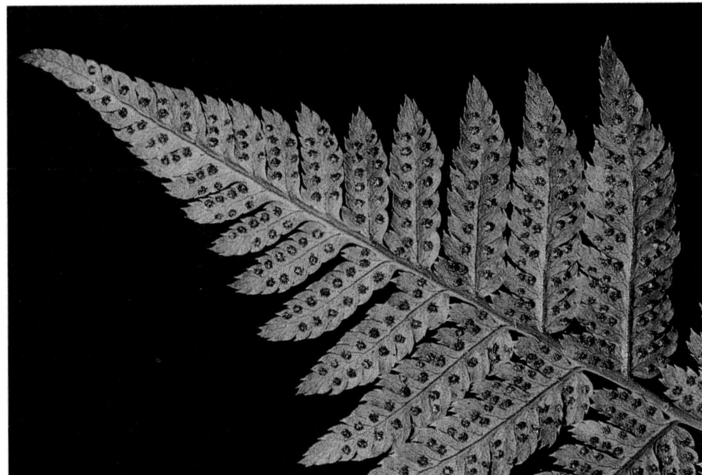

▲ **The brown patches on the underside of this fern leaf are the sporangia which produce the spores. The plant is a long beech fern growing in Michigan, USA.**

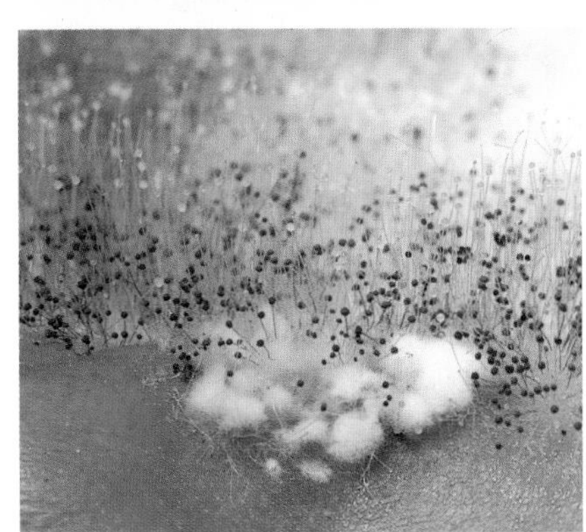

◀ **This patch of mould, many times magnified, is growing on a papaya fruit.**

Sport

When the FA Cup Final takes place towards the end of the British football season, thousands of spectators turn up at Wembley Stadium to cheer on the teams and many millions more watch the match on television. The same is true of many famous sporting events, such as cricket's Test Matches, the Wimbledon tennis tournament, the American football Superbowl, the baseball World Series, the Tour de France cycle race, and the Olympic Games. However, for every person who watches sport, there are many more who take part in it for the fun and excitement it offers.

Everyone needs to exercise regularly to stay healthy, and one of the most enjoyable ways to exercise is to take part in organized sport. Throughout history, people have done this, from the original Olympic Games of ancient Greece to the wide range of sporting activities available to us today. Nearly all children join in sports, and many people do so all their lives.

Amateurs and professionals

People who take part in sport just for fun and who do not get paid for it are called 'amateurs'. Some sports, such as Rugby Union, will only allow amateurs to play and have strict laws against paying anyone.

Those who make a living from sport are called 'professionals'. Professional sport is big business, and some of the most popular stars can earn huge amounts of money from displaying their skills to the fans.

How to get involved

Schools and youth clubs offer many chances to participate in the most popular sports. However, they may not be able to cater for the whole range of activities. You may need to join a club or go on a course to take part in some of the sports listed. Ask your PE teacher at school for information about how to get involved in the sport of your choice. Then go out and enjoy yourself. ■

► These are the main types of sports split into different groups. There are other ways of grouping them. This is just one way which may help you to choose those that interest you. Some people enjoy team games, others prefer individual competitive sports. There is an article on each of these sports, or one closely relating to it, in this encyclopedia except those which are marked with an asterisk*.

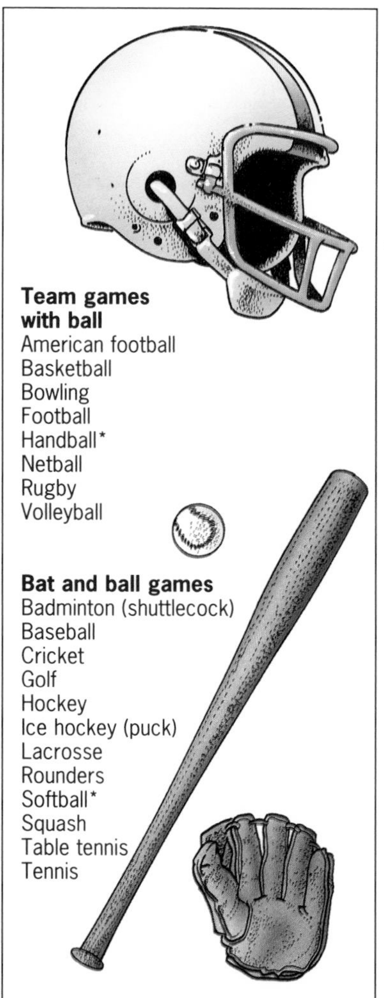

Team games with ball
American football
Basketball
Bowling
Football
Handball*
Netball
Rugby
Volleyball

Bat and ball games
Badminton (shuttlecock)
Baseball
Cricket
Golf
Hockey
Ice hockey (puck)
Lacrosse
Rounders
Softball*
Squash
Table tennis
Tennis

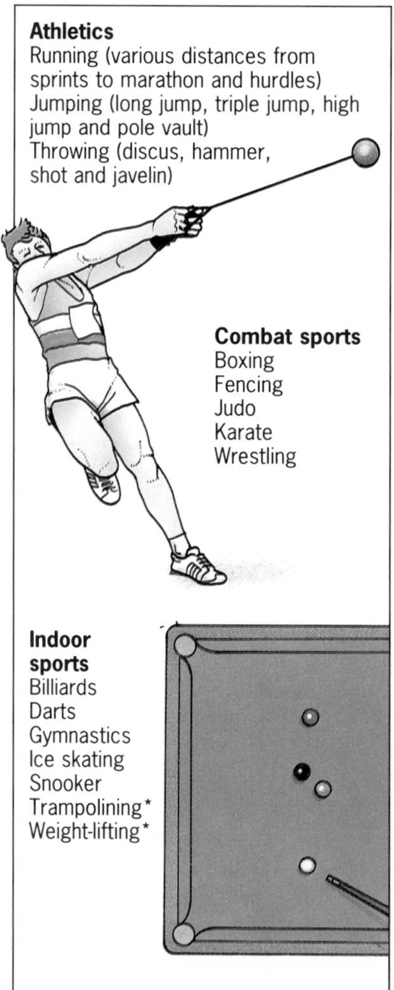

Athletics
Running (various distances from sprints to marathon and hurdles)
Jumping (long jump, triple jump, high jump and pole vault)
Throwing (discus, hammer, shot and javelin)

Combat sports
Boxing
Fencing
Judo
Karate
Wrestling

Indoor sports
Billiards
Darts
Gymnastics
Ice skating
Snooker
Trampolining*
Weight-lifting*

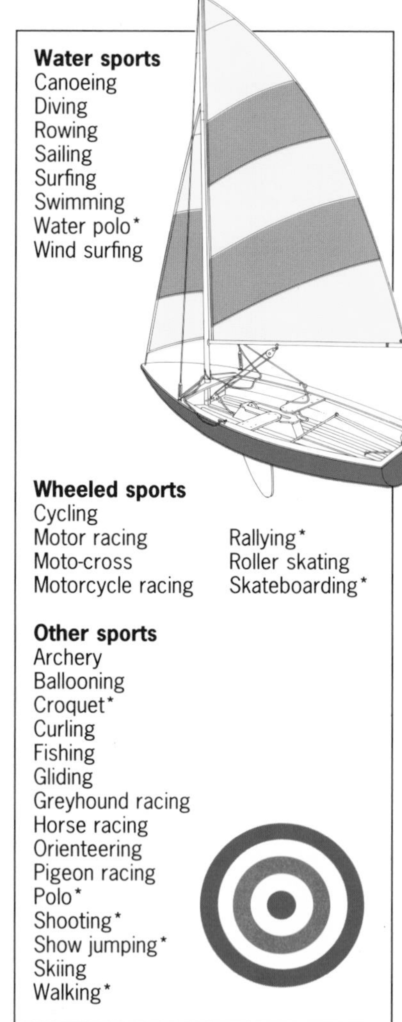

Water sports
Canoeing
Diving
Rowing
Sailing
Surfing
Swimming
Water polo*
Wind surfing

Wheeled sports
Cycling
Motor racing
Moto-cross
Motorcycle racing
Rallying*
Roller skating
Skateboarding*

Other sports
Archery
Ballooning
Croquet*
Curling
Fishing
Gliding
Greyhound racing
Horse racing
Orienteering
Pigeon racing
Polo*
Shooting*
Show jumping*
Skiing
Walking*

See also
Olympic Games

Biography
Sports special

Springs

In a clockwork motor, a coiled-up strip of steel slowly unwinds to turn the wheels.

You can use springs to store energy for a short or a long time. This energy can be allowed to escape quickly or slowly from the spring. As it does so, it can move something or drive a piece of machinery around. Clocks and watches were once driven by coiled-up springs. And springs like this are used in the 'clockwork' motors in some toys. A spring is usually made of a special type of steel so that it will return to its original shape, however much it has been squeezed, bent or stretched. The steel in the spring must also not crack or break after it has been bent a large number of times. The metal spring may be a thin flat strip, a wire or a rod. It can have many different shapes, such as those in the drawing.

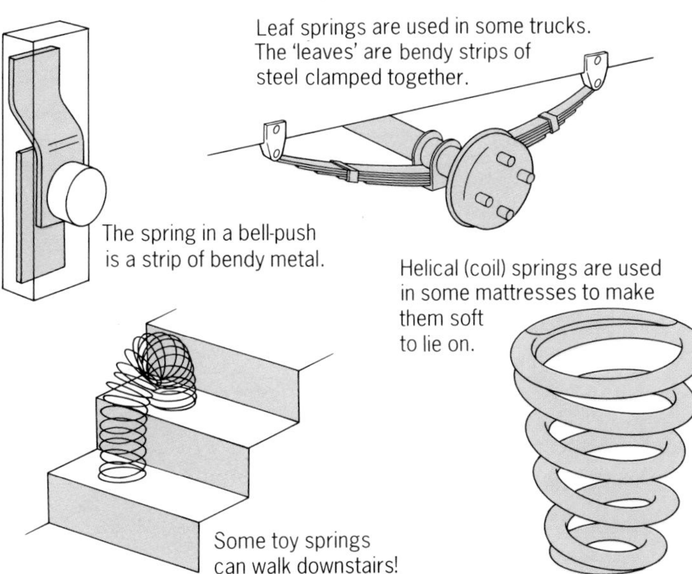

Leaf springs are used in some trucks. The 'leaves' are bendy strips of steel clamped together.

The spring in a bell-push is a strip of bendy metal.

Helical (coil) springs are used in some mattresses to make them soft to lie on.

Some toy springs can walk downstairs!

Springs can be designed so that when they are released they return to their original shape so quickly that they shake or vibrate, and this can be put to good use. Guitar strings are springs which vibrate when you pluck them. A piece of rubber can behave like a spring. So can air which is trapped inside a container. The air in a ball makes it springy, so that it bounces. In vehicles, metal springs are fixed between the wheels and the body. They absorb the jolts when the wheels travel over a bumpy road. ■

See also
Locks and keys
Motor cars

Squash

front-wall
side-wall
back-wall
1·8 m
4·6 m
2·1 m
6·4 m
9·7 m
4·3 m
the 'tin', 48 cm high

Service box 1·6 m square on each side of the court. The server must have at least one foot inside the service box.

▲ **The squash court, with the player on the right about to serve. In America squash is played on a narrower court with a much harder ball.**

This is a variation of an older game called 'racquets'. It is played in an enclosed court, usually by two players, with a soft ball and a strung racket. Squash is a very energetic game, requiring quick bursts of speed and energy to get to the falling ball or to intercept a hard shot. Players score points by hitting shots that their opponents are unable to return. Players must hit the ball before it bounces twice, and must return it so that it hits the front wall. When the ball is in play it can bounce from all four walls.

Because of the four-walled court, the game is not easy to watch and has never been an important spectator sport. Transparent courts are specially built for big tournaments, however, and the game is sometimes shown on television.

Squash is one of a group of games which grew up out of 'hitting against the wall' games in English public schools in the 19th century. ■

Squash is also called squash racquets.

The American version of squash uses a harder ball.

▲ **Squash rackets are made of wood, fibreglass or carbon graphite, and the balls are made of hollow rubber.**

See also
Biography
Sports special

Squids

Distribution
In the sea, mainly in the open oceans. Some live at very great depths.
Smallest squid
Sandalops pathopis, a deep sea squid, is one of the smallest, measuring about 2·5 cm.
Largest squid
Giant squids, *Architeuthis* sp., sometimes become stranded. The largest measure about 20 m overall. Parts of the arms of still bigger squids have been found in the stomachs of sperm whales, but are unknown as complete animals.

Phylum Mollusca
Class Cephalopoda
Order Decapoda
Number of species
About 350

Squids are relatives of the snail, but they have no shells. Instead they have a stiff, horny support inside their bag-like bodies. This is called the pen. As squids also have ink sacs, they are sometimes called the pen and ink animals. The head, with its large eyes and big brain, is attached at the front of the body bag. Eight long arms surround the mouth, and there are also two even longer tentacles.

Squids live mostly in the open ocean. They propel themselves with jets of water. Some move so quickly that they can become airborne and skim over the waves for a distance of 20 m (60 ft) or more. Squids feed mainly on fish, which they catch with their long tentacles. Like the arms, these carry suckers, which often have claws to help hold the slippery prey. Squids are themselves the food for many kinds of animals. Giant squids which live in the deep sea are an important part of the food of sperm whales.

In the darkness of the deep sea squids often use brightly coloured light organs to signal to each other and dazzle attackers. Usually there is at least one light organ near to the eyes, so that the squid will not be blinded by the light which may be produced by a hunting fish. ■

See also
Molluscs
Oceans and seas
Octopuses

Squirrels

Distribution
Throughout the world except for Australasia, Madagascar and some deserts
Largest Alpine marmot up to 90 cm long including tail
Smallest African pygmy squirrel, total length as little as 11 cm
Number of young 4 or 5
Lifespan Up to 10 years

Subphylum Vertebrata
Class Mammalia
Order Rodentia
Family Sciuridae
Number of species 67

See also
Rodents

Unlike most small mammals, squirrels are active during the daytime. Their eyesight is better than that of other rodents and they are able to judge distances very well as they climb and leap in trees.

Tree squirrels feed on nuts and fruits and sometimes gnaw at trees to get at the sap. Like many rodents, squirrels store surplus food, usually by burying it. They forget where they make their larders, but they have a good sense of smell and are able to find nuts even under 10 cm (4 in) of soil. Tree squirrels make secure nests in hollow trees and also dens among the branches, called dreys.

Red squirrels were once far more numerous in the British Isles than they are now. Disease, clearance of forests, and competition from the larger grey squirrel, which was imported from America at the end of the 19th century, have made them now quite rare.

Flying squirrels are small relatives of the tree squirrels. They are able to glide rather than fly, but they can steer to avoid branches. They also have many relatives which burrow. These are called the ground squirrels and include prairie dogs. ■

▶ **Tree squirrels have very sharp claws well adapted for tree-climbing. They always climb down head first using the claws of the hind feet as anchors.**

Sri Lanka

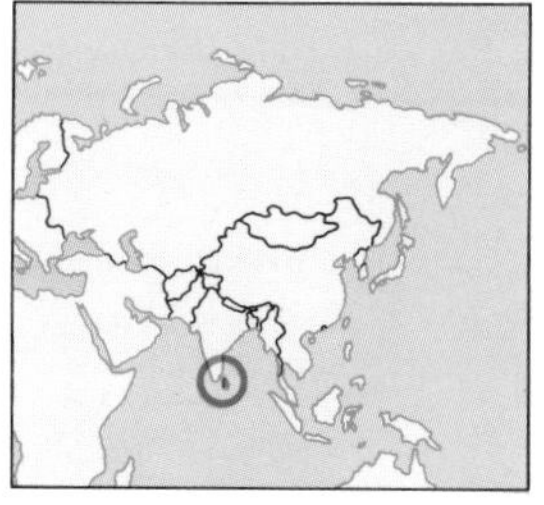

Area
65,610 sq km
(25,332 sq miles)
Capital
Colombo
Population
15,837,000
Language
Sinhalese, Tamil, English
Religion
Buddhist, Hindu, Muslim, Christian
Government
Parliamentary republic
Currency
1 Sri Lankan rupee = 100 cents

Sri Lanka is a tropical island country off the south-east tip of India. Most of the island is lowland, with a mountainous area in the central south. One of the peaks, called Adam's Peak, has a small hollow at the summit which is said to be a footprint. The mountain is visited by pilgrims from Sri Lanka's three main religions: Buddhists, Hindus and Muslims.

Large tea plantations grow on the mountain slopes. Women pick the green leaves and throw them into the baskets they carry on their backs. The leaves are dried, cut and packed and exported all over the world. Sri Lanka also exports rubber, coconuts and gemstones such as sapphires, rubies, topaz and garnets. Most people eat rice, but the country does not grow enough of its own. The streets of Colombo are busy and colourful, but there are many poor people. Some children even have to live in the streets begging, polishing shoes or selling cigarettes and plastic combs for money to survive.

► **A crowded Colombo street scene with jewellery shops advertising in English as well as in Sinhalese.**

See also
Asia
British empire
Buddhists
Commonwealth
Gems
Hindus
Muslims
Tea

Flashback

People have lived on Sri Lanka for 5,000 years. Traders have visited the island for centuries. It was called Taprobane by the Romans, Serendip by Arab merchants, Ceilão by the Portuguese, and the British, who captured it from the Dutch in 1796, called it Ceylon. The island became independent from the British in 1948 and the name has been changed to Sri Lanka which means 'Resplendent Land'. Tension between Tamil Indians who settled in the north and native Sinhalese has led to violent conflict. ■

Stained glass

Stained glass artists work with glass, lead and light. The artist plans the window carefully, drawing a full-scale design, called a cartoon, which shows the positions of the lead lines and the colours of the glass pieces.

In the Middle Ages, the stained glass master used glass made in his own workshop. Nowadays artists can choose from glass which has already been coloured (by mixing metal oxides with the molten glass mixture), blown and flattened into sheets.

Following the cartoon, the artist cuts the glass. Some pieces have designs painted on them, and these pieces are fired to fix the paint.

Once the glass is ready, the artist starts to lay out the network of leads. Following the outline of the cartoon, he bends the leads and slides the glass pieces into place. In this way, a complete panel is built up piece by piece.

When the artist is satisfied with the whole panel, he solders the leads together and fills any gaps with cement. If the panel is a large one, the leads are strengthened with tie-bars. Then the panel is ready to be fixed into its window-frame. ■

▲ **The network of leads from the window in Canterbury.**

▲ **In the Middle Ages, windows acted as picture books for a congregation, many of whom could not read. This 13th-century panel comes from a window in Canterbury Cathedral. It illustrates the parable which Jesus told of the sower who went out to sow seeds on different kinds of soil.**

See also
Cartoons
Cathedrals
Churches
Glass
Middle Ages

Biography
Becket
Fleming
Jacob

Stalactites and stalagmites

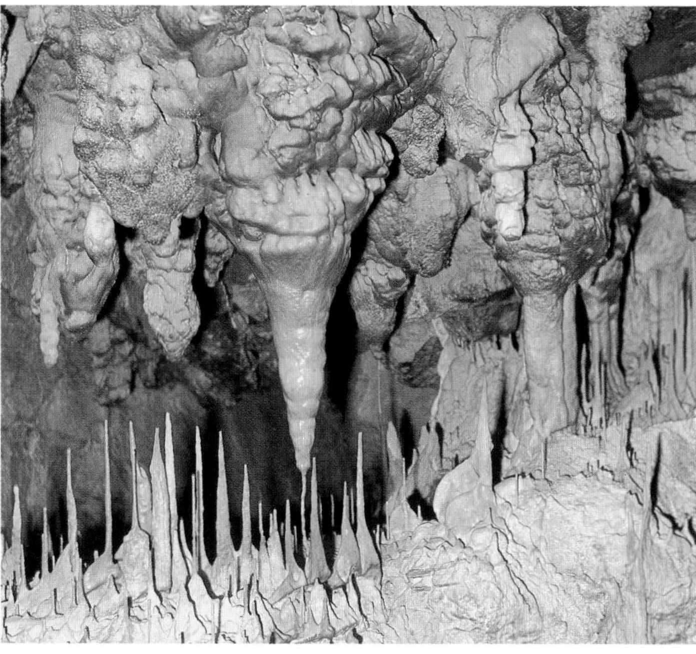

▲ Some of the stalactites in this cave in Romania have joined with the stalagmites to form strange-shaped crystalline pillars.

Stalactites and stalagmites are found in many limestone caves. Stalactites hang down from the ceiling as thin stone columns. Stalagmites rise from the floor as pillars of stone. Sometimes they join together to form a column of rock stretching from ceiling to floor.

How to remember the difference
Stala**c**tites **c**ling to the **c**eiling. Stala**g**mites **g**row from the **g**round.

The rock which forms stalactites and stalagmites is sometimes called 'dripstone'. This gives you a clue about their formation. Limestone is made mainly of a chemical called calcium carbonate. When rain-water seeps through cracks in limestone, it dissolves some of the calcium carbonate. So the water dripping from a cave roof contains a lot of this chemical.

Longest unsupported stalactite
7 m long, County Clare, Irish Republic

Every time a drip forms, some of the water is evaporated and a tiny deposit of calcium carbonate is left on the cave roof. These grow very, very slowly to form stalactites. The drips that reach the cave floor deposit calcium carbonate there, which gradually piles up to form stalagmites. If the cave stays undisturbed for thousands of years, huge and spectacular formations can grow. ■

Tallest stalagmite
Probably La Grande Stalagmite, Aven Armande Cave, near the Tarn Valley, France, 29 m high

Stamps

Postage stamps are used to show that the cost of sending a piece of mail has been paid. Modern stamps have an adhesive backing and are perforated so that they can be separated without tearing. Individual countries have their own national stamps. The designs on postage stamps can be used for a variety of purposes: to honour the country's leader or national heroes, to commemorate or celebrate a special event, or to show aspects of the history or geography of the country. They also show how much each costs.

Rowland Hill was a major figure in the postal reforms that took place in England, and he suggested that the first stamps should show Queen Victoria. He thought this image would be harder to counterfeit (forge) because so many people would recognize their queen.

► This stamp collection is based on the theme of famous people.

When mail goes through the postal system, the adhesive stamps are cancelled with an inking stamp so that they cannot be re-used. These cancelling stamps will show the date on which they were used, and they may also give a slogan or message.

Companies which send a lot of mail often use franking machines instead of stamps. They pay a sum of money to the post office and the machine will frank envelopes or labels until that amount of money is used up. People can also buy envelopes and other stationery in which the price of postage is included.

Flashback

Adhesive stamps were used by various postal services from the mid-17th century onwards. The introduction of the Penny Black and Twopence Blue in Britain in 1840 marks the beginning of their regular use. The first Penny Black was issued on 1 May 1840 and was valid for postage on 6 May. The first Twopence Blue was delivered by the printers on 8 May 1840.

► A letter sent from Ceylon in 1883.

◄ British one and two pence stamps, dating from the 19th century.

See also
Postal services

Biography
Hill, Rowland

In May 1981, $1 million was paid for a rare stamp: the only known example of the Alexandria *Blue Boy* on cover.

Philately

Many people enjoy philately (the study of stamps). Most philatelists collect stamps according to a chosen theme: perhaps old stamps, stamps of a particular country, or stamps that depict a particular item such as trains or birds. The value of stamps varies a great deal depending on their condition and their rarity. ■

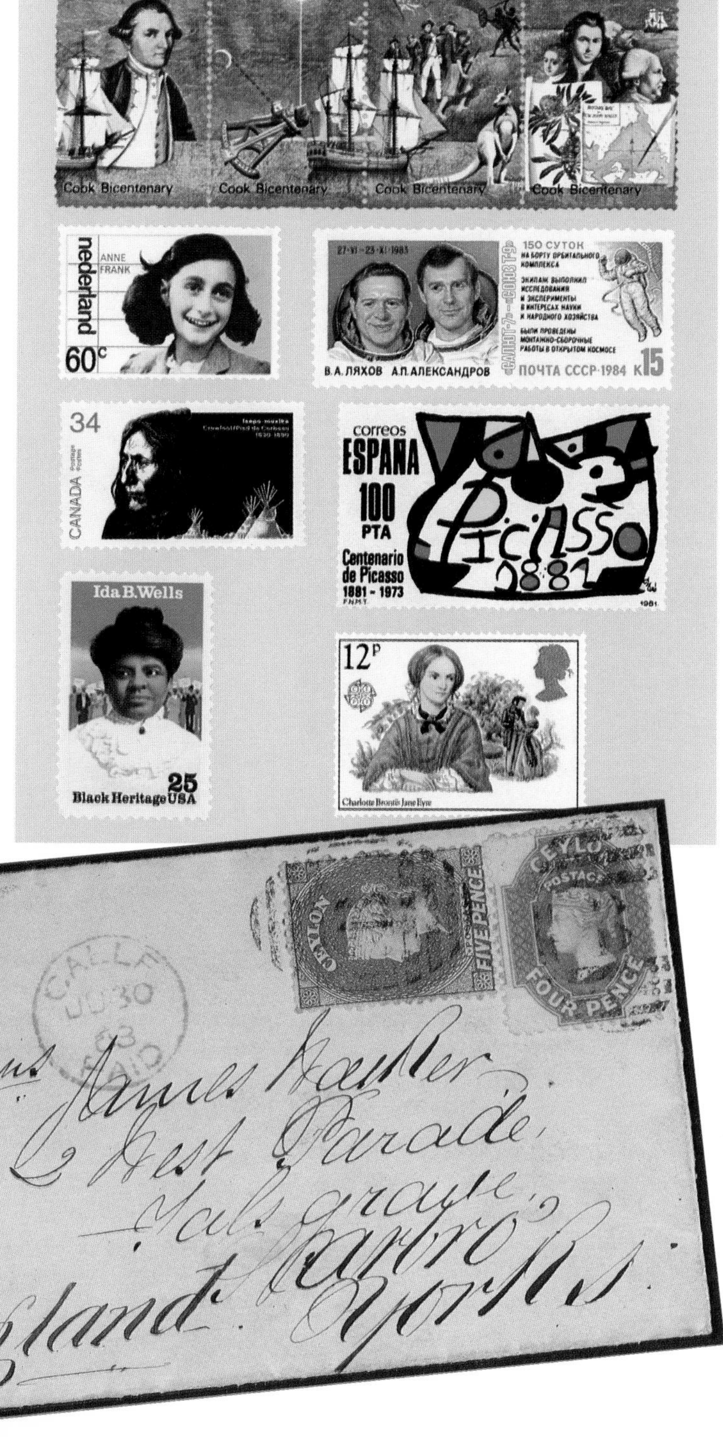

Starfish

Starfish are not fish, but they live in the sea and are star-shaped, with arms that branch out from the central disc of their body. Most have five arms, but some have many more. Often their outer skin is rough or spiny, and inside they have a skeleton of jointed rods, which strengthens and supports them.

▼ Starfish cannot see but they are able to detect changes in light and dark. This starfish has the tips of its arms slightly turned up as it is testing the amount of light with light-sensitive cells.

In grooves on the underside of a starfish's arms you can see a large number of pale, waving tube feet. These are like balloons pumped full of sea water. Each tube foot has a sucker on the end, so that it can hold onto food, or the sea-bed as the starfish moves about.

You can see a starfish's mouth in the middle of the underside of its body. Most starfish are flesh eaters. Some take very small prey, but others feed on quite large animals, such as mussels. They do this by pulling the two parts of the mussel shell open, using their strong tube feet. If a starfish is attacked, it can recover from serious injuries, and can regrow whole arms, provided that part of the central disc of the body survives. Because of this you can often find a starfish with one or more arms much smaller than the others. ■

Distribution
Only in the sea, but at all depths and on all sorts of sea-bed
Largest starfish
About 1 m in diameter
Smallest starfish
About 5 mm in diameter
Number of young
Varies, but some starfish spawn up to 1 million eggs in a season.
Lifespan
Variable, but most live for several years.

Phylum
Echinodermata (number of species about 5,400)
Class
Asteroidea
Number of species
About 1,600

See also
Invertebrates

Stars

◀ **The light from red and blue stars, reflecting off the gas clouds around them make this part of the sky unusually colourful. The brightest star at bottom left is Antares. Just to the right of it is a globular star cluster called M4. Above Antares you can see dark dust clouds blotting out the light from stars behind.**

The brightest star in the sky is Sirius, sometimes called the 'Dog Star'. The nearest star (apart from the Sun) is Proxima Centauri, which is 4·3 light years away. It belongs to a triple star, Alpha Centauri. The other two stars are only slightly further away.

There are about 5,780 stars that can be seen by eye without a telescope. About 2,500 are visible from one place on the Earth at any one time (on a clear dark night).
A supergiant star where the Sun is would swallow up the planets out as far as Mars.

On a clear, dark night you can see hundreds of twinkling stars in the sky. These stars are huge glowing balls of gas like our Sun but they are fainter because they are so much further away. The light from even the nearest stars takes years to reach us. We look up at the stars through air that is constantly blowing about, so their light is unsteady and they seem to twinkle.

A star shines because nuclear energy is given off as hydrogen gas particles crash into each other in the centre of the star. Scientists call what happens nuclear fusion.

Our Sun is one ordinary star among millions. They are all speeding through space but look still to us because they are so far away. The patterns they make in the sky stay the same. You might sometimes see what people call 'shooting stars' flash across the sky. They are not really stars at all but meteors, which are chunks of rock and bits of dust falling into our atmosphere.

How stars are made

Stars are being created all the time. They start off as clumps of gas and dust in space. Once the material begins to collect, the force of gravity makes it pull together even more strongly. In the middle it gets warmer and denser until the gas is so hot and squashed up that nuclear fusion can start. When this happens, a new star is born.

Astronomers look for new stars in the gas clouds of space. Often, lots of stars form near to each other in a giant cloud and make a cluster. The smallest stars contain about one-tenth the amount of material in the Sun. The biggest may be fifty times more massive than the Sun.

Star colours

If you look carefully at the bright stars, you might notice that some of them look quite red while others are brilliant white or bluish; our Sun is a yellow star. The colours show up even better on photographs.

The stars shine with different colours because some are hotter than others. The Sun's surface is about 6,000°C. The red stars are cooler and the blue-white ones hotter, at about 10,000°C or more. The colours are the same as you see when a piece of metal is heated up in a furnace. It first glows red-hot, then brighter and yellower until it is white-hot.

Giants and dwarfs

Although the stars are so far away that they look only like points of light, even in the world's biggest telescopes, astronomers have worked out that stars cover a huge range of sizes. They often call the large ones 'giants' and the small ones 'dwarfs'.

The Sun is a smallish star, though some are even smaller. The unusual kind of star called a white dwarf has a diameter less than one-hundredth that of the Sun. In contrast, there are some truly immense stars that have puffed themselves out till they are several hundred times the Sun's size. The bright red star called Betelgeuse in the constellation of Orion is about 500 times bigger than the Sun. If Betelgeuse were at the middle of the Solar System, it would swallow up the Earth and reach nearly as far as Jupiter.

Star clusters

Stars often form together in families, called clusters. One of the easiest to see is called the Pleiades or Seven Sisters and is in the constellation of Taurus, the Bull. There are six bright stars and many more come into view in a telescope. Photographs of the Pleiades show up the shining gas between the stars. There are many other beautiful clusters similar to the Pleiades, each with a few hundred stars in it.

There is also another kind of star cluster where many thousands of stars are packed together into a tight ball. They are called globular clusters because of their globe-like shape.

Double stars

The Sun is a single star on its own, but that is quite unusual among the stars. Most are in pairs. The force of gravity keeps them together and they orbit round each other like the planets going round the Sun. The brightest star in the sky, Sirius, is a double. The nearest stars to the Solar System, Proxima Centauri and its two partners, make a triple star called Alpha Centauri. There is a famous 'double double' of four stars in the Lyre.

Sometimes the two stars in a double cross in front of each other. This blocks out some of the starlight and makes the pair look fainter for a short time. The best-known double like this is called Algol, 'the winking demon'.

Variable stars

You might imagine that the stars are all shining steadily, but many of them go up and down in brightness. They are called variable stars. Some change in a regular way but others suddenly get brighter or fainter unexpectedly. They can vary because the star pulses in and out or because it lets off a bright flare. Some variable stars are doubles with material flowing between the two.

Some stars vary dramatically, like Mira (its name means 'wonderful'), which can sometimes be seen by eye then fades out of view. Others, such as the Pole Star, change so slightly that it is hardly noticeable to ordinary observers.

The planets, which are much nearer the Earth, shine with a steadier light than the stars.

▼ The Pleiades, a cluster of several hundred stars. They formed out of a cloud of dust and gas about 50 million years ago. The blue haze is starlight reflected off the remaining part of the cloud.

▲ **The Helix Nebula. The star at the middle of the pink ring has blown off a shell of glowing gas into space.**

► **A stellar explosion. The bright yellowish star at the top left is a supernova – a star that blew up in 1987. Before, it was even fainter than the other stars in the picture. It got very bright suddenly, then gradually faded away again.**

See also

Astronomers
Celestial sphere
Constellations
Galaxies
Gravity
Meteors
Nebulas
Nuclear power
Pulsars
Sun

Biography
Brahe
Kepler

How stars change

Stars do not live for ever. They make nuclear energy from the hydrogen gas in their cores where it is very hot, but a time comes when all the fuel is used up. When this happens the star changes and eventually it dies. Old stars swell up into red giants. They can blow off some of their gas into space, like a big smoke ring. Astronomers can see stars like this at the centres of shells of glowing gas.

The Sun is already about 5,000 million years old and is reckoned to be about half-way through its life. In the far future, the Sun will become a red giant and swallow up the planets near to it.

After that, it will shrink until all its material is squashed into a ball about the size of the Earth. It will then be a white dwarf and gradually fade away. Stars rather more massive than the Sun finish up with a tremendous explosion, called a supernova.

Supernovas

When a supernova goes off, it shines as brightly as millions of Suns put together for a few days. The inside of the exploded star that is left becomes a bleeping radio star, called a pulsar.

Nearby supernovas in our own Galaxy are rare. Only three supernovas have ever been recorded: by Chinese astronomers in 1054, by Tycho Brahe in 1572 and Kepler in 1604. Astronomers can spot them quite often in distant galaxies because they are so bright.

In 1987, a supernova exploded in a galaxy very near to our own called the Large Magellanic Cloud, which can be seen from countries in the southern hemisphere. It was very bright, so astronomers could study this important event carefully.

Star names

Many of the bright stars have their own names. Most of them have been handed down to us from Arab astronomers of centuries ago. Arabic names often start with the two letters *Al*, such as Altair, Aldebaran and Algol. Others come from Greek or Latin, such as Castor and Pollux, the 'heavenly twins' in the constellation Gemini.

Stars are also called after the constellation they are in, with a Greek letter in front. Alpha Centauri, the nearest star, is one example.

Fainter stars do not have names. Astronomers know them just as numbers in catalogues. ■

Stargazing

You can start on any clear, dark evening, so long as you have a safe place near home. Try to keep out of street and house lights; then your eyes get adapted to the dark and you see more stars. See what patterns you can imagine in the stars. Notice bright ones and faint ones. See if you can find some red stars. You will find some star charts in the article: Constellations.

Starvation

Deaths from starvation

1235
London, about 20,000
1333–1337
China, many million
1600
Russia, about ½ million
1769
France, about 5% of people
1845–1849
Ireland, about 1 million
1876–1878
India, about 5 million
1899–1900
India, over 1 million
1921–1922
Ukraine, over 1 million
1928–1929
China, several million
1932–1934
Ukraine, about 5 million
1941–1944
Siege of Leningrad, 1 million
1967–1969
Nigeria (civil war), 1½ million
1968–1974
Sahel countries, ½ million

Food is the most basic human need, and yet at least 500 million people (one-tenth of the world's population) suffer from hunger. Most of them live in the Third World, and many of them are children and young people. Every year about 15 million children die of hunger and related causes. They are starving to death.

Starvation occurs when a person has nothing to eat. During the first few days a starving person suffers from severe hunger pains. Gradually these pass, and the person gets progressively weaker as the body uses up its store of fat and energy. Body weight drops, the limbs shrivel and ultimately the person dies.

Starvation and poverty are closely linked. Between the 1970s and 1980s the number of starving people in the world doubled, made worse by widespread drought in Africa. Aid in the form of loans to Third World countries is often seen as a solution, and many international organizations work hard to try to relieve hunger. But many people believe that mass starvation can only end if land is used more carefully to grow food and if the resources and wealth of the world are shared out more fairly. ■

See also
Drought
Famine
Floods
Malnutrition
Third World

States

The word 'state' is often used as another word for 'country' or 'nation', but it has a special meaning as a division of a country with a federal government. The states of the United States of America and those of Australia are good examples of this meaning. States like these have a good deal of independence from the national government, and often collect their own taxes and make their own laws. The provinces of Canada and the republics of the Union of Soviet Socialist Republics are also states. ■

See also
American Constitution
Countries
Nations

Statistics

Every day, people collect more and more information about the world. They keep records of the weather, price rises, sports results, population changes, and so on. Information like this is called data. Statistics is the branch of mathematics that deals with data, particularly in the form of numbers.

In statistics, numbers are collected and organized in such a way that people can make sense of them, draw conclusions, and make predictions from them. For example, scientists study statistics, looking for patterns in past data, when making forecasts for the weather in the future, or when trying to predict when the next earthquake is likely to occur.

A table of statistics might give you the populations of cities of the world or the distances of planets from the Sun. Tables deal with all sorts of data, but they often have one feature in common: the data is organized so that you can compare things. Statistics may also be presented as graphs so that you can compare things easily.

Statisticians have methods of comparing two sets of figures to see how likely it is that the difference between them, or the relation between them, is an accident. For instance, if the probability of the figures being so different by chance is less than 5%, the difference is **significant at the 5 per cent level**. A biochemist testing a new fertilizer would sow crops with and without it and compare the results like this.

Statistics need to be handled with some caution, because a single statistic often summarizes a wide range of values. For instance, according to official government statistics, the average weekly spending on holidays for each household in the United Kingdom in 1984 was £4.28. But we know that holiday spending occurs at a few specific times of year, and not at a steady weekly rate throughout the year.

Statistics need careful interpretation. The way in which the information was collected can give a false view of what is happening. Trying to find out the country's favourite sport by asking 100 people at a Wimbledon Tennis Final would not give a true picture. To make proper sense of statistics, you need to find out what lies behind them. ■

See also
Averages
Graphs
Probability

Steam-engines

The first steam-powered machine was made by the Greek scientist Hero in about AD 100. It was a tiny ball-shaped boiler with nozzles sticking out of its sides. Jets of steam from the nozzles made it spin round when the water boiled.

Steam-engines were the first fuel-burning engines to be invented. During the 18th and 19th centuries, they were the main source of power for industry. With coal as their fuel, they drove machinery in factories and later powered ships and trains. Today, there are very few steam-engines left. Other types of engine have taken over.

How they work

1712 Thomas Newcomen builds an atmospheric engine. It is the first practical steam-engine.
1765 James Watt repairs Newcomen's engine and improves it.
1782 Watt invents his sun-and-planet gear, a type of crank which turns up-and-down movement of a piston into rotation.
1804 Richard Trevithick builds the first steam locomotive.
1960 Britain's last steam locomotive is built.

The oldest steam-engine still working is on the Kennet and Avon Canal in England. It was built by Boulton and Watt in 1812.

Most steam-engines use the pressure of steam to push a piston up and down a cylinder. The steam is made by boiling water over a fire of burning coal or oil. Steam from the boiler is let into the top of the cylinder by a valve. The steam expands and pushes the piston down. When the piston reaches the bottom, the valve changes position. Now, the valve lets the first lot of steam escape and feeds fresh steam into the *bottom* of the cylinder. This pushes the piston back up. When the piston reaches the top, the valve changes position again, the piston is pushed down . . . and so on. The up-and-down movement of the piston is turned into round-and-round movement by a crank. The crank moves a heavy flywheel which keeps the engine turning smoothly. The flywheel can drive other wheels or machinery.

Steam-engines work best with high-pressure steam. To withstand the pressure, the boiler, pipes and cylinders have to be very strong. In some engines, there is a condenser to collect and cool the escaping steam. The steam condenses (turns into water), goes back into the boiler and is used again. With a condenser, a steam-engine can work for longer without running out of water.

Flashback

The first practical steam-engine was built by Thomas Newcomen in England in 1712. It produced up-and-down motion and was used to pump water from mines. In Newcomen's engine, steam trapped in a cylinder was cooled by a spray of water. This made the steam condense and created a vacuum in the cylinder. The natural pressure of the atmosphere pushed the piston into the vacuum. Newcomen's engines were sometimes called atmospheric engines because of the way they worked.

James Watt made the big breakthrough in steam-engine design. He built an engine which used steam pressure to push the piston. It also had a separate condenser for cooling the steam. Within five years, Watt had developed engines which could produce rotation and drive machinery. His engines provided much of the power for Britain's mills and factories during the Industrial Revolution.

During the 19th century, the design of steam-engines improved and they became widely used. They powered the locomotives of the new railway system. They hauled coal from mines and worked the huge hammers that shaped metal. They drove the traction engines used for threshing and ploughing. And they moved ships across the sea.

By 1900, internal combustion engines and electric motors were starting to replace steam-engines. They gave more power for their size and did not need huge supplies of coal and water. Today, most factory machinery is driven by electricity, and trains are diesel or electric. However, in most electric power-stations, the generators are turned by huge steam turbines. ■

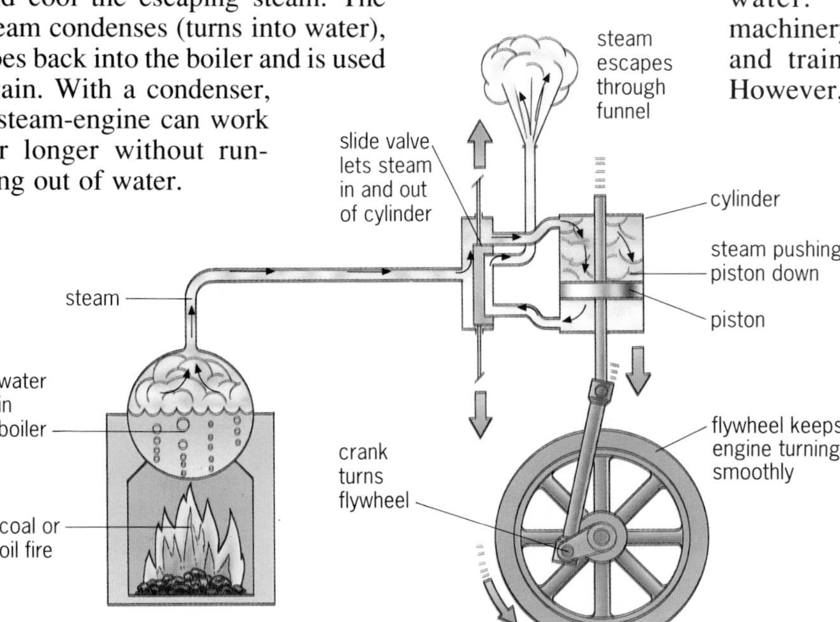

◀ **In a steam-engine, steam pressure is used to move a piston up and down a cylinder. The up-and-down movement is changed into round-and-round movement by a crank.**

See also
Agricultural revolutions
Engines
Industrial Revolution
Internal combustion engines
Locomotives
Railways
Turbines

Biography
Hero of Alexandria
Newcomen
Stephenson
Trevithick
Watt

Stick insects

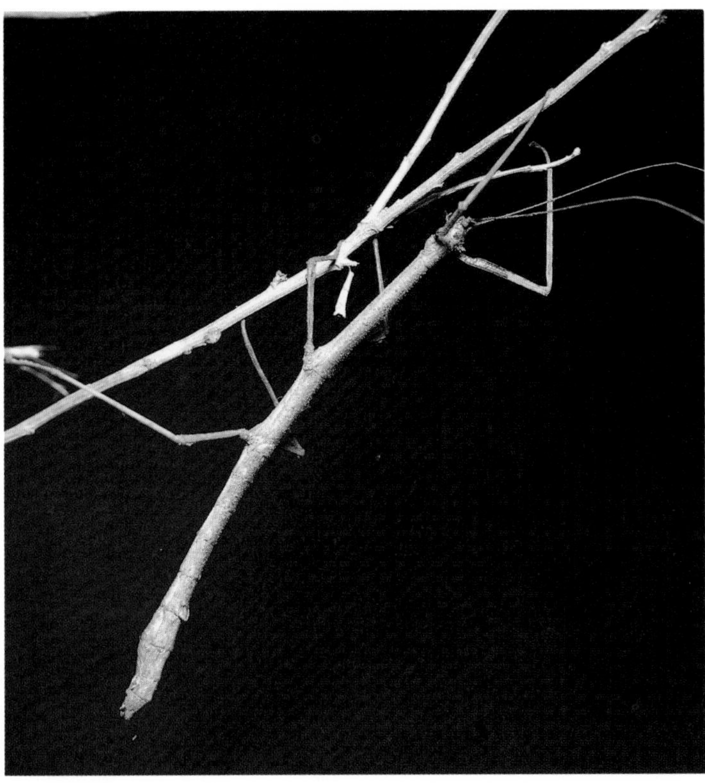

▲ **The perfectly camouflaged stick insect will not be seen by birds or other small predators.**

Distribution
Almost all warm countries, especially in south-east Asia
Size
Up to 25 cm long, the longest of all insects but very narrow
Food
Plant food, each species normally eating only one kind of plant
Phylum
Arthropoda
Class
Insecta
Order
Phasmida
Number of species
About 2,000 species, most of which are stick insects, but with about 25 broad-bodied insects that look very much like leaves. These are called leaf insects.

See also
Camouflage
Insects

The body of a stick insect is long and twig-like. Stick insects are usually coloured green or brown and are often covered with bumps or spines.

This makes them match the stems of their food plants so that it is almost impossible to see them. They normally sit quite still during the daytime and feed and move about at night.

In many kinds of stick insects the males are very rare, and the females lay hard-shelled, seed-like eggs without mating. This method of reproduction is called parthenogenesis. The eggs may take over a year to hatch, but when they do so, more females are born.

Some kinds of stick insect are kept as pets. Their cage needs to be in the warm, but out of direct sunlight. They must have fresh leaves to eat.

When changing the food plants you must be careful not to throw away the insects. They are so well camouflaged it is easy not to notice them. ■

Stomachs

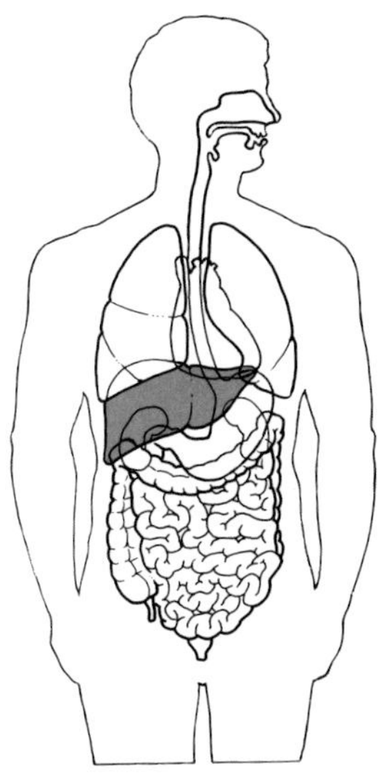

When you swallow your food, it passes down your gullet into your stomach. The stomach is a strong, muscular bag which expands as more food passes into it. It is found just under the diaphragm at the top of the abdomen.

Food begins to be broken down and digested whilst in the stomach. The stomach adds acid to the food, which helps to kill bacteria in it. This provides the right acidic conditions for the working of the stomach's own digestive enzyme, called pepsin, which is secreted into the food by the stomach wall. Pepsin begins the digestion of proteins, such as meat and eggs. The muscles in the stomach wall make it contract and churn, squeezing the food up with the acid and pepsin until it forms a runny mush. This passes into the small intestine for further digestion. An adult's stomach holds about one litre of food. Liquids start to drain out within 10 minutes. Meat and vegetables drain out in about an hour, but fats can take up to 30 hours. The stomach is usually empty after 6 hours. Then its walls contract and you feel hungry again.

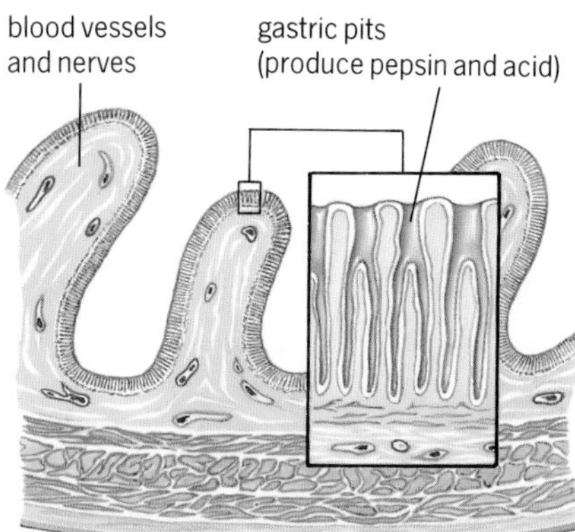

▼ **The stomach wall is folded to give it a large surface area for digestion. It is covered with holes called gastric pits, which produce acid and the digestive enzyme pepsin.**

Stomach ache

We tend to call any pain in the abdomen 'stomach ache'. Such pains are often nothing to do with the stomach at all. A true stomach ache can be caused by too much acid in the stomach, or by eating too much food. ■

See also
Cattle
Digestive systems
Enzymes
Human body
Muscles

Stone circles

There are more than 900 stone circles in Britain. One of the most impressive is at Callanish on the island of Lewis in the Outer Hebrides.

The great henge at Avebury, Wiltshire in southern England has three stone circles inside it. The largest in Britain, of 98 stones, is just inside the ditch.

The largest trilithon at Stonehenge stands 7·7 m high.

The oldest drawing of Stonehenge is from a 14th-century manuscript. It was thought then that the stones had been transported to Salisbury Plain from Ireland by the magic of the wizard Merlin.

See also
Archaeologists
Prehistoric people

The lives of prehistoric peoples all over the world depended on their surroundings, their environment. Hunters needed good supplies of food to kill or gather. Farming peoples and their animals relied on the weather to ensure that supplies of crops would survive.

Today we find it difficult to understand the religious beliefs of people who have left no written record of what they thought. Some of the first farming peoples (neolithic) built structures which must have been gathering places for the community to use for ceremonies. There were **henges,** which were enclosures surrounded by a bank on the outside and a ditch on the inside. Avebury in Wiltshire is a good example. A *cursus* was a great earth monument consisting of two parallel banks and ditches.

Stone circles were built in Europe from about 3000 BC to about 1200 BC. The circles vary in size (in fact some are not proper circles) and the stones used are of different sizes. People in the recent past have given the name 'megalithic' to the stones used, from the Greek meaning 'big stone'. Some of the stones are massive. Like the great earth monuments of the prehistoric period, building them must have required great effort involving the whole community.

There are often other types of stone structures associated with stone circles. Standing stones and stone rows can be found in many parts of western Europe. The most spectacular example is at Carnac in Brittany, France, where nearly 3,000 single stones were placed in ten to thirteen rows. One massive stone weighs 345 tonnes.

What were they used for?

Because no records survive from the prehistoric period, archaeologists have to interpret the evidence they collect. Careful calculations show that most stone circles were constructed by people who knew how to measure. An engineer, Professor Alexander Thom, suggested that they were built with a standard measurement of 2·72 ft (0·829 m) but this does not apply to all the circles in Britain.

We do believe that the circles were built as ceremonial or religious monuments. Some experts believe that some circles were constructed to make observations of the planets and stars. Stonehenge is a good example of this. Placing the stones very carefully, perhaps after years of observation, would give the early farmers a sort of calendar. They might watch the Sun or Moon rise over a certain stone and know exactly what time of year it was. These calculations would tell them when seasons, and the ceremonies which went with them, were approaching.

Excavations at many stone circles have revealed burials of pieces of human bone and broken pottery as if some sort of ritual had taken place. Archaeologists often find the remains of burning, too. There are a good many puzzles and problems which archaeologists have not solved.

▼ Castlerigg in Cumberland, one of the most impressive stone circles in the north of England.

Stonehenge

The stone circles at Stonehenge in Wiltshire probably form the most famous prehistoric ceremonial site of all. Even today enough of the circles survive to build up a picture of what it was once like.

The first ceremonial construction was a henge built some time between 3100 and 2100 BC. A large circle was enclosed by a bank and ditch and two stones were placed upright to mark the entrance. About 30 m (100 ft) from this entrance a much larger stone, now called the Heel Stone, was put up.

About 500 years later, the first stone circle was built inside the henge. Eighty-two stones were placed in two rings, one inside the other (called concentric circles). The most amazing thing is that these bluestones were probably brought to Wiltshire all the way from the Prescelly Mountains in South Wales. It must have been an enormous effort to drag, and carry on rafts, stones weighing as much as 4 tonnes each.

The circle we see today was built about 1500 BC. Nearly 80 stones were brought about 30 km (20 miles) to form a special circle of uprights with large capping stones. These local stones, called sarsen stones, also formed five separate 'arches' we call *trilithons* (Greek for 'three stones').

What was it for?

Even at its earliest period archaeologists think that Stonehenge was used to observe the movements of the Sun and Moon. Just inside the henge circle over 50 pits were dug. Some contained pieces of flint or red clay; perhaps they were offerings. Later some of these holes were used to hold the cremated remains of people. It is clear that Stonehenge was an extremely important religious site, perhaps the most important in Britain. ■

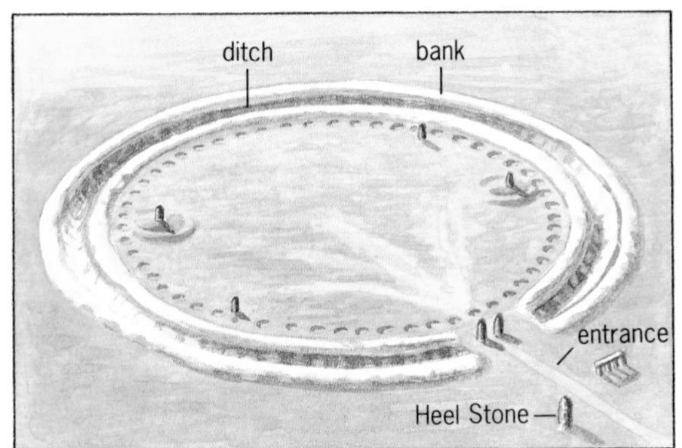

◀ Stonehenge in about 2500 BC. The Heel Stone is placed so that the Sun rises over it on Midsummer Day. This stone weighs over 20 tonnes.

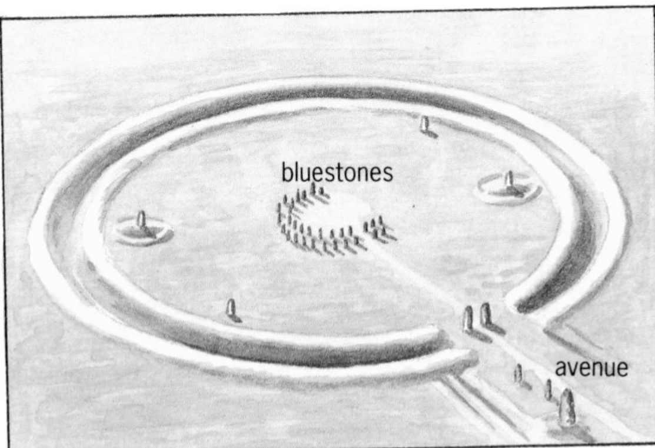

◀ The bluestones formed two uncompleted circles in the centre of the henge. At this time two rows of upright stones were also put up, running from the entrance.

▼ The sarsen stones were shaped by 'cutting' each edge with round hammer stones. This alone must have taken months of work. Even after 1500 BC there were slight improvements made to Stonehenge.

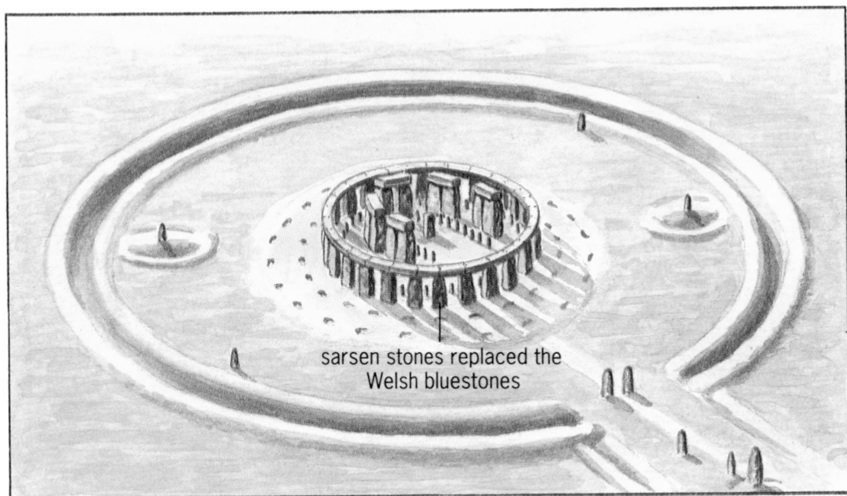

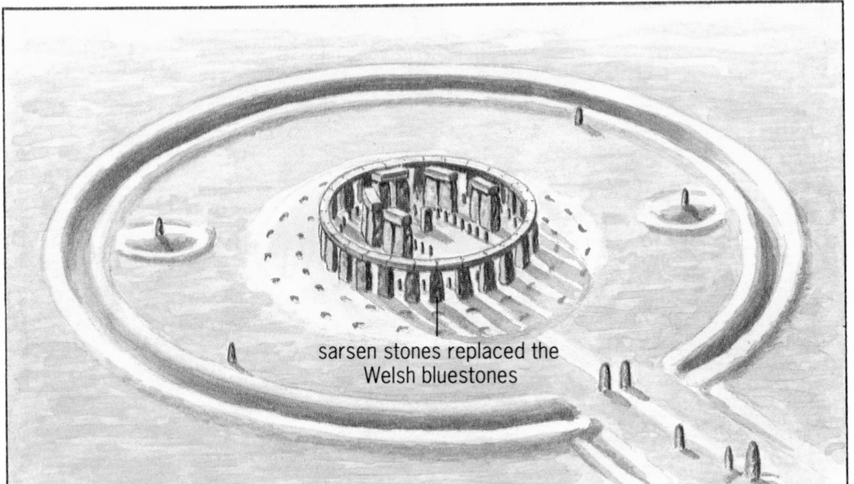

A The huge stone is rolled into its hole.

B It is pulled upright by ropes and a movable wooden frame.

C Once the stone was upright the hole could be filled, often with the round hammer stones.

D To form each trilithon the capping stone needed to be raised. At first it could be levered onto timbers.

E As it got higher, a stronger framework of timbers had to be built.

F Once at the top of the uprights the 7 tonne capping stone could be levered across into position.

Streams

There are many different kinds of streams. Mountain streams rush down steep valleys, foaming over rocks and waterfalls. Lowland streams wind in and out through farmland, flowing slowly between flower-lined banks. Woodland streams are clogged with fallen leaves and shaded by overhanging branches.

Streams do not contain so much water as rivers, but they can have a powerful effect on the landscape. Rocks and pebbles roll down the mountain slopes into the fast-flowing mountain streams, bouncing along the stream bed and scouring it deeper.

Stream flow

The speed at which the water flows depends upon the gradient (slope) of the stream bed: its height above sea-level and its distance from the sea. The steeper the gradient, the faster the flow. The stream flows more slowly near its banks. In some streams the amount of water varies from one season to another. Some are fed by snow melting in the mountains in spring, and shrink or freeze over in winter, or dry up in summer.

The stream environment

Because streams are quite shallow, the water contains plenty of oxygen. It also contains nutrients (substances that provide nourishment or food) dissolved from the surrounding land. Streams have many different habitats for plants and animals. Animals that can swim live in the open water; others cling to the rocks, shelter under boulders, or hide in the gravel or mud of the stream bed. Many live among the underwater plants near the banks. Birds and mammals visit the stream to drink or to hunt for food.

Plants

The stream banks are home to many plants. Mosses and liverworts cling to the stones. Moisture-loving plants such as ferns benefit from the spray. In fast-flowing streams there are few plants living in the water, but in slower streams plants such as pondweeds and waterlilies can take root in the mud. In very slow streams, duckweed floats on the surface. Snails and other invertebrates graze on the underwater plants. The flowers on the banks attract insects, which in turn are food for frogs, toads and newts, whose tadpoles live in the stream.

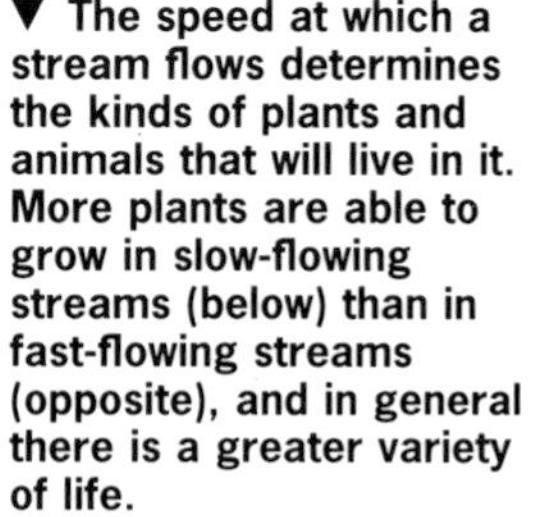

▼ The speed at which a stream flows determines the kinds of plants and animals that will live in it. More plants are able to grow in slow-flowing streams (below) than in fast-flowing streams (opposite), and in general there is a greater variety of life.

Slow-flowing stream

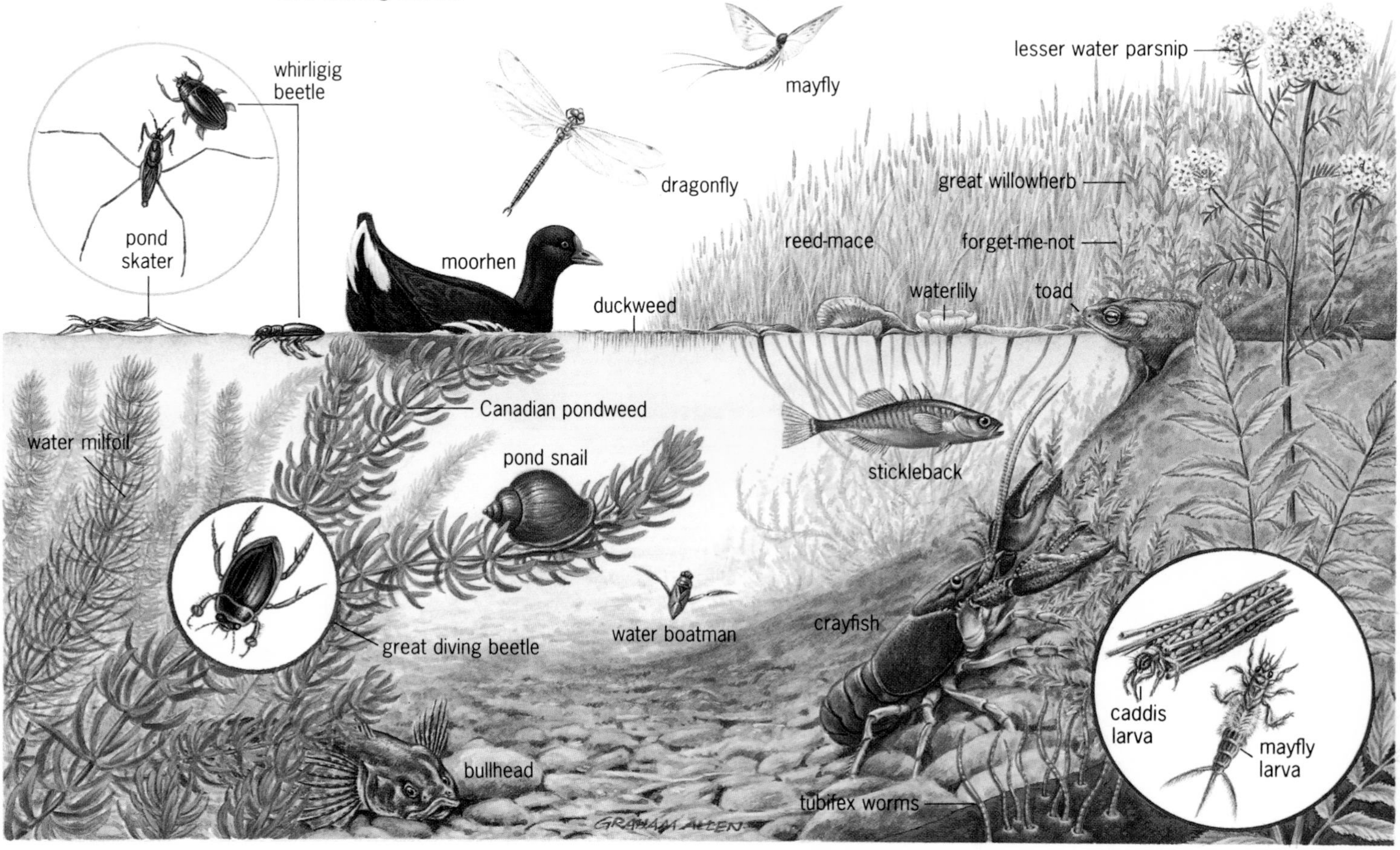

Fish

Streams are home to many small fish, including the young of larger species. The fish usually swim against the current, facing upstream, so that they are not swept away. Fish like sculpins and bullheads stay near the bottom. They have eyes near the top of their heads to spot prey in the water above. Some fish, such as loaches and lampreys, have suckers for clinging to the rocks.

In clear water, the fish have large eyes and good vision for finding their food. But in muddy waters, they have to rely on other senses. Their eyes are often smaller, and they use the lateral line system (sensory cells situated just under the skin on their sides) to sense vibrations in the water. Some use smell and taste, and may have fleshy whiskers called barbels on their chins which act rather like tongues for tasting. A few, such as the electric catfish, use weak pulses of electricity to locate, and sometimes stun, their prey.

When breeding, fish like salmon and trout lay their eggs in hollows in the gravel, then cover them with stones to prevent them being washed away. Other fish, such as sticklebacks, make nests of weed to hold their eggs.

Fast-flowing stream

Stream bed

Where water flows over stones, the friction of water against rock slows down the water immediately next to the rock. This layer of slow-moving water is called the boundary layer. Freshwater limpets cling to stones by suction, even in fast-flowing water. The larvae of mayflies and stoneflies have flattened bodies, so that they stay within the boundary layer. Some caddis-fly larvae build cases of tiny stones to weigh themselves down. Others spin nets to trap food.

The gravel of the stream bed is home to many different invertebrates, such as insect larvae, mites, shrimps and other tiny crustaceans. Where the stream bed is covered in soft mud, there are burrowing worms.

Fish and crayfish hide among the larger stones, waiting to ambush their prey. Some, like the bullhead, are camouflaged to match the stream bed.

Fast and slow streams

Fast-moving water can carry a greater load of sand and stones than slow-moving water. Where streams slow down, they drop their sand and gravel. Slow-flowing streams therefore have muddier beds and banks, with more pondweed and other aquatic plants. Water boatmen, pond skaters and whirligig beetles can survive here without being swept away. ■

See also
Fish
Invertebrates
Ponds
Rivers
Water birds

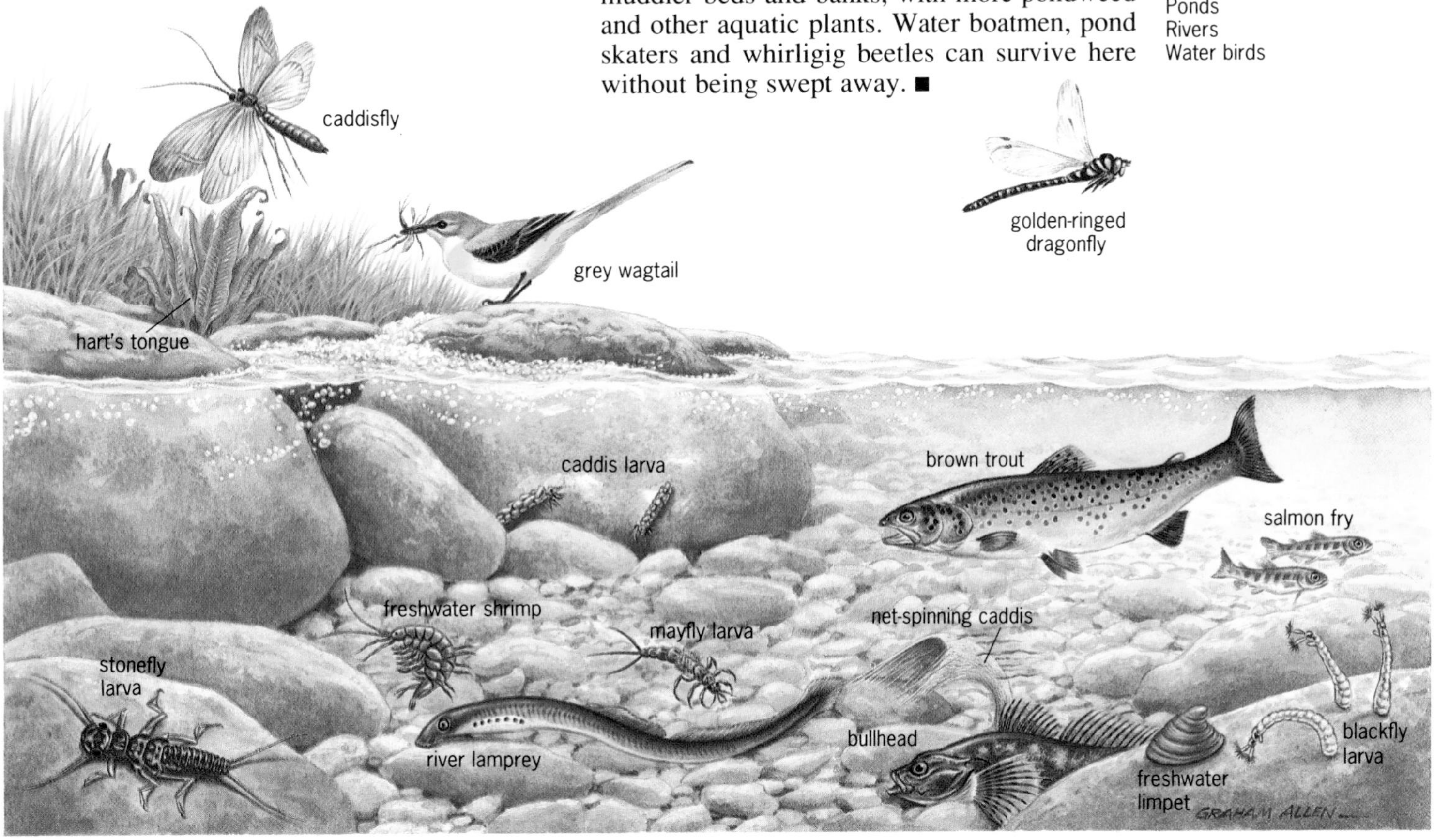

Stuart Britain 1603–1714

The Tudors had ruled before the Stuarts.

1603 **James I** (James VI of Scotland)

1605 Gunpowder Plot

1620 Pilgrim Fathers

1625 **Charles I**

1642 Civil War

1648 2nd Civil War

1649 Charles I executed

1650 **Commonwealth**

1653 Cromwell Lord Protector

1655 Jamaica captured from Spaniards

1660 **Charles II** Restoration of monarchy

1665 Great Plague

1666 Fire of London

1685 **James II**

1688 **Mary II and William III** Glorious Revolution

1690 Battle of the Boyne William III defeated James II in Ireland

1692 Massacre of Glencoe

1694 Mary II died

1702 **Anne**

1707 Union of England and Scotland

1710 St Paul's cathedral completed

1714 Death of Queen Anne

The next king was George I. There is an article on Georgian Britain.

◄ Sir Richard Saltonstall may have had this picture painted to tell the story of his family, with two scenes in one picture. The pale ghost-like lady in bed is his first wife Elizabeth. She is dying, and stretches out her hand to her two children who are painted at the age they were when she died. Richard is seven and still wears skirts like his three year-old sister Anne; he will soon be old enough to be dressed like his father. The lady with the new baby is probably his second wife Mary and their son Philip.

The family in the picture lived in England in the early 17th century at a time when there were so many difficulties between the king and Parliament that they led to civil war. English people fought each other; neighbours, friends and even members of the same family sometimes found themselves on opposite sides.

Sir Richard Saltonstall, the father in the picture, owned land and a big house in Chipping Warden, Northamptonshire. Many of the ordinary people who lived near by worked for him, and rented their houses and any land they had from him, so he influenced their lives in many ways.

Many powerful landowners like Sir Richard sat in Parliament. When the king summoned Parliament they would go to Westminster to make laws, and agree to taxes. They were worried about the way the Stuart kings, James I and Charles I, were using their power. Kings still believed their power came from God, and that they should not share it with anyone. Parliament did not always agree. There were two great problems: money and religion.

James I and Charles I were often short of money. When they had it, they were extravagant. So they often asked Parliament for extra taxes. But MPs wanted to control how the king spent his money, as this would give them a lot more power. They often refused to grant taxes if they did not like what the king and his advisers were doing. When Charles I found ways of raising money without asking Parliament, there was even more trouble.

Many MPs were Puritans who wanted the Church of England to have plainer services and churches. The Puritans hated and feared Catholics. Catholics were the bogymen of Stuart England, especially since the Gunpowder Plot of 1605. In fact, this was very unfair as most English Catholics just wanted to worship freely, and get on quietly with their lives. Charles I had a Catholic wife, and liked elaborate church services. This made Parliament afraid he was going to make England Catholic. They wanted to have much more say over religion.

Civil War

The English Civil War was fought because of these problems. From 1642 to 1646, Cavaliers (for the king) fought Roundheads (for Parliament). When Parliament's New Model Army won the war, many Roundhead soldiers had very new ideas. Some of them, called Levellers, even wanted ordinary people to share in governing the country. Oliver Cromwell and the other army leaders did not agree with these ideas, but when Charles I started fighting again in 1648 in alliance with the Scots, they decided they no longer wanted to be ruled by a king. In 1649, Charles was put on trial and executed.

For the next eleven years, England did not have a king. It was called a 'Commonwealth'. From 1653, Oliver Cromwell ruled as Lord Protector. He kept England peaceful, and made it strong abroad. The Levellers' movement was broken up by 1649, but Cromwell did allow people to worship in the way they wanted (except Catholics). However, he too found it difficult to get on with Parliament, and had to use the army to help him rule. This was unpopular. Taxes were heavy because the army cost a great deal, and landowners did not like soldiers interfering in their local area.

Restoration of a king

When Cromwell died, most people wanted the old familiar way of doing things. In 1660, Charles I's son Charles II was invited back from exile and crowned as king. This was the Restoration. Charles II had to be careful not to offend Parliament, though there were still no rules about how much power he should have.

The Glorious Revolution

When James II became king his ways upset many people. He was Catholic, and he tried to rule without Parliament. His reign lasted only three years. In 1688 he was forced to escape into exile in France. Parliament asked his Protestant son-in-law and daughter, William and Mary, to become joint king and queen. They agreed to share their power with Parliament, and this peaceful change was called the Glorious Revolution.

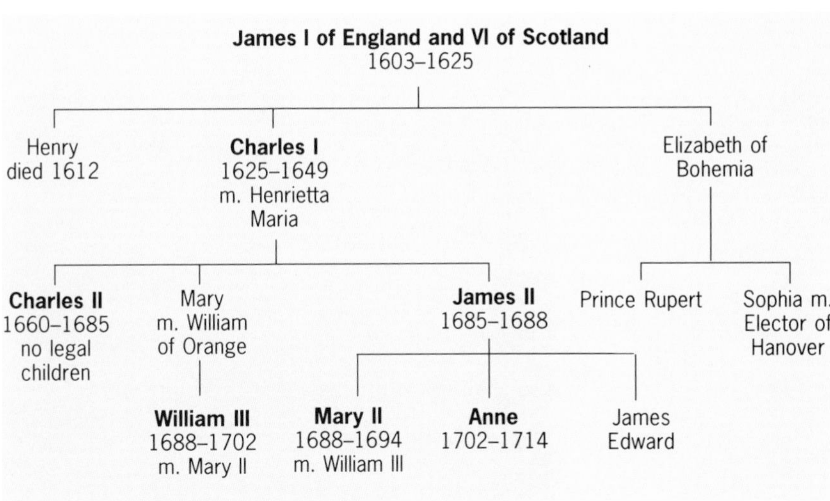

By the time of the last Stuart, Queen Anne, rulers of England had become 'constitutional monarchs'. This meant they had to keep rules made by Parliament, especially over money and religion. The rich landowners and wealthy merchants in Parliament had much more say in running the country, and became even more powerful and prosperous. Queen Anne still had power but she could not do exactly as she liked.

Ireland was governed by English rulers. Most Irish were Catholics, except in Ulster where Protestant English and Scots settled. By 1714 the Irish owned only 7 per cent of the land of Ireland. The rest had been taken by English Protestants.

Scotland had the same Stuart kings as England, but remained a separate kingdom until the Act of Union in 1707 which formed the United Kingdom. After the Glorious Revolution many Highlanders became Jacobites, who supported the exiled James II and his descendants.

Wales was ruled in the same way as England, with similar law courts and counties.

◀ The execution of Charles I, 30 January 1649. This was the only time an English king has been put on trial and publicly executed. Many Roundheads who did not like the way Charles I had ruled were horrified at his death. But Oliver Cromwell and other leaders of the New Model Army believed that the execution was the only way to bring peace to the new Commonwealth of England.

► **London after the Great Fire. Many churches and a new St Paul's Cathedral were designed by Christopher Wren. Fine houses, with large recently invented sash windows, were built for the wealthy.**

Famous books
King James Bible 1611
Book of Common Prayer 1662
Pilgrim's Progress 1678

Population
In 1600 the population of England was about 4,100,000.

By 1700 it was about 5,300,000.

The widening world

By the end of the 17th century, great changes had taken place in Stuart England, but change was slow for ordinary people, who had no property. They still could not vote or sit in Parliament. Times were often hard, especially when there was a bad harvest. In the early years of the century people sometimes died of starvation. During the Civil War, if they lived near any fighting, that meant trouble, too. Soldiers took crops, animals, and equipment, and often brought disease with them. By the end of the century, the country was generally more prosperous. Slightly fewer people died young, so the population continued to increase.

London

London was the biggest city in Britain, with a population of about half a million. Buildings spread outside the old city walls. Slums full of filthy tumbledown houses grew up to the north; the rich built grander houses to the west. There were fashionable new coffee houses, bull-baiting rings, bear-baiting pits, and theatres. When the Thames froze hard in 1685, there was a Frost Fair on the ice.

London was an exciting, busy place, but there were problems too in its crowded streets. Traffic jams of carriages, carts, and animals were common. The smoke from coal fires polluted the air. Disease spread easily. The Great Plague of 1665 was the last of several outbreaks of bubonic plague. Fire was a common danger; the most famous and devastating one was in 1666.

London was always full of merchants and traders from abroad, and there were other foreigners who settled there. Oliver Cromwell allowed Jews to live and work in England in 1656. Huguenots (French Protestants) came as refugees from France where they had been persecuted for their beliefs. They worked as silk-weavers, clock-makers, doctors and silversmiths. Rich people often had African servants, bought from English merchants, who profited from the slave trade.

Trade

Trade grew enormously. At the beginning of the century, England had only one important industry, the woollen cloth trade. Corn often had to be imported to feed everyone. By 1700 enough corn was grown to export some, and new goods, including tobacco, tea, coffee, and chocolate, were imported. Much more sugar was coming into the country, and some of it was refined in London. Cotton, silks, fine china, dyes, and jewels came from the East. Trade led to wars with Dutch and French rivals and to colonies in North America and the Caribbean. The East India Company, which brought many of the luxury goods from the East, established settlements in India too. In the next century these colonies grew into an empire. ■

 **See also**
American colonial history
Cavaliers
English Civil War
Fire of London
Glorious Revolution
Gunpowder Plot
Huguenots
Ireland's history
Pilgrim Fathers
Puritans
Quakers
Roundheads
Scotland's history
Slave trade
Welsh history

Biography
Anne, Queen
Charles I
Charles II
Cromwell
Fox
James I
Marlborough
Mary II
William III
Wren

Scientists
Boyle
Harvey
Hooke
Newton

Authors
Bunyan
Milton
Shakespeare

Submarines

Submarines are ships which can travel under water as well as on the surface of the sea. Most are naval vessels, but some are used for engineering and exploration.

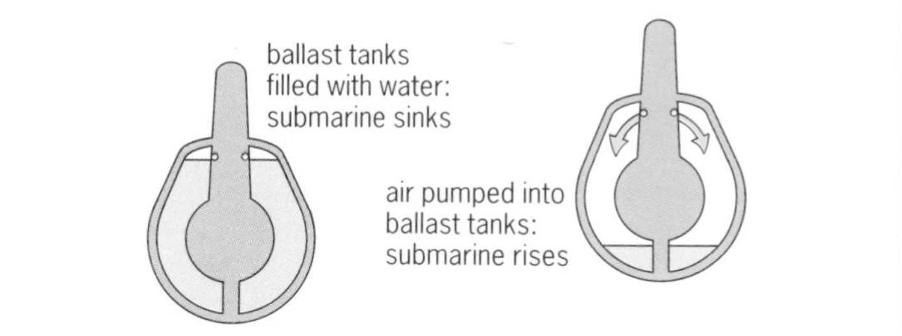

▲ A submarine can float or sink by emptying or filling its ballast tanks.

Diving and surfacing

Submarines have long hollow tanks on either side of the hull. These are the ballast tanks, which can be filled with air or water. To dive, the tanks are filled with water. Then the submarine is driven forward by its propeller, and the hydroplanes, which are like the tail on an aeroplane, force the submarine downwards. For the submarine to surface, the water in the ballast tanks has to be blown out by compressed air.

The world's biggest submarines are the Russian Alpha Class. They weigh about 10,000 tons and have an underwater speed of more than 60 km/h (40 mph).

Submarines cannot use diesel and petrol engines when submerged, because these use up too much air and give out exhaust fumes. Instead, small submarines use electric motors and batteries. Larger ones are nuclear powered.

Submarines for exploration

In 1959 the American submarine *Skate* travelled under the Arctic ice and actually surfaced at the North Pole.

In 1960, the submarine *Trieste* reached a record depth of 11,000 m.

These special submarines, or mini-subs, are of many different sizes and shapes. Within the hull there is a spherical cabin built of very thick metal. The crew look out through windows, and use powerful lights because there is no sunlight at great depths. These mini-subs are very useful for helping to position and repair oil rigs, exploring sunken wrecks and searching the sea-bed for valuable minerals. There are often movable arms attached to the hull which can hold tools or pick objects up. Divers cannot work at the enormous depths which these mini-subs can reach.

Flashback

The first vessel which could travel submerged or on the surface was built by a Dutchman who propelled it by oars from Westminster to Greenwich on the River Thames in 1620. Many people tried to improve on this idea until, in 1878, John Holland built his *Holland I* and *II*. The modern submarine is descended from these vessels. By 1914 there were nearly 400 submarines in existence. Submarines did not change much until the first nuclear submarine was built in 1954. ■

The first nuclear submarine, the USS *Nautilus*, was built in 1954.

▼ Mini-subs like this are used for exploration and oil rig maintenance. They can work at much greater depths than a diver.

See also
Divers
Navies
Nuclear power
World War II

Sudan

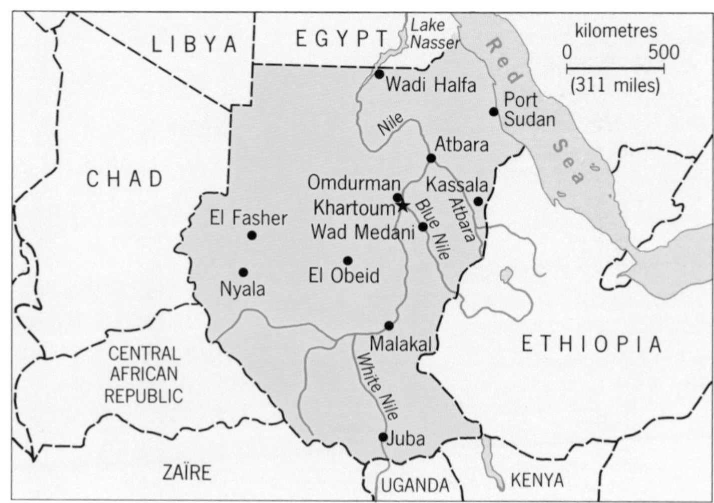

Area
2,505,800 sq km
(967,500 sq miles)
Capital
Khartoum
Population
22,350,000
Language
Arabic, English, Nubian
Religion
Muslim, Traditional, Christian
Government
Republic
Currency
1 Sudanese pound = 100 piastres = 1,000 millièmes

Sudan is the largest country in Africa. It stretches from the Sahara Desert almost to the Equator. The north is very dry. The capital, Khartoum, gets less than 160 mm (6·3 in) of rain a year on average. But it can still be flooded when the Blue and the White Nile overflow.

Without the Nile, northern Sudan would be total desert. There is a narrow strip of farmland, about 100 m (300 ft) wide, on each side of the river. Most of the people in the north are Muslims who speak Arabic. Travelling south, the countryside gradually changes. More grass, with bushes and small trees, grows in the semi-desert. Then the baobab trees appear. They can store water in their trunks. Further south, as the rainy season gets longer there is taller grass and more trees. A region called the Sudd has permanent swamps, and floating vegetation blocks the river channels. Cattle-herding is very important to some tribes in this area. Near the border with Uganda and Zaïre there is tropical forest.

In the south many people are Christians. They speak a variety of African languages, not Arabic. Many do not like being ruled by the Arab north and are fighting for independence.

Sudan is a very poor country. Some of the neighbouring countries are also suffering from civil war, and people have fled for safety to refugee camps. Sudan cannot afford to look after them, but the number of refugees is growing because of drought and war. ■

See also
Africa
Drought
Nile
Refugees
Sahara

Suffragettes

▼ Suffragettes often interrupted politicians' speeches, shouting 'Votes for Women' and waving banners and placards. They organized meetings and demonstrations, especially in London.

Suffrage means the right to vote. British women at the beginning of the 20th century did not have this right. 'Suffragists' were already working peacefully for 'Votes for Women'. But Mrs Emmeline Pankhurst believed there must be 'Deeds, not Words'. In 1903 she founded the Women's Social and Political Union. Many middle-class girls, living rather boring lives at home, became suffragettes. They chained themselves to the railings of 10 Downing Street. They burned empty buildings and letter-boxes and smashed shop windows. Emily Davison threw herself under the king's horse at the Derby, and died.

Suffragettes were very determined and, when in prison, many refused to eat. The government did not want them to die, so they were forcibly fed. This was horribly painful, and suffragette posters made sure everyone knew about it. In 1913, the 'Cat and Mouse Act' allowed suffragettes on hunger strike to leave prison, but put them back there when they were better. Neither side would give in.

In 1914 World War I changed everything. Suffragettes backed the war. Women proved they could do all kinds of work. In 1918, women over 30 got the vote. In 1928, the age was lowered to 21, the same as for men.

So did the suffragettes or the war bring 'Votes for Women'? Perhaps it was both. ■

Suffragists
National Union of Women's Suffrage Societies (NUWSS): founded 1897
Leader Millicent Fawcett
Colours Green and white. Red was added later.

Suffragettes
Women's Social and Political Union (WSPU): founded 1903
Leaders
Emmeline, Christabel and Sylvia Pankhurst, Emily Davison
Colours
Green — **G**ive
White — **W**omen
Violet — the **V**ote

See also
Edwardian Britain
Victorian Britain
Women's movements

Biography
Pankhursts

Sugar

Sugar is made both from sugar cane and sugar beet. Sugar cane grows in tropical countries such as the islands of the Caribbean, Brazil and India. Sugar beet grows in temperate areas such as Britain. The process used to extract sugar is similar for both cane and beet, and the refined white sugar made from each is exactly the same. This sugar is ground to give finer sugars such as castor and icing sugars. It is also compressed into sugar cubes. Some refined white sugar is coloured with molasses to make soft brown sugar.

Some sugar-cane-growing countries make brown sugars such as muscovado, Barbados and demerara from unrefined raw cane sugar. These sugars have more flavour than ordinary soft brown sugar. Molasses and black treacle are by-products of the cane-sugar refining process.

Sugar is pure sucrose, which is a carbohydrate. It provides energy and flavour, but does not provide any body-building foods. Sugar is used to sweeten foods and to make sweets and chocolate. Most experts agree that sugar is partly to blame for tooth decay.

Flashback

Sugar cane was cultivated in India in prehistoric times. The Indians discovered how to extract sugar crystals from it. Sugar was known in Europe in the Roman period but was rare and expensive for many centuries. Christopher Columbus took the plant with him to the West Indies in 1493. It grew so well there that huge plantations were set up by Europeans. The plantations were worked by African slaves, and the owners made so much money that sugar was known as 'white gold'. During the Napoleonic wars the supply from the Caribbean to Europe was cut. More and more sugar beet was grown and sugar was extracted from the beet. ■

sugar cane
sugar beet
cane cut and crushed
roots sliced up and soaked
sugary liquid
molasses from sugar cane
sugary liquid boiled and condensed
sugar crystals separated from liquid
sugar

◀ Sugar cane is cut and crushed. Sugar beet is sliced up. The strips are soaked and a sugary liquid extracted. This liquid is boiled and condensed by evaporation. Sugar crystals separate from the liquid in centrifugal machines.

Naturally occurring sugars
Fructose found in honey and some fruit
Glucose found in most starchy foods
Lactose found in milk
Maltose found in barley malt
Sucrose found in sugar cane and beet and in maple syrup

Honey was used for sweetening before sugar became common.

See also
Caribbean history
Chocolate
Food
Nutrition
Slave trade

Sumerians

The Sumerians are famous for their skill at inventing and their great discoveries. They were building cities by about 3800 BC. Archaeologists have carried out excavations at Ur, Uruk, Eridu and Lagash. At one time there were about 50,000 people living in the city of Uruk. The Sumerians lived in the southern part of Mesopotamia near where the rivers Tigris and Euphrates met. They were farming peoples and the land they worked was very productive because it was watered by the two rivers.

Wealth from their farming allowed their architects to construct huge and elaborate palaces and temples. To honour their gods they built *ziggurats*, huge pyramid-shaped temples. At Ur the ziggurat was built for Nanna, the moon god.

The most important Sumerian city was Ur. It was excavated by a British archaeologist, Sir Leonard Woolley, between 1922 and 1934. In the Royal Cemetery he excavated a number of objects of gold and precious jewels. Some of the things he uncovered can be seen in the British Museum, London. ■

See also
Ancient world
Mesopotamia
Writing systems
Biography
Abraham

The Sumerians invented the *cuneiform* kind of writing.

Abraham lived in Ur in about 1800 BC.

◀ This gold helmet probably belonged to a Sumerian prince called Meskalam-dug. It was buried in one of the graves in the Royal Cemetery at Ur. The helmet was hammered out from a single sheet of gold alloy. The holes around the edge were to hold the padded lining.

Sun

► A total eclipse of the Sun in 1980. The Moon blots out the light from the Sun's yellow disc. All you can see is the faint white haze around the Sun, called the corona.

Distance from the Earth
149,600,000 km
(93 million miles)
Equatorial diameter
1,392,000 km
(865,000 miles)
Rotation period
27¼ days
(as seen from Earth)
Mass
332,946 x Earth
Volume
1,303,946 x Earth
Surface temperature
6,000°C
Core temperature
16 million°C

The Sun gets 4,000 million tonnes lighter every second as it generates nuclear energy from hydrogen. It takes light 8·3 minutes to travel from the Sun to the Earth.
The Sun is 5,000 million years old.
In 5,000 million years the Sun will become so bright that it will be impossible for anything to live on our planet.

The Sun is an ordinary star, like the ones you can see at night, but for us and all the things that live on the Earth it is very special. Without the heat and light energy from the Sun, there would be no life. Even things we get from the ground and burn to get energy, such as coal, gas and oil, are the remains of plants and animals that grew in sunlight millions of years ago. People have always recognized how important the Sun is and they often worshipped it as a god.

Energy from the Sun

The Sun is a giant ball of hot gas, 150 million km (93 million miles) away. It measures as much across as 109 Earths side-by-side and could hold more than a million Earths inside its volume. Near the outside of the Sun the temperature is about 6,000°C but in the centre it is more like 16 million °C. In the Sun's hot core, enormous amounts of energy in the form of heat and light are produced by a process called nuclear fusion. This energy makes the Sun shine.

As well as heat and light, the Sun gives out X-rays and ultraviolet rays that are harmful to life. Most get soaked up in our atmosphere and do not affect us. Sunlight is very strong and **no one should ever stare at the Sun or look at it through any kind of magnifier, binoculars or telescope**. Your eyesight would be badly affected or you could even be blinded. Even with dark sunglasses or film it could still be dangerous to look at the Sun, so it is best not to risk it at all. Astronomers study the Sun safely by looking at it with special instruments.

► This special picture of the Sun was taken in 1973 from Skylab, a space station in orbit round the Earth. It shows up the 'graininess' of the Sun's surface and a giant plume of gas erupting from a solar flare.

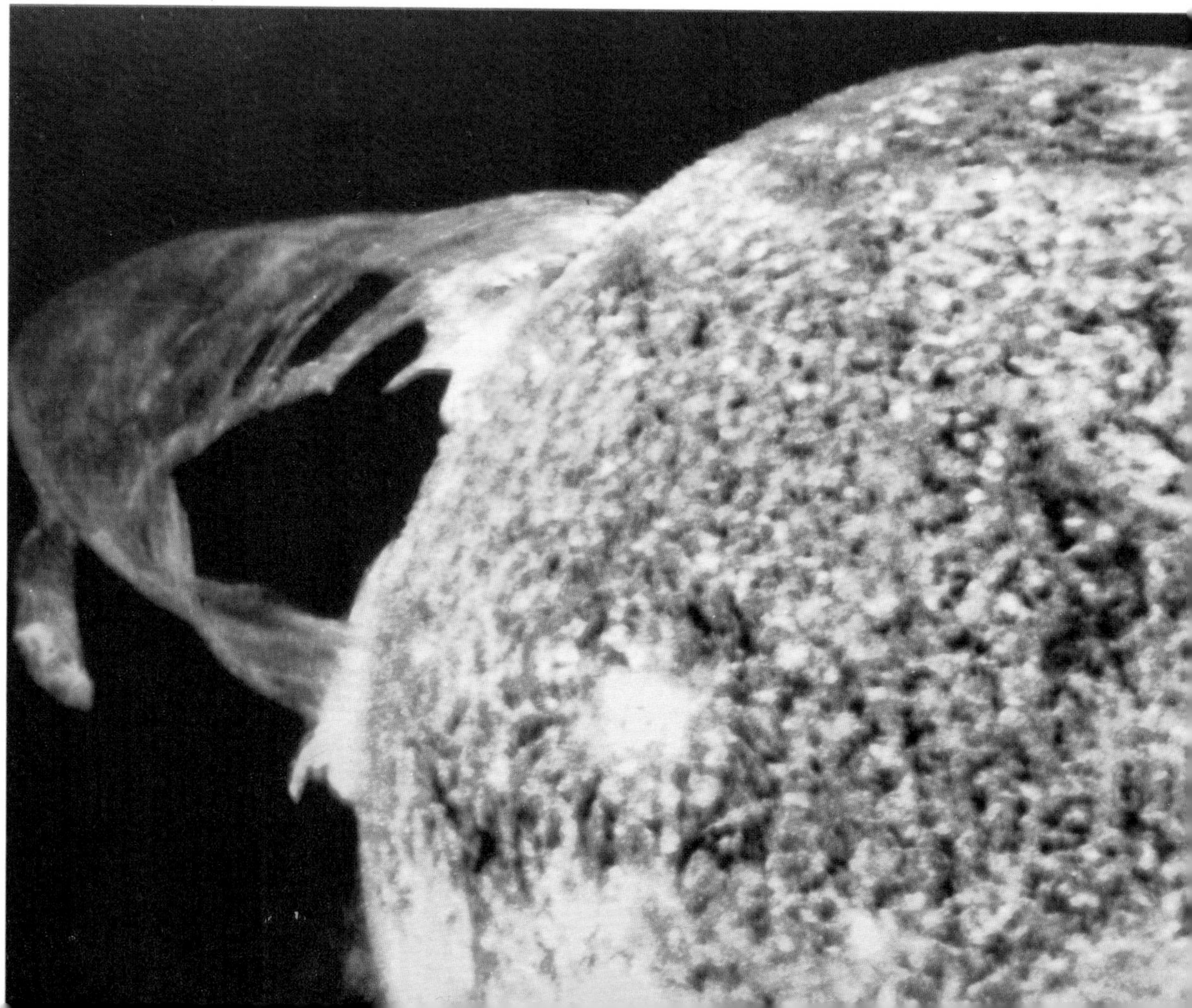

See also
Atoms
Aurora
Eclipses
Energy
Seasons
Solar System
Stars

Sunspots

Close-up pictures of the Sun show that it looks like a bubbling cauldron as hot gases gush out then fall back. Some of the gas is streaming away from the Sun all the time into the space between the planets. The faint halo of glowing gas round the Sun only comes into view in a total eclipse.

Sometimes there are dark blotches on the Sun's yellow disc. These sunspots can be many thousands of kilometres across and last for several weeks. The average number of spots on the Sun goes up and down over about eleven years. When there are a lot of spots, the Sun is active in other ways too.

Action on the Sun

Giant tongues of hot gas leap out violently from the Sun to heights of 1 million km (620,000 miles) or more. They are called prominences. Near to sunspots, flares like enormous lightning flashes can burst out. Particles shot out from the Sun take about two days to travel through space to the Earth. When they reach us they cause the lights in the night sky called the aurora and can interfere with radio signals on the Earth. ■

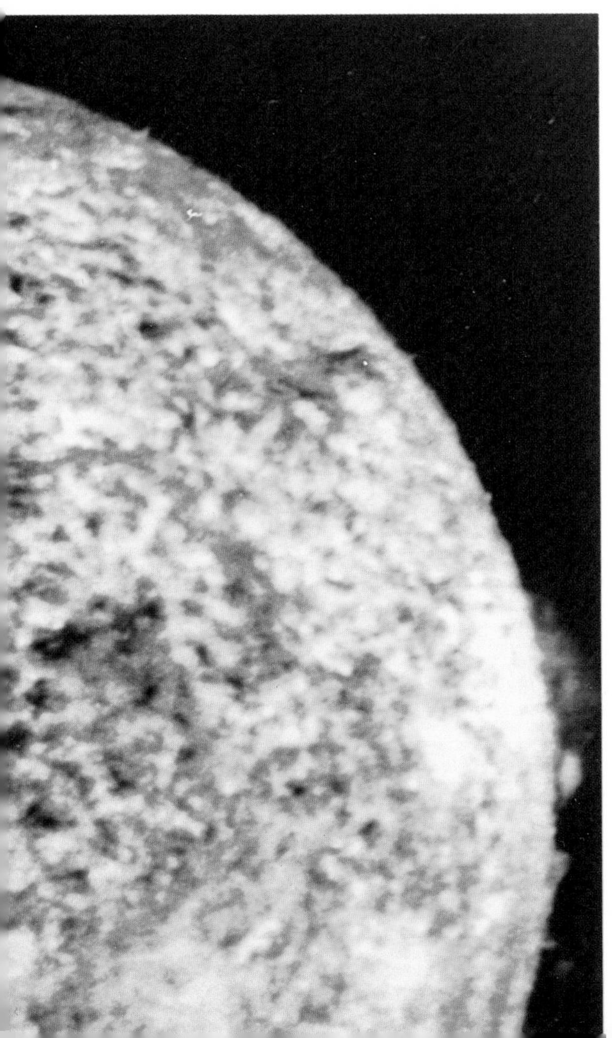

Superconductivity

At very cold temperatures strange things happen. Normally when an electric current goes along a wire the power which comes out of the end is less than the power put in. This is because power is wasted pushing the current through the wire. We say that the wire has resistance. But at very low temperatures resistance disappears and the wire becomes 'superconducting'. Then an electric current sent round a wire circle would continue flowing for hundreds of thousands of years without showing any loss of power.

Most metals become superconducting within a few degrees of absolute zero. This is the coldest possible temperature, at –273°C below the freezing point of water.

◀ A magnet floats freely above a piece of superconducting material which has been cooled by liquid nitrogen.

In 1987, there was tremendous excitement when scientists produced a substance that became superconducting at about 100 degrees above absolute zero. Now they are searching for substances which are superconductors at ordinary temperatures. This will mean that machines like computers can work even faster and use less power. It will mean that the huge electromagnets used in body scanners in hospitals will need much less electricity. And it will help the engineers who are developing magnetic levitation (maglev) trains. These trains 'float' just above their track, and scientists have discovered that magnets will float in mid-air just above a superconductor because the materials repel each other. ■

See also
Cold
Electricity
Heat
Magnets
Temperature

Supernatural

Many things happen that we cannot explain. The everyday experiences that we do understand we refer to as 'natural'.

Super is a Latin word meaning 'above'.

Some other things that happen seem so extraordinary that we say they are above or beyond the natural. This is what the word supernatural means.

Until the last few centuries there was much that people could not explain. They produced supernatural explanations and believed in ghosts and spirits and magical powers.

Most people today believe that there must be a natural explanation for everything, even if we do not know it yet. ■

See also
Ghosts
Thunderstorms

Superstitions

Superstitions are things we do to try to stop bad luck happening to us. Thousands of years ago people thought gods lived in trees and so they stroked the trees to keep the gods on their side. Today some people still 'touch wood' for luck.

Two hundred years ago public hangings used to be common in England for quite ordinary crimes. Once the noose was put round the neck, the ladder to the scaffold was knocked away. Ladders were a reminder of what could happen, so superstitious people avoided walking under them. The world is often a frightening place and we want to control what happens to us. But following superstitions is irrational and has no effect at all. ■

Surfing

▲ When a surfer launches from the peak of a wave and drops down its face, this is known as 'taking the drop'. The timing of this manoeuvre is vital, and it often takes considerable nerve on the part of the surfer.

Surfing is the sport of riding towards the shore on the face of a wave by standing on a surfboard. Surfboards are made of light, hard, plastic foam, covered with resin and fibreglass.

The size and shape of a wave depend largely on the land it travels over. For surfers, the 'tube' is the most exciting shape of all. This happens when a wave curls over to form a tube. The surfer tries to ride into and through the tube.

An expert surfer is skilful and daring, and must have a wonderful sense of balance. He or she tries to catch an unbroken wave and then slides down its face. To continue his ride, the surfer must keep away from the white water where the wave breaks. The basic surfing position is with one foot in the centre of the board, the other pressing down at the back. But by changing the position of the feet and body the surfer can change speed and direction, either dramatically or subtly.

The best surfing and the biggest waves are found off the beaches of Hawaii in the Pacific Ocean. World championships are held there regularly. ■

▼ Surfing through the tunnel formed by a breaking wave is called 'tube riding'. When fully inside the tube the surfer is completely hidden from viewers on the beach by the falling lip of the wave.

Surgeons

The first recorded surgical operation done under anaesthetic was to remove a cyst from a man's neck. This took place in Georgia, USA, in 1842. The surgeon used ether as the anaesthetic.

Some illnesses cannot be treated by medicine. Instead they need surgery. Surgery is a way of treating disease or injury by carrying out operations, usually under anaesthetic. Most operations are carried out in hospitals by surgeons, specialists who have had many years of training after qualifying as doctors.

There are many different kinds of surgeons. **General** surgeons deal with a whole range of routine operations. These include sewing up a bad cut, the removal of an appendix and the removal of gall bladders. **Neuro**-surgeons are concerned with surgery of the nervous system and care of head injuries. **Orthopaedic** surgeons operate on bones and joints. Their work includes setting broken bones, correcting birth defects, and hip replacement surgery. **Cardiac** surgeons specialize in heart surgery. This ranges from correcting inherited disorders to replacing diseased heart valves and doing heart transplants. **Plastic** surgeons specialize in 'plastic surgery'. This does not mean that they use plastic. They reconstruct or replace parts of the body that are damaged by burns for instance, with skin from another part of the body that is undamaged. **Ophthalmic** surgery is concerned with the eyes, and **ENT** surgery with the ears, nose and throat. In 'spare-part' surgery, doctors replace or repair parts of the body with artificial limbs.

The most surgical operations done in one working day were 833 cataract operations performed by Dr M. C. Modi in India.

The smallest surgical instruments are used for eye operations and have blades only 0·3 mm long.

Flashback

During the Middle Ages, surgery was primitive, dirty, painful and dangerous. Little was known about how the body worked, and surgery was commonly carried out by barber-surgeons. During the 16th century dissection became part of medical training and doctors learned more about the body. A French surgeon, Ambroise Paré, who lived from about 1510 to 1590 is often called the father of modern surgery. He was the first to make use of the new knowledge. ■

See also
Anaesthetics
Artificial limbs
Hospitals
Operations
Transplants

Biography
Lister

Surinam

Surinam is a small country on the north-east coast of South America. Most of the people live on the coastal plains, while inland the Guiana Highlands rise from savannah grasslands and dense jungles. The climate is tropical with temperatures on the coast averaging 26 to 27°C (80°F) all year round. Surinam heavily relies on bauxite (aluminium ore) which is by far the most important export, but it has oil and timber resources that have not been exploited. The country was a Dutch colony for 161 years until independence in 1975. Many of the people are descended from Indonesians from the Dutch East Indies, transported to work in the sugar plantations. ■

Area
163,265 sq km
(63,037 sq miles)
Capital Paramaribo
Population 384,000
Language
Dutch, English, Hindi, Javanese, others
Religion
Christian, Hindu, Muslim
Government Republic
Currency
1 Surinam guilder (florin) = 100 cents

See also
South America

Surveyors

When a new map is made or an old map brought up to date, measurements have to be made of the positions of all the important things, such as hills, houses, bends in the road, churches, and so on. Making these measurements is called surveying. The measurements are all reduced by the same amount so that they can be shown inside the boundaries of the map. For example, 1 km (⅗ mile) on the ground might be shown as 1 cm (⅖ in) on the map.

People who do surveying are called surveyors. To help surveyors, many hills have a short concrete pillar at the top. This is called a triangulation pillar and it has a level metal plate set into it. From it, a surveyor can use a special type of telescope, called a theodolite, to measure the directions and levels of other triangulation pillars, landmarks and everything in sight. By moving from one triangulation pillar to another, the whole country can be surveyed. Theodolites are also used for much smaller surveys, such as the route of a new road or the site of a new house. ■

See also
Architects
Maps
Roads

Survival

See also
Bears
Camels
Conservation
Endangered species
Extinct animals
Zebras

Biography
Darwin

Survival is the everyday business of all living things. Everything, whether plant or animal, is suited (adapted) to a particular way of life. Zebras, for example, are adapted to life in grasslands. Their adaptations include a stripy coat which makes them difficult to see, and living in a herd where they are safer than if alone. A polar bear is adapted to life in a very cold harsh habitat by its thick white coat, keeping it warm and camouflaging it against the snow. The camel is adapted to desert life, as it can go for long periods without drinking. You can imagine what would happen to a zebra stranded on the coast of Iceland, or a polar bear left in a desert: both would die.

There is no creature without its natural enemies. These may be other creatures which want to eat it; so survival for lions means death for some zebras. Or it may be the climate which is the enemy. Drought kills many zebras and lions. Any animal which is born better able to withstand these natural enemies has a greater chance of surviving to be an adult and produce young. Only the strongest and healthiest animals will survive to breed. This is known as 'survival of the fittest'. The parents will pass this 'fitness' to their offspring in their genes. Because of this, eventually the whole species may change to be better adapted to their environment.

Conservation

Humans have destroyed many habitats and the plants and animals which lived in them, so more species have become extinct in the last 500 years than in all of the previous 2,000 years. Today very many more are in danger of extinction. To improve the survival chances both of individuals and of whole species, conservation societies have been set up. Their aim is to prevent the destruction of habitats and extinction of threatened plants and animals. ■

► Meerkats standing in the early morning sun in the Kalahari Desert. These animals can stand for hours scanning the horizon for anything which may threaten their survival. They often act as a group : one stands on watch while the others feed.

Swaziland

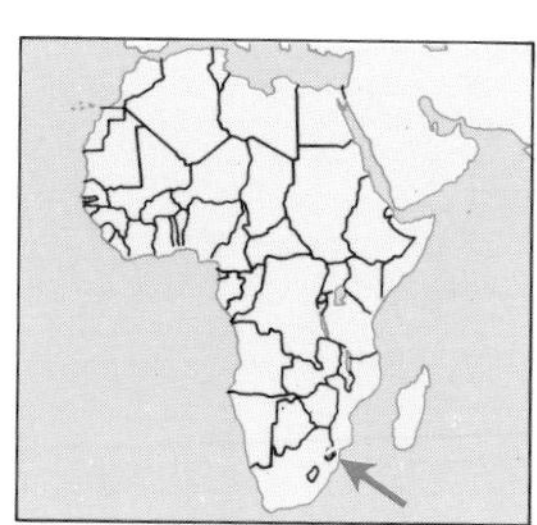

See also
Africa

Sandwiched between South Africa and Mozambique is the small but beautiful kingdom of Swaziland. Its king is called the *Ngwenyama*, which means 'lion'. Swaziland contains high plains, called the high veld, in the west, with lower plains in the centre. The Lebombo plateau, an upland region, runs along the eastern border.

The Swazis speak a language called siSwati. They are mostly farmers, who grow maize and rear cattle to feed themselves, and may also grow tobacco and cotton to sell. The main crops are sugar cane and citrus fruits. The cultivation of these is controlled by large commercial companies. Timber and asbestos are also exported. On special occasions, such as royal ceremonies, the Swazis wear traditional clothes, made of animal skins and brightly coloured cloth. On these occasions spectacular dances are performed.

Swazis began to settle in what is now Swaziland nearly 200 years ago, founding the kingdom which survives to this day. Swaziland was a British protectorate from 1902 until 1968, when it became an independent monarchy. ■

Area
17,400 sq km
(6,700 sq miles)
Capital
Mbabane
Population
731,000
Language
English, siSwati
Religion
Christian, Traditional
Government
Monarchy
Currency
1 emalangeni = 100 cents

Sweden

Sweden is the fourth largest country in Europe. Over half its land surface is covered with dense forest, mostly pines, and it has over 95,000 lakes. Most of the country is fairly flat, but there is a long chain of mountains in the north-west where Sweden borders Norway. There are thousands of islands off the coast.

Sweden is a large country with a great many natural resources, including timber and valuable mineral deposits especially iron ore. However it has a population smaller than that of greater London. There are very few large cities and there are long distances between them. In parts of central and northern Sweden you could drive for a whole day and pass only a handful of other vehicles. Because of this, Sweden is rich in wildlife. Elk live in most parts of the country. Wild bears can be found in the forests of central Sweden.

The average winter temperature in Kiruna in Swedish Lapland is –15°C (+5°F), where the winter snow can stay for up to 200 days. At midwinter in Kiruna there is no daylight at all. But in the summer, temperatures rise to over 15°C (60°F), and in June and July the Sun never sets completely. This is why Sweden is one of the countries known as 'The Land of the Midnight Sun'.

Because of the resources Sweden possesses, its people have a very high standard of living. Their homes are usually well designed and built to keep out the winter cold. Almost all Swedish families have a car and most Swedes still prefer to buy a Swedish-made car, a Saab or a Volvo.

Sports

Skating and skiing are popular pastimes in Sweden and the national sport is ice hockey. Swedes also enjoy visiting the countryside. Berry and mushroom picking are very popular in the late summer and early autumn months. Most Swedes live within 10 km (6 miles) of a lake, so it is not surprising that water sports and pastimes are very popular, especially sailing and fishing.

Flashback

In the 17th century the Swedish kings ruled an empire which included Finland and parts of Denmark, Germany and Poland. During the 18th century the country produced some of the most famous European scientists, including Celsius, whose name is used for the temperature system. In the 19th century Sweden became a developed industrialized nation. Norway, which had been part of it since 1814, finally became independent in 1905. Sweden did not take part in either of the World Wars and has remained a neutral country. ■

Area
449,964 sq km
(173,732 sq miles)
Capital
Stockholm
Population
8,358,140
Language
Swedish, Finnish, Lappish
Religion
Christian
Government
Parliamentary monarchy
Currency
1 Swedish krona = 100 öre

See also
Europe
Midnight Sun

Biography
Linnaeus
Nobel
Sports special:
Borg

▼ The city of Stockholm is situated on 20 islands and peninsulas beside the Baltic Sea.

Swimming

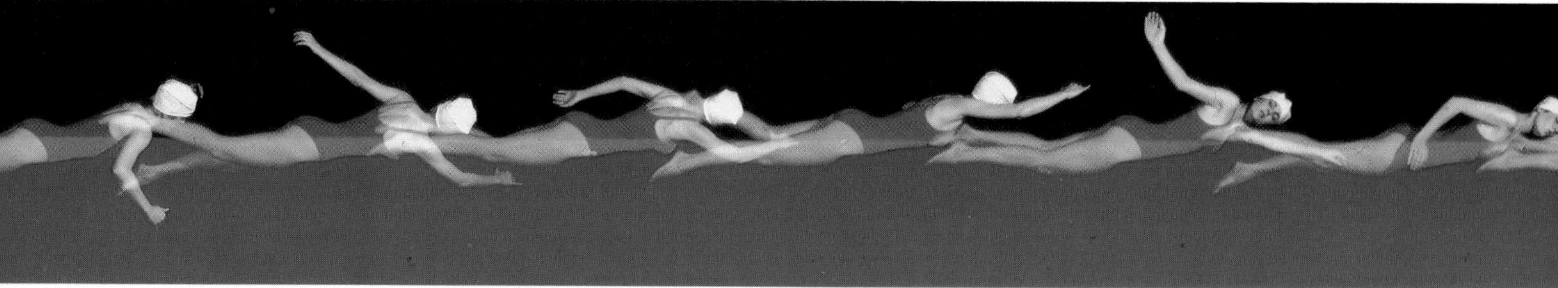

▲ **The crawl is the fastest stroke. It was developed early in the 20th century by an American swimmer, Johnny Weissmuller.**

The fastest human swimmers on record are Matthew Biondi, who swam 50 m (55 yards) at a speed of 8·13 km/h (5·05 mph), and Yang Wenyi, at 7·21 km/h (4·48 mph).

The greatest distance swum in a single continuous swim was 481·5 km (299 miles) by Ricardo Hoffman in 1981, in the River Paraná, in Argentina.

Record holders in the animal world include:
sailfish 109 km/h (68 mph)
killer whale 55 km/h (34 mph)
leatherback turtle 35 km/h (22 mph)
gentoo penguin 27 km/h (17 mph)

See also
Fish
Sport

Swimming is the way in which an animal pushes itself through water. A wide variety of animals can swim, including hedgehogs, cows and even moles. Fish, whales, dolphins, seals, penguins and millions of aquatic insects and microscopic animals spend much of their lives in the water and have to swim in order to hunt for food. Animals such as antelopes and reindeer swim across rivers as they migrate, or when escaping from predators.

The basic principles

In order to swim, an animal must push the water back (to move forward) and down (to stay afloat). Simple wave-like movements of the body can achieve these thrusts, but often fins or paddles are used as well. Many animals, such as frogs, turtles and water beetles, keep their bodies stiff, but use their legs to provide the thrust.

Often the animal's feet, or sometimes whole legs or arms, are shaped like paddles to provide a greater surface area to push against the water. Turtles and seals have flippers; dolphins and whales use their large tail flukes. Fish have fins, and ducks, seagulls and otters have webbed feet. Many small shrimps and water insects have fringes of stiff bristles on their legs which have the same effect.

In order to offer little resistance to the water, the bodies of swimming animals tend to be streamlined, that is they are more or less torpedo-shaped. The water can flow smoothly round them. This is why many marine animals have very small ears or no external ears at all. Fish are covered in slime to help them slip through the water.

Different techniques

When swimming, the animal needs to thrust against the water as well as maintaining as good a streamlined shape as possible. Like rowing a boat, the 'paddles' are spread out against the water when pushing, but folded close to the body when gliding forward. Human swimmers have several different ways of doing this.

In breast-stroke the feet provide most of the thrust. They are brought together in a scissors motion, producing a rather jerky movement. In a good breast-stroke, the head is level with the water on the forward stroke. This brings the face into the water, but improves streamlining.

In the crawl, the body lies flat on the surface of the water, and both arms and feet provide thrust. As one arm pushes against the water, the other is brought close to the body to improve streamlining. The legs kick up and down. This is a very fast stroke, popular in competitions. It is also used for long-distance swimming.

In back-stroke, swimmers lie on their backs. Their arms reach alternately above their heads, and enter the water level with the shoulders. This stroke is used in competitions, and for relaxing.

Butterfly-stroke is used only for competitions. It resembles the up-and-down motion of dolphins. The arms are brought forward above the water, and the legs kick up and down.

Swimming for sport

A variety of strokes are used in organized sport. Straight speed trials are popular, usually involving the crawl. Style may also be judged, points being awarded for the correct positioning of body and limbs, and for the smoothness of the motion. The less the water is disturbed, the less resistance it offers to the swimmer. Long-distance swimming is popular, with swimmers attempting to cross well-known stretches of water such as the English Channel.

Because the body is partly supported by the water, it is a good form of exercise for the elderly and the disabled, putting minimal strain on their limbs yet offering a chance to practise bending them, and at the same time exercising the heart and lungs. ■

Switzerland

High mountains make up more than half of this small inland European country. They are the Swiss Alps, which attract many tourists in winter for skiing and in summer for mountaineering and sightseeing. Cattle are taken up to the high Alpine pastures in spring and summer while grass in the valleys is cut for hay. Their milk is used to make famous cheeses such as Gruyère and Emmental. The milk is also used in the Swiss chocolate industry.

Engineering in the Alps

The Alps are the site of many fine engineering projects. Fast-flowing mountain rivers have been dammed to generate hydroelectric power. This energy for towns and factories all over Switzerland is very important because the country has no coal or oil. Major road and rail routes linking northern and southern Europe cross the Alps.

Fast and efficient electric railways use long tunnels and amazing loops and bridges. Swiss engineers invented the rack railway to take trains up steep slopes, and these mountain railways are very popular with tourists.

Industry and wealth

Near the French border is a lower range of mountains called the Jura. The Swiss clock and watch industry is centred on Neuchâtel at the foot of the Jura. For centuries, skilled people have made valuable products such as watches, but Switzerland has to import nearly all the raw materials that are used.

Large towns and cities with factories and offices are in the lower land between the Jura and the Alps. Machinery, locomotives, tools, textiles, and many items for the optician's and the chemist's shop are made here.

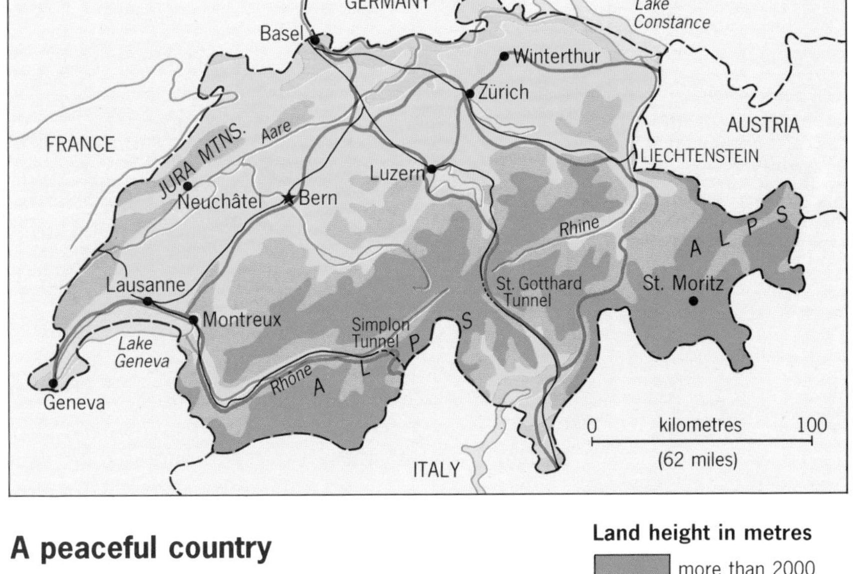

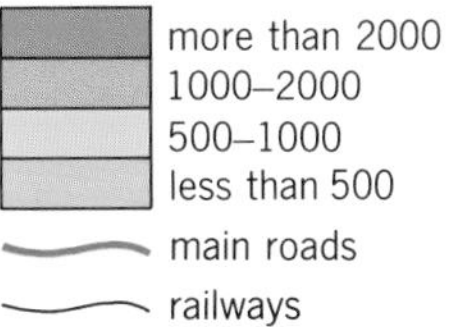

A peaceful country

Switzerland has been a neutral country since 1815. This means it remained peaceful when the rest of Europe was at war. It is also a country with four national languages. The headquarters of some United Nations and many other international organizations are in Bern and Geneva. The International Red Cross was founded here and its badge is the Swiss flag with the colours reversed. ■

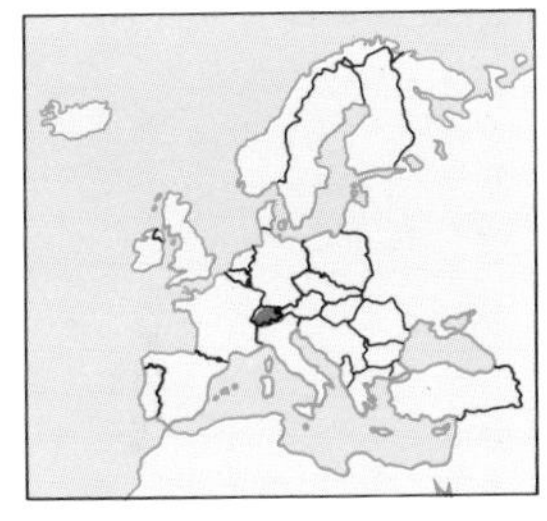

◀ Modern roads climb the Alpine passes, but deep snow and avalanches often close them in winter. Today, the most important roads and railways go through long tunnels which can be kept ice-free all year. This is the entry to the St Gotthard Tunnel.

▶ Summer in the Bernese Oberland. Cattle can be seen grazing on the meadows to the right of the photograph.

Area 41,293 sq km (15,943 sq miles)
Capital Bern
Population 6,523,400
Language
German, Swiss German, French, Italian, Romansch
Religion Christian
Government
Federal parliamentary republic
Currency
1 Swiss franc = 100 rappen or centimes

See also
Alps
Dams
Europe
Railways

Biography
Jung

Symbols

Flower language

Red rose symbol of love
Lily symbol of purity
Laurel symbol of victory
Rosemary symbol of remembrance
Peony symbol of marriage
Lotus symbol of wisdom

Have you ever wondered why we throw confetti over a bride at her wedding? Some people throw grains of rice instead. They are repeating a symbol that is thousands of years old. Grain is important. It will grow into next year's plants that feed us. By throwing grain over a bride we show that we wish her to have plenty of everything. A symbol is something that represents something else. Quite ordinary objects, pictures, clothes, colours, and actions may be symbolic.

► **In ancient Egypt cats were considered special and were often commemorated in works of art.**

Pictures

This symbol, which is Chinese, says a very great deal. It tells us that there are two forces in the universe: the female and the male. The female symbolizes the night, the Earth, and is called yin. The yang symbolizes all that is high: mountains, the sky, light itself. Each has in it a small part of the other. Together they form the indivisible force of life.

▲ **The Chinese symbol of yin and yang.**

Actions

At the last supper before Christ died, he washed the feet of his apostles. By this symbolic act he showed that he loved and served them, and that they in turn should love and serve others. The cross, which for the Romans was a symbol of shame, became the symbol of all Christians.

Objects

The same object can be either ordinary or symbolic. For instance, a cat can be a symbol for magic, since European people used to believe that witches turned into cats. In ancient Egypt the cat was considered so special that if you killed one, you yourself could be sentenced to death. This was because the cat symbolized Isis, the Mother goddess, and people needed her protection against evil.

For Jews, Christians and Muslims the rainbow in the sky is the reminder that God created it after the great flood, as a symbol of the everlasting bond between himself and all life on Earth.

Cat On the continent of Europe and in the USA, a black cat is considered unlucky. In Britain it stands for good luck.

Tiger stands for speed and power.

Oil used to anoint a king or queen at a coronation symbolizes the giving of wisdom through the grace of God.

Swastika a prehistoric, universal symbol of creative force; in Sanskrit it means 'so be it'. It was also used as a symbol by the Nazis in Germany.

Wheel in Buddhism, represents the unending cycle of birth, life and death.

▲ **The fish was an early, secret symbol for Jesus.**

► **The dove is a symbol of peace.**

Colours

Any colour can be used as a symbol. The colour white may symbolize purity, and is worn by brides in Christian countries; but a white bird may symbolize the soul of a dead person or, in the case of the dove, the spirit of life and of peace. In ancient Rome a white mark on a boy's foot was a sign that he was for sale as a slave. ■

Red danger, passion
Green hope
Blue harmony, coolness
Purple royalty

See also

Flags
Graphic Design
Icons
Maps

► **The rainbow symbolizes hope.**

Symmetry

► Compare the two sides of the line of symmetry in this butterfly.

A butterfly is a beautiful example of symmetry in nature. Draw a dividing line down the middle, and each part and pattern on one side of the line is the same shape and size and in the same position as on the other side. An animal or an object is symmetrical when exactly similar parts face each other on either side of an imaginary centre line. This dividing line is called the line of symmetry.

We are almost symmetrical about a line that goes straight down the middle of us. We might have a few pimples and spots on one side of the line of symmetry and one arm might be a bit longer than the other. But we are generally symmetrical.

◄ This rug, designed and made in the Punjab state in India, has a partly symmetrical pattern. The large hens face each other in a symmetrical way but the rows of smaller birds are not symmetrical.

▼ The view of the piazza (square) from St Peter's basilica in Rome. The curved buildings on either side are exactly similar. Symmetry is a feature of the classical style of architecture which was revived at the time of the Renaissance and continued to influence architects in Europe through the 17th, 18th and early 19th centuries.

Something to do

Are faces exactly symmetrical? To find out, stand a mirror on a photograph of someone's face. Place the mirror so that half the face and its reflection make up a whole face. Does the person look any different?

Try the test on some words to find out if they are symmetrical. Here is one to start you off: MUM.

Sometimes things have more than one line of symmetry. Take the capital letter H. It has two lines of symmetry. Some things do not have a line of symmetry but if you turned them round a little they would look just the same.

See also
Kaleidoscopes

Symphonies

See also
Classical music
Orchestras

Biography
Beethoven
Brahms
Dvorak
Elgar
Haydn
Mendelssohn
Mozart
Prokofiev
Schubert
Tchaikovsky

Other symphony composers
Berlioz
Bruckner
Mahler
Nielsen
Schumann
Sibelius
Vaughan Williams

Symphonies are pieces of classical music for orchestra. Most symphonies are divided into 'movements': individual sections which follow one another to make the complete symphony. Usually there are four movements. The outside movements balance each other, so that the symphony usually begins and ends in a similar mood. The inside movements make a contrast. One is usually slow, and the other is lively, often in a dance-rhythm, like a scherzo or minuet. Some composers write symphonies where the order of movements is altered, or they leave some movements out, run movements together, or even write one-movement symphonies. But the symphony is always a major item in any concert. A symphony may take between fifteen minutes and an hour to play. ■

Joseph Haydn wrote 104 symphonies: he is known as 'the father of the symphony'.

Symphonies are usually known by a number (Beethoven's Symphony No. 7), but some symphonies have names: Mozart's 'Prague' and 'Jupiter' symphonies; Beethoven's 'Eroica', 'Pastoral' and 'Choral' symphonies; and Prokofiev's 'Classical' Symphony.

Synagogues

Synagogue comes from a Greek word meaning 'gathering'. Greek-speaking Jews 2,000 years ago were already using it to mean synagogue.

The place where Jews gather together for study and prayer is called a synagogue. Another name for it is the school or house of meeting. Jews think that it is important to study and discuss religion as well as to worship. Study includes learning Hebrew, the language of the Jewish Bible.

The first five books of the Old Testament of the Bible are a translation of the Hebrew Torah. To Jews it is much the most sacred part of the Bible, given by God directly to Moses. The whole Torah is read aloud in every synagogue in the course of the year, one portion on each Sabbath. After this there is another scriptural reading called *haphtarah*, from the Prophets.

The focus of a synagogue is the scrolls of Torah (teaching or law). These are placed in beautifully decorated covers in a cupboard or alcove which is called the Holy Ark. The ark is at the end of the synagogue which faces Jerusalem. A light usually burns in front of the ark as a symbol of the presence of God. The first ark was a portable chest for the Ten Commandments given to Moses.

Another important part of a synagogue is the *bimah* (reading desk), which is usually in the centre. At the main point in a service, everyone stands while a scroll is carried from the ark to the reading desk and a member of the congregation reads the portion of scripture for that week. Synagogues can be decorated with abstract patterns or symbols but Jews do not make statues or paintings of God or their great prophets.

The main services are on Friday night and Saturday (the Jewish Sabbath), and at festivals. They are led by a rabbi (teacher) or any learned person appointed by the community. In Orthodox (traditional) synagogues women sit separately and rabbis are always men.

Flashback

Synagogues probably began during the exile of the Jews in Babylon in the 6th century BC when Jews could not visit Jerusalem and the first Temple in Jerusalem had been destroyed. When the second Temple was finally destroyed by the Romans in AD 70, synagogues and homes became the main centres of Jewish worship. ■

▼ **This illustration shows the interior of a modern synagogue.**

1 Ten Commandments
2 rabbi's seat
3 pulpit
4 Holy Ark
5 bimah (reading desk)

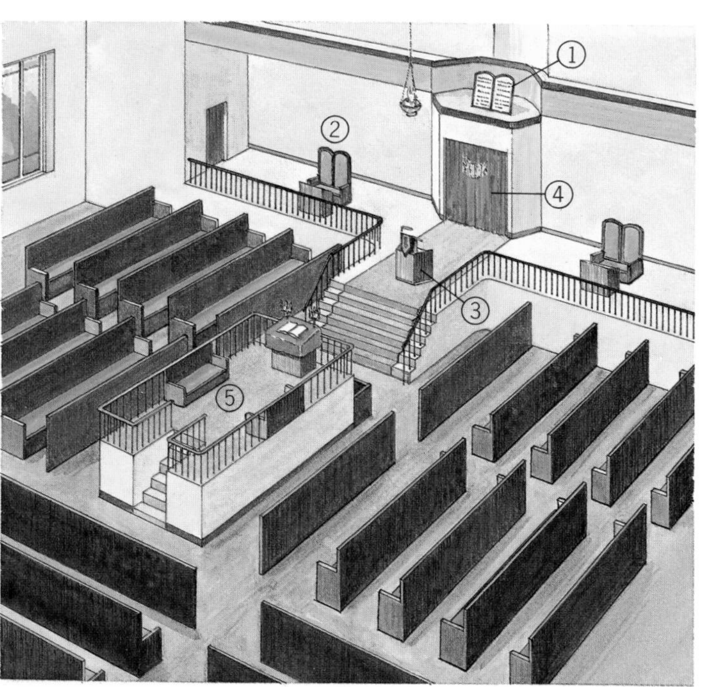

See also
Bible
Festivals
Jews
Temples

Synthetic fibres

Fibres are long, thin, hair-like threads which we use to make fabrics. There are three types of synthetic fibres. The first is made from a substance known as cellulose, found in plants. The second is made mainly from oil. The third is made from minerals.

Cellulose fibres

The fibres of rayon are made of cellulose obtained from wood pulp. First, the cellulose is dissolved by various chemicals. The liquid is then pumped through fine tubes or holes, known as spinnerets, into another chemical solution. There it solidifies into fine threads. These threads are then twisted together to make the rayon yarn. Rayon has the advantage that it dyes easily.

Fibres from plastics

Fibres are made from plastics by melting or dissolving the plastics and then forcing them through spinnerets to make fine threads. Plastic fibres include nylon, polyester and the acrylics, and are sold in the shops under several names including Terylene, Dacron and Acrilan.

Fibres from minerals

Glass fibres are made by melting glass in a tank with many tiny holes in it. The glass is forced out of the holes, and it turns into fine fibres. This fibreglass is used for insulating buildings and making certain kinds of curtains. When stuck together with a synthetic resin, fibreglass is used for making the hulls of boats and the bodies of a few kinds of cars. ■

Asbestos fibres are used to make the special fireproof clothing worn by firemen.

Acrylic fibres feel soft like wool, and they are used to make blankets and winter clothes.

See also
Asbestos
Fabrics
Fibres
Oil
Plastics
Wood

Syria

Syria is an Arab republic at the eastern end of the Mediterranean Sea. Its capital, Damascus, is said to be the oldest city in the world that has been in continuous use. The old market, called a *souk*, is one of the most bustling and colourful in the Middle East. In the centre is a large mosque which dates from soon after the birth of Islam in the 7th century. Damascus was then at the heart of the Arab empire. Syria is a Muslim country, although there is a small Christian community. If you drive north from the capital you come to the village of Maaloule where the people still speak Aramaic, the language spoken by Jesus.

Syria's south-western neighbour is Israel, with whom Syria has fought two wars. Huge sums of money have gone into buying Soviet weapons in preparation for another possible war. In 1967 Israel captured the Golan Heights in southern Syria which command the road north to Damascus.

Syrians work in a variety of jobs, but the largest number work in farming. They grow cereals, vegetables and many kinds of fruit. An oil industry is being developed. In country areas you will still see the simple, loose robes worn by young and old people alike. In the cities it is more common to see European-style clothes.

Flashback

Syria has seen many armies march over its land. In the Middle Ages crusaders passed through on their way to the Holy Land. From the 16th century Syria was ruled by the Ottoman Turks. In 1918, after World War I, it came under French control. It became independent in 1946. There were many turbulent changes of leadership in the years that followed until President Assad took power in 1971. ■

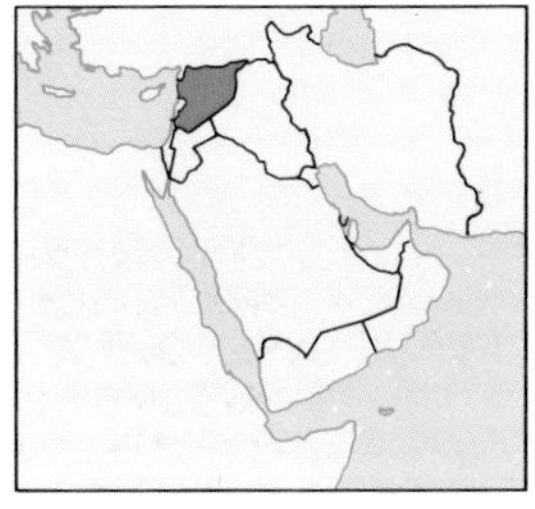

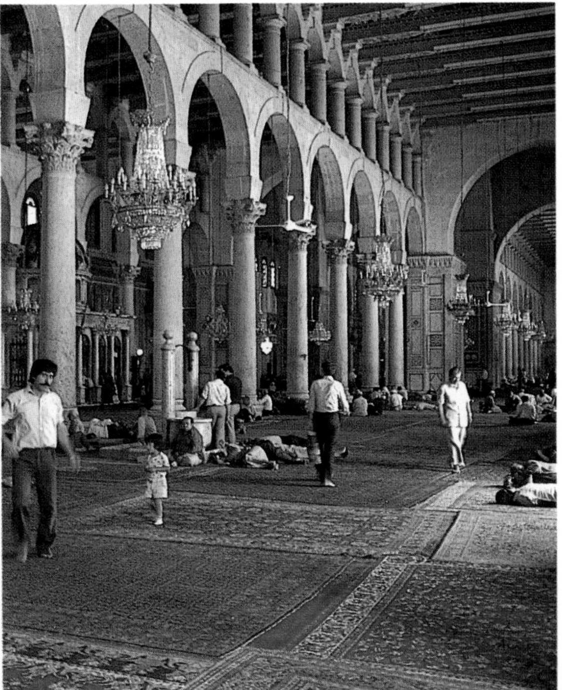

▶ **Rich carpets cover the floor of the magnificent Umayyad Mosque in Old Damascus.**

Area
185,180 sq km
(71,498 sq miles)
Capital
Damascus
Population
11,338,000
Language
Arabic, French, Kurdish, Armenian, others
Religion
Muslim, Christian, Jewish
Government
Republic
Currency
1 Syrian pound = 100 piastres

See also
Arabs
Crusades
Israel
Middle East
Muslims
Ottoman empire

Table tennis

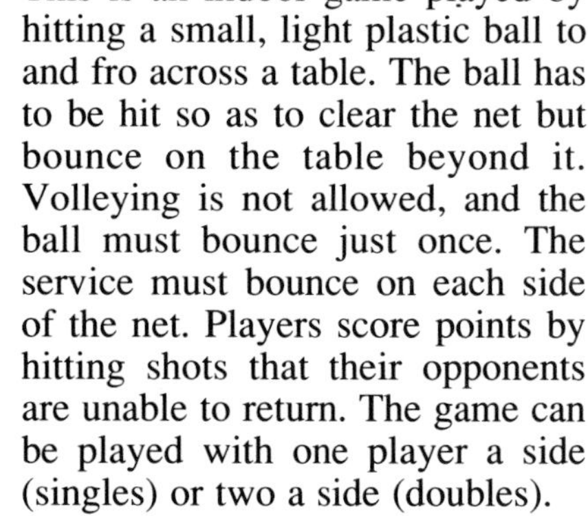

A white line 2 cm wide marks the edges of the playing surface. For doubles a 3 mm wide centre line divides the table into halves.

The game was invented in England at the beginning of the 20th century as an after-dinner game. It was called 'ping-pong', a trade name. The name 'table tennis' took over in the 1920s as the game became more widespread and more athletic.

This is an indoor game played by hitting a small, light plastic ball to and fro across a table. The ball has to be hit so as to clear the net but bounce on the table beyond it. Volleying is not allowed, and the ball must bounce just once. The service must bounce on each side of the net. Players score points by hitting shots that their opponents are unable to return. The game can be played with one player a side (singles) or two a side (doubles).

The bat is made of wood covered with rubber. The rubber can be fairly thick so that it grips the ball to put spin on it.

The ball can just be tapped to and fro, but the secret of good fast play is to be able to hit hard, controlling the ball by putting spin on it with the bat. Because the ball is very light, spin greatly affects both its flight through the air and its bounce on the table. The receiving player has to judge the spin which is on the ball and respond by hitting it correctly. ■

See also
Tennis

Tadpoles

Subphylum Vertebrata
Class Amphibia

Tadpoles hatch from eggs laid by amphibians, such as frogs and toads. They are not like their parents, which are mostly land-living creatures with legs, able to breathe dry air. A tadpole swims with wriggling movements of its tail, and it uses gills to take oxygen from the water.

As a tadpole grows, small lumps appear on its sides, about two-thirds of the way along its body. These develop into hind limbs. Soon after this, front limbs also sprout. In frogs and toads the long tail shrinks and disappears. So do the gills, as lungs develop for breathing.

See also
Amphibians
Frogs
Metamorphosis
Newts
Salamanders
Toads

Many tadpoles feed on tiny water plants, but the adults eat other animals, so the digestive system must also change. The change to the adult form is called metamorphosis. In some species it occurs a few weeks after hatching, but in some cool parts of the world it may be three years before metamorphosis occurs. ■

▼ Axolotls are the tadpoles of a certain type of salamander. They are unusual in that many axolotls remain tadpoles all their lives but are still able to breed.

Taiwan

Taiwan is an island in the Pacific Ocean about 120 km (75 miles) from the south-east coast of China. It is a mountainous island with the highest peak, Yu Shan, rising to 3,997 m (13,113 ft). Taiwan lies on the Tropic of Cancer and has a warm, humid climate for most of the year.

Rice is the most important food crop, but tea, sugar cane and bananas also grow well in the high temperatures, good rainfall and fertile soil.

Taiwan has modern cities, factories and motorways. Its industry and economy have been growing very fast in the last 25 years. Electronic goods, clothing and footwear from Taiwan are exported all over the world and the hard-working Taiwanese have a high standard of living.

Flashback

Taiwan, which used to be called Formosa, was at one time part of China. It was occupied by the Japanese from 1895 to 1945. When Jiang Jieshi (Chiang Kai-Shek) fled from China in 1949 two million Chinese followed and Jiang set up an independent government on the island. ■

Area 36,174 sq km (13,967 sq miles)
Capital Taipei
Population 19,650,000
Language
Mandarin Chinese, Hokkien, Hakka, others
Religion Buddhist, Confucian, Taoist, Christian
Government Republic
Currency 1 new Taiwan dollar = 100 cents

See also
China
Biography Jiang Jieshi

Tanks

A tank is a fighting vehicle protected by thick armour. It is like a moving castle, and runs on tracks not wheels so that it can travel across rough and soft ground. There are two types of tank, large heavy battle tanks and smaller faster reconnaissance tanks used for scouting.

Performance

Tanks are fast-attack weapons. They can travel across ditches and rivers. Some can even travel short distances under water. Others are used to clear paths through minefields. A tank has one main gun mounted on a turret that can turn right round, so it can fire in any direction. Their armour is of steel plate. This can be more than 12 cm (4½ in) thick at the front. Half a tank's weight is armour. To save weight it is thinner on the sides and back. This protects tanks against small bullets, but even thick armour can be pierced by modern shells. The Russian T-12 antitank gun fires shells which can go through 41 cm (16 in) of armour.

Flashback

The first tanks were used in 1916 in World War I. They were slow and unreliable but were very useful for moving across muddy ground and bursting through barbed wire and trenches. The tank was developed in Britain and France from the idea of the new tracked farm tractors. Tanks helped the Allies to win the campaign of autumn 1918. ■

British Challenger Tank 1988
Weight 60 tonnes
Maximum speed 56 km/h (35 mph)
Gun bore (width of barrel tube) 120 mm (4·7 in)
Crew 4
Engine Rolls Royce Condor diesel

British Mark V Tank 1916
Weight 29·5 tonnes
Maximum speed 7 km/h (4½ mph)
Guns two 6-pounders
Crew 8
Engine Ricardo petrol engine

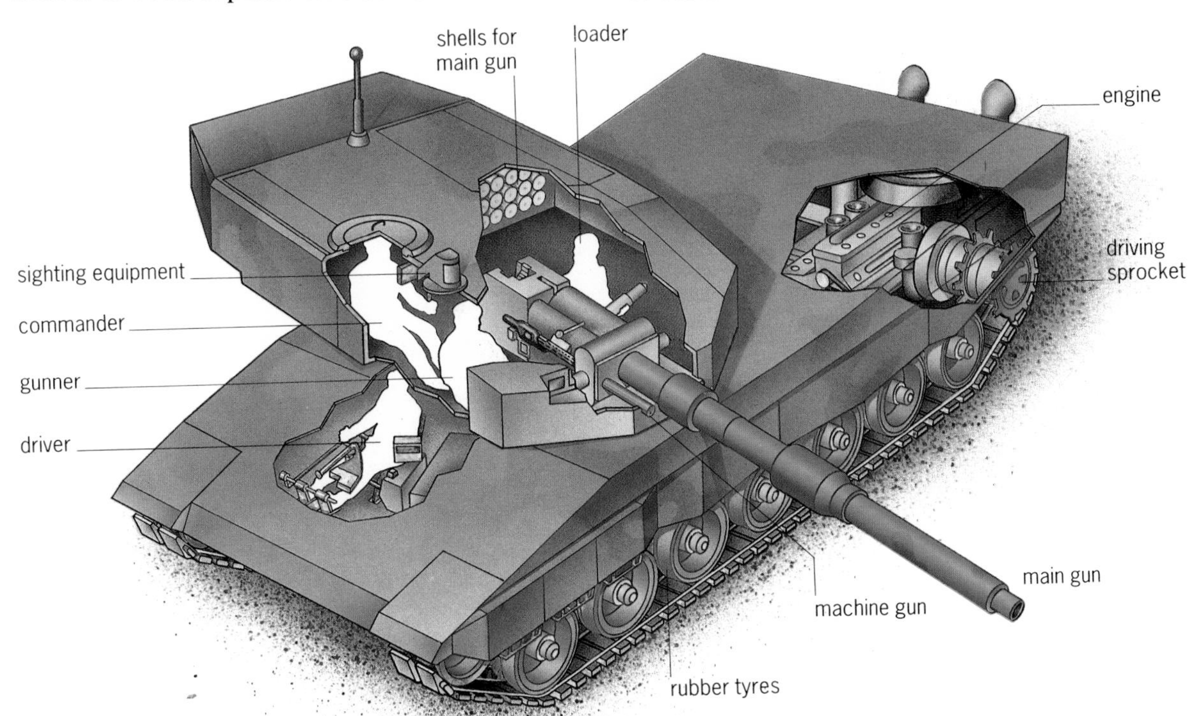

◀ Layout of a modern tank. The driver sits at the front. The weapons are mounted in a rotating turret which also houses the rest of the crew. The engine is at the rear of the tank.

See also
Guns
Weapons

Tanzania

► **A herd of wildebeest grazes in the foreground of Kilimanjaro.**

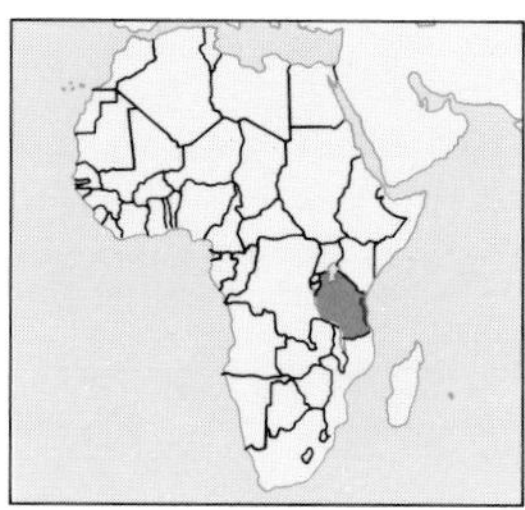

Area
945,050 sq km
(364,886 sq miles)
Capital
Dodoma
Population
22,430,000
Language
Swahili, English, others
Religion
Christian, Muslim
Government
Republic
Currency
1 shilling = 100 cents

► **These villagers are winnowing millet.**

See also
Africa
Evolution of people

Biography
Leakey
Nyerere

The name Tanzania was made up in 1964 when the large country of *Tan*ganyika, on the mainland of East Africa, united with the small island state of *Zan*zibar, which also includes the island of Pemba. Tanzania is a beautiful country. Many wild animals, including antelopes, buffaloes, elephants, giraffes and zebras, roam freely across its huge national parks.

Landscape and climate

Tanzania contains Kilimanjaro (5,895 m, 19,340 ft), Africa's highest mountain. This mountain is near the Equator, but it is always capped by snow and ice. Tanzania also contains part of Lake Victoria, Africa's largest lake, and part of Lake Tanganyika. But most of Tanzania, apart from the offshore islands and the narrow coastal lowlands, consists of high plains covered by grass and woodland. Tanzania has a tropical climate. Near the coast, it is very hot throughout the year. The dry high plains are cooler. The rainiest places are in the north and in the mountains.

The people and how they live

About 120 languages are spoken, and so to be widely understood Tanzanians use a second common language, Swahili. Many Tanzanians also speak English. Most Tanzanians are farmers. The chief food crop is maize, but some farmers grow such crops as coffee, cotton, sisal (used to make rope) and cashew nuts for sale. Tanzania produces some diamonds. The main industrial city is the port of Dar es Salaam.

Flashback

Olduvai Gorge in northern Tanzania is of scientific interest. Here, in the 1960s, Louis and Mary Leakey dug up fossils of creatures that lived two million years ago. These remains are probably those of the ancestors of modern people.

In the late 18th century, Tanzania was a source of slaves. Many slaves were sold in a market on Zanzibar until it was closed in 1873. Germany ruled mainland Tanganyika from 1891 until World War I, when British troops invaded the country. British rule continued until the country's independence in 1961. ■

Taoists

See also
China's history
Confucians
Symbols

Tao (dao) is a Chinese word which means 'the way'. It is used both for the way to live your life and to express religious belief in the Truth (God). Taoists base their ideas and practices on the teaching of Lao Zi, who lived in the 5th century BC. His ideas were written down in the book called the *Dao De Jing*.

Taoism, like Confucianism, has influenced most Chinese people, whether or not they call themselves Taoists. It teaches harmony and balance between all opposites; these are called the yin and yang forces. We can learn from observing nature that a way can always be found by going gently and without using force. ■

Tapestries

The so-called *Bayeux Tapestry* is really an embroidered picture. It is not woven as is a true tapestry. It can still be seen today at Bayeux in northern France.

Tapestries are woven pictures or patterns often used as wall hangings. They are made on a loom, and the pattern is woven into the textile by the weft threads. A high warp loom has the warp threads, which are neutral in colour, hanging vertically. The weft threads, in various colours, are woven backwards and forwards across parts of the warp to make the pattern.

Arras in Flanders was famous for tapestries in the late Middle Ages. In England tapestry was called arras.

Some tapestries made in the Middle Ages are quite like larger versions of miniature paintings from illuminated manuscripts. Later, artists such as Raphael painted 'cartoons' as designs for tapestry weavers to follow. The finest tapestries were made in workshops in France and Flanders. In 1662 Louis XIV, King of France, developed the Gobelins workshop in Paris into a factory for making tapestries. ■

See also
Allegories
Weaving

Biography
Raphael

▲ This tapestry named 'Sight' is one of a set of six, called the Lady and the Unicorn, woven in the late 15th century. It would have brightened a castle room. Tapestries with thousands of flowers in the background are known as 'mille fleurs'.

Tapeworms

Distribution
Throughout the world
Smallest species
Echinococcus granulosus, about 8 mm long, is one of the smallest species.
Largest species
Diphyllobothrium latum, which infects humans, may be 20 m long. Whales have even larger tapeworms.
Number of eggs
Very large in all species. The rat tapeworm may produce 250,000 eggs a day, or about 100 million in the course of its life.

Phylum
Platyhelminthes (flatworms)
Class
Cestoda
Number of species
About 2,500

Tapeworms get their name because they are long and flat, like a tape measure. Adult tapeworms cannot see, smell or hear. They have no way of escaping from enemies, or of catching food. They are parasites and live protected inside the intestines of their final vertebrate hosts. Here they are surrounded by digested food, which is taken in through the body wall.

Adult tapeworms are made up of many body sections produced at the front end of the worm. The mature sections at the end of the worm are full of eggs. These are passed out in the faeces of the host animal. When the eggs are ingested (eaten) by an animal such as a pig they hatch into larvae. The larvae develop a sac around themselves in the muscle. If the muscle (meat) is eaten by humans and other vertebrates the adult worms may develop. Cooking meat kills the larvae. ■

See also
Invertebrates
Parasites
Worms

Tasmania

Tasmania is an island off south-eastern mainland Australia. The climate is cool and wet. It has many mountains, forests, lakes and orchards and only a small population. It is famous for the apples it produces.

Once, Tasmania was joined to mainland Australia, but about 12,000 years ago the level of the seas rose and it eventually became an island. Wallabies, possums, Tasmanian devils, penguins, seals, and many species of snakes are some of the animals native to Tasmania. Its first inhabitants were Tasmanian Aborigines, a slightly different people from mainland Aborigines. Tasmania was named after the Dutchman Tasman who was the first European to visit it in 1642. In 1803 the first British settlers arrived. Their numbers rapidly increased and they eventually destroyed the Aborigines. ■

Area
68,330 sq km
(26,382 sq miles)
Capital
Hobart
Population
433,300
Government
Part of the Federal government of Australia

See also
Australia

Biography
Tasman

Taxes

The governments of countries need money to spend on things that benefit the whole country and are generally best provided by the government on behalf of all the people. Such things might include hospitals, defence (the army, navy and air force), schools, road building and much more. To get the money it needs, a government passes laws saying how much money individual people and businesses have to pay in taxes to the government.

One of the main kinds of tax is income tax. People have to pay to the government part of their income if they earn more than a certain amount. In most countries, a tax is added onto the price when goods and services are sold. This tax is called Value Added Tax (VAT) in Europe and sales tax in the United States. Sometimes governments get taxes in other ways. They may make businesses pay part of their profits in tax, or they may tax wealth which is inherited. ■

See also
Customs and excise
Government

Tea

Tea is made from the dried young leaves of a small bush which grows mainly in the subtropical areas of south-east Asia. It is a hardy evergreen plant which will grow at up to an altitude of 2,000 m (7,000 ft). It likes an even rainfall and ground that is easily drained. Tea grows less quickly in the higher areas and this produces the best quality. India, China and Sri Lanka are the best-known tea-growing areas, but tea is also grown in Taiwan, Bangladesh and parts of Africa.

► The Japanese have a special tea ceremony. An honoured guest and the host or hostess follow a set of traditional rules. Powdered green tea is whisked into boiling water using a bamboo whisk.

Growing teas

Tea bushes are grown together in plantations. The bushes must be three years old before they can be plucked. They are pruned from two years on, to make sure that they produce plenty of leaves and that they grow to the right shape for easy plucking. Tea picking is a highly skilled job done mainly by the women.

Some teas like Assam, Darjeeling and Ceylon or Sri Lankan are sold on their own. Others are blended. English breakfast tea is a blend of Assam and Ceylon tea. Earl Grey is a blend of black China and Darjeeling tea flavoured with bergamot, a delicate citrus oil.

► Tea is picked by hand. The women on this estate in Sri Lanka will pick just one bud and the first two leaves of each young shoot.

Types of tea

There are two main types of tea. One of them is green tea, which is picked and quickly and fully dried. It has a greenish colour and a mild flavour. It is very popular in China and Japan.

Black tea is darker in colour and stronger in flavour. This is the favourite type of tea in Europe. The leaves are only partly dried. They are then put into rolling machines which break up the leaf cells. This releases the natural juices which give tea its special taste. It also gives a twist to the leaf.

After rolling, the leaves are spread out in a damp atmosphere and left to ferment to a bright coppery colour. The fermented leaf is dried in hot air, to become our familiar black tea.

The next stage is to grade the leaves for size. Very often the names of types of tea describe their size and appearance. Examples are Orange Pekoe, Broken Pekoe, and Pekoe Fannings. The final stages are tasting and blending. ■

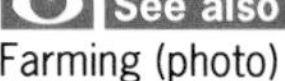

See also
Farming (photo)

Teachers

Not all adults who work in schools are teachers, and some teachers do not work in schools. However, we usually think of a teacher as someone in charge of a class in school, and this is what most teachers actually do.

Training

In most countries, young people who want to be teachers have to go to college or university after leaving school. They learn more about one or two subjects, and also study the history and workings of schools and how children learn. This is called studying 'education'.

Part of their training course usually involves teaching practice. Student teachers spend part of their time in schools watching how other teachers take their classes and also teaching some lessons themselves. They are guided and supervised by their college tutors, and partly by the staff of the school where they are on practice.

In Britain every new teacher has to have a degree from a university or polytechnic. In some countries only the teachers of older pupils need a degree qualification. Teachers of infants and juniors may have a different type of training in a special college.

Flashback

In Western countries the profession of qualified teachers has grown up as schools have developed. In Britain, when schools began to be established for poor children in the early 19th century there was a shortage of teachers. So a system of using monitors was started. The children assembled in groups in a huge school hall, and each group was taught by a monitor, usually a boy of about 14, who listened to the teacher and repeated the information to the group. In 1846 a better system was organized. Pupil teachers, aged from 16 to 18, worked as apprentices in the elementary schools. They had to be tested, and they often went to a Teacher Training College as well. This system lasted until there were enough Teacher Training Colleges for students to do all their training there.

The first training college started near Glasgow in 1836. Shortly afterwards two were founded in London, and others followed. ■

See also
Schools

Technology

Cars, concrete and batteries are all examples of technology. So are bricks, bridges and computers. Technology is about making things which can do useful jobs. Sometimes scientific discoveries lead to new technology. For example, when X-rays were discovered, people soon realized that they could be used to take see-through photographs of bones. At other times, scientists do research so that new technology can be developed. Before the space shuttle could be built, scientists had to find materials which could stand the heat of re-entering the Earth's atmosphere.

Technologists

People who produce new technology are called technologists.

Materials technologists develop new plastics, fabrics, metals and building materials.

Food technologists find new ways to prepare, store and pack food.

Information technologists deal with computers and their uses.

Engineers are technologists. They produce cars, planes and ships, as well as roads, bridges, chemical factories and machinery.

Alternative technology

Modern technology uses lots of energy. Metals have to be melted, bricks have to be baked and engines and power-stations need fuel. Many people think that we waste too much energy. We could use bicycles rather than cars. Wind could turn our generators. And we could build with local clay, wood and stone instead of transporting bricks over huge distances. These ideas are sometimes called alternative technology. They are widely used in many African, Asian and South American countries.

Flashback

Prehistoric people were making simple stone tools over a million years ago. These were the first examples of technology. By 4000 BC, the plough and the wheel had been invented and people were starting to use metals. The age of modern technology began in the 18th century, when the first steam-engines were used to drive machinery. By 1900, power-stations were being built. These led to the world of electricity and electronics we know today. ■

The first

1290	Mechanical clock (the Chinese had water clocks in the 7th century)
1712	Steam-engine
1790	Wrist-watch
1804	Railway locomotive
1826	Photograph
1839	Pedal bicycle
1876	Telephone
1879	Electric light bulb
1885	Petrol-driven car
1894	Radio signals
1903	Aircraft
1926	Television
1946	Electronic computer
1957	Space satellite
1959	Hovercraft
1971	Pocket calculator
1971	Digital watch
1975	Home computer
1982	Compact-disc player

See also
Energy
Engineers
Farming
Industrial Revolution
Industry
Information technology
Materials

Teeth

► The root is attached to the jawbone by cement and tough fibres. The crown is protected by an outer layer of enamel, the hardest substance in the body.

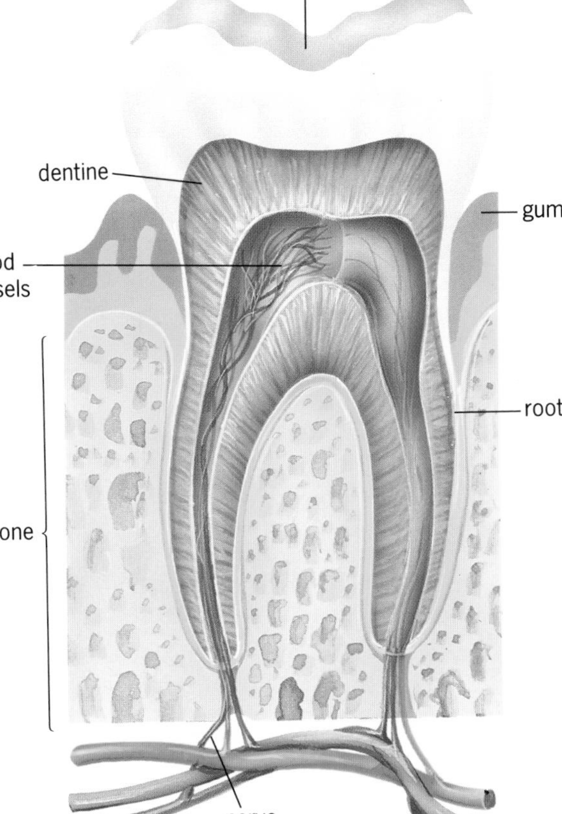

See also
Dentists
Mouths

▼ Teeth develop inside the jawbones before birth and first appear at about five months of age. By about six years children have 24 teeth. Twenty of these are milk teeth, and these fall out between seven and eleven years. They are replaced by larger permanent teeth.

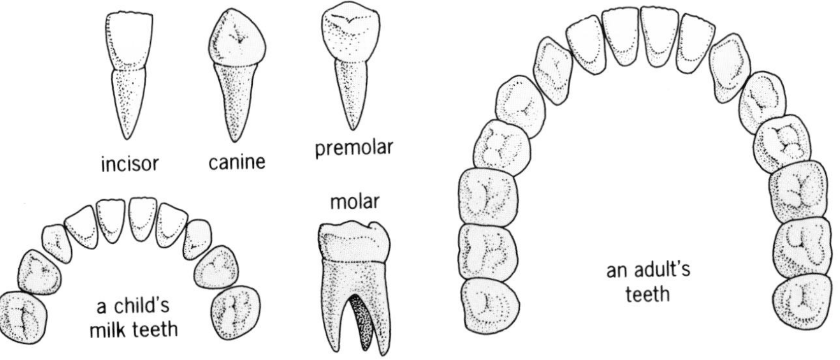

Most animals with backbones have teeth. They are used for holding, cutting and chewing food, so they have to be very strong. The part of a tooth that you can see is called the crown. Below the crown, hidden in the gums, is the tooth's root. This fixes the tooth firmly into the jawbone.

Most of the tooth is made of hard material called dentine. The crown is coated with an even harder material called enamel. Inside the tooth is a cavity filled with pulp. The pulp consists of blood vessels and nerve fibres.

A baby is born with no teeth showing. Hidden in the gums are tiny growing tooth buds. The baby has two sets of buds. The most rapidly growing set are the first, or milk teeth. These appear during the first five years. Then they fall out and are replaced by the second, or permanent teeth. These should last all your life.

Special teeth

In most animals teeth are specialized for different jobs. Our upper and lower front four teeth have straight chisel-shaped ends. They are called incisors and are used for slicing mouth-sized pieces from food. On each side of the incisors is a single pointed tooth. This is the canine tooth. The canines are more developed in meat-eating animals and are used for puncturing the skin of their prey. Our back teeth, behind the canines, are broad-topped and bumpy. These are called molars. When you chew, you rub the upper and lower molars together, grinding up food into small pieces for swallowing.

In plant-eating animals the molars are large and have many ridges to enable them to grind up large amounts of tough grass and leaf material. Meat-eating animals also have special molars for chewing meat with the sides of their jaws. The edges of these teeth slide past each other like blades of shears.

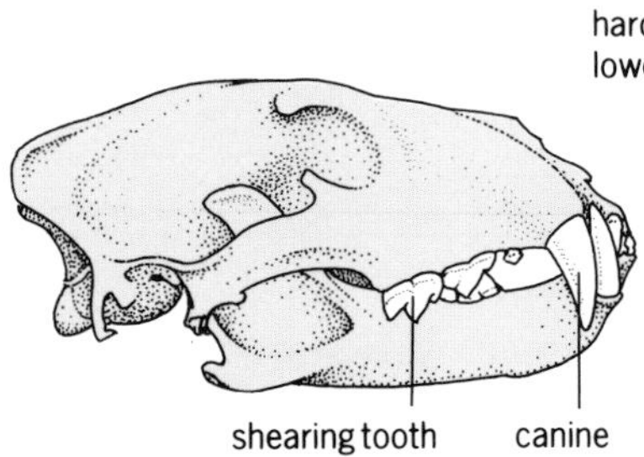

▲ Lion (carnivore)
Carnivores have long canines to kill prey, and hold onto them. Massive shearing teeth crack bones and cut flesh.

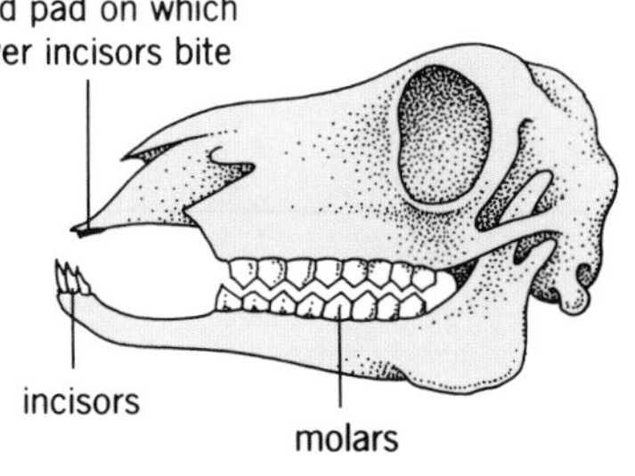

▲ Sheep (herbivore)
Herbivores cut grass by moving their chisel-edged lower incisors sideways across a thick pad on the upper jaw.

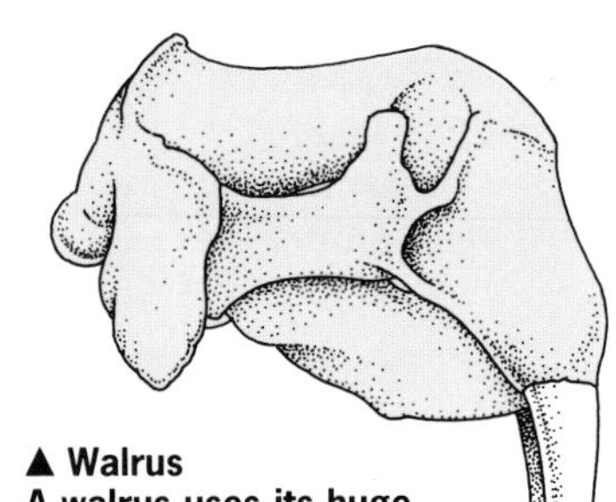

▲ Walrus
A walrus uses its huge, tusk-like upper canines to dig up shellfish from the sea bottom, or to stab to death larger prey like seals.

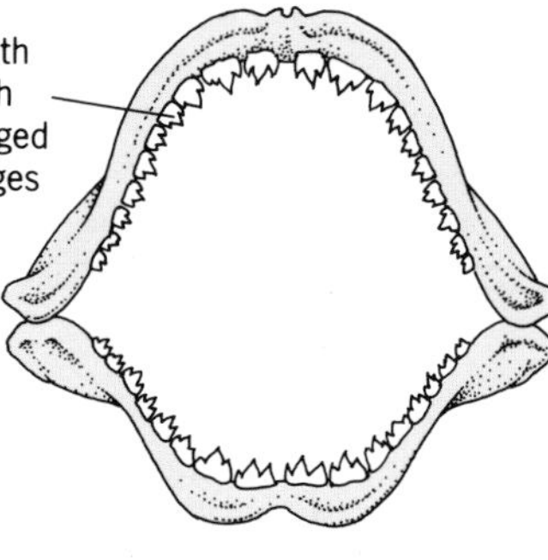

▲ Shark
The jagged teeth cut through flesh like a chainsaw and hold prey firmly in the mouth.

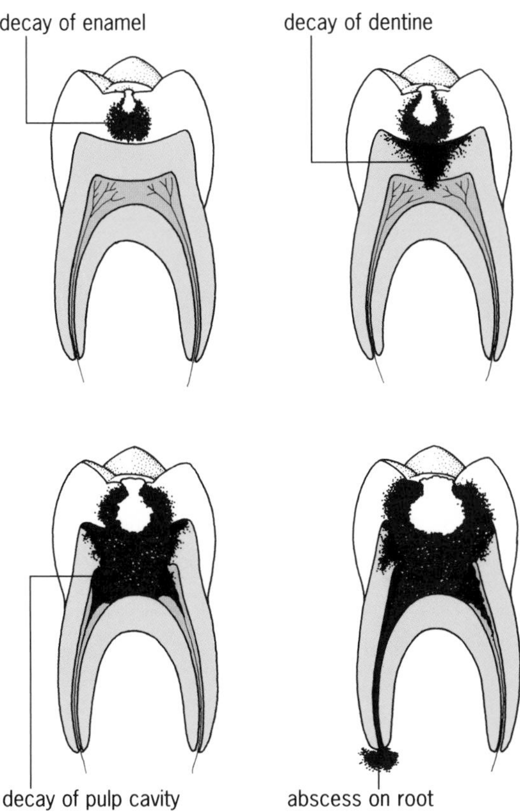

Tooth decay

If you eat too much sugar and do not clean your teeth regularly you will get tooth decay.

Tooth decay occurs when small pieces of food, trapped in the teeth, are broken down by bacteria that live in the mouth. This produces acid which slowly damages the hard enamel coating the crown. Then it attacks the softer dentine, causing a hole or cavity. This results in toothache.

Apart from avoiding too much sugar, the best way to prevent tooth decay is by carefully brushing your teeth after every meal and before you go to bed. ■

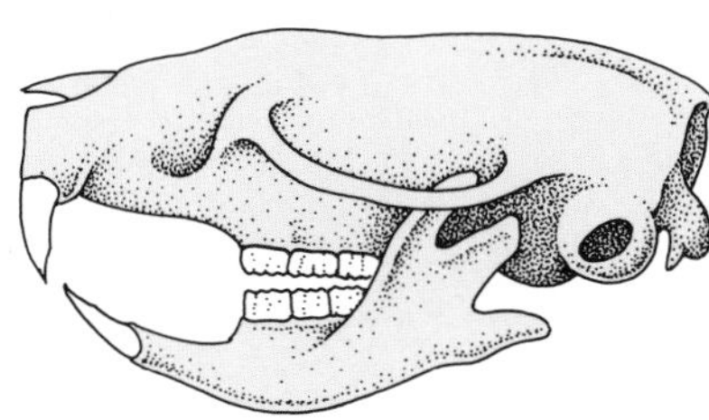

▲ Rat (rodent)
Rodents have long incisors with sharp edges, like chisels, for gnawing.

Telegraphs

Until telephones appeared in the 1870s, telegraph was the only way of sending messages quickly over long distances. The first practical electric telegraphs were made in the 1830s. They worked by sending electric signals along wires. At the far end, magnetic needles spelt out the message by pointing at letters.

Before telegraph was developed, the only quick method of sending signals across country was by lighting bonfires on hilltops.

It was the arrival of the railways which put inventors to work on electric telegraphy. Signalmen needed a reliable method of passing on information about trains.

The word *telegraph* is based on two Greek words: *tele* meaning 'far off' and *graphia* meaning 'writing'.

Morse code

Some of the early electric telegraphs needed a different wire for each letter of the alphabet. However, in 1838, Samuel Morse invented a system for sending signals along a single wire. Morse used short and long bursts of current, sent one after another in different combinations.

At the end of the wire, the bursts of current passed through an electromagnet. This moved a pen which marked out a series of dots and dashes on paper tape. The different combinations of dots and dashes were a code which stood for different letters (and numbers). Morse code was widely used by ships when radio telegraphy became available in the 1900s. And it is still used in emergencies today. It can be received as bleeps on a radio speaker, or as flashes of light from a lamp or torch.

The Morse code

A	.-	N	-.
B	-...	O	---
C	-.-.	P	.--.
D	-..	Q	--.-
E	.	R	.-.
F	..-.	S	...
G	--.	T	-
H	....	U	..-
I	..	V	...-
J	.---	W	.--
K	-.-	X	-..-
L	.-..	Y	-.--
M	--	Z	--..

Telegrams, telex and beyond

Telegrams are messages sent by telegraph, printed on paper and then delivered by a messenger. The first public telegram service was set up in Britain in 1843. By 1900, more than 80 million telegrams were being sent every year. Telegrams are still used for communication overseas, but most people rely on the telephone for quick, long-distance communication.

The word *telegraph* was thought up by a French clergyman, Claude Chappe. In 1793, he designed a system of tall towers with movable arms. The arms were set in different positions to show the different letters of the alphabet. In this way, messages could be sent across country from one observer to another.

Telex is a system of sending printed messages by telephone. It was first developed in the early 1930s. The message is typed on the keyboard of a teleprinter. This sends signals by telephone to another teleprinter which prints out the message.

Since telex first appeared, electronics has made many other developments possible. Fax machines can copy whole documents, including pictures, and send them by telephone. With electronic mail, computers are linked by telephone or satellite so that a message left on one computer can be read on another. ■

See also
Codes and ciphers
Communication
Computers
Electronics
Information technology
Radio
Sign language
Wire

Telephones

The very first words spoken over a telephone were: 'Mr Watson, come here, I want to see you!' They were spoken by Alexander Graham Bell, calling his assistant in the next room.

Telephone conversation takes about a quarter of a second to travel from Britain to America. Calls are sent via a satellite 36,000 km (22,000 miles) above the Atlantic Ocean.

See also

Fibre optics
Information technology
Microphones
Microwaves
Radio
Telegraphs

Biography
Bell

A telephone lets you talk to people who are far away. It is the most widespread means of long-distance communication and there are over 525 million telephones throughout the world.

How does a telephone work?

When you telephone a friend, you probably use a handset with a separate mouthpiece and earpiece. As soon as you lift the handset off the base, your telephone is automatically connected to the local exchange. The exchange sends a dialling tone which means you can dial or tap in the number you want. The dialling unit sends out a series of electrical signals. These correspond to the number you enter and the exchange automatically connects you to the telephone line of your friend. Your friend's telephone will then ring.

Uses of the telephone

Emergency services such as fire, police and ambulance can be rung using a special priority number. In Britain, the number is 999. Businesses use telephones to communicate with customers and suppliers, but they also use them to link staff who are working in different rooms. People use mobile phones to make and receive calls in cars and trains or when walking. The phones are linked to the exchange by a network of radio transmitters and receivers. Computers in different places use telephones to send data to each other. Each computer is connected to the telephone by a device called a modem. This sends computer signals down the telephone lines instead of ordinary conversation.

Flashback

The first telephones were built in 1876 by Alexander Graham Bell in the USA. He demonstrated them by speaking to his assistant in the next room. In Bell's early designs, the earpiece was also the mouthpiece. The first telephone exchange was opened in 1878 in Connecticut, USA. It had just 21 customers. The connections were made by an operator who had to listen to the calls to find out when they had ended. Automatic telephone exchanges, without operators, were first built in the late 1890s. Customers could call each other up by pressing buttons or turning a dial on the telephone. The first transatlantic telephone service was set up in 1928. Conversations were carried by radio signals. ■

▼ When you speak into a telephone, the sound is changed into electrical signals. In your friend's telephone, electrical signals are changed back into sound.

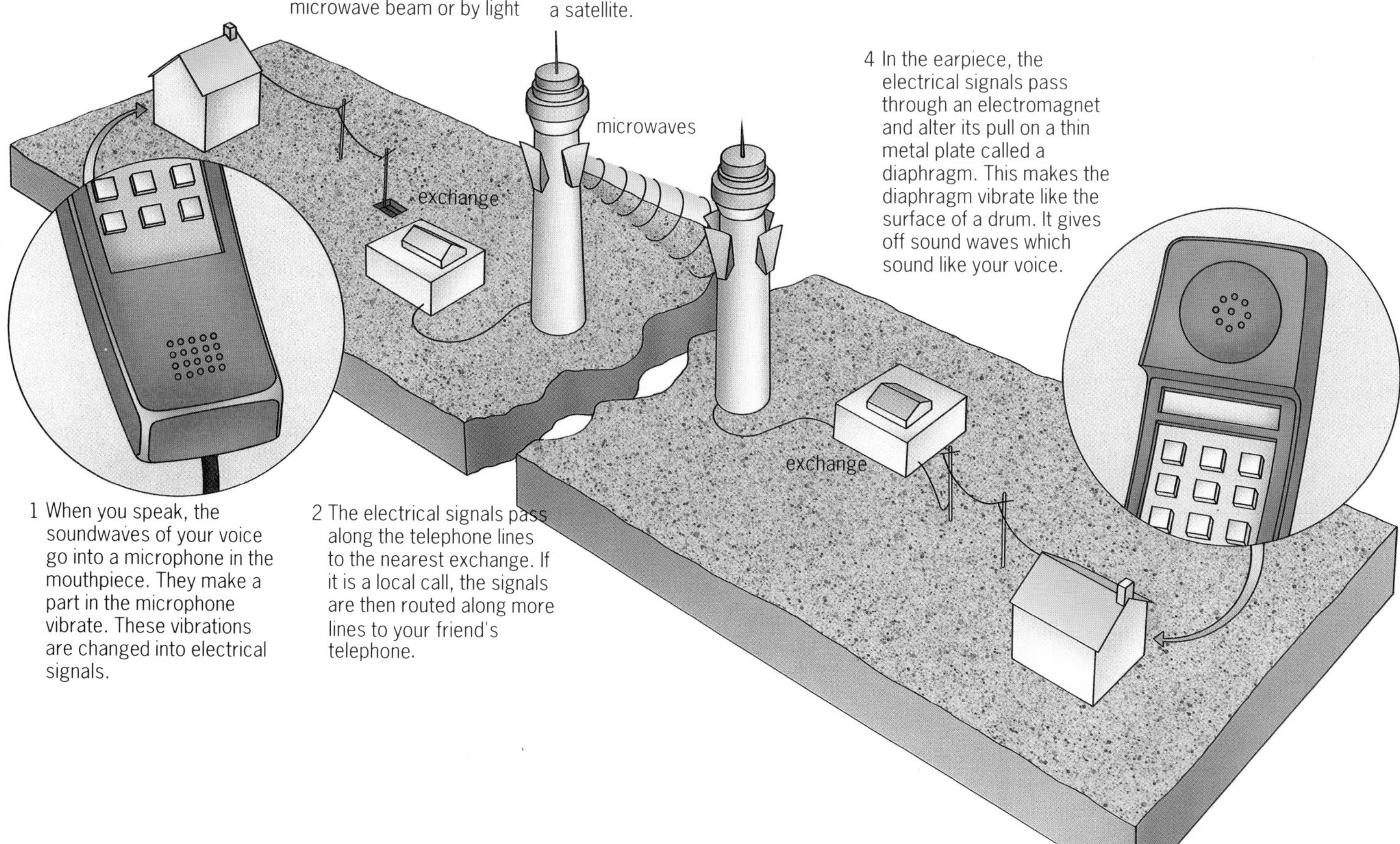

Telescopes

When you look through a telescope, distant things seem nearer and bigger. Telescopes also help you see things that are too faint to see by eye alone. They can collect light, rather as a bucket collects rainwater, and then funnel the light into your eye. Astronomers use telescopes to explore the sky.

Telescopes from lenses and mirrors

The simplest telescope is a tube with a lens at each end. This kind is called a refracting telescope. The lens at the front collects the light. The one you look through is called the eyepiece. It magnifies the image of what you are looking at. Many telescopes are made so that the eyepiece can be changed. A stronger one gives you more magnifying power.

A telescope that uses a curved mirror to collect the light is called a reflector. The main mirror concentrates the light onto another small mirror which then reflects it into an eyepiece. Really big telescopes are always reflectors because it is impossible to support large lenses so that they do not bend under their own weight. The bigger a telescope's collecting mirror or lens, the fainter the things it can see and the stronger the magnifying power you can use with it. Astronomers like telescopes with mirrors that are as big as possible.

Giant telescopes are built on huge mounts with drive motors for moving them. A back-garden telescope usually has a small stand that keeps it firm and lets you point it anywhere by hand.

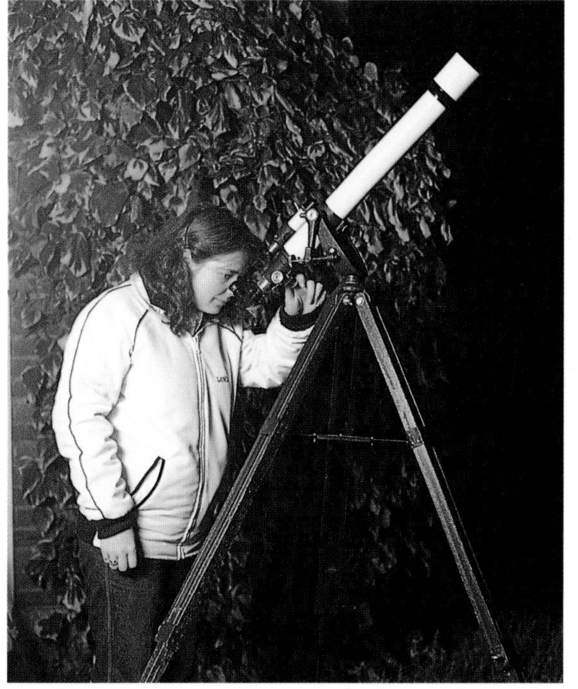

◀ **A reflecting telescope.**

The **largest reflecting telescope** with a single mirror is at Mount Semirodriki in the USSR and has a mirror 6 m across.

The **largest refracting telescope** is at the Yerkes Observatory in the United States of America. The lens is just over 1 m across.

The **largest radio telescope** is built in a natural hollow in the ground at Arecibo in Puerto Rico in the Caribbean. It is 300 m across.

Flashback

No one knows for sure who invented the telescope. In 1608, three Dutch spectacle-makers all claimed that they had made the first working telescope out of two lenses. Hans Lippershey is usually said to have been the first. The next year, news of the invention reached the astronomer Galileo Galilei in Venice. Soon he had worked out how to build one for himself and turned it on the sky. In 1672 Sir Isaac Newton announced that he had made the first working telescope to use a curved mirror for collecting light. ■

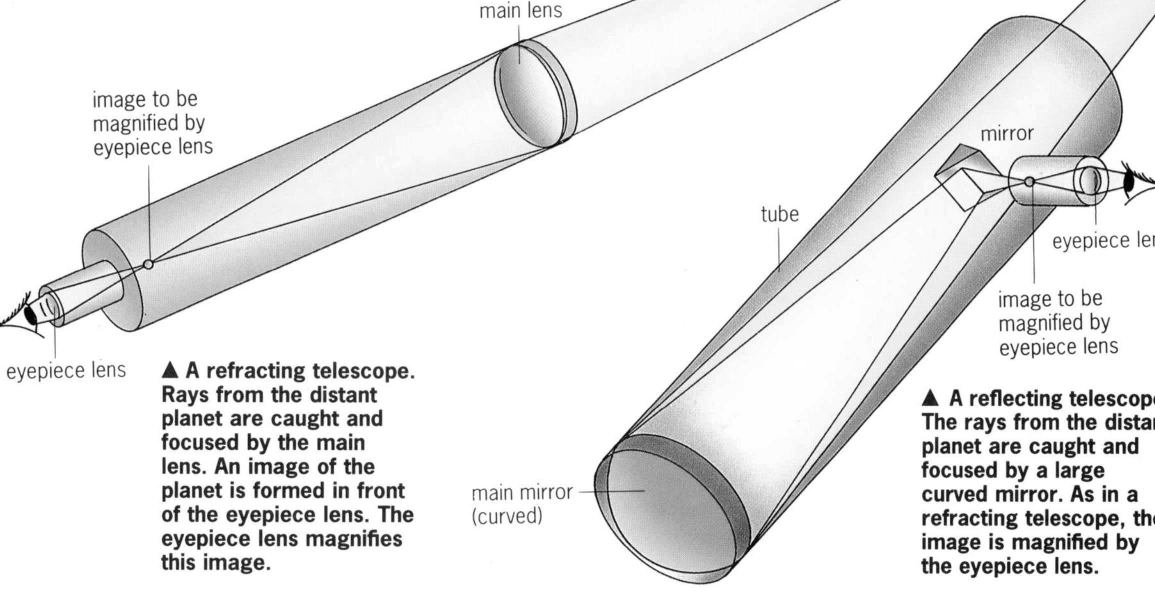

▲ **A refracting telescope. Rays from the distant planet are caught and focused by the main lens. An image of the planet is formed in front of the eyepiece lens. The eyepiece lens magnifies this image.**

▲ **A reflecting telescope. The rays from the distant planet are caught and focused by a large curved mirror. As in a refracting telescope, the image is magnified by the eyepiece lens.**

The Hubble Space Telescope was designed to detect objects 25 times fainter than the dimmest seen with telescopes on the ground. It has a main mirror 2·4 m across and was launched into Earth orbit in April 1990.

See also
Astronomers
Lenses
Observatories

Biography
Galilei
Huygens
Newton

Television

Television (TV for short) is a way of sending pictures so that events happening in one place can be seen somewhere else. A TV camera changes the pictures into signals. The signals can be transmitted (sent) using radio waves in much the same way as sounds are sent by radio. When a TV set receives the signals, it uses them to make pictures on its screen.

▼ **The picture on a black-and-white TV screen is made up of hundreds of horizontal lines which change between light and dark along their length. The lines are made by a beam of electrons which strikes the back of the screen and makes it glow.**

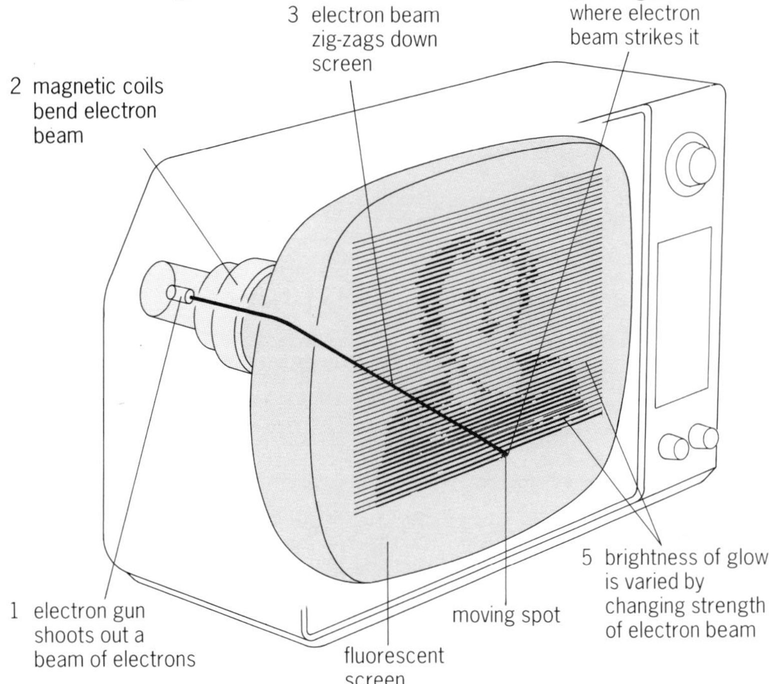

Making the pictures

The 'moving' pictures on a TV screen are not really moving at all. What you actually see is lots of still pictures flashing on the screen one after another. This happens so quickly that it looks like continuous motion. Films in the cinema use the same effect.

In Britain, TV pictures have 625 lines. 25 complete pictures are put on the screen every second.

In the USA, TV pictures have 525 lines. 30 complete pictures are put on the screen every second.

Many small, portable TV sets give black-and-white pictures. The main part of the set is the picture tube. At the narrow end of the tube there is a 'gun' which shoots out a beam of electrical particles called electrons. At the wide end there is a screen with a phosphor coating on the inside. The phosphor glows where the electron beam strikes it. This produces a spot of light.

To make a picture, the electron beam is pulled by electromagnets so that it zigzags its way down the screen. At the same time, the strength of the beam is varied so that the spot glows brighter or dimmer. The result is a picture made up of hundreds of horizontal lines. Along each line, the white bits are where the beam is at full strength. The 'black' bits are where the beam is so weak that the screen does not glow at all. When the picture is changed it is not changed all at once but bit by bit. Making the electron beam zigzag over the screen is called scanning.

Sending the pictures

A TV camera uses lenses to pick up an image, just like an ordinary camera. However, a TV camera does not have film in it. Instead each image falls on a light-sensitive plate. A beam of electrons scans the plate, just as in a picture tube. This makes the plate give off a tiny, varying current. So, line by line, the picture is changed into electrical signals.

The signals from a TV camera are transmitted in a similar way to radio signals, by modulating (varying) radio waves. UHF (ultra high frequency) radio waves are used for TV transmission. UHF waves cannot bend round hills or large buildings, so, for good reception, a TV set needs an aerial which points straight at the transmitter.

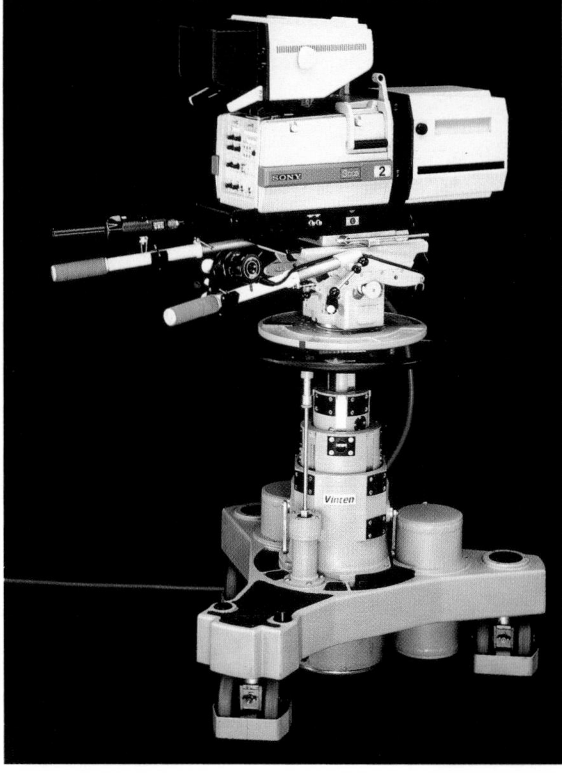

► **A television studio camera. The operator can see what is being filmed in a small TV screen on top of the camera.**

red picture

green picture

blue picture

pictures combine to give full colour picture

◀ A colour TV picture is really three separate pictures, one on top of the other. When you look at the screen, you see the three pictures as a single picture in full colour.

How a colour picture is made

Your eyes can be made to see any colour, including white, by mixing red, green and blue light together in the right proportions. Colour TV uses this idea. A colour TV set gives you separate red, green and blue pictures on top of each other on the same screen. When you see the three pictures together, they look like a single picture in full colour.

Before signals can be transmitted, a colour TV camera has to split each picture into separate red, green and blue pictures. It does this using mirrors, filters and three different light-sensitive plates.

A colour TV set uses three electron beams to produce the red, green and blue pictures. The screen is covered with thousands of tiny phosphor strips which glow red or green or blue when a beam strikes them. Behind the screen there is a special grid called a shadow mask. This makes sure that only one of the beams can strike the red strips, one beam the green strips and one the blue. If you look at a colour TV screen through a magnifying glass, you can see the red, green and blue strips grouped in threes all over the screen. See if you can work out which strips are glowing if the screen looks white when you stand back from it.

Flashback

In the early 1900s, engineers realized that it might be possible to send pictures using radio waves. However, it was not until 1926 that John Logie Baird gave the first public demonstration of television in London. The Baird system was quite different from the electronic picture tubes and cameras of today. His picture scanning was done mechanically using a huge spinning disc with holes in it for the light to pass through. His first images were of poor quality and had only 30 lines. By the time the BBC started regular television broadcasts from Alexandra Palace, London, in 1936, a fully electronic television system had been developed. Pictures at this time were all in black and white. The first programme in colour was transmitted by CBS in the USA in 1951. ■

◀ A family watching colour television in 1954.

Closed-circuit television
The signals from the camera are sent straight to a TV set and not transmitted. Security cameras in shops use closed-circuit television.

The average British viewer spends more than 25 hours a week in front of a television set.

The largest TV screen in the world was built by Sony for an international exhibition in Tokyo. It measured 45 m by 24 m.

The tallest television transmission mast in the world is at Fargo, North Dakota, USA. At 628 m, it is just over twice the height of the Eiffel Tower.

2,500 million people (about half the world's population) watched live or recorded transmissions from the 1984 Olympic Games in Los Angeles.

See also
Cameras
Colour
Electronics
Information technology
Lenses
Microwaves
Radio
Satellites
Video

Biography
Baird

Temperature in °C

15 million — centre of sun
6000 — surface of sun
2800 — bulb filament
1500 — iron melts
800 — electric fire
200 — hot frying oil
100 — boiling water
45 — Death Valley USA
37 — body temperature
0 — melting ice
-80 — South pole
-200 — air turns liquid
-273 — absolute zero: coldest possible temperature

Absolute zero is the lowest possible temperature that can exist. The Kelvin scale measures temperatures using absolute zero as its starting point. On this scale absolute zero is 0 K and water freezes at 273 K.

The lowest temperature yet reached was $3x10^{-8}$ K (3 hundred-millionths of a degree) above absolute zero.

See also
Cold
Heat
Thermometers

Temperature

The temperature of an object tells us how hot it is, but this is not the same as the amount of heat the object contains. A red-hot spark from a fire is much hotter than a cup of tea, but the cup of tea is larger and has more heat in it.

We use thermometers to measure temperature. They are marked with a scale showing the degree of hotness. Most countries use the Celsius scale (sometimes called centigrade). On this scale the numbers were chosen so that water freezes at 0 degrees and boils at 100 degrees. Sometimes weather forecasts and cooking temperatures are given in degrees Fahrenheit. On this scale, water freezes at 32 degrees and boils at 212 degrees. On a warm day the temperature will be about 20°C (68°F). ■

▲ Death Valley, California, USA, one of the hottest places on Earth. Temperatures can reach 45°C or more.

▲ Lake Baikal, Siberia. In Siberia, one of the coldest places on Earth, temperatures can fall below -50°C.

Something to do

Our skin has special detectors in it so that we can get a good idea of the temperature of something without using a thermometer. But we can easily trick ourselves. Get three bowls of water: one with cold, one with warm, and one with hot water (as hot as you would use for washing up). Put one hand in the hot water and the other in the cold. Now put them both in the warm water. What does it feel like?

Temples

Members of most religions like to have special buildings for worship. Some of these buildings are basically large halls with enough room for people to pray together and listen to teaching. Synagogues, mosques, Baha'i houses of worship and Quaker meeting-houses are like this.

Temples are different from meeting-houses in the following way. A temple usually contains something which helps members of the religion to feel that God is present there to a greater extent than in other places. They might call a temple a sacred or holy place or even the house of God. Each community will try to make their temple the most beautiful building they can afford. Temples can be very old and elaborate, or small, new and built for a local group. Some Christian churches are like temples and some are more like meeting-houses.

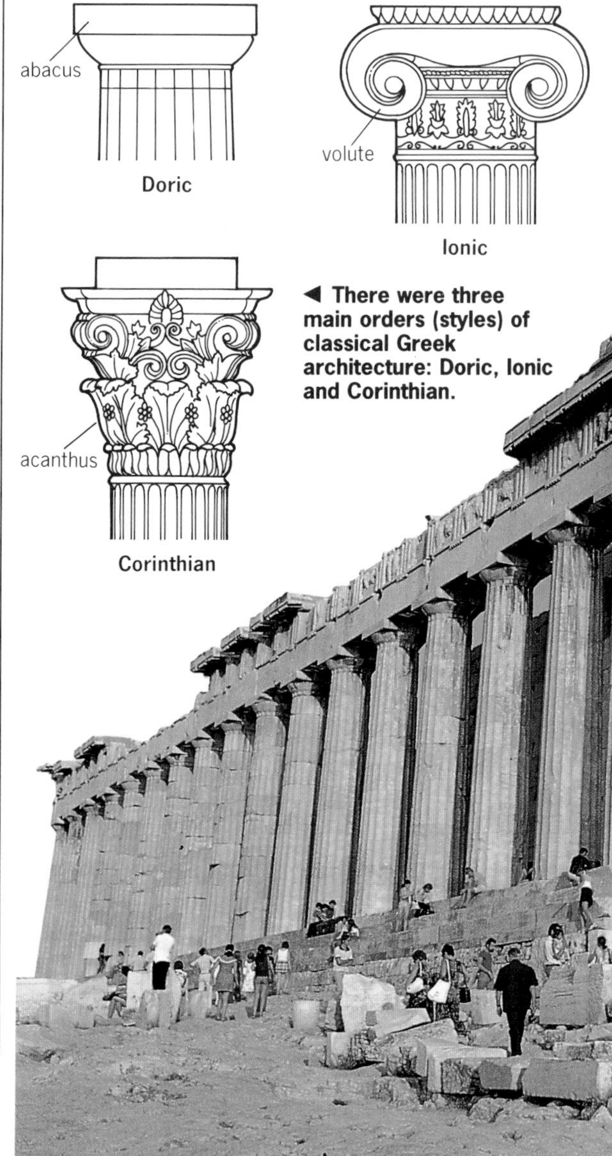

◀ There were three main orders (styles) of classical Greek architecture: Doric, Ionic and Corinthian.

The Greeks and Romans built temples to contain statues of their gods which were specially made and blessed (consecrated). Priests organized the offerings and ceremonies that took place. These classical temples with their elegant columns and stone carvings have influenced architects, especially at the time of the Renaissance and during the 18th century in Europe and North America.

Hindu temples can be small shrines, housing an image of God. Many of the great Hindu temples are built in India with towers to look like the Himalayan mountains, the home of the gods. There is often a series of courtyards and halls but the most important part is the shrine room for the image of God. Images help Hindus to feel a close relationship with God as they can bring their offerings and say their prayers in front of them. Brahmins (priests) look after the temple and perform rituals for the people.

Buddhists place statues of the Buddha in their temples. Sometimes the statue and a small model stupa may contain relics (remains) of the Buddha. These help people to feel close to him. They bring offerings of flowers and sometimes fruit to the temple and try to follow the example of the Buddha by looking at the peacefulness of the image and meditating in front of it.

▼ The Parthenon, a temple dedicated to Athene, the goddess of wisdom. The Parthenon was built in the Doric style in the 5th century BC. Inside the temple was a statue of Athene made of gold and ivory.

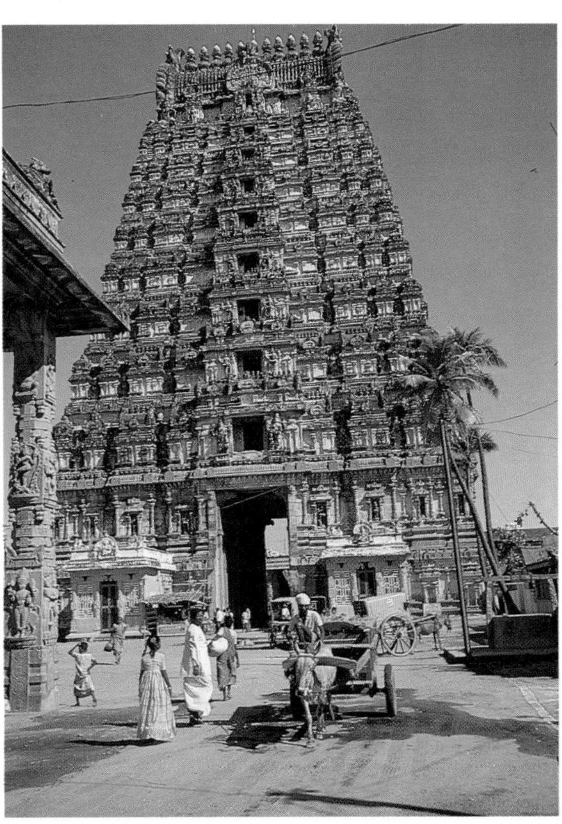

◀ A Hindu temple in south India. Here we can see an elaborately carved tower and images of the gods high on the walls.

▲ A Buddhist temple built in the 11th century AD at Byodo, near Nara, Japan. Inside the main building is a large statue of the Buddha.

Flashback

The Holy of Holies inside the temple in Jerusalem, which was destroyed by the Romans in AD 70, contained the Ten Commandments which Jews believe God gave to Moses on Mount Sinai. This place was so sacred for Jews that only the High Priest went into it, once a year on the Day of Atonement. The rest of the people worshipped in various outer rooms and courtyards. ■

See also
Buddhists
Greek ancient history
Hindus
Priests

Tennis

▼ **A modern tennis racket and ball. The head of the racket is strung with animal gut or an artificial material such as nylon. Racket frames were traditionally wooden, but in recent years aluminium and carbon graphite rackets have become very popular.**

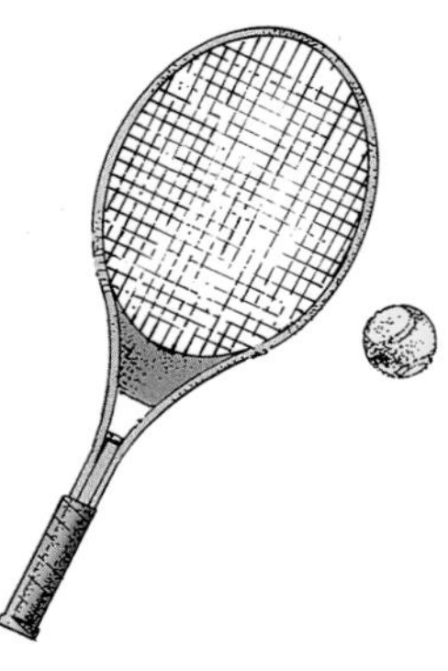

Tennis is a racket and ball game played indoors or outdoors on a grass, clay, wood or synthetic surface. Games can be played between two opponents (singles) or between two pairs of players (doubles).

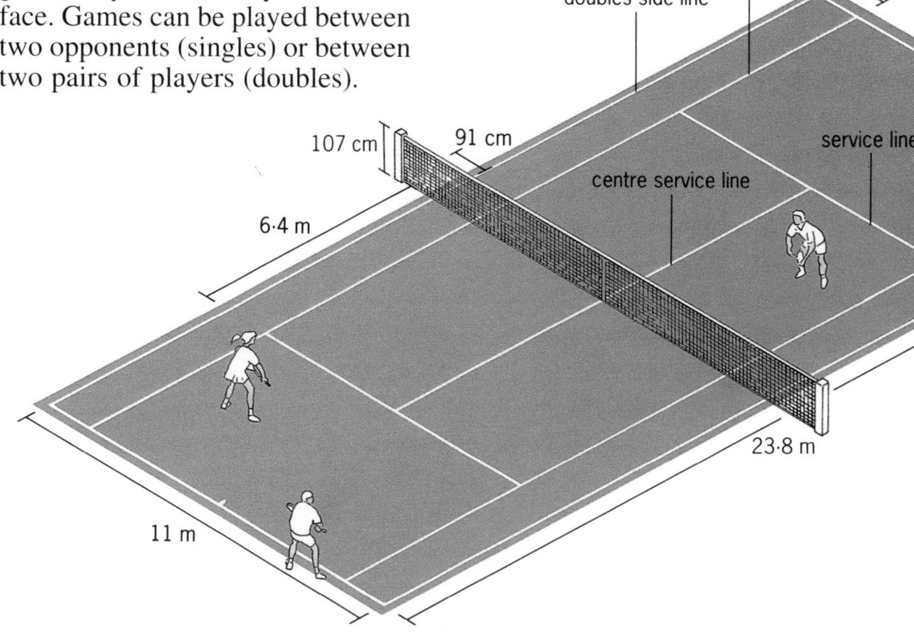

◀ **The court, with doubles players, at the moment of service. The server throws the ball up and hits it over the net with an overhead stroke. The ball must bounce in the service court diagonally opposite.**

Tennis balls are made of rubber and covered with wool or manufactured fibres. In major tournaments the balls are replaced at the end of the first 7 games and every 9 games thereafter. This is because they change shape and pressure when hit, and are likely to bounce differently.

The ball is put into play by 'serving'. This is a shot from behind the baseline which must bounce in the opponent's service court before being returned. A service into the net or outside the receiver's service court is called a fault. If a server steps over the baseline or walks or runs before hitting a ball while serving, this is called a foot fault. If the server commits two faults in succession the opponent gains a point. Otherwise, the players then play a 'rally' until one of them fails to hit the ball, lets it bounce twice, or hits it into the net or out of court, and so loses a point.

In order to win a game, one side must score four points and lead by at least two points. The first point is called 15; the second, 30; the third, 40; and the fourth, game point. A score of zero is called love. Six games are needed to win a set, provided that there is at least a two game lead. If not, a 'tie break' game can be played when the game score is 6–6. Then the first side to win two sets (or three in some tournaments) wins the match.

Flashback

'Real tennis' began as a game played inside French monasteries in the Middle Ages. It was called 'real' (royal) because kings played it. In England, in Tudor times, King Henry VIII liked to play the game at Hampton Court, where he kept a professional player on hand to play.

In the 19th century some people took tennis outdoors and invented 'lawn tennis'. Rules were drawn up for a tournament at Wimbledon in 1877, and that remains the world's most famous grass court championship. Until 1968 it was for amateur players only, but since then amateurs and professionals have played against each other in all the major Open championships.

Any player who wins the US, French, Australian and Wimbledon Opens in the same year achieves the 'Grand Slam'. Only five players have done this: Don Budge (1938), Maureen Connolly (1953), Rod Laver (1962 and 1969), Margaret Court (1970) and Steffi Graf (1988). ■

The first Wimbledon tournament was held by the All-England Croquet Club to raise money to repair their pony-roller. A profit of £10 was made. In 1988, the total prize money at the Wimbledon championships was over £2½ million.

The 'tie break' was introduced to most tournaments in the 1970s after some amazingly long matches. At Wimbledon in 1969 Gonzales defeated Pasarell 22–24, 1–6, 16–14, 6–3, 11–9. Nowadays when the game score reaches 6–6, players have a 'tie break' game. They swap service every two points and the first to win seven points takes the game and set, as long as there is a two point lead. If not, the tie break continues until a two point lead is established.

See also

Biography
Sports special

Termites

Termite mounds can be immensely strong. When they are built on ground needed for cultivation, sometimes even bulldozers cannot flatten them and explosives are needed to level them.

The termite queen can lay one egg a second, but only for a short time.

Phylum
Arthropoda
Class
Insecta
Order
Isoptera
Number of species
About 1,700

Termites live only in the warmer parts of the world. Some kinds make very large nests, which may be 7 m (23 ft) in height and house over 1 million insects. At a certain time each year, numbers of winged termites emerge. After a brief flight they lose their wings and each male pairs with a female. The termite nest includes a queen, who is the mother of all of the insects in the nest, and a king, who is their father. The queen's body, swollen with eggs, may measure 10 cm (4 in) in length. She cannot move, but all her needs are attended to by her worker children.

The young termites hatch out as small replicas of their parents. They eat only plant materials and because of their numbers they may be pests, damaging crops or the timbers of buildings. The termite is the longest lived insect. The queen usually lives for 15–20 years, but there are records of termites living up to 50 years. ■

See also
Ants
Bees
Grasslands
Insects

Terrapins

Distribution
Fresh water in Europe, Asia, Africa and America
Largest
Alligator snapper, usually grows to about 72 cm long and weighs about 90 kg
Smallest
American mud terrapins, shell length about 10–15 cm

Subphylum Vertebrata
Class Reptilia
Order Chelonia
Number of species
About 150 (belonging to several families)

Terrapins live in fresh water. They have flatter shells than their land-living cousins, the tortoises, so they can lie almost unseen on the bed of a pond or stream. They can hold their breath for a long time, and some species have pointed snouts so that they are barely visible when they come up for air.

They are flesh eaters. Some, like the alligator snapper, lie in wait for unwary fish or smaller creatures. It lies with its mouth open, and at the back of its tongue there is a small worm-like organ. If a fish tries to eat this 'worm', the snapper has an easy meal. Other species are hunters, some even being powerful and quick enough to catch ducks. Unlike most other reptiles, terrapins use their forelimbs to hold large or struggling prey. ■

See also
Reptiles
Streams
Tortoises
Turtles

Territory

Territory is the name given to an area that an animal defends as its living space. It may occupy a far larger space, known as its home range, in which it feeds or hunts, but this is not defended. In any one habitat, no two animal species live in exactly the same way, so fighting over territories occurs only among animals of the same kind. You can see this easily in a garden or a park in springtime, when the birds are taking up breeding territories. Members of the same species, such as robins, fight for possession of an area in which they can rear a family, for each territory contains the essentials of food, shelter and nesting sites. Territories prevent overcrowding, for an animal which cannot get a territory, or is pushed out and has to make its territory in an unsuitable area, will probably not be able to breed. But as each kind of bird or other animal has different needs for food and nesting places, the territories of different species overlap. ■

Human beings are territorial animals. What is your territory? What is your home range?

See also
Habitats

Terrorists

People who use violence or threaten to kill people to make a political gain are called terrorists, because they try to create terror. This fear may lead people to pressurize a government into agreeing to the terrorist demands.

Terrorist methods include bombing, shooting, taking hostages, and hi-jacking vehicles, and most victims are civilians. The Irish Republican Army has used terrorism to further its aim of uniting Northern Ireland with the Republic of Ireland. From the 1950s to the 1990s many countries were terrorist targets of the Palestine Liberation Organization. The PLO aimed to achieve an Arab state in Palestine. Some governments have been accused of state terrorism – using terrorists against opposing governments. ■

Airports have been terrorist targets in many countries. Security is one way of combating this terrorism, particulary searching people's luggage for weapons and explosives. Ways of searching include X-ray machines, metal detection equipment, and even dogs which can sniff out explosives.

Textiles

The word textile comes from the Latin word *texere*, which means 'to weave'.

► **Weaving a carpet on a ground loom in Rajasthan, India. Notice the geometrical shapes woven into the design of the carpet.**

The word textile originally meant a fabric made by weaving. Today, all types of fabric are considered textiles, including those produced by knitting and felting. Textiles are made of either natural fibres, such as wool, cotton, silk and linen, or from synthetic fibres, such as nylon or rayon. Textiles are chosen according to their use. For instance, hard-wearing fabrics are selected for furnishings, while softly draping fabrics are chosen for clothing.

Textile design

Textile designers create fabrics with new patterns and colour combinations. When starting to design a fabric, the designer has to consider a number of things, including colour, the type of fibre used, the texture (or 'feel') and pattern required, and how the fabric is to be manufactured.

A range of design techniques are used in textile production, some of them requiring a high level of skill. Patterns can be woven into the fabric, or dyed or printed on it using techniques such as batik, tie and dye, and silk-screen printing. Or they may be sewn on in a form of collage. ■

▼ **Producing a batik design in Java, Indonesia. Batik is a method of decorating textiles with dye. First a design is made on a piece of fabric. Those parts which are not to be dyed are covered with wax. The fabric is then dipped into the dye. The wax-coated areas do not absorb the dye and the wax is then removed by boiling the cloth. This process can be repeated to obtain different shades or to apply new colours.**

◄ **The blue and cream design on this shawl was produced by silk-screen printing. This involves squeezing ink or paint onto a piece of fabric through a piece of silk stretched tightly across a frame. The designer uses stencils, glue or lacquer to mask out the parts of the design that are not to be printed.**

◄ **This woven design is made of wool and features a purple chevron (V-shaped stripe).**

When designing a woven textile it is important to remember that the colours used never actually mix. They are seen as spots of colour and show up more clearly when a thick yarn is used. When thin yarn is used, or when seen from a distance, the colours seem to blend. For example, blue and yellow may appear as green.

◄ **This design of amaryllis flowers was produced using a decorative method called appliqué. Appliqué is a form of collage and involves sewing or sticking cut-out shapes of fabric onto a background cloth.**

See also

Cotton
Embroidery
Fabrics
Fibres
Knitting
Sewing
Spinning
Synthetic fibres
Tapestries
Tie and dye
Weaving
Wool

Biography
Ashley
Morris
Rivera

Thailand

Thailand is a country in south-east Asia. It is a tropical country of mountains, jungles and rainforests, although much of the rainforest has been cut down in recent years. The central area is a flat, damp plain criss-crossed with irrigation canals (*klongs*) and ideal for growing rice, which is the staple food. Thailand is the world's leading exporter of rice. The climate is hot and sticky most of the year round. During the rainiest season, between May and October, more than 1,500 mm (59 in) of rain may fall. A 'cool' season lasts from November to February, but even during this time average temperatures are about 26°C (79°F).

Bangkok is the capital of Thailand, a busy city of over 5 million people. This is where the King and Queen of Thailand have their Grand Palace. Although Bangkok's streets are full of cars and modern buildings the city's 300 Buddhist temples, many with curved roofs in orange and green tiles, give Bangkok a distinct atmosphere. Most Thais are Buddhists, and a majority of the men spend some part of their lives as monks learning about their religion in one of the country's 27,000 'wats' (temples). Monks in orange robes can be seen walking the streets as they do all over Thailand.

Flashback

There has been a country called Siam for over 700 years, and remains of more ancient cities date back to at least AD 500. The Thai people have been invaded by the Burmese and others, but theirs is the only country in south-east Asia which has never been a European colony. In 1939 the name was changed from Siam to Thailand, which means 'land of the free'. ■

Area
514,820 sq km
(198,773 sq miles)
Capital
Bangkok
Population
53,700,000
Language
Thai
Religion
Buddhist
Government
Monarchy
Currency
1 baht = 100 satang

◄ Workers stand on bamboo scaffolding to polish the stupa (shrine for relics) of Wat Phra Keo, a Buddhist temple in Bangkok.

See also
Asia
Buddhists
Kings
Palaces
Rice

Theatres

Theatres are buildings put up especially for plays, ballet or operas to be performed in. They have to do several things. They must be big enough to hold a lot of people, and let them see and hear clearly. They must allow actors to get on and off the stage easily. And there must be room to store all the things like scenery and costumes which are needed when you put a play on. If they look splendid and have comfortable seats, so much the better.

Theatres today

Theatres today are built in all shapes and sizes. Some of them have the audiences sitting all round the actors, like a circus. Some of them have a 'picture-frame' for the action to take place in; and some of them have the audience sitting in curved rows rising up around the stage. Some theatres, like the Swan Theatre in Stratford-upon-Avon, have been built to look like theatres of the past. The Swan Theatre has a stage very like the ones Shakespeare's plays were first seen on, but it is a modern theatre none the less.

Most theatres have what is called the Green Room. This is a room in which the actors wait before they go on stage. Originally it is said that the room was painted green because green is a soothing colour. Green, it was believed, would calm the nerves of the actors before they performed. In theatres nowadays the room is not always green, but it is still called the Green Room.

Japanese theatre

In Japan, people developed a particular kind of theatre for staging the ancient drama called the *No*. The masked actors entered the plain, square stage across a structure like a little bridge from the Mask Room. There was no scenery, but sometimes simple objects like a bell or a tree were brought on to indicate where the action was taking place.

▼ An artist's reconstruction of a scene from *A Midsummer Night's Dream* at the Globe Theatre, London in Shakespeare's lifetime. The groundlings are standing around the stage. The actor playing Bottom is wearing an ass's head mask.

▲ The famous theatre at Epidaurus in Greece. This theatre was built around 200 BC and seats more than 12,000 people. It has a neutral 'backdrop' of beautiful mountains. You can still sit here in the open air to watch a play, just as audiences used to do in the days of ancient Greece.

Greek theatres

The first theatres in Europe were built in Greece about 2,500 years ago. They were open to the sky, and often built against a hillside, with rows of stone seats rising up around a circular space for acting. This space was called the *orchestra*, which originally meant dancing-floor. Behind the orchestra was a building called the *skene*, from which our word scene comes. Sometimes the skene contained a crane for flying the actor playing a god or goddess onstage.

Shakespeare's theatre

Another famous theatre was also open to the sky. This was the theatre that William Shakespeare wrote his first plays for, in the reign of Queen Elizabeth I. It was built in the shape of a circle surrounding the stage. In one of his plays, Shakespeare calls it a 'wooden O'.

The stage was bare, but there was a balcony above it where actors could play scenes on the battlements of a castle or in the upper window of a house. The building behind the stage was called the 'tiring house'. The actors would use it as a dressing room.

The audience would stand on the ground around the stage. They were sometimes called groundlings. Richer people could pay more money and sit in the galleries going all the way round the theatre.

The theatre goes indoors

If people wanted to put on a play with scenery, they had to have a different kind of building. In the early years of the 17th century a kind of play called a masque was popular. This had a lot of spectacular scene-changes, with clouds floating to and fro across the stage and gods flying past in chariots. Masques were often set to music as well. A play like that would be ruined by bad weather, so this sort of play was performed in great halls with roofs, including Whitehall in London.

The stage was differently shaped from that of Shakespeare's time. Very often the designer who painted and arranged the scenery wanted the audience to look at it as if it was a picture, from the front and not from the side. So they built a frame around the stage and sat the audience in front of it, all looking the same way. This frame was called a proscenium.

In the limelight

To put on a play indoors you need lights. At first people used candles, but they were not very bright, and sometimes theatres caught fire. Gas lighting was used in Britain in the reign of Queen Victoria. This provided the footlights and also limelight, a bright light used for the spotlights. We still use the expression 'in the limelight' when we are talking about someone being the centre of attention. But there was still a fire risk. Covent Garden, London, was twice gutted by fire in the early 19th century. Once electric light started to be fitted after 1887, theatres became safer.

The scenery used in Victorian theatres was very complicated. Some theatres even managed to have horses racing on rollers. But it took so long to set up the stage for such plays that audiences got tired of them. Early this century the first cinema films were being made and they were much more realistic than any play could be.

Changes and fashions

Whatever theatres are like in the future, they will still have to do the things theatres have always done; and sometimes the simplest way of doing them is the best. In general, people seem to prefer the simple way of staging things, and have left special effects to the cinema. ■

See also
Ballet
Drama
Greek ancient history
Masks
Mime
Operas
Pantomimes

Biography
Shakespeare

Many actors believe it is bad luck ever to mention the title of Shakespeare's play *Macbeth*. They always refer to it as 'the Scottish play' or some other form of words that does not mention the title.

▼ A spectacular scene from Beethoven's opera *Fidelio* at the Royal Opera House, Covent Garden. The triumph of good and justice over evil is being represented by doomed figures hanging from wires from the ceiling, or 'flies'. The orchestra is playing in a 'pit' just in front of the proscenium stage.

Thermometers

Digital thermometer any thermometer which displays its readings using numbers

Maximum and minimum thermometer records the highest and lowest temperatures reached over a period of time

The first thermometer was invented by Galileo Galilei in 1592. Known as a thermoscope, it used the expansion of water to measure temperature.

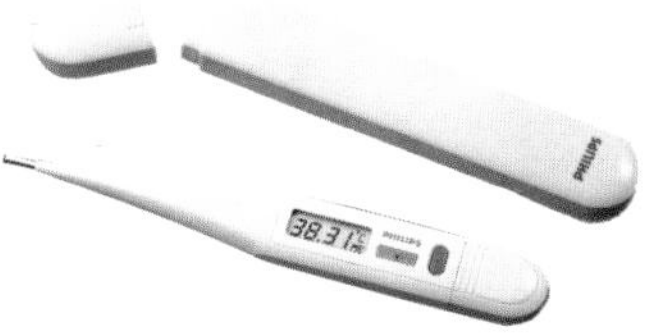

► **Some thermometers are just a row of squares printed on a strip of paper. The squares are treated with special chemicals so that they change colour at different temperatures. The green rectangle indicates a temperature of 36°C, which is just below normal (37°C).**

See also
Cold
Heat
Temperature
Thermostats

Biography
Galilei

Thermometers measure temperature (hotness). Some depend on the fact that liquid mercury or alcohol expands when heated. The more the temperature rises, the more the liquid in the bulb in the end of the thermometer expands and moves up the narrow tube. The position of the liquid gives the temperature on the scale. Others are electrical. They have a tiny probe connected by wires to a measuring unit. When the temperature changes, the flow of current from the probe changes. Electrical thermometers are widely used in industry. One of their big advantages is that the measuring unit can be placed well away from the probe. Often, the reading appears as a number, like the numbers displayed on a calculator. ■

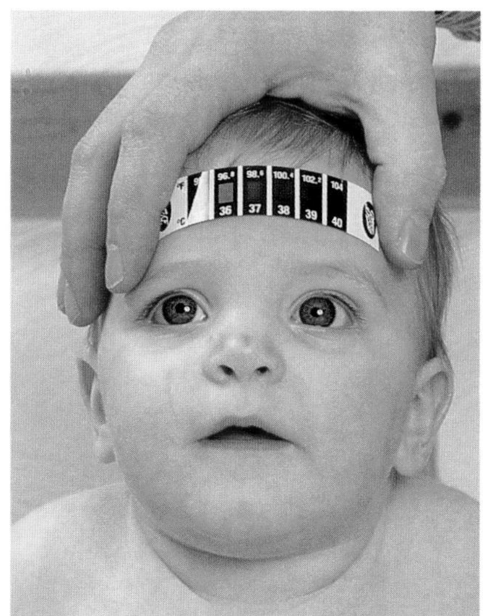

Thermostats

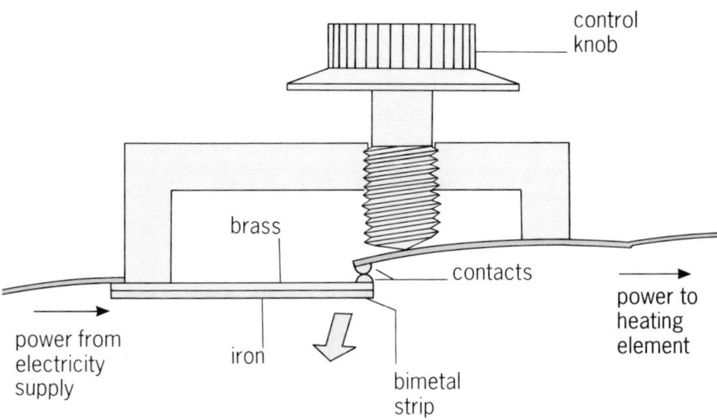

▲ **Bimetal thermostat. When the temperature rises, the bimetal strip bends. This separates the contacts and cuts the power. Turning the control knob alters the temperature needed for the contacts to separate.**

Most irons, ovens and refrigerators have a thermostat in them. Its job is to keep the temperature steady by automatically switching the power on and off. For example, when an iron is just hot enough, the thermostat cuts the power. It brings the power back on again when the iron cools. You can see the light going on and off as the thermostat does its job.

Many thermostats have a tiny bimetal strip in them. This is two strips of different metals stuck together. When the bimetal strip warms up, one metal expands more than the other. This makes the bimetal strip bend. The contacts move apart and the power is cut. When the temperature falls, the bimetal strip straightens and the contacts touch again.

Not all thermostats are electrical. Some gas ovens have a thermostat which controls the flow of gas. ■

Part of your brain acts as a thermostat, helping to control your body temperature.

The first thermostat was patented by Andrew Ure in Scotland in 1830. Bimetal thermostats were first used on electric irons in 1924.

See also
Central heating
Electricity
Heat
Metals
Refrigerators
Temperature
Thermometers

Third World

The Third World is the name given to countries which are trying to develop their economies. The rich nations of Western Europe, North America and Australasia make up the 'first world'. The USSR and Eastern Europe (formerly communist) are the 'second world'. People argue about whether communist countries such as China and Cuba are 'second' or 'third' world. The third world includes about 120 countries, with more than half the world's population.

Most Third World countries are in the tropics or the southern hemisphere. They prefer to use the phrase 'The South', pointing out that apart from Australia and New Zealand, the richer countries are in 'The North'. ■

The term 'third world' originated in the 1950s during the Cold War; it was used to cover those countries which did not belong to the Western powers or the communist bloc.

See also
Developing countries

Thunderstorms

Thunderstorms come from the biggest clouds in the sky. The clouds are called cumulonimbus and have a wide flat top and a narrower bottom. They bring heavy rain and often there is thunder and lightning.

Thunderstorm clouds have electrical charges. At the top they are positive, while at the bottom the charge is negative. The ground below a thunderstorm is also positive. When all these charges build up there is a lightning flash which very briefly lights up the sky. Thunder is the noise we hear when the air in front of a stroke of lightning is rapidly expanded because of the great heat. Thunderstorms have bigger raindrops than other clouds. This is because the raindrops move up and down inside the cloud again and again, and each time they do another circuit inside the cloud they collect more water. When the drops are very big they are too heavy to stay in the cloud. Sometimes the air in the cloud is cold enough for the raindrops to freeze, and then they fall out as hailstones. ■

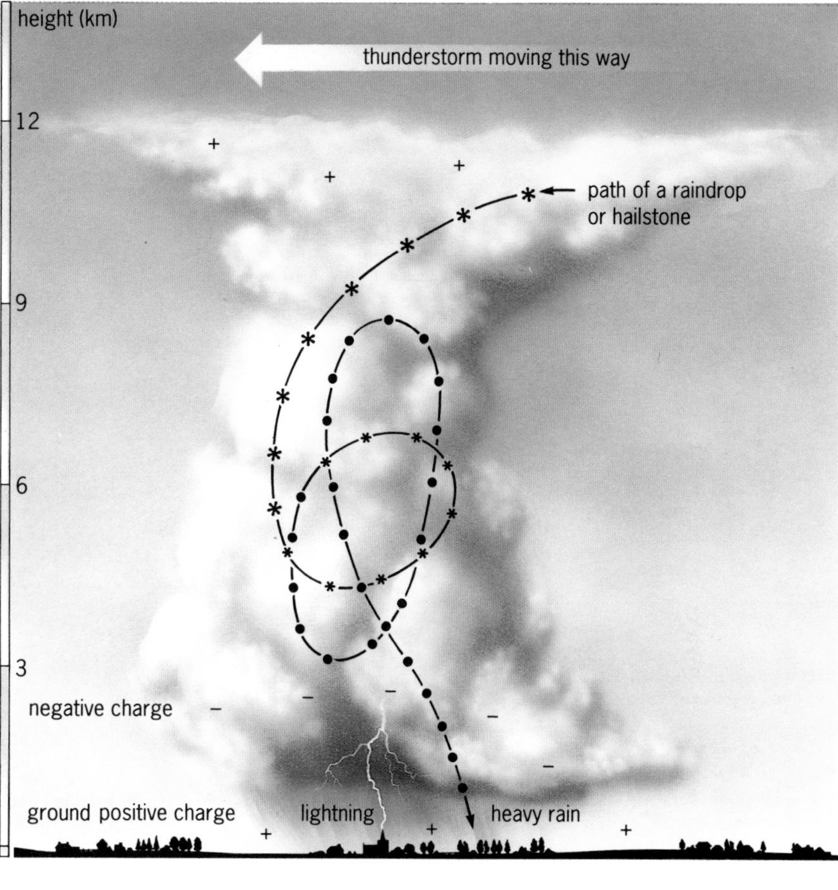

See also

Clouds
Monsoon
Rain

Biography
Franklin, Benjamin

Tibet

Tibet lies to the north of the Himalaya Mountains in Central Asia. Much of the region is a plateau which is over 4,000 m (13,000 ft) above sea-level, the largest and highest plateau in the world. The landscape is barren, very dry and very cold. Much of it is uninhabited. About half of the small population herd yaks, sheep and cattle. In many parts of Tibet the yak is the only pastoral animal that can live in the harsh conditions. It is used for transport, meat and milk, and yak butter is drunk in Tibetan tea with salt.

Tibetans are Buddhists and the most senior Buddhist monk, the Dalai Lama, used to be ruler of the country. In 1950 Chinese troops invaded; later they destroyed hundreds of ancient monasteries and murdered many of the monks. The Tibetans rebelled in 1959 but were defeated. The Dalai Lama fled to India with many of his followers and set up a government in exile there. China regards Tibet as part of the People's Republic of China. Most Tibetans regard the Chinese as occupiers. Since 1978 the Chinese have allowed more freedom to practise religion and some temples have been restored. ■

Tibetan refugees live in India and in several western countries including Britain, France, Switzerland and the USA.

Area 1,221,600 sq km (471,660 sq miles)
Capital Lhasa
Population 1,970,000
Language Tibetan, Chinese
Religion Buddhist
Government Autonomous region of the People's Republic of China

◀ The Potala, in Lhasa, was the Dalai Lama's residence until 1959 when he left Tibet for exile in India to escape from Chinese rule.

See also

Asia
Buddhists
China
Himalayas

Biography
Dalai Lama

Tides

Timing the tides
High tides are 50 minutes later each day.

Highest tidal range
At the Bay of Fundy in Canada, the sea-level can rise more than 15 m between low and high tides.

At high tide, the sea rises high up the beach. At low tide, it falls low down the beach. This happens because the Moon's gravity tries to pull the Earth and its oceans towards it.

The sea nearest the Moon is pulled most strongly so it bulges slightly towards the Moon. The sea furthest from the Moon is pulled less than elsewhere, leaving another bulge here, too. There are high tides at the two bulges and low tides in between. As the Earth spins on its axis, places move in and out of the bulges and their sea-level rises and falls.

Most places have two high tides a day, but the shape of the coastline can affect the rise and fall of the water. In enclosed seas like the Mediterranean the tides are usually too small to notice. Between the Isle of Wight and Portsmouth in southern England there are four high tides a day.

▼ **The Moon's gravity makes two bulges in the Earth's oceans (greatly exaggerated in the diagram). As the Earth spins, places get high and low tides as they move in and out of the bulges.**

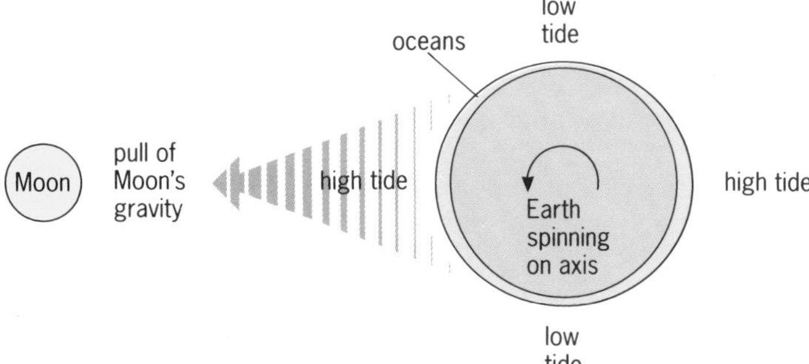

The Sun's gravity also pulls on the oceans. Twice every month, the Sun, Moon and Earth are lined up. Then the Sun's pull adds to the Moon's pull, making the rise and fall of the sea more than at any other time. These tides are called spring tides, though they do not only happen in the spring. In between, there are neap tides when the change in sea-level is least.

High tides send a tidal wave, called a bore, up some rivers. On a spring tide, the Severn bore in England can reach a height of over 2 m. ■

See also
Gravity
Moon

Tie and dye

Tie and dye is a way of making patterns on cloth by tying some areas so that dye does not mark them. Each method of tying produces a different design. Cloth can be knotted, sewn or have small objects tied into it. It may also be bunched, twisted or folded, and then bound tightly.

After binding, the cloth is dipped in dye. The patterns after dyeing will be like ripples of small lines and spaces. It may then be tied some more and dipped in a new dye colour, or it can be tied in another way before re-dyeing. The more tying and dyeing done on one piece of material, the more complicated the pattern becomes.

Something to do

Find some suitable clean cloth and then knot and tie it. If you have some interesting pebbles, or unusually shaped buttons, try twisting some of them into the cloth. If each twist is held firmly in place with an elastic band, this will make a pattern of small circles.

Select your colours, and consider how they will contrast on the finished cloth. Buy some packets of cold-water dye. Follow the instructions on the packet carefully. Make up the dye only when you have prepared the cloth.

Soak the tied cloth in the dye for the length of time recommended on the instructions. Then remove it and leave to dry. When dry, undo the knots or elastic bands and rinse in cold water to let any loose dye run away. Dry and iron the cloth.

Flashback

There are records of tie and dye being used to decorate cloth from the 7th century in India and Japan and from the 10th century in China. In South America the Inca people were using tie and dye before the 15th century. ■

▼ **Knots tied in a piece of cloth.**

▲ **Cloth can be wrapped round a button or pebble and held by an elastic band.**

See also
Dyes

Tigers

Distribution
India, China, Siberia, Indonesia
Size
Head and body length 140–280 cm; tail length 60–90 cm
Weight
180–360 kg
Number of young
3–4 cubs
Lifespan
In captivity up to 26 years, about 15 in the wild

Subphylum Vertebrata
Class Mammalia
Order Carnivora
Family Felidae (cat family)
Number of species 1

Tigers are big cats of forest country. At one time they were found throughout much of eastern and southern Asia, but now they survive mainly in India and Sumatra. The biggest tigers come from the forests of Siberia.

Male tigers live alone in large territories, though these may overlap the living areas of several females. They warn other males away by roaring when near the boundaries of their living areas. They are chiefly active at twilight or at night, using their sight and sense of hearing rather than smell, to stalk their prey. They may travel up to 20 km (12 miles) in a night and can leap as much as 10 m (30 ft) in a single bound. They are good swimmers and can climb quite well. Their main food is large mammals such as wild pigs, buffalo and deer. But in spite of their size and strength, tigers fail in about 90 per cent of their hunts. Tigers rarely attack humans, but those that do often get a taste for it.

Tiger cubs can be born at any time throughout the year. They do not hunt for themselves until the age of about eighteen months, and they stay with their mother until they are two or three years old. ■

▼ Indian tiger threatening. Its powerful front legs, muscular shoulders and long back legs adapted for leaping, make it a superb hunter of large prey.

◀ Siberian tiger drinking. After a kill the tiger will often drag its prey near to water so that it can drink whilst eating.

See also
Cats
Cheetahs
Jaguars
Leopards
Lions
Pumas

Timber

Timber is wood which is useful. Carpenters recognize two main types: hardwood and softwood.

Softwood comes from coniferous trees, which are mostly evergreen, have needle-like leaves, and can survive long, cold winters. Foresters plant conifers because they grow quickly. Softwood timber is useful for building, for packaging (crates and pallets for example) and for chipboard. Chipboard is made out of wood chips mixed with glue and pressed together.

Hardwood comes from deciduous trees (those that lose their leaves each year). Temperate hardwoods include oak, beech and ash. Tropical hardwoods include teak, mahogany and rosewood. Hardwoods are very tough and make good furniture as well as special items such as boats and cricket bats. Hardwood timber can also be sliced into veneers to cover softwood chipboard for cheap furniture. Huge areas of tropical forest are being chopped down because hardwood timber is valuable. ■

See also
Conifers
Forests
Trees
Wood

Time

The world's first public time signal was a red ball on top of the Royal Observatory at Greenwich, put up in 1833. It was dropped from the top of a pole at 1 p.m. precisely every day.

We all know what it means to say that time is passing by, but it is very hard to say exactly what time is. We notice natural things around us change with time: plants and animals, the seasons and weather, the Sun, Moon and stars. Anything that changes regularly can be used as a clock to keep track of time. Now that people all round the world are in contact through telephones, television and fast air travel, it is important that everyone agrees to keep to the same standard time and measure it in the same way.

Days and hours

The day is the most important period of time for us. Our daily pattern of sleeping, eating and working is almost built-in as a kind of natural clock.

The large publicly displayed clocks built, for example, on cathedrals from the 14th century onwards, helped spread a sense of time among people.

We divide days up into 24 equal hours. Hours have not always been equal. Before mechanical clocks came into use in the 14th century, an hour was one-twelfth of the period of daylight, so in winter hours were shorter than in summer. The number 24 has been handed down from the distant past. It might have been any number. The ancient Babylonians based their numbers on units of 60, rather than tens like us, and it is from them that we got 60 minutes in an hour and 60 seconds in a minute.

12-hour clock	24-hour clock
1pm	13.00
2pm	14.00
3pm	15.00
4pm	16.00
5pm	17.00
6pm	18.00
7pm	19.00
8pm	20.00
9pm	21.00
10pm	22.00
11pm	23.00
12pm	24.00
1am	01.00
2am	02.00

and so on.

Days start at midnight and we use a.m. and p.m. to show whether a time is before or after midday. They are short for the Latin words *ante meridiem* and *post meridiem.* The 24-hour clock is often used instead to avoid confusion: 1.00 p.m. is called 13.00, 2.00 p.m. becomes 14.00 and so on.

Standard time

Noon (midday) at a particular place occurs when the Sun gets to its highest point in the sky. Countries further east are already into the afternoon or evening, while people living further west still have not reached midday. As the Earth spins, places across the world, from east to west, have noon one after another.

Spacetime
In Einstein's theory of relativity neither space nor time could exist without each other. Time became the fourth dimension (there being three dimensions of space: length, breadth and height).

If everyone measures time from when it is noon where they are, at every longitude the time is different. People used to reckon time locally in that way, but as travel got more common, especially when the railways were built in the 19th century, having everyone using different local times became very confusing indeed. So, in 1880, the whole of Britain adopted the average local time at Greenwich (where the Royal Observatory was) as its standard time, Greenwich Mean Time (GMT). At an international conference in 1884, the world was divided up into 'time zones', each about 15 degrees of longitude wide, though the exact divisions were set to be convenient for the country and state boundaries. The standard time in each zone differs from the zones either side by one hour.

If you travel to another country you usually have to alter your watch. The further you go,

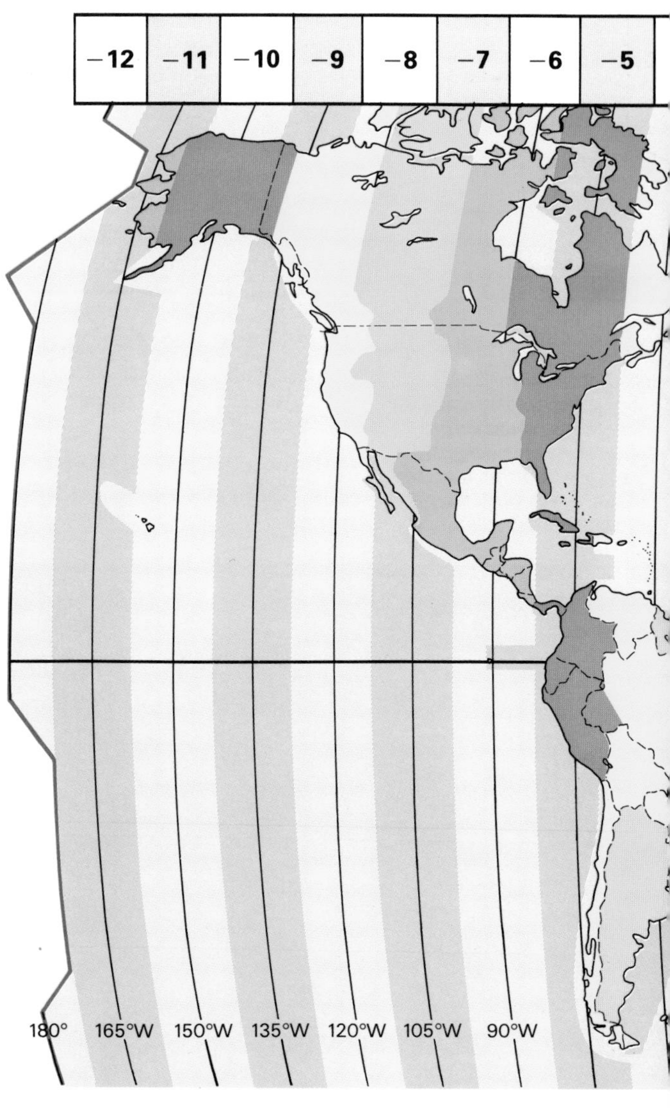

east or west, the bigger the time change. Travelling by air, you can cross several time zones in just a few hours. When you arrive your body has to adjust. Long-distance travellers sometimes suffer from tiredness, called 'jet-lag', as they get used to the time change.

Daylight-saving time

During World War I (1914–1918) Britain and the USA set their clocks one hour ahead of their usual standard times. The idea of this was to give extra time for working in the evening when it was light and so save electricity. It is much easier to get everyone to change their clocks than to persuade them to get up and go to work an hour earlier! Britain still goes onto British Summer Time (BST), one hour ahead of GMT, during the summer months. The government announces the days on which the clocks are to be changed.

Measuring and keeping time

Anything that happens at regular intervals or at a steady rate can be used as a clock to measure time. It could be the burning of a candle, the swing of a pendulum or the natural vibrations of tiny atoms and molecules.

The spin of the Earth gives us our day. Astronomers keep a check on the Earth's rotation speed by watching the stars travel across the sky at night. It used to be the main way of keeping standard time accurate. Today, though, 'atomic clocks' have taken over as the best time-keepers.

International atomic time is kept by special clocks in laboratories round the world. These are the clocks that are used to give the time pips broadcast by radio services and the speaking clock service on the telephone, so that anyone can set a clock accurately. ■

In ancient Egypt short intervals of time were measured by the flow of water through a hole at the bottom of a vessel; the inside of the vessel was marked with a scale of hours. The Egyptians also used sun dials to measure hours; these were more accurate than their water clocks.

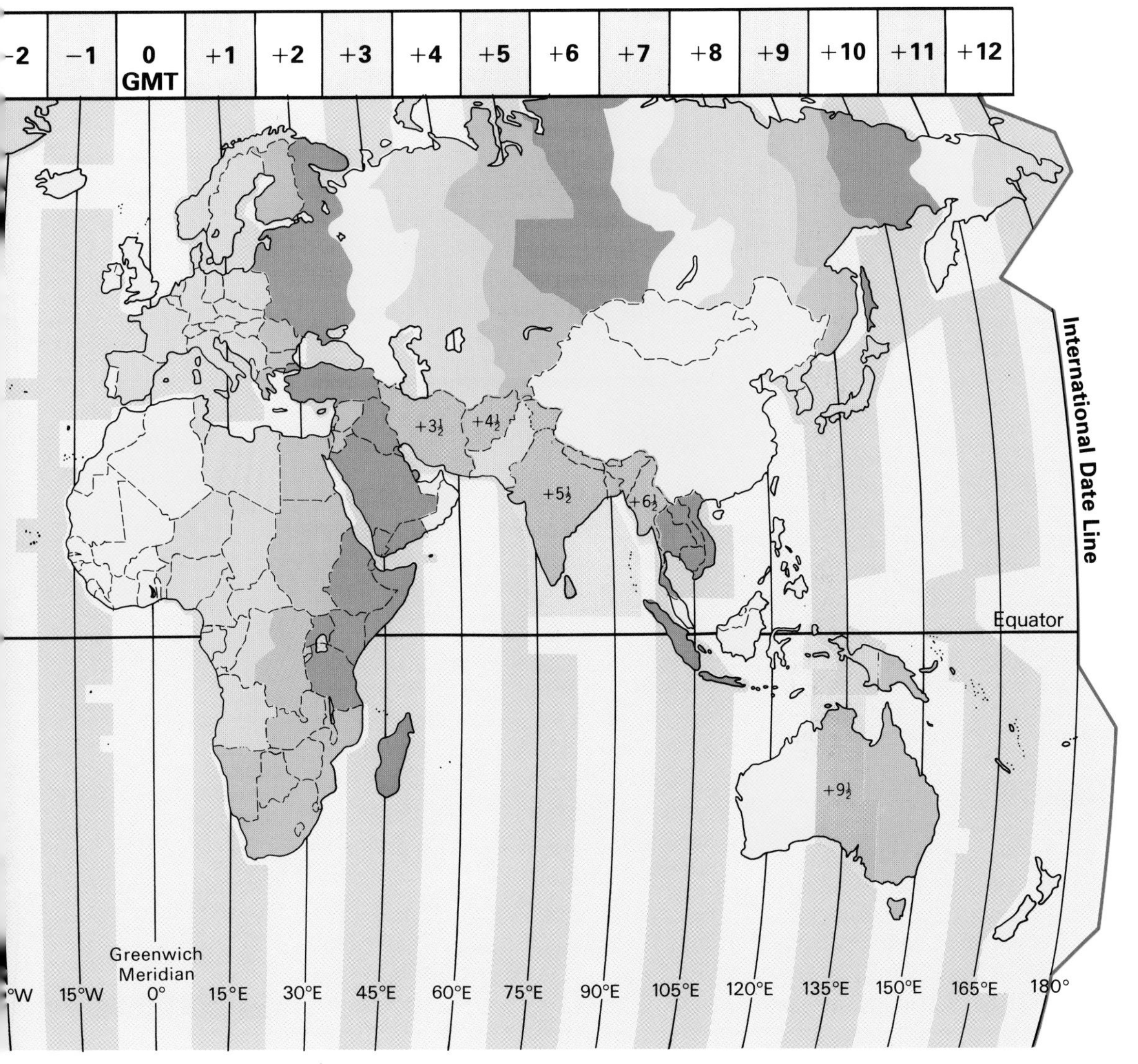

◀ The world is divided into 24 time zones, each about 15° of longitude wide. When you travel west you put your watch back an hour for every time zone you cross and when you travel east you add an hour. The International Date Line is the 180° line of longitude which marks where one day ends and another begins. Travelling from east to west across the line you go forward one day, and travelling west to east you go back a day. The line has been adjusted so that it does not cross a country.

See also
Calendars
Candles
Clocks and watches
Day and night
Latitude and longitude

Biography
Einstein

Tin

Tin is a soft, silvery-white metal. It does not rust or corrode, and is mainly used in tin-plating. The 'tin cans' in which many foods are packed are not really made of solid tin but of thin sheets of steel coated with tin. The tin stops the cans from rusting. The other main uses for tin are in the solders used for joining soft metals and wires, and for making alloys such as bronze and pewter.

Pure tin is found in nature, but it is usually made from tin ores, especially cassiterite. Most of the world's tin ore comes from Malaysia, Bolivia and the USSR. At one time Cornwall in England was an important source. ■

See also
Alloys
Metals

Toads

Largest
Marine toad: length up to 23·8 cm; weight about 1·3 kg
Number of eggs laid
About 3,000 for common toad
Lifespan
May be over 30 years

Subphylum Vertebrata
Class Amphibia
Order Anura (frogs and toads)
Number of species
About 380

Toads are tailless amphibians like their relatives the frogs, but with shorter legs and warty skins. They go in water only to breed, returning every spring to the best places, using their excellent homing instincts. In some areas yearly toad watches are organized to protect breeding toads as they cross roads.

Toads are most active at night, when they hunt worms, grubs and any insects that they can catch. Only moving prey attracts the toad's attention. It is caught on the toad's long tongue, which it flicks out and back into its mouth in less than one-tenth of a second. ■

See also
Amphibians
Frogs
Newts
Salamanders
Tadpoles

Tobacco

Tobacco is a leafy plant which originally came from South America. It was first grown commercially in Virginia in the 17th century from seeds imported from Trinidad and Venezuela. Today it is grown in any area which has a high humidity,

◀ The flowers of the tobacco plants have been pinched out at an early stage. This makes the leaves grow larger before they are picked.

high temperature and plenty of rainfall.

Tobacco contains the drug nicotine. This kills insects that eat the plant but when smoked or chewed by people acts as a drug. The leaves of the plant are harvested and tied to long sticks. They are then placed in curing barns where the leaves are heated and dried. Cured tobacco is rolled into cigars, or shredded and blended to make different brands of cigarettes and pipe tobacco. ■

In many countries a tax is imposed on the sale of tobacco. This tax can bring in quite a lot of revenue.

See also
Smoking

Togo

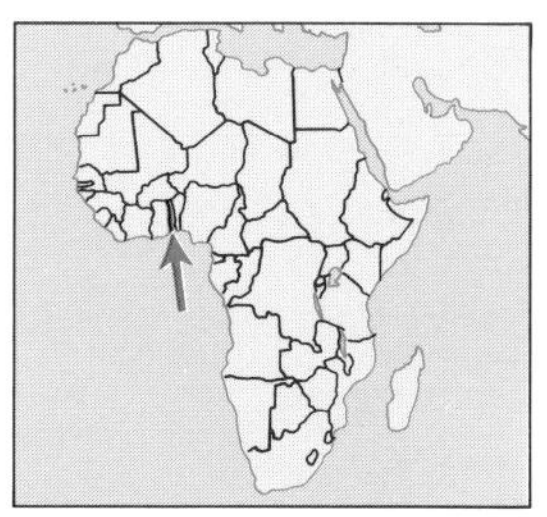

Area
56,785 sq km
(21,925 sq miles)
Capital Lomé
Population 3,110,000
Language
French, Ewe, Kabré, Gurma
Religion
Traditional, Christian, Muslim
Government Republic
Currency 1 (CFA) franc = 100 centimes

The West African country of Togo is long and narrow with a short coastline. Grassy plains and hills cover much of this hot, rainy land. Mountains rise in the centre.

Most of the Togolese live by farming. Many northerners are Muslims, who dress in flowing white robes. The southerners usually wear Western clothes. Togo produces phosphate rock (which is used to make fertilizers), cotton and coffee.

Germany ruled Togo before World War I, when it was taken by Britain and France. The British part joined with Ghana in 1957. The French part became independent in 1960. ■

See also
Africa

Tolpuddle Martyrs

Tolpuddle is a quiet little village in Dorset. In 1834, it became famous.

Times were bad everywhere for ordinary people. Some working-class leaders had just formed a trade union for all workers: the Grand National Consolidated Trades Union (GNCTU). Its aim was to win better conditions peacefully. But it terrified employers and the government.

In Tolpuddle, six farm labourers decided they must try to improve their very low wages. They were hard-working and law-abiding; their leader was George Loveless, a Methodist preacher. They formed a trade union, with an entrance fee of one shilling. Members swore an oath to be loyal to each other. Local landowners got to hear of it. Trade unions were not against the law. But they used a law which forbade secret oaths. In 1834 magistrates in Dorchester sentenced the Tolpuddle men to seven years' transportation to Australia. This was a terrible punishment: they had to leave their families behind with no money.

The GNCTU held a huge protest meeting in London. Many better-off people felt that the Tolpuddle men had not had a fair trial. In the end, the government brought back the six men before their sentence ended. In Dorchester, people raised money to give them a new start. So this story has a happy ending. The GNCTU did not survive, but people still remember 'the Tolpuddle Martyrs'. ■

The six farm labourers who became known as the Tolpuddle Martyrs were George Loveless, James Loveless, James Brine, Thomas Stansfield, John Stansfield and James Hammet.

George Loveless at his trial: 'My Lord, if we have broken the law, it was not done intentionally. We have injured no man's character, reputation, person or property. We were uniting together to preserve ourselves, our wives and our children from utter degradation and starvation. We challenge any man to prove that we have acted different from that statement.'

They returned to England two years after their trial. Five of the six later emigrated to Canada.

See also
Trade unions

Biography
Owen, Robert

Tombs

Tombs are special places for the burial of the dead. The earliest tombs were natural rock caves. Later, people cut chambers into rock, such as the tomb where according to tradition Jesus was buried.

The Egyptians built pyramids above ground as tombs for their kings and nobles. The most elaborate underground tombs were the catacombs of ancient Rome where early Christians buried their dead.

Famous tombs include those of the Unknown Soldiers in Westminster Abbey, London, beneath the Arc de Triomphe in Paris, and in Arlington Cemetery, Virginia, in the USA. ■

The tomb at Mount Li, where Zeng, the first emperor of China, was buried was so large that there was room for 8,000 life-size soldiers made from terracotta pottery.
See **China's history** for a photograph of the soldiers.

◀ The tomb of Lenin in Moscow. Thousands of people have filed past the glass-covered coffin which contains his embalmed body.

See also
Burial mounds
Cemeteries
Churchyards
Pyramids

Biography
Lenin

Tonsils

If you open your mouth, look in a mirror and say 'aah', your tongue will flatten and you will be able to see the back of your throat. On either side of the back of your tongue you will be able to see a small, usually wrinkly, bump. These are your tonsils. They are made of lymphatic tissue. This contains large numbers of the white blood cells that can protect you against germs.

When you get an infection, extra protective cells in the tonsils make them enlarge and they can become painful. If they get permanently enlarged doctors sometimes suggest that they should be taken out. ■

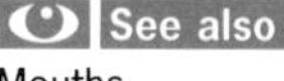

See also
Mouths

Tools

Scissors are tools. So are drills, spades and tin-openers. A tool is any device which helps you do a job. At home, people use tools for preparing food, putting up shelves, doing the gardening and mending the car. The type of tool depends on the job to be done. Hand tools use the force of your muscles. Power tools are driven by another energy source, such as electricity or compressed air, to make jobs even easier and faster. Much larger machine tools are used in factories for cutting and shaping metals, plastics and other materials. Machine tools can make lots of identical parts one after another. Often they are controlled by computer. ■

A heavy metal head gives most force when hammering, but a wooden or plastic head is less likely to damage the material being struck.

Some cutting tools have a sharp, smooth blade. Others have a jagged blade with tiny teeth along the edge.

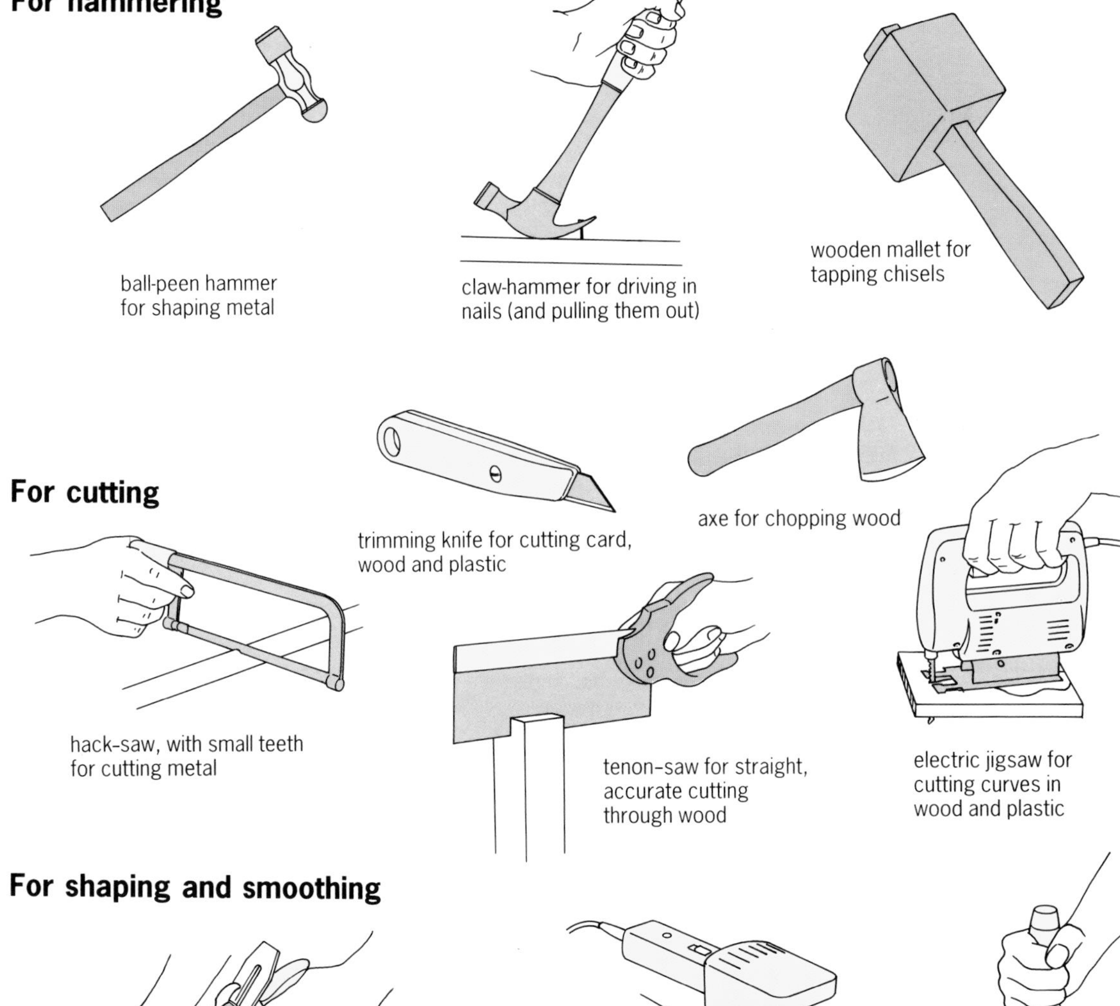

Some shaping and smoothing tools cut into the material with a sharp edge. Others have hundreds of tiny points to rub the material away.

For shaping and smoothing

glasspaper

plane for smoothing wood

chisel for shaping wood

electric sander for smoothing wood

file for smoothing edges or widening holes in metal

Hand drills have gearwheels to make the bit turn faster. Electric motors turn very fast anyway, so electric drills have gearwheels to slow the bit down.

Before materials are cut, drilled or fixed, it is important to check that all sizes and positions are correct.

A high gripping force can be produced by lever action or by turning a screw thread.

Nuts, bolts and screws have special tools to turn them. Tools like this must fit properly to give a firm grip, so they are made in a range of sizes.

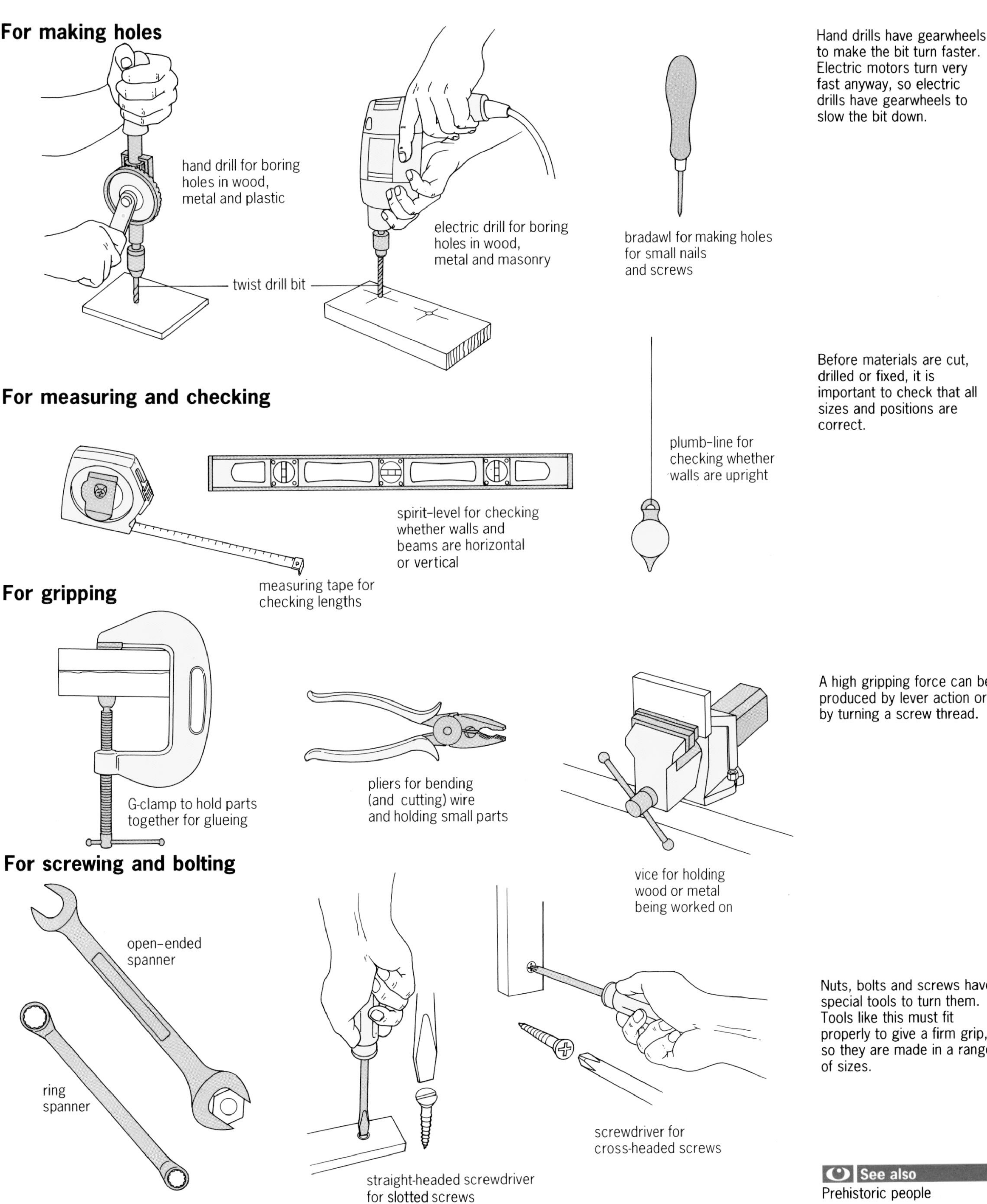

See also
Prehistoric people

Torches

The word torch comes from the Latin *torquere* meaning 'to twist'. The first torches were made of twisted hemp.

People have always found it convenient to be able to carry light around with them. The Romans twisted fibrous hemp or flax into a brand that could easily be held. Dipping it in oil or fat made it burn brightly. Oil lamps and lanterns replaced this simple torch, and a modern torch is powered by electricity, using electrical cells put together in a battery. Some torches are rechargeable. Some are designed to flash, or give coloured light as a warning. Some have small fluorescent tubes, giving longer battery life. ■

See also
Batteries

▼ A torch powered by a battery.

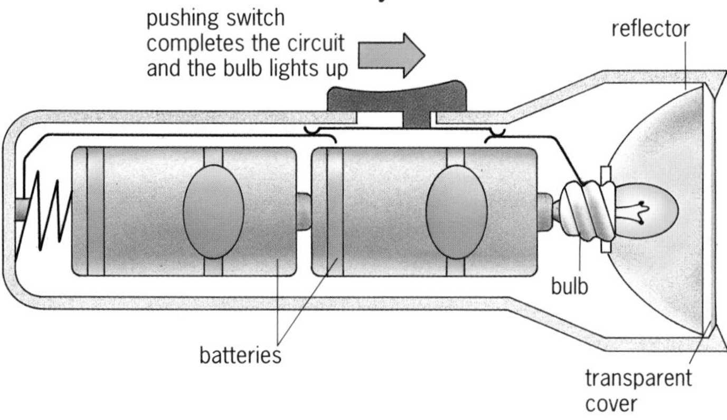

Tortoises

◀ Tortoises, like this giant tortoise from the Galapagos Islands, feed on plants and can go for long periods without water. They live only in warm parts of the world.

Tortoises are land-living armoured reptiles. They are well protected against enemies, but their domed shells are heavy, so they are slow-moving creatures. They protect themselves by pulling their heads, tails and legs into their shells. To breathe, tortoises must pump air into their lungs using special muscles since, like turtles, their shells stop their rib cages expanding.

At one time giant tortoises were found on many remote tropical islands. Unfortunately, most of these are now extinct, but the few that survive are carefully preserved. Many other species of tortoise are threatened by damage to the environment or hunting. ■

Distribution
Warm parts of the world
Largest
Aldabra giant tortoise: shell length of up to 1·4 m; weight up to 254 kg
Smallest
Madagascar spider tortoise: shell length about 15 cm
Lifespan
Greek tortoise up to 115 years. Giant tortoises at least 180 years
Subphylum Vertebrata
Class Reptilia
Order Chelonia
Family Testudinidae
Number of species
About 80

See also
Armoured animals
Endangered species
Galapagos Islands
Reptiles
Terrapins
Turtles

Tornadoes

Tornadoes are especially common in the southern states of the USA, where they are known as 'twisters'.

A tornado is sometimes called a whirlwind. It is a terrifying wind which destroys everything in its path. It looks like a violent, twisting funnel of cloud which stretches down from a storm-cloud to the Earth.

A tornado is narrow and rushes across the land at speeds of 30 to 65 km/h (20 to 40 mph). The wind twists up within the funnel at speeds of up to 650 km/h (400 mph). It sucks up dust, sand, even people and animals like a giant vacuum cleaner and dumps them where it dies out.

A tornado is quite different from a hurricane. It is smaller, faster and more violent. Tornadoes are most frequent far inland, unlike hurricanes. ■

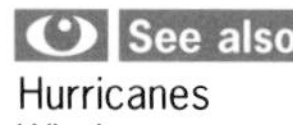

See also
Hurricanes
Wind

Tourists

More than 40 million West Germans were travelling abroad each year for their holidays by the end of the 1980s.

Tourists are people who travel within a country or to another country for recreation. Some people go for holidays in the sun, and the two most visited countries in the world are Italy and Spain, where there is plenty of hot weather.

Other people prefer to spend their time sightseeing, visiting buildings, monuments and museums. Over 90 per cent of the tourists who go to London find their way to Piccadilly Circus.

Tourism is big business now, creating lots of jobs for people who provide accommodation and services for holiday-makers. By the late 1980s, more than 16 million tourists were visiting Britain each year and spending over £7 billion there. ■

See also
Holidays

Town planning

Most towns and cities are growing. In some places new buildings are simply added, but in many countries a builder must get permission from the local authorities. These authorities try to control the changes in the settlement by planning. Although we talk of 'town planning', the same phrase is used for planning in a city. Town planners do not just control the construction of new buildings or roads. Many towns and cities grew up before cars were invented, for example. Roads that were meant for horses and carts may not be suitable for cars and buses. Town planners may decide to make a road wider, or make it one-way, or forbid parking to keep the traffic moving.

Old towns

If you were to see a street plan of the Italian city of Bologna you would notice that the central area is criss-crossed by roads in a pattern of squares. This grid layout was planned and built 2,000 years ago by the Romans.

The Italian seaport of Venice is another planned city. The settlement was built on wooden foundations driven into the mud of a lagoon. It is a series of small islands all connected by bridges. Each island has its own church and central square. In modern times the town planners of Venice have had to face a new problem. The first town was built a few centimetres above the high tide level, but the heavy buildings have been slowly sinking into the mud over hundreds of years. New defences against the sea have been planned and built to stop flooding, and the pumping of water from below the ground, for drinking and industry, has been banned because this was making the buildings sink faster.

▲ A three-dimensional plan of new flats and houses. Plans like these are often displayed in public libraries or in Town Halls so that people can get an idea of a planned new development.

New towns

As in Roman times, some modern towns have been completely planned before any building has begun. In Britain, a series of New Towns were planned and built in the 1940s and 1950s. They were designed to take population from overcrowded cities like London and Glasgow. East Kilbride, in Scotland, is a typical New Town, started in 1947. An area was planned to be the town centre and around it are a number of neighbourhoods. Each neighbourhood contains the buildings for everyday needs, such as schools, shops, churches, doctors' surgeries and meeting halls. Areas were set aside on the northern edge of East Kilbride for industry, since each New Town was planned so that there would be employment for everyone living there. ■

Although old countries do have planned cities they are more common in younger countries where there may be more space, such as Washington, DC, USA, Adelaide and Canberra in Australia, and Abuja in Nigeria.

◀ This aerial photograph of housing for employees working on the Taipu Dam in Brazil shows the neat geometric pattern of a planned settlement.

See also

Cities
Roman ancient history

Toys

The biggest toyshop in the world is Hamleys in London, which has been going for more than 200 years. It has been on its present site since 1901. The shop has 4,180 sq m of floorspace on six floors. During the Christmas rush, Hamleys employ about 300 people to help sell their toys.

Toys are playthings that have been used throughout the centuries by children, and adults too, for fun and entertainment. They come in all shapes and sizes. Even something as simple as a stick or a round stone can be used by children as a toy. Many toys, games and sports have developed from the use of such everyday items by children.

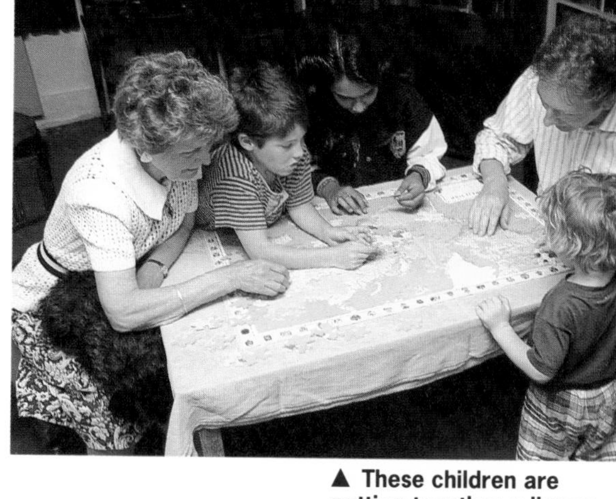

▲ These children are putting together a jigsaw puzzle of a map of the world.

► This wooden rocking horse was made in the 17th century for quite a small child. It is very strong and simple. Rocking horses like this one continued to be made for many years.

▲ A traditional wooden toy village made some time between 1920 and 1930 in Germany. The children who played with it probably added other small toys when they set it out. Their grandparents could have played with a village just like it.

▲ Meccano is just one of the wide range of construction sets that give children the chance to build their own models.

◄ Electronic toys like these robots can be built using microchip technology.

► Model railways have been around almost as long as the real railways and provide hours of fun for children – and adults. A steam locomotive stops at a model country station.

Some of the best-loved toys are dolls and teddy bears. These are miniature versions of humans and animals. Teddy bears were given their name after the American President Theodore (or Teddy) Roosevelt. When he was president at the beginning of the 20th century, a cartoonist drew him refusing to shoot a bear cub which had walked into his camp while he was on a bear-shooting expedition. A sweetshop owner asked if he could call his new toy after him, and he agreed. Soon toy manufacturers saw the opportunity to make money by selling 'Teddy bears' to children. Many children keep their teddy bears or other toy animals until they are adults.

Some toys help children to learn skills that will help them in later life. Puzzles and board games sharpen children's minds and teach them to think quickly. Construction kits, such as Lego and Meccano, give children the chance to use their hands to build models of vehicles and buildings.

▲ A lady called Miss Miles furnished this dolls' house in the 1890s. It must have taken her several months. She bought the house in a toyshop and a carpenter added the small rooms to the side.

Toys and technology

In the early days of toy-making, most toys were simply carved from wood. From the 16th century onwards, such toys were made in Germany and sold in many other countries. Quite young children were given jobs in the toy industry, assembling and painting these toys.

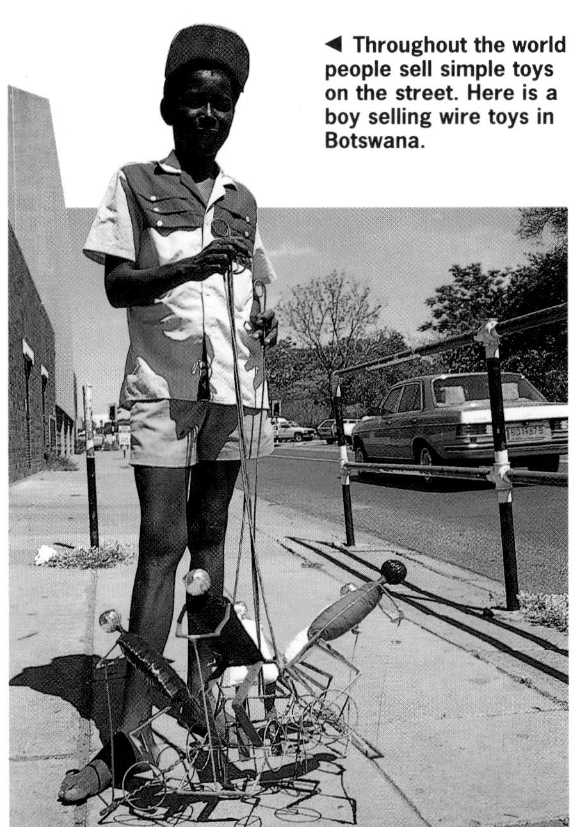

◀ Throughout the world people sell simple toys on the street. Here is a boy selling wire toys in Botswana.

However, toy-making has always kept up with advances in technology and scientific knowledge. As makers of clocks and watches learnt how to use balances and counterbalances, the pendulum and springs, these ideas were introduced into toy-making. Mechanical toys were made for royal children in Europe as early as the 18th century, and later they were mass-produced for many more children.

After the railways had appeared, clockwork was used to power model railways. In Britain the firms of Hornby and Triang produced very popular models, but one of the best in the world was the firm of Marklin in Germany. At the beginning of the 20th century they produced models of Stephenson's 'Rocket', the first train to run on a public railway. In 1984 one of these models was sold at Sotheby's in London for £25,500.

Later in the 20th century, batteries and electricity began to be used as well as clockwork for toys. Now there are many toys and games which use the same microelectronic technology which has been developed by the computer industry.

▲ A teddy bear made in about 1935 by the German firm of Shuco. It is made from fur fabric, with felt pads and glass eyes. Many others just like it would have been made in the same factory.

Where toys are made

Many of the toys today are made in the Far East, particularly in Hong Kong and Taiwan. In these countries toys can be mass-produced at prices that millions of families throughout the world can afford. However, there is sometimes a danger that cheap toys will be unsafe for small children, so many countries now set safety standards and have campaigns to warn parents and children about dangerous toys. ■

See also

Board games
Dolls
Models

Biography
Roosevelt, Theodore

Tracks and signs

Many animals are shy, and distrust human beings. Often the only way to know that they are about is to find their tracks. By becoming a nature detective and studying these tracks, you will be able to find out a great deal about the animals without disturbing them.

► Having cracked the nut open, this red squirrel will discard the shell. If you find empty shells you can tell which animal has been eating the nuts by the way the shell has been opened.

Usually creatures take the same routes through their territories, so they make pathways through the grass or woodlands. The size of a path is often a clue to the type of animal. Obviously, the run made by a vole will be smaller than that of a badger or a deer.

Sometimes, when the ground is soft, or after a fall of snow, you will be able to see footprints. Each kind of animal makes a different sort of footprint, so you can identify the creature just from this. The first thing to do is to count the number of toe marks on each footprint. Badgers and otters have five toes on each foot. Dogs and cats have four. Cattle and sheep and deer walk on the tips of two toes, while horses and ponies leave the mark of the single toenail which forms the hoof on each foot. The distance between the footprints will tell you whether the animal was walking or running along the track. The footprints are spaced further apart when running.

When an animal leaves its den, it often grooms itself. You may find tufts of a deer's hair caught in a rubbing post, or the scarred tree that badgers have used for cleaning their claws.

When they feed, animals leave clear marks of their presence. Squirrels crack nuts with their powerful teeth, while mice and voles nibble them open. Deer and other large plant eaters often browse on the lower branches of trees, or they may eat the bark. Each kind of animal has its own way of feeding. Look at the height from which the food was taken and see if you can find toothmarks, for these may tell you the size of the creature. Some animals make food stores. What has been hidden, where and how will again be clues to particular species.

The tracks and signs of birds and smaller animals are usually more difficult to find. The exception is the nests of birds and some insects, but these should always be left completely alone unless you are absolutely sure they are deserted. Some birds, including hawks, owls and gulls, form pellets of the indigestible parts of their food. These are not at all unpleasant to handle and can tell you exactly what the bird has been eating. You may find that they contain the tiny bones of birds or mice and the wing cases of beetles. ■

▼ This owl pellet, from a short-eared owl, has been opened up to show what the owl has eaten. The small bones and grey fur are probably from a mouse or a vole.

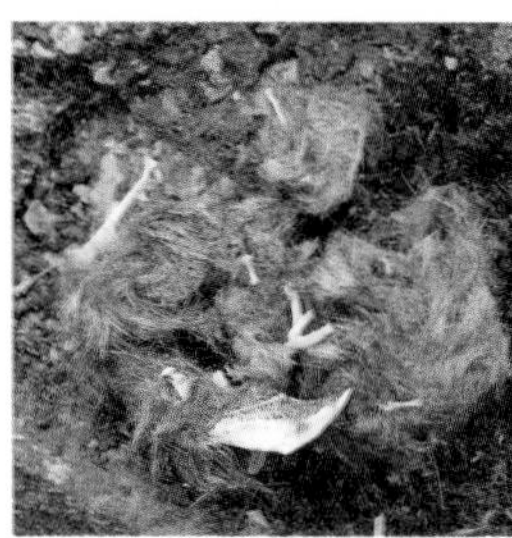

► Look for tracks in wet mud (often found near gates and paths) and fresh snow. Dog and fox tracks are similar, but dogs often have their toes spread apart.

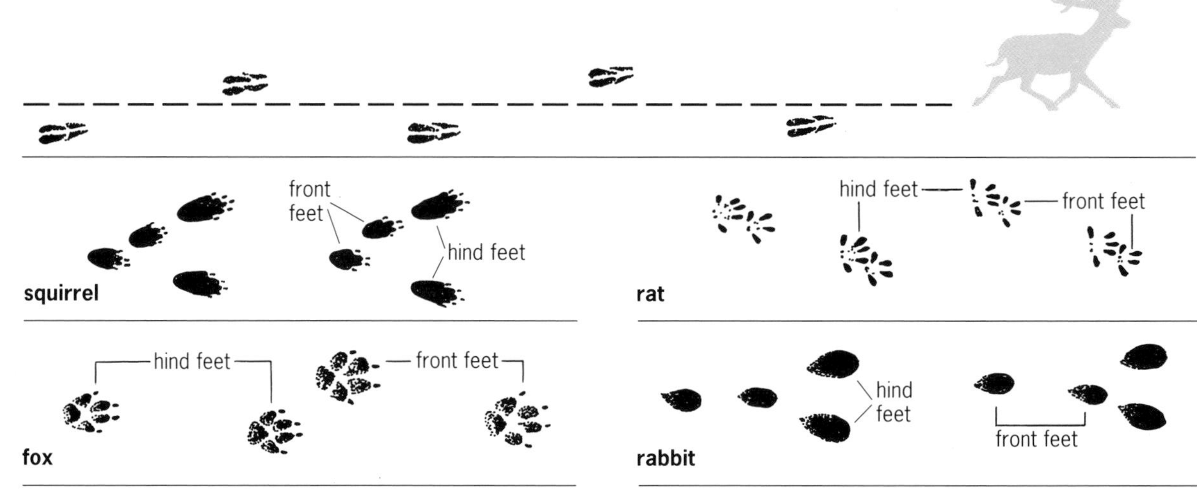

 See also
Birds
Deer
Mice
Squirrels
Voles

Trade

Have you ever swapped something of yours for something else your friend had? If so, you were trading. Trade takes place when people exchange things. These days, most trade involves money, but when things are swapped directly for other things we call it barter.

The last time you bought a bar of chocolate, yours was the last in a whole series of trades. Before it was sold to you, the chocolate was bought from a wholesaler by the shopkeeper. In turn, the wholesaler bought it from the manufacturer, who paid people to make the chocolate bar. And before that, the ingredients, like cocoa beans, sugar and milk, had to be bought by the manufacturer.

All over the world, people trade. In the Sahara Desert, nomads make salt which they take on their camels to markets south of the desert. Here they trade their salt for food. Millet, which is a type of grain, and sugar are at the top of their shopping list.

It is not just individual people and businesses who trade. Countries trade too. A country sells the things it produces and, with the money it earns, it buys the things it needs. Some Middle Eastern countries sell oil to many parts of the world and buy cars, machinery and food.

Transport is vital to trade. Without ships, aeroplanes and trucks, it would be impossible to move all these goods around the world and trade would grind to a halt. ■

When countries trade with each other this is called 'international trade'. **Exports** are products which are sold abroad to customers in other countries. **Imports** are products which are bought from other countries.

See also
Businesses
Markets
Shops
Slave trade
Spices
Transport
Wool

Trade unions

Workers often find that they have to band together to talk to their employers if they want to get the best possible wages and working conditions. Such groups of workers are called trade unions. There are trade unions in every country and every industry, but they are strongest in factories and offices and weakest amongst people who work on the land.

Employers need their workers if their firms are to make money. Workers need employers to pay their wages. Both sides make use of this fact when they bargain about wages or working conditions. If talks between employers and trade unions break down, the trade unions may threaten to stop working (strike) to make the employers agree to their demands.

Different kinds of unions

There are four main kinds of trade union. Craft unions are formed by people who have the same skill, like printers or electricians. There are many such unions in Britain. Industrial unions recruit all the workers in a particular industry, such as mineworkers or metalworkers. Such unions are the rule in Germany. General unions represent workers in many different industries, and may also concentrate on unskilled workers. They are common in many developing countries, and the largest unions in Britain are of this type. Finally, white collar unions represent non-manual administrative, clerical, supervisory, professional and technical workers. In some countries, trade unions have very little freedom to carry out their activities. In Poland, South Africa and several South American countries trade union members have had to struggle to make their voice heard.

Federations of unions

It is often useful for unions to act together, so they have formed national and international associations. The national association in Britain is the Trades Union Congress (TUC), founded in 1868. Most of the unions are linked to it, representing many millions of workers. A similar body in the USA is the American Federation of Labor and Congress of Industrial Organizations (AFL-CIO). Australia has the Australian Council of Trade Unions (ACTU).

Flashback

Life was hard for workers during the early part of the Industrial Revolution. Many factories were dirty, crowded, badly lit and poorly ventilated. Men, women and children were expected to toil for up to sixteen hours a day, six days a week. It was conditions like these that led to the growth of trade unions in Britain.

At first trade unions were banned by law in Britain. They became legal in 1824, and gained strength only slowly. A major step was when they helped to form the Labour Party at the beginning of the 20th century, but they often came into conflict with the government, especially in the 1926 General Strike. They were at their most powerful from the 1940s to the 1970s, but declined in influence and membership in the 1980s. ■

The largest trade union the world has known is Solidarnosc ('Solidarity'). When it was formed as a free trade union in communist Poland in 1980 it soon spread throughout the country and gained 8 million members. Even though it was banned by the government in 1981, it remained so popular that it won the free elections in 1989 after turning from a trade union into a political organization.

Germany has the Deutscher Gewerkschaftbund (DGB), German Federation of Trade Unions. In France the main federation is the Confédération Générale du Travail (CGT).

See also
British history 1919–1989
Factory reform in Britain
Industrial Revolution
Tolpuddle Martyrs
Victorian Britain

Trams

► **Trams, like this one in Amsterdam, are used in many European cities.**

Trams are passenger-carrying vehicles that run on rails laid in the street. The top of each rail is level with the surface of the road so that other vehicles can cross the rails without any difficulty. Today there are trams in many European towns. Modern trams are quiet, comfortable and fast, but the old trams were noisy and slow and got in the way of other vehicles. Most British towns replaced trams with buses in the 1940s.

Horse-drawn trams started in the USA in about 1830 and in Britain in 1858. Within about fifteen years almost every city in Europe was using them. Two horses could pull a tram carrying about 40 passengers. In some places, the horses were replaced by steam tram locomotives pulling up to four tramcars. Since about 1900, trams have been driven by electricity collected from overhead wires by an arm on the top of the tram. ■

Transformers

Step-down transformer
A transformer which *decreases* voltage (and increases current). It has *fewer* turns on the secondary coil than on the primary.

Step-up transformer
A transformer which *increases* voltage (and reduces current). It has *more* turns on the secondary coil than on the primary.

Electric model train sets run on low-voltage electricity. Mains electricity, on the other hand, is high voltage. It is pushed out with too great a force for the trains. With a transformer, a model train set can still be run from the mains supply. This is because the transformer reduces the voltage to the right level. Transformers for reducing mains voltage are also used in radios, television sets, cassette players, battery chargers, and mains adaptors for computers.

Some transformers increase voltage. There are huge transformers like this at power-stations. They increase the voltage before the power is fed to the overhead lines. But they do not give something for nothing. When a transformer increases voltage, it reduces the current. In other words, the electricity is pushed harder but less of it flows. This means that thinner power lines can be used.

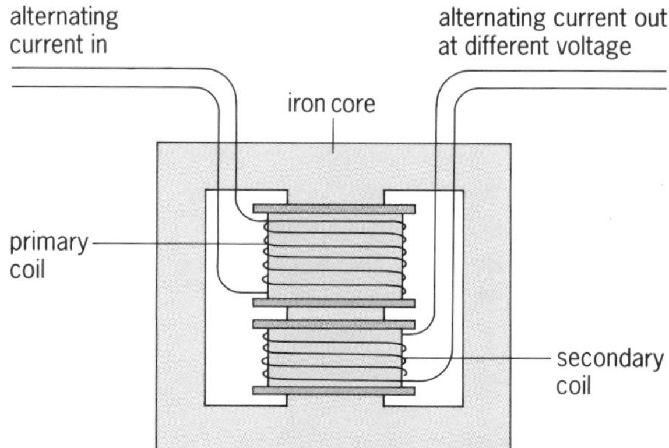

► **A transformer has two coils wound round an iron core. When alternating current is passed through the primary coil, the secondary coil delivers alternating current at a different voltage.**

► **Step-up transformer at a power-station. It transfers power to overhead cables in the form of a much smaller current at a greatly increased voltage.**

How a transformer works

Transformers will only work with alternating current (a.c.). This is the sort of electricity you get from the mains. It flows backwards, forwards, backwards . . . and so on. Inside a transformer, there is a core of iron with two coils of wire wrapped round it. When alternating current is passed through one coil, called the primary, it sets up a changing magnetic field in the iron. This changing field generates a voltage in the second coil, called the secondary. The more turns there are on the secondary, the higher the voltage produced. ■

See also
Electricity
Electricity supply

Biography
Faraday

Transistors

Transistors are used in radios, TVs and other electronic equipment. They control and change the flow of electric currents. In a radio, for example, they amplify the tiny changing currents called signals. They boost them so that the signals are strong enough to make the radio give out sound. Most transistors are made from a material called silicon. Silicon is a semiconductor. It is not a good conductor of electricity, but it is not an insulator either.

▲ **These are transistors. Inside each case is a specially treated crystal of silicon, with three connecting leads attached.**

Flashback

Before transistors were invented, their jobs were done by electronic valves. These were large, made of glass and broke easily. Only when transistors became available was it possible to make electronic equipment which was small and portable. The first transistor was made in 1947 at the Bell Telephone Laboratories in the USA. It was made of germanium, another semiconductor. At one time all transistors were made separately.

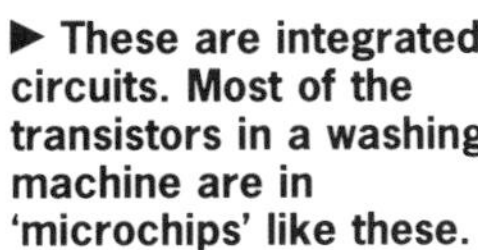

▶ **These are integrated circuits. Most of the transistors in a washing machine are in 'microchips' like these.**

Nowadays they can be made with thousands of other electronic components on a small slice of silicon. The result is a complete electronic circuit ready to be used. It is called an integrated circuit or chip. ■

See also
Electronics
Radio
Silicon

Transplants

Transplant surgery is the replacement of a damaged human organ by another one during an operation. The healthy organ has usually come from someone who has died and has donated the organ for this use. Over recent years the number of types of organ that can be transplanted in this way has increased.

Corneas (the transparent fronts of eyes) can be replaced when they become cloudy and cause blindness. Kidneys which stop working can also be replaced. Transplant operations have also been carried out with hearts, lungs and livers, but the success rates for these are not very good.

Everyone has two kidneys but can survive with only one. It is possible for close living relatives to donate kidneys for transplant.

Finding enough donors of organs is often a problem. In some countries people carry donor cards which say that they would like to donate their organs for transplants after they die. This is necessary, because the organs have to be removed from the donor's body very soon after death so the organs themselves stay alive.

Rejection

The body of a patient receiving a transplant recognizes that the organ is made of different cells to its own. It often tries to 'attack' the transplant with its own immune system. This can cause destruction of the transplant and is called 'rejection'. Scientists and doctors are constantly searching for ways of stopping this happening. One way is to make sure the two sets of cells are as chemically similar as possible. Another is to find drugs which can dampen down the patient's natural immune defences against the transplant. Blood transfusion is a special sort of transplant. There are only a few human blood groups so a blood bank can supply the correct blood to anybody needing blood after an accident or major operation. Blood transfusion services collect new blood from donors to keep fresh supplies in stock. ■

Before making a transplant, tests must be made on both the donor organ and the patient's body to make sure that they are similar.

See also
Kidneys
Operations

Transport

See also
Acid rain
Greenhouse effect
Ozone
Pollution
Rockets
Space exploration

Humans have always been trying to find better ways of moving themselves and their goods around. Nowadays, most countries are criss-crossed with road and rail networks. Ships carry enormous cargoes from country to country. Aircraft can carry passengers faster than the speed of sound and space shuttles can, at enormous expense, transport a very few people into space.

Road

A car is a convenient way of getting around if only a few people want to travel. It can take you exactly where you want to go. Buses and coaches are a cheaper way of carrying lots of people but they can only be boarded at set stops and certain times. In small countries like Britain, trucks (lorries) are the main method of transporting goods. The goods being carried are called freight.

For fast, long-distance travel, cars, trucks and coaches need motorways to travel on. Some of these have three or more lanes in each direction.

See also
Bicycles
Motor cars
Motor cycles
Roads

Rail

Railways are the main freight carriers in large countries like the USA where huge distances have to be covered. For passengers, high-speed trains are a convenient way of travelling between large cities. They avoid tiring journeys on crowded roads and the problem of finding somewhere to park when you arrive. For those who want to take their vehicles, motorail services carry cars as well as passengers. Most cities have stations near the centre and many people use local trains to get to work. Building railway lines across cities has always been difficult. In some cities, the problem has been solved by putting the lines underground.

See also
Locomotives
Railways

Air

Flying is easily the fastest way to travel long distances. A cruise liner can sail across the Atlantic in three and a half days. Concorde, flying supersonic, can cross it in three and a half hours. One problem with flying is that airports are often a long way from city centres. Completing your journey by car or bus can make the total travel time much longer. Some cities have fast rail or helicopter links into the city centre. Others are building airports much closer in. These are designed for new, quiet aircraft which can take off and land from short runways.

Flying is an expensive way of moving freight. Very little freight goes by air compared with land and sea.

See also

Aircraft
Airports
Gliders
Balloons and airships
Helicopters

The future

Already, more than 700 million passengers travel by air every year. And the number could double within ten years. For faster travel, spaceplanes are being developed that can carry passengers at more than five times the speed of sound. But planes like this burn huge amounts of fuel and may harm the atmosphere. In the future, most land, sea and air vehicles are likely to be quieter, use less fuel and cause less pollution.

Sea

Ships carry nearly all the freight that has to travel overseas. Some, like supertankers, are designed to carry one type of cargo. Others carry containers which are packed with goods before they reach the docks and can fit straight on the back of a truck.

Most people use ships only for ferry crossings. Many ferries carry vehicles as well as passengers. Ro-ro (roll on, roll off) ferries are designed for quick loading and unloading of vehicles. Hovercraft are used on some ferry services. They float on a cushion of air and can travel faster than ships. ■

See also

Boats
Docks
Hovercraft
Sailing ships
Ships
Yachts

Trees

▶ **The left half of the illustration shows an oak tree in the summer months when the twigs are covered in leaves. The right half of the same picture shows the tree in winter when the leaves have fallen and the branches and twigs look bare.**

Trees are the largest land plants. Their strong, woody trunks support a mass of branches with buds producing leaves, the food factories of a tree. If you look at trees in winter you will see that some are bare and have lost their leaves. These are deciduous trees sometimes called the broadleaves. Others are covered with a mass of dark green foliage; these are the evergreens. Trees are giant forms of two main plant groups: the flowering plants and the conifers (cone-bearers).

Leaves

This leaf is one of thousands that cover an oak tree in summer. Each leaf plays its part in making food for the tree by providing a suitable site for photosynthesis. Light energy from the Sun powers this process, so each leaf needs to be in a position to receive the maximum amount of light.

If you sit under a tree in summer and look up at the leaf canopy you will see the pattern made by the spreading leaves. They allow very little light to penetrate between them.

▼ **The male flowers of the oak are catkins which produce pollen. The female flowers have red stigmas to catch the pollen. After the ovary has been fertilized by the pollen, it swells and grows into an acorn.**

male flowers (catkins)

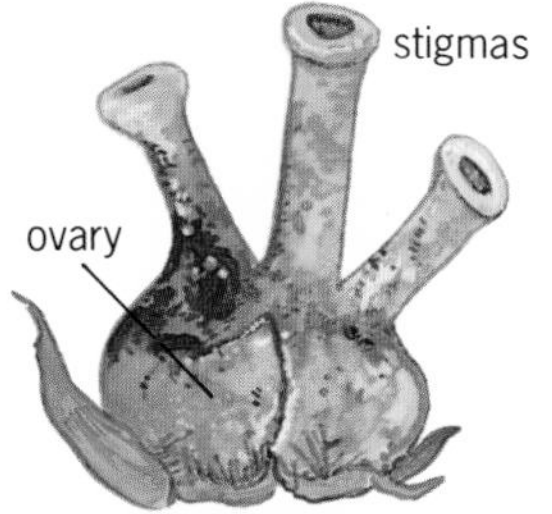

female flowers, enlarged

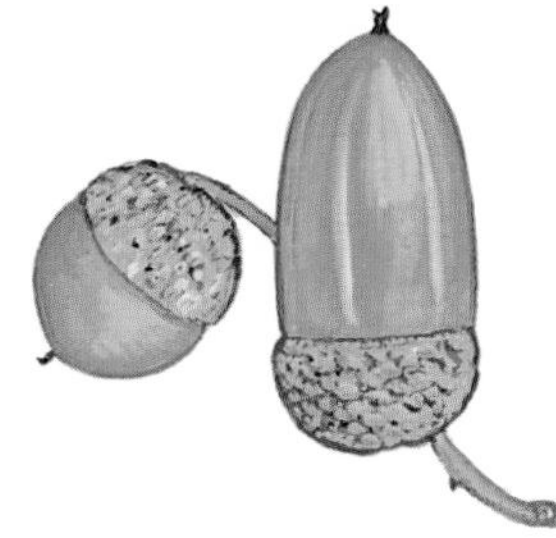

acorns

Flowers and fruit

Most people recognize an acorn, the fruit of an oak tree, but have you seen its flowers? These dangle from new buds like yellowy-green catkins. They appear in early May before the leaves, and the male and female flowers are separate. You can recognize the male catkins by the clouds of yellow pollen they produce. Female

oak tree in summer

oak tree in winter

flowers, each with three dark red stigmas, develop on spikes growing from buds at the end of a shoot. After wind pollination each ovary grows into an acorn, held in its own little cup.

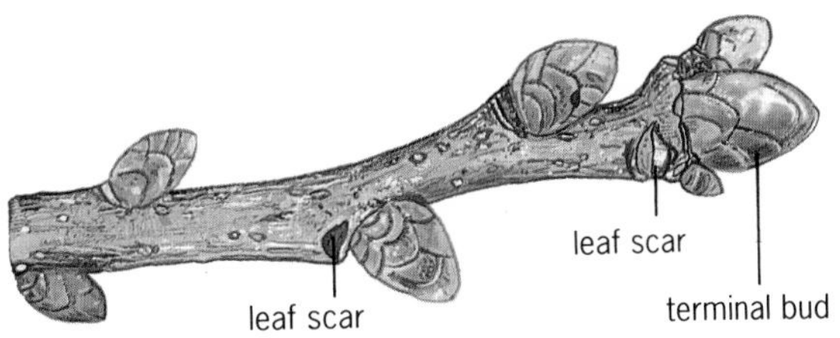

◀ **Twig from an oak tree in winter.**

Twigs

At the end of each twig and spaced along its length are buds. These will produce new leaves and flowers in the following season. Buds survive the harsh weather of winter so that the tree can grow again the next year.

Take the bud from the end of a twig and peel off each scale. These protect the tiny leaves and flowers in the middle. At the tip of each twig is a large terminal bud. This produces all the new growth that twig will make in the following season. Smaller buds beside it and along the length of the twig will grow into side shoots. On the stem below each bud is a crescent-shaped scar where a leaf was attached in the previous year.

Bark

Bark is the rough, grooved surface layer which covers the trunk and branches of a tree. It protects the living part of the tree's structure and the tubes through which water, mineral salts and food travel between the roots and leaves. New bark grows on the inside and dies as it gets pushed further out by later growth. As the girth of the tree increases, the rigid bark often cracks forming grooves.

Roots

Roots spread from the base of the trunk through the soil like underground branches. They have two basic functions. One is to form a secure anchor so that the tree does not topple over. The other is to absorb water and mineral salts from the soil. Roots are growing most of the time and only stop when it gets too cold. In some trees such as beech, birch and spruce the roots never grow very deep. Others like oak and pine are deeper rooting. They are very stable but difficult to transplant.

▼ **One way of recognizing different species of trees is by the patterns made by grooves in the bark.**

oak bark

ash bark

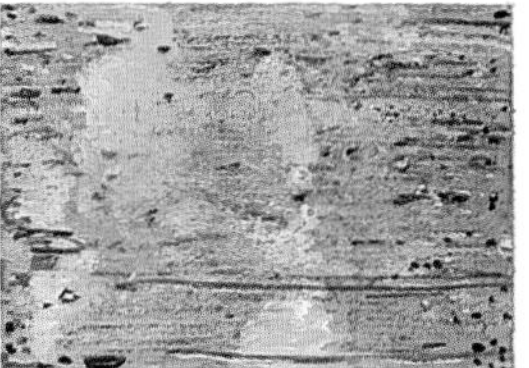

beech bark

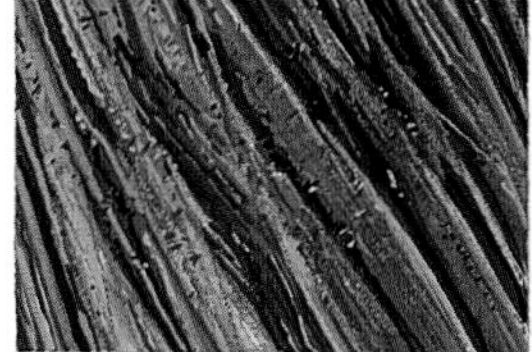

sweet chestnut bark

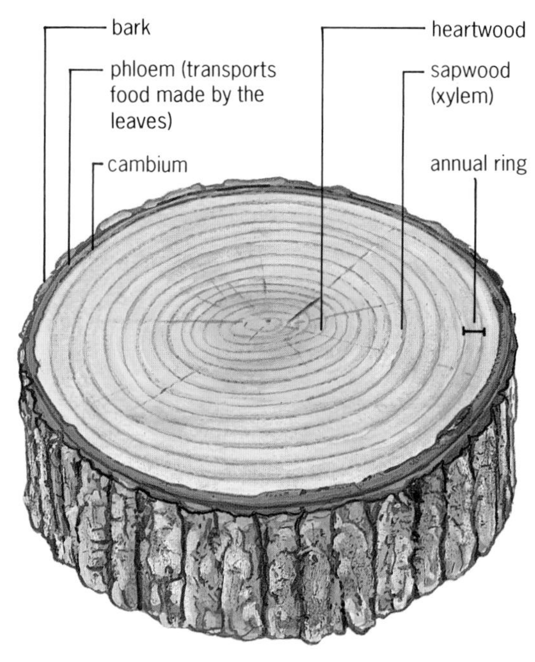

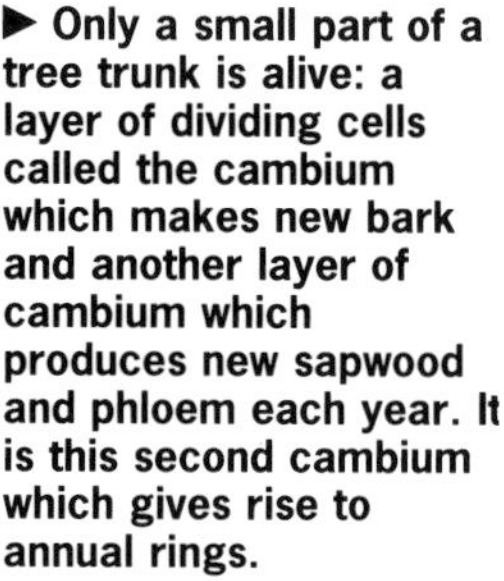
▶ Only a small part of a tree trunk is alive: a layer of dividing cells called the cambium which makes new bark and another layer of cambium which produces new sapwood and phloem each year. It is this second cambium which gives rise to annual rings.

How a tree works

The water and mineral salts that the tree needs are carried by a system of tubes called the sapwood. Each season the tree produces new sapwood to carry sap to the buds ready for the new crop of leaves and flowers.

Working leaves continuously lose water by a process of evaporation called transpiration. Water, replacing that lost, moves up through the tree in a continuous column from the roots. Sap, carrying food made by the leaves, is transported down the tree in another set of tubes called the phloem. This food is taken to where it is needed or stored in the trunk or roots.

How trees grow

Trees increase in size as the branches and roots divide and grow longer spreading over a greater area. Trees also increase in girth, that is the diameter of the trunk and branches get larger each growing season.

Just inside the bark is a damp layer. This is one of the few living parts of the trunk, a layer called the cambium. Cambium cells are able to divide adding new wood cells (xylem) to the inside and new phloem to the outside. At the end of the season the sapwood cells are filled with waste products and become part of the dead centre of the tree, the heartwood. Bark is produced by another ring of cambium cells outside the phloem.

Growth rates

At the beginning of each season the cambium produces new sapwood. These large tubular cells supply water to the opening buds. As the season progresses, there is less need for new cells so fewer and smaller cells are produced. You can recognize these different rates of growth as the annual rings seen in the cut surface of a tree trunk or branch. The smaller, close-packed cells make a lighter coloured wood than the larger cells produced at the beginning of the season.

Hard and soft wood

Deciduous trees like oak, beech and ash are quite slow-growing. After 20 years they may only be 4 m (13 ft) high and reach a maximum of 13 m (43 ft) in 150 years. Conifers grow much more quickly reaching a height of 10 m (32 ft) in 30 years. Different rates of growth produce different types of timber. Slow growers have a denser wood called hardwood whereas fast growers produce a lighter timber called softwood.

▼ Silhouettes of a selection of mature trees shown in winter.

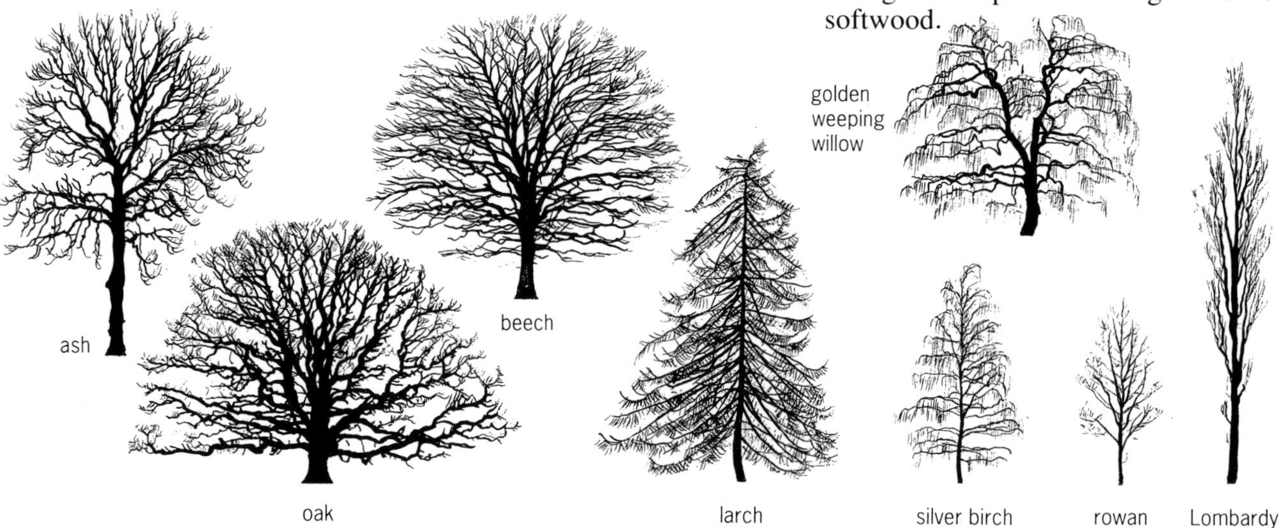

Coppicing and pollarding

To increase the amount of timber some trees are coppiced. This involves cutting down the young trees to soil level. The stumps are left to sprout new shoots in the following spring. These grow for ten years, then they are cut and the cycle starts again. Hazel and sweet chestnut are the commonest coppiced trees. Hazel is used for firewood, fencing and charcoal, and chestnut for furniture and fencing.

Pollarding is similar to coppicing but the shoots are cut 2 m (6 ft) above ground level. This creates a short trunk topped by a mass of shoots, out of reach of grazing animals. Willows growing around meadows were often pollarded and the cut branches woven into baskets or wattle fencing.

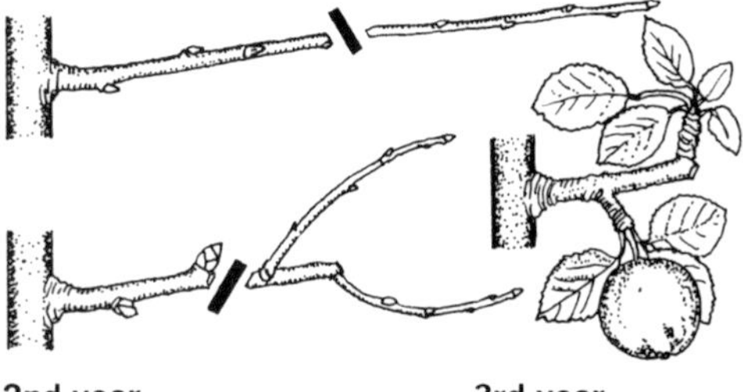

◀ **Apple and pear trees are pruned to increase their yield of fruit. By pruning away the growth buds, the flower buds develop and each produces a fruit.**

Pruning

This is the trimming of branches on fruit trees to encourage them to produce more flowering shoots and fruit. Some, like apples and pears, are trained against wires or a wall to form espalier or cordon fruit trees. These provide a large crop of fruit which is easy to pick. Topiary is a type of pruning in which evergreens, such as yew, are trimmed to form interesting shapes for decoration.

◀ **Giant sequoias in the Mariposa Grove in Yosemite National Park, California, USA. The size of the person sitting by the tree gives an idea of the enormous girth and of the height of the trees.**

Giant conifers

Giant sequoias, like those in the photograph on the left, are conifers which grow in the mountains of California. They are not as tall as their close relatives the redwoods, which can grow over 90 m (300 ft), but their trunks are much larger.

The largest living tree is a giant sequoia called the 'General Sherman'. It is 83·8 m (274·9 ft) tall and measures 31·4 m (103 ft) around its base. As well as being the world's largest living thing it is also one of the oldest things on Earth, being between 2,200 and 2,500 years old. ■

See also
Conifers
Flowering plants
Forests
Leaves
Photosynthesis
Roots
Timber
Wood
Woodlands

Trigonometry

Trigonometry is the branch of mathematics which deals with the links between lengths and angles in triangles and other figures. When some measurements are known, others can be calculated.

One important idea in trigonometry is that similar triangles have sides whose lengths are in proportion. The red and green triangles here have the same angles. The red triangle has a base twice the length of the green triangle. It also has twice the height.

See also
Geometry
Mathematics
Surveyors

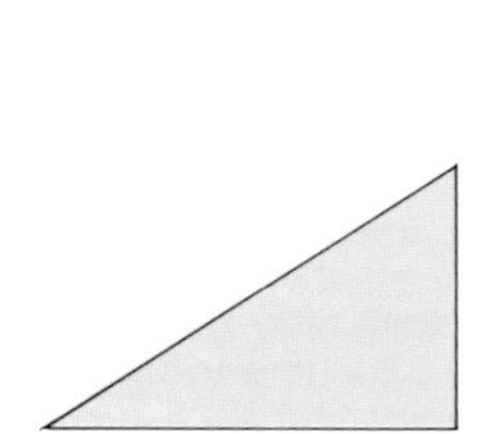

The idea of proportion is very useful for measuring the height of something whose top you cannot reach. Try using it to find the height of a lamp-post. Stand exactly 10 m from the lamp-post. Ask a friend to hold a stick upright exactly 1 m in front of you. Make two marks on the stick so that, looking with one eye, the top mark lines up with the top of the lamp-post and the bottom mark lines up with the base. Measure the height between the marks. The lamp-post is ten times this height. ■

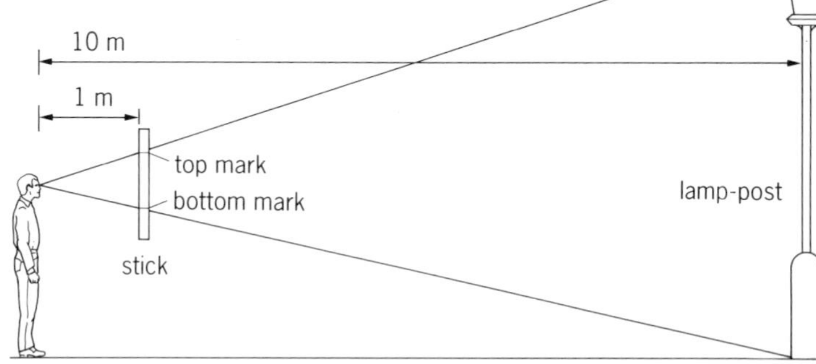

Trinidad and Tobago

Columbus sailed past Trinidad in 1498. He named the island after three mountain peaks.

Trinidad and Tobago is a twin-island country in the Caribbean and a member of the Commonwealth. Oil and natural gas are extracted in Trinidad and from the shallow seas around the island. Money from oil exports made Trinidad and Tobago into a prosperous country in the 1970s. Some of the oil wealth was used to build up other industries, making steel, chemicals and other goods, and to modernize farming.

▼ A game of hockey on the savannah, in Port of Spain, the capital of Trinidad.

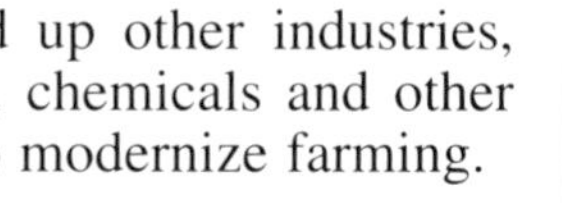

Tobago is much quieter than Trinidad. It has a beautiful coastline with fine coral reefs, and attracts many tourists from Trinidad and elsewhere.

Trinidad and Tobago is sometimes called the 'Rainbow Country', because so many different peoples have made up one nation. First there were American Indians from South America, then Spanish, French, and British settlers, who brought in slaves from Africa to work on their sugar and cocoa plantations. In the 19th century there were contract labourers, mostly from India, but also from China and the Portuguese island of Madeira. This century, there have been many migrants from other Caribbean islands. This mix of cultures can be seen in the annual carnival, with its calypsos, steel bands and costume bands. ■

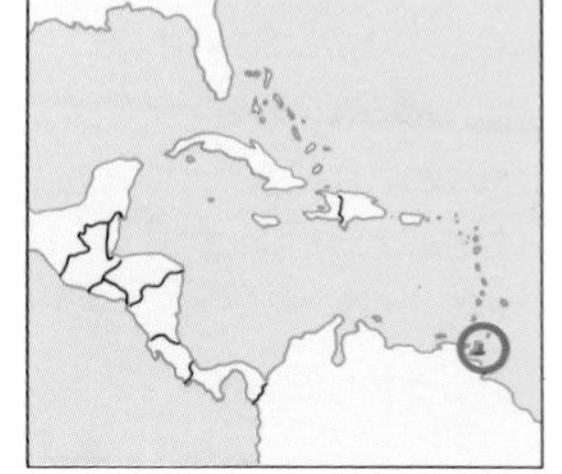

Area
5,130 sq km
(1,981 sq miles)
Capital
Port of Spain
Population
1,185,000
Language
English, Hindi, French, Spanish
Religion
Christian, Hindu, Muslim
Government
Parliamentary republic
Currency
1 Trinidad and Tobago dollar = 100 cents

See also
Caribbean
Caribbean history
Carnivals

Trojan War

In the times of the ancient Greeks there was a city of Troy on the eastern coast of the Aegean Sea in the land that is now Turkey. About a hundred years ago the ruins of this city were discovered and excavated. It had probably been destroyed by Greeks about 1210 BC. There is a legend that the city states of Greece combined to send a vast fleet to attack Troy. Many stories grew up around this Trojan War and some of them have come down to us through the poems of Homer and Virgil.

How the war began

Three goddesses argued about who was the most beautiful and asked a mortal, Prince Paris of Troy, to choose. Paris chose Aphrodite and she rewarded him by saying that he could marry Helen, the loveliest mortal woman in the world. But Helen was married already, to King Menelaus of Sparta in Greece. Paris kidnapped her and took her to Troy. The Greeks sent an army to win her back, and the Trojan War began.

Hector and Achilles

The war lasted for ten years. Neither side could win. The two most powerful warriors were Achilles of Greece and Hector of Troy. No one else could beat them, and they refused to fight each other. Then Patroclus, a friend of Achilles, put on Achilles' armour and challenged Hector, pretending to be Achilles. Hector killed Patroclus, and Achilles was so angry that he fought Hector, killed him and dragged his body behind a war-chariot, three times round the walls of Troy. Achilles was later killed by an arrow in the one unprotected spot on his body: his heel.

The wooden horse

Not even Hector's death ended the war. The walls of Troy were too strong for the Greeks, and the Greek army was too big for the Trojans to defeat. Then a Greek warrior called Odysseus (Ulysses) thought of a trick to beat the Trojans. The Greeks built a huge wooden horse, and filled its hollow inside with soldiers. Then they left it outside the walls of Troy and pretended to sail away. The Trojans were overjoyed. Thinking that the Greeks had fled, they dragged the horse into Troy as an offering to the goddess Athene, who had helped them in the war. That night, the Greeks sailed back to Troy, and Odysseus and the other soldiers in the horse slid down on ropes and threw open the city gates. The Greeks poured in, and captured the city.

Aeneas and the survivors

The Greeks killed all the Trojans they could find, and burned the city. But that was not the end of Troy. A band of Trojan refugees escaped. Led by Prince Aeneas, they sailed south to found a new city. But they were blown off course by storms and faced terrifying supernatural monsters. Eventually they landed at Carthage in North Africa, where Aeneas fell in love with Queen Dido. The gods led them at last to Italy. Here they settled on the banks of the River Tiber, not far from the place where Romulus later built a new city: Rome. ■

Greeks
Agamemnon (leader of the army), Achilles, Ajax, Diomedes, Menelaus, Odysseus
Trojans
Priam (King of Troy), Aeneas, Antenor, Glaucus, Hector, Paris

Homer's long Greek poem, the *Iliad* (which means 'poem about Troy'), is nearly all about a few days in the last year of the war. Virgil's long Latin poem, the *Aeneid* (which means 'poem about Aeneas'), describes the fall of Troy and Aeneas' later adventures.

◀ The climax of Homer's *Iliad* is the single combat between Achilles and Hector. Here Achilles, wearing helmet, shield and sheathed sword, lunges forward with his spear to deal a finishing stroke to Hector who, already wounded, gives ground.

See also
Greek ancient history
Greek myths
Odysseus

Biography
Homer
Virgil

Tropics

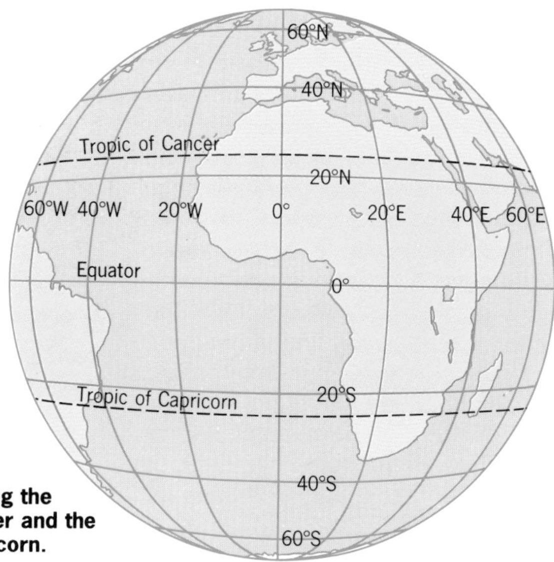

► Globe showing the Tropic of Cancer and the Tropic of Capricorn.

You will find two tropics marked on any globe or map of the world: the Tropic of Cancer at 23½° north of the Equator; and the Tropic of Capricorn at 23½° south of the Equator. These imaginary lines mark the places furthest away from the Equator where the Sun is overhead. It is directly overhead at the Tropic of Cancer at midday on 21 June, and at the Tropic of Capricorn at midday on 22 December each year. The area between these two lines is called the tropics.

It does snow in the tropics. Kilimanjaro, Africa's highest mountain, has snow all year. So do the highest peaks of the Andes in tropical South America.

Tropical areas are hot all through the year. It is the rainfall that varies, and gives the seasons. At the Equator, there is plenty of rain every month. At the edges of the tropics some areas are desert. In between, there are large areas with a wet season at the hottest time of the year, and a dry season when it is slightly cooler.

Trees lose their leaves in the dry season in the savannah.

Places nearer the Equator have a long wet season and a short dry one. Tall trees grow as well as grass. But nearer the deserts, there is a short, wet season and a long dry one. Trees get fewer and further apart and there is more grass. It grows tall and lush in the wet season, but it is brown and dry when there is no rain. This landscape of tropical grassland and trees is called savannah. ■

See also
Equator
Grasslands
Latitude and longitude
Seasons

Trucks

Trucks (lorries) are large vehicles used for carrying goods by road. The heaviest can weigh 40 tonnes or more. Most are powered by diesel engines and can have as many as sixteen gears.

Trucks are often built with the same basic cab and chassis (frame), but different bodies are bolted on depending on the load to be carried. Special trucks can tip, carry liquids in a tank or keep food refrigerated.

Some trucks are in two parts. The front part, with the engine and cab, is called the tractor unit. This pulls the rear part, a trailer which carries the load. Trucks like this are known as articulated trucks, because the whole unit bends where the two parts join. As the parts can be separated, the trailer can be loaded before the tractor unit comes to collect it.

flat bed truck

truck with rubbish skip

tipper

tanker for bulk liquids, powder or grain

truck with drawbar trailer

articulated truck with container

▼ A mammoth Caterpillar dump truck for use in quarries and open cast mines.

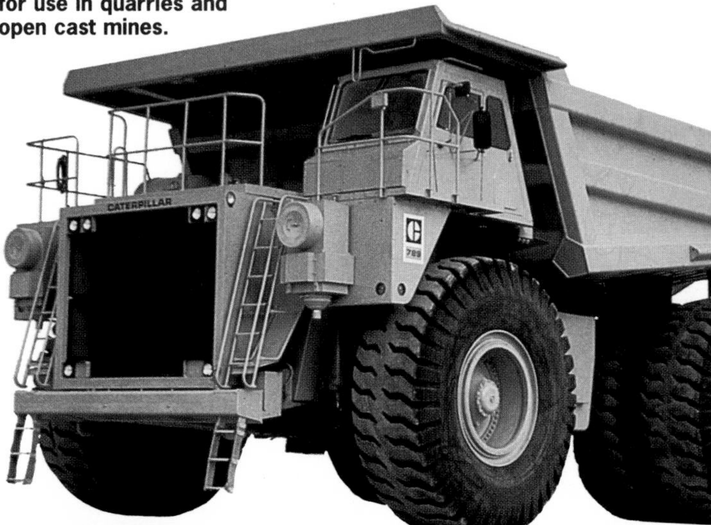

▼ Special trailers are made to carry very long loads. The longest load ever moved was a gas storage vessel, 83.8 m long.

Longest truck
The Arctic Snow Train, originally built for the US Army, is 174 m long and has 54 wheels.

Very large trucks are sometimes called juggernauts. Juggernaut is a name of a Hindu temple and god whose image is traditionally carried in a huge, unstoppable chariot.

Most trucks are owned by haulage companies and hired out with their drivers. Some travel abroad or carry containers to and from the docks. Bigger trucks may have a bed, a basin and even a microwave oven so that the driver can live in the cab on long journeys.

Flashback

Trucks, powered by steam or electricity, first appeared in the 1890s. Trucks with petrol engines were introduced in the early 1900s and were widely used during World War I (1914–1918) for carrying supplies. During the 1920s, reliable diesel engines became available. These proved to be more economical and long-lasting than petrol engines and have been used on trucks ever since. ■

See also
Docks
Internal combustion engines
Transport

▼ **An American articulated truck made by White's.**

Tubers

Tubers are underground stems or roots which swell up to store food. With stored food the plant can survive the winter. Some perennial flowering plants, such as dahlias, produce root tubers which can be dug up in autumn and stored through winter. The following spring they can be split and planted to increase the number of plants grown.

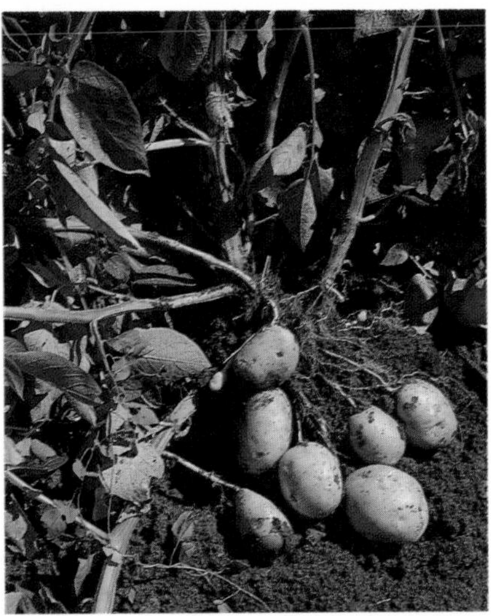

◀ **Potato tubers.**

Other tubers, like potatoes, develop from special underground stems. Gardeners encourage these to grow by piling up the soil around the potato plants. This keeps out the light and stops them becoming green and poisonous. Extra food produced by the leaves in summer travels down the veins into these special stems. The tips swell with stored food to form potatoes.

Many tubers provide animals, including humans, with a vital part of their diet. ■

Something to do

Look carefully at a potato and see if you can recognize the features that make it part of a stem. At one end there is a group of 'eyes'. The central one has a larger bud, the terminal bud. With a closer look at the 'eyes' you will see that the 'eye' is a bud and the 'brow' above is a scale leaf scar. ■

See also
Bulbs and corms
Flowering plants
Roots

Tudor England 1485–1603

► A Flemish painter, called Joris Hoefnagel, painted this picture in 1571. The tall man dressed in black and standing behind the two violinists may be his self-portrait.

Richard III was the last English king of the Middle Ages.

1485 Henry Tudor became **Henry VII** after winning battle of Bosworth

Rebellions suppressed

1509 **Henry VIII**

1513 Scots defeated at Flodden

1529 Trouble over Henry's divorce

Cardinal Wolsey dismissed

1534 Henry VIII Supreme Head of the Church of England

1536–1540 Monasteries destroyed

1538 English Bible printed

1547 **Edward VI**

1549 First English Prayer Book

1553 **Mary I**
Catholic Church restored

1558 **Elizabeth I**
Church of England

1568 Mary, Queen of Scots imprisoned

1577– 1580 Drake's voyage round the world

1587 Mary, Queen of Scots executed

1588 Armada defeated

1596–1603 Rebellions in Ireland

1601 Poor Law

1603 Death of Elizabeth

The next king was James I (Stuart). There is an article on Stuart Britain.

This picture shows a fête, or perhaps a wedding, in the village of Bermondsey in the time of Elizabeth I. It gives us many clues about what it was like to live in Tudor England. Most people lived in villages. Although Bermondsey was near London, it was right in the country then; now it is just part of the great city.

Houses were generally built of wood and plaster. Poor cottages were often much smaller than the ones in this picture. Only the church and the manor house were made of expensive stone or brick.

Knowing your place

In Tudor England, people accepted that they had their place in the world. The richest people in this village are probably the sober group coming out of the church. They own the land, and employ most of the other people in the picture. Rich people at court wore grander clothes in bright colours, like the important visitor arriving on horseback on the left. The well-dressed musicians are probably a travelling group. Like almost everyone else in the picture they are not top people and have to work for their living. The plainly dressed men, and women with aprons, may run small farms or be skilled cobblers, thatchers or carpenters. The busy servants (four carry huge pies) are the poorest people in this picture.

Women in Tudor England

Girls were not free to run their own lives, and parents usually chose their husbands. But, if this is a wedding, the bride in this picture is probably a widow. She is wearing black and her three children (including a baby) are behind her. She is a good catch if she has money of her own from her first husband, and this time she can choose for herself.

Growing up in Tudor England

About one baby in five died before its first birthday. Clothes were heavy and complicated. Rich toddlers (both boys and girls) wore long dresses till they were about six. From then on they looked like miniature adults, if portraits like Lady Jane Grey's are anything to go by. Girls usually prepared for marriage by helping their mothers at home. Boys often went to 'grammar' schools, where they learned a great deal of Latin grammar, religion, and usually arithmetic and geography. Poor children seldom went to school. They worked alongside their parents as soon as they were old enough, at home and in the fields. Parents and teachers seem to have been very strict, and beating was a common punishment. But it may not always have been as bad as it sounds. Sir Thomas More only beat his children in fun with a peacock feather.

Health

Diseases were often killers and spread rapidly. Outbreaks of bubonic plague spread by rat fleas were common (London had a bad one in 1563). In wartime many more soldiers and sailors died from diseases like typhus than from battle wounds. A dangerous kind of influenza called the sweating sickness swept through Tudor England several times. Doctors usually treated disease by bleeding the patient, or giving purges (medicines to cause vomiting and diarrhoea), which cannot often have helped to cure them, though some medicines made from herbs were very good. Old people who had survived all these dangers were often tough and energetic, like Elizabeth I herself.

Crime and punishment

There were no policemen in Tudor England, so catching criminals was usually a matter of luck. The worst crime was treason, plotting against the king or queen. The punishment for this was public execution: beheading by an axe if you were a noble, or hanging, drawing (pulling out the intestines) and quartering (cutting off the legs and arms) if you were unlucky enough to be an ordinary person. Murderers and thieves were hanged if they were caught. Poverty was a great problem, and there were harsh punishments for wandering beggars, especially in towns. At best they were put in the stocks, or whipped out of the town so that they became someone else's problem. But by 1601, the new Poor Laws gave some help to people who were poor because they were too old, too young, or too ill to earn a living.

Entertainments

Going to the theatre was new and fashionable. Earlier, plays had been acted in the street or in rich people's houses. The Globe Theatre was a very exciting place to visit in Elizabeth I's time. Both rich and poor marvelled at the comics, the ghosts, murders and tragic deaths in plays by an actor called William Shakespeare.

Football was a terrifying game played in the streets, with no rules and goals often more than a mile apart. Stool-ball was rather like cricket, and archery, wrestling and bowls were popular. The rich enjoyed hunting, jousting and royal tennis. Quieter games were chess, nine men's morris, backgammon (found amongst sailors' belongings on the *Mary Rose*) and different kinds of card games.

Tudor England: time of change

The population was increasing in spite of so much disease. This was hard for ordinary people. Food prices went up because there were more people to feed. Wages did not go up because employers had no difficulty in finding people to work for them. There was more unemployment because there were not enough jobs for everyone.

Printed books first appeared in England when William Caxton set up his printing press in Westminster in 1476. Books became cheap and easy to buy. We do not know how many more people learned to read, but ideas and information spread more quickly. Printed pictures began to appear too. By 1600 most English villagers had seen a picture of Elizabeth I, even if they could not read.

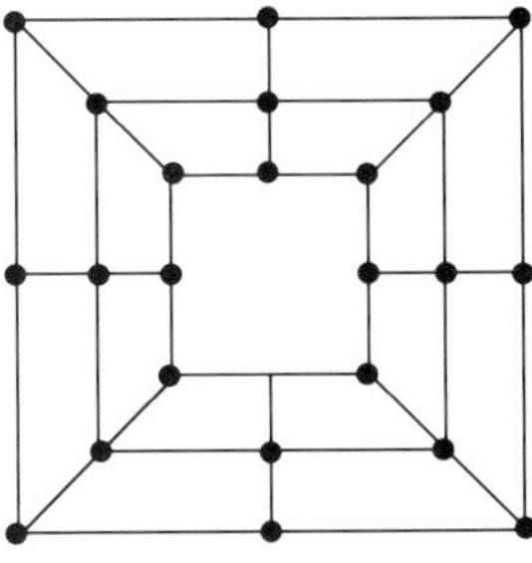

Nine men's morris is a board game for two players. Each has nine counters, and takes it in turn to put a counter on one of the circles. The aim is to get three counters in a straight row, and to stop your opponent doing so. When you make a row of three, you can remove one of your opponent's counters, as long as it is not already in a row of three. When you have used all your counters, you must move one of your counters from circle to circle along the lines, even if it means breaking up a row of three. (Still play in turns.) If you can remove all your opponent's pieces, you have won.

▼ London in 1600: a much bigger and more crowded city than in 1500. The circular Globe Theatre is near the middle in the foreground. The flag flies to show a play is going on. Old St Paul's is the biggest church in the background, and London Bridge with its narrow arches is on the right. The river was always busy. People often preferred a boat trip to a journey along the city's dirty, crowded streets.

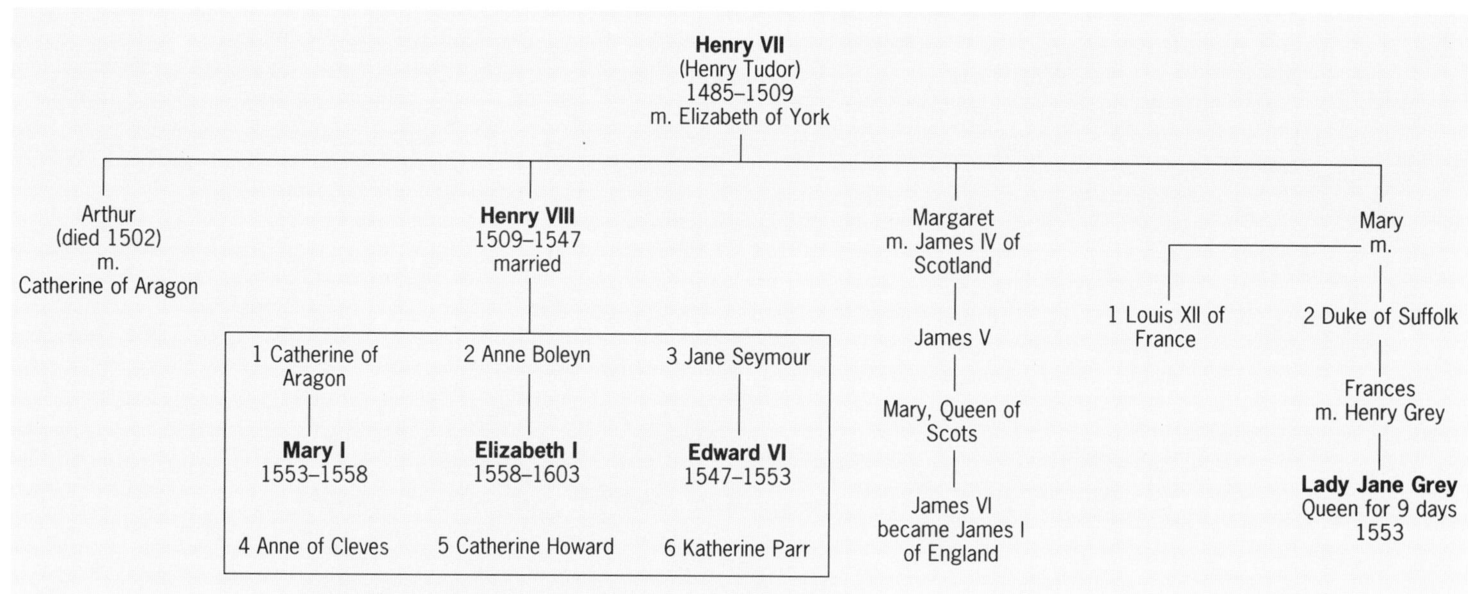

► Lady Jane Grey, aged 13. Jane was Protestant. When Edward VI died, the Protestants knew they would lose power if Catholic Mary became Queen. So at 16 Jane was made Queen, but after nine days she was deposed and executed for treason.

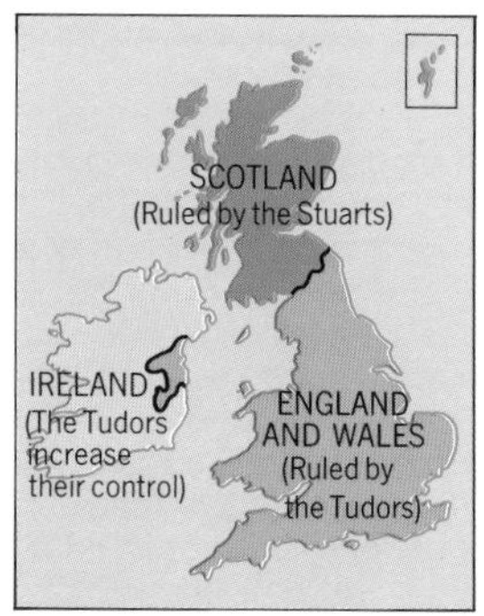

The Church changed as the Reformation spread to England. Henry VIII quarrelled with the Pope and in 1534 made himself Supreme Head of the Church of England. Between 1536 and 1540 he destroyed all the monasteries (over 800) and sold most of their lands. The English Bible was printed, and became a best-seller. Under Edward VI, Protestant changes altered the parish church. Statues and pictures disappeared, and there was a new English service.

Mary I brought back the old Catholic faith, and persecuted Protestants. Elizabeth's Church of England aimed to be a 'middle way'. Probably people's beliefs changed more slowly. In Elizabeth I's reign, when Mary, Queen of Scots and the Spanish Armada were serious dangers, there were harsh laws against English Catholics, and they became very unpopular.

The Tudors tried to control more of the British Isles. There were wars with Scotland. Henry VIII's minister, Thomas Cromwell, gave Wales the same local government as England, and made English the official language there. The Tudors tried to strengthen English rule in Catholic Ireland by giving land to English settlers, but there were several serious rebellions.

New goods like tobacco and potatoes appeared as English sailors and explorers travelled new routes, and trade increased. Rich people could buy luxuries such as silks, spices, cotton, furs and carpets more easily. Some people went to make a new life in North America: the beginning of colonies. But for ordinary people, work, food, houses and entertainments were much the same as they had been for centuries. ■

See also
Armada
Explorers
Ireland's history
Mary Rose
Poor Laws in Britain
Protestants
Reformation
Scotland's history
Theatres
Welsh history

Biography
Drake
Edward VI
Elizabeth I
Henry VII
Henry VIII
Mary I
More
Ralegh
Shakespeare
Wolsey

Tundra

Tundra is the kind of vegetation that grows in some of the coldest areas of the world. The word comes from the language of the Sami (Lapp) people, who live in the far north of Norway, Sweden and Finland. This is part of the vast area of tundra which surrounds the Arctic Ocean. Other areas occur at the edge of Antarctica, and just beneath the snowline on high mountains.

Tundra plants have to withstand long, cold winters and grow during very short summers, when the temperature hardly rises above 10°C. Although the snow and ice melt from the surface during the summer, the ground beneath remains permanently frozen. Water cannot drain away, so it collects in lakes, pools and marshes. Trees cannot grow in the frozen soil, so the tundra is a treeless wilderness: marshy in summer and snow-covered in winter.

Plants and animals of the tundra

Plants that can survive include reindeer moss, many grasses, and plants which can produce flowers and seeds in a very short time. Some animals, like polar bears and caribou, survive by hibernating or moving away for the winter. Animals that are active all through the year change their colour to match the landscape. The arctic fox is white in winter and brown in summer. Birds like the snow-goose and the arctic tern breed in the tundra, where there are plenty of insects and fish in the summer. They migrate to warmer areas in winter. But sea animals and fish survive in the oceans. ■

▲ Though the summer season is short, flowers bloom in the tundra. Here are rhododendrons flowering in Lapland.

See also
Arctic Ocean
Canada
Finland
Norway
Sweden
Union of Soviet Socialist Republics
Wetlands

Tunisia

Tunisia is a small Arab country on the Mediterranean coast of North Africa. Most of the country is lowland, rising to the Atlas Mountains in the north-west. Evergreen oaks and cork trees grow on the hills. Wheat, grapes and olives grow well in the Mediterranean climate in the north where the majority of the people live.

To the south lies the Sahara Desert. Here date palms grow in the oases, and phosphates are dug from ancient dried up lakes. Both are valuable exports. Oil and natural gas are found deep under the desert and are more than enough for Tunisia's own needs.

Flashback

Carthage, now a suburb of Tunis, was once the home of Hannibal, who in 218 BC took elephants as well as an army from Spain over the Alps to try to conquer Rome. Later Tunisia became part of the Roman empire. There are ruins of Roman aqueducts, towns and villas scattered over the country. Many of these buildings had splendid mosaic floors which have been preserved in the dry climate.

In the 7th century AD Muslim Arabs conquered North Africa, and from the 16th century Tunisia was part of the Ottoman empire. It was ruled by France from 1881 until 1956, when it became independent. ■

Area
164,150 sq km
(63,378 sq miles)
Capital
Tunis
Population
7,205,100
Language
Arabic, French
Religion
Muslim, Jewish, Christian
Government
Parliamentary republic
Currency
1 dinar = 1,000 millimes

See also
Africa
Muslims
Ottoman empire
Roman ancient history
Sahara

Biography
Hannibal

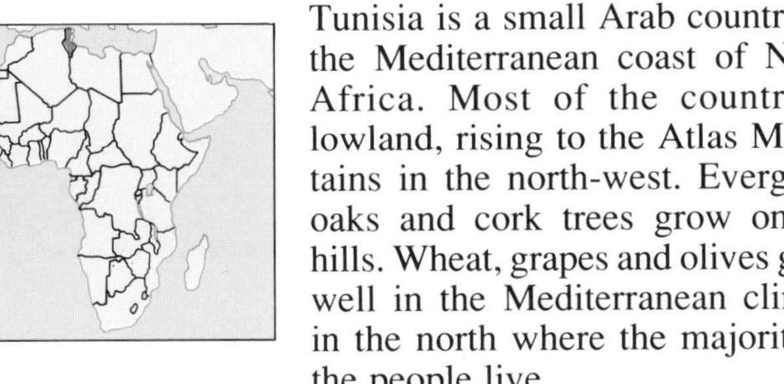

Tunnels

London's Underground
Over a million people use London's underground trains every day.
The longest tube tunnel is 28 km (17 miles) long and runs from Finchley to Morden. During World War II, Londoners used the tube tunnels to shelter from bombs.

Tunnels are underground passages that have usually been made for a particular purpose. Some are very large and have been built for canals, railways or roads. They enable us to travel under cities, rivers and even seas. Some provide a route through hills and mountains, making journeys shorter. Before the tunnel under Mont Blanc was opened in 1958, it was impossible for vehicles to cross the Alps from the Chamonix valley in France to Italy. Miners dig tunnels to obtain coal, metals, diamonds and gold. A network of small tunnels under cities is used to carry water, sewage and cables.

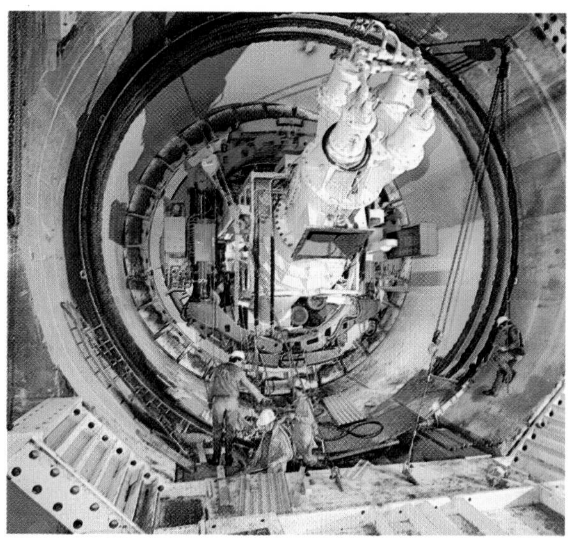

► The Channel Tunnel project is the largest civil engineering project this century. Eleven tunnelling machines have been used to dig the 50 km (31 miles) of tunnel.

Constructing tunnels

Building tunnels is difficult and dangerous. Keeping water out and supplying fresh air is often a problem. Early tunnels were dug by hand. Explosives became available in the 17th century and made the removal of rock easier. To prevent tunnels from collapsing they have to be supported by hydraulic jacks or lined with metal or concrete sections. Tunnelling machines were invented in the 19th century. Today's tunnelling machines have huge, very hard drilling bits that remove large amounts of rock at great speed. Robot 'moles', controlled from the surface, are being developed, and lasers may be used in the future. ■

See also
Canals
Explosives
Mining
Railways
Roads

Turbines

The first practical steam turbine was built by Charles Parsons in England in 1884.

A windmill is a type of turbine. So is a water-wheel. Turbines are huge wheels with fan-like blades or vanes on them. When a stream of moving liquid or gas strikes them, they spin round. Most turbines are turned by air, water, steam or hot gas. They have a shaft through the middle which is used to drive other machinery.

► A low pressure steam turbine rotor to be used in a power-station.

Ninety-five per cent of the world's electricity is made using turbines.

Types

There are two main types of turbine. Radial flow turbines work like water-wheels, where the water hits the edge of the wheel. Axial flow turbines work like windmills, where the blades face into the wind. Modern axial flow turbines can have hundreds of blades.

Uses

Turbines have many uses. Water turbines drive the generators in hydroelectric power-stations. They are turned by water rushing from a river or dam. Steam turbines are spun round by jets of steam from a huge boiler. They drive the generators in coal, oil, gas and nuclear power-stations. They also turn the propellers in some ships. Gas turbines are used in jet engines. They are pushed round by the jet of hot gas which shoots out of the back of the engine. They are used to turn the compressor which sucks in air at the front of the engine. Some people call the whole engine a 'gas turbine'. ■

See also
Electricity supply
Hydroelectric power
Jet engines
Nuclear power
Steam-engines

Turkey

Turkey is a country at the eastern end of the Mediterranean Sea. A small part, called Thrace, is in Europe, but most of the country is in Asia. Dividing the two parts is a strait called the Bosporus. The Asian part, called Anatolia, has a high central plateau surrounded by mountains. Mount Ararat, the highest peak at 5,165 m (16,945 ft), is supposed to be the resting place of Noah's Ark, as told in the Bible. The central area is largely agricultural, growing cereal crops, but many small boys watch over sheep grazing in the dry countryside. The shepherd boys have dogs that help drive off the wolves.

Turkey's biggest city, Istanbul, bridges the Bosporus and is the only city to be built in two continents. It is a lively city with a busy port. Turkey is a Muslim country, and on Istanbul's skyline you can see many towers and minarets of mosques such as the Blue Mosque and the Mosque of Suleiman the Magnificent.

Flashback

From the 15th century, Turkey was ruled by the Ottomans, a Turkish tribe. By the 16th century the Ottoman empire included a large part of Europe and the Middle East and most of North Africa. The capital was Constantinople, today's Istanbul. The Ottoman empire slowly declined over the next 400 years and finally came to an end after World War I. The father of modern Turkey was Mustafa Kemal Atatürk, a general who changed the alphabet to a Latin script and made Turkey more westernized. ■

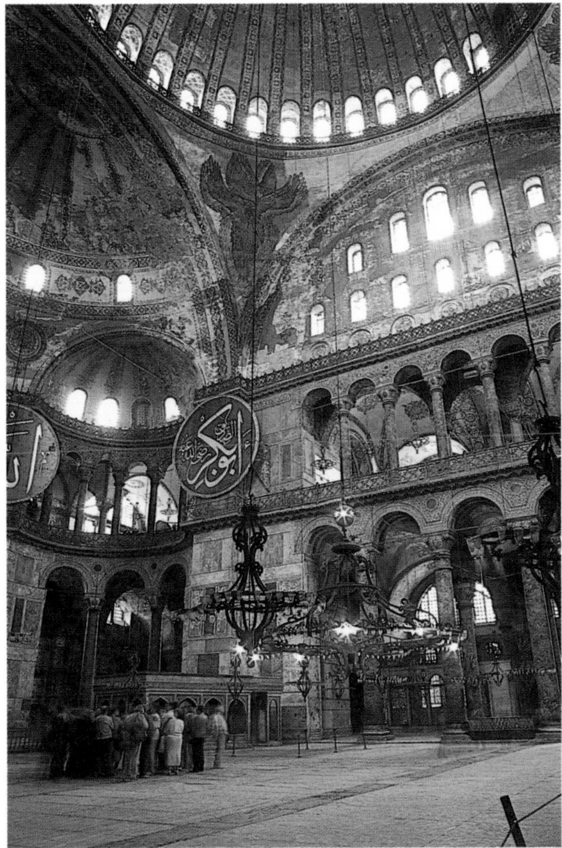

◄ **Inside the Sulimanye mosque, Istanbul.**

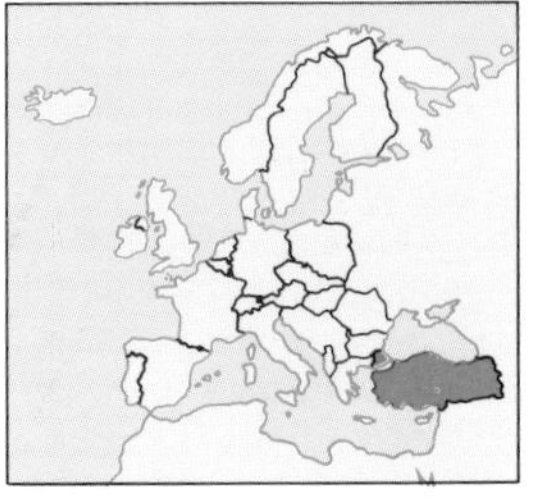

Area
779,452 sq km
(300,948 sq miles)
Capital Ankara
Population 50,670,000
Religion Muslim
Government
Parliamentary republic
Currency
1 Turkish lira = 100 kurus (piastres)

See also
Asia
Europe
Kurds
Mediterranean
Middle East
Mosques
Muslims
Ottoman empire

Biography
Atatürk
Suleiman I (the Magnificent)

Turtles

The word 'turtle' is sometimes used for all of the shelled reptiles. These include the land tortoises, the freshwater terrapins and the sea turtles. Their shell is made of horny plates covering bone. On the inside of this, their backbone, ribs and some other bones are attached. This makes them very stiff and slow-moving creatures.

All of the turtles have toothless jaws, edged with sharp bone to chop up their food. The largest turtles, the great sea turtles, feed on many sorts of marine plants and animals, including jellyfish. They spend most of their lives at sea, but during the breeding season they visit shallow water to mate, then at night the females come ashore to lay their eggs. They take most of the night to dig a pit and lay up to 200 eggs. These take about three months to hatch. The young turtles then dig their way out of the nest and go down to the sea. They have many predators, including humans, and large numbers are killed before they are old enough to breed. ■

◄ **Green turtle, having come ashore at night to lay its eggs, digs a nest.**

Distribution
Mainly in warm oceans, nesting on tropical shores
Largest
Leathery turtle: measures over 2 m in length and weighs over 500 kg
Lifespan Up to 50 years

Subphylum Vertebrata
Class Reptilia
Order Chelonia
Number of species 8

See also
Armoured animals
Reptiles
Terrapins
Tortoises

Industry
In 1900 many millions of men and women laboured long hours at heavy jobs in mines, quarries and factories. Conditions were often dangerous. Many such jobs are now done by machines.

Travel
1n 1900 long-distance travel had to be done by rail or by ship. In towns there were trams or horse-drawn vehicles, and some travelled by bicycle. For many families a long journey was a rare and exciting event.

Communications
At the beginning of the century all contact between separated families and friends was by letter. Telephones and telegraph were already being used by businesses.

Twentieth-century history

The world has changed more in the 20th century than in any other century. Since 1900, people have conquered the air and explored space. Radio and television have brought distant peoples together. Diseases have been brought under control. Many more children are educated. But although there have been wonderful inventions and discoveries, many nations are still poor. Famine and disease afflict millions.

Beyond the suburbs of some of the world's big cities there are slums and shanty towns. In 1990 about 30 million children had no settled homes and were living on the streets. Throughout the century people have been made homeless by wars and by disputes over land, and many children are born to live out their lives in squalid refugee camps. When we say that we now have television, video, cars and comfortable homes, we really mean that some of us have these things. And, of course, many of the century's great inventions have brought death and danger with them.

Population

The world's population in 1900 was 1,550 million. A quarter of the world's people lived in Europe. By the end of the century the world's population may reach over 6,000 million, and many more people live outside Europe. In China alone there are over 1,000 million people. The world cannot get bigger to make room for extra people. There is only one Earth to give us food from its soil and materials from its mines.

► **The waterfront of Singapore in the early years of the century.**

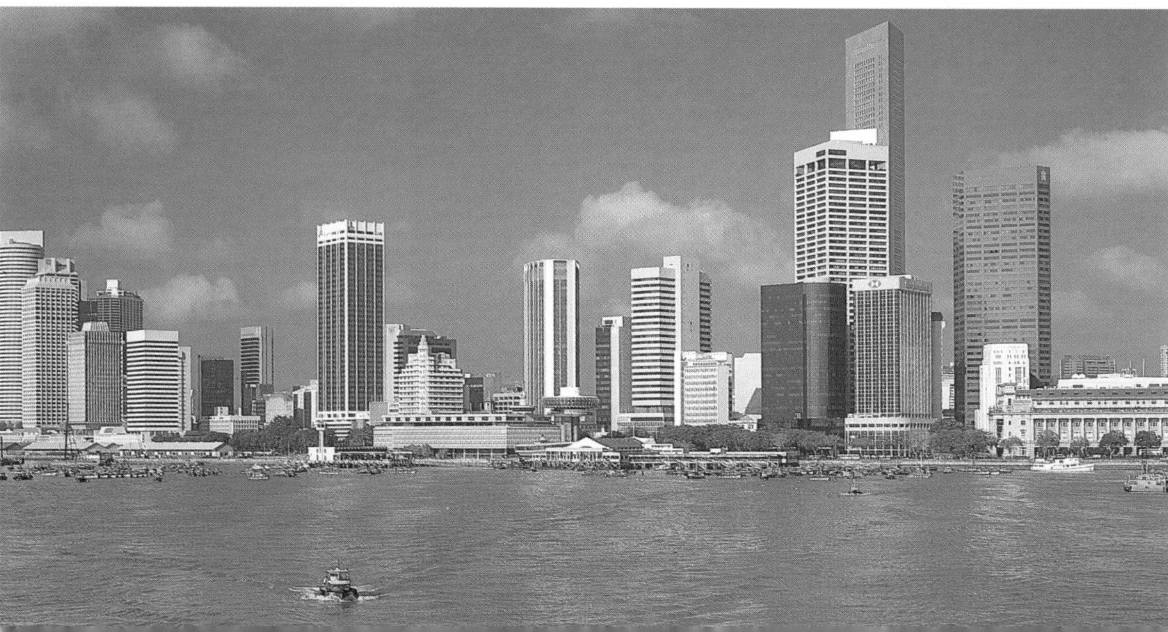

► **By 1987 Singapore city had grown enormously and the skyline had completely changed.**

Cities

◄ This photograph was taken in the East End of London in 1912. All over Europe and North America there were communities so poor that they could not afford shoes for their children. At this period there was no Welfare State. The gap between rich and poor was enormous.

In 1900 most of the world's people lived in small villages. Even important cities were not nearly so big as they are now. Through the century people have moved into the cities. Nearly all the world's towns and cities have spread outwards into the country and upwards into the sky. Urban living has been made possible by better transport and better building methods. For some, town living is convenient and pleasant. The shops are near by, there are places to go for entertainment. For a poor person, though, a town can be a grim and violent place.

Technology

Today, if your family can afford these things and chooses to use them, you can get a meal from the freezer, cook it in seconds in the microwave and put your plate in the dishwasher. Then you can phone up a friend and decide either to go to a film or stay in and watch the video.

The technology that makes this possible has developed since 1900. At the beginning of the century, in Britain, Europe or North America, a family's washing would be done by mother, or by a servant if the family had enough money. She would wash by hand, in tubs, using water heated on a stove and carried in buckets. Food would be prepared in the house and cooked on a coal or wood stove. For most of the world's people, of course, life is still like that.

Ease of travel and ways of keeping in touch have also made it possible for people to live a long way from their work. Some people travel 100 miles to work every day, and very many travel 20 or 30. Computer links mean that some people can do their work at home. A journalist or an accountant can work on a computer and then send the results down a line to the office or to a colleague also working at home.

The global village

In 1900 'the ends of the earth' seemed far off. Distant people were strange folk in books and magazines. America was a week away from Europe by ship; Australia was a five-week journey. Now Australians, Americans, Chinese, Japanese, Argentinians are bound close together by air travel and by telephone, radio and television. We all know much more about each other. All of this ought to make us feel friendly and united: one people on the Earth. But does it?

◄ This photograph was taken in a West African village in 1911. Women use long sticks to pound grain into flour. At this time the vast majority of Africans lived in villages and worked on the land, growing food or herding animals.

◄ African family watching the television in Harare, the capital city of Zimbabwe. For those who can afford to buy consumer goods, furnishing and entertainment are now quite similar the world over.

Children and teenagers

In 1900 few people went to school. Even in industrial Western countries such as Britain, France and the USA, most children went to school for only a few years. Now, all over the world, there are schools for most children, and in Western countries the majority stay at school well into their teens. In poor countries, education is highly valued, and governments try hard to provide it. The world is much more complicated now, and people need to be educated to cope with it. In 1900 a person could get by and do various jobs without being able to read, and many had to do so. Now a non-reader in a Western country has serious problems in dealing with everyday life.

By the 1990s a supersonic aircraft could fly from New York to London in less than three hours. Even the journey from America to Australia can be done in less than fifteen hours.

In 1900 you were either a child or an adult. Now people from 13 to 18 have their own entertainment scene: music, clothes, films, clubs. Although the idea of the 'teenager' is a Western one, television and travel have spread it throughout the world, even into countries where adults are still faithful to their traditional way of life.

The phrase 'Cold War' was first used in 1947 by Bernard Baruch, an adviser to the American President.

Empires break up

From space the globe looks the same now as it did in 1900. A map of the world however looks very different. During the first half of this century Britain, France, The Netherlands and other European countries had empires which stretched across the world.

Most of Africa, the Caribbean, Oceania, and huge areas of Asia were colonized and ruled by Europeans. Before 1914 much of the Middle East was part of the Ottoman empire. Gradually these empires disintegrated and the power of the European states grew less.

New nations

Many new nations have come into being and some ancient ones have regained their independence. In 1947 India and Pakistan became independent countries within the Commonwealth. In Africa France gave independence to Morocco and Tunisia in 1956 and the following year Britain gave independence to Ghana. Over the next ten years many more independent African states were formed but often these new nations were born after conflict. The struggle of the Jewish people for a homeland created the new state of Israel.

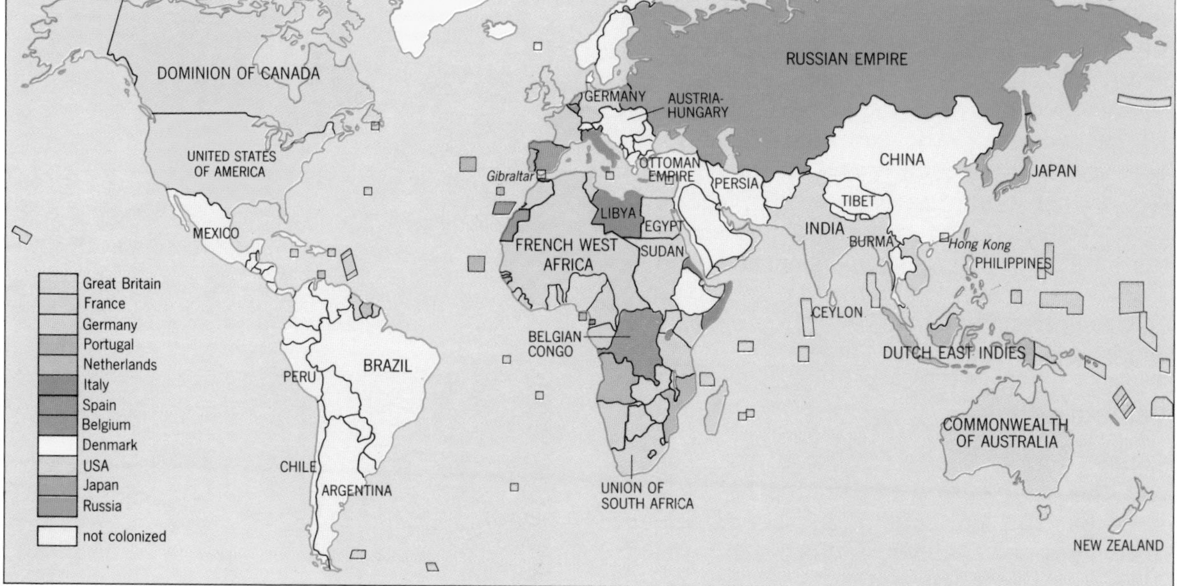

► In 1900 the European powers ruled over large parts of the world. The French, Dutch, Belgians, Germans, Portuguese, Spanish and British all controlled colonies overseas.

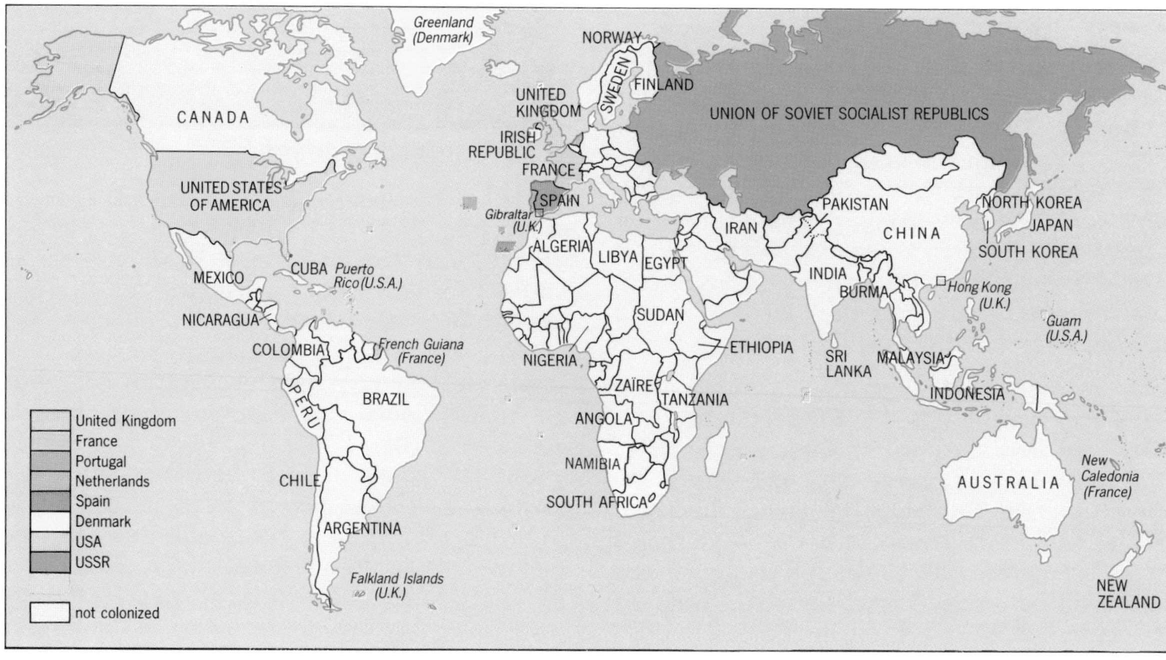

► By 1990 there were many more independent countries. The European empires had gradually broken up. New nations had formed and ancient ones regained their independence.

Conflicts and war

The 20th century has seen two world wars. Each of them deeply affected the nations which took part. World War II, particularly, showed how tremendously strong the USA and the USSR had become. After that war, Europe lost its world leadership to these two countries.

After World War II, the USA and the USSR were suspicious of each other, even though they had fought on the same side. Each country believed that the other wanted to dominate the world. The Americans and other people with democratic governments feared that the USSR would use its power to force more nations to adopt a communist form of government. This led to hostility, refusal to trade and a lot of threatening behaviour. This post-war period was called 'the Cold War' and it went on, sometimes very cold, sometimes a little warmer, right up to the late 1980s.

◀ Weapons were more destructive than ever. In the Vietnam War napalm bombs were used. These children were running to save their lives after being burnt by napalm in 1972. The naked girl recovered after several skin grafts but suffered pain for years afterwards.

After World War II and the atomic bomb, another world war seemed unthinkable. There were many smaller conflicts, however. The Korean War (1950–1953) and the Vietnam War (1963–1975) were both caused by suspicion between communist and non-communist countries. Most other recent conflicts have been either caused by or affected by the same suspicions. The fighting between Jews and Arabs in the Middle East seems at first to have no connection with the Cold War, but in fact the USA wanted to preserve Israel as a friend so that the USSR would not dominate the area.

Suspicion between communist and democratic nations poisoned the second half of this century. It caused billions of pounds to be spent on weapons. It caused concrete and barbed-wire barriers to go up between countries. It split Europe into two blocs: the western democratic countries and the communist eastern bloc. This division lasted until the collapse of the communist governments in eastern Europe in the revolutions of 1989.

Democracies, dictators, communists

All through the century, we have seen countries changing their methods of government. Some, including the USA and the United Kingdom, are proud of their democracy; democracy means that everybody votes and everybody has a chance of standing for election to Congress or Parliament. Some, like Italy and Spain and Germany, for a long time had dictatorships.

Others became communist, with a strong belief in control of production and distribution of goods by the central government. Each country has thought its own ideas to be the best, and this has often led to conflict and sometimes to war. No system is perfect, however, and what suits one country might not suit another.

Energy and food

Since 1900 we have used more and more energy, getting much of it from coal and oil taken from the earth. We have also needed to grow much more food to feed the increased population. The struggle for food and energy is perhaps the most important struggle of all. Countries which have oil under their land have become rich. Countries which have problems growing food have become poorer. But farmers can produce enough food for all the people of the world and there are surpluses of most cereal crops. There are plenty of sources of energy, including nuclear power and wind, water and tidal power. Technologists are able to solve most problems of supply. They cannot solve problems of inequality of wealth.

Unsolved problems

A hundred years ago, when people looked into the future, they hoped for a better world in which there would be no more disease and no more war. Now we see that, as some problems are solved, others take their place. New diseases claim lives. Famine still strikes. Wars still break out when countries cannot solve their problems peacefully. People are not perfect, and the world may never be perfect. But, at least, there was no major world war between 1945 and 1990. ■

◀ In 1985 a huge televised pop concert, Live Aid, raised money for the starving in African countries. Teenagers and others across the world enjoyed the same music and shared their concern for the poor.

See also

Aircraft
British history 1919–1989
Cities
Cold war
Communists
Democracy
Dictators
Farming
France's history
German history
Industry
Japan's history
Nuclear power
Pop and rock music
Population: human
Radio
Russia's history
Schools
Spain's history
Television
Transport
United Nations
USA: history
Vietnam
World War I
World War II

By the fourth quarter of the twentieth century, oil-rich countries such as Saudi Arabia had an income per person as high as that in Europe, America or Japan.

Type

This encyclopedia has been set in two typefaces. The main text has been set in 11 pt Times Roman, a serif face. The headings, marginal notes and captions have been set in News Gothic, a sans serif face. The main headings are set in bold in 18 pt. The margin notes are set in 8 pt.

Type is the term used to describe letters, numbers or any character used in printing. Originally each letter was cut out of a piece of wood or metal, but today most type is produced using a typesetting machine which is very similar to a word processor.

There are hundreds of different typefaces, but most fit into three categories; serif, sans serif (without serifs) and script.

serif — ascender
gh
serif
72 points
x-height
xy
descender

serif sans serif script
typo gra *phy*

Each typeface can be set in a range of different styles,

Roman *Italic*
Bold ***Bold italic***

and in different sizes. Type is measured in points; there are 72 points in 25·4 mm (1 inch). ■

Typewriters

See also
Word processors

Typewriters let you write letters and articles as if they were printed. Some typewriters are powered by electricity. Others are manual; they work using the downward force of your fingers. A manual typewriter has lots of long, thin hammers (called type bars) with the shape of a different letter on the end of each one. When you press a key, the hammer flips up and hits an inky ribbon against the paper. In some electric typewriters, the letters are all on a single 'golfball' which rotates into position before hitting the ribbon. Many typewriters have now been replaced by word processors. ■

The first typewriters to go on sale were made by the Remington company in the USA in 1874.

The world's smallest typewriter was only 16 cm square and weighed 90 g.

▼ Most typewriters, computers and word processors have a 'qwerty' keyboard like this. The name comes from the first six letters on the top row.

Tyres

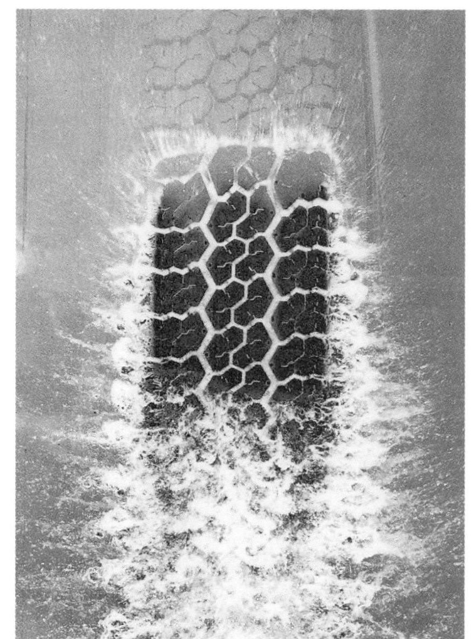

◀ This photograph taken from under a wet glass plate shows, as the car drives over, how the tyre sprays water away and lets the rubber grip the road.

A tyre is a band of rubber or metal, put around a wheel to strengthen it, to prevent it jarring, and to help the wheel grip the road. Most tyres are air-filled and are made of rubber or synthetic plastics that behave like rubber. They are strengthened with cords.

Each car tyre has a tread pattern moulded into it, which is important in wet weather, as it clears water from under the tyre's 'footprint' while the car goes along. The water sprays out through 'sipes' (slits), and the tyre grips dry road. The pattern is not so important for driving on a dry road; but bald tyres are dangerous. Some cars have 'runflat' tyres, filled with foam. When punctured, they can still be used, slowly.

In snowy countries, tyres have studs in the tread for grip; or the driver may fit a chain belt over the tyre.

Flashback

Metal cart tyres were heated to expand them, and slipped onto wooden cartwheels. When the wheel was plunged into water the metal shrank onto the wheel, holding it together. Solid rubber tyres were used on early cars and bicycles, but it was Robert Thomson, in 1845, who invented the air-filled (pneumatic) tyre, and John Boyd Dunlop, in 1888, who developed it. ■

See also
Motor cars
Wheels

Biography
Dunlop

UFOs

The name 'unidentified flying object' or UFO was first used by the United States Air Force in 1953. Before that time most people spoke of 'flying saucers' or, in the Soviet Union, 'flying sickles'.

The letters 'UFO' are the initials of the words 'unidentified flying object'. A UFO might be anything someone sees in the sky and cannot explain. The kinds of things people claim to see are mysterious lights or 'flying saucers'.

Most sightings can probably be explained quite easily, either as natural things such as clouds or lightning, or as man-made things such as aircraft, satellites or scientific balloons.

Some people imagine that UFOs are signs of living visitors from space. Others have deliberately set out to create a hoax by faking photographs and telling lies. So far, no one has produced evidence that will satisfy the majority of scientists that life exists beyond the Earth. ■

Ulster

Ulster is a former province in the northern part of the island of Ireland. To the north-east is a large lake called Lough Neagh, while to the north and north-west rise the mountains of Antrim and Derryveagh.

The region was colonized by Britain in the 16th and 17th centuries. In 1920, six of Ulster's nine counties remained part of the United Kingdom and were called Northern Ireland. The other three counties became part of what is now the Irish Republic.

For hundreds of years there have been problems between the two main religious groups: Catholics and Protestants. Some want Ulster to be reunited as part of the Irish Republic, others want it to remain divided and partly in the United Kingdom. ■

The six counties of Ulster which form Northern Ireland are Antrim, Down, Armagh, Londonderry, Tyrone and Fermanagh.
The three in the Republic of Ireland are Monaghan, Cavan and Donegal.

See also
Ireland's history
Irish Republic
Northern Ireland

Uganda

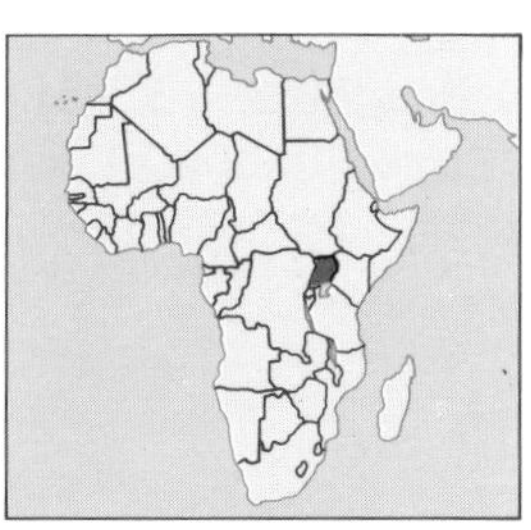

Area
236,036 sq km
(91,259 sq miles)
Capital
Kampala
Population
16,398,000
Language
English, Swahili, Luganda, Nyankole, others
Religion
Christian, Muslim, Traditional
Government
Republic
Currency
1 Uganda shilling = 100 cents

Water covers about a sixth of Uganda. The largest area of water is Lake Victoria, Africa's largest lake, which Uganda shares with Kenya and Tanzania. The northern outlet of Lake Victoria is part of the River Nile.

Most of the north consists of high plains, the centre is marshy, and the south contains Lake Victoria. In western Uganda there are high mountains and a long, deep valley, with several lakes.

About 40 languages are spoken in Uganda. One of them, Luganda, is spoken by the Baganda of central and southern Uganda. Most of the Baganda are farmers, and the women do most of the farm work. They grow plantains, a type of banana, which are picked when they are green. They steam and mash the plantains and eat them with spicy stews. Many farmers also grow coffee, cotton and tea to sell. Some of the people in the dry north are nomads, who rear cattle.

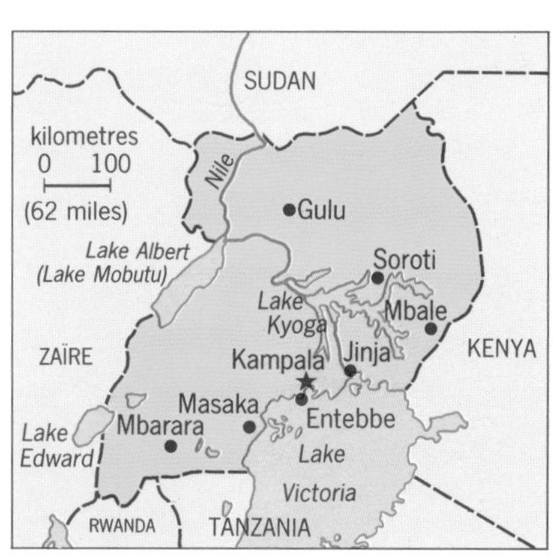

Flashback

When Europeans first came to East Africa, Uganda consisted of several kingdoms. The most powerful was Buganda, the land of the Baganda, which was ruled by a king called the Kabaka. Britain ruled Uganda from 1894 until 1962. In 1963 the Kabaka of Buganda became president of Uganda, but after disputes with the government he was dismissed. In 1967 all the kingdoms, including Buganda, were abolished. ■

See also
Africa
African history

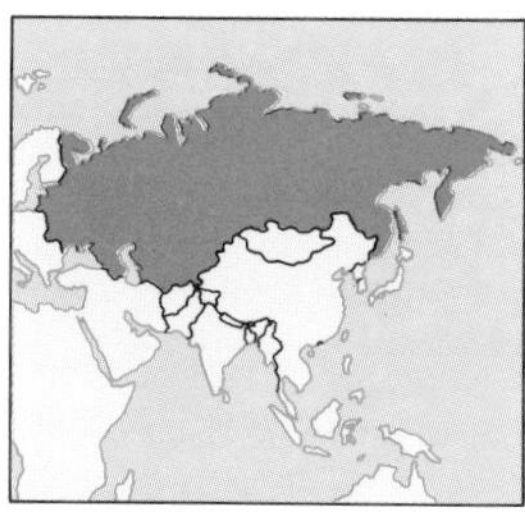

Area 22,402,000 sq km (8,649,461 sq miles)
Capital Moscow
Population 286,700,000
Language Russian, Ukrainian, Belorussian, Georgian, Estonian, Latvian, Lithuanian, Armenian, Turkic
Religion Christian, Muslim, Jewish, Buddhist
Government Communist federal republic
Currency
1 rouble = 100 copecks

Union of Soviet Socialist Republics

The USSR is the biggest country in the world. The initials USSR stand for the Union of Soviet Socialist Republics. On the news you will often hear it called the Soviet Union for short. Soviet means 'council' and in 1989 socialist councils governed the fifteen republics which made up the whole Union.

The country covers nearly one-sixth of the Earth's land surface and lies partly in Europe but mostly in Asia. From east to west it is more than 9,000 km (5,600 miles) and crosses eleven time zones. While people are eating their breakfast in the European part of the USSR, in the Asian Far East they are sitting down to dinner at the end of the same day. You can take a train all the way. The journey takes about a day to cross from the European border to the capital, Moscow. In Moscow you would buy a ticket to Nakhodka and climb aboard for the longest train journey in the world, all of it in the Russian Republic, arriving six days later at the Sea of Japan.

▼ In Moscow, St Basil's Cathedral looks like a fairytale castle in the night sky.

The USSR has the third largest population of any country. Only China and India have more people. Sometimes people call the USSR 'Russia', but Russia is, in fact, just one of the republics. It is by far the largest, and Russians make up about half of the population of the whole country. The official language of the USSR is Russian, too, but there are more than a hundred other languages spoken.

If you live in the Ukraine in the south-west, your mother tongue is probably Ukrainian. Estonians in the north-west speak Estonian. Uzbeks, Kazakhs and others speak languages related to Turkish. People who belong to these different nations are proud of the language and culture of their own ethnic group and many want independence from central government in Moscow.

Religion is also important to some groups, although for over 60 years the communist government stopped people from worshipping freely. Christians mostly belong to the Russian Orthodox Church. The second largest religious group is the Muslims. Most of the USSR's Muslims live in the Caucasus and the Central Asian part of the country, in Kazakhstan, Uzbekistan and other republics on the borders with Iran and Afghanistan. Many of these peoples are strongly influenced by Persian (Iranian) culture. There are Buddhists in Siberia and there is a large Jewish population in the USSR, which has been persecuted for many years.

Mountains

The European and Asian parts of the USSR are separated by the Ural Mountains. The Urals are not very big mountains. The highest point is Mount Narodnaya which is less than 2,000 m (6,500 ft) high. The USSR's largest mountains are on the southern borders. The Caucasus Mountains, between the Black Sea and the Caspian Sea, contain Europe's highest peak, Mount Elbrus, an extinct volcano. But the highest mountain in the USSR is called Communism Peak. Communism Peak lies in the Pamir Mountains near the border with Afghanistan and China.

Central Asia: seas, plains and desert

Lake Balkhash in Soviet Central Asia is a great freshwater lake. It is frozen for five months of the year, but provides a quarter of all the trout eaten in the USSR. In winter, Lake Balkhash suffers from terrible blizzards blown from the

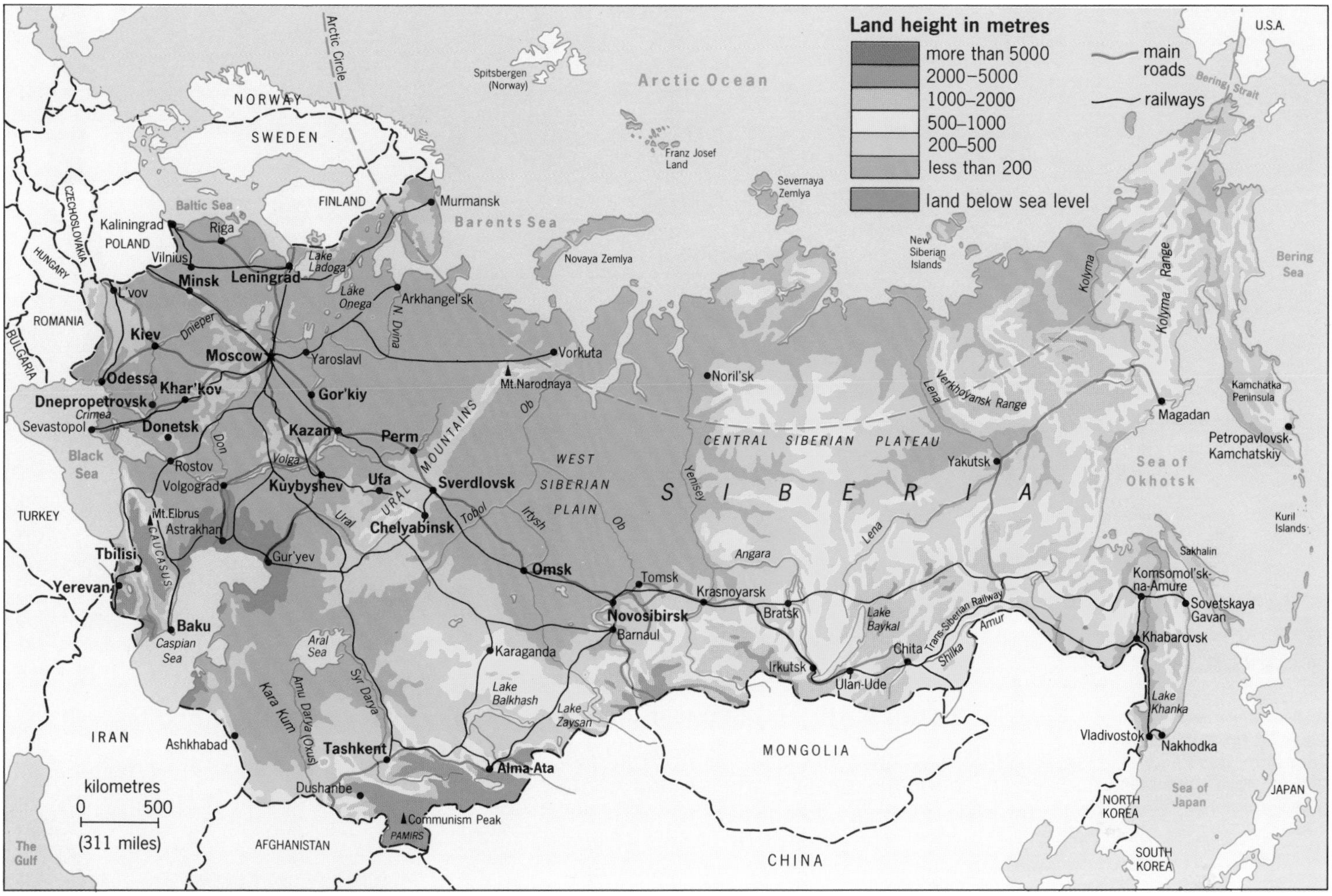

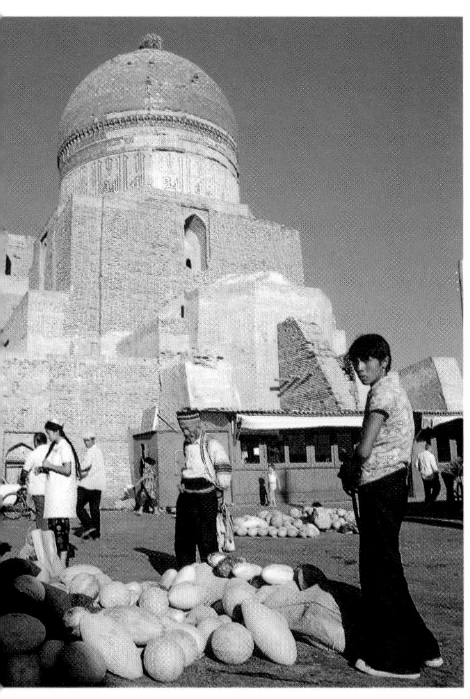

▲ **Melon sellers show their wares in front of a mosque in Uzbekistan.**

mountains on the nearby border with China. The winds in these mountains are so fierce that in one mountain pass, called the Dzungarian Gate, no trees can grow.

Lake Balkhash is in Kazakhstan, a vast area of flat grassy plains where much of the USSR's wheat is grown. To the south and west of Kazakhstan are two of the world's largest inland seas: the Aral Sea and the Caspian Sea. But in recent years both these seas have been shrinking, as water has been taken from their tributary rivers for agriculture and industry. To the east of the Caspian Sea are the deserts of Soviet Central Asia. One of these deserts is known as Karakum, which means 'black sands' in the Turkmen language. It is a great sandy desert with dark-coloured dunes.

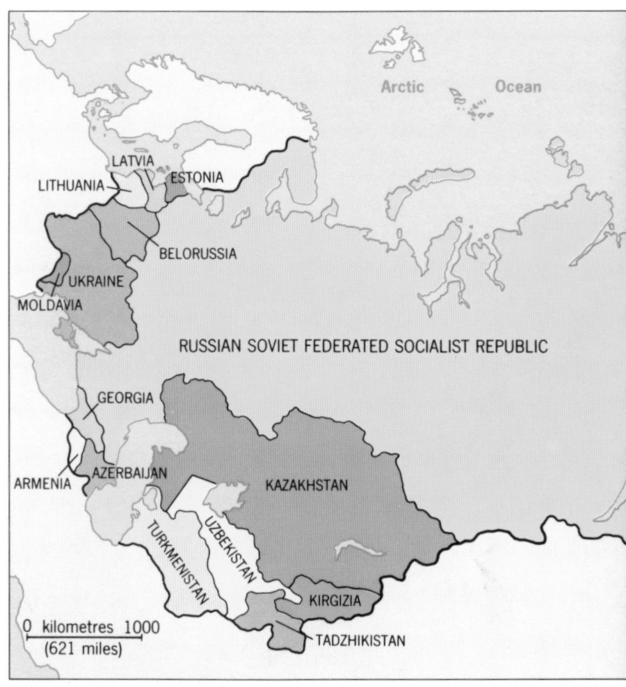

▲ **Map showing the republics of the USSR.**

▲ A winter scene in a Siberian town. Daylight hours are short. The temperature stays below freezing for months on end.

Siberia: frozen earth and deepest lake

The largest region in the USSR is Siberia, which stretches from the Urals to the Pacific coast region. The northern parts of Siberia are in the Arctic Circle. Here areas of the Arctic Ocean are permanently covered in ice and snow. South from the Arctic coast is a vast area of tundra, where it is so cold that the soil is always frozen solid and the only things that can grow are mosses, lichens, grass and small trees. South of the tundra lies the taiga, the largest area of coniferous forests in the world. If you were to take your train journey across the USSR in spring as the snows are melting, you would see Siberia turning from a frozen land to one of green birch and larch trees and swamps. During the summer it gets unpleasantly hot and the marshes are plagued by mosquitoes.

Siberia has some mighty rivers. The River Ob flows north into the Arctic Ocean. The Ob and its chief tributary, the River Irtysh, which rises in northern China, are 5,570 km (3,460 miles) long, the world's fifth longest river. In the south-east of Siberia is a land of steep mountains and deep valleys. Lake Baykal, the world's deepest lake, is in one of these valleys. At its deepest point it is 1,741 m (5,712 ft) deep. Over 300 rivers flow into the lake, but just one flows out. The Trans-Siberian Railway runs along the southern shore of Lake Baykal. The lake used to be famous for its crystal clear waters but is now badly polluted. Smoked sturgeon, a fish from Lake Baykal, may be on the menu in the railway restaurant car. The tiny eggs of these sturgeon are called caviare, and this is a great delicacy served in restaurants all over the USSR. To the east of Siberia is a great peninsula the size of Britain called Kamchatka. Kamchatka has a cold and wet climate and is a land of active volcanic mountain ranges.

Europe

Much of the European USSR is a great low-lying plain, with a cool dry climate. In the south, the area around the Black Sea is popular for holidays. Its climate does not get the winter snows that the rest of the USSR does, and the summers are dry and sunny. In the streets of Moscow snow lies on the ground for five months every year, and the region around the capital is marshy in many parts during the summer.

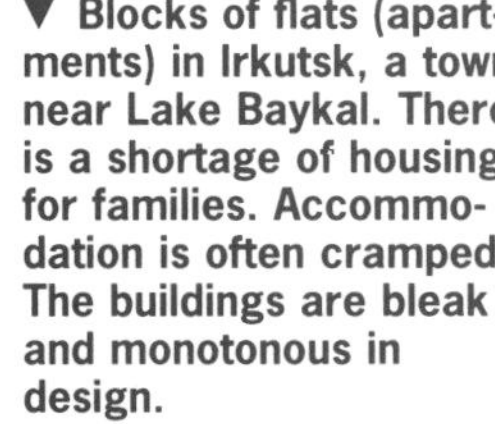

▼ Blocks of flats (apartments) in Irkutsk, a town near Lake Baykal. There is a shortage of housing for families. Accommodation is often cramped. The buildings are bleak and monotonous in design.

Moscow

About 75 per cent of the USSR's population live and work in the European part of the country. A walk around Moscow, the USSR's capital, shows some interesting contrasts. Many of the buildings are very bleak and drab blocks of flats. At the centre of Moscow is Red Square, about the size of Trafalgar Square in London. To one side is the Kremlin, the centre of government, rather like a great fortress with high yellow walls. In front of the Kremlin stands the Lenin Mausoleum, where the body of the USSR's first communist ruler lies. The tomb is guarded around the clock and every day long queues of people gather to look at the body. Large areas of the square are roped off, and policemen sternly blow their whistles if you cross the ropes. Smoking is forbidden in Red Square.

Shop windows in Moscow and many other cities are not as well designed as in Britain or North America. For a long time queues of people have been a common sight outside the shops, as the goods inside them are often in short supply. Meat can be difficult to find, but there are always vegetables. A family sitting down to dinner in Moscow may have bread with vegetables such as beetroot and cucumbers and potatoes.

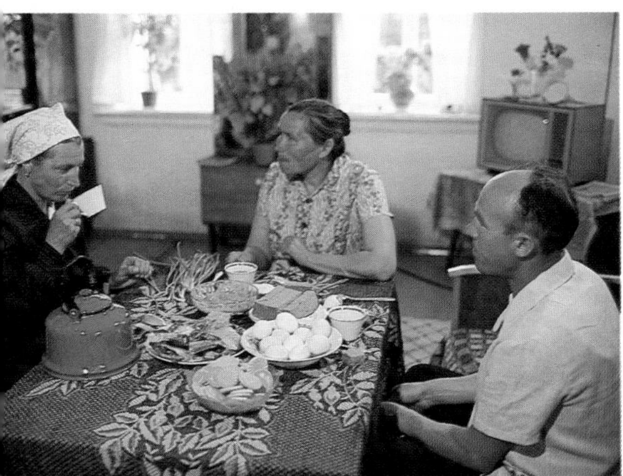

◀ These workers are eating lunch in their home. On the table are plates of hard-boiled eggs, smoked fish, bread and biscuits. Tea is drunk at most meals.

Farms and fish

Much of the agricultural land in the USSR has been owned by the state since the 1920s. Many farms are known as 'collective farms'. On these farms the workers are required to produce a certain amount of food that they must sell to the state at a fixed price. Any extra food can be eaten on the farm or sold in local markets. Farm workers also produce food on their own plots of land which they can eat or sell. In recent years the government has been trying to get more food into the shops to shorten the queues.

The USSR is also one of the greatest fishing nations of the world. Soviet fleets catch fish all over the world as well as from their own lakes and seas.

Industry and resources

The USSR is a great industrial nation. It produces all sorts of goods that are sold inside the country and in eastern Europe. The country contains large deposits of nearly all the minerals used in modern industry. It produces over a quarter of the total world production of asbestos, chromium ore, gold, iron ore, manganese ore, mercury, potash and sulphur. There is also plenty of coal, oil, natural gas and sites for hydroelectric energy.

The big problem with these vast reserves of minerals and energy is that many are located in very remote parts of Siberia. The government pays extra money to encourage people to move to these areas to work in the mines, because these are not pleasant parts of the world in which to live and work. The winters are very hard, bitterly cold, and in northern Siberia the Sun may shine only for an hour or so each day for months on end. Sunshine gives important vitamins to the skin and body, so children have to stand around ultraviolet lights for a certain time each day at school to make up for the lack of sunlight. The cold also makes the mining difficult. Special machinery is needed to work in the freezing conditions, and all buildings must be heavily insulated to keep warm. Frozen ground tends to bulge after it is disturbed. In some Siberian cemeteries coffins buried in the summer are pushed to the surface again the following winter.

Education

Children may go to nursery school from the age of three, or as young as six months if both parents are working. But compulsory schooling starts at age seven and lasts for eight years. Children go to the same General Educational School. For the first three years in the Primary classes, they wear uniform: white shirts and black shorts for boys, and lace aprons and white bows in their hair for girls.

There is no streaming or selection, but there are specialized secondary schools for music, ballet, art, engineering, technical and other subjects. Most children, however, go to the local General School for the full eight years. They can stay on for two more years from the age of fifteen to seventeen, if they choose, and can then go on to University. ■

▲ The fruit market at Frunze in Kirgizia in the south of the USSR.

See also
Asia
Christians
Communists
Europe
Muslims
Russia's history

United Arab Emirates

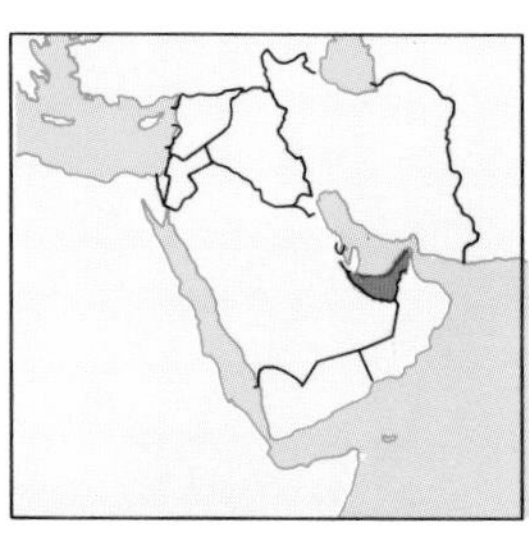

Area 83,600 sq km (32,280 sq miles)
Capital Abu Dhabi
Population 1,600,000
Language Arabic, English
Religion Muslim, Christian
Government Federation of sheikhdoms
Currency 1 UAE dirham = 1,000 fils

The United Arab Emirates (UAE) is a grouping of seven small Gulf states on the northern tip of south-east Arabia under one national flag. They are: Abu Dhabi, Dubai, Sharjah, Ras al-Khaimah, Fujeirah, Umm al-Quwain and Ajman. Each is led by a sheikh from a ruling family. Abu Dhabi is a major oil producer and is the leading power within the UAE. Until the 1960s this remote area of desert and rugged mountains was home for just a small number of fishermen and traders. After the discovery of oil, modern cities sprang up. The UAE was created in 1971 after British forces left the Gulf. ■

See also
Arabia
Arabs
Muslims
Oil

United Kingdom

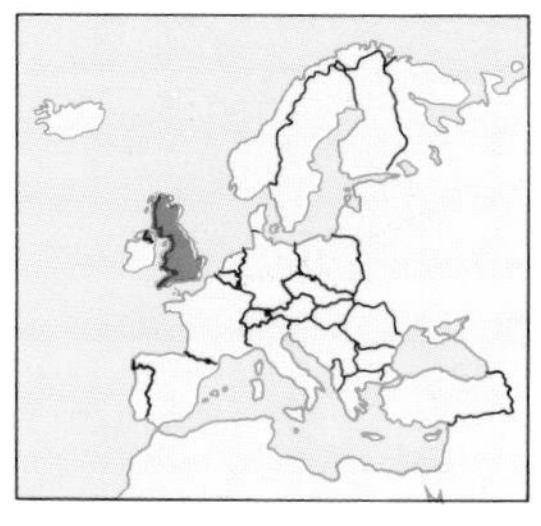

Area 244,046 sq km (94,227 sq miles)
Capital London
Population 56,972,700
Language English, Welsh, Gaelic
Religion Christian, Jewish, others
Government Parliamentary monarchy
Currency 1 pound sterling = 100 pence

The United Kingdom is a country in north-west Europe. It is often called simply the UK, but the full name is the United Kingdom of Great Britain and Northern Ireland. It is made up of the kingdoms of England and Scotland, the Principality of Wales and the Province of Northern Ireland.

The king or queen is Head of State but entrusts the running of the country to the Government and its ministers. The Channel Islands and the Isle of Man are dependencies of the British Crown but they have their own laws and taxes. The national flag of the UK is the Union Jack.

Flashback

The British Isles were invaded by Celts, Romans, Saxons, Vikings and Normans. Each group of settlers brought their own language and culture. Wales resisted Norman rule but was eventually conquered and united with England in 1282. In 1603 James VI of Scotland became James I of England. England and Scotland have had a common parliament since 1707. In 1801, Ireland was united with the rest of Britain to form the United Kingdom of Great Britain and Ireland. After World War I, southern Ireland broke away to form a separate country, the Irish Republic. ■

See also
British Isles
Commonwealth
England
European Community
Northern Ireland
Scotland
Wales

United Nations

Nearly all the countries in the world belong to the United Nations (UN). The purpose of this body, founded in 1945, is to maintain international peace and security. It provides a place where countries can discuss problems of all kinds.

Every country has a seat in the General Assembly, which meets for three months every year. Day-to-day problems of peace-keeping are handled by the Security Council, which meets all the year round.

The Security Council has five permanent members, China, France, the USSR, the UK and the USA, and ten members who are elected for two-year terms. A secretary-general and a secretariat handle administration.

Much of the work of the UN is carried on by its specialized agencies. These agencies cover such matters as food and agriculture, health, labour, civil aviation and shipping, international postal services, education and finance.

Specialized agencies

FAO Food and Agriculture Organization
ICAO International Civil Aviation Organization
ICJ International Court of Justice
IDA International Development Association
IFC International Finance Corporation
IFAD International Fund for Agricultural Development
ILO International Labour Organization
IMF International Monetary Fund
ITU International Telecommunication Union
UPU Universal Postal Union
UNESCO UN Educational, Scientific and Cultural Organization
UNHCR UN High Commission for Refugees
UNICEF UN International Children's Emergency Fund
World Bank
WHO World Health Organization
WMO World Meteorological Organization

Flashback

A similar body called the League of Nations was founded in 1919, after World War I. It was unable to keep peace and World War II broke out in 1939.

The idea for the United Nations arose from the allies who united to fight against Nazi Germany and Japan. In 1942, 26 of the allies signed a 'Declaration by the United Nations' promising to work for world peace and prosperity. ■

United Nations' Day is October 24.

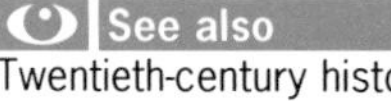
See also
Twentieth-century history

United States of America

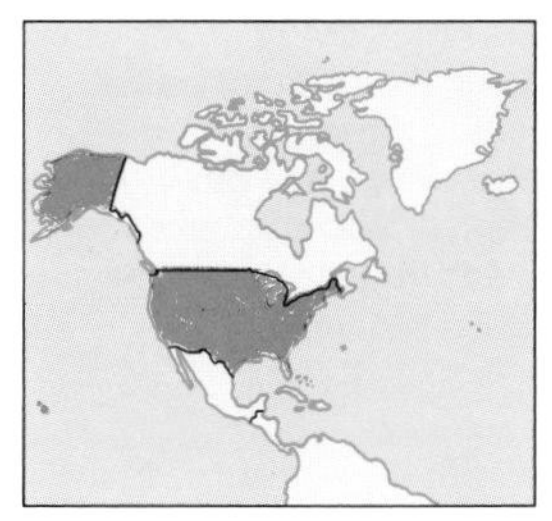

During this century the USA has become the richest and most powerful country in the world. It is the fourth largest country by both land area and population. The USSR, Canada and China have more land, and China, India and the USSR have more people.

The USA is often called just the United States, or more simply 'America', and the people 'Americans'. But this is a mistake, since 'Americans' could be any people living in North, South or Central America, from Canadians to Brazilians.

Forty-eight of the USA's fifty states are together in the main landmass between Canada and Mexico. Alaska, the 49th state, is separated from the rest by Canada. Hawaii was the last state to be made part of the USA. It is in the Pacific Ocean, over 3,700 km (2,300 miles) west of California.

Although the USA has a federal government that organizes the whole country, each state also has its own government and these state governments make their own laws. In the states of California, Florida and Kentucky, for example, the death penalty can be given for very serious crimes, but in Iowa, Maine and Minnesota it cannot. Alcoholic drinks are not allowed to be sold in parts of Alabama and Georgia. The public holidays vary from state to state and the things students learn in school are not always the same in every state.

CONN.	CONNECTICUT
DEL.	DELAWARE
MARY.	MARYLAND
MASS.	MASSACHUSETTS
MISS.	MISSISSIPPI
N.H.	NEW HAMPSHIRE
N.J.	NEW JERSEY
PENN.	PENNSYLVANIA
R. I.	RHODE ISLAND
VER.	VERMONT
W. VA.	WEST VIRGINIA

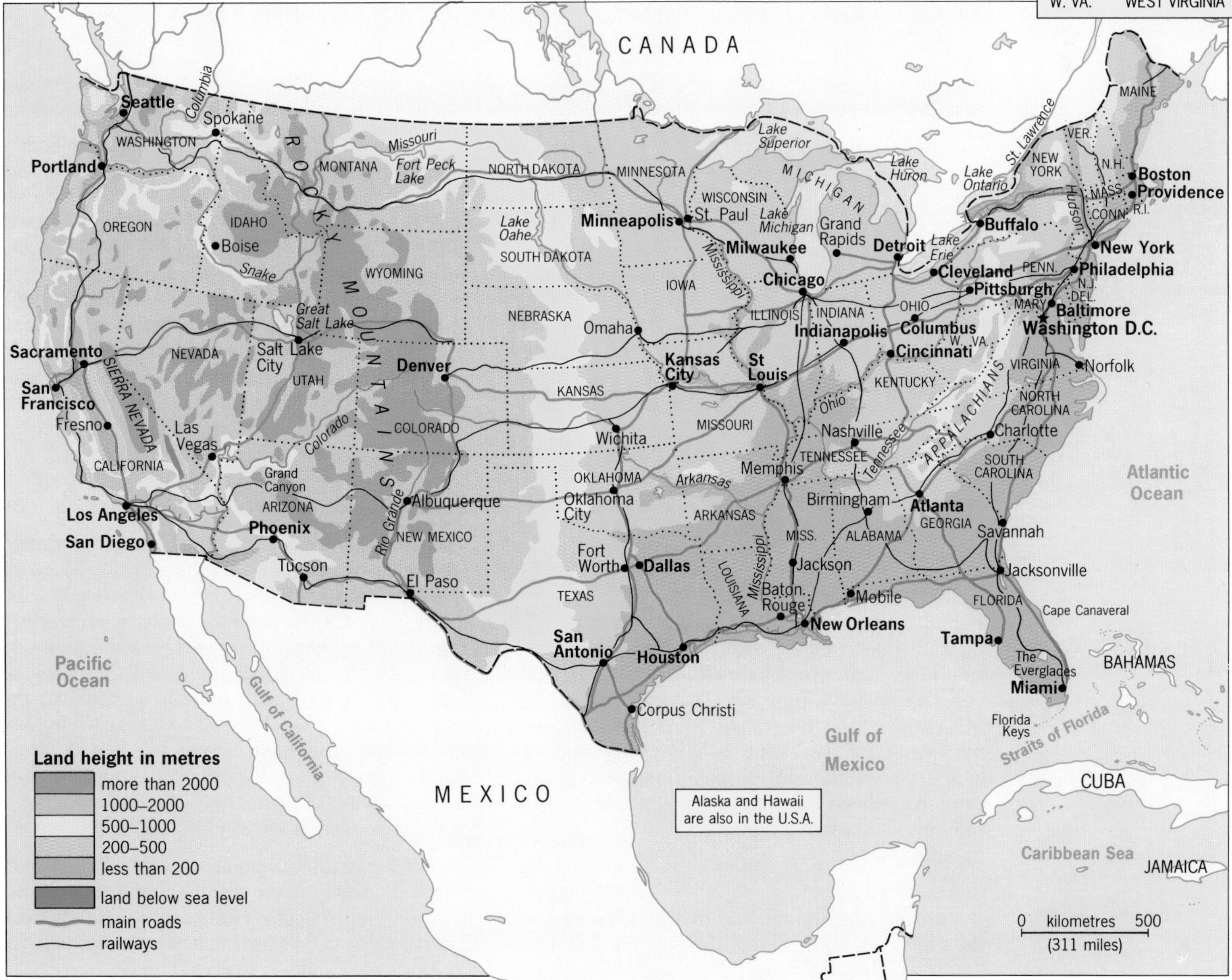

Land height in metres

- more than 2000
- 1000–2000
- 500–1000
- 200–500
- less than 200
- land below sea level
- main roads
- railways

Alaska and Hawaii are also in the U.S.A.

0 kilometres 500 (311 miles)

▶ **Wheatfields in Montana look like a brown and golden patchwork quilt. Summers are dry and dusty. You can see the dust thrown up by the automobile.**

Area
9,372,614 sq km
(3,618,787 sq miles)
Capital
Washington, DC
Population
238,740,000
Language
English, Spanish, German, Italian, others
Religion
Christian, Jewish, Muslim, others
Government
Federal parliamentary republic
Currency
1 dollar = 100 cents

The mainland area of the USA is nearly 40 times the size of the United Kingdom. It is so large that there is a time difference of eight hours between its westernmost point in Alaska and the most easterly spot in the state of Maine. The country includes regions with almost every type of landscape and climate on Earth. In the south-west the states of Arizona and New Mexico have large areas of desert. In the north-west the states of Washington and Oregon have vast forests of beech, chestnut, maple, pine trees and Douglas fir. Some of the southern states, such as Louisiana, have large areas of swamp land, whereas in the states of the north-east, such as Maine, forests of oak, chestnut and yellow poplar trees abound.

Rivers

The Missouri River is the largest river in the USA. It rises in the northern state of Montana and flows into the Mississippi which in turn flows south to the Gulf of Mexico. Together, the Mississippi-Missouri make the fourth longest river system in the world. Both these rivers have had serious floods in the past, and now many dams have been built along their course which can help to control the flow of water.

Another of North America's major rivers, the Colorado River, rises in the Rocky Mountains in the state of Colorado and flows south-west to the Gulf of California in Mexico. On the way the river flows through a spectacular gorge known as the Grand Canyon. Each year nearly three million people visit this canyon in the desert to marvel at the mighty work of nature. It is 350 km (220 miles) long and at its deepest point the river is 1,870 m (6,135 ft) below the surrounding landscape. In some places the gorge is 29 km (18 miles) wide. Downstream of the Grand Canyon the Colorado River is dammed by the Hoover Dam. The waters of the Colorado are used for many irrigation schemes in south-western USA, and arrangements have been made so that there is enough water left in the river for Mexico to use when it crosses the border.

Earthquakes and volcanoes

The Colorado River forms the boundary between the states of Arizona and California. Much of California suffers from earthquakes. If you were to fly over California you could see clearly a line in the landscape from San Francisco, a city on the Pacific coast, all the way to the Gulf of California. This line is a fault line, called the San Andreas Fault. One of the worst earthquakes caused by movements along the San Andreas Fault happened in 1906 in San Francisco. The earthquake and fires that were started by it destroyed much of the city and killed 700 people.

A more recent earthquake, in 1989, killed over 80 people and another could happen at any time. But the warm sunny climate and the beautiful San Francisco Bay make it worth the risk for millions of people to live in the area.

The whole west coast of North America is at the edge of two of the great plates which cover the Earth: the Pacific Plate and the North American Plate. This means that in addition to earthquakes, it is a zone of volcanic activity. In fact, there are not many active volcanoes in mainland USA, but one exploded unexpectedly in the state of Washington in 1980. This was Mount St Helens. The eruption was very violent. It blew the top 400 m (1,300 ft) off the mountain. Sixty-five people were killed and forests were destroyed by the blast up to 20 km (12 miles) away.

Landscapes

Mountains dominate the landscape of the western states but large parts of the middle of the USA are vast, flat plains. Two hundred years ago these plains were grasslands where thousands of buffalo grazed. Today there are few buffalo in the USA. Most of them have been shot for their meat and skins. The grasslands have been ploughed up and planted with crops, especially wheat. The USA is the world's largest exporter of wheat. The Appalachian Mountains have some important coal deposits and are heavily forested. They stretch up to the St Lawrence River in Canada. This river drains into the Atlantic Ocean from a series of five connected lakes known as the Great Lakes. One of these lakes, Lake Michigan, lies totally within the USA, while the other four are shared by the USA and Canada, the border running through their waters. The south-east of the USA, around the Gulf of Mexico, has a humid and subtropical climate. The peninsula that sticks out from this part of the country is the state of Florida. In the south of the state is a subtropical wilderness known as the Everglades, an area of wetlands which includes forests, and swamps with alligators and elegant white birds called ibises.

People

The people of the USA are descended from peoples who migrated to the USA from all over the world. The USA is young for a country and much of the population has grandparents and other relatives who live in other continents including Europe, South America and Asia.

There are also many black Americans whose ancestors lived in Africa and were brought to what is now the USA as slaves. All these people have migrated to the USA to live in the last 400 years. But this land was the home of American 'Indians' for over 25,000 years before people began to arrive from Europe and Africa.

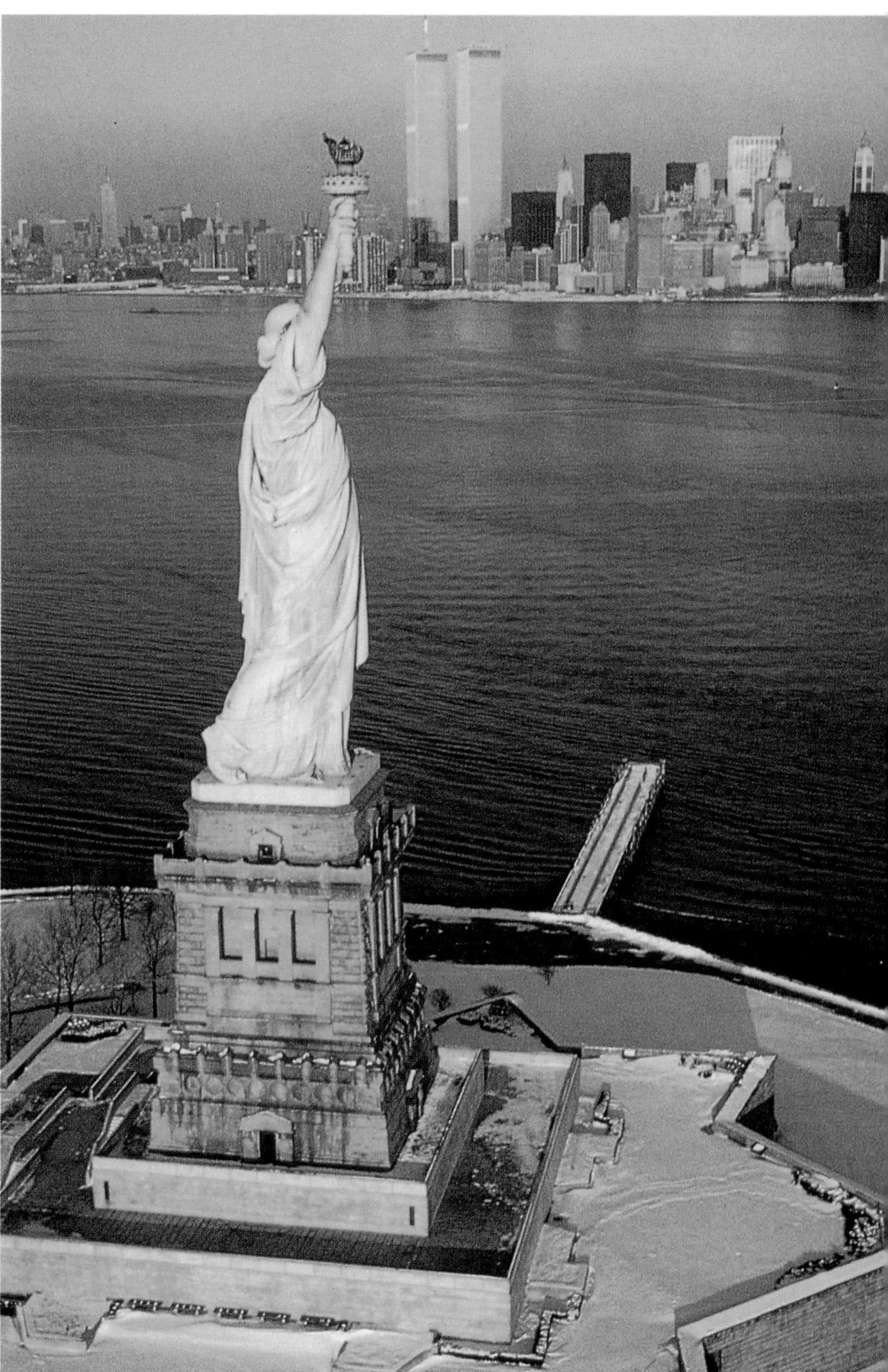

▲ The Statue of Liberty, a symbol of freedom and hope to immigrants arriving by sea from Europe, was a gift from France in 1886.

Cities

Many of the people arriving in the USA in the last 100 years have landed in New York, today the USA's biggest city. One of the first sights seen by the people crowded onto the ships was the Statue of Liberty, a figure of a woman holding a burning torch to the skies, at the entrance to New York harbour.

► Central Park becomes a winter playground in the shadow of Manhattan Island skyscrapers in New York.

Although English is the official language of the country, many other languages are spoken. New York has a number of areas where people have decided to live together because they all originally came from the same country. One part is known as Little Italy. Here people speak Italian. Another area is called Chinatown, where the signs to the shops and restaurants are written in Chinese and the shops sell many Chinese products. The person behind the counter is usually of Chinese descent and speaks Chinese as well as English. Similar areas can be found in many cities. Miami, a city in Florida, has a large population from Cuba who speak Spanish and read local newspapers printed in Spanish. These and other Spanish-speakers are called Hispanics, and most are from Mexico, Puerto Rico and other countries in Central America. Large populations of Hispanics live in Los Angeles, San Francisco and other Californian cities. Cleveland, Ohio, has more people of Hungarian descent than any other city outside Hungary's capital Budapest.

▼ Street vendors in New York.

Communications

Communications inside the USA are extremely good. On average there is one telephone for nearly every person. Most families have a car and some have two or even more. In many cities people can drive to a bank and get money from a machine through the window of their automobile. There are drive-in shops and fast food restaurants selling hamburgers and milk shakes. There is an excellent air transport network in the USA. If you add up the distances flown by all the aeroplanes in the USA the distance is over 4,000 million km (2,500 million miles) each year. This is more than ten times as far as the aeroplanes of any other country.

▲ Minnie Mouse at Disney World, Florida. Since Walt Disney made the first Mickey Mouse short cartoons in the 1920s Disney productions have developed into a multi-million dollar industry including books, music, toys, films, videos, and theme parks. Disney cartoon characters are popular throughout the world.

Leisure

Almost every home has at least one TV set, and there is a wide variety of channels which can be watched by paying a fee to receive them from a satellite or through a special cable. Some channels present nothing but music. Others show films, and some show news 24 hours a day. Television is one way in which the USA's culture is exported all over the world. Coca-Cola is another popular American export. The drink was invented in the USA and today it is drunk in nearly every country.

Farming and industry

The USA produces all kinds of agricultural goods. It is a major world producer of maize, soya beans, tomatoes, oranges, peaches, cheese, beef and chickens. The country has deposits of most of the minerals useful to modern society. It mines more coal, copper, gypsum, salt, phosphates, and sulphur than any other country. The aluminium and iron and steel industries are among the biggest in the world.

◀ New York's Shea Stadium, homeground for the baseball team the New York Mets.

Education

At age six children enter the first grade of elementary schools and stay there up to the age of 12 (sixth grade). Secondary education is usually divided into junior (grades 7–9) and senior (grades 10–12) high schools, but in some communities there is a single high school. After graduating from high school over 60 per cent of students go to college. Every state in the USA has at least one university, and in total there are over 3,000 universities and colleges in the country.

The USA has produced some great scientists. They have won more than twice as many Nobel prizes as any other country. Scientists in the USA were the first to build an atom bomb and the first to build a spaceship able to take a man to the Moon and back in 1969. ■

See also
Afro-Americans
Alaska
American Indians
Earthquakes
Geological time (photo)
Grasslands
Hawaiian Islands
Hispanics
Mississippi River
North America
Plate tectonics
Rocky Mountains
USA: history

▼ Cowboys have been the inspiration for many American films. A skilled cowboy can lasso a moving horse or calf with his rope.

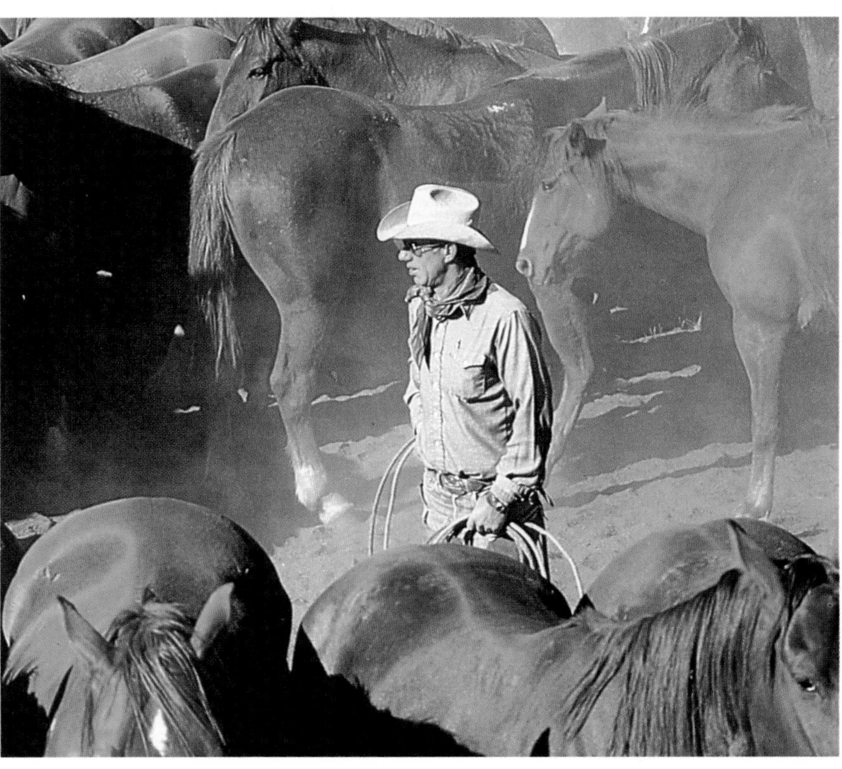

USA: history

The history of North America goes back over 25,000 years, for the ancestors of the American Indians have lived there at least as long as that. The history of European exploration and settlement dates back over 400 years. But the history of the United States of America only started in 1776 when the first thirteen of the states which had been colonies declared themselves independent of Britain. They soon found that they needed a central government as well as the governments of each state, and so agreed to join together as a 'federal' country. A group of politicians drew up a constitution, and George Washington became the first president.

By 1803 four new states had joined the USA. In that year the size of the USA doubled when the third president, Thomas Jefferson, bought France's Louisiana Territory (the Louisiana Purchase). This extended the western frontier from the Mississippi River to the Rocky Mountains. Sixteen years later the USA bought Florida from Spain. Between 1783 and 1840 pioneer settlers opened up the new territories. The population grew rapidly, as thousands of new immigrants came from Europe.

▼ This bar graph shows how the population has grown.

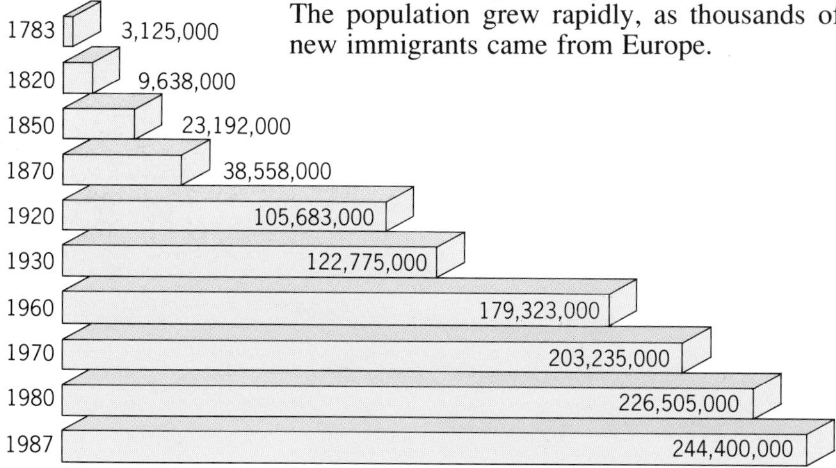

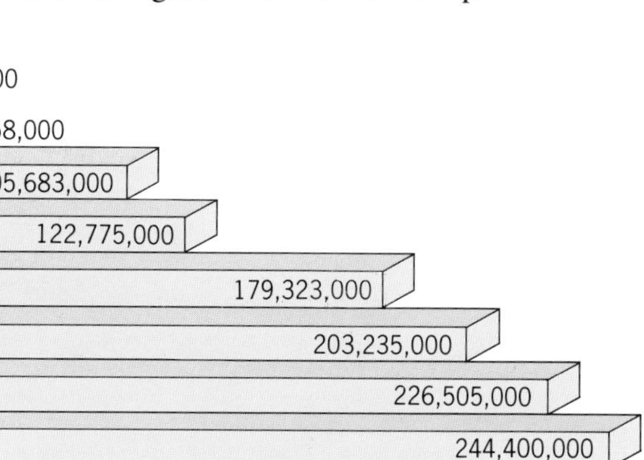

The land of opportunity

During the second half of the 19th century, several million Europeans flocked to the USA. Men, women and children, travelling in great discomfort, crossed the heaving ocean in steam and sailing ships. The journey took about 40 days, and one person in ten died on the voyages. Yet for most it was the land of opportunity. Some immigrants bought land and started farming. Others looked for work in the cities, where life for the newcomers was often tough. There was unemployment and overcrowding. But the USA became a land of inventions and machines, which gradually created more jobs.

► A family of immigrants from Germany arrive at Ellis Island in 1905. Ellis Island in New York harbour was the reception centre for immigrants from 1892. More than 12 million people landed there between then and 1921 when immigration was restricted and quotas fixed.

► Two railway companies, the Union Pacific starting from the west coast and the Central Pacific starting from the River Missouri laid track for six years until the two railway lines met in the middle of the prairie. The final spike, made of gold, was driven home at Promontory, Utah, in 1869.

The development of telegraphs and railways made communications easier. The first railroad to cross the continent was opened in 1869.

For the native Indian peoples and for the black slaves working on the cotton plantations of the South, life was as harsh as ever. Indians were forced westwards and constantly harassed as European settlers took over their ancestral lands. Although slavery was abolished as a result of the American Civil War of 1861–1865, black people did not have equal rights and opportunities.

Throughout the century American territory expanded. The USA annexed Texas in 1845, and took a vast area in the south-west from Mexico as a result of war in 1848. The states of California, Arizona, and New Mexico were formed from these lands. Britain ceded land in the north-west, and the USA bought Alaska from Russia in 1867. This was the period when the West was populated, with range wars, cowboys, and gold rushes.

Work and freedom

The years of the 1890s and 1900s brought enormous changes to the USA and its people. The new Americans were immigrants from southern and eastern European countries, such as Italy, Sicily, Greece, Russia, Poland and Hungary. Many of the eastern Europeans were

Jews, escaping from persecution. Other immigrants left the poverty of their rural homelands for dirty, overcrowded tenements in cities such as Chicago and New York. Some slum areas became terrorized by organized gangs. The majority of Americans lived in rural rather than urban areas and there was still plenty of land where farmers could expand. But few of the new immigrants became farmers once they were in America.

Meanwhile, the flow of American inventions had become a flood: the sewing machine, the typewriter, barbed wire, the telephone, electric light, the combine harvester and dozens more. They brought increasing prosperity to the American people.

At the end of the century, in 1898, the USA fought against Spain and gained Puerto Rico, Hawaii and the Philippines. In 1917 the USA entered World War I, joining Britain and France against Germany and its allies.

Boom and bust

After World War I the government introduced quotas to slow down the rate at which immigrants were entering the country. Many black Americans from the southern states moved north to find work.

In 1919 an act was passed banning the sale of alcohol; this was known as 'prohibition'. But it did not stop people drinking. 'Bootleggers', people who made and sold alcohol illegally, supplied drinks in secret rooms called 'speakeasies'. Prohibition ended in 1933.

The 1920s were a boom time. A lot of people made money on the stock market. Then in 1929 the stock market crashed and the Great Depression began. Millions of people were without work. A government programme called the New Deal provided help and jobs, but the depression lasted until World War II began and the demand for arms created new jobs. The USA entered the war in 1941, and played a major part in gaining victory over Germany and Japan, in alliance with Britain and the USSR.

▲ **Martin Luther King, leader of the Civil Rights movement, addresses a huge crowd from the steps of the Lincoln Memorial in Washington, 28 August 1963. In the background is the Washington monument.**

The USA had become one of the superpowers. Their great rival was the Soviet Union, in the Cold War and the space race. The Moon landing in 1969 gave people a new pride in their country. There was plenty of work, and people had more possessions such as TVs and washing machines. Black Americans began the Civil Rights campaign, a fight for equality.

New racial problems flared as immigration speeded up. This was especially caused by the arrival after 1980 of more than 6 million Spanish speakers (Hispanics), mainly from Mexico. English is still the official language spoken all over the USA, but many children are brought up to speak Spanish at home and among their friends. ■

See also
Afro-Americans
American Civil War
American colonial history
American Indians
American Revolution
American West
Cowboys
Hispanics
Slaves
United States of America
Biography
Eisenhower
Kennedy
King
Nixon
Reagan
Roosevelt, F. D.
Roosevelt, Theodore
Wilson
Reformers
Carnegie
Rockefeller
Roosevelt, Eleanor
Scientists/technologists
Bell
Edison
Franklin, Benjamin
Lindbergh
Wright brothers

Universe

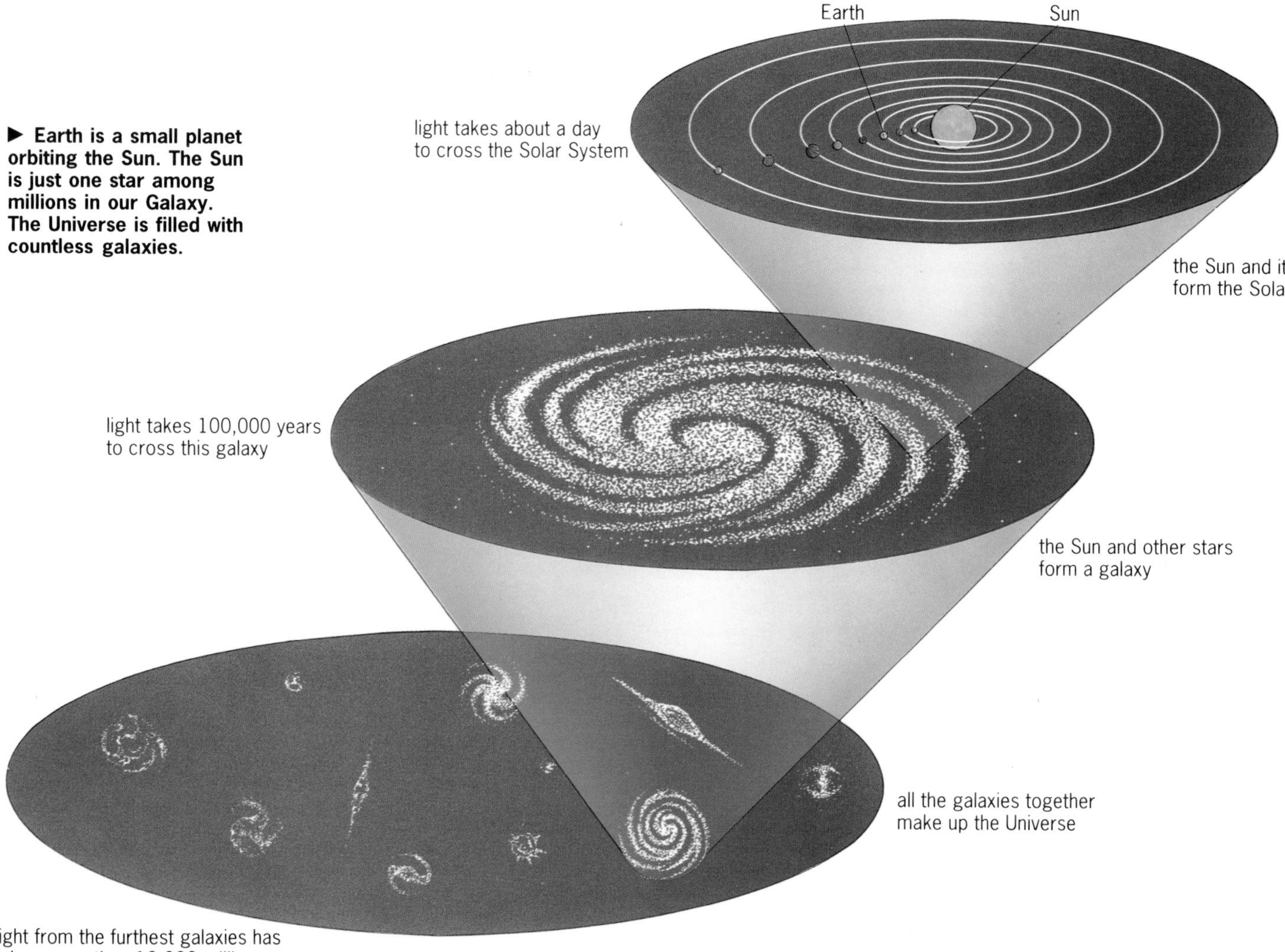

Earth

Sun

light takes about a day to cross the Solar System

the Sun and its planets form the Solar System

light takes 100,000 years to cross this galaxy

the Sun and other stars form a galaxy

all the galaxies together make up the Universe

light from the furthest galaxies has taken more than 10,000 million years to reach us

► Earth is a small planet orbiting the Sun. The Sun is just one star among millions in our Galaxy. The Universe is filled with countless galaxies.

We use the word 'Universe' to mean everything that exists, from the Earth out to the most distant parts of space that astronomers can possibly see. People used to think that the Earth was the centre of the Universe. Although the Earth is important to us, we know now that it is a little planet going round the Sun, which is just one of millions of ordinary stars in our Galaxy.

The Universe contains countless galaxies of stars. The furthest ones we can see are so distant that their light takes thousands of millions of years to reach us. This delay means that we are seeing them now as they actually were long ago. When we look deep into space, we look a long way back in time as well.

We can also tell that the galaxies are rushing apart and that the ones furthest away are going the fastest.

Light travels at nearly 300,000 km (186,000 miles) every second. Yet light from the furthest known galaxies has taken more than 10,000 million years to reach us.

See also
Astronomers
Big bang
Cosmology
Galaxies
Light years
Solar System

The edge of the Universe

The most distant galaxies we know about are travelling at $\frac{9}{10}$ of the speed of light. Astronomers keep finding more distant ones, but there is a limit to how far we could ever see, even with incredibly powerful telescopes. If there is anything beyond our Universe, we can never know what it is.

Beginning and end

Astronomers have worked out that the Universe we know started thousands of millions of years ago. It is changing and getting bigger all the time as the galaxies rush apart. Thousands of millions of years in the future, the stars may stop shining and perhaps the Universe will get smaller again. ■

Universities

Some old universities with dates when they started

Bologna	1088
Oxford	about 1150
Paris	about 1150
Cambridge	1209
Vienna	1365
St Andrews	1411
Glasgow	1451
Dublin	1591
Harvard	1636

A university is one of the places people can go to if they want to carry on studying after they finish school. A university has three main purposes. The first is to give its students qualifications which will help them to earn a living. The second is to give them a better understanding of the arts and sciences, and to widen their views of life. The third is to undertake original research.

When students complete their studies they graduate. If they pass their final examinations, they are awarded a degree, a certificate to say that they have successfully completed their studies. Until then, students are called undergraduates. They may then go on to post-graduate studies and do research which can help to increase our knowledge and understanding of the world.

One of the most ancient European universities is at Bologna, Italy. But the first universities began elsewhere. In ancient Egypt, there was a famous one at Heliopolis. The Roman empire had universities at Rome, Athens, Rhodes and Alexandria. Later, there were Muslim universities at Cairo, Timbuktu, Fès and Salerno. ■

Some degrees awarded to university students in Britain are:

first degrees
BA Bachelor of Arts
BSc Bachelor of Science

postgraduate degrees
MA Master of Arts
MSc Master of Science
PhD Doctor of Philosophy

Similar degrees, with slightly different names, are awarded in other countries.

See also
Colleges

Uruguay

Uruguay is one of the smallest independent countries in South America. It lies in the south-east of the continent, on the wide estuary of the Río de la Plata on the Atlantic Ocean. Montevideo, the capital, is the hub of the nation. About half of all Uruguayans live there.

Much of Uruguay is grasslands. Summers are warm and winters mild. Only one-tenth of the land is cultivated. The rest is used for cattle and sheep. Millions of animals are herded by cowboys called *gauchos*. The nation's main exports are canned and frozen meat, hides, leather goods, and wool. Farmers grow wheat, maize, rice, olives, grapes, and citrus fruits. Uruguay's fine beaches attract many thousands of tourists.

Uruguay was South America's first welfare state, and in the first half of the 20th century the standard of living became high. But after World War II there was much violence and lawlessness. The army took control and many terrorists were arrested and tortured. Government by civilians returned in 1985. In spite of high inflation, Uruguay remains one of the most prosperous countries in South America. ■

Area
186,925 sq km
(72,171 sq miles)
Capital Montevideo
Population 2,964,000
Language Spanish
Religion Christian
Government
Parliamentary republic
Currency
1 new peso = 100 centésimos

Uruguay became an independent republic in 1830, after being held in turn by Argentina and Brazil.

▼ A cattle market in Uruguay.

See also
Cowboys
Grasslands
South America
Spanish colonial history

Utopias

Utopias are perfect countries that do not exist. The name *Utopia* (which means 'no place') was invented by Sir Thomas More for the title of a book he wrote in 1516. His book tells the story of a traveller to an imaginary land. In this way More could tell his readers what he believed the world should really be like, if only people were perfect. The book was so popular that many people have copied the idea. A lot of science fiction stories take the opposite idea and make up imaginary, terrible worlds. ■

The full title of Sir Thomas More's book was: *On the Highest State of a Republic and on the New Island Utopia.*

See also
Biography
More

Vaccinations

See also
Germs
Immunity

Biography
Jenner
Montagu
Pasteur

The 'jabs' that doctors give you to prevent you getting diseases are called vaccinations or immunizations.

These contain either harmless, dead germs or substances extracted from them. They work by getting your body's natural defences against germs to behave as if you have been invaded by a disease-causing germ when in fact you have not. Your body starts producing antibodies which kill germs, and protective white blood cells to combat that type of infection.

When later in life you really do meet some germs of that sort, your body can destroy them immediately and you do not get sick. ■

Vacuums

The first vacuum flask was made by James Dewar in 1892.

A vacuum is a completely empty space from which even the air has been removed. Scientists cannot make a complete vacuum; there is always a little air left. The best vacuum we know is in space, though even here there are some particles of gas and dust.

Often when we say vacuum we mean a partial vacuum, where most of the air has been removed. The pressure of the atmosphere will push air or liquid into a vacuum if it can. This happens when you suck a drink up through a straw. The sucking removes air from your mouth and makes a partial vacuum. The atmosphere pushes on your drink, forcing it up the straw and into your mouth.

Vacuums are needed in some electrical equipment. There is a vacuum inside a television tube.

Vacuum flask

A vacuum flask (Thermos flask) uses a vacuum to keep drinks hot or cold, because heat cannot travel very well through a vacuum. The drink is poured into the flask, which has double walls of glass. The air between the walls has been pumped out leaving a partial vacuum. Very little heat can get across the vacuum, and the walls have a shiny coating to reflect this back.

So for several hours your drink stays almost as hot or cold as it was to begin with.

▼ In a flask there is a partial vacuum between the two glass walls. This, along with the shiny surfaces and the stopper, helps to keep the heat in or out.

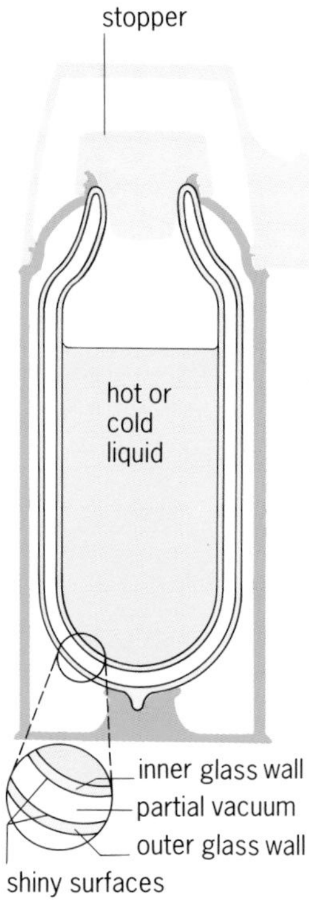

See also
Atmosphere
Heat
Pressure

Vacuum cleaner

A vacuum cleaner picks up dust and dirt from furniture and floors. Its motor turns a fan, making a partial vacuum inside the cleaner. The air outside rushes in, bringing with it the dust and dirt near the opening. This is all sucked up a tube into a bag, where the dirt is trapped while the air escapes. Some cleaners are pushed across the floor and have a spinning brush which loosens the dirt so it can be picked up easily. Others suck up the dirt with a nozzle at the end of a long, bendy tube. ■

The first vacuum cleaner was made by Hubert Booth in 1901. It was pulled by a horse and parked outside the house. A long tube was then passed into the house to clean the carpets.

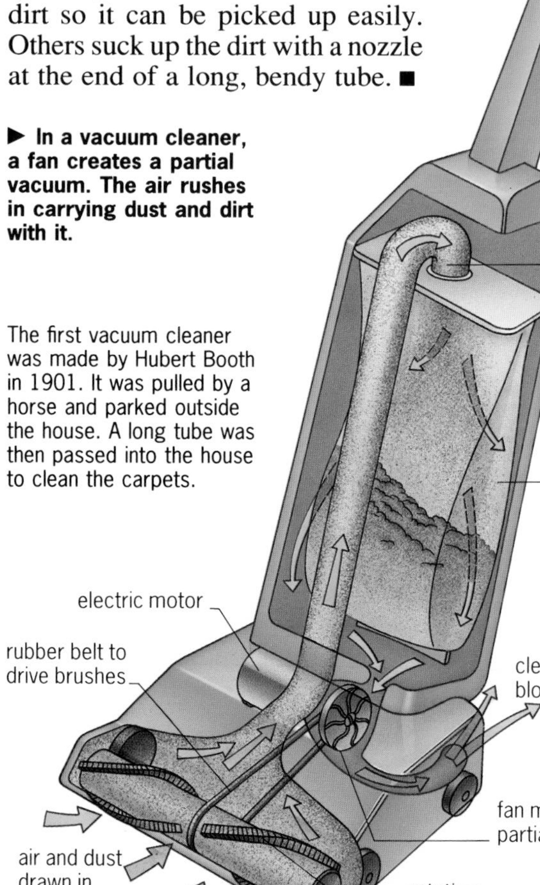

► In a vacuum cleaner, a fan creates a partial vacuum. The air rushes in carrying dust and dirt with it.

Valleys

Valleys are formed by the action of rivers or glaciers, wearing away the rocks. As the water or ice flows down from the mountain tops it carves out valleys, leaving ridges of rock in between and giving the mountains their shape.

River valleys

Rivers flowing down steep gradients (slopes) have great cutting power. Rocks and boulders roll down the valley sides into the river and are bounced along its bed, cutting deep into the rocks. River valleys high in the mountains are steep-sided. If you see them in cross-section, they look V-shaped.

Further down the river course, the gradient of the river bed is less, the river flows more slowly and cuts less deeply. It develops a more winding course, flowing around obstacles and cutting a wider valley, like a shallow U.

The river flood-plain has a very slight gradient and may appear almost flat. Some river flood-plains are hundreds of miles wide.

Glaciated valleys

Glaciers can erode valleys much more powerfully than rivers. The ice may be hundreds of feet thick, so a great weight presses down on the valley floor. Rocks and boulders become stuck in the ice on the bottom of the glacier. The ice pushes them along like a giant piece of sandpaper. Glaciated valleys are U-shaped in cross-section, with very steep sides and flat bottoms. After the ice has melted, the rivers that flow down these valleys look much too small for them.

▲ The Colorado River has cut steeply into the rising mountains, forming the spectacular Grand Canyon in the USA. Because of low rainfall the sides of the gorge have weathered little.

Where tributary glaciers enter the main valley they form 'hanging valleys'. Because these glaciers are smaller, their valleys are not cut so deep. They are seen high up the main valley sides. Picturesque waterfalls often cascade from these hanging valleys after the ice has retreated.

◄ A river in Wales is dwarfed by its large valley. The U-shape tells us that a glacier once gouged out its channel along here.

The deepest known canyon is in the Andes mountains in Peru. It is called El Cañón de Colca and is 3,223 m deep.

Gorges

Where the river follows a line of weakness in the rocks, such as a fault, it may cut a very deep valley with almost vertical sides, called a gorge. Gorges also form in desert areas where rainfall occurs very rarely in the form of heavy thunderstorms. The soil has been baked hard by the Sun and very little water can soak in, so huge volumes of water run off the surrounding land, forming 'flash floods' so powerful that they carry large boulders with them and cut deep gorges called wadis.

The longest fjord is the Nordvest Fjord of Scoresby Sound, Greenland. It extends 313 km (195 miles) inland.

Some of the most spectacular gorges are the canyons of the United States, including the Grand Canyon, 1·6 km (about a mile) deep. Here, the mountains were rising as the rivers were cutting down.

Dry valleys and drowned valleys

In some parts of the world, especially where there is limestone or chalk, there are valleys which contain no water. These dry valleys were formed at a time when the climate was much wetter, as at the end of the last ice age. Their rocks are very porous, and water quickly sinks down into them. When there was more rainfall, the water level in the rocks remained above the valley floor, so the rivers flowed. Today, the water is much deeper and only underground rivers occur.

Where coastlines are sinking or sea-levels rising, valleys may be drowned, forming long inlets of the sea called rias. Rias are found on the south-west coast of England. Where deep glaciated valleys are drowned, they form fjords with very steep sides and extremely deep water.

Rift valleys

Some of the widest valleys in the world are the rift valleys. These were formed when huge blocks of rock moved relative to each other: either the blocks on either side of the valley were raised up to form mountains, or the block

► The slow progress of this river in Germany has allowed time for the valley sides to weather. The result is a wide valley with gently sloping sides.

There are valleys on the sea-bed as well as on land. The deepest underwater canyon is south of Western Australia. It is 1,800 m deep and 32 km (20 miles) wide.

in the middle dropped down to form the valley floor. The great Rift Valley of Africa and the Great Glen of Scotland were formed in this way.

Life in valleys

The climate in a valley is usually much milder than in the hills around it. The valley sides provide shelter from wind, and often the mountains themselves receive much of the rainfall or snowfall, leaving the valleys short of rain. Because the valley floor is lower than the hilltops it is warmer. South-facing valley slopes get more light and are usually warmer than north-facing slopes, and often have different vegetation.

In some valleys there are special mountain winds which blow down the valley bringing warm or cold air at certain times of year. When frost and fog form, the cold air sinks, and valleys often have more frost and fog than the mountains above.

In mountain valleys near the sources of rivers the soils are usually thin and not very fertile. Sheep farms are more common than crops. Where the slopes are very steep, farmers may build terraces to prevent the water and soil rushing away down the slope. Where there is no farming the slopes may be wooded. The trees help to anchor the soil and prevent it being washed away in heavy storms. They also help to prevent avalanches of snow or mud crashing into the valley and villages below. There are often trees and shrubs near the river, benefiting from the extra moisture.

In many mountain areas, such as the Alps and Himalayas, cattle are moved up to high alpine pastures in spring as the snow melts, and brought back to the shelter of the valley floor in winter to be fed on hay.

In valleys near the river mouth the soil is thicker and the valley floor contains sediments brought down by the river. Good crops can be grown in these fertile sediments.

In lowland valleys flooding may be a problem if the river is suddenly made bigger by seasonal rainfall or melting snow. Settlers have to find the right balance between controlling the damage done by the water by building higher dikes and banks, and benefiting from the rich silt that is left behind by the floods. In many parts of the world today, flooding is being made much worse because forests are being cut down in the hills. With no trees to soak up the water, more of it rushes into the rivers, together with the soil.

Valley settlements

In mountain regions the valleys are the main areas where people live. This is because the climate is sheltered and the soils are thicker. The valleys provide routes for roads and railways, and larger rivers can be used for transport, too. Large settlements often occur where one or more valleys meet, encouraging trading.

Where springs emerge on the valley slopes there may be a line of villages which date back to times when spring water was the main source of water for drinking. In valleys with fair-sized rivers water power may be used to generate electricity for industry.

Communications between valleys may be difficult in mountain country. Roads and railways have to climb winding mountain passes, or pass through expensive tunnels. The hills may also interfere with radio and television reception. ■

Death Valley in California is the deepest valley in the western hemisphere. At the lowest point it is 86 m below sea-level. It is 209 km (130 miles) long and 10–23 km (6–14 miles) wide.

Transhumance is the word used for the seasonal moving of stock between high and low pastures.

See also

Erosion
Fjords
Flood-plains
Floods
Geological time
Glaciers
Mountains
Rivers

Valves

▼ **One-way valve on a bicycle tyre. Air pressure in the tyre normally keeps the valve closed. But pressure from a pump will open the valve so that air flows in.**

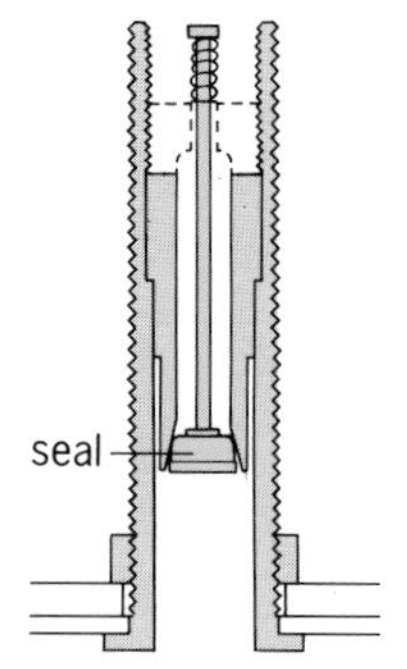

valve held closed by pressure of air inside tyre

valve opened by pressure of air from pump

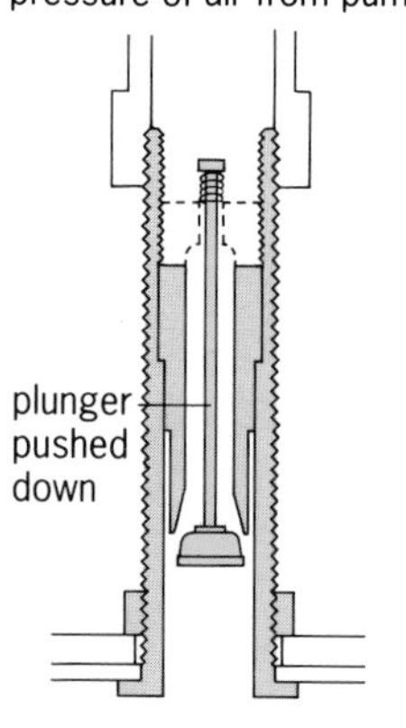

You use a valve to control the flow of hot water through a radiator. A tap is a type of valve which controls the flow of water into a sink. In a car engine, valves open and shut to let gases in and out of the cylinders. All valves do the same type of job. They control the flow of something, usually a liquid or a gas.

Some valves work automatically. The thermostatic valves fitted to some radiators are like this. Their job is to keep a room at a steady temperature. If the temperature starts to rise, the valve closes and the flow of hot water stops. When the room has cooled a little, the valve opens again.

Some valves allow a flow in one direction only. A bicycle tyre has a one-way valve in it. When you pump up the tyre, the valve lets the air in but stops it getting out again. You have one-way valves in your heart so that blood is drawn in and pumped out in the right direction. And there is a one-way valve in the top of a pressure cooker. It lets the steam out if the pressure inside is too great.

Not all valves deal with liquids and gases. Thermionic valves were once used in radios and computers to control the flow of electric currents. They did the jobs which are now done by transistors and microchips. ■

See also
Central heating
Electronics
Hearts
Internal combustion engines
Plumbing
Pumps
Steam-engines
Thermostats
Transistors

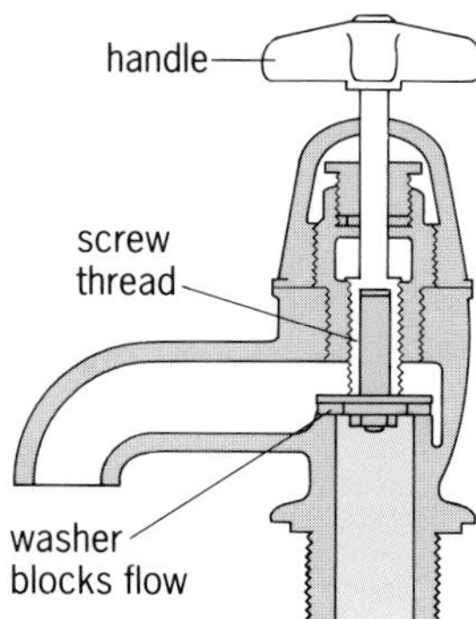

▼ **When a tap is closed, a rubber washer blocks the flow of water. Turning the handle raises the washer so that water can flow.**

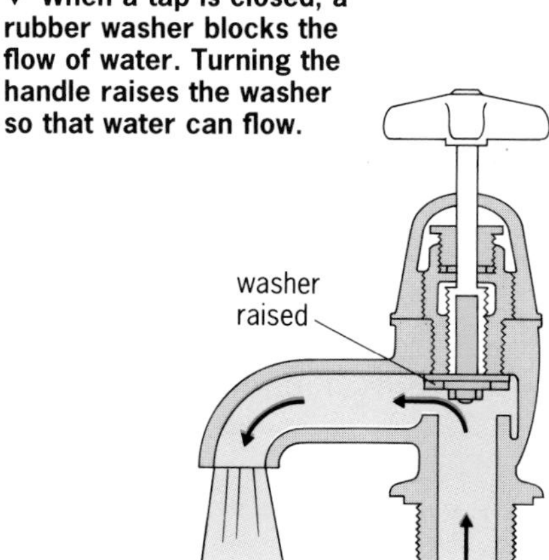

Vatican

▲ **The Swiss Guard wear their brightly coloured ceremonial uniform as they prepare to welcome distinguished visitors to the Vatican.**

The world's smallest independent country is also a palace and a city. It is the Vatican, which occupies 44 hectares (109 acres) in the Italian capital, Rome. It is the headquarters of the Roman Catholic Church, and the home of the Pope.

At the heart of the Vatican is St Peter's Basilica, the world's largest Christian church. Inside the Vatican Palace are the living quarters of the Pope and the offices where the officials work. The palace includes chapels, a library and museums.

As well as being head of the Roman Catholic Church the Pope is also the head of state of the Vatican. But he leaves the government to a commission, headed by a cardinal.

Vatican City State has its own coins, stamps, postal service, telephone exchange, radio station and daily newspaper. It has its own small 'army' of soldiers called the Swiss Guard, who maintain order and protect the Pope. About 1,000 people live in the Vatican.

Vatican City State has been an independent country since 1929. It is all that is left of the Papal States, a large area of central Italy which was ruled by the Popes until 1870. ■

Vatican City is so small that you can walk round its boundaries in less than an hour.

Nearly all its citizens are priests or nuns.

Area
0·44 sq km
(0·17 sq mile)
Population
1,000
Language
Italian
Religion
Christian
Government
Ecclesiastical state (government of Roman Catholic Church)
Currency
Vatican City lira

See also
Christians
Italy's history
Popes

Biography
John Paul II

Vegetables

Vegetables include many hundreds of edible plants. Some vegetables such as potatoes and aubergines are always cooked. Others like lettuce and radishes are eaten raw. Some can be eaten either way. These include carrots, celery, spinach and green peppers.

The edible part of a plant may be those parts which grow underground, like roots, tubers, bulbs and rhizomes. Or they may be the stems, leaves, flowers and fruit which grow above the ground. The idea of fruit as a vegetable may cause some confusion. Courgettes, tomatoes, peas and aubergines are seen as vegetables by the cook and as fruit by the botanist. A stem vegetable which is used as a fruit and served as a dessert is rhubarb.

All fresh vegetables contain vitamin C. Dark-green leaves, tomatoes and peppers have the largest amounts. Since vitamin C is gradually lost during storage, preparation and cooking, the sooner the vegetable is eaten after it is picked the better. Green and orange vegetables contain vitamin A. All vegetables are low in energy but high in dietary fibre. ■

flowers cauliflower

stems celery

leaves lettuce

roots carrot

See also
Food
Market gardens
Nutrition
Pulses

Vegetarians

Vegetarians are people who do not eat meat or fish. Some believe that killing animals is morally wrong, while others will not eat meat because of their religious beliefs. Many simply believe that it is much healthier to avoid eating meat.

Vegetarians can obtain all the nutrients they need from vegetables, cereals, pulses, fruit, nuts, eggs and dairy products such as milk, butter and cheese. The strictest vegetarians will only eat food which comes from plants, and exclude eggs and dairy products from their diet. These people are called vegans. ■

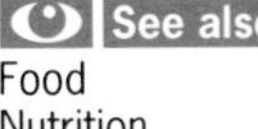

See also
Food
Nutrition

Venezuela

In 1499 Amerigo Vespucci, an explorer from Venice, saw American Indian huts on stilts in a gulf on the Caribbean coast of South America. The waterways between the huts reminded him of Venice, so he named the land Venezuela which in Spanish means 'Little Venice'.

In the north-west, a branch of the Andes Mountains forms a string of snow-capped peaks. Further west, lowlands surround Lake Maracaibo. The llanos (grassy plains) cover the centre of the country, where the mighty River Orinoco divides Venezuela in two. Thousands of cattle are raised on the llanos. The mysterious, densely forested Guiana Highlands rise in the east. There, the Angel Falls, the highest waterfall in the world, plunges 979 m (3,212 ft) down into the green wilderness below.

Many Venezuelans have both Amerindian and European ancestors. Spain ruled Venezuela until the War of Independence, led by Simón Bolívar, finished in 1823.

Venezuela was a poor farming nation until the early 1900s. Then oil was found beneath Lake Maracaibo, and Venezuela quickly became the richest country in South America. But the wealth was not distributed to everyone and many Venezuelans remained very poor. Then in the 1980s the world price of oil fell. Venezuela borrowed heavily and was faced with huge debts. ■

Area
912,050 sq km
(352,144 sq miles)
Capital
Caracas
Population
17,323,000
Language
Spanish
Religion
Christian
Government
Parliamentary republic
Currency
1 bolívar = 100 céntimos

See also
Andes
South America
Spanish colonial history

Biography
Bolívar
Vespucci

▼ Some of the 10,000 derricks of Venezuela's rich oilfields are silhouetted against the setting Sun on Lake Maracaibo.

Vertebrates

You can see how the vertebrata fit in with other Phyla (groups) in the chart in the article on Animals.

Phylum Chordata
Subphylum Vertebrata

The word 'vertebrate' comes from the Latin word for a backbone, so vertebrates are animals with backbones. The bodies of all vertebrates are supported by backbones and the other bones in the skeleton. The ribs and the skull also protect the body's organs.

There are many more kinds of invertebrates (animals without backbones) than vertebrates, but the vertebrates are almost all bigger and more complicated. There are five big classes of vertebrates.

Fish are cold-blooded and live in water. They breathe by means of gills, and in most cases the females lay large numbers of eggs, which are not usually cared for.

Amphibians are cold-blooded and hatch from eggs as tadpoles. These live in water, later changing into adults that generally live on dry land. They have a soft, moist skin and usually stay near water.

Reptiles are cold-blooded and most spend all their lives on land, though some, like crocodiles, live in water. The females lay shelled eggs, and when the young hatch they look like small adults.

Mammals are warm-blooded, so they can be active even in cold parts of the world. A few kinds lay eggs, but in most cases the young are born alive and fed on milk.

Birds are warm-blooded, feathered animals with wings. Birds lay eggs, and the young are kept warm and cared for. ■

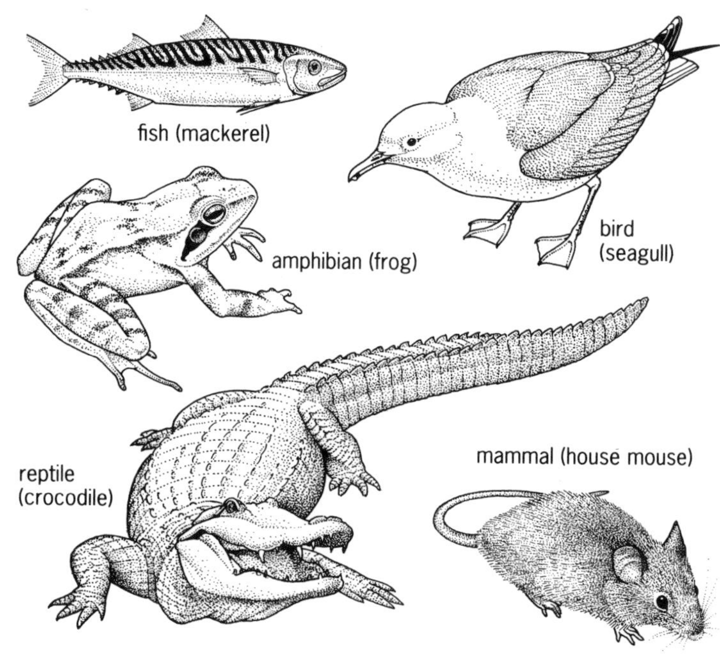

See also
Amphibians
Animals
Birds
Fish
Human body
Invertebrates
Mammals
Reptiles
Skeletons
Warm-bloodedness

Veteran and vintage cars

Until 1896, cars could be driven on British roads only if someone walked in front with a red flag. The London to Brighton veteran car rally is held every year to celebrate the ending of this law.

Veteran cars are those built before 1918. Vintage cars are those built between 1918 and 1930. Old cars built after 1930 are also of great interest to collectors and enthusiasts.

Some, like 1930s Aston Martins, are known as post-vintage thoroughbreds. More recent cars, like the E-type Jaguars of the 1960s, have also become collectors' items. These are sometimes called classic cars. ■

The first petrol-driven cars were built by Karl Benz and Gottlieb Daimler in 1885 and 1886.

► **1901 Napier**

▼ **1910 Austin**

See also
Internal combustion engines
Motor cars
Motor sports

Veterinary surgeons

Veterinary comes from a Latin word *veterinae* meaning 'cattle'.

Veterinary surgeons are animal doctors. Human doctors deal only with people, but veterinary surgeons (or vets, as they are often called) look after many different types of animals. In towns, vets often work in a 'small animal practice'. This means that they care mainly for pets. In the country, vets often have a 'large animal practice' and are concerned with farm animals and horses.

Like human doctors, vets use modern drugs and techniques for curing sick animals. They give many animals injections to protect (immunize) them against illness, just as doctors immunize children against measles and other diseases.

Being a vet is a hard job. An animal that is ill is often frightened and may bite. Also a vet has to be ready day and night to attend a sick or injured animal.

Many people think that they would like to be a vet. But the training is difficult and takes five years to complete. In spite of this, there is great competition for college courses in vet training.

If you would like to work with animals but do not succeed in getting one of the few college places, you could become a veterinary nurse. This means helping the vet, just as hospital nurses help doctors. ■

Viaducts

A viaduct is a long bridge, often with a series of arches, crossing a valley or marshy ground. It may carry a railway, or a road. It may be very high, like those 100 m (300 ft) high across Swiss valleys, or low and long, like the North Circular road across Lea marshes near London which rests on 600 concrete columns. ■

See also
Aqueducts
Bridges

Vibration

Vibration is the scientific word for what happens when anything wobbles or shakes. If you 'twang' your ruler over the edge of a table you make it vibrate. When something that is wobbling makes the air near it vibrate we may get a sound.

The clatter when someone drops a pile of plates, has irregular vibrations. But if you play a note on a musical instrument the vibrations are very regular.

Scientists call the number of complete vibrations every second the frequency. For example, if you play the note A above middle C on a piano, the piano string will have a frequency of 440 vibrations every second. In scientific language we would say 440 hertz (Hz).

Vibrations do not have to be in solid things. If an electric current oscillates (vibrates) it sets the electric and magnetic fields round it wobbling too, and the wobbles travel as waves, called electromagnetic waves. They could be radio waves that have frequencies of hundreds of thousands of vibrations each second. They could be microwaves in which the frequency might be as high as 2,000 million. In a microwave cooker these vibrations make the atoms in the food wobble at the same frequency so it gets hot very quickly.

If you push a child on a swing at exactly the right frequency you can easily build up a big swing. Pushing at the right frequency is called resonance. If it occurs in a building or a bridge or some other structure it can cause damage and this is one of the things designers must take into account.

In 1940, the Takoma Narrows Bridge in the USA was set into resonant vibration by the wind blowing across it (like the reed in a musical instrument) and was destroyed.

If a delicate wine glass is tapped, it vibrates and produces a lovely, clear note. If a singer can produce a very pure, loud sound, on exactly the same note, resonance can make the glass shatter. ■

See also
Microwaves
Musical instruments
Radio
Sound
Waves

Victorian Britain

► The opening of the Great Exhibition in Hyde Park.'The sight . . . was so magical – so vast, so glorious, so touching. The tremendous cheering, the joy expressed on every face, the vastness of the building . . . God bless Albert, and my dear country, which has shown itself so great today' (Queen Victoria's diary, 1 May 1851).

On the platform are Queen Victoria and her husband Prince Albert, their eldest children (Bertie and Victoria), and the Queen's mother. Hing See, a Chinese sea captain looked so important that he was included in the front row below the platform, although he had not been invited.

Britain in 1851

May 1st, 1851, was an exciting day for many people in Victorian Britain. Queen Victoria, with Prince Albert by her side, opened the first Great Exhibition of industry from countries all over the world. Over half the exhibitors were British, because Britain in 1851 was the leading industrial nation of the world.

Population of England
1801 8,300,000
1851 16,811,000
1901 32,528,000

► Over 6 million people visited the Great Exhibition, many on the new railways. Railway building changed the environment, as motorway building does now. In 1872 Gustave Doré, a Frenchman, drew this London scene of slum houses under a railway bridge, with another railway beyond.

Britain and her empire

The Great Exhibition showed the vast wealth of the British empire. In 1851 Britain ruled over millions of people. Many Victorians worked in India as soldiers, traders and government officials. Victorian explorers were beginning to go deep into Africa. Most Victorians believed that their empire was good for everyone who lived in it. But few of them understood the different cultures they met.

Scotland, Wales and Ireland were part of the British empire. Sometimes English people did not understand their problems either. Ireland especially was an unhappy place. Her people were the poorest in the British Isles. Most were Catholic. Some already wanted Ireland to be free of Britain. But Ulster in the north was different. More Protestants lived there, and they were more prosperous; they wanted to stay British.

Country life

Landowners had been the richest and most powerful people in Britain for centuries. This was still true in Victorian Britain. The squire who lived in the big house in a village usually

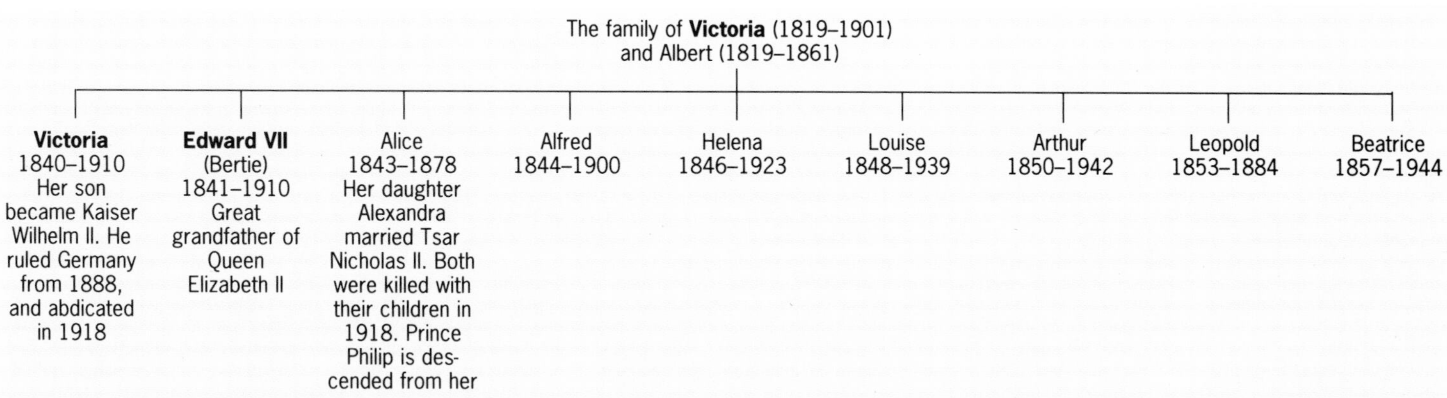

owned the villagers' homes, and employed most of them to work on his land. A good squire who looked after the villagers, and helped in hard times, could be like a kind father, but a father who had to be obeyed. Owners of small farms were often prosperous and quite independent. Ordinary villagers lived in damp, cold houses with no indoor water supply, and could be very poor.

Things began to change about 1880. Cheap wheat poured in from the USA and Canada; meat could now be frozen, so that could be imported too. Margarine was invented, and was cheaper than butter. All this hit British farming. Landowners did less well, wages fell, and there was more unemployment. Even more people left to find jobs in towns.

Town life

In 1801, 20 per cent of Britain's people lived in towns. By 1901, it was 75 per cent. London especially was like a great octopus with its tentacles reaching out into the surrounding country. Life in the slums of big cities was grim. Although the population as a whole was going up, more babies died young in the cities than anywhere else. But rail travel made it easier for the better-off to get to work. So suburbs grew up on the edge of towns, with bigger houses, trees and gardens. By 1901, people could shop in the new department stores in city centres. Big cities like Birmingham had fine new town halls, libraries, art galleries and parks.

Women's lives

Women did not have the vote, and had few rights. A working-class woman lived a hard life. She usually had a large family and lived in a small, cramped house. Everyday jobs like washing clothes were very hard work. She often had to earn money as well to make ends meet: sewing shirts or making matchboxes for very low pay. Richer women had different problems. Most were just educated for marriage. When they did marry, they became dependent on their husbands. But in spite of the difficulties, some women began to find new opportunities. Better schools gave girls the chance to do more. The first woman doctor, Elizabeth Garrett Anderson, began work in 1865. About ten years later, the first women studied at Oxford and Cambridge Universities. Some began to work for 'Votes for Women', though Queen Victoria called it 'mad, wicked folly'.

The Victorian Sunday

In many better-off Victorian homes, and some poorer ones, there were family prayers each morning. Sunday was a special day, and usually the family went to church more than once.

1837 **Victoria** becomes Queen
1840 Victoria and Albert marry
1851 Great Exhibition
1854 Crimean War
1857 Indian 'Mutiny'
1865 First woman doctor began work
1867 Workers in towns got the vote
1870 Education Act
Trade Unions legal
1875 Public Health Act
1884 Workers in country get vote
Irish demand Home Rule
1892 Keir Hardie elected MP
1899 Boer War
1901 Death of Victoria

◀ This picture and verse, 'Preparing for Sunday', appeared in a children's magazine in 1868:

**Haste! Put your playthings all away,
Tomorrow is the Sabbath Day.
Come bring to me your Noah's Ark,
Your pretty tinkling music cart;
Because, my love, you must not play,
But holy keep the Sabbath Day.**

Factories and cities

More industry meant more cotton mills, bigger coal mines and more factories all over the country. Cities grew fast. Some were new. By 1880 the industrial town of Middlesbrough with 50,000 people had grown up on the River Tees. In 1830 there had been one farmhouse there. This huge change in people's lives brought problems. Employers did not often fence off machinery or make factories and mines healthy places to work. There were no rules about hours of work or wages. Workers' houses were built as cheaply as possible, huddled together with no taps or toilets indoors. They soon became slums. Filthy drains were often close to pumps providing drinking-water. Cholera, spread by infected water supplies, was a new disease in Britain and became the 'Victorian Plague'. Not only the poor suffered. Prince Albert died of typhoid in 1861, caught from the drains in Windsor Castle.

▼ This picture appeared in 1866 and was called *The Black Country round Wolverhampton.* The reason for the name is obvious. Coal was the fuel for furnaces and the steam-engines which drove factory machines. Its smutty smoke caused air pollution. Thick greenish fogs, nicknamed 'pea-soupers', were quite common in Victorian cities.

Strikes

It was hard if you were very poor to do anything about these problems. But gradually workers realized that if they joined a trade union, they could help each other, and perhaps force their employer to improve things. In the late 1880s, strikes by the 'Match Girls' and the dockers were both successful, partly because newspapers reported their terrible problems. But strikes were very risky. Employers tried hard to make strikes illegal, and often 'locked out' strikers, so they lost their jobs. Then their families could starve.

Reforms

Many Victorians worked hard for reform. In 1837, only rich people could vote and be Members of Parliament. By 1884 most men over 21 could vote. So MPs had to win ordinary men's votes if they wanted to be elected. By 1901 there were even a few working-class MPs, though MPs were still not paid.

Many people began to realize that rules were needed to make towns healthy, and workplaces safe. Parliament passed laws enforcing clean water supplies, proper drains and dustbin collections. Cholera disappeared. There were laws which stopped children working in mines

◀ In the hot summer of 1858 the River Thames, London's chief sewer and main source of drinking-water, became so smelly that people called it 'the Great Stink'. This photograph shows the modern sewage system being built in 1862. It carried London's sewage right away from the city, and was complete by 1865.

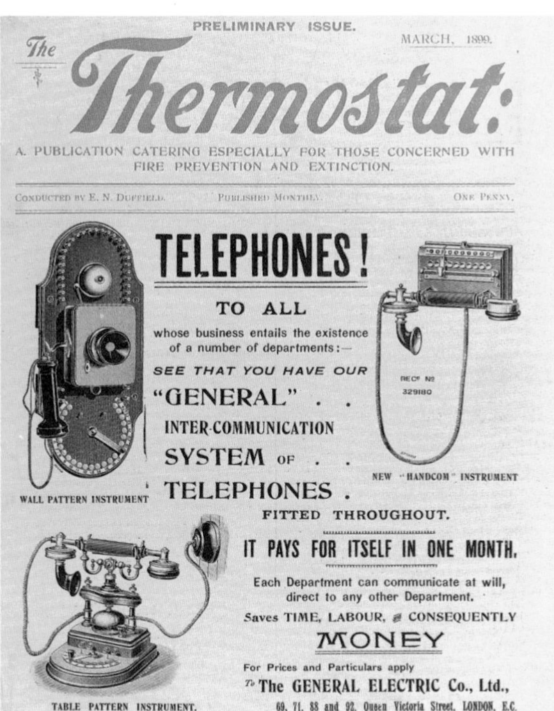

and factories. By 1878, a factory worker's day was limited to ten hours, and there were rules about safety at work. Married women gained some rights. They could keep their own property, and husbands had to pay for their keep if there was a divorce. Things improved, but poverty and disease did not disappear.

Schools for rich and poor

Rich boys usually went to 'public' schools which were not public but fee-paying. These improved after Dr Arnold reformed Rugby School, and other schools copied his ideas. The North London Collegiate School was one of the first to provide a good education for girls. Britain was slow to provide schools for all its children. After 1870 there were 'elementary' schools for 5- to 10-year-olds. By 1901 these schools were free for everyone up to 12. But the difference between schools for rich and poor remained.

Emigration and immigration

Some people left the crowded cities of Victorian Britain to make a new life. They went mainly to Canada, Australia and New Zealand. Emigrants from poverty-stricken Ireland went to the USA, with bitter memories of British rule. Some Irish became 'immigrants' in British cities like Liverpool and Manchester. Russian and Polish Jews arrived in London in the 1890s, escaping from persecution at home. There were already some black people in Britain.

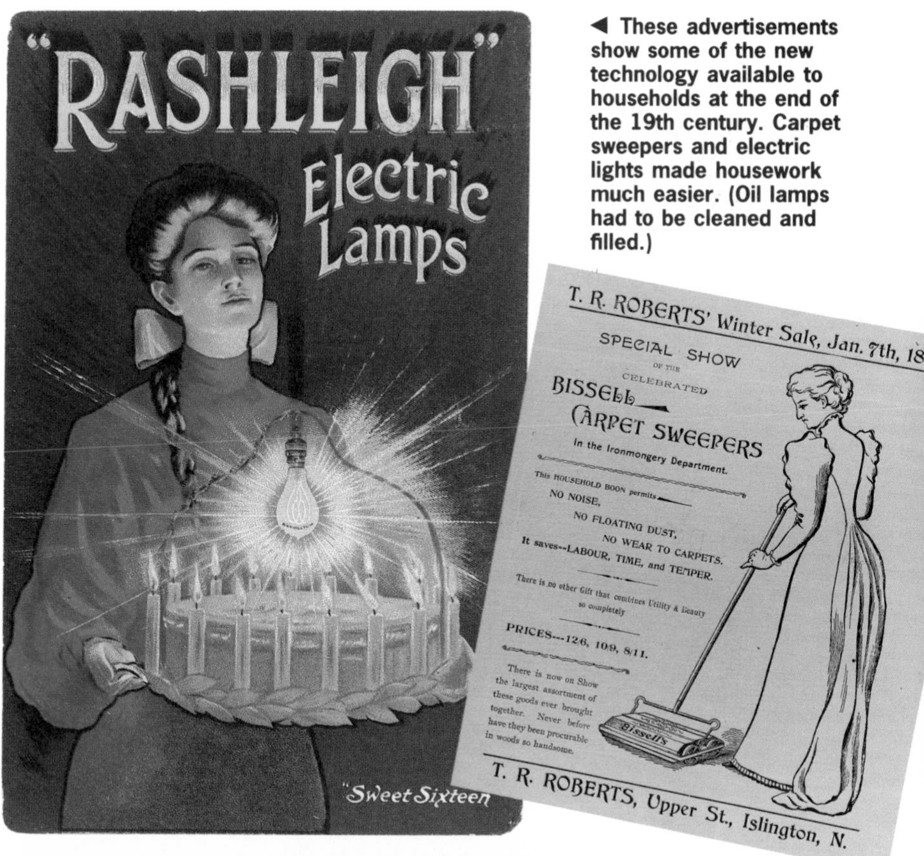

◀ **These advertisements show some of the new technology available to households at the end of the 19th century. Carpet sweepers and electric lights made housework much easier. (Oil lamps had to be cleaned and filled.)**

Fun and games

The rich enjoyed the London Season, a whirligig of balls, banquets and theatres. Music halls were much cheaper and provided the pop music of the time. At home, magic lanterns (simple slide projectors) were very exciting. The first cinemas in the 1890s showed short silent films and were called bioscopes. Rail travel made outings to the seaside or to London Zoo easy. People went to football matches, and to horse-races. County cricket began, and W. G. Grace was a national hero. Lawn tennis was becoming popular by 1901. ■

See also
Boer War
British empire
Colonies
Crimean War
Factory reform
Ireland's history
Parliaments
Police
Tolpuddle Martyrs
Trade unions

Biography
Garrett Anderson
Victoria

Famous politicians
Disraeli
Gladstone
Hardie
Peel

Reformers
Barnardo
Fry
Nightingale
Shaftesbury

Authors and poets
Brontës
Brownings
Carroll
Dickens
Eliot, George
Kingsley, Charles

Video

▲ **Hand-held video camera.**

With a video game you can fight space invaders on a screen. With a video recorder you can record television programmes and play them back later. With a video camera you can take moving pictures and see them on TV. The word video describes many things. In all of them, pictures are stored or handled electronically.

Video recorders

Video recorders use the same basic idea as cassette players which record sound. The signals are stored on magnetic tape. The tape is on reels in a cassette which fits into the machine. Tiny parts called heads can record, play back or wipe out signals on the tape.

Many more signals are needed for storing moving pictures than for storing sounds. In the first video recorders, the tape needed to store all these signals was so long that it had to run through the machine at very high speed. On modern tapes, the signals are stored in diagonal tracks which lie side by side along the tape. Wider tape is needed for this, but its length is less and it can move more slowly.

See also
Cassette players
Electronics
Lasers
Recording
Television

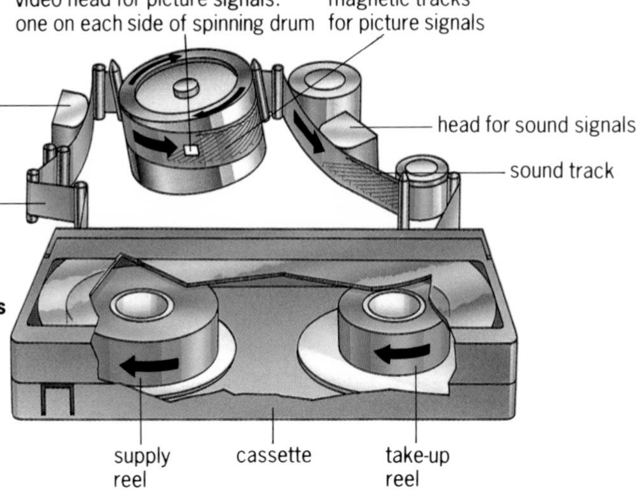

► **When you put a cassette in a video recorder the tape moves slowly past a spinning drum with recording/ playback heads in it. Picture signals are recorded on the tape in diagonal stripes.**

When you load a cassette, levers inside the machine pull out a large loop of tape and wrap it half-way round a metal drum. The drum spins very fast. It is set at an angle, so that as the tape moves slowly past it, two heads in the spinning drum keep moving over the tape in diagonal lines. The same heads are used for recording and for playback. Camcorders are video cameras with a small video recorder built into them. You can record your own moving pictures and play them back later through a television set.

Video discs

Some compact discs (CDs) have pictures recorded on them as well as sounds. The signals are stored as tiny pits on the surface of the disc and 'read' by a laser. The recording quality is very high, but the system cannot be used for making recordings at home. CDs which give pictures as well as sounds are sometimes called CDV discs. CDV stands for compact disc video.

Video games

Video games give you action on the screen which you can control yourself, including space invader attacks, Grand Prix races and sports contests. The games themselves are stored on tape, disc or computer microchip, in the games machine. The most advanced video games are not really games at all. They are used to train fighter pilots and astronauts. ■

Vietnam

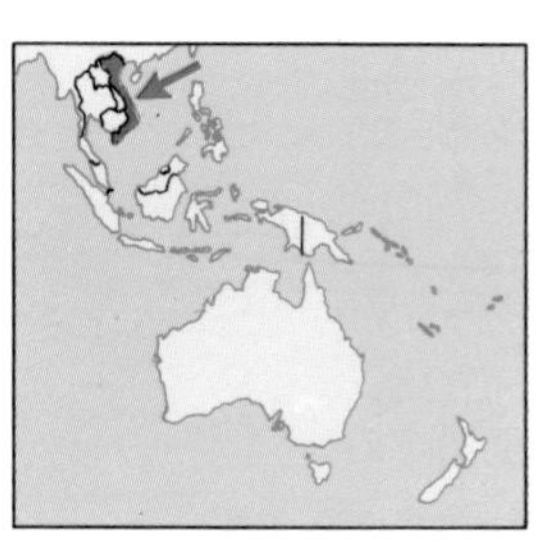

Vietnam, in south-east Asia, is a long narrow country shaped like a tall letter S. The widest part is in the north, bordering China, and includes the delta of the Red River, so-called because it carries away so much red soil. From there to the Mekong River delta in the far south is about 1,600 km (1,000 miles). A beautiful coastline with sandy beaches stretches the length of the eastern side of the country while a mountain range climbs up into Laos on the west. Near the centre the distance from east to west is only 50 km (30 miles) and the mountains come close to the sea.

Climate

The north and the south of Vietnam have different climates, though everywhere it is usually damp and humid. The north has four seasons, with cool winters and hot summers. If you travel south, once you are over the high Hai Van Pass you are in a sunny land, warm to very hot all year round. In the mountains it rains a lot, but near the coast it can be very dry. Yet almost every year typhoons roar in from the east causing havoc as wild seas break down the defences, surge up the rivers and flood land with salt water that destroys crops and spoils soil.

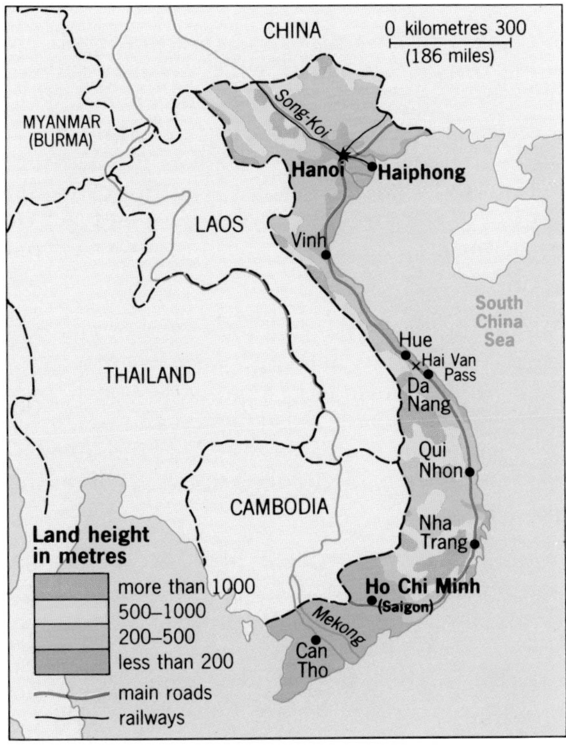

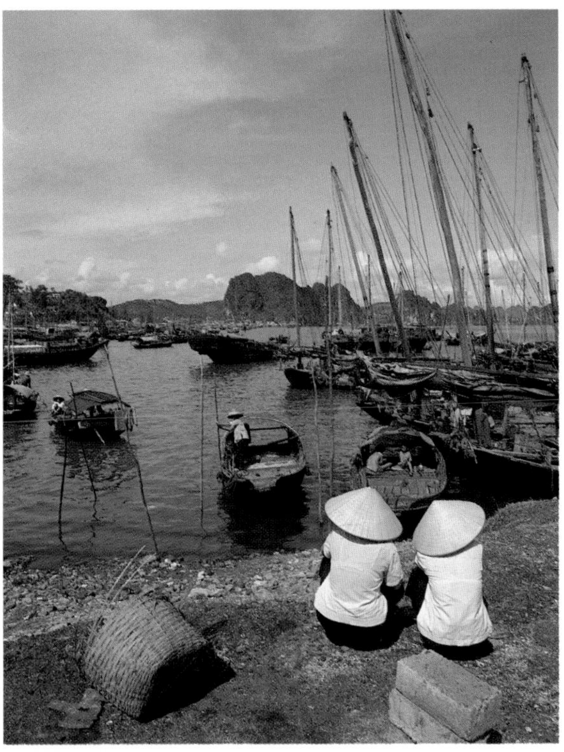

In Vietnamese, the Red River is the Song-Koi.

◀ Fishing boats in north Vietnam. The refugee 'boat people' have sailed to Hong Kong in boats similar to these.

Hats and hard work

It is a typical sight to see Vietnamese people in their large, round, conical straw hats working hard in the paddy fields. Less than a third of the country can be used for agriculture, because of the mountains and the coastal sands. But nearly three-quarters of the population work on the land. Rice, maize and sweet potatoes are the most important crops. Peanuts grow well too, especially in the central provinces. Fishing and forestry are also important. Many trees are being planted to replace 70,000 sq km (over 25,000 sq miles) destroyed by war and by people cutting wood for their fires.

Flashback

Temples, pagodas and stone sculptures from an ancient Buddhist kingdom called Champa are evidence of the great antiquity of civilization in the area now known as Vietnam. For many centuries the Chinese controlled the country until an independent Vietnamese kingdom, Annam, arose. For just over 60 years this land was part of Indo-China under French control. A war of independence resulted in 1954 in the formation of two separate countries, North Vietnam and South Vietnam. North Vietnam had a communist government led by Ho Chi Minh. Elections had been promised at the 1954 Geneva Conference. Almost certainly the communists would have been voted into power in the south, too. Elections were never held.

From the early 1960s the USA sent troops to defend the south from communism. American forces fought against communist guerrillas, the Vietcong. American bombers attacked the north and neighbouring Cambodia. Millions of tons of bombs were dropped; people were burnt by napalm; forests and crops were destroyed by chemicals which caused trees to lose their leaves. Eventually the Americans realized that they could not win, and by 1973 had withdrawn. Three years later North and South Vietnam joined as one nation under a communist government. ■

Area
329,556 sq km
(127,242 sq miles)
Capital
Hanoi
Population
64,500,000
Language
Vietnamese, Chinese, French, English, others
Religion
Buddhist, Christian
Government
Republic
Currency
1 dong = 10 hao = 100 xu

◀ Workers potting rice seedlings which will eventually be transferred to paddy fields. Rice, the major crop, grows best in the fertile river deltas. Most land is farmed by village co-operatives.

See also
Asia
Refugees
Twentieth-century history (photo)

Biography
Ho Chi Minh

Vikings

In the Middle Ages the word Viking meant a robber who came by sea, a pirate. Today we use Viking as the name of Norse peoples who lived in the Scandinavian countries of Norway, Denmark and Sweden. In their own countries they were farmers. In the 8th century AD they began to look for more land. They made raids across the seas and settled in other countries. They were great traders, too, reaching as far east as Byzantium (Istanbul) and westwards across the Atlantic to Newfoundland.

▼ **The Vikings made their journeys between the years 780 and 1100.**

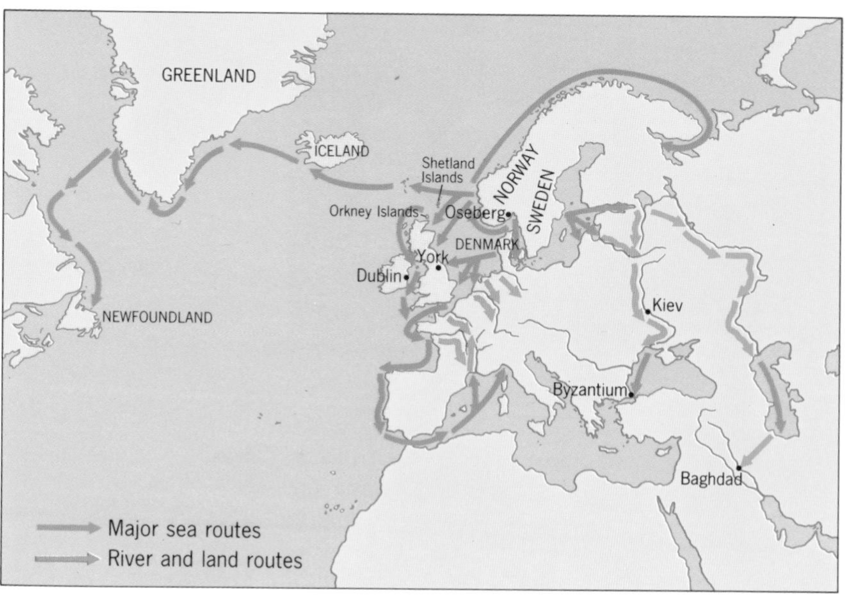

▼ **Archaeologists found the remains of Viking houses at Jorvik still standing over a metre high. From these remains, and all the other evidence, they have been able to rebuild part of Coppergate in York: 'the street of the wooden-cup makers'.**

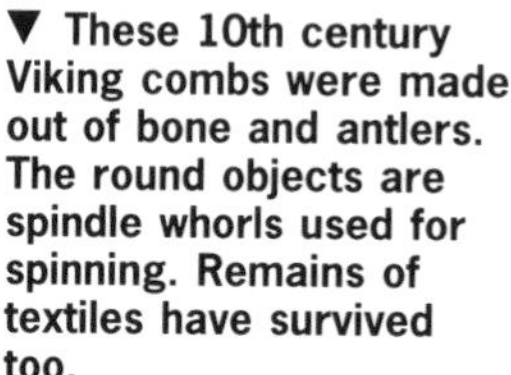

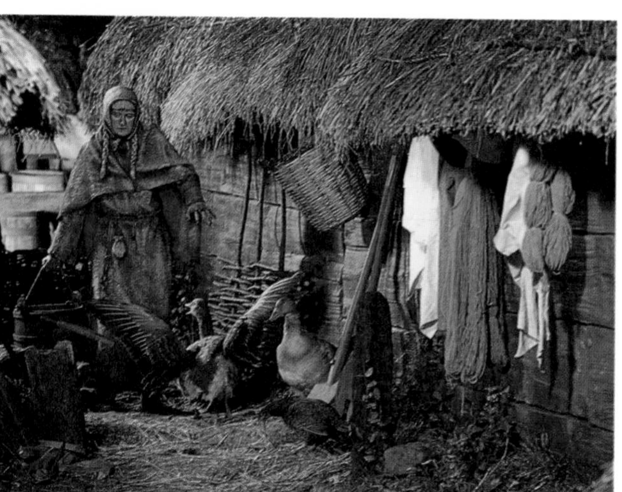

▼ **These 10th century Viking combs were made out of bone and antlers. The round objects are spindle whorls used for spinning. Remains of textiles have survived too.**

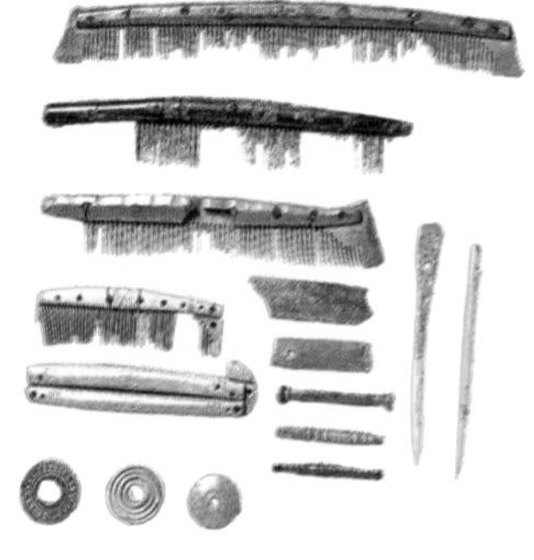

Everyday life

Most Vikings were farmers and they built the same sort of farmhouse wherever they settled. The most important part was the great hall. In earlier times this was where the family lived, ate and slept. Later the hall was divided into eating and sleeping rooms. The house would often be smoky inside because cooking was done over an open fire in the middle of the room.

Viking farmers grew all sorts of crops to eat: wheat, oats, barley and vegetables like cabbages, beans and carrots. They kept cattle, sheep, pigs and chickens but they also hunted animals, birds and fish. Some of this food would be smoked in the roof of the hall, dried or salted to eat during the winter.

Viking men and women liked bright clothes and decoration and jewellery. Women often wore headscarves, an ankle-length dress of wool or linen, with an overdress held on by great brooches. They might also wear necklaces, bracelets and rings. Men wore woollen trousers with a tunic or shirt on top.

Jorvik, a Viking town

In AD 866 some of the Vikings who had settled in East Anglia marched north and took over the Anglo-Saxon capital of Northumbria, then called *Eoforwic* (previously the Roman city of *Eburacum*). The Vikings called it *Jorvik*. Recently archaeologists have discovered some of the houses of Viking Jorvik in modern York. They were not as big as the farmhouses, just one-room wooden houses. It was a rich town, though, full of merchants and craftspeople. The Vikings ruled Jorvik for nearly 90 years. Their last king, Eric Bloodaxe, was thrown out by the English in the year 954.

Merchants and traders

One writer said that Jorvik was 'filled with treasures of merchants from many lands'. The Vikings were famous for the goods they made themselves and for their trade with far-off countries. They traded as far north as Iceland and with the Lapps (for ivory and furs), as far south as Baghdad (for silk and spices) and into Russia (for slaves and furs). In towns, craftspeople made a variety of products, for example: pots and pans for the kitchen, clothes and jewellery, tools and weapons of bronze and iron. They exchanged goods but they also minted their own coins.

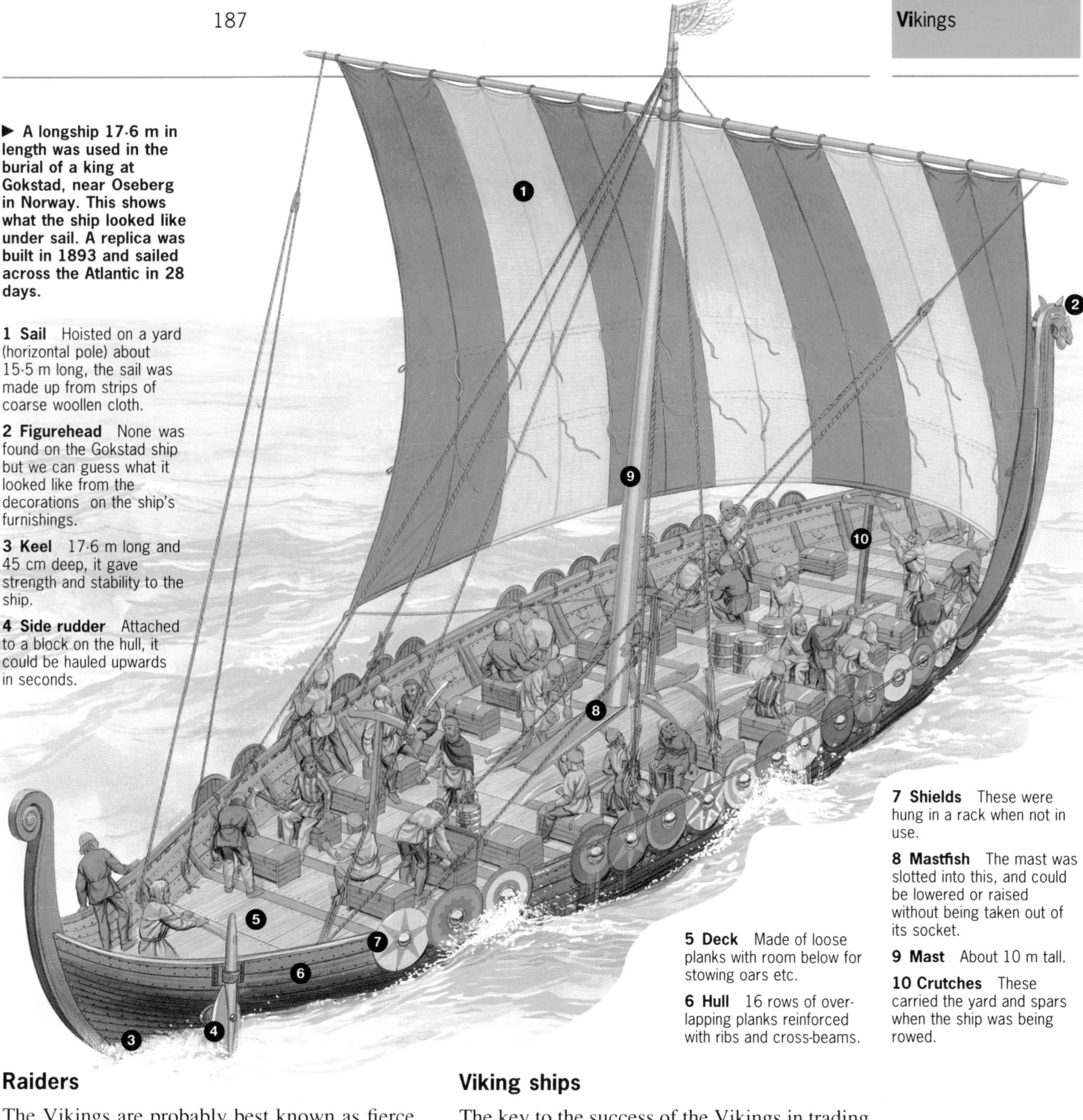

▶ **A longship 17·6 m in length was used in the burial of a king at Gokstad, near Oseberg in Norway. This shows what the ship looked like under sail. A replica was built in 1893 and sailed across the Atlantic in 28 days.**

1 Sail Hoisted on a yard (horizontal pole) about 15·5 m long, the sail was made up from strips of coarse woollen cloth.

2 Figurehead None was found on the Gokstad ship but we can guess what it looked like from the decorations on the ship's furnishings.

3 Keel 17·6 m long and 45 cm deep, it gave strength and stability to the ship.

4 Side rudder Attached to a block on the hull, it could be hauled upwards in seconds.

5 Deck Made of loose planks with room below for stowing oars etc.

6 Hull 16 rows of overlapping planks reinforced with ribs and cross-beams.

7 Shields These were hung in a rack when not in use.

8 Mastfish The mast was slotted into this, and could be lowered or raised without being taken out of its socket.

9 Mast About 10 m tall.

10 Crutches These carried the yard and spars when the ship was being rowed.

Raiders

The Vikings are probably best known as fierce raiders of other peoples' lands. They first invaded Britain in AD 793 when they attacked the island of Lindisfarne off the Northumbrian coast. Raiders would be looking for rich plunder, but also for slaves.

Slaves, called *thralls*, worked on the farms for freemen, called *karls*. More important than freemen were the rich landowners who were also chieftains. They were called *jarls*. Warriors on raiding parties were heavily armed with swords, shields, spears and axes. They wore helmets and chain mail.

Viking ships

The key to the success of the Vikings in trading and raiding was the ship. Shipbuilding was a very skilled craft. Of course, other peoples, such as the Anglo-Saxons, had ships. The Vikings, however, built fast, strong ships that could withstand even an Atlantic crossing. In about AD 1000 Leif Ericsson explored Newfoundland in North America.

The Vikings built not only 'longships' for raiding (one was known to have held 200 fighting men), but also wider, deeper ships called *knarrs* for trade, and little rowing boats called *faerings*. Ships had both oars and sails. ■

See also

Anglo-Saxons
Archaeologists
Ireland's history
Norse myths
Russia's history

Villages

► A small village with slate roofs and whitewashed walls nestles in a valley in Cumbria in the north-west of England.

Villages are settlements in the country. Villages are different from towns or cities because they are smaller. Fewer people live in a village and there are fewer roads and buildings. Villages are traditionally places where farmers live so that they are close to the land they work on. Not all the people living in villages are farmers. Others provide services to farmers and their families, such as a few shopkeepers and a doctor.

Villages in India

In India, three out of every four people live in villages. Most of these people work in agriculture. Many farmers have a small piece of land, perhaps two hectares (five acres). Others do not own land, but rent it from a landlord. The rent they pay may be cash or some part of their harvest. Other agricultural workers in Indian villages get work from day to day, on a landlord's land. Their payment may be food and a place to sleep.

Agricultural workers usually live in a small hut, often with just one room where the family lives, eats and sleeps. Some farmers keep a cow, if they can find enough fodder to feed it. The cow's dung is collected and dried in the sun and used as fuel for a fire where meals are cooked. Otherwise women and children spend time searching for firewood.

▼ A small village high above the river is home for the farmers who work the terraces on this Indian mountainside.

Commuting

In Europe some villages have changed from places where the main work is farming. Village houses have been bought by people who work in cities and each day travel into the city by car or train. These 'commuters' have decided that they would like to live in the country, away from the noise and dirt of the city. This often means that they spend a longer time each day getting to their place of work, but they consider this extra time to be worth while because of the benefits of living in the peace of the countryside.

Flashback

Many villages in Europe are hundreds of years old. If you look on a map at the distribution of buildings that make up a European village you may notice some interesting patterns. Many villages are built in a line stretched out along a road or a river. Others are very compact, where all the houses have been built close together because in times gone by they were more easily defended against attack. In hilly areas villages were often built on hill slopes, so leaving the level land for farming. Most villages had a number of farms, each with the piece of land where the farmer worked, and usually a bigger manor house where the landowner lived. Also there was a church and sometimes an open space or village green. Most of these parts of the old village survive in the villages of today. In England the village green is the traditional spot where the village cricket teams play their matches. ■

Viruses

Diseases such as flu, colds and cold sores are caused by viruses, and so is AIDS. Distemper in dogs and seals is a viral disease, and so are a number of plant diseases like tobacco mosaic disease.

Viruses cause diseases in animals or plants. They are so small that scientists measure them in millionths of a millimetre. Viruses are either rods or spheres in shape.

Viruses are not cells and scientists are uncertain whether they are living things. They consist of a coat of protective protein which surrounds the material they need to reproduce (DNA or RNA). They can only reproduce inside the cells of the living things they infect. They take over those cells and turn them into virus factories which produce hundreds of new viruses before the cells are killed. ■

See also
Cells
Diseases
DNA
Germs

Vitamins

The word vitamin comes from the Latin word *vita* meaning 'life'.

Vitamins are chemical substances that are essential for life and health. They exist naturally in a wide variety of foods. The body uses these vitamins to perform important chemical processes. The amounts needed to keep a person alive and well are extremely small and can be obtained from a normal, balanced diet. There are thirteen major vitamins: A, C, D, E, K and eight different B vitamins. ■

See also
Food
Nutrition
Vegetables

	Found in	Used for
A	Carrots, milk, butter, eggs, fish-liver oils, liver, green vegetables	Keeping skin and bones healthy, fighting disease and infection
B	Yeast, wholemeal bread, nuts, peas, beans, fish, meat, eggs, milk, cheese, green vegetables	Helping the body to release energy from food for growth, keeping skin and nerves healthy
C	Oranges, lemons, limes, tomatoes, black currants and green vegetables	Helping wounds to heal, keeping blood, gums and teeth healthy, protection against colds
D	Liver, butter, cheese, eggs, fish. Also made in the body by the effects of sunlight on the skin	Keeping bones and teeth strong and healthy. Important in childhood
E	Wholemeal bread, brown rice, butter and green vegetables	Believed to help cell growth and wound healing
K	Green vegetables and liver	Clotting blood

Vivisection

More than 100,000 animals die in British laboratories each week.
About 100 million animals probably die each year in laboratories throughout the world.

Vivisection is the use of live animals in experiments. It is found in medical research and the testing of weapons, pesticides, cosmetics and toiletries.

Laws controlling vivisection vary between countries, but most require a licence of some kind. In Britain vivisection is regulated by the Home Office and in the United States of America by the Department of Agriculture. Licences are not needed for experiments on animals without backbones.

Many people believe that all or some vivisection is unnecessary. The demand for household products, cosmetics and toiletries that have not been tested on animals is increasing. ■

Voice

Many animals use special sounds to communicate with each other. These sounds are called the animal's voice.

Our voice is much more complex than those of any other animals, because of the languages we speak. We make sound with a group of organs based in the throat and mouth. We change that basic sound by changing the shape of our mouth and, most importantly, by moving our tongue very quickly and precisely. Our spoken languages would be impossible without our thick, quick-moving tongues.

In other animals different sound-producing organs may be used. Crickets 'sing' by rubbing their wings together rapidly, and frogs have special air sacs in their throats to amplify their croaks.

The voice of an animal may be used to attract mates, warn off rivals and defend territory boundaries. The song of a songbird like a blackbird or thrush may perform all these functions. ■

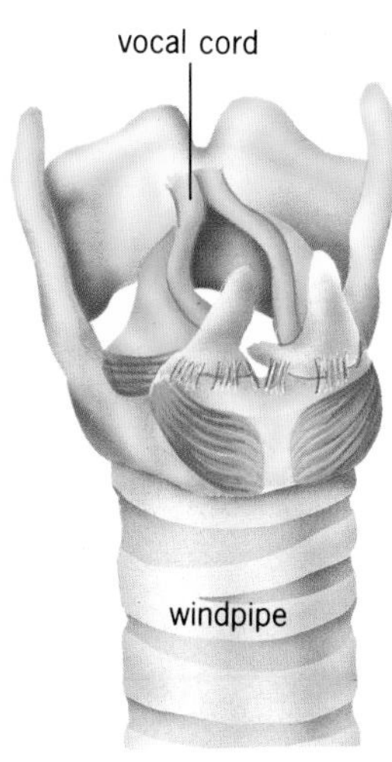

▲ The larynx (voice box) is a thickened part of the windpipe. It contains flaps called vocal cords. Air forced out over the vocal cords produces the basic sound of our voice.

See also
Communication
Crickets
Frogs
Languages
Singing and songs
Sound

Volcanoes

Vulcano is an Italian island which has given its name to all other volcanoes.

Mauna Loa is the world's largest volcano. It reaches 4,170 m above sea-level, but its base is on the Pacific Ocean floor, 5,180 m below sea-level.

A volcano is a mountain or hill made of lava which comes from deep beneath the Earth's surface. When a volcano erupts, lava and ash build up to make a cone. Some volcanoes give off clouds of ash and gas when they erupt. Others have streams of red-hot lava pouring down their side. Volcanoes can form on land or on the ocean floor. Some undersea volcanoes grow high enough to reach above sea-level and become islands.

► Kilauea is a small volcano on the slopes of the much larger Mauna Loa in Hawaii. Most of the time the lava swirls and seethes in the fire pit, but occasionally it erupts explosively.

The birth of a volcano

It is not often anyone can see a volcano begin and then grow. In Mexico, in 1943, some villagers were worried by earthquakes. Then a crack appeared across a cornfield and smoke gushed out. The crack widened, and ash and rocks were hurled high into the air. Soon, red-hot lava poured out. After a week, a volcano 150 m (500 ft) high stood where the cornfield had been, and the villagers had to leave. Mount Paricutin grew to 275 m (900 ft) in a year, and to 410 m (1,345 ft) after nine years.

How a volcano grows

The molten rock deep beneath the Earth's crust is called magma. It forces its way up through cracks and weak spots in the Earth's crust and spills out as lava. As magma rises, gases separate out from the molten rock. These gases may collect near the surface and cause a great explosion. On Martinique, in the Caribbean, 20,000 people were killed by an explosion of hot gases and ash when Mont Pelée erupted in 1902.

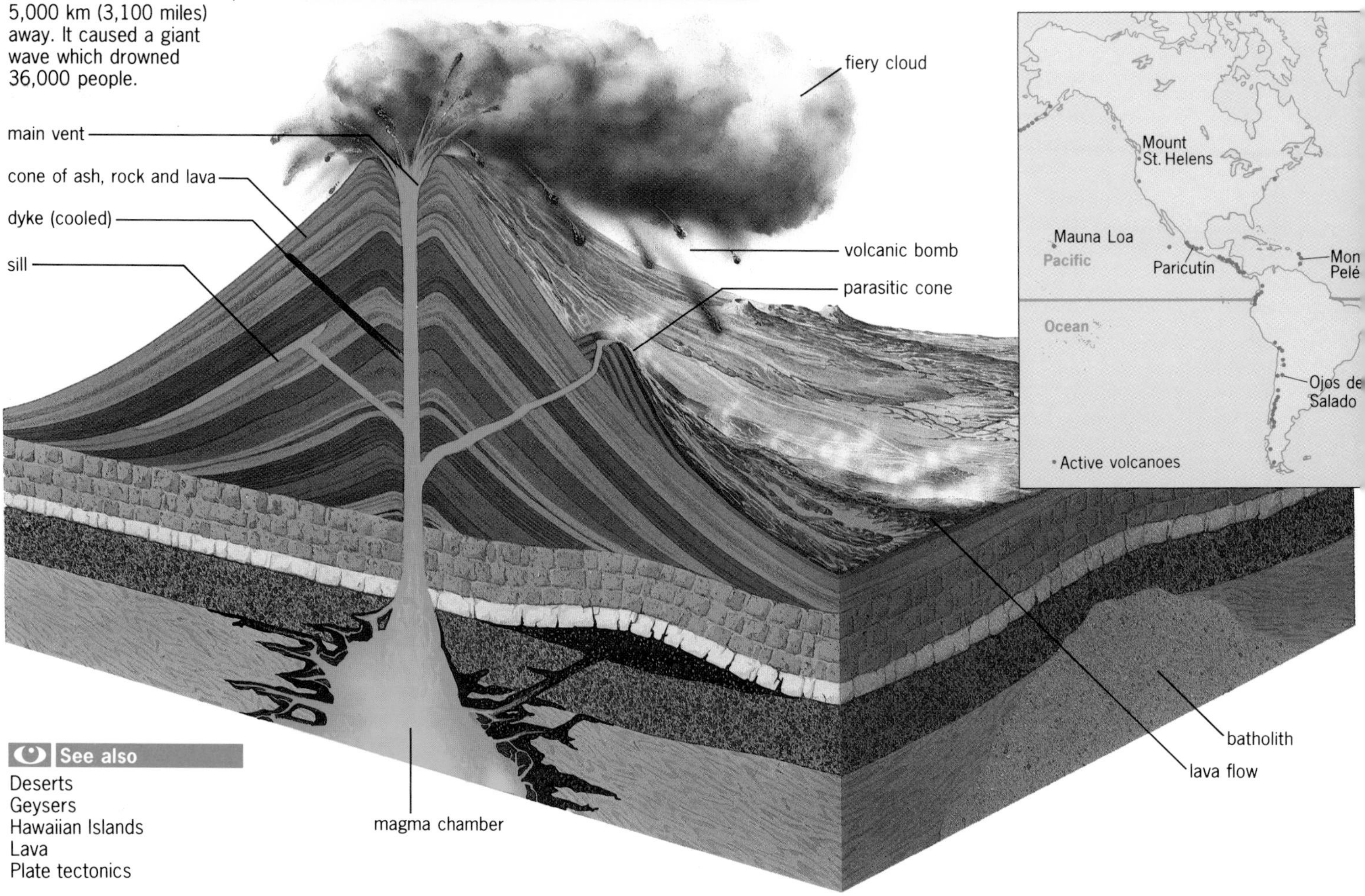

The biggest explosion ever recorded was when Krakatau in Indonesia erupted in 1883. It was heard in India and Australia, 5,000 km (3,100 miles) away. It caused a giant wave which drowned 36,000 people.

fiery cloud
main vent
cone of ash, rock and lava
dyke (cooled)
sill
volcanic bomb
parasitic cone
magma chamber
batholith
lava flow

Mount St. Helens
Mauna Loa
Pacific
Ocean
Paricutin
Mon Pelé
Ojos de Salado
• Active volcanoes

See also
Deserts
Geysers
Hawaiian Islands
Lava
Plate tectonics

When a volcano erupts, pieces of broken rock and ash are often thrown out with the lava. Large lumps are called 'volcanic bombs'. As the rock and ash cool, they make layers of solid rock. When Vesuvius, in southern Italy, erupted in the year AD 79, the town of Pompeii was completely buried under volcanic ash. Further round the Bay of Naples, Herculaneum was buried by mud which swept down the side of the volcano. Today, the remains of both towns have been dug out for all to see.

Dormant and extinct volcanoes

Volcanoes eventually die. A volcano that has not erupted for a long time is said to be dormant. There is always the danger that a dormant volcano may suddenly erupt. When people think a volcano has finally died, then it is called extinct. Gradually, the volcano will be eroded. The softer rocks are worn away first, and in some places the only part left is the hard plug which filled the vent of the volcano.

There are about 700 active volcanoes in the world today, including some that are under the

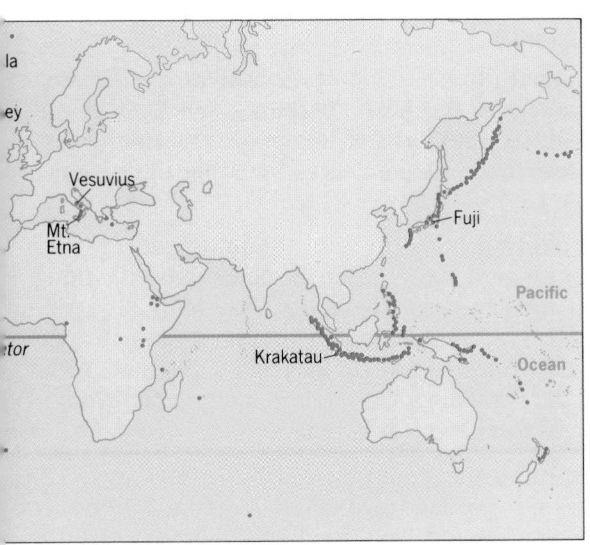

sea. The map shows that most of them are arranged like beads on a string. Notice how many volcanoes surround the Pacific Ocean. The areas with volcanoes are also the areas which suffer from earthquakes. This fact helped scientists come up with the theory of plate tectonics. They believe that the Earth's crust is broken into huge slabs, called 'plates'. Most of the world's volcanoes occur where plates meet, which is where magma can rise to the surface. A few, such as in Hawaii and the Canary Islands, occur above 'hot spots' where magma seems to pierce through a plate. ■

Voles

◀ The bank vole is a common species over most of Europe and Asia. Like most voles it is often active during the daytime. It lives among rough vegetation or burrows in the surface of the soil. It makes stores of food, sometimes hiding its larder in an old bird's nest.

Voles may be mistaken for mice, but differ in having short tails and faces with small eyes and ears. They often feed on very tough plants. To deal with this, most voles have teeth which continue to grow throughout their lives, keeping pace with the wear caused by such a harsh diet. Voles rarely live for more than one year, but most females produce several litters of young in this time. Most are eaten by foxes, owls or other predators but sometimes enough survive to cause a huge increase in numbers. They live in northern parts of the world.

Some northern voles are known as lemmings. These animals often have huge increases in population, which then crash to a low level again. ■

Distribution
North and Central America, Europe and Asia
Largest
Musk-rat, head and body length up to 32·5 cm
Smallest
Head and body length less than 8 cm
Number of young
Up to 12
Lifespan
Between 1 and 2 years

Subphylum Vertebrata
Class Mammalia
Order Rodentia
Number of species 110

See also
Rodents

Volleyball

This is a game for six players a side. Each team tries to hit or knock the ball with hand or arm (or any part of the body above the waist) over the net so that the opposing team is unable to return it or prevent it from hitting the ground.

Each team can hit the ball a maximum of three times before sending it back across the net, but they cannot catch or hold the ball.

The game was invented in 1895 in America by a games instructor called William Morgan. He wanted a game for people who did not want to play basketball. ■

A leather ball is used, similar to a soccer ball but lighter.

See also
Basketball

Wading birds

Subphylum
Vertebrata
Class
Aves
Order
Charadriiformes
Number of species
Over 200

Birds that feed in wet places need to be specially equipped. Long legs allow them to wade into water, and long bills help them to pick up small creatures, even those hiding in mud.

In Britain most 'waders' are sandpipers and their relatives. In North America these are called 'shorebirds', and 'waders' means herons and egrets.

▲ **Marbled godwit with the typically long legs and long beak of the wading birds.**

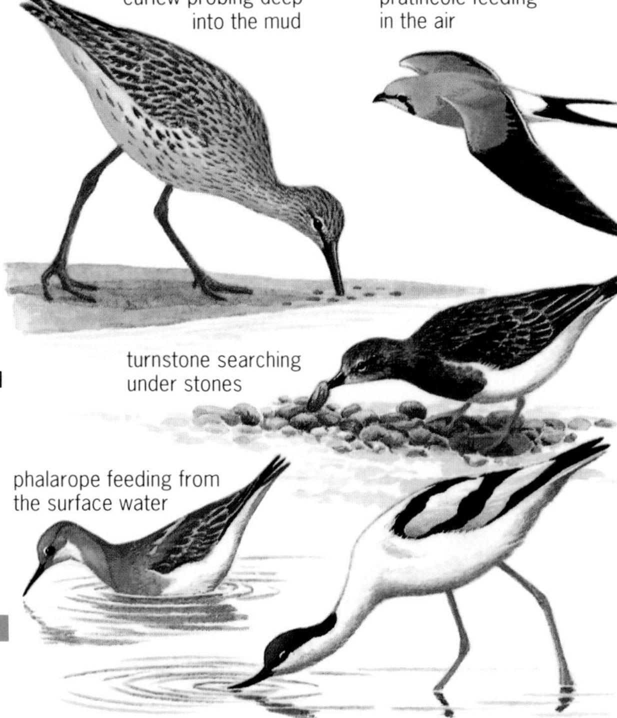

► **Wading birds find food in many different ways.**

See also
Birds
Migration
Water birds

The long and the short

Herons are large with long necks, legs and toes for climbing in trees and among waterside plants. They eat animals, often fish, which they grasp in their dagger-like bills.

Shorebirds spend much of the year near water. Many are at home in open spaces and breed on the northern tundra.

Size and feeding methods vary. Snipe have extremely long, straight bills and probe deep into the mud for worms. Oystercatchers have long, strong bills for prising open mussels, clams and other shellfish.

Avocets have long up-swept bills which they sweep from side to side as they search for tiny creatures to eat. Plovers have short, stubby bills. They run, stop, bend and seize their prey from the surface.

Flight for survival

Many waders, or shorebirds, live in the far north where food is plentiful in summer. The summer is short, but there is very little darkness and the young grow fast. Before the Arctic winter returns the birds must fly south. For some, like the ringed plover, which breeds over a wide area, the most northerly breeding birds make the longest journeys and winter farthest south. They 'leap-frog' the southerly breeding birds, which move hardly any distance.

Family groups do not migrate together. Often one parent leaves when the chicks are still young. If food is short this action may help the young survive. With some species, such as the redshank, the female leaves and the male looks after the young. On migration often the juveniles will form their own flocks.

Some waders make remarkable journeys. The lesser golden plover flies from Siberia to Australia and New Zealand. Others near by in Arctic Canada winter in South America and fly the shortest route, which is mostly over sea, a continuous journey of 3,800 km (2,400 miles).

Safety in numbers

Outside the breeding season many of these species form large flocks. They feed on estuaries where food is plentiful, and numbers may build up to thousands. As they search for food they all spread out over the mud. As the tide comes in they are driven off their feeding grounds and onto high-tide roosts where they wait, saving their energy, until the tide starts to fall again. ■

Wales

Wales is a principality of the United Kingdom, in north-west Europe.

Mountains

Wales is mostly mountainous and the highest Welsh peak is Yr Wyddfa (Snowdon). Instead of climbing it, many people prefer to use the narrow gauge railway that runs to the very top. Beneath the peaks of Snowdonia are great caverns and quarries from which slate has been mined. The 'great little trains' which took the slate to the coast for export now carry three-quarters of a million tourist passengers a year.

Wales is wet. Fast-flowing mountain rivers are used to turn turbines to make hydroelectricity. The power-station at Maentwrog uses water from an artificial lake at Trawsfynydd. The lake water is also used to cool the reactors of a nuclear power-station. Water from Llyn Brenig and other lakes in mid Wales goes by pipeline to Birkenhead, Liverpool, Birmingham and other English cities.

Industries

South Wales is industrial Wales: a landscape of long streets, terraced houses, and hillside chapels. There are far fewer working coal-mines now than there were in the first half of this century. New factories stand on or beside the derelict sites of 19th-century copper furnaces. The tradition of metal working and engineering continues. Factories make cars, refrigerators and machines. There are offices, too. The government department that issues licences for drivers and vehicles is at Swansea.

Cardiff is the capital city of Wales. It has government offices and one of the finest Norman castles in Britain.

Welsh people like singing and their choirs, especially male voice choirs, are famous. Voices are raised too at the Welsh National Stadium, the home of Welsh rugby football. About half a million people in Wales speak Cymraeg (Welsh), as well as English. A few speak only Cymraeg. Road signs and official documents are in both languages. The Eisteddfod is an annual festival of Welsh culture. ■

Area
20,761 sq km
(8,016 sq miles)
Capital
Cardiff
Population
2,791,851
Language
Cymraeg (Welsh) and English
Religion
Christian
Highest peak
Yr Wyddfa (Snowdon)
1,085 m
Largest lake
Llyn Tegid (Bala)
4·38 sq km (1·69 sq miles)
Longest river
Usk

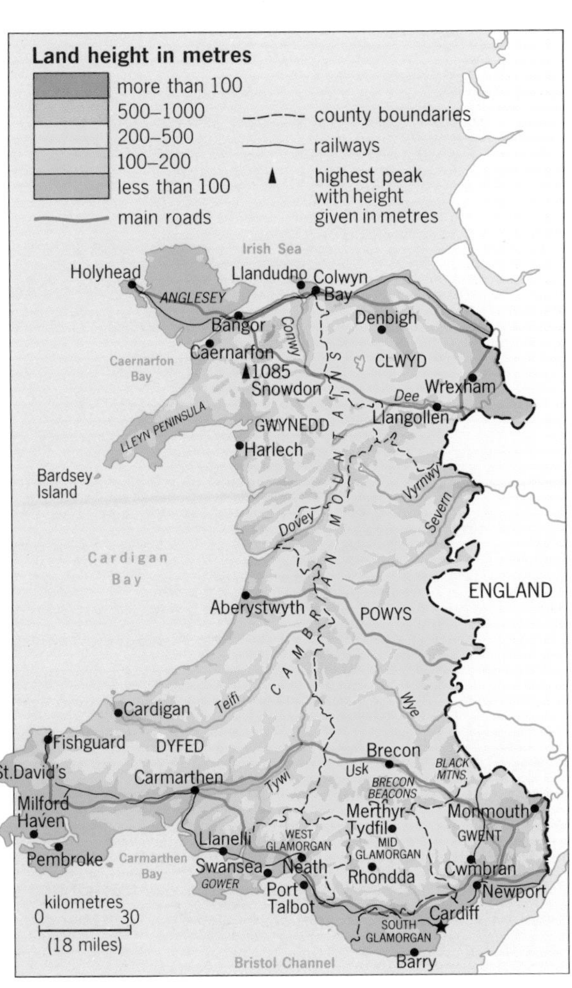

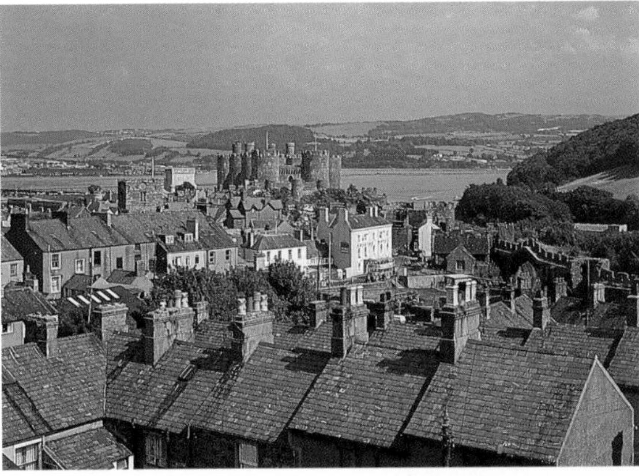

◀ Conway, north Wales. In the background is the River Conway.

▲ A bilingual sign with the harp, symbol of Wales.

◀ The Clywedog dam on the river Severn in central Wales. For 25 years slightly under half the water collected in Wales for public supply has been consumed in England.

See also
British Isles
Castles
Celtic history
Eisteddfod
Europe
United Kingdom
Welsh history

Warm-bloodedness

Warm-blooded animals can survive in cold parts of the world. Birds and mammals live in the Arctic, which reptiles and amphibians (cold-blooded animals) cannot do.

Highest mammal body temperature
41°C in the dromedary, a type of camel

Human beings, like all other mammals and the birds, are warm-blooded. This does not mean that we never feel cold, but that we have a kind of thermostat in our brains, which keep our bodies at about the same temperature (37°C, 98·6°F) all of the time. Because of this our bodies can go on working at a steady rate, digesting food and giving the same amount of energy, whether our surroundings are cold or hot. Warm-blooded animals are protected against the climate in a number of ways. Human beings, whales and seals have an insulating jacket of fat under their skin. Mammals in general have hair or fur which also insulates them against heat and cold, while birds have feathers for the same purpose. Warm-blooded animals also shiver, which produces extra heat in the muscles.

If we get too hot our blood flows close to the surface of our skin and we cool off as we lose heat like a radiator. Many other mammals, such as dogs and rabbits, have very thin fur on their ears and they lose heat from these areas in the same way. ■

Warsaw Pact

See also
Cold war
NATO
Twentieth-century history

Albania withdrew in 1968.

The Warsaw Pact was signed in 1955 as a treaty of friendship and a military alliance between the USSR and seven countries of Eastern Europe: Albania, Bulgaria, Czechoslovakia, East Germany (the German Democratic Republic), Hungary, Poland and Romania. All these countries had communist governments at that time. The Western powers had already founded NATO and the two alliances opposed each other throughout the Cold War which lasted till the late 1980s. In November 1990 the six countries of the Warsaw Pact (Germany was by then reunited) signed a treaty of disarmament with members of NATO and other European states. ■

Wars of the Roses

Lancastrians in power

Yorkists in power

The Wars of the Roses were civil wars fought in England between 1455 and 1485. The leading families on either side were called Lancaster and York. Their badges were a red rose for Lancaster and a white rose for York. So, many years later, their struggle became known as the Wars of the Roses. Supporters of the two families often changed sides: it just depended on which seemed to be stronger at the time.

A war of changing fortunes

The trouble began in the reign of Henry VI, a Lancastrian. He was a weak king, and suffered from attacks of madness. So, after the battle of St Albans in 1455, his relative Richard of York was made protector of England. Henry's wife, Queen Margaret, seized power again for the Lancastrians. But in 1461 Richard of York's son, Edward, defeated the Lancastrians at Towton. He was crowned King Edward IV, and ruled with only one interruption until his death. His brother then became King Richard III. Richard was unpopular with Yorkists and Lancastrians alike and in 1485 the Lancastrian Henry Tudor defeated him at Bosworth Field and became King Henry VII. He married a Yorkist princess, to help to bring the two families together. Slowly the kingdom became more peaceful, but the danger of more fighting was never far away. ■

See also
Biography
Richard III

Washing machines

Washing machines were once equipped with a mangle. This had two rollers which squeezed the water out of wet clothes. Later, twin-tub machines were made, with one tub for washing and another for spin-drying.

The first electric washing machine was made in 1906.

Just putting dirty clothes in water will not get them clean. They need to have water forced through the fibres of the cloth. Most washing machines work by swirling the clothes in water in a revolving metal drum. Detergent is used to get the water more deeply into the fabric. It also removes the grease.

Most washing machines are automatic. They can be left to do the whole wash by themselves. Often, they are controlled electronically. You choose from a range of different programs so that the machine hot-washes cotton clothes or cool-washes delicate woollens. It mixes hot and cold water to the right temperature, gives the clothes a long or short wash, rinses them, then spins out most of the water. Some machines tumble-dry as well. ■

See also
Detergents
Household equipment

▼ In this machine, the dirty washing goes in the revolving drum. Here it is washed, rinsed and spun almost dry.

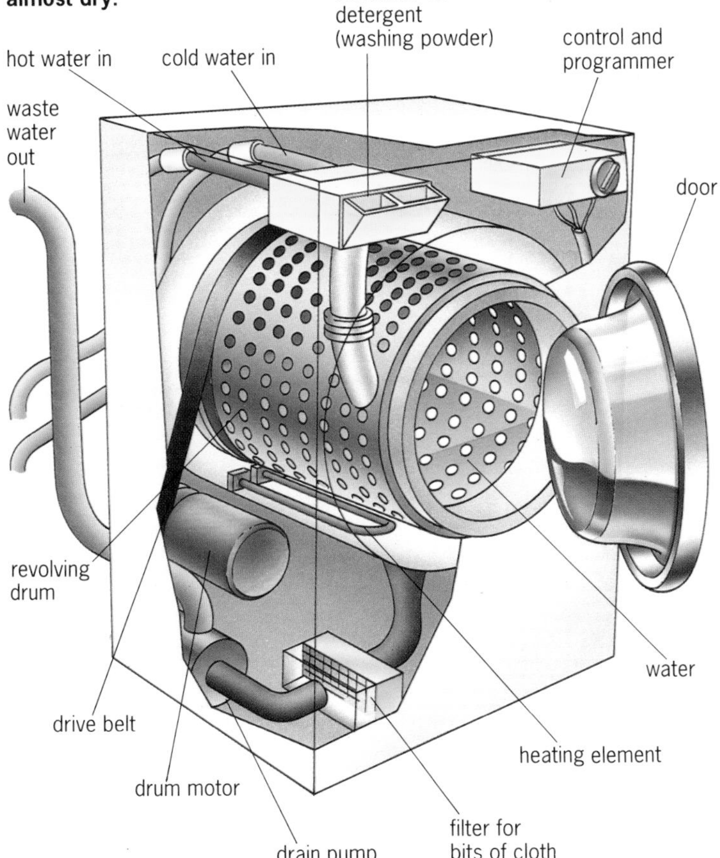

Wasps

Wasps are insects with yellow and black stripes. These bright colours act as a warning that the wasp can protect itself with a sting.

Many wasps live in family groups which are all the offspring of one female, called the queen. These are called social wasps. Their nests are formed of a kind of paper. The wasps make this by chewing up dead wood and mixing it with their saliva. The cells of the wasp's nest are hexagonal and the nest is formed in a series of floors, connected to each other by paper pillars. The grubs living in the nest are fed on the flesh of other animals, particularly insects. Early in the summer, when many grubs are being reared, wasps are very useful animals, as they kill many pests for food. The adults themselves need sugars for energy and feed only on nectar, fruit and tree sap. Most adults are sterile female workers but by late summer fully sexed males and females have been produced. These breed, and then the whole colony, which might number 50,000 wasps, dies with the arrival of cold weather. Only the young mated queens survive in hibernation, to emerge next spring.

As well as the social wasps, there are many species which do not live in family groups. ■

▼ These large wasps are called paper wasps. The sterile female workers continue to enlarge the nest that their mother the queen wasp began. The queen wasp will lay an egg in each hexagonal cell.

Distribution
Worldwide
Largest social wasp
The hornet *Vespa crabro* grows up to 3·5 cm
Phylum
Arthropoda
Class
Insecta
Order
Hymenoptera
Number of species
About 17,000

See also
Bees
Insects

Waste disposal

► This incinerator in the London suburb of Edmonton uses the heat from burning rubbish to generate electricity.

Every home produces vast quantities of tin cans, packaging, waste paper, glass and other rubbish. Britain alone throws out about 70 million tonnes of waste a year, which is more than 1 tonne for each person in the country. If this rubbish is not disposed of carefully it can become a health hazard. Rotting rubbish not only looks and smells unpleasant, it also acts as a breeding ground for flies, rats and other carriers of disease. In addition, waste can pollute the air, water and soil.

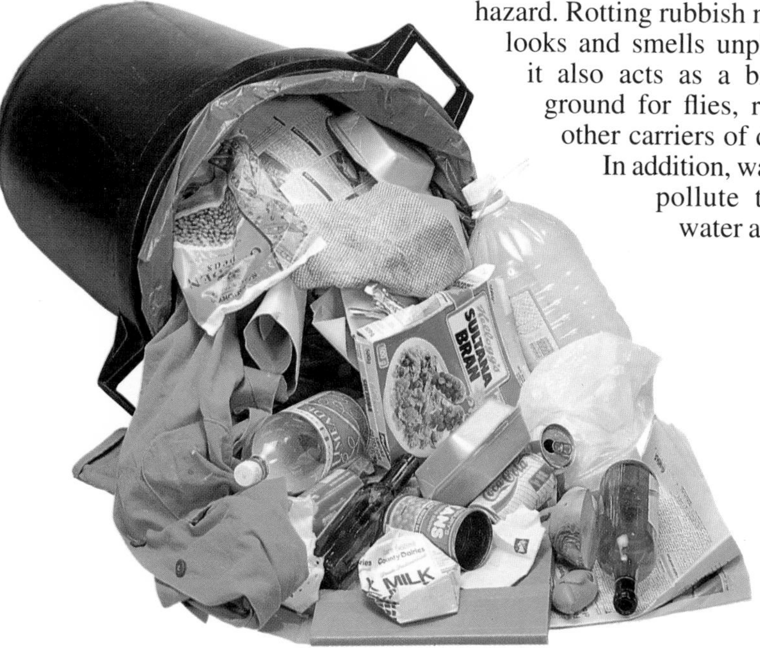

▲ Many of the things in household rubbish like aluminium cans, newspaper, cardboard boxes and glass can all be recycled, as can cloth, which can be made into paper or into new fabrics. Vegetable matter can be used as compost.

Tipping

The easiest and cheapest method of disposing of rubbish is to tip it into a hole in the ground. In some areas there are many large holes caused by quarrying and open-cast mining, and these are often used for waste disposal.

During tipping, each layer of rubbish is covered with soil, so that in section the tip looks like a giant layer cake. Care has to be taken to see that rain-water running off the tip does not enter rivers, since such water often contains poisonous substances.

Reclaiming land

Tipping can be used to reclaim waste land or marsh land. Once the hole is filled to the desired level, it can be capped with soil and used for planting crops or trees. It takes a long time, though, before the reclaimed land can be used for building. This is because the land may sink as the buried rubbish rots.

Almost 80 per cent of Britain's rubbish is disposed of by tipping. However, in many places there is now a shortage of suitable places where tipping can occur.

Burning rubbish

In some areas, waste is disposed of by incineration (burning). This has the advantage that it greatly reduces the volume of the waste material. Nine cubic metres of household waste are reduced to one cubic metre of ash, which can be tipped. Further, the ash is clean and germ-free.

Making electricity from rubbish

In some towns the heat produced by burning waste is used to generate electricity. A massive incinerator in the London suburb of Edmonton, for example, burns some 400,000 tonnes of rubbish a year and uses the heat to generate electricity. In other places, waste is ground up and turned into solid fuel pellets. These can be used in boilers instead of coal or coke.

Making compost

The incinerators used to burn rubbish are large and expensive, and they produce smoke that can pollute the air. One alternative is to grind up the rubbish and turn it into compost for use by farmers and gardeners. Great care has to be taken, though, to see that the compost does not contain poisonous materials.

Recycling materials

It has been estimated that 60 per cent of the materials we throw away could be sorted and recycled (used again). New glass, for example, can be made from old, while new paper can be made from waste paper. Recycling waste saves raw materials and fuel, and causes less pollution. ■

See also
Pollution
Recycling

Wastelands

If there is land which we cannot farm, or find any obvious productive use for, we label it wasteland. That is a mistake. The frozen 'wasteland' of the polar regions provides a home for specially adapted wildlife: polar bears in the Arctic, and penguins in the Antarctic. The hot, dry 'wasteland' of the Sahara Desert is home to a whole range of plants and animals too, and there are groups of people who have found a way of living in these hostile places. The Inuit (Eskimos) can build shelters from blocks of snow, and hunt through the ice for fish. The Bushmen of the Kalahari know just which spot in the dry sand to dig a hole and find water.

Industrial wasteland

In the less remote parts of the world, most so-called 'wasteland' has been made unproductive by the actions of people. Mining and quarrying have left great scars in the landscape. All kinds of waste materials have been dumped to form mountainous waste tips, and land has been poisoned, too, with chemicals from industry.

A great deal of new wasteland was created in Europe and North America during the 19th and early 20th centuries. Now mining, dumping and chemical pollution are creating new wasteland in the Third World countries.

Wasteland within towns is usually land which has been used in the past, often for buildings, and where these are no longer needed, and get knocked down, the land is abandoned.

Wasteland wildlife

There are special plants and animals that can make their home on this kind of wasteland. Most of the plants have seeds which will blow in on the wind, the fluffy down of willows, dandelions and thistles for example; the super-light seeds of silver birch, and the winged 'helicopter' fruits of sycamore and ash trees. The dust-like spores of fungi and mosses are often the first to colonize when new wasteland is created. Many of the wasteland flowers are very colourful. They need to attract insects to the new habitat, and urban wastelands are very good places to see butterflies, bees and moths. Flocks of small birds fly from site to site, feeding on the masses of seed they find there, and many wild creatures such as foxes and hedgehogs often use the shelter of wasteland to hide from people during the daytime.

Uses for wasteland

People have found all kinds of 'unofficial' uses for wasteland in towns. Lots of children play on them. When local people are short of land, they often use wasteland to make temporary gardens, or even set up city farms.

Very often, urban wasteland is used for dumping rubbish, but if the edges are kept clean and tidy, people will respect the wasteland, and nature will quickly take over and create a new green space where children can play, wildlife can live, and where the trees and bushes can help clean up the air, slow down the wind, and improve the way the city feels. ■

See also
Deserts
Flowers
Wildlife

▼ Wastelands in London: flourishing great bindweed (left) and home for a red fox cub (right).

Water

Water expands when it freezes, and can break pipes.

Almost three-quarters of the Earth's surface is covered with water, and in places the oceans are miles deep. Frozen water forms the ice-caps at the North and South Poles; and snow covers the highest mountain ranges the whole year round. In the sky, massive clouds of water vapour bring rain to us; and where the rain falls and the rivers flow, plants and animals thrive. Without water there would be no life on our planet.

H_2O

The freezing point of water was taken as the bottom of the Celsius (centigrade) scale of temperature, so that water freezes at 0°C. The boiling point of water was taken as 100°C.

Like many other substances, water is made up of molecules. These are so small that even the smallest raindrop contains billions. Every molecule of water consists of two atoms of hydrogen stuck to a single atom of oxygen. Scientists say that the chemical formula for water is H_2O.

Water and you

Two-thirds of your body is water. Most of your blood is water. Every organ of your body: brain, heart, liver, muscles, contains water. Press your skin and feel how bouncy it is compared to pressing a sheet of paper. Skin is like a layer of tiny water-filled balloons.

Every day your body loses lots of water. About a litre goes down the toilet. Another half a litre disappears as sweat and in the air you breathe out. On a cold day you can see this water vapour in your warm breath. On hot days sweating helps keep you cool. The moisture (sweat) that seeps through pores (small holes) in the skin then evaporates into the air, taking with it some heat from the body.

See also

Atoms
Cells
Cold
Heat
Hydroelectric power
Ice
Liquids
Molecules
Photosynthesis
Plants
Steam-engines
Water cycle
Water power
Water sports
Water supplies

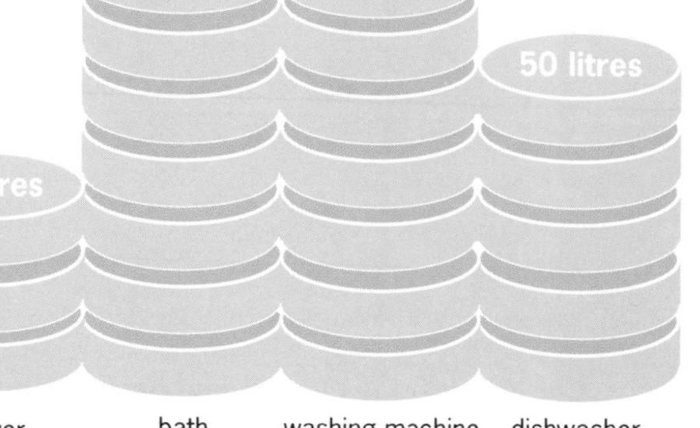

► A family of four uses about 3,500 litres of water every week. The bar graph shows how much water can be used each time in washing and other activities.

Unlike camels which can store many gallons of water in their tissues, we have no store of water and must replace what we lose each day. We need a litre and a half (2½ pints) of water every day to stay alive. Much of that water can come from the food we eat. Many vegetables and fruit are three-quarters water, and even a slice of bread is one-third water.

Plants and water

Plants need water to grow. They use water and other chemicals to make the substances needed for new plant growth. They use water to carry substances between their roots and leaves. And they use the pressure of water in their cells to stay firm and rigid. Without water, plants wilt.

Plants usually take in water through their roots and lose it through pores in their leaves. Plants which must survive in deserts have a waxy coating on their leaves to stop water escaping.

Different kinds of water

There is not just one kind of drinking water. It can taste completely different depending where you live.

The water that comes out of the tap has had a long journey that begins as rain falling through the air, washing over rocks and flowing along rivers. On its travels, the rain-water dissolves gases from the air and many different substances from the rocks. The kind of drinking water we end up with depends very much on what is in the local rocks.

Where there are chalk and limestone rocks, these dissolve in the rain and join with the dissolved gas, carbon dioxide, to form a substance called calcium bicarbonate. This and other similar chemicals produce 'hard' water which leaves a hard, yellowish deposit in the bottom of kettles called 'limescale'. It is difficult to make a good lather with soap in hard water. Water that does not have these particular substances is called 'soft'. But it still has lots of different chemicals in it. Really pure water has no trace of anything in it. It is called distilled water and is tasteless and unpleasant to drink.

Water at home

You use ten litres (2·2 gallons) of water every time you flush a lavatory, and more than seven times that amount to have a bath. Using a washing machine needs at least 100 litres (22 gallons). If a house catches fire the fire brigade might pump thousands of litres on the flames. ■

Water birds

Many birds live on or near water. Here we look more closely at those which are not sea birds, waders, or ducks, geese or swans, but nevertheless feed in lakes and rivers.

Birds which find food regularly in water need to use special methods. A heron will use its long legs to wade into the water and wait patiently until a fish comes within reach. An osprey dives into the water, talons first, to seize its prey. Wagtails run along river banks or flit from stone to stone to catch flies.

Colourful fishers

There are over 80 kinds of kingfishers but many do not catch fish at all. They are all large-headed birds, with strong bills, short necks and short tails. Most are found in tropical forests, where they feed on ground-living creatures as well as fish.

The brilliantly coloured kingfisher of Europe and Asia nests in river banks at the end of 50 cm (20 in) tunnels which it digs with its bill and feet. It catches fish by hovering or diving into water from an overhanging perch. Fish are swallowed whole, generally head first so the scales and fins slip down the throat easily.

A secret life

Members of the rail family are often very secretive and some are nocturnal. Although a few live in dry places, most are water or swamp birds and prefer to remain hidden than to fly.

Perhaps the least shy rail is the coot. It is black with a white bill and forehead. It swims and dives to pull up water plants. Its feet are 'lobed', which means that the toes have round flaps of skin which help it to swim.

Masters of the deep

Fish-hunting under water is highly specialized, but the divers (called 'loons' in North America) and grebes have mastered the art.

Divers have long, straight, pointed bills and long bodies with rather small wings. The legs are set so far back on the body that the bird is awkward on land. Normal hunting time under water is between 30 and 60 seconds.

Many of the grebes have crests or tufts on their heads. They have many of the same features as the divers, but the smaller species are more likely to hunt insects.

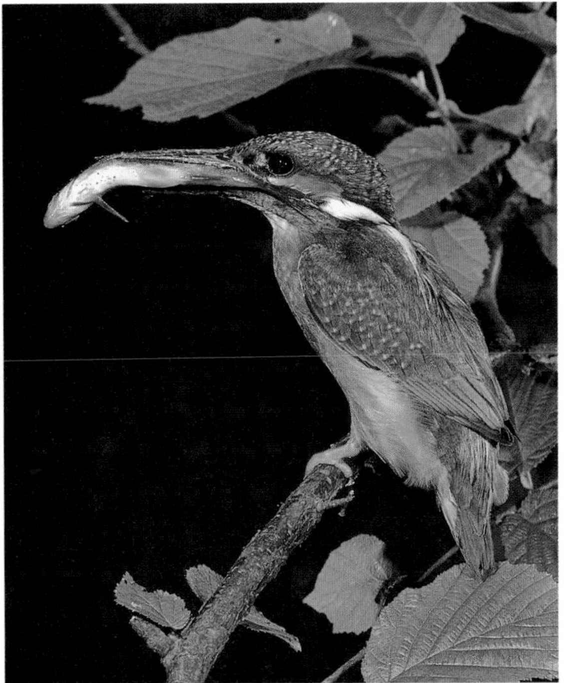

◄ **Kingfisher, the only European species, with fish.**

◄ **Dipper diving in stream to feed on insect larvae and other water-living invertebrates.**

Walking under water

Dippers are rather like large wrens, except that they are never found far from water. They have developed the most unusual feeding method.

Their food consists of many kinds of water creatures living in fast-flowing rivers and streams. To feed, the dipper will wade into shallow water. In deeper water it will first wade and then dive to the bottom. To stay submerged the bird flies against the current and the pressure of water helps to keep it under the water. ■

Subphylum
Vertebrata
Class
Aves
Orders
Ciconiiformes (herons)
Coraciiformes (kingfishers)
Gaviiformes (divers)
Gruiformes (coots and rails)
Passeriformes (wagtails, dippers)
Podicipediformes (grebes)

See also
Ducks, geese and swans
Sea birds
Streams
Wading birds

Water cycle

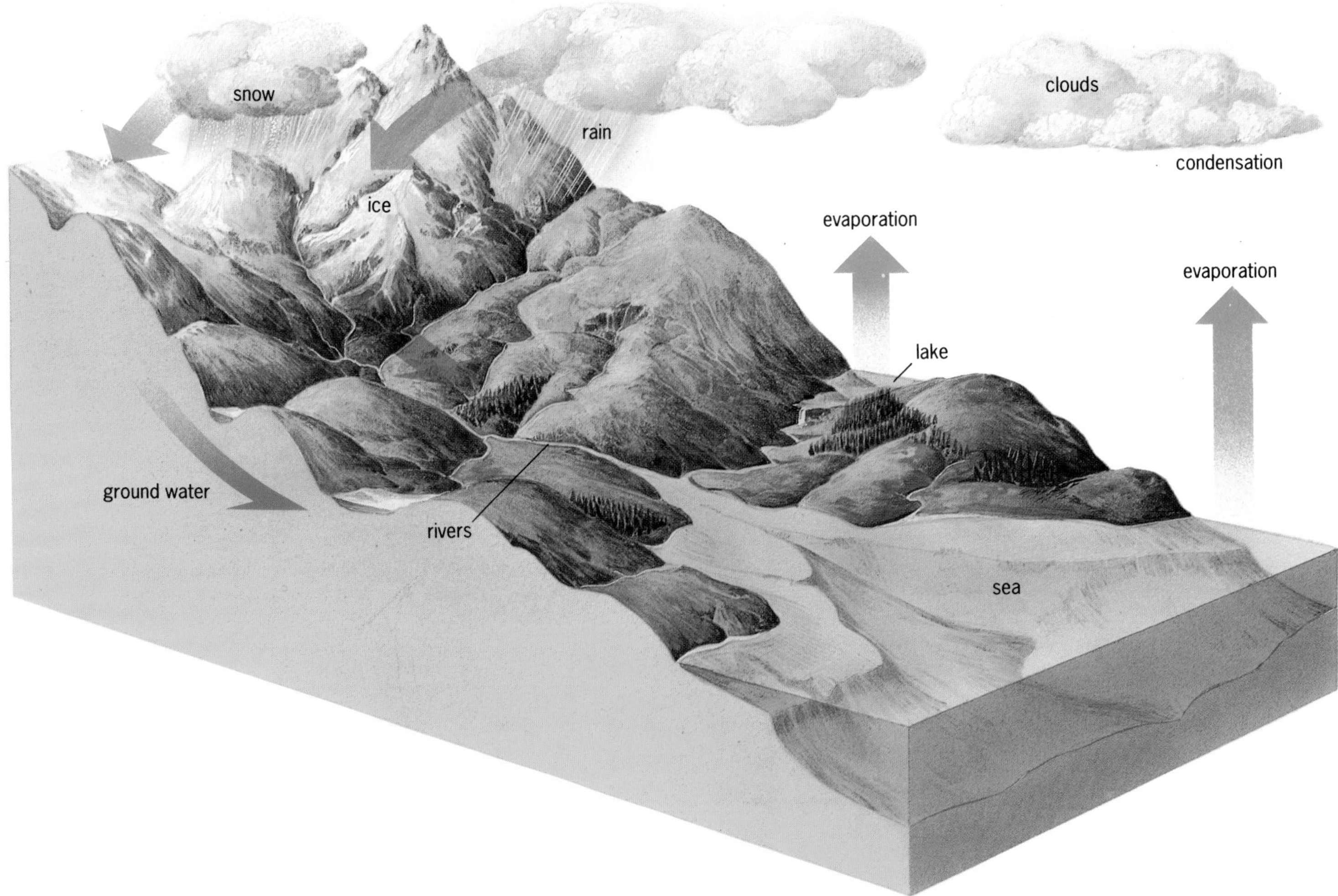

▲ **Water is never used up, it just goes round and round this cycle. It is a remarkable fact that the oceans hold about 97 per cent of the world's water. A further 2 per cent is frozen in the polar ice-caps. This means that only about 1 per cent of the world's water is going round the water cycle at any one time.**

You may sometimes wonder what happens to all the water that falls on the land. Much of it flows down to the sea in streams and rivers. Some soaks into the ground, but will eventually come to the surface as a spring, or seep back into rivers or the sea. Some stays as ice for a long time, but eventually melts and also flows to the sea. But where does the rain and snow come from in the first place? The warmth of the Sun evaporates water from the sea, from rivers and lakes, and also from the soil and plants on the land. The water is turned into water vapour, which is one of the invisible gases that make up the air we breathe.

Air is moving about all the time. If it rises high up into the atmosphere, or if it comes into contact with a cold area, it will cool down. Cool air cannot hold as much water vapour as warm air, so some of the water vapour will turn into tiny droplets of water. When this happens on the cold window of a room at home, we call it condensation. In the sky, the tiny water droplets form clouds; near the ground we call them fog, mist or dew. If the tiny water droplets combine, they will fall to earth as rain, or as hail or snow if they are frozen. The land is watered again.

Pollution

So water is constantly being recycled in a process called the water cycle. The cycle is kept going by the Sun's energy. In some parts of the cycle the water is a liquid (rain), in other parts it is a gas (water vapour) or a solid (ice). Each part of the cycle depends on the other parts, which is why any interference by people, such as pollution, is a danger. Polluting gases that are added to the air in one place join the water vapour and are carried to another place. Then the rain becomes acid, making the water of streams and rivers acid. This in turn, affects rocks and soil, plants and fish and other animals. ■

See also
Acid rain
Air
Clouds
Rain
Snow
Water

Waterfalls

Spectacular waterfalls occur when a large river plunges into a gorge or falls from a high plateau. The world's highest falls are the Angel Falls in Venezuela. The Carao River falls 979 m (3,212 ft) over the edge of a high plateau of hard rock.

▲ **The Iguaçu Falls, on the border of Brazil and Argentina. The river plunges 80 m (about 260 ft) down a crescent-shaped cliff which is half as wide again as the Niagara.**

What makes a waterfall

The rocks in the bed of a river are worn down slowly by stones and grit that are rolled along the water. Large rivers will flow across many different kinds of rock. Some rocks are tougher than others so do not erode quickly. Others will be worn away quite easily. When a river flows over bands of hard then softer rock there will probably be one or more waterfalls or rapids where the different types of rock meet. The river will plunge off the resistant rock, and wear away the softer rock underneath even faster. The river will undercut the hard rock on top of the falls. Sometimes there is a hollow with a ledge wide enough for people to walk behind the waterfall.

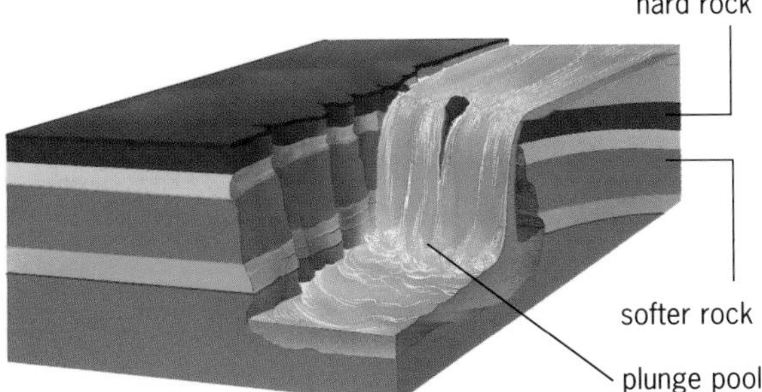

▲ **Waterfalls form in river valleys where there are bands of hard and soft rocks. The hard rock resists erosion while the softer rock beneath is eroded away.**

At the Niagara Falls, on the boundary of Canada and the USA, there is a flat layer of resistant limestone on top of a much weaker rock called shale. The river erodes the shale more quickly, and big blocks of undercut limestone crash down from the edge of the falls. This happens most often in the centre of the river where the water flows most powerfully. This erosion has caused the marvellous Horseshoe Falls, the Canadian part of Niagara.

The Niagara Falls have been wearing away the rock so that they have been getting nearer to Lake Erie by more than a metre a year for thousands of years. In Africa the spectacular **Victoria Falls** flow through a gorge 80 km (50 miles) long.

▲ **The Niagara Falls on the USA side. Behind the thundering curtain of water lies a cavern, the Cave of the Winds.**

The highest waterfall in Europe is in Norway. The Utigard Falls are 800 m (2,600 ft) high. Water from the Josterdal Glacier falls in Nesdal which is far below. The sides of Nesdal were worn away by a glacier and are very steep.

Mountain rivers often have lots of waterfalls. The water rushes down steep hillsides, tumbling over boulders and rocky ledges in a series of small falls. Waterfalls are not so common at the coast, though they do happen when a river falls over into a sea. ■

See also

Erosion
Rivers
Zimbabwe (photograph of Victoria Falls)

Water power

► **The Guri hydroelectric dam on the Caroní River in Venezuela is one of the world's largest dams.**

Water always flows from a higher point to a lower point. This movement of water can be used as a source of energy. It can be the gentle flow of a river, or water falling from a great height as in a waterfall or from a dam. The never-ending movement of waves at sea and tides can also be harnessed to provide energy. Unlike many other sources of energy, water does not get used up and there will always be a cheap and constant supply of moving water on the earth.

Hydroelectric power

Electricity is generated when water drives a machine called a turbine which is connected to a dynamo. Turbines are more efficient versions of earlier water wheels. They are designed to take as much energy from the moving water as possible. Hydroelectric power-stations are often built in hilly regions where there is lots of rain. A lake or reservoir provides a store of water high above the generating station. The amount of power available depends on the height the water falls. A dam is often needed to increase the size of a natural lake. Water flows from the reservoir down to the turbines through strong steel pipes or tunnels.

1850 James Francis invents an efficient turbine

1882 Water power used to generate electricity in Appleton, Wisconsin

1896 Britain's first water-powered generating station built at Foyers on Loch Ness

1966 Tidal power-station built in Brittany, France

1980s The Grand Coulee project on the Columbia River in the United States and the Krasnoyarsk project in the USSR provide over 6 million kilowatts of power each

1990s Itaipú project of Brazil and Paraguay will produce over 12 million kilowatts

► **A water wheel near Murcia in south-east Spain. Water wheels are one of the oldest forms of water power, believed to have been developed in about 100 BC.**

Some hydroelectric power-stations are on river systems and are built inside or at the bottom of a specially constructed dam.

Tidal power

Tides provide another source of moving water that can produce power. A dam is built across the mouth of a river in a place where the height between low and high tide is great. Water rushes through tunnels in the dam as the tide rises and flows out of them when the tide turns. Turbines are turned by this flow and electricity generated. Unfortunately, high tide comes at different times each day and providing electricity when it is most needed is difficult.

Scientists are exploring ways of using the up-and-down movement caused by waves in open sea as a reliable and cheap source of power.

Flashback

The earliest water wheels were invented by the Greeks in about 100 BC. They were placed horizontally in the water flow. The Romans used vertical water wheels to provide the power to mill grain. There were two common types of vertical wheels. An overshot wheel turned when water fell onto it from above. In contrast, an undershot wheel was placed in a fast-flowing stream to turn it. During the Industrial Revolution large water wheels provided power for factories. ■

See also
Dams
Hydroelectric power
Industrial Revolution
Turbines

Water sports

Most people live near water, whether it is a river, a canal, a reservoir, a lake or the sea. Water provides all sorts of opportunities for recreation, but it is vital to learn to swim before you take up any water sport. It could save your life one day.

Indoor water sports

A swimming pool is where most children have their first experience of water sport. Many pools run 'parent and toddler' sessions where infants can get used to the water even before they can walk. Once they have learnt to swim, children may want to compete in races in one of the four main strokes: breast-stroke, back-stroke, butterfly and freestyle (or front crawl).

Another event is synchronized swimming, where women competitors perform ballet routines in the water in time to music. In water polo two teams of seven players try to score goals by throwing a ball into their opponents' net. Springboard diving takes place from a flexible board 3 m (10 ft) above the water, while highboard diving is from a platform 10 m (33 ft) above the pool, which must be at least 4·5 m (15 ft) deep.

▲ The start of a 100 m breast-stroke race. This is a match between competitors from Germany and Italy.

Getting involved in indoor water sports

Of course, it would not be possible to have all these events taking place in the pool at the same time, but if you go to your local pool, the attendants should be able to give you the information you need about the activities on offer there.

▲ Close racing between dinghies of the same type. The helmsman controls the mainsail and rudder, while the crew controls the jib sail and hangs on a trapeze to balance the boat.

Outdoor water sports

Many people prefer to enjoy water sports out in the open, in a boat or on a board. Some, like canoeists and rowers, use only their own muscle power to get along. Others, like sailors and surfers, rely on wave and wind power. Windsurfers combine the ideas of surfing and sailing to steer their wind-powered sail-boards at high speed across the water.

Others prefer to explore the world beneath the waves by diving with the aid of 'Self-Contained Underwater Breathing Apparatus' (hence called *scuba* diving). All of these activities are likely to be on offer at coastal resorts, but many windsurfers and water-skiers also use inland waters. Whatever the sport, though, you must know how to swim. ■

◀ In white-water or wild water canoeing competitors canoe down a mountain river course about 3 km (2 miles) long. Helmets are worn to protect the canoeists if they capsize.

See also

Canoes
Divers
Rowing
Sailing
Surfing
Swimming

Biography
Sports special

Water supplies

In Europe, an average family uses over 500 litres of water each day.

At home, we need water for drinking, cooking, washing, cleaning, and flushing the lavatory. In factories, huge amounts of water are needed for manufacturing things.

Where our water comes from

All our water comes from rain (or snow in the winter). Most of this rain falls in hilly areas. Some evaporates, some sinks into the ground, and some runs into streams and rivers. The water can be collected in various ways. A stream or river can be dammed to make an artificial lake called a reservoir. A well can be dug and underground water pumped up. Or water can be taken straight from a river.

Before the water leaves the waterworks, chlorine gas is bubbled through it. This kills any bacteria not removed by filtering. In some areas, fluoride is also added to the water to help prevent tooth decay. The water is now clean, but not quite pure. For example, in some areas it may have tiny amounts of rock dissolved in it. This is harmless, but you can see it slowly building up as scale ('fur') in a kettle.

Pumping and storing

Water from the waterworks is pumped through pipes to storage tanks. The tank supplying your area may be on a hill or at the top of a tall tower. The height of the tank gives the water the steady pressure which pushes it along the pipes to your taps.

Recycling water

Used water from homes and factories usually passes to a sewage works for cleaning. It may then be pumped into the sea or returned to a river. The water from some large rivers is taken out and used several times on its journey towards the sea. For example, a glass of water from a tap in London may already have passed through six or seven people. ■

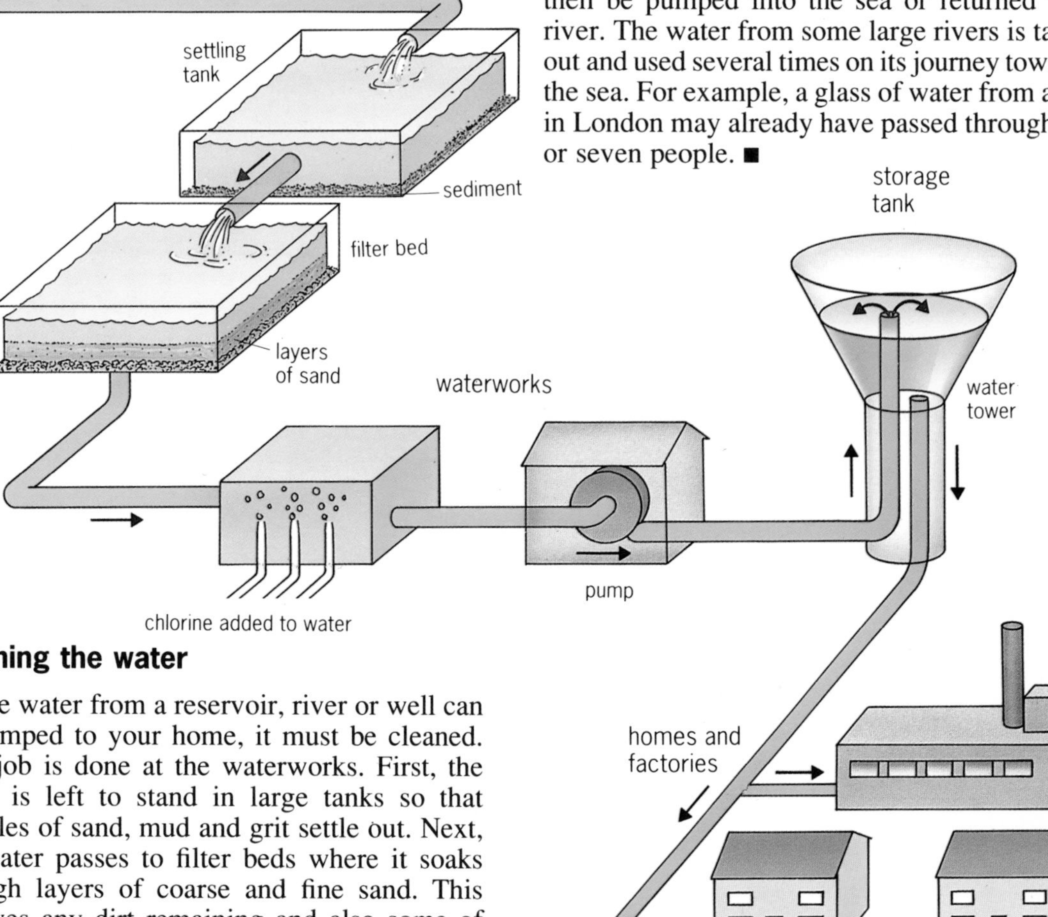

► **Water from the reservoir is cleaned at the waterworks. It is pumped to a storage tank which supplies homes, factories and other buildings in the area.**

Cleaning the water

Before water from a reservoir, river or well can be pumped to your home, it must be cleaned. This job is done at the waterworks. First, the water is left to stand in large tanks so that particles of sand, mud and grit settle out. Next, the water passes to filter beds where it soaks through layers of coarse and fine sand. This removes any dirt remaining and also some of the bacteria. Some waterworks use a faster method of filtering. They clean the water in large, closed metal drums filled with sand and a chemical jelly.

See also
Dams
Fluoride
Pollution
Rain
Rivers
Sewage
Water
Wells and springs

Waves

The word 'waves' might make you think of the sea, but you can have waves in all kinds of things. Suppose a line of children wait for a bus. Ian is late and dashes up and crashes into Julie who is at the end of the line. Julie bumps Ben, who bumps Michelle and so on down the line. The 'bump' is a wave travelling along the line. When it has passed by, all the children are back in the position where they started.

If you drop a stone into a pond, waves spread out in circles and you can see the movement outwards. A toy boat floating on the surface may go up and down, but it does not move outwards with the wave.

If the wave is started by something that is wobbling in a regular way the scientific name for the wave is 'periodic'. For example, the sound wave made by a tuning fork is periodic. The air is alternately squashed and expanded and the squashes travel out as a wave. We can measure three things about such a wave. Its speed is the speed at which any one squash is travelling along. Its frequency is the number of wave crests that pass a particular point every second. Its wavelength is the distance between two crests.

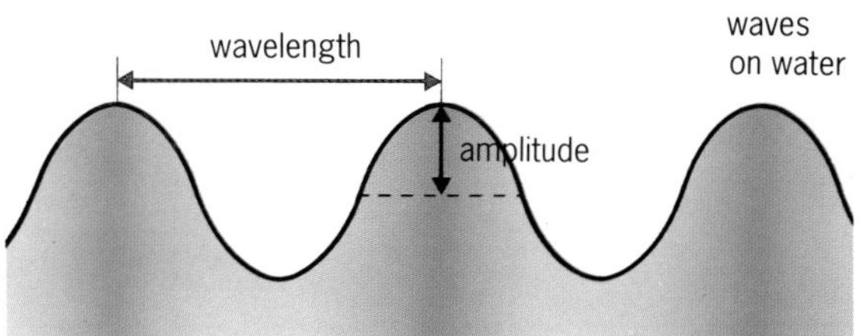

waves on water

wavelength

amplitude

◀ **With some waves, the wobbles make squashes which travel along. With other waves, the wobbles make up-and-down movements which travel along.**

Scientists measure frequency in hertz (Hz). If 10 waves are passing every second the frequency is 10 Hz.

▼ **Some typical measurements of common waves.**

	frequency	wavelength	speed
sound	30–20,000 Hz	10 m–15 mm	300 m/sec
medium wave radio	1 million Hz	300 m	300 million m/sec
light	600 million million Hz	1/2,000 mm	300 million m/sec
X-rays	2,400,000 million million Hz	1/8,000,000 mm	300 million m/sec

You know that a magnet or an electric current has a field round it. You can see the lines of the field if you scatter iron filings on a piece of paper. If the current wobbles, waves travel along these lines. We call them electromagnetic waves. Light, radio, ultraviolet and X-ray waves are all of this kind. ■

See also
Colour
Light
Microwaves
Radiation
Radio
Vibration
X-rays
Biography
Maxwell

Wax

Waxes are naturally white or yellow fatty substances. There are many different kinds of wax. Some are made by plants or animals, and others are made from minerals. All waxes soften and melt when heated and burn with a sooty yellow flame. Waxes do not dissolve in water, and they form a waterproof layer when spread on a smooth surface.

Mineral waxes

Candle wax (paraffin wax) is a mineral wax. It is made from crude oil or shale. It melts at quite a low temperature: about 50°C (120°F). When liquid, it can be coloured and poured into moulds to make candles and waxwork figures. Paper is sometimes coated with this wax to make airtight bags for foods, such as cornflakes, which must be kept crisp. Most ordinary polishing waxes contain paraffin wax.

Animal waxes

Beeswax is the most common animal wax. It is made by bees when they form the tiny cells in which they store honey. When full, each cell is sealed with a wax cap. Beeswax, like paraffin wax, is used for polishing wood. Even we humans make waxes. A yellow waxy substance is made in our ears. This helps to stop dust and dirt from entering them.

▲ **Bees make honeycombs with beeswax. They seal each cell with a cap of beeswax when it is full of honey.**

Vegetable waxes

Vegetable wax is formed in the bark of some trees. One kind, called carnauba wax, comes from the bark of the Brazilian palm tree. Carnauba wax is sometimes used for polishing leather to make it waterproof. ■

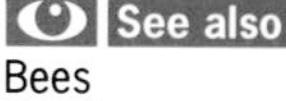
See also
Bees
Candles

Weapons

Modern weapons are very powerful and complicated. Although guns carried by soldiers are very similar to those used in World War I, most other weapons have changed a lot. Guided missiles can hit aircraft travelling at over 1,800 km/h (1,100 mph). They can even hit other missiles. Large rockets can carry nuclear bombs half-way around the world to their targets. Tanks can travel at over 60 km/h (37 mph) across rough ground, firing as they go.

► In addition to guns, modern armies have a range of other weapons available to them, including missile launchers like this one.

Gunpowder was discovered in China nearly 1,000 years ago.

More ships of the Spanish Armada in 1588 were lost due to bad weather than were destroyed by English cannon fire.

▲ The longbow was the main weapon for English soldiers from the time of William the Conqueror to the reign of Elizabeth I. It was made of yew, about 1·8 m long and had a range of 180 metres. English bowmen won victories at Crécy, Poitiers and Agincourt and fought from shipboard against the Spanish Armada.

▲ Muskets were used by infantrymen in Europe from the 16th to the 19th centuries. Soldiers in the English Civil War were armed with muskets. The musketeer fired from a rest stuck in the ground. Gunpowder and padding were poured down the barrel, together with a bullet. The fuse was lit with a glowing match, rather like a firework.

Many different weapons are carried by ships and aircraft. A modern warship has large and small guns, guided missiles, torpedoes and depth charges to defend it. This use of many weapons together is called a weapons system. The tank, ship or aircraft that carries the weapons to the place where they may be used is called a weapon delivery system. Most modern weapons have several parts: a guided missile usually needs a launcher with radar and a computer to guide it to its target.

Flashback

Hands and feet were the first weapons, but these were not much use against sabre-tooth tigers or mammoths. So prehistoric people learnt to use sticks and stones as weapons, then pointed sticks as spears and sharpened stones as knives and axes. Bows were used as much as 20,000 years ago to fire arrows further and more accurately than a man could throw a spear. When metal-working developed, bronze daggers replaced flint ones, but arrowheads of flint or bone continued to be used even in the Iron Age. Swords were made of bronze and later of iron.

The Greeks and Romans used large catapult-like weapons to throw huge rocks at enemy castles. The chariot was one of the first weapon delivery systems; it was used by the ancient Egyptians at least 3,000 years ago.

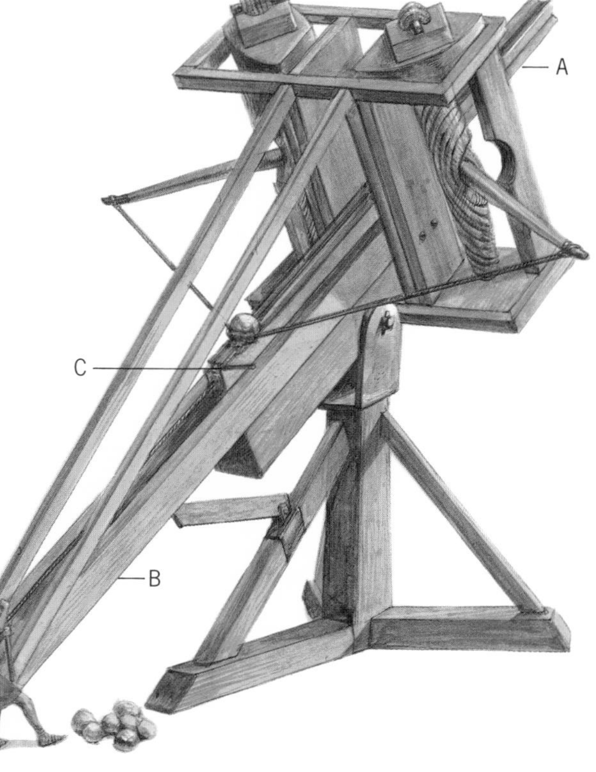

► Catapult used by Roman soldiers to throw stones of about 12 kg. Larger catapults could throw stones of up to 50 kg. The slider (A) was pulled back along the stock (B) bringing the bowstring with it. A trigger (C) released the bowstring.

See also
Armies
Armour
Battles
Bombs
Guns
Missiles
Tanks
World War I
World War II

Biography
Edward III (illustration of longbow)

▲ Cannon like this '6-pounder' were used in the 18th century, drawn onto the battlefield by horses. A powder charge with cannon balls was rammed down the barrel, then lit with a long match.

Gunpowder

Until gunpowder was discovered, weapons could only cut or hit. Cannons, guns and bombs all use the explosive power of gunpowder. Cannons and guns appeared in Europe in the 14th century, but they were inaccurate, took a long time to load and had the unfortunate habit of blowing up in your face. The English longbow was still better than the early guns.

The cannon was improved in the 16th century, but even so was still not very effective. The development of the musket in the 16th century greatly improved the gun. The musket's bullet could penetrate a soldier's armour, but muskets took a long time to load. Knives, called bayonets, were added to the gun's barrel so that they could be used as spears as well.

The rifled barrel

In the 19th century a new development, the rifled barrel, made the gun much more accurate. This made bullets spin in flight, and so they could travel in a straighter line, and further than those fired by older guns. A musketeer would be lucky to hit a man at 100 m (110 yards). But marksmen using the new rifles could easily hit such a target over 1,000 m (1,100 yards) away.

In World War I aircraft and tanks were first used to carry weapons. By the end of World War II the invention of the long range rocket and the nuclear bomb changed the face of warfare. ■

Weasels

Members of the weasel family are generally long-bodied, short-legged hunters. They live in many ways: the martens, for instance, are tree climbers, the otters are swimmers and the badgers are diggers. In Europe the animal known as 'the weasel' is the smallest of all the family. Females weigh as little as 25 g (1 oz) and are said to be able to squeeze through a wedding ring! They are often active during the daytime, for though they hunt mainly by scent, they have good senses of hearing and sight.

Weasels feed mainly on small rodents, and in the northern part of their range they are tiny enough to be able to chase mice and voles down their tunnels. Further south they tend to be larger and rely on catching bigger animals.

The prey is killed with a bite to the base of the skull. When food is plentiful it is sometimes stored. Young weasels may remain with their mother after they are weaned, and can sometimes be seen hunting together. ■

Largest member of the family
Sea otter, which may weigh up to 45 kg
Smallest
Weasel (least weasel), females may have a head and body length of as little as 11·5 cm and weigh as little as 25 g.

Subphylum Vertebrata
Class Mammalia
Order Carnivora
Family Mustelidae (weasel family)
Number of species in family 64 (16 are very similar to the weasel)

See also
Badgers
Otters
Skunks

▼ One of the smallest of the carnivores, the European weasel is able to catch and kill prey much larger than itself.

Weather

Rain, clouds, sunshine, wind: the conditions in the atmosphere and their day-to-day changes make up the weather. Knowing what the weather will be like saves money and can also save lives. Is it safe to climb the mountain tomorrow? Do we need to grit the roads tonight? Will it be dry enough to harvest the crop this week?

Weather recording

Weather stations on land need to be on open sites, away from buildings and trees which can influence the accuracy of readings. Observations must be precise and presented in a standard way so they can be compared with those taken at other sites. Most observations are made at ground level, but instruments can be carried into the atmosphere by balloons which transmit readings back to Earth by radio.

rain gauge

Rainfall is collected in a rain gauge. Rain falling into the funnel trickles into a jar. At the end of the day the jar is emptied into a measuring cylinder marked in millimetres.

Maximum and minimum temperature are measured with a Six's thermometer. This is filled with alcohol and mercury. When the temperature rises the alcohol in the left-hand part of the thermometer expands and pushes the mercury up the right-hand part. A metal marker shows the position of the highest temperature. When the temperature falls, the alcohol contracts and the mercury is pulled in the opposite direction. Another marker shows the position of the mercury at the lowest temperature.

maximum and minimum thermometer

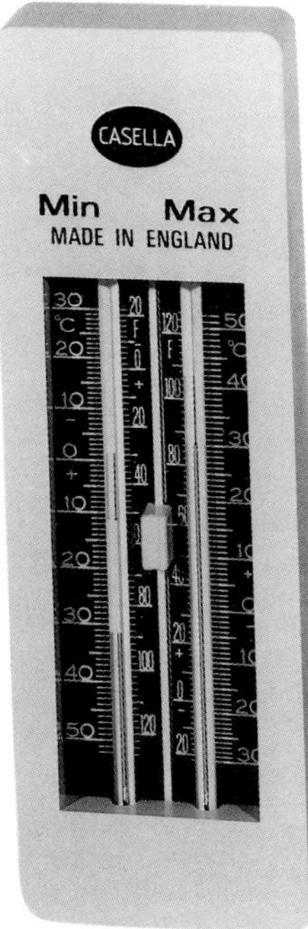

wind vane

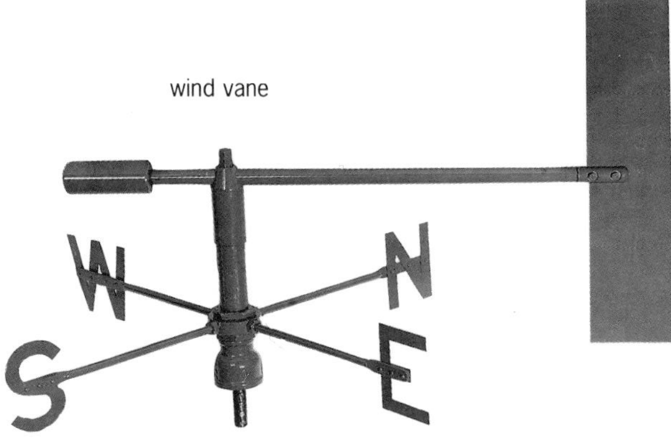

Wind direction is measured by a wind vane. The arrow of the wind vane always points to the direction from which the wind is blowing: the north wind blows from the north (not towards the north).

Wind speed is measured by an anemometer. The faster the wind, the faster the cups spin. A meter records wind speed in metres per minute.

Sunshine: the number of hours a place receives sunshine can be measured by a strip of sensitive card. The Sun's rays are focused onto the card by a glass ball and burn the card. The length of the burn shows the number of hours of sunshine.

sunshine recorder

barograph

Air pressure can be measured with a barograph. In the centre of this instrument is a metal box containing very little air. When the air pressure changes, the top of the box bends and this movement is recorded by a pen on a rotating drum.

Weather forecasting

Accurate weather forecasting depends on an accurate supply of information about weather conditions all over the Earth. Forecasters have to know what is happening over the whole planet, because today's weather in America could affect the weather in Europe a week later. Thousands of separate pieces of weather information are collected several times a day from weather stations on land, from ships and from aeroplanes. This data is fed into a giant communications network called the Global Telecommunications System. The information is sent round the world at great speed by satellite, radio and cable. Weather forecasters in every country take from the system the data they need to make their own local forecast.

The information is first mapped on a synoptic chart which shows the overall weather situation. Using their knowledge of how the atmosphere behaves and with the help of computers which show what happened last time when there were similar conditions, meteorologists make their forecasts. These must then be turned into maps and descriptions of what the weather will be like for the next 24 hours, for newspapers, television and radio.

Synoptic comes from a Greek word meaning 'looking together', and means 'looking at the whole situation at the same time'. A synopsis is a short summary that gives you an overall view of a situation or a story.

How accurate are the forecasts? They are becoming more accurate as time goes by, especially for short periods ahead. Weather is complex, and long-range forecasting is still difficult.

Weather and people

People have always made up sayings about the weather. Some are nonsense, but others are based on good observations. Many sayings are based on what the sky looks like. 'Red sky at night, shepherds' delight' is not always true, but 'Red sky in the morning, shepherds' warning' is usually reliable.

Scientists who study the weather are called meteorologists. Meteorology comes from two Greek words meaning 'study of what is high in the air'. (The word meteor originally meant anything unusual that appeared in the sky).

Many weather rhymes relate to farmers or sailors, because they are usually more aware of the sky and winds than people who live in towns. If it rains on St Swithun's day (15 July), there is supposed to be rain for the next 40 days. Keep a record to see if this is true!

It is likely that the weather affects people's moods. The warm, dusty sirocco wind of the Mediterranean or the Mistral wind which blows down the Rhône Valley in France are famous for making people irritable. ■

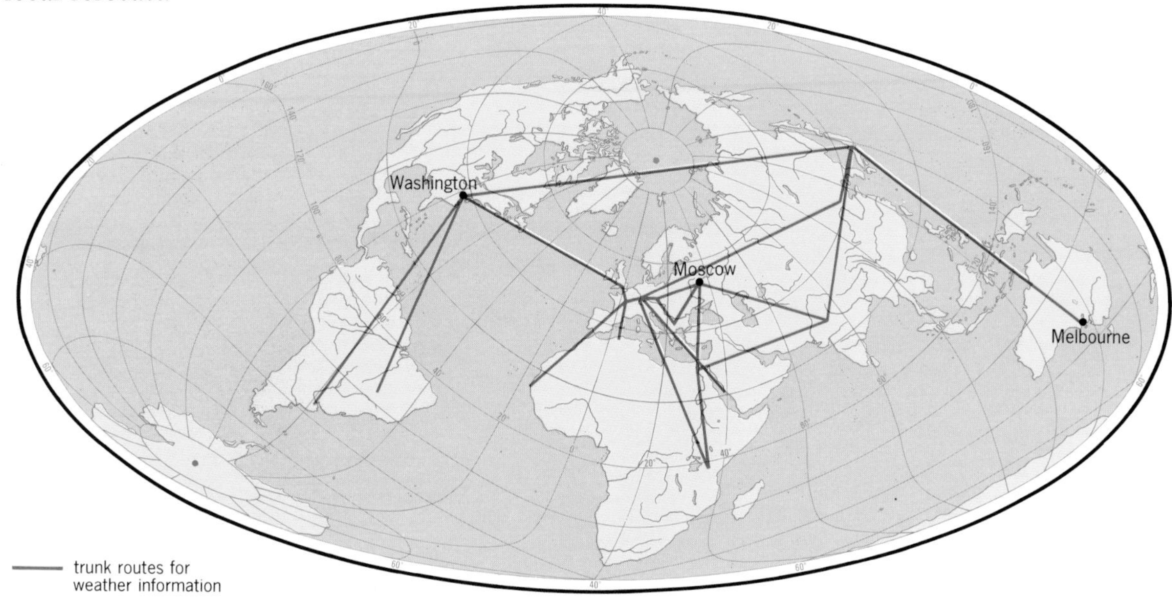

◀ The Global Telecommunications System supplies weather forecasters with accurate information on weather conditions all over the world.

See also
Barometers
Climate
Clouds
Cyclones and anticyclones
Depressions
Fog
Frost
Rain
Snow
Sun
Thunderstorms
Tornadoes
Wind

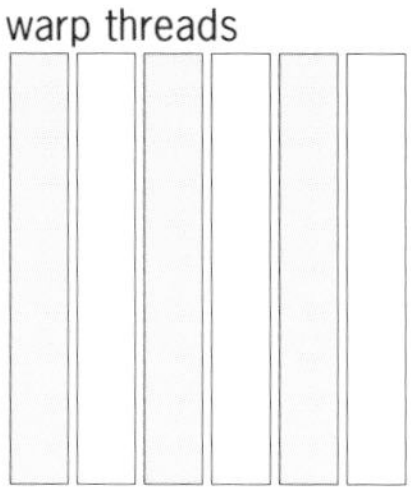

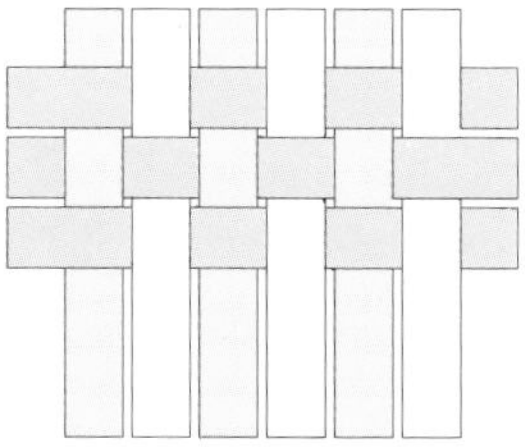

Weaving

warp threads

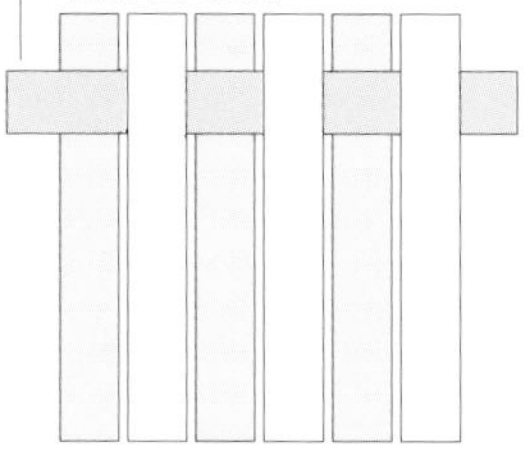

weft threads

You can see how weaving is done by using strips of paper. Cut out thin strips of paper about 1 cm (0·4 in) wide and 10 cm (4 in) long. You will need three white strips and three coloured strips.

Lay them alternately on a sheet of paper. Fix them together across the top with sticky tape. These represent the **warp** threads. Now cut ten more strips in another colour, 1 cm (0·4 in) wide and 8 cm (3 in) long. These are the **weft** threads.

Lift up all the white strips. Slide in a strip of paper.

Lift up all the coloured strips. Slide in a strip of paper.

Keep going to the end.

Weaving on a loom

To weave with threads you need a loom. This is a frame which will hold a set of threads, the warp, so tightly that you can weave a second set of threads, the weft, across and through them. To make it easier to weave the weft threads through the warp, the end of the weft is tied onto a short stick called the shuttle.

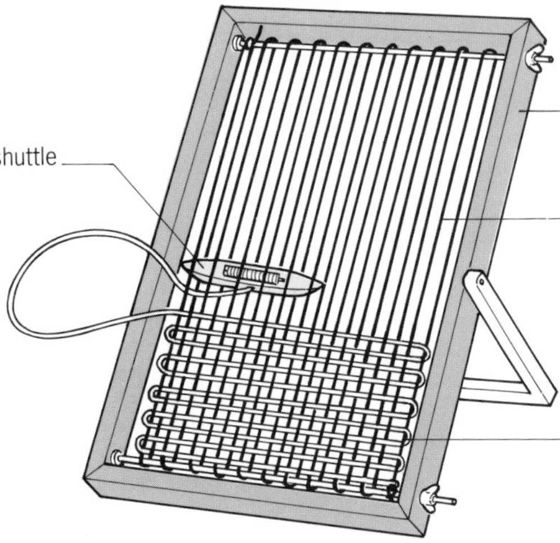

frame

shuttle

warp threads

weft threads

Types of loom

The weaving of threads together to make cloth is a very ancient craft. It was developed by people who lived before about 6000 BC. Early weaving frames were made of wood. The warp was weighed down with heavy wooden bars and large pebbles.

A **ground loom** is pegged into the ground. The weaver often sits on top of the finished weaving and uses a forked beater to force the threads down tightly. Looms like these are still used by nomads in Iran and Jordan. When they move camp, the loom can be rolled up and carried on camels or mules.

The **frame loom** is used for small weavings, especially tapestry pictures. The warp threads can be picked up with the fingers, and the weft threads are passed under two threads at a time. The length of the weaving cannot be greater than the length of the loom.

Backstrap looms are used all over the world. The weaver ties one end of the loom around the waist. The other end can be tied to a tree or a door knob. The weaver leans backwards to keep the warp threads tight. The weaver raises the alternate warp threads by using a heddle.

Today most fabric is woven in factories using mechanical looms. These power-driven looms can make thousands of yards of fabric a day. Many different kinds of cloth can be made. Some is **flat weave**, like tweed and sheeting. Another method is called **pile weaving**. Little tufts or loops are woven into the fabric. Towelling and velvet are made like this, and so are some carpets. ■

▼ This Mayan woman in Guatemala is weaving using a backstrap loom.

See also

Tapestries
Textiles
Wool

Weddings

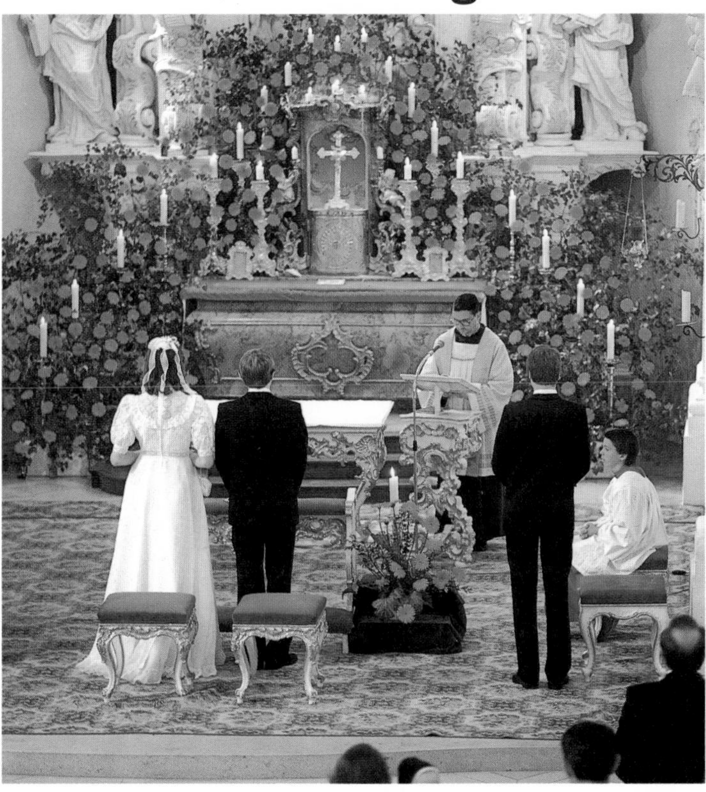

▲ **This Roman Catholic couple make their marriage vows at the church altar with the blessing of the priest. The bride wears white as a symbol of purity.**

A wedding is the rite or ceremony that takes place when a woman (the bride) and a man (the bridegroom) get married. Because it is a celebration, people like to wear their best clothes, and over the last century it has become common in Western countries for brides to wear elaborate white dresses. After the ceremony there is often a feast for families and friends.

A wedding may take place in a registrar's office or a place of worship such as a church or temple. People of different religions have different customs to show the importance of what is happening. Eastern Orthodox Christians crown the bride and groom, who are like a king and queen on their wedding day. Hindu couples walk seven times round a sacred fire to show their unity, and the Sikh bridegroom leads his bride round the Sikh holy book, which will be at the centre of their lives together. The Jewish bridegroom crushes a glass under his foot to show that love is finely made and easily destroyed. ■

▼ **This wedding is taking place in a Registrar's office. This is a legal not a religious ceremony.**

► **At a Sikh wedding both the bride and bridegroom wear red. Red is the colour also worn by Hindus when they get married. Here the couple walk together round the Holy Book, which will help them in their lives together.**

See also

Marriage
Rites and rituals

Weeds

▲ **Although they are very attractive, these poppies at the edge of a cornfield are looked upon as weeds by farmers.**

Weeds are any plants growing where they are not wanted. A rose bush in the middle of a vegetable patch is a weed! Most weeds are quick growing plants able to produce a large quantity of seeds in a very short time. Usually the seeds are easily spread: think of a dandelion clock with each fruit having its own tiny parachute to carry it away on the slightest breeze. Some weed flowers will go on setting seed even after they have been pulled up. In groundsel, a common garden weed, the flowers will make a mass of hairy seeds on the compost heap if put there and not destroyed. Other weeds, such as creeping buttercup, produce shoots which root wherever they touch the ground. With these runners the plant spreads very quickly. Some weeds, such as convolvulus, have to be removed from the soil completely. Any remaining fragments of stem will grow into whole new plants.

Control of weeds

The best way to control weeds is to dig them up and kill them before they have time to spread. This is why a gardener hoes the ground between plants. Any weeds are uprooted or sliced off at ground level by the sharp edge of the hoe. In the past children were paid to pull wild oats in corn fields. More recently weeds have been killed by chemicals called herbicides. Selective weedkillers will kill only weeds and not crops. There is now concern about harmful effects these chemicals might have on wild plants and animals. ■

See also
Flowering plants
Gardens

Weight

Astronauts floating around in space are weightless because they cannot feel the effects of gravity. Here on Earth, we can measure the force of gravity pulling us towards our planet. Scientists call this force weight. They measure all forces in newtons, so they measure weight in newtons as well. Our weight depends on where we are because the pull of gravity gets less if we move further away from the centre of the Earth. The Earth bulges out slightly at the equator. A girl weighing 200 newtons at the North Pole would weigh about one newton less if she moved to the equator, and less again if she then climbed a high mountain.

On Earth, every kilogram of mass weighs about 10 newtons.

Weight of an apple: about 1 newton.
Weight of an average 10-year-old: about 300 newtons.

In shops, the 'weight' of things is usually shown in kilograms or pounds, though these really measure mass. Mass is the amount of matter in something. It stays the same wherever it is. There is a connection between mass and weight because the more matter there is in something, the more strongly it is pulled to the Earth by gravity. ■

Kilograms and pounds really measure mass, not weight.

See also
Forces
Gravity
Mass
Measurement

Welfare State

A Welfare State is a country where the government takes responsibility for the well-being of its citizens, in such matters as old-age pensions, unemployment pay and health care. Such government care is sometimes called social security.

The Welfare State has its origins in the accident, sickness and old age insurance introduced by the German chancellor Otto von Bismarck in the 1880s. In Germany the term used is 'Welfare Society'.

The term came into use in Britain in the 1940s, when a plan for care 'from the cradle to the grave' was carried out by the Labour Government of 1945–1951. The scheme was drawn up by the social reformer William Beveridge (later Lord Beveridge) in 1942, during World War II. It is funded partly by National Insurance contributions and partly through taxes. Most developed countries now have some form of social security. ■

National Insurance contributions are sums of money paid by employers and their employees to cover the cost of social security schemes such as pensions and unemployment benefits.

See also
British history 1919–1989
German history
Pensions

Wells and springs

A well is a deep hole dug or drilled in the ground to obtain water or oil. This article deals with water wells. Oil wells are described in the article on oil.

Permeable and impermeable rocks

Some of the rain that falls on the land finds its way into rivers and streams and flows down to the sea, and some evaporates back into the atmosphere, but a lot sinks into the ground. The water soaks easily through rocks such as sandstone or chalk. These rocks are said to be permeable. But clay, for example, stops the water sinking any further, and is said to be impermeable. The water that goes into the ground sinks until it reaches either a layer of clay or some other impermeable rock, or a rock that cannot soak up any more water. The level in the ground below which water collects is called the water table.

Wells and the water table

If a hole is dug deep enough to reach below the water table, water will seep from the surrounding rocks into the well. The water table is not always at the same level. In dry weather it may fall, and a well may empty, while in wet weather the water table will be much nearer the surface and the well will be full. Before water pipes were invented, every village had its own well.

Artesian wells

Sometimes a layer of water-holding rock is sandwiched between two layers of impermeable rock. London is built in a giant saucer-shaped hollow over rocks like this. At one time, if a well was dug down to the water table under London, water was squeezed so hard that it came out of the well like a fountain. A well like this is called an artesian well. In London, so many artesian wells have been bored to provide water for all the people that the water table has fallen and its pressure has decreased. Now the water has to be helped to the surface by pumps.

Underground water is particularly important in dry areas where rain is infrequent. Water from artesian wells has made it possible for cattle and sheep farms to be set up in the dry interior of Australia.

Springs

A spring is the name given to any natural flow of water out of the ground. Springs are often found where permeable rocks lie above impermeable ones, particularly at the foot of steep slopes. Long ago, villages frequently grew up around large springs, and many of our largest rivers begin their lives as springs.

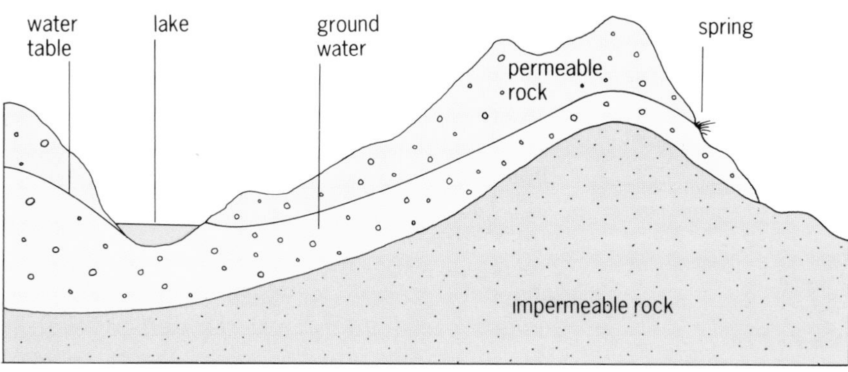

▲ The depth of the water table depends on the climate and the rocks underground.

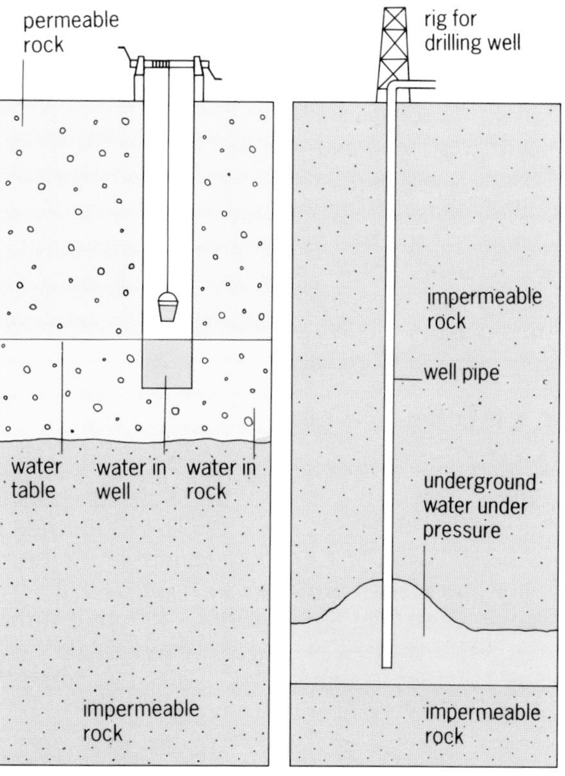

▲ Water collects in the bottom of the well and has to be drawn or pumped up to the surface.

▲ In an artesian well, the pressure underground forces water up a pipe to the surface.

At many points in the Sahara Desert, water-bearing rocks come to the surface. These places are called oases.

The practice of dropping a coin into a well and making a wish probably began with the belief that wells are holy.

Holy and wishing wells

Many years ago, people used to think that the way water rose to the surface in wells and springs was miraculous or magic. Many wells were thought to be holy or lucky. The Celts of western Europe frequently built altars and made sacrifices at wells, while the Romans dedicated their wells to goddesses. ■

See also

Oases
Oil
Pumps
Rivers
Rocks
Water
Water cycle
Water supplies

Welsh history

One of the chieftains who resisted the Romans was Caractacus (or Caradoc). He was eventually captured and taken to Rome, where he behaved with such dignity that he was not put to death.

Burial chambers thousands of years old have been found by archaeologists but little is known about life in Wales until the coming of the Celts from Europe some time after 700 BC. The Celts built hillforts such as Dinorben (Clwyd) for protection just as they did in the rest of Britain. When the Romans invaded after AD 54 they found it very hard to crush the Celts of Wales. The mountains always made Wales a very difficult place to conquer.

Hywel Dda means Hywel the Good. He was the only Welsh ruler to issue his own coins.

The Romans built a huge fortress at Isca (Caerleon) in south Wales and smaller forts dotted around the country. At first the Celts fought back fiercely, but in time those in the south were attracted to Roman ways of living. Here Romans built villas and a large town named Venta Silurum (Caerwent). But they never totally conquered the mountainous areas. By the time the Romans left Wales around AD 390, Celtic and Roman ways had merged together in some inland parts of Wales and people had been converted to Christianity.

A Christian and independent country

Offa, the king of Mercia from 757 to 796, built a huge earthwork dyke to separate Mercia from Wales. This can still be seen in places today.

1 March is a special day in Wales. It is St David's Day and it reminds the Welsh people of the period 1400 years ago when David struggled to keep Wales a Christian country at a time when the rest of Britain had been overrun by pagan Angle and Saxon tribes. Although some of these invaders attacked around the coasts they found the mountains of Wales too difficult an enemy to conquer.

After the Romans left, Wales remained independent for over 800 years, but was not a united country. There were many local rulers who fought one another and often tried to grab more land. Sometimes a strong ruler like Hywel Dda (died 950) forced other leaders to obey him, but usually fighting started again once the strong ruler died. One of the problems was the custom of dividing land between all the sons when the father died. Yet there were many things which kept Wales together. There was the love of the Welsh language and poetry and the laws which had been gathered at the time of Hywel Dda.

When the Normans reached Wales in 1076 they succeeded in conquering only the flat areas of the south and parts of the borders. They could not defeat the rulers or princes in the mountains. At times, usually when the Normans quarrelled among themselves, princes such as Owain Gwynedd (1100–1170) and Llywelyn the Great (1172–1240) gained control of large parts of Wales.

Loss of independence

The greatest struggle was between Llywelyn ap Gruffudd and King Edward I, who decided to deal with the Welsh once and for all. After a long war Llywelyn was killed in 1282 and Edward began to rule the lands of the Welsh princes himself. He built a series of vast castles and proclaimed his eldest son the Prince of Wales. The lands he seized became known as the Principality of Wales (a title which is still used in this century).

▶ Caerphilly Castle was built in about 1270 to protect the English Earl of Gloucester's territories from attack by the Welsh princes.

For years afterwards the Welsh people dreamt of freedom from English rule. Owain Glyndwr fought the English between 1400 and 1413, but was finally defeated. Harsh laws were passed and the Welsh had to pay even heavier taxes.

Union with England

Still the Welsh dreamt of freedom, and many thought that day had arrived when a Welshman, Henry Tudor, became King of England in 1485. But Henry VII showed little interest in the land of his birth. Yet things were beginning to change.

Some of the richer Welsh landowners wanted to follow English customs and they begged Henry Tudor's son, Henry VIII, to change the way Wales was ruled. So in 1536 the English parliament passed the Act of Union. From then on Wales was divided into thirteen counties, had the same laws as England and elected members to the parliament at Westminster. The Act said that the Welsh language was not to be used for official business, and many of the landowners began to forget the Welsh language and customs.

The Welsh language

Y BEIBL CYSSEGR-LAN. SEF YR HEN DESTAMENT, A'R NEWYDD.

Imprinted at London by the Deputies of CHRISTOPHER BARKER, Printer to the Queenes most excellent Maiestie.

1588.

The Bible shown here was the first Bible translated into Welsh (Cymraeg) by Bishop William Morgan in 1588. The fact that the Bible could be read in Welsh did more than anything to keep the Welsh language alive. Welsh, one of the oldest languages in Europe, might have disappeared if people had not grown to love the language of the Welsh Bible. Today, over 500,000 people still speak Welsh and many more want to learn it.

Chapels

From the 16th century onward, Welsh people increasingly took an interest in religion. Over 80 per cent of all the Welsh books published were about Christianity. Many of the Welsh people were Nonconformists, that is Protestants who did not agree with the Church of England. By 1900 there were more than 5,000 chapels in Wales. Most of these chapels used Welsh in their services and this greatly helped to preserve the Welsh language.

▲ **In 1910 these women and girls at Aberdare carried coal home from the tips to use while their menfolk were on strike.**

Coal-mines and industry

Up until the year 1800 most of Wales was a country of small farms and villages. But changes were beginning. Ironworks opened around Merthyr Tydfil in the south and thousands of people migrated from rural Wales and from Ireland and England looking for work. Later, after 1850, even larger numbers of people moved to the coal-mining valleys to find work. Although mining was very dangerous, people could earn higher wages than in the country, and some found town life more exciting. By 1913, Cardiff, Barry, Newport and Swansea had grown into large ports sending coal all over the world. In north Wales too, the slate quarries employed many people. Life was also getting better in the countryside. New roads and railways meant that farmers could get their goods to market.

In Welsh, the principality of Wales is called Cymru.

Unemployment and new industry

After World War I, demand for coal, steel and slate fell sharply. Many people who worked in these industries became unemployed and were forced to leave Wales. This was especially so in the 1930s, when over 250,000 people left Wales to find work. In 1914 there were 250,000 miners in Wales. In 1990 there were fewer than 4,000.

But things in Wales are changing. A number of foreign firms have moved into Wales bringing new jobs to replace those lost in the coal-mines. Great efforts are also being made to strengthen the language. More people are attending Welsh classes; schools teaching in Welsh have been opened; the Eisteddfod has never been more popular and there is now a separate Welsh-language television channel. ■

See also
Castles
Celtic history
Eisteddfod
Hillforts
Normans
Protestants
Roman Britain
Wales

Biography
David, Saint
Edward I
Glyndwr
Henry VII
Lloyd George
Llywelyn ap Gruffudd
Llywelyn the Great
Morgan, William

West Indies

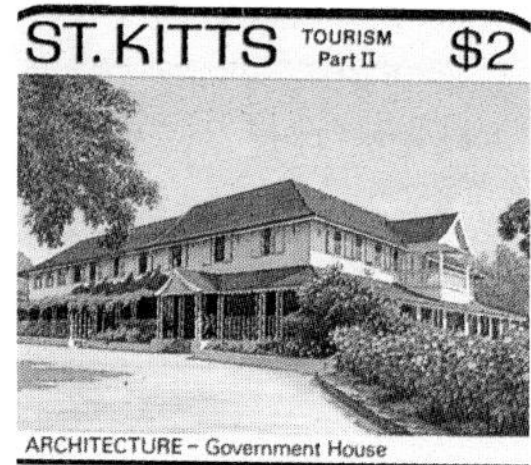

The chain of islands to the north and east of the Caribbean Sea is often called the West Indies. This is because Christopher Columbus thought he had found an Atlantic route to the 'Indies' in Asia when he reached the Caribbean in 1492. But many people today call them the Caribbean Islands.

The islands stretch for over 3,000 km (1,900 miles) from the coast of Mexico, past the southern tip of the USA, to Venezuela. The largest island, Cuba, is over 1,100 km (700 miles) long, and has a population of ten million. There are more than 20 other independent or self-governing countries in the region, and hundreds of other smaller islands, many of which are uninhabited.

Cuba, the Dominican Republic and Puerto Rico are Spanish-speaking. They have more inhabitants than all the other Caribbean countries put together.

People in Haiti, Martinique and Guadeloupe speak French or a local language called Creole. Haiti has been independent since 1804. The other French-speaking islands are Overseas Departments of France. They are governed in much the same way as the French mainland and are part of the European Community, but the way of life is distinctively Caribbean.

The Netherlands Antilles consist of three islands off the coast of Venezuela: Curaçao, Aruba, and Bonaire, where people speak Dutch or a language called Papiamento, and three smaller islands, Saba, Statia and part of St Martin, where Dutch is the official language but most people speak English. These islands are self-governing, but are linked to the Kingdom of The Netherlands.

Most of the other islands are independent English speaking countries, which were once ruled by Britain and are now members of the Commonwealth. These islands are grouped together in the Caribbean Community (Caricom). The most important Caricom island countries are Jamaica, Trinidad and Tobago, and Barbados. Belize and Guyana on the mainland of South America are also part of Caricom. Many of the Caricom islands are very small; but they have well-established democratic governments. In the past, most people in these islands were very poor. Today, the islands are much more prosperous. Many people still earn their living from farming, but tourism, manufacturing, mining and banking are increasingly important.

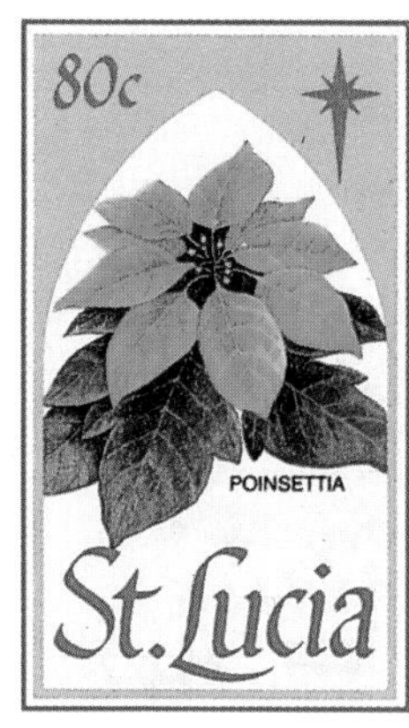

Windward Islands

Grenada, St Vincent, St Lucia and Dominica are known as the Windward Islands. They are mountainous, volcanic islands. Much of the land is covered with forests, and there are beautiful, fast-flowing rivers and streams. There are many small farmers, and bananas have long been an important export crop. They all have a thriving tourist industry. Many people on St Lucia and Dominica speak Creole, because these islands were once ruled by France.

Leeward Islands

To the north of the Windwards are the Leeward Islands: Antigua, St Kitts, Nevis, Montserrat and Barbuda. Antigua is a drier island. The land is not so good for farming, but there are beautiful sandy beaches. More than 100,000 tourists visit the island every year. Nearby St Christopher and Nevis is a twin-island country. Both islands are volcanic. The larger island is usually called St Kitts. With only 45,000 people, it is the smallest independent country in the Caribbean.

Some of the smaller islands: Montserrat, Anguilla, the British Virgin Islands, the Turks and Caicos Islands, and the Caymans, are still British Dependent Territories. The United States Virgin Islands and Puerto Rico are linked to the USA. ■

Dominica
Area 751 sq miles
(290 sq miles)
Capital Roseau
Population 76,000

Grenada
Area 344 sq km
(133 sq miles)
Capital St George's
Population 112,000

St Lucia
Area 616 sq km
(238 sq miles)
Capital Castries
Population 138,000

St Vincent and the Grenadines
Area (St Vincent)
344 sq km (133 sq miles)
Capital Kingstown
Population 104,000

Antigua and Barbuda
Area (Antigua) 279 sq km
(108 sq miles)
Capital St John's
Population 80,000

St Christopher and Nevis
Capital Basseterre
St Kitts 168 sq km
(65 sq miles)
Population 35,700
Nevis 93 sq km
(36 sq miles)
Population 9,400

Montserrat
Area 106 sq km
(39 sq miles)
Capital Plymouth
Population 11,850

See also
Afro-Caribbeans
Bahamas
Barbados
Caribbean
Caribbean history
Commonwealth
Cuba
Dominican Republic
Haiti
Jamaica
Puerto Rico
Trinidad and Tobago

Biography
Bogle
Columbus
Garvey
Marley
Seacole
Toussaint l'Ouverture

Wetlands

Wetlands are damp, marshy areas where water lies on the surface in many places, often forming lakes or large pools. There are many different kinds of wetlands. Some are formed naturally, while others are the result of human activities. Wherever water is trapped by rocks or impermeable (water-resistant) soil, wetlands form.

Wetland wildlife

Wetland ground is soft, so many small invertebrates (animals without backbones) live in it. These are food for other animals, such as shrews, frogs, toads, and wading birds (shore birds) such as sandpipers and curlews, which probe in the soft mud with their slender bills. Other birds, such as kingfishers and herons, feed on fish in the shallows, or on frogs and toads.

Insects thrive in wetlands. Mosquitoes and dragonflies lay their eggs in the water and hunt for food over the surrounding land. Insect-eating warblers and flycatchers nest near by, and seed-eating birds are attracted by the seed heads of the reeds and rushes. Wetlands also attract large mammals to drink. Deer, antelope, foxes and, in the African savannah, lions and even elephants visit wetlands at dawn and dusk to drink.

Because of their abundant food, wetlands are important stopover places for millions of migrating birds all over the world. The birds can pause to feed and maybe breed, roosting in safety on the water, out of reach of foxes and other predators.

Flood-plains and estuaries

Where rivers meander slowly over large flat flood-plains, the water often becomes trapped in pools and lakes, especially where the river spreads out to form a fan-shaped delta where it enters the sea. As the river slows down, it drops its load of sediment, forming muddy banks. River estuaries are usually muddy, as sediment is dropped when the river meets the still water of the sea. Estuaries are often lined with salt-marshes, home to many invertebrates and wading birds.

◀ A wet tundra landscape in the interior of Alaska in July. Sedges and other flowering plants have a short flowering season in the Arctic summer.

Tundra wetlands

In the far north, over the vast treeless plains of the tundra in Canada, Alaska, the USSR and Scandinavia, the soil is frozen not far below the surface. When the snow melts in spring, the water cannot drain away through the frozen soil, so it lies in great pools on the surface. Here mosquitoes and other insects breed, attracting millions of migrating birds from countries further south.

▼ Lake Nakuru in East Africa supports a huge population of water birds.

▶ Egrets and other waders in the swamps of Florida, USA. This is a habitat rich in wildlife.

Mangrove swamps

In tropical countries the coasts are often fringed with mangrove swamps. Mangroves are trees adapted to live in salty, wet places. They have aerial roots which stick up from the mud like knobbly knees. These roots take in oxygen from the air in order to breathe, as there is very little oxygen in the wet mud in which they live. As the mangrove leaves fall into the mud they rot, enriching the mud with minerals.

Mangrove swamps are home to many different animals. Fiddler crabs scuttle about the mud, scavenging the dead remains of plants and animals. Mudskippers skitter over the mud on their front fins. These little fish can stay out of water for long periods, breathing a mixture of air and water stored in their gill chambers. In the Sundarbans mangrove swamps of Bangladesh and India, tigers hunt deer and pheasants.

Millions of invertebrates live in the rich mud, and the warm, shallow waters form a nursery for the young of many ocean fish. Crocodiles or alligators lie in wait for them. The fish, frogs and other food attract colonies of birds, such as storks, ibises and herons.

▼ The Okavango Swamps is a vast area of marshland in the north-west of Botswana in southern Africa. This is natural wetland formed where the Okavango River divides into small streams.

Artificial wetlands

Some wetlands are made by human activity. Disused gravel pits fill with water, and marshes develop around the edges of reservoirs. The many thousands of square kilometres of flooded rice paddies in warm countries are home to fish, egrets and herons. The famous bird reserve at Bharatpur in India was originally created to attract birds for shooting. Some artificial wetlands are also valuable nature reserves.

Ever-changing wetlands

The margins of wetlands are always changing. Where rivers drain into the still waters of lakes or the sea, they drop their sediment, and the mud gradually builds up the banks. The original margin of the water is now dry land, and new species of plants start to grow there. In temperate regions, reeds soon give way to grasses and rushes, and water-tolerant trees such as alder start to take root. As the land is built up further by mud, and wind-blown soil becomes trapped in the new vegetation, other species such as oak and maple can grow. Along the coasts, salt-marshes gradually extend seawards. Some wetlands are constantly shrinking as they become silted up. But new ones form where rivers change course or become blocked by landslides or dams.

Destruction of wetlands

In recent years, wetlands have been disappearing at an alarming rate. Many have been drained so that the land can be built on or farmed. Others have been filled in as rubbish dumps. Some have become polluted as the rivers that feed them have picked up pesticides and other chemicals from farms and factories.

While the loss of wetlands has devastating effects on the local wildlife, it can be disastrous for humans, too. Wetlands often act as buffers to river floods. They soak up the water and let it drain out gradually, so lessening the effect of the flood further downstream. Where farmers have drained lands for cultivation, often villages and farms further downriver have been flooded and crops lost.

Wetlands can also act like a water filter, removing many of the impurities from the water that passes through them. In some places loss of wetlands has led to poor-quality drinking water for local cities.

Wetlands protect the coast

At the coast, the loss of wetlands can be much more serious. In many parts of the tropics, cutting down mangroves for timber or to make fish farms has resulted in severe damage to villages further inland during tropical storms and hurricanes. Expensive artificial barriers and other forms of protection have had to be built. The loss of mangroves can also reduce fish catches, since many commercially caught fish use mangrove swamps as nurseries.

Wetlands of international importance

Destruction of wetlands in one part of the world can have serious effects on the wildlife in another part of the world. The numbers of small migrating birds reaching northern Europe in spring have been considerably reduced since extensive wetlands just south of the Sahara have been drained to provide grazing for cattle. The birds have lost their last vital stopover point for feeding and drinking before crossing the Sahara, and so many now perish on the journey. Some important wetlands are now protected by international agreements.

Managing wetlands

In many parts of the world, conservationists are persuading governments to set aside wetlands for wildlife and for people to visit. But simply leaving wetlands alone is not enough. Many would gradually silt up and disappear. Their water supply must be carefully controlled. Sometimes grazing animals such as sheep or horses are brought in at certain times of year to prevent tree seedlings becoming established. Setting up only part of a wetland as a nature reserve may not be enough to save it. If surrounding areas continue to be drained, the water in the nature reserve will drain into these areas and be lost anyway. This has happened in the Somerset Levels in England, an area of wet peatlands rich in rare plants and in insects.

Extra funds for conservation can sometimes be brought in by allowing tourists into the wetlands. In the Everglades in Florida, USA, many kilometres of wooden walkways direct people along restricted tracks which do not damage the habitat. ■

See also
Conservation
Forests
Migration
Moors and heaths
Rivers
Tundra
Wading birds
Water birds

▼ A drainage ditch in the Somerset Levels in the west of England. For centuries farmers living in this low-lying area have experienced flooding. Recently peat has been cut so extensively that the habitat for birds and other wildlife has been destroyed.

Whales

▲ **Pilot whales usually swim in large schools.**

Whales are mammals. They are warm-blooded, air-breathing creatures, which produce living young and feed them on milk. Whales are also very intelligent. Yet they live all their lives in water, and die if they are forced onto dry land, for their weight crushes their lungs. The term 'whale' is generally used for creatures more than 10 m (30 ft) long, but dolphins and porpoises are also whales.

Breathing

All whales are streamlined. They swim using a horizontal tail fin called a fluke and a pair of large flippers near the front of the body. Inside these flippers are bones similar to those of your arms and hands. Whales have no hind limbs at all. Their skin is very smooth. Unlike most mammals, which have hair or fur, whales have at most a few short, bristly hairs round their jaws. They are kept warm by a layer of blubber beneath the skin. In a big whale, this can be 60 cm (2 ft) thick.

Toothed whales have one nostril; baleen whales have two. The nostrils are on top of the head and called a blowhole. This is the first part of the whale to surface. Air breathed in goes down to the lungs; from there oxygen gets taken into the blood, which carries it to the muscles. A whale can carry enough oxygen in this way to last over an hour under water. When it comes to the surface, it needs to breathe deeply. As it does so it throws out of its blowhole a foam from its lungs. This foam contains trapped nitrogen from the air. This is mainly what can be seen when a whale 'blows'. The whale does not breathe water out of its blowhole, as a whale with water in its lungs would drown, just like any other mammal. Because it can remove the nitrogen from the air it breathes, a whale can dive deeply and come to the surface quickly. This would kill human divers.

Sight and sound

Whales' eyes are not large, and since they close their nostrils when they submerge, a sense of smell would be of little use to them. Their smooth bodies have no visible ears, but they do actually hear very well indeed. They use sounds we call whale songs, to communicate with each other. Some whale songs carry many hundreds of kilometres under water. They use sound to locate obstacles and food (echolocation). Loud bursts of sound are also used to disable prey. Most whales feed on fishes or squid, but the largest species feed on krill. ■

Distribution
All of the oceans of the world. Most stay in deep water and rarely come near to the land.
Largest
Blue whale: 25–33 m, females slightly larger than males; weight 100–120 tonnes, record weight about 180 tonnes
Number of young 1
Baby whales are suckled for several months at least. Females produce a baby every other year, or every third year.
Lifespan
Fin and blue whale thought to live for over 110 years

Subphylum Vertebrata
Class Mammalia
Order Cetacea
Number of species 38 (not including dolphins)

► **Humpback whales feeding off the shores of Alaska.**

See also
Dolphins
Endangered species
Krill
Mammals
Porpoises

Wheels

Wheels make it much easier to move or turn things. Without wheels, everything would have to be dragged or carried around. At one time, most wheels were made of wood. Nowadays, they can be made of steel, aluminium light alloy, or plastic. It depends on the job which the wheel has to do.

Most of the wheels you see around you are on the roads or railways, but almost every machine or instrument with moving parts has wheels in it. Grinding wheels are used for sharpening tools. Potters' wheels are used for turning soft clay so that it can be moulded into round pots. Ferris wheels carry you high above the ground at a fair.

Wheels have a rod through the middle called an axle. If the wheel rubs against the axle, there is friction. This makes the wheel more difficult to turn and wears out the materials. Oil or grease helps to reduce friction. But most wheels also have bearings to reduce friction even more. Usually, the bearings are tiny metal balls or rollers which fit between the wheel and the axle.

Flashback

We will probably never know who invented the wheel. The idea may have come from the use of tree trunks as rollers to carry heavy loads. Instead of having to put the rollers under the load, it might have seemed a good idea to fit slices of tree trunk to rods sticking out of a platform. By about 3200 BC, solid wooden cart-wheels were being used in Mesopotamia. By about 2000 BC, wheels with wooden spokes had been developed. ■

The wheels on furniture and supermarket trolleys are called castors. They swivel so that they always point in the direction you are pushing.

◀ Main wheels on the undercarriage of an airliner. Each wheel may have to support a load of over 20 tonnes.

See also
Machines
Pottery
Pulleys
Turbines
Water power

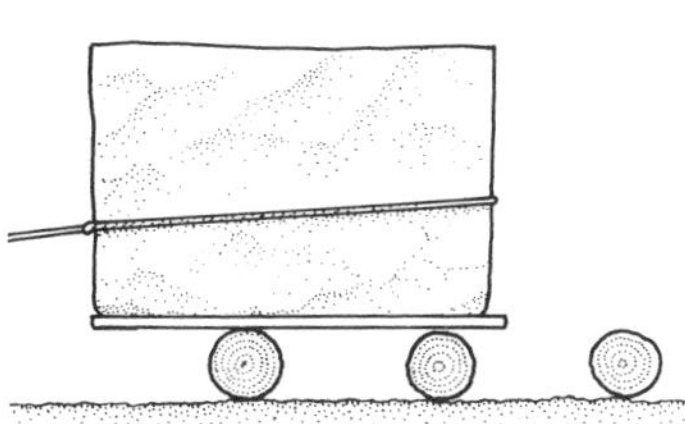

Before the wheel was invented, heavy loads were moved using tree trunks as rollers. But someone had to pick up the rollers at the back and move them round to the front.

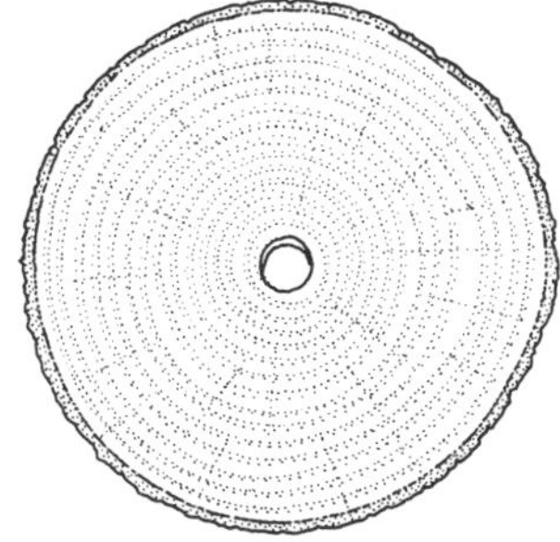

The first wheels were probably slices of tree trunk. If a hole was made in the middle, a rod, called an axle, could be pushed through.

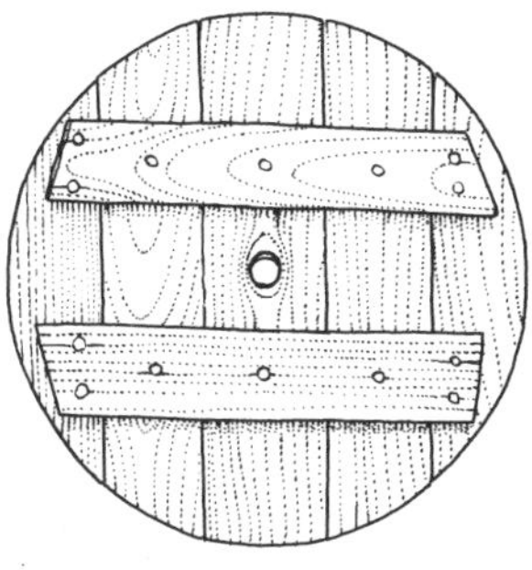

Bigger wheels were made by cutting short planks of wood and fixing them together. A knot-hole in the middle made an ideal place for the axle to go.

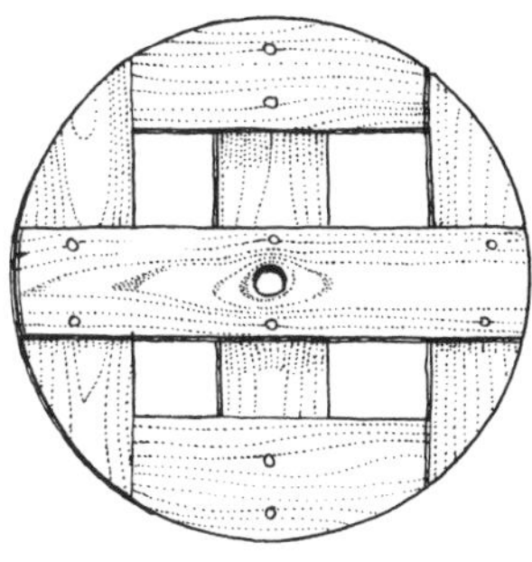

It was found that, by leaving out some of the middle pieces, wheels could be made lighter but just as strong.

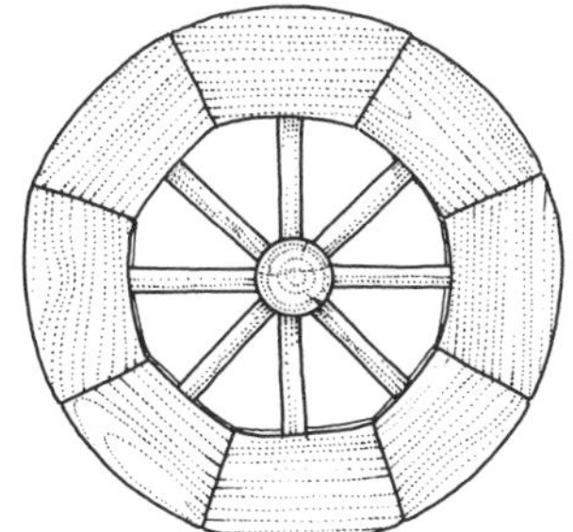

The next step was to make the rim (edge) of the wheel with shaped pieces. These were connected to the centre by thin wooden strips called spokes.

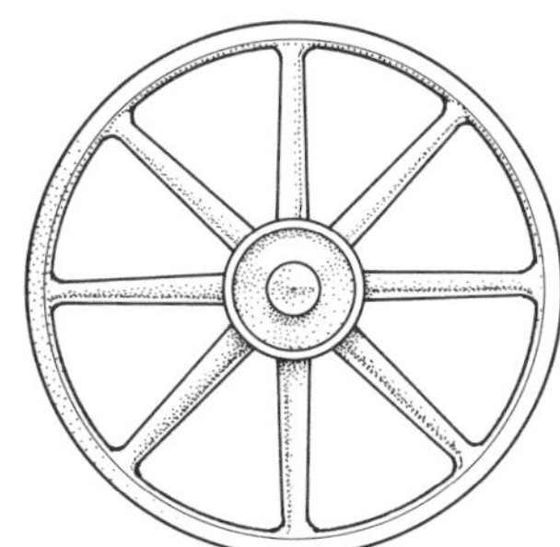

During the Industrial Revolution, iron became plentiful and wheels could be cast in iron. They were hard-wearing but brittle and the spokes often broke.

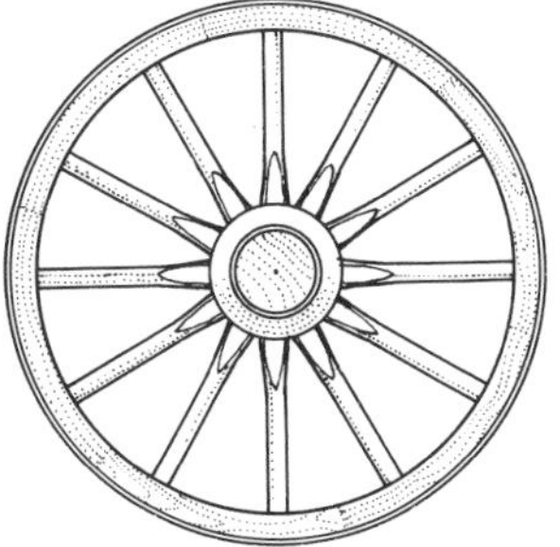

A strong, less brittle wheel could be made of wood with a thin strip of iron fixed all the way round the rim.

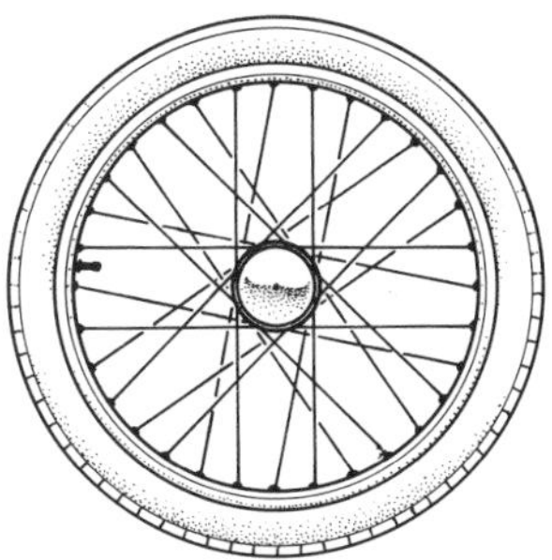

Tight wire spokes helped to make wheels lighter and stronger. Rubber round the rim gave a softer ride. Later, air-filled rubber tyres made the ride softer still.

Wildlife

The word 'wildlife' means all of the plants and animals in the world which are not tame or domesticated. Nobody knows how many different kinds there are but many will have become extinct before we are even aware of their existence.

If you were to travel about the world, you would notice a change in the kinds of plants and animals as you went from one area to another. This is partly because of climate and environment and partly because the big landmasses of the continents are separated from each other by water. The plants and animals in each one have evolved over millions of years and adapted to their separate environments.

Bio comes from the Greek word *bios* meaning 'life' and so biogeography is the geography of living things.

The world can be divided into several biogeographical zones. Each zone tends to have many plants and animals not shared by the others, although they often have related species. Even when the same habitat exists in different zones there are different animals occupying the same niche or way of life. For example the prairies of North America and the steppes of eastern Europe and Asia are both grasslands with hot summers and cold winters. In the steppes susliks and marmots live in basically the same way as the related prairie dogs of North America.

In a few cases the same animals may be present. This happens in northern North America, northern Asia and Europe. If you were to take a trip round these cold regions you would find reindeer (caribou), wolverines and brown bears in the whole area, although many of the small animals are different. The reason for this is that until about 10,000 years ago there was a land bridge between north-east Asia and Alaska. Animals were able to move from one great landmass to the other. Now the sea has broken through that bridge and American and Asiatic animals are quite separate. But they have not been apart from each other for long enough to have changed very much.

It is easiest to see the biggest differences in wildlife among the mammals. Birds, which can fly, often move between two or more zones during migration, and some kinds, such as the swallow and the peregrine falcon, are found in almost all regions. Even plants can travel between zones as their seeds can be carried by birds (stuck to their feet, beaks or feathers and in their droppings), or by wind or water.

The main animal and plant zones of the world

The northern Old World area (Palaearctic zone) includes the whole of Europe, North Africa as far as the Sahara and Asia to the southern edge of the Himalayas. Animals found in no other zones include Asiatic asses such as onagers, camels and yaks. Some, such as Przewalski's wild horse, are now found only in zoos.

The northern New World area (Nearctic zone) includes all of North America and its nearby islands. The animals are in many cases like those of Europe and Asia, but those found nowhere else include pronghorns (deer-like animals), skunks, racoons and the strange, rare mountain beavers (true beavers live in both the northern zones).

South America and its nearby islands (Neotropical zone). South America was a separate landmass until about 10 million years ago. It has many animals which are not found anywhere else, including sloths, armadillos, New World monkeys and unique rodents including guinea pigs. Many other creatures which once lived in South America died out when it became joined to North America. Animals moved in both directions across the land bridge. Very few South American animals succeeded in their new habitat, though the Virginia opossum and the nine-banded armadillo managed to survive in the north. Some North American animals, such as the jaguar, moved south and these invaders took over from similar original inhabitants. South America has some of the strangest living and fossil mammals to be found anywhere in the world.

Africa south of the Sahara (Ethiopian zone) is a great landmass which is the home of many animals that have become extinct in Europe and Asia. They include hippopotamuses, giraffes and many species of antelopes. In the past, relatives of these animals lived in Europe, but were forced southwards as the climate changed.

Southern Asia (Oriental zone) contains some animals related to other creatures found in warm climates. These include some monkeys, which are similar to those found in Africa, and the orang-utan which is an ape related to the gorilla and chimpanzee. Animals found nowhere else include giant and red pandas, gibbons and their close relatives the siamangs.

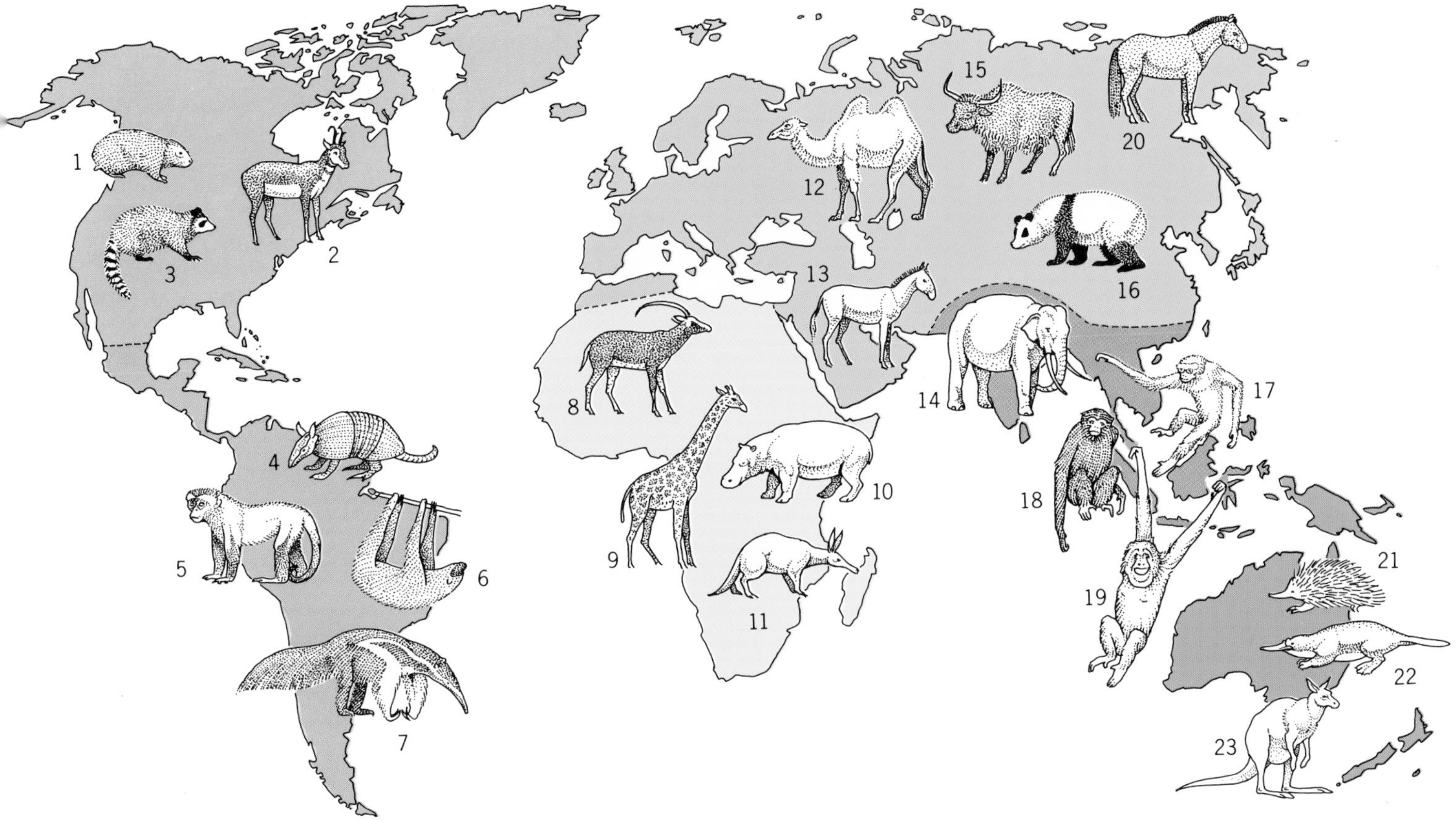

Australia and nearby islands (Australasian zone). Australia is sometimes called the island continent, because it is separated by sea from all of the other great landmasses. As a result the animals that were there about 100 million years ago, when it first became isolated from the rest of the world, have evolved without any competition from other species. They include animals which scientists think must be like the very earliest of all mammals: the platypus and the spiny anteater (echidna). These lay eggs, like reptiles, instead of producing living young as all other mammals do. But the babies are still fed on milk, like those of all other mammals.

Almost all of the rest of the native mammals of Australia are marsupials. They include kangaroos and wallabies, wombats, possums, koalas and many others. Only a few small rodents, bats, the dog-like dingoes and humans are like mammals in the rest of the world. Australasia includes New Guinea and some other islands which stretch towards south-east Asia. The line separating them from the Oriental zone islands was first charted by an explorer and naturalist called Alfred Russel Wallace, and is called Wallace's Line.

▲ The world can be divided into biogeographical regions (zones). Each zone contains wildlife not found anywhere else.

nearctic

neotropical

palaearctic

African (Ethiopian)

Oriental

Australasian

1 mountain beaver
2 pronghorn
3 racoon
4 armadillo
5 capuchin monkey
6 tree sloth
7 giant anteater
8 roan antelope
9 giraffe
10 hippopotamus
11 aardvark
12 Bactrian camel
13 onager
14 Asian elephant
15 yak
16 giant panda
17 gibbon
18 siamang
19 orang-utan
20 wild horse
21 spiny anteater
22 duck-billed platypus
23 kangaroo

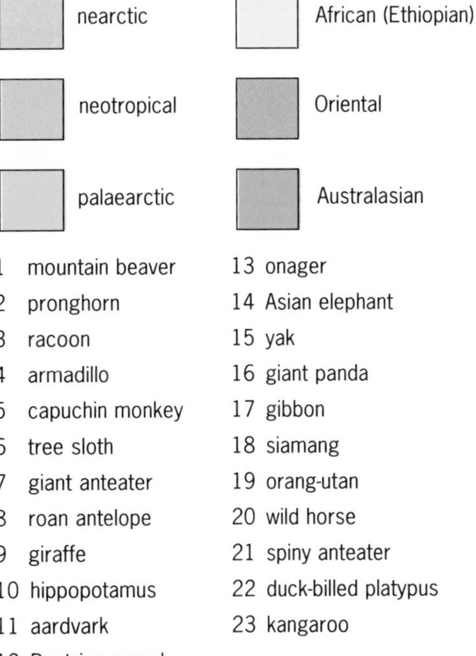

Island animals

See also
Conservation
Continents
Galapagos Islands
Islands
Marsupials
Platypuses

The isolated islands of the world are mostly formed by volcanoes which have erupted in the middle of the oceans. They include the Galapagos Islands, the Hawaiian Islands, the Seychelles and many others. They do not make a single biogeographical zone, but they are of great interest to biologists because the animals found there usually got there by accident. Once there, they were usually unable to escape and evolved over thousands of years into strange forms unknown elsewhere.

There are very few mammals on isolated islands as, unlike birds, they cannot be blown off course, nor are they likely to survive long spells at sea. On some islands there are no mammals at all, but there may be reptiles, some of which are very large as they have less competition than there would be on the mainland. Giant tortoises were at one time found on many islands. Birds and insects may get blown to islands. Those that stay may change, and often the survivors become large and flightless, such as the dodo or the Gough Island rail. Such animals are at risk when their island homes are discovered by humans. Like the dodo, they may become extinct because they are attacked and their habitat destroyed.

▼ **An iguana from the Galapagos Islands.**

Animals taken about the world by human beings

In the past, when human beings explored the world, they often took animals from home with them. Sometimes this was to make sure that they had food in their new lands, sometimes they wanted beasts of burden, or maybe they just wanted to have something which reminded them of home. Horses were taken to South America by the Spanish conquistadores, and rabbits and foxes were taken to Australia. Goats, pigs and camels have all become wild in many places far from their original homes. Often the newcomers do a great deal of damage to the environment, sometimes causing the original animals to become very rare or even extinct.

Sometimes animals are introduced into new lands as a natural solution to biological problems, such as pests on crops. This usually involves introducing a natural predator or parasite to the pest, and it is called biological control.

If your greenhouse is full of greenfly and you do not wish to spray your plants with insecticide you can gather as many ladybirds as you can find and put them in the greenhouse. The ladybirds will eat the greenfly.

Myxomatosis is a very infectious disease that occurs naturally in some South American rabbit species, usually causing death. The disease was deliberately introduced into Australia and western Europe to reduce the numbers of wild rabbits.

Biological control has not only been used to kill pests. In Australia local dung beetles were unable to cope with disposing of all the dung produced by newly introduced cows. Dung beetles from Africa were introduced to help with the problem.

Conservation

Today humankind controls almost all of the earth. Too often this control results in harm to the environment, by pollution, or destruction of forests or wetlands. Often the harm is unintentional. But habitats have evolved over millions of years; once destroyed, and their plant and animal inhabitants extinct, they cannot be replaced. We should think before we destroy, for only by conservation of wildlife can we keep the variety and richness of the world. ■

Wind

Wind is air moving. If you pick up a magazine and move it back and forth in front of you then you will feel the air on your face: a slight wind. Flapping the magazine needs energy. If you flapped for an hour your arms would get very tired. Wind also needs energy and this energy comes from the Sun.

Sunshine warms and cools different parts of the air. When the Sun warms the ground, the air above it rises up and cooler air flows in to take the place of the air which has risen. This flowing air is the wind.

You can feel wind on the ground and high up in the air. Weather forecasters use the scale of winds shown below, called the Beaufort scale.

Special winds

Many winds have names. Among the most constant winds are the 'Trade Winds'. These winds blow towards the tropics and blow most of the year round. They were called the Trades in the times when much world trade was done by sailing ships. Ships always tried to avoid other areas in tropical oceans where winds hardly ever blow. These are called the 'Doldrums'.

A breeze is a light wind. Where the land and the sea meet, for example, you get land and sea breezes in summer. This is because the air is hotter over the land than the sea by day and cooler over land than sea at night. So the winds blow from the sea to land during the day and from land to sea at night.

In southern France a wind called the 'Mistral' often blows in March and April. It is a cold, northerly wind, which can blow for several days. In the USA a wind called the 'Chinook' is a warm, dry wind that blows down the eastern slopes of the Rocky Mountains.

When the Chinook starts to blow, the temperature rises quickly, sometimes by as much as 22°C (40°F) in five minutes. These winds often make snow thaw rapidly. The word Chinook means 'snow eater' in a local Indian language. ■

See also
Depressions
Hurricanes
Monsoon
Tornadoes
Weather

0 Calm

1 Light air

2 Light breeze

3 Gentle breeze

4 Moderate breeze

5 Fresh breeze

6 Strong breeze

7 Moderate gale

8 Gale

9 Strong gale

10 Storm

11 Violent storm

12 Hurricane

◀ **The Beaufort Scale, including calm (with no wind) and twelve different wind speeds.**

Beaufort number	km/h	mph
0	below 1	below 1
1	1-5	1-3
2	6-11	4-7
3	12-19	8-12
4	20-28	13-18
5	29-38	19-24
6	39-49	25-31
7	50-61	32-38
8	62-74	39-46
9	75-88	47-54
10	89-102	55-63
11	103-117	64-73
12-17	over 117	over 74

Wind power

In 1840, there were around 10,000 working windmills in England and 8,000 in Holland.

The wind can be very destructive. Gales can uproot trees and lift tiles off roofs. But the wind can also be put to work. Sailing ships and yachts have sailed round the world on wind power alone. And windmills have used the power of the wind for grinding corn and pumping water. Today, aerogenerators are using the wind's energy to generate electricity. Unlike oil and gas, the wind is one source of energy which will never run out.

▶ **Tower mills like this were once used to pump water from low-lying land. They were also used to drive grinding stones, saws and other machinery.**

See also
Greenhouse effect
Pollution
Turbines

Aerogenerators

Most aerogenerators have a tall, slim tower with huge blades like an aircraft's propeller mounted on top. The blades can be over 20 m (65 ft) long. As they spin in the wind, they turn a generator which produces electricity. Aerogenerators are placed on exposed, windy sites often in large groups called wind farms. Unlike fuel-burning power-stations, they do not pollute the atmosphere, but the force of the wind is unpredictable and few sites in the world are suitable.

Windmills

A hundred and fifty years ago, there were thousands of windmills across The Netherlands and the fens of eastern England. Many were used to drain water from low-lying land. Very few remain today, but some have been kept in working condition. They have vanes (sails) which turn a shaft. This is connected by gearwheels and another shaft to a pump, a stone for grinding corn, or some other machinery. When the wind changes direction, the sails must be turned so that they face into the wind. In post mills, the whole building turns on a vertical post. In later designs, called tower mills, only the top part of the tower turns. The main tower, made of wood or bricks, is fixed.

Windmills around the world

Windmills are still used in many parts of the world for pumping water from wells and drainage ditches. Some have fabric or slatted wooden sails. Others are made by cutting an old oil drum in half and attaching the two parts to a vertical shaft. In Australia and America, one common type of windmill has a tall, framework tower. The rotating part has lots of steel blades with a tail vane to turn it into the wind. ■

▼ **These aerogenerators are positioned on high ground in California to catch the maximum wind force. Many hundreds of aerogenerators are needed to produce as much power as a single power-station.**

Wine

Grape vines are grown and wine is made in the temperate and Mediterranean climates of the world. In the northern hemisphere, this includes most of central and southern Europe, and California and Oregon in the United States. In the southern hemisphere, wine is made in Australia and New Zealand, South Africa, Chile and Argentina.

Wine is an alcoholic drink usually made by fermenting grape juice with yeast so that it is chemically changed. The yeast grows on the sugar in the grape juice and produces alcohol, and carbon dioxide gas which is lost to the air. Country wines may also be made with other fruits, vegetables and flowers such as red currants, cherries, beetroot, cowslips, dandelions and elder flowers.

Wine-making

Red wine comes from black grapes. White wine comes from white grapes or from black grapes with the juice extracted before the skins can stain it.

To make the wine the grapes are crushed and in the case of red wine the juice (called must) is left in contact with the skins. Yeast is added and the juice ferments. The wine is then filtered and stored in vats or barrels to mature it. Finally it goes into bottles.

▲ After the grapes have ripened in the summer sun they are picked by hand.

Flashback

Wine-making first started in ancient Persia, but the wine and its secrets were soon transported along the Mediterranean coast. The Greeks and Romans both made wine, and the Romans established some of the earliest vineyards in France and Germany. ■

See also
Alcohol
Farming
France
Yeasts

Winter sports

The main competition for winter sports is held every four years as the Winter Olympic Games. The events include the biathlon (skiing and shooting), bobsleigh, luge, ice hockey, ice skating and skiing.

Winter sports take place on ice or snow. Skating, skiing and ice hockey are the most popular of winter sports. Bobsleigh, tobogganing, and ice yachting are also winter sports. The first two are adaptations of the great winter pastime of sledging.

Tobogganing

Anyone riding a sledge over snow is tobogganing, but as a sport it is divided into two types, called lugeing and Cresta tobogganing. Both involve sliding down ice-covered tracks on small sleds.

Luge sleds are made of wood with steel runners and a fibreglass seat. Riders lie almost flat on their backs. Mechanical braking and steering is not allowed; steering is by leg pressure on the front runners and a hand rope. There are events for one- and two-man teams, and winners are decided by taking the lowest total time for a certain number of runs down the course. Speeds can reach 120 km/h (75 mph).

Cresta tobogganing takes place on the Cresta Run, a winding, steeply banked channel of ice built by the St Moritz Tobogganing Club, Switzerland. The single rider lies chest down. Speeds can reach 135 km/h (84 mph).

Bobsleigh

In the middle of the 19th century, British tourists started sled-racing on snowbound mountain roads in the Alps. Three racing sports emerged: lugeing, Cresta tobogganing and bobsleigh.

Bobsleighs also began as sledges, but they are now streamlined machines made of steel and aluminium with mechanical brakes and steering. They are guided down specially prepared tracks of ice with banked bends. Four-man bobs are slightly faster than twos, and speeds exceed 135 km/h (84 mph).

Ice yachting

This is travelling across ice in craft with runners and sails. The techniques are like those of ordinary sailing. ■

See also
Curling
Ice hockey
Ice skating
Olympic Games
Skiing

Wire

Wire is made by pulling a metal rod through a series of moulds called dies. These have tiny, funnel-shaped holes in them which get smaller from one die to the next. As the rod passes through the dies it is squeezed into a thinner and thinner shape. Some wire is made of steel. It can be stiff and springy or pliable and bendy, depending on the thickness and the type of steel used. Wire can be chopped up to make pins, needles and nails and it can be bent into springs. It can also be woven into netting for fencing. Wire for fences is usually galvanized, which means that it is coated in zinc to stop it rusting. When wires are twisted or plaited together, they make wire rope. This is much stronger than ordinary rope and is used for the cables in cranes and lifts. You pull on thin wire cables when you move the brake levers on your bike. Wire cables hold up radio and TV masts. In suspension bridges, the roadways are hung from wire cables.

The other main use of wire is for conducting electricity. The power cables in houses are made of copper wire, coated in plastic for insulation. Wire is also used for carrying signals between telephones, though this job can now be done more efficiently by optical fibres carrying pulses of laser light. ■

Fly-by-wire
A system used in some aircraft where the pilot's controls send signals to a computer which controls the plane.

In southern Africa, dies were being used to make wire over 1,600 years ago.

See also
Cables
Copper
Fibre optics
Flight
Springs
Telegraphs

Witches

Female
Witch or sorceress
Male
Wizard, sorcerer or warlock

Witches in stories have pointed hats and black cats, and ride broomsticks through the sky. They chant magic spells. They are wicked women, unless their spells go wrong, and then they are people to laugh at.

If you had lived 400 years ago you would not have thought witches were a joke. Almost everyone believed that some women were the servants of the Devil. If they cursed you, trouble would follow and you might even die.

It was usually poor old women who were accused of being witches. Because they were poor they often begged from their neighbours. Sometimes the neighbour refused to give them anything. The old woman might go away mumbling to herself. The neighbour would feel guilty because it was everyone's duty to help the poor. Perhaps then one of the animals became ill, or one of the children. Why did it happen to them? Had they been cursed? What had the old woman mumbled? The woman might be taken to court and accused of being a witch. One way of testing a witch was to tie her up and throw her in a river or pond. Only the guilty would float because water rejected evil (so people thought). So the innocent drowned and those who floated were then killed. In Europe witches were burnt; in England they were hanged.

During the 17th century, witch-hunting became a mania. In parts of Germany there were a hundred burnings a year. In England over 200 women were hanged in just two years, 1645 to 1647. Matthew Hopkins, the 'Witch-Finder General', was partly responsible. Parliament paid him £1 for every town he visited looking for witches.

As scientific knowledge increased, belief in witchcraft faded, and there were few trials after 1700. In Salem, USA, thirty people were executed for witchcraft in 1692. Only five years later, the judge and jury publicly admitted their mistake and begged forgiveness. Many people in Europe used to believe in a 'witches' sabbath'. This was a night-time gathering of witches, often in a bleak or mountainous place. It was believed to take place on a special date, like the night before May Day or Hallowe'en (31 October). ■

A witch who does good, like healing sick people, is often called a white witch.

A coven is the name given to a group of witches, usually twelve in number.

Last English execution: Alice Molland, Exeter, 1684

Jane Wenham (Walkern, Hertfordshire) was sentenced to death in 1712 but was given a royal pardon.

Witch laws were abolished by Act of Parliament in 1736.

Wolves

► **Usually only one female in a pack produces cubs and all members of the pack help to feed and rear them, bringing them meat from kills made many kilometres away.**

Number of young
4–7 suckled for about 5 weeks and then fed and cared for by all members of the pack.
Lifespan
About 10 years in the wild, 16 years in captivity.

Subphylum Vertebrata
Class Mammalia
Order Carnivora
Family Canidae (dog family)
Number of species 2

See also
Dogs
Foxes

Wolves live in packs the size of which depends on food availability. The pack centres around the breeding pair (which mate for life) and can contain up to twenty members. Because they hunt as a group, wolves are able to kill animals larger than themselves, and feed mostly on deer, usually preying on the weaker ones. After making a kill, a wolf can eat about 9 kg (20 lb) of meat. The pack will finish the carcass completely. ■

Wombats

Distribution
Mainly in New South Wales, Tasmania and Victoria
Size Head and body length up to 115 cm
Weight Up to 39 kg
Number of young 1
Pouch life about 6 months. Remains with mother for about 11 months more.
Lifespan 5 years in the wild; up to 20 years in captivity

Subphylum Vertebrata
Class Mammalia
Order Marsupialia
Family Vombatidae
Number of species 3

► **When a common wombat is attacked it turns its back on its attacker as the skin on its rump is extremely thick. It also kicks out with its hind legs.**

See also
Australia
Kangaroos
Koalas
Marsupials

Wombats are pouched mammals whose closest relative is the koala. Unlike koalas they live completely on the ground and burrow. Each common wombat has several burrows which it may share with other wombats, but each wombat has its own separate feeding area.

Wombats are active at night, when they emerge to feed on grasses, or sometimes the roots of trees and shrubs. They may have to travel several kilometres in search of food. ■

Women's movement

For many centuries there have been people who want women to have the same rights as men. From about 1850 there were campaigns in both the USA and Britain for married women to be able to own their own property, instead of everything belonging to the husband when they married. Women also took part in the anti-slavery movement and other public activities. They were refusing to stay at home as they were expected to do.

Two thirds of the world's work is done by women; they earn less than 70 per cent of male earnings and they own less than 7 per cent of the world's wealth.

In 1893 New Zealand became the first country to give women the right to vote in elections. Women elsewhere then demanded this right. In Britain, many women joined the Suffragette movement to force Parliament to agree to their demands. By the end of the 1920s, the right to vote had been won by women in Australia, Canada, Finland, Germany, Britain, Sweden, the USA and other countries.

After this, women's organizations campaigned for such things as help with child care. Then in the 1960s, the women's movement grew even stronger when the women's liberation movement started in the USA. Feminists, who believe in equal rights for women, began to work for equal pay, equal education and equal opportunities for women.

In the 1990s, the women's movement has changed emphasis and women's groups are now an accepted part of society. In business, sport, music, in the trade unions and in many other areas, there are women's organizations who meet regularly and give positive advice and support to each other.

Substantial achievements have been made, but many women believe that they will only become completely equal when men do their fair share of work in the home. Then women will be free to work away from the home and will therefore have more power over their own lives. ■

See also
Peace movement
Suffragettes

Biography
Pankhursts

Wood

See also

Conifers
Finland (photo)
Forests
Furniture
Materials
Paper
Timber
Tools
Trees

Wood is one of our most useful materials. It is strong, but can easily be cut and carved into various shapes. Most wood comes from the trunks of trees. Each year, as a tree grows, it makes a new layer of wood around itself. If a log has been cut through, you can see these 'annual rings'.

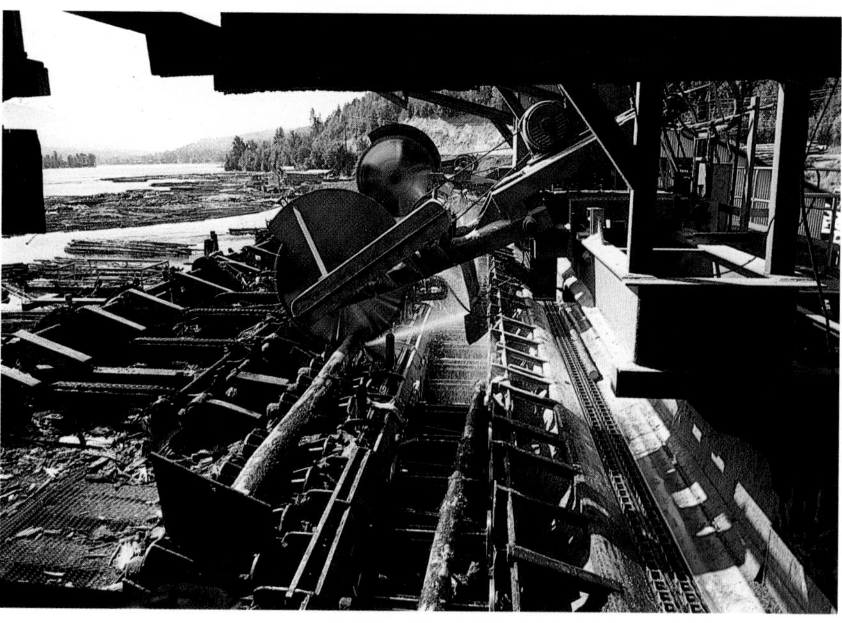

▲ Timber being cut into regular lengths at a sawmill in British Columbia, Canada.

The structure of wood

Wood is made up of millions of minute tubes that run along the length of the trunk of the tree. When the tree is alive, these tubes carry sap up from the roots to the leaves of the tree. The wood (timber) from each species of tree is different in colour, hardness and pattern ('grain').

Felling and transporting timber

Foresters use power saws or large machines which can cut and trim a tree trunk in seconds. In some countries the logs are pulled to the nearest river and floated downstream to the sawmills, but most timber is transported by special lorries or trains.

At the sawmill

At the sawmill large saws slice the logs into planks. Before the wood can be used it must be seasoned (dried), otherwise it will twist or shrink. Sometimes the planks are seasoned in the air. More often this is done in a special building called a kiln, where warm air is blown over the planks to dry them quickly.

Manufactured wood

Not all logs are cut into planks. Some are turned against a sharp blade so that thin sheets, called veneers, are peeled off. Several veneers may then be glued and pressed together to make plywood, which is stronger and cheaper than solid woods of the same thickness. If the veneers have been cut from a rare or expensive log with an attractive grain, they may be stuck onto plainer pieces of wood or chipboard and used to make furniture.

Blockboard is another manufactured wood, often used for making doors. Blocks of soft wood are glued together between two sheets of veneer. Blockboard is rather like a wooden sandwich.

None of the sawdust and small pieces of wood from the sawmill is wasted. The small pieces of wood are cut into tiny chips which, together with the sawdust, are sprayed with glue and pressed into sheets to make chipboard. This is often found, covered with veneers or plastics, in kitchen fittings and furniture.

Carpentry

Cabinet makers and carpenters make things from wood. They select the type of wood to use depending on the nature of their task. Hardwoods come from deciduous trees (those that shed their leaves each year). They have beautiful patterned grains and polish up well, so they are used in good quality furniture. Hardwoods include oak, walnut and mahogany. Softwoods, from coniferous (evergreen) trees, are used mainly in building. They are easy to saw, drill, chisel and plane, and they include pine and cedar. ■

► There are 3 main types of manufactured wood; plywood, blockboard, and chipboard.

Plywood is made by sticking together thin sheets of wood.

Blockboard is made by sticking together lengths of wood and then sandwiching them between two thin sheets of wood.

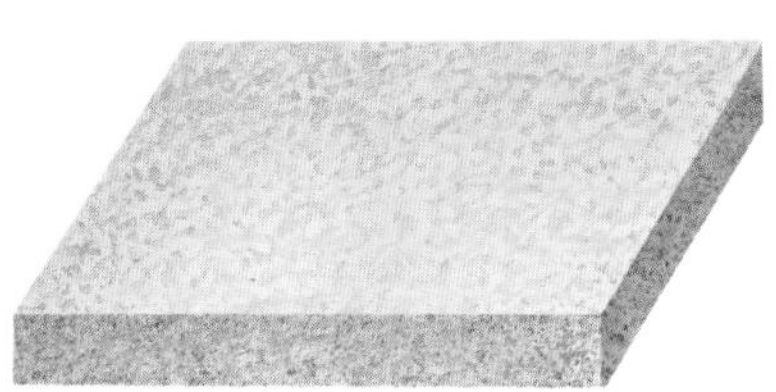

Chipboard is made from tiny pieces of wood mixed with glue, then pressed into large boards.

Woodlands

◀ **Beech woodland in spring. Bluebells flower on the woodland floor before most light is blocked out by the thick summer foliage.**

Woodland is the name often given to small patches of forest. Usually these are in areas where human beings have cut down most of the trees, as in Britain or much of north-west Europe. Woodlands in such places are oases in which the natural wildlife of the region can survive.

Within a wood, trees are the dominant plants. In cool parts of the world there may be several species in the same wood, but in the forests of the tropics there may be more than 100 species in a small region, while in the cold forests of the north there may be only one species. Beneath the canopy of the branches few other plants can thrive. Even so, in deciduous woodlands, where the trees drop their leaves in winter, there may be a shrub layer, formed of small, bushy trees, such as hawthorn, holly or dogwood. At ground level there are plants that flower in the spring. These grow and bloom before the trees have put on their leaves, while there is still enough light on the ground.

The trees give shelter and food to many kinds of animals. Deer are the largest creatures in woodlands in cooler countries. They browse on the leaves and eat the bark of many kinds of trees. Many of the inhabitants of woodlands can climb, such as squirrels, and many can glide or fly. Yet others, such as shrews, scuttle and tunnel among the fallen leaves, while some, such as badgers, dig deep safe burrows underground.

The trees themselves are the home for a host of tiny animals. Insects feed and take shelter among the leaves, and their grubs often burrow deep into the wood. Most woodland insects are marvellously camouflaged so that they are very difficult for us, or the birds that prey on them, to see. In spite of this, they are eaten by many woodland birds. Woodpeckers winkle wood-boring grubs from their tunnels, while warblers pick aphids and similar tiny insects from leaves. Small birds and some small mammals are food for predators such as owls and foxes. The fruits of the trees are eaten by squirrels and mice, while in autumn some bigger creatures such as wild boars become fat on a diet of acorns.

When a tree dies, its remains decay and are returned to the soil by insects which eat the wood, helped by fungi and a host of bacteria. The space and light given by the tree's fall make it possible for there to be new growth of the many plants and animals for which the woodlands are home. ■

Over 300 species of animal probably depend, completely or in part, on the European oak. These include deer, many kinds of birds, and insects such as the purple hairstreak butterfly and the small insects which make at least ten different sorts of galls.

If people's activities were to stop this afternoon, today's woods would spread and in 200 years great forests would stretch throughout Britain, and across most of Europe and North America.

See also
Forests
Timber
Trees
Wood

Woodlice

Distribution
Worldwide, in suitable damp places
Size
Between 5 and 15 mm

Phylum
Arthropoda
Class
Crustacea
Order
Isopoda
Number of species
About 4,000 isopods, mostly water-living or parasitic forms

Woodlice have armoured bodies and seven pairs of walking legs. They are not insects, but crustaceans. Woodlice live in damp places, because they breathe through gills which can only work if they are moist.

Woodlice feed mainly on rotting plants. They protect themselves from enemies, such as spiders and centipedes, by producing a sticky fluid or rolling themselves into a tight ball. Female woodlice lay up to 200 eggs, which they carry with them. The baby woodlice also often stay with their mother for some weeks after hatching. They take about two years to become fully mature. ■

See also
Crustaceans
Invertebrates

Woodworms

► A woodworm beetle.

Size of beetle
About 4·5 mm long (full-grown grub is about 7 mm long)
Number of eggs laid
Up to 80, usually less
Lifespan
About three years as a grub (dry wood is not very nutritious). The adult survives for only a few weeks.

Phylum
Arthropoda
Class
Insecta
Order
Coleoptera
Species
Anobium punctatum

Woodworms are not true worms, but the grubs of a small beetle. They eat dry wood, which has usually been dead for years. In the wild, they act as recyclers, breaking down the remains of dead trees and returning them to the soil. The adults, called furniture beetles, sometimes fly into houses and lay their eggs on furniture, or any other wood. The grubs that hatch out tunnel into the wood, and eventually destroy it.

Many kinds of insect grubs feed on timber, but they generally prefer damp wood, so are not as important in our homes as the woodworm. ■

See also
Beetles
Insects
Larvae

Wool

Wool comes from sheep, goats, llamas and some other animals. It grows from follicles in the animal's skin just like the hair which grows from our skin. It has some unusual qualities which make it a very useful fibre. Its cells still carry on trying to stay in balance with the surrounding moisture even when the wool is no longer alive and growing. This is why wool is said to breathe. It absorbs and evaporates moisture. It is also soft but strong and resists dirt, static and tearing.

Raising and shearing sheep

Many countries have sheep and produce wool, but four countries dominate the world trade in wool. They are Australia, New Zealand, South Africa and Argentina. These countries export more than half their wool to countries in the northern hemisphere.

The woolmark is the International Wool Secretariat's symbol for products made from pure new wool. It is one of the world's best-known trade marks. Four hundred million labels are applied every year.

The fleece is removed from the animal with special clippers. This is called shearing. The shearer aims to remove the fleece in one piece. This usually takes about five minutes. After the fleece has been shorn it is examined for quality and then graded. The sheep will grow a new coat for the following winter and can be shorn again.

▼ To make woollen yarn the fibres in a sheep's fleece have to be combed by a carding machine. They are then twisted so that they form a strong, continuous strand.

Woollens and worsteds

Two kinds of yarn are made from wool for weaving and knitting. Woollens are spun from fibres which vary in length and are jumbled up together. Worsteds are spun from combed wool. Combing removes the shorter fibres and leaves the longer ones lying parallel to make a smoother and more even yarn.

Flashback

From ancient to medieval times the spare moments of the women of the house were often spent spinning. Weaving was considered to be more difficult and was left to men who specialized in the art.

In Britain in the Middle Ages the wool trade was concentrated in southern England, the Cotswolds, Devon and East Anglia. Trade in wool and cloth with Flanders and France made huge fortunes for the wool merchants. Powerful Weavers' Guilds were set up in many towns. By the 15th century, sheep-farming had spread in Yorkshire, and wool was made in Derbyshire and Yorkshire as well as in the south. Three hundred years later in the Industrial Revolution these counties began to take over as the centres of cloth manufacture. This came about because they had plenty of fast-running water which could be used to power some of the new machines. ■

The Lord Chancellor in Britain's House of Lords sits on a seat called the Woolsack. It is made of wool covered with red cloth, and is said to have been introduced in the 14th century to remind people of the importance to England of the wool trade.

See also
Farming
Goats
Llamas
Sheep
Spinning
Textiles
Weaving

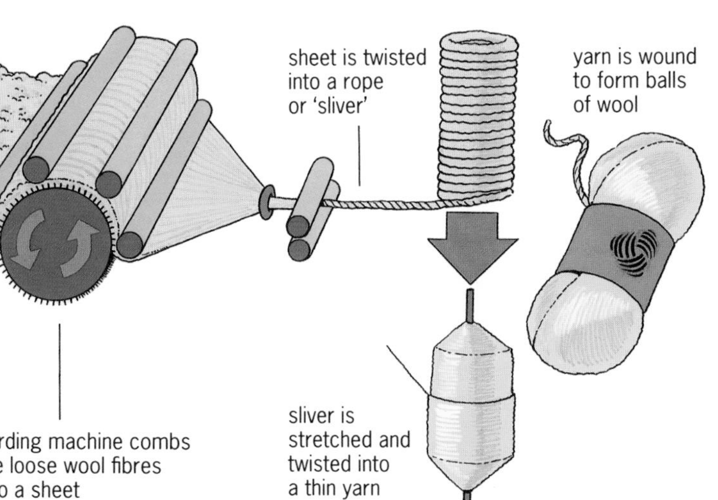

Word processors

A word processor is a computer which can be used as a typewriter. You type at the keyboard and the words appear not on paper, but on a screen. By using special keys, you can change the words and move them about. You can even store or save the words on cassette or computer disc and get them back again whenever you like. When your work is finished and there are no more changes to make, an electronic printer prints out the words on paper.

In offices throughout the world, reports and letters are prepared using word processors. Most of the articles in this encyclopedia were prepared in this way. The authors wrote their articles on word processors and altered them until they were happy with the results.

Some word processors can handle pictures as well as words. Journalists use these to design and prepare whole pages for magazines and newspapers. This is sometimes called desk-top publishing. At the printer's, signals from a word processor can be sent straight to the machine which makes the printing plates.

Mail order companies and many other organizations use word processors for sending out 'personal' letters. Everyone gets the same basic letter, but the word processor changes the name and address each time so that every letter looks as though it has been typed specially for that person.

Many word processors are just ordinary desk-top computers with a special program in them for word processing. Some have special spelling and grammar checkers. Some even 'learn' words you use a lot and complete them as soon as you have begun to type them. Most word processors plug into the mains electricity. But some run on batteries and are small enough to be used on trains and planes. ■

WYSIWYG
(pronounced WIZZY-WIG) 'What You See Is What You Get'. A word processor that shows on the screen exactly what will appear when printed.

WIMP
(Window Icon Mouse Pointer) Word processors sometimes use a **mouse,** a small device that does the same job as a joystick or a keyboard. When you move the mouse about on your desk, a pointer moves about on the screen. You use the pointer to make changes to the words.

Text
Words and numbers on a screen.

Graphics
Pictures on a screen.

See also
Computers
Information technology
Printing

World history

	before 10000 BC	10000	9000	8000	7000
Asia	• Hunter-gatherers • From about 50,000 BC people were spreading through all continents with a variety of tools – knives, axes, scrapers, harpoons, needles	• Hunter-gatherers • Earliest pottery in Japan, flourishing coastal culture based on fishing	• Hunter-gatherers	• Rice farming in Thailand	• Rice and millet farming spreads
America and Oceania	• Hunter-gatherers • Cave drawings in Australia from about 20,000	• Hunter-gatherers • Sledges and canoes used	• Hunter-gatherers	• Hunter-gatherers	• Hunter-gatherers • Farming settlements in New Guinea
Africa and Middle East	• Hunter-gatherers • Engravings in south-west Africa from about 27,000	• Hunter-gatherers • Wild wheat gathered in Palestine • Domestication of dogs (wolves)	• Rock paintings in Sahara • Farming of cereals • Domestication of sheep and goats • Site of Jericho occupied • Pottery made in Syria • Wheat and barley ground on querns	• Farming skills spread through Middle East	• Wheel invented • Pottery and textiles used in Anatolia (Turkey) • Cattle domesticated • Jericho and Çatal Hüyük walled towns
Europe	• Hunter-gatherers • Cave paintings from 30,000 • Female figurines of Great Goddess made across continent	• Hunter-gatherers • Cave paintings • Bow invented • Sledges and canoes used	• Hunter-gatherers	• Hunter-gatherers	• Farming in Balkans and Greece • Domesticated sheep and goats • Cattle and pigs domesticated
Britain	• Hunter-gatherers • Cave dwellings	• Hunter-gatherers • Evidence of canoes for fishing and early trading	• Hunter-gatherers	• Hunter-gatherers	• Hunter-gatherers
		10000	9000	8000	7000

Archaeologists are working all the time and digging up new evidence. They often disagree on the period when new technology first developed so the dates given here are only approximate.

This represents 1,000 years: a millennium

6000	5000	4000	3000	2000
Asia				
• Farming in China and India • Pottery made in China	• Farming spreads in Huang He (Yellow River) valley, China • Wheat, barley, rice cultivated • Horses domesticated on steppes	• Ploughs used in China • Bronze worked in China and Thailand • Decorated pottery made in Japan • Jade worked in China	• Silk weaving in China • Cities of Harappa and Mohenjo-daro in Indus valley (now Pakistan) • Cotton grown in Indus valley	• Xia dynasty • Shang dynasty • Cities in China • Aryans invade north India • Hindu religion develops • Rice cultivated in Korea
America and Oceania				
• Hunter-gatherers	• Maize cultivated in Mexico • Hunter-gatherers	• Pottery made in Guyana and Ecuador • Llamas domesticated in Andes	• Ceremonial centres built in Peru • Melanesian islands settled	• Metal working and cotton weaving in Peru • Olmec culture in central America • Burial mounds in Mississippi valley
Africa and Middle East				
• Farming settlements in Mesopotamia • Copper used	• Sails used on Nile • Plough invented • Bronze worked and cast • Vines and olives cultivated	• Hieroglyphs in Egypt • Farming in central Africa • Cuneiform writing in Sumeria • Cities in Sumeria • Wheeled vehicles • Pottery in Sudan and East Africa	• Egyptian Old Kingdom ruled by Pharaohs • Pyramids built • Sumerian civilization • Cities in Iran • Troy founded	• Middle and New Kingdoms in Egypt • Hittite empire • Hammurabi king of Babylon • Jewish religion develops • Exodus of Jews from Egypt
Europe				
• Copper and gold worked	• Megalithic tombs and standing stones • Flint mines • Horse domesticated in Ukraine	• Farming along Danube • Copper working spreads • Ploughs drawn by animals • Wheeled vehicles • Vines and olives cultivated around Mediterranean	• Sails used on Aegean Sea • Bronze worked in Crete • Megalithic tombs spread • Ox-drawn wagons and ploughs	• Minoan civilization on Crete • Mycenean civilization in Greece • Bronze begins to give way to iron
Britain				
• Farming and fishing	• Early megalithic stones and tombs • Stone circles on uplands • Farming spreads to uplands	• Farming spreads • Circles built at Avebury • First circle made of wood at Stonehenge	• Megalithic burial mounds and stone circles • First stone circles built at Stonehenge • Bronze worked	• Stonehenge rebuilt • Farms on uplands abandoned
6000	5000	4000	3000	2000

	1000	800	600	400	200 BC
Asia	• Zhou dynasty in China • Mahabharata composed in India	• Taoism founded in China • Zhou dynasty establishes legal system	• Iron working in China • Kongzi (Confucius) lived • Gautama Buddha lived	• Zhou dynasty ends • Qin dynasty • Great Wall of China • Alexander the Great of Macedon invades India • Ashoka, emperor of India	• Han dynasty • Roman envoys to China • Buddhism spreads to south-east Asia and China
America and Oceania	• Chavín village culture in Peru Pottery and cotton made • Settlements in Polynesia	• Olmec civilization in Mexico	• Hieroglyphic system of writing develops in Mexico	• Early Maya culture in Guatemala • Olmec civilization ends	• Foundation of Teotihuacán in Mexico
Africa and Middle East	• Kingdom of Kush in Africa • Assyrian empire • Phoenician alphabet • Kingdom of Israel • Carthage founded	• First coins in Lydia (Turkey) • Babylonian empire of Nebuchadnezzar • Assyrians conquer Israel • Zoroastrian religion in Iran	• Persian empire ruled by Cyrus, Darius and Xerxes • Persians conquer Egypt • Old Testament of Bible completed • Jews exiled to Babylon	• Nok culture in Africa • Carthage powerful • Persian empire conquered by Alexander the Great • Egypt ruled by Ptolemy dynasty	• Carthage destroyed and Syria, Palestine, Egypt conquered by Roman armies • Jesus born
Europe	• Celtic tribes migrate to Germany and France • Etruscans settle in north Italy	• Greek alphabet develops • Homer's poems composed • Rome founded	• Greek city states • Athens defeats Persians • Pericles lived • Socrates lived • Parthenon and other temples • Roman republic founded	• Philip of Macedon conquers Greece • Alexander the Great rules Greece and conquers Persians • Plato lived • Romans conquer Etruscans, rule all Italy and conquer Spain	• Greece ruled by Romans • Romans conquer Gaul • Civil war between Roman rivals • Augustus first Roman emperor
Britain	• Ox-drawn plough used • Bronze worked	• Celtic tribes invade and settle • Iron worked	• Hillforts built	• Trade increases with continent of Europe	• Belgae settle in south • Romans invade
	1000	800	600	400	200 BC

This represents 200 years: two centuries

	1 AD	200	400	600	800
Asia	• Han dynasty in China • Paper invented in China Magnetic compass used • Emperors in Japan	• Gupta empire, India • Great Wall of China built	• Sui dynasty, China • Horse collar harness used • Mathematics develops in India	• Tang dynasty, China • Block printing invented in China • Kyoto capital of Japan	• Song dynasty, China • Gunpowder invented in China • Khmer empire in south-east Asia • Fujiwara family dominates Japan • Burma unified
America and Oceania	• Pyramids, palaces, temples built in Peru	• Maya civilization in central America	• Teotihuacán temples in Mexico • Complex cities and temples built in Mexico	• Maya astronomical congress	• Vikings sail to North America • Toltec civilization in northern Mexico
Africa and Middle East	• Iron working in Zambia • Jesus crucified • St Paul's missions • New Testament written • Jews expelled from Jerusalem	• Ethiopians become Christians • Text of Bible agreed • Byzantium becomes capital of Roman empire	• Sassanid empire in Persia • Byzantine empire powerful	• Muhammad founds Islam • Text of Koran established • Muslims conquer north Africa • Umayyad caliphs rule from Baghdad • Arabs develop algebra	• Bantu tribes move into south Africa • Muslim religion spreads • Abbasid caliphs rule
Europe	• Roman empire most powerful • Emperors Trajan and Hadrian • Christianity spreads	• Franks, Huns, Goths, Vandal tribes attack Roman empire	• Roman empire in west collapses • Dark Ages	• Spain conquered by Muslims • Charles Martel defeats Muslims near Poitiers, France • Vikings raid and trade in France, Russia and Mediterranean	• Vikings settle Normandy, France • Charlemagne emperor • Magyars settle Hungary • Bulgars and Russians become Christian • Kingdom of Poland established
Britain	• Romans conquer Britain	• Villas built • Saxon raids begin • Christian missionaries in Britain	• Romans leave • Angles, Saxons, Jutes settle England • Celts retreat to Wales and Cornwall • Irish missions to Scotland	• Angle and Saxon kingdoms • Christianity spreads • Christians accept authority of Roman Church	• Vikings raid and settle Danelaw • Alfred defeats Danes • England unites into one kingdom

1 AD | 200 | 400 | 600 | 800

	1000	1100	1200	1300	1400
Asia	• Song dynasty • Movable type printing • Muslim conquests in north India	• Song dynasty • Khmer empire powerful in south-east Asia • Many kingdoms in India	• Genghis Khan extends Mongol empire • Kublai Khan conquers China, Burma, Korea, founds Yuan dynasty • Marco Polo in China	• Ming dynasty in China • Tamerlane extends Mongol empire in central Asia • Muslim sultans rule north India • Black Death	• Ming dynasty • Mongols defeated by Ivan III of Russia • Vasco da Gama to India
America and Oceania	• Polynesian Maori settle in New Zealand • Chimú civilization in Peru	• Inca empire develops • Aztecs move into Mexico	• Easter Island statues • Aztec empire develops in Mexico	• Aztec empire powerful	• Inca empire powerful • Cabot in Newfoundland • Columbus in Caribbean
Africa and Middle East	• Zimbabwe • Kingdom of Ghana, West Africa • Turks invade Byzantine empire and occupy Palestine	• Turks conquer Egypt • Turks attacked by Christian crusaders	• Empire of Mali, West Africa • Mongols attack Baghdad • Turks defeat crusaders and rule Palestine	• Empires of Benin and Mali in West Africa powerful • Ottoman Turks conquer Anatolia and the Balkans • Black Death	• Songhai empire in West Africa • Portuguese explore coast of Africa • Ottoman Turks capture Constantinople 1453
Europe	• Normans rule Sicily and south Italy • Roman Catholic and Greek Orthodox churches split 1054 • First universities • First crusade	• Romanesque architecture • Cistercian monasteries • Crusades establish Christian state in Palestine	• Gothic architecture • Franciscan and Dominican friars founded • Golden Horde of Mongols conquer Russia • French kingdom expands • Christians defeat Muslim states in Spain	• Black Death • Hundred Years War • Venice, Florence, Genoa powerful city states	• Printed books made • Renaissance in Italy • Muslims driven from southern Spain • Russians drive out Mongols
Britain	• Norman conquest 1066 • Domesday Book	• Henry II rules Angevin empire in France • Norman (Romanesque) architecture	• Edward I conquers Wales, builds castles • Early English (Gothic) architecture	• Scots defeat English at Bannockburn 1314 • Black Death • Peasants' Revolt 1381 • Decorated (Gothic) architecture • Chaucer	• Wars of Roses • Perpendicular (Gothic) architecture
	1000	1100	1200	1300	1400

This represents 100 years: a century

	1500	1600	1700	1800	1900
Asia	• Ming dynasty ends • Babur founds Mughal empire, north India • Sikh religion founded	• Qing (Manchu) dynasty in China • Dutch found empire in East Indies • Taj Mahal built	• Qing (Manchu) dynasty • Chinese export porcelain, silk and tea to Europe • Dutch trade increases • British fight French for control of India	• Opium war • USA forces trade with Japan • Britain founds Singapore and takes Hong Kong • India part of British empire • Independence movement starts in India	• China becomes republic 1911, communist 1949 • Japan defeats Russia 1905 • Rise and fall of Japanese empire • India becomes independent 1947 • Vietnam War
America and Oceania	• Aztec and Inca empires conquered by Spaniards • Spanish capture Caribbean islands and establish colonies • Magellan's fleet sails round world	• Europeans found colonies in north America • Slavery grows in America	• British defeat French in Canada • American Revolution and Declaration of Independence • Cook explores coasts of Australia and New Zealand • Australia settled by convicts	• Spanish and Portuguese colonies independent • USA expands by Louisiana Purchase and Mexican wars • Civil War • Slavery ends • Australia and New Zealand settled	• USA becomes world power • Technological revolution in industry, transport and com-munications • Civil rights and black power movements • Caribbean countries independent
Africa and Middle East	• Slave trade from West Africa to Caribbean and America begins • Suleiman the Magnificent rules Ottoman empire	• Slave trade expands • Dutch settlers (Boers) in South Africa	• Asante kingdom in West Africa • Slave trade continues	• Europeans explore and colonize Africa • Slave trade abolished • Boers fight British in South Africa • Ottoman empire declines	• African states gain independence • South African policy of apartheid • Ottoman empire ends • Turkey and Arab states independent • Israel founded
Europe	• Reformation • Protestants break from Catholic Church • Wars of Religion • Ivan the Terrible rules Russia	• Dutch fight Spaniards and gain independence • French power grows under Louis XIV • Spanish power declines	• Russian power grows under Peter the Great and Catherine the Great • Poland partitioned • French Revolution 1789	• Napoleonic wars • Russian empire expands • Crimean War • Italian unification • German unification • Industrialization and growth of railways	• World War I 1914–1918 • Russian revolution 1917 • USSR • World War II 1939–1945 • Communist domination of eastern Europe 1945–1989 • European Community
Britain	• Tudors fight Irish kings • Protestant Church of England founded • Shakespeare	• English colonists to North America and Caribbean • Civil War • Ireland conquered • St Paul's Cathedral built	• Union of England and Scotland 1707 • Agricultural and Industrial revolutions • Parliament's power grows • Canals constructed	• Emigration to USA and colonies • Industrialization and growth of cities • Empire powerful • House of Commons' power grows • Crimean War	• World War I • World War II • Colonies become independent members of Commonwealth • Welfare State developed • Industrial power declines • Joins European Community
	1500	1600	1700	1800	1900

World War I

Military loss of life

Germany	2,000,000
Russia	1,700,000
France	1,358,000
Austria-Hungary	1,200,000
UK	761,213
Italy	460,000
USA	114,095

Over 6 million people died of Spanish influenza.

World War I was also called the 'Great War'. It started in August 1914 and ended in November 1918. For four years it was the biggest and most terrible conflict between nations that the world had ever seen. Millions of soldiers, sailors and airmen were killed and wounded. Large numbers of civilians were killed, injured or made homeless. Even though later wars were in some ways more terrible, and even though we now have the fear of nuclear war, we still remember the Great War as a particularly terrible and tragic happening. Many nations were involved.

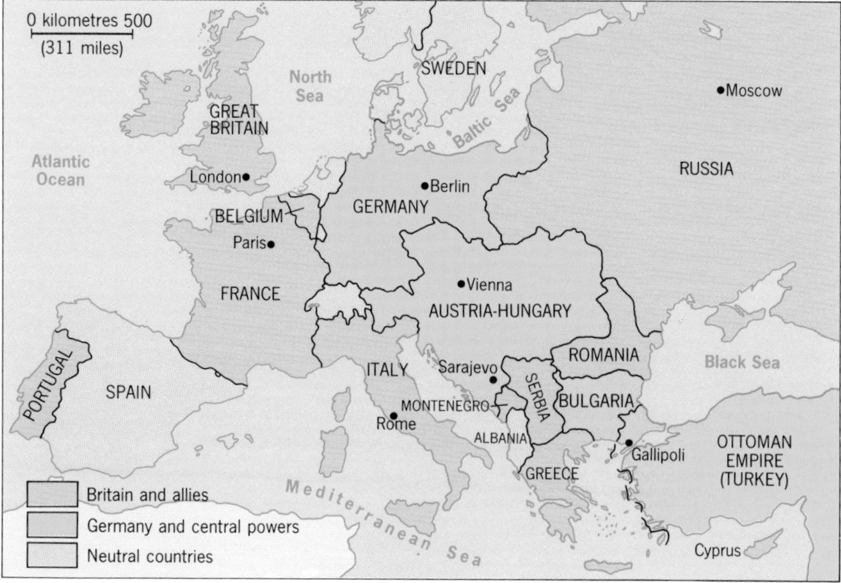

▲ Germany and the central powers fought against Britain, France, Russia, and their allies.

Assassination!

No war has just one simple cause. World War I came after many events which showed that countries were jealous of each other's power. Germany and Britain each wanted an empire and a big navy. Austria and Russia wanted to take over weak countries in the Balkan region of Europe. France wanted to win back land lost in a war against Prussia in 1870. Sooner or later there was bound to be conflict. The spark which set it all off was when the Archduke Franz Ferdinand, heir to the throne of Austria, was killed by a Serb on 28 June 1914. Austria threatened her small neighbour Serbia, which Russia supported. Germany sided with Austria. France backed Russia and Britain was friendly with France. By 4 August much of Europe was at war.

Britain and allies
British empire
Russia
France and empire
Romania
Belgium
Italy
Serbia
Japan
Portugal
USA (from 1917)

Germany and central powers
Austria-Hungary
Bulgaria
Ottoman (Turkish) empire

The war starts

For many years the Germans had known what they would do if war broke out. They would first attack France by passing through Belgium. In this way they would bypass the defences along the French border. Belgium was 'neutral', which means that it said it did not want to be involved in any war. Germany intended to ignore this and gain the advantage of surprise. The plan was to knock France out quickly and then turn to deal with Russia.

The plan only partly worked. The German armies swept through Belgium into France, but they were held by the British and French, and the armies dug in, facing each other in positions which were to stay the same for almost four years.

The Western Front

Where the German armies met the British and French a 'front' developed which stretched from the Channel to the Swiss border. Each side dug trenches which were difficult to capture. To make progress, soldiers had to leave their trenches and run across open ground towards men firing rifles and machine-guns. Neither side was able to break through into the countryside beyond. Huge numbers of men and guns were used to fight the long battles on the Western Front, and there were millions of casualties.

The Eastern Front

There were other fronts. Most important was the Eastern Front, where the Austrian and German armies faced the Russians. This front too eventually became bogged down. Many millions of Russian soldiers were killed or wounded, and even though the Russians began to be successful in 1916, the war had been too much for a country already in crisis. The casualties and the great hardship caused to the Russian people added to their discontent. In 1917 the Russians rebelled against the tsar and set up a republic. After the Bolshevik revolution in October, the government abandoned the fight.

A world at war

In Italy the Germans and Austrians faced the Italian army, and in the Middle East the British army and troops from Australia and New Zealand (Anzacs) fought the Turks, who were on the side of Germany and Austria. This was a world war. Troops came from Canada, India and other countries of the British empire to fight alongside the British and French. In the spring of 1917 the United States of America declared war on Germany and sent money, munitions and eventually reinforcements to the allies in Europe.

◀ **The purpose of digging a trench was for protection from enemy gunfire. The trenches on both sides stretched from the Channel to the frontiers of Switzerland. They became water-logged and muddy. Soldiers ate, slept and stood guard in mud. To attack they had to go over the top and face the lethal power of machine-guns.**

The war at sea

Before the war Britain and Germany had each tried to build a huge fleet of warships. When war started, each side was reluctant to risk its fleet in a big battle for fear of losing it. There were lots of skirmishes, but only one real sea battle with battleships slugging it out. This was at Jutland in the North Sea in 1916. Even then, there was caution on both sides and the result was not decisive.

The most effective sea warfare was the German submarine, or 'U-boat', campaign against cargo and passenger ships. Britain depended on importing food and goods, and the U-boats had a very serious effect on British shipping all through the war.

◀ **Ships of the British Grand Fleet. Battleships blockaded German ports to prevent food and other supplies from getting through. The Germans were desperately short of food by 1918.**

The war in the air

All the main countries had aeroplanes. They were used at first for spotting and scouting. Then the 'scouts' started to shoot at each other, and air 'dogfighting' began. Both sides dropped bombs on each other's armies, and also on cities. The Germans used big hydrogen-filled airships called Zeppelins to attack British and French cities. They also bombed London with Gotha bombers. By the end of the war it was clear that air power would be vital in the years to come.

Zeppelins were used by the Germans to bomb British and French towns, and both sides used aeroplanes for bombing raids. Over 1,000 British civilians were killed in air raids.

The end

When war started in August 1914, people said 'It will all be over by Christmas'. In the end the war was won by a long, hard and expensive trial of strength. The British and French and their allies gained the victory simply by wearing down the enemy. The entry of fresh troops from America in 1917 was crucial in the final victory.

The end came in November 1918. An 'armistice' (end to the fighting) with Germany was called for at 11 a.m. on 11 November, the eleventh hour of the eleventh day of the eleventh month. The guns stopped and all went quiet. ■

See also

Armies
Balloons and airships
Canada's history
German history
Russia's history
Twentieth-century history

Axis countries
Bulgaria
Finland
Germany
Hungary
Italy
Japan
Romania
Thailand

Allied countries
Australia
Belgium
British empire
Canada
China
Czechoslovakia
Denmark
France
Greece
The Netherlands
New Zealand
Norway
Poland
South Africa
United Kingdom
USA
USSR
Also countries in South America and the Middle East

World War II

After defeat in World War I, Germany lost lands which had belonged to her in 1914. The countries which had defeated Germany were determined to keep her weak, without powerful armed forces. Many Germans resented this. So when Hitler and the Nazis came to power in the 1930s they gained popularity by saying that Germany should get back the lands it had lost, and take over other neighbouring lands where there were German-speaking people. The Nazis also set about rearming Germany. German expansion into neighbouring countries eventually led to war.

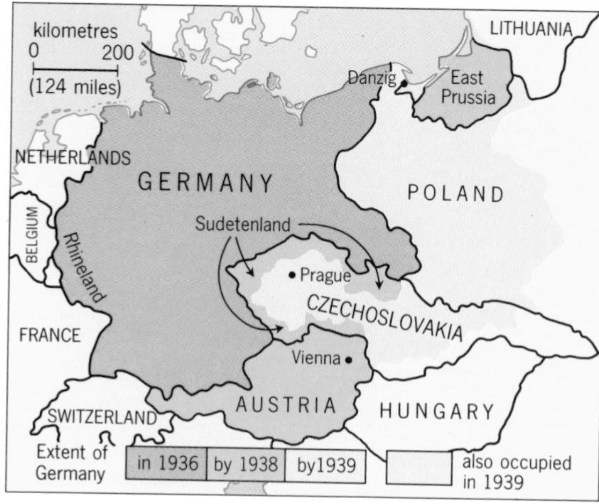

A step too far

Germany began its expansion in 1936 by reoccupying the Rhineland. Then in 1938, German soldiers marched into Austria, which was made part of Germany. This was called the 'Anschluss'. The next country to be taken over, in 1939, was Czechoslovakia, where there were many German-speaking people. Throughout the 1930s, too, Hitler had been building up the German armed forces.

▼ German troops marched into Prague in March 1939. The year before Hitler had annexed the Sudetenland, an area of north-western Czechoslovakia inhabited mainly by German people. Britain and France accepted the German takeover of the Sudetenland at Munich in September 1938.

Britain and France allowed each of these things to happen without much protest. The policy of doing this was called 'Appeasement'. It was hoped that when Germany regained her 1918 position, she would stop threatening other countries. Then in 1939, Germany threatened to occupy Poland. This was a step too far for Britain and France, who warned that there would be war if Poland was invaded.

War breaks out

In August 1939, the German Nazi government made an agreement with the Soviet Union. This took Britain and France by surprise, because Nazis and communists had seemed natural enemies. The agreement meant that if war came, the Germans would not have to fight Russia on the eastern front. Then in September 1939, German troops marched into Poland. They used the tactic called 'Blitzkrieg', or 'lightning war'. Troops and tanks moved quickly, backed up by very effective dive-bombing. Hitler probably thought that the British and the French would once more allow Germany to have her way. But they responded by declaring war.

Britain and France could do little to help the Poles, who were quickly defeated. The British army went to France and waited for months for the Germans to attack. In spring 1940 the German army invaded Norway, Denmark, France, Belgium and The Netherlands, and the British army had to retreat in ships and small boats from the French port of Dunkirk. Germany was soon in control of most of Europe, and Britain stood alone, in danger of invasion.

USSR: the Great Patriotic War

In June 1941, with western Europe under Nazi rule, the Germans invaded the Soviet Union, breaking the agreement made in 1939. German troops drove deep into Russia and besieged Leningrad and Stalingrad. Russian losses were enormous, and civilians endured great hardships.

The Germans had expected a quick victory, but the Russians resisted with determination, and the Russian winter killed many German soldiers, unprepared for such cold weather. In January 1943 the Germans were defeated at Stalingrad and over 90,000 German soldiers became prisoners. This was the beginning of the end for the Nazis, though two years of war were still to come.

The Soviet Union suffered terribly in World War II. There were millions of civilian casualties, and Russians were badly treated by German troops. Only by knowing this can we understand some of the actions of the Soviet Union after the war.

Global war

Even more than World War I, World War II was a truly global war. Japan allied itself with Germany and eventually overran several British and French colonies in the Far East. In December 1941 a surprise Japanese air raid destroyed American ships at Pearl Harbor Naval Base in Hawaii, in the Pacific Ocean. After this attack, the USA entered the war on the side of Britain and the USSR.

Fighting went on across the Far East, the Pacific, the Atlantic Ocean, the Middle East and North Africa. American, Soviet, British and Commonwealth forces, together with 'Free' forces of people from France and other countries in German hands, fought against Germany, Italy and Japan in a terrible and costly conflict.

Armaments on land

The main land weapon was the tank. Commanders tried to get their armies into positions where the tanks could be given freedom to travel across the countryside against the enemy. Great tank battles were fought, especially in Russia and the deserts of North Africa. There were also heavy guns, but at the heart of the army there was still the infantryman marching with rifle and bayonet.

In the air

Commanders tried to get air supremacy, which meant that their aircraft could roam the skies attacking targets at will. The 'Battle of Britain' was a battle for the skies over southern Britain in 1940. Had the RAF lost, a German invasion would have been possible. Small fighter aircraft battled each other, and big bombers penetrated deep into enemy territory.

At sea

By 1939 the big battleship was already becoming old-fashioned, because it was too easily attacked from the air. Aircraft carriers and submarines became the most important fighting ships. Submarines ranged far from home, attacking cargo ships and battleships. The Germans had a large and very effective fleet of submarines or 'U-boats'.

War dead

USSR	20,000,000
Poland	4,300,000
Germany	4,200,000
China	2,200,000
Japan	1,200,000
France	600,000
USA	406,000
UK	388,000

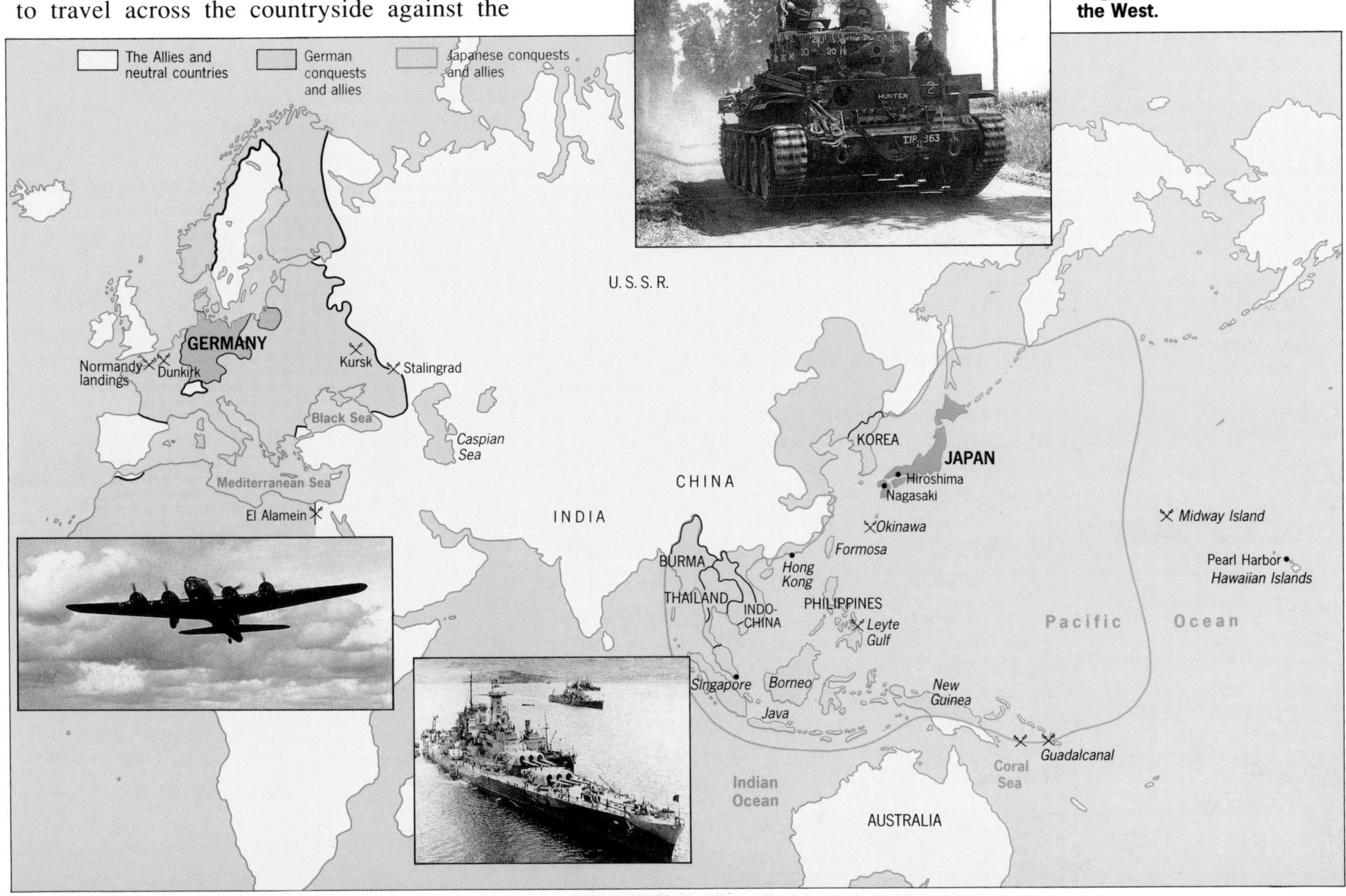

▼ The Japanese conquests were greatest by August 1942. The Germans were still advancing up to November 1942. By the end of that year the allied reconquest had begun in the Pacific and the West.

The Nazis believed Jews to be inferior. When they captured a country, they sought out Jews and deported them to the concentration camps and death camps which they built in Germany and eastern Europe.

The British and American air forces throughout the war flew more and more bombing missions against Germany, attacking factories and also civilian areas so as to sap German morale. In February 1945, Dresden was almost obliterated, with many thousands of deaths.

As the great armies battled to and fro, millions of people were forced from their homes and took to the roads with their possessions. Many never succeeded in returning home, and children lost contact with their families. This Italian family was lucky.

► The banner of victory hoisted over Stalingrad (now Volgograd) in January 1943. The city had been besieged for over 6 months and street fighting had reduced it to rubble before the German army surrendered. This was the turning point of the war. See the article called Battles for map.

German defeats
Battle of Britain
August–September 1940
El Alamein, North Africa
October–November 1942
Stalingrad, Russia
November 1942–January 1943
Kursk, Russia
July 1943

Japanese defeats in Pacific
Coral Sea
May 1942
Midway Island
June 1942
Guadalcanal
Winter 1942–Spring 1943
Leyte Gulf
October 1944
Okinawa
April–June 1945

See also
British history 1919–1989
German history
Hiroshima
Holocaust
Japan's history
Russia's history
USA: history

Biography
Attlee
Churchill
Hitler
Mussolini
Roosevelt, F. D.
Stalin

Victory

Once the Soviet Union and the USA were in the war, the defeat of Germany, Italy and Japan was only a matter of time. From early 1943, the Soviet Red Army rolled the Germans back towards their border and then pressed on to Berlin. In 1942 the American navy won important battles in the Pacific, and American forces began to recapture the Pacific islands taken by the Japanese. In November 1942 the British defeated the Germans and Italians at El Alamein in North Africa, and in 1943 allied troops crossed the Mediterranean to invade Italy itself. Then in June 1944 came the long awaited 'Second Front': the invasion of northern France by British and American troops on 'D-Day'.

Now Germany was under pressure from east, west and south. Gradually her troops were pushed back to Berlin, and Germany surrendered in May 1945. The Japanese surrendered in August after American planes dropped atomic bombs on the cities of Hiroshima and Nagasaki. The first atomic bomb destroyed over 13 square kilometres of the city of Hiroshima and killed nearly 80,000 people instantly. The scale of destruction shocked people on both sides of the war.

After the war

In the autumn of 1945, the world was in a desperate condition. European cities lay in ruins. Millions were homeless. Japan was laid waste by firebombs and two atomic bombs. Germany was occupied by British, French, American and Russian troops ('the Allies'). Everyone was grateful for peace, of course, and countries began to pick themselves up, though for some it was a long process.

Many of the effects of World War II have lasted for nearly half a century. Until the autumn of 1990 Germany was divided into two separate states and Berlin was a divided city. The history of the world since 1945 can only be understood if we first understand World War II. ■

▲ Commandos landing on 6 June 1944 (D-Day) on a beach in Normandy, northern France. British and Canadian troops landed on the eastern beaches and Americans landed to the west.

Worms

Largest earthworm
The giant Australian earthworm, over 3 m long
Smallest worm
A water worm, about 6 mm long

Phylum
Annelida
Class
Oligochaeta
Number of species
Over 2,500

Very many kinds of long, thin animals without backbones are called 'worms', but the word is most often used for earthworms.

An earthworm has a head and a tail end, but most of its body is made up of segments which are very similar to each other. Each of these segments has a small number of stiff hairs on it. These grip the sides of the worm's tunnel so it is very difficult to pull the worm out.

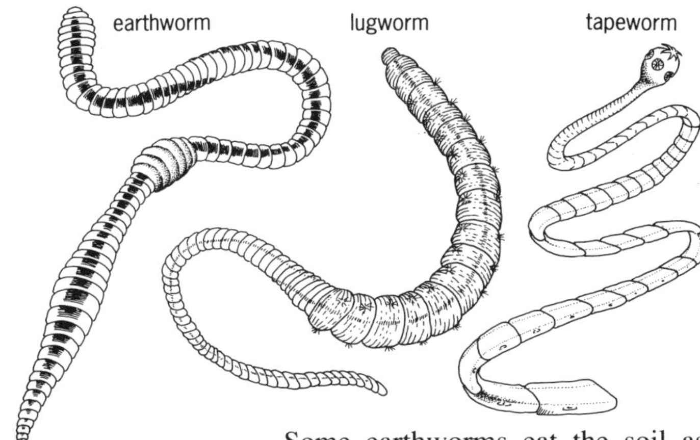

▲ **The earthworm with its marine relative the lugworm and a tapeworm, which is unrelated.**

Some earthworms eat the soil as they burrow, and digest tiny scraps of plant and animal material that they get from it. Other kinds feed on leaves that they pull down into their burrows.

There are huge numbers of earthworms in the soil. An area the size of a football pitch could be the home to half a tonne of earthworms, and in very rich farmland there could be 24 times as many.

The worms' burrows allow air and rain to reach the roots of plants. Their droppings, which are the wormcasts you can see on the surface of the ground, contain minerals which fertilize the soil. As well as this, worms are important as the chief food of many animals, including birds, moles and badgers. Some tropical relatives of the earthworms can grow into two new worms if the animal is cut in two. In the cooler parts of the world a worm may be able to regrow one part of itself, but not both. ■

See also
Invertebrates
Soil
Tapeworms

Worship

When you concentrate your words, actions or thoughts on God, you are worshipping him. You can do this with other people in a church, synagogue, gurdwara, mosque or temple. You can do it at home on your own, or by the way you lead your whole life. If you use words, either out loud or in your head, this is called praying. You can also worship God by making offerings. This can be food for people in need or flowers to make a place of worship beautiful. You can also offer your time to God. The word 'worship' means acknowledging the worth of someone or something, usually the highest reality. ■

See also
God

Wrestling

Wrestling is an unarmed combat sport in which two people struggle to throw one another onto the ground. The sport is one of the oldest and most basic, and dates back to at least 3400 BC. In Greco-Roman wrestling you are not allowed to hold the body below the waist or use your legs to hold or trip your opponent. Free-style wrestling does not have these restrictions. In both styles a competitor fights an opponent of similar weight. Some 'holds' earn technical points, a 'fall' brings immediate victory. A fall is achieved by pinning your opponent's shoulders to the ground for one second.

In Japanese sumo wrestling, two giants weighing at least 130 kg (20 stone) try to push each other out of the ring. ■

See also
Judo

Biography
Sports special

▼ **Sumo wrestlers.**

Writing systems

We send language messages in two quite different ways: we say them or we write them. We write ideas or words down when we want either to keep them and remember them later, or to let someone else read them at a later time or in a different place. Writing is a way of recording and storing words and ideas. Famous books, the country's laws, scientific discoveries, letters to friends: these are all written down, to be read or remembered for various purposes later.

► The Sumerians wrote their signs on blocks of wet clay and then let the clay dry in the sun. The clay blocks became very hard and were stored. Some have survived over 4,000 years.

Before writing

Many early peoples kept an 'oral' record of the great events of their history or beliefs. This means that some people learnt the record by heart (perhaps in a long poem) and recited it to others in their society. The poem about the great war between the Greeks and Trojans called the *Iliad* is an example of this. It was recited for a long time before it was finally written down.

Pictograms and ideograms

Pictograms are an early form of communication. Pictures of objects, such as a circle for the Sun, represented the object itself. In ideograms the whole idea of the word is explained in a shape rather like a picture. The Chinese and Japanese use ideograms instead of using an alphabet.

We use signs for mathematical ideas such as + = ÷ x, and for money: £ and $. These are similar to ideograms.

Cuneus means wedge in Latin.

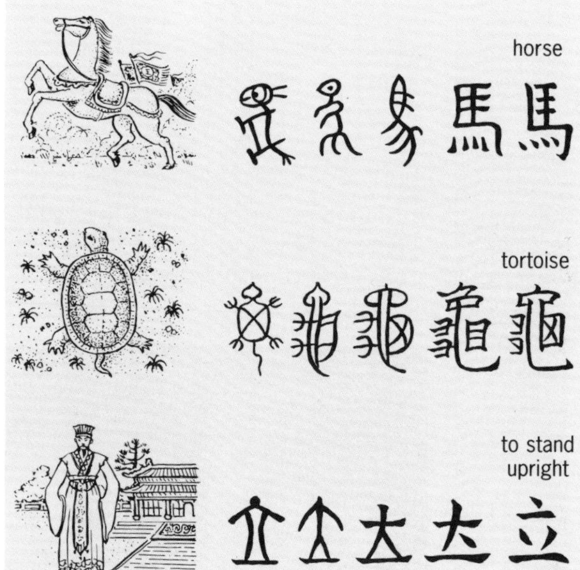

► Chinese ideograms. The earliest forms were simple but recognizable drawings. Over the centuries they changed into stylized shapes that are easy to write.

Early writing systems

The earliest true writing was developed by the Sumerians in the land of Mesopotamia (now Iraq). The earliest examples found come from Tell Brak and are dated to about 3250 BC. The language was discovered on a very large number (over 250,000) of clay tablets. They used wedge-shaped signs on the tablets to develop a type of writing known as cuneiform. Cuneiform was used for about 3,000 years.

From about 3100 BC the ancient Egyptians developed a different form of writing called hieroglyphics. Their writing system used pictures at first, but the pictures did not enable them to explain complicated ideas. They developed a system which used picture-signs to represent sounds. The Egyptians carved and painted these hieroglyphs on stone, but they also wrote with rush pens on papyrus, a sort of paper made from crushed reeds.

The first proper alphabet to be used was developed in Syria in the 15th century BC. ■

See also
Alphabets
Braille
Calligraphy
Communication
Hieroglyphics
Sumerians

X-rays

X-rays are a kind of energy which can be both useful and dangerous. They are waves like radio waves and light but they have much more energy. They travel at the same speed as light, but can go right through some solid things which light cannot penetrate. The Sun and stars produce X-rays, but our atmosphere protects us from these. The X-rays used in our hospitals, factories and laboratories are produced using X-ray tubes.

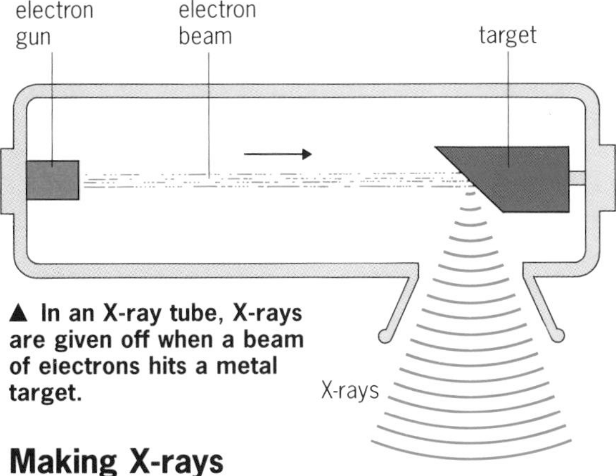

▲ **In an X-ray tube, X-rays are given off when a beam of electrons hits a metal target.**

Making X-rays

Electricity is lots of tiny particles called electrons. In an X-ray tube, a beam of electrons is shot out from an electron gun at one end. The electrons travel down the tube, gaining speed all the time as they are pulled towards a metal target by a very high voltage. When the electrons smash into the target, some of their energy is changed into the penetrating radiation called X-rays. The tube has no air in it because this would disturb the beam. The target gets very hot under the electron bombardment. In some tubes, it is cooled by passing oil through it.

Using X-rays

Doctors and dentists use X-rays to take pictures of broken bones and growing teeth inside your body. X-rays make shadow pictures because they go through soft parts of your body, like skin, but are stopped by the hard bones or teeth. Doctors also use much stronger X-rays to treat cancers. These are carefully measured and aimed to kill the cancer without damaging the rest of the body. In industry, X-rays can check inside machinery for cracks or faults. At airports, they are used by security staff to check luggage for weapons and bombs. Scientists use X-rays to study how atoms are arranged inside solid materials like crystals. Astronomers can learn more about the stars by studying the X-rays that come from them. The X-rays are detected by satellites.

Dangerous X-rays

X-rays with high energies can damage the cells in our bodies, so they must be used carefully, especially by people who work with them all the time. A screen, often made of lead, protects nurses and dentists while an X-ray picture is taken. Lead also shields your body when your teeth are X-rayed.

Flashback

Wilhelm Röntgen discovered X-rays in 1895. He was experimenting with a beam of electrons in a glass tube when he noticed that invisible rays were escaping from the tube. He found that these X-rays, as he called them, would go right through some solid materials. Very soon doctors were using them to look at broken bones. Now doctors use computers to build up very detailed X-ray pictures of the inside of a patient's body. ■

X-rays from space
Some X-rays come from the clouds of dust and gas left when a star explodes. Other X-rays can show astronomers where black holes might be.

TV screens and computer VDU screens give off X-rays because they have electron beams striking them. However, the amount of radiation is far too small to be dangerous.

See also
Radiation
Scanners

Biography
Röntgen

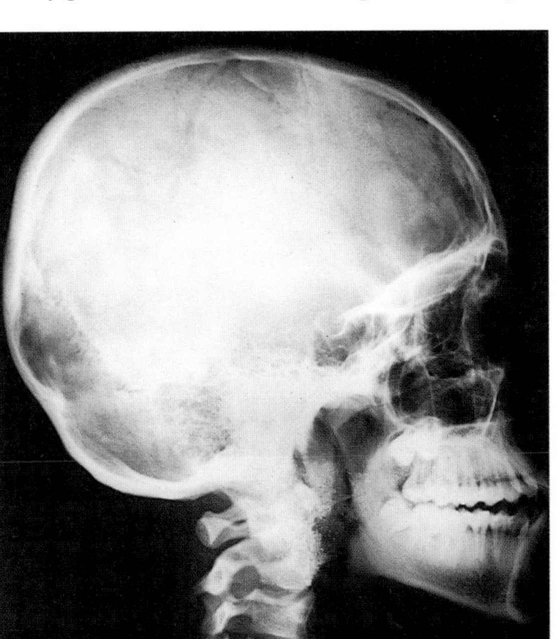

◀ **X-ray of a normal human skull.**

▼ **X-ray machines are used at airports to check the contents of bags to prevent passengers taking weapons or bombs onto an aircraft.**

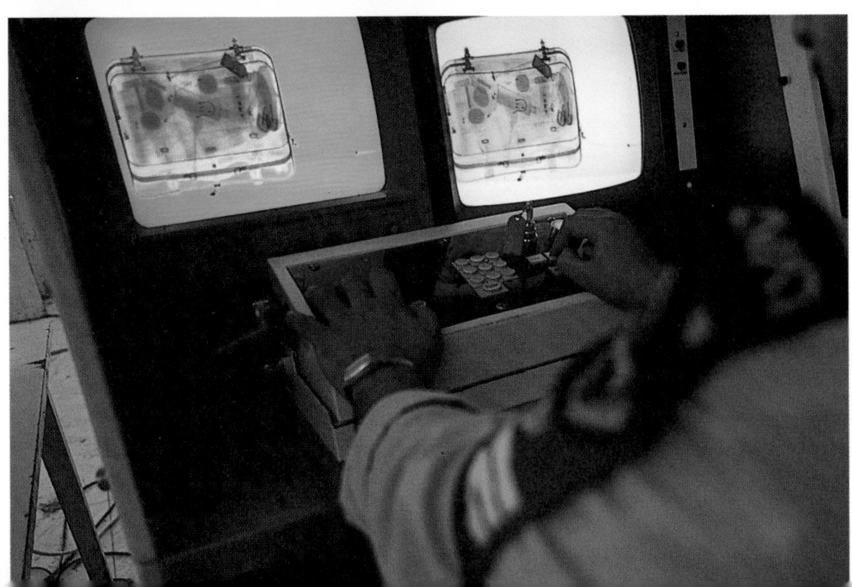

Yachts

Yachts are boats or small ships used for leisure. There are sailing yachts which have sails and motor yachts which have an engine, but sailing yachts are much the more popular of the two types. The smallest yachts are also called sailing dinghies. Most have a crew of one or two. The biggest ocean-racing yachts may have a crew of more than twenty. The person who steers the yacht is called the helmsman and those who help to adjust the sails are the crew.

The word comes from the old Dutch word *jaghtschip* meaning 'pursuit ship'.

burgee
mast
stay (rope supporting mast)
jib (front sail)
jibsheet (rope for holding jib)
mainsail
boom
mainsheet (rope for holding boom)
tiller
rudder
centreboard

◀ **A sailing dinghy is a small yacht, normally sailed by a crew of one or two.**

See also
Boats
Sailing
Sailing ships
Water sports

Racing yachts

These have hulls and sails which are designed to make the yacht go fast. The hulls are shaped so that they will move through the water with least effort. And there is a keel or a centreboard to stop the yacht being blown sideways when sailing across the wind. The sails are made of strong lightweight synthetic materials, like nylon and Terylene, of as large an area as possible. A big yacht will go faster than a small one, so yachts are grouped in classes such as Firefly, Enterprise, Mirror, or Lark. All the yachts in one class are the same size, so they can race against each other with an equal chance of winning. When yachts of different classes race each other, each one is given a handicap. The yacht with the lowest handicap starts first and the one with the highest handicap last. If the handicaps have been worked out correctly then all the yachts have an equal chance of winning.

Cruising yachts

These are slower and much more comfortable than the racing yachts. They often have a small outboard or inboard motor which makes it easier to enter and leave harbour and can be used if the wind drops. ■

Spinnaker
Big, bulging sail used to give a yacht extra speed when the wind is behind it.

Catamaran
A yacht with two hulls joined by a platform which carries the mast.

Trimaran
A yacht with one main hull and two smaller hulls, one either side.

Yeasts

 See also
Beer
Bread
Enzymes
Wine

Yeasts are found growing wild in the soil, on the skins of fruit and in dust. Wild yeasts have been cultivated and their properties used in baking, brewing beer and wine-making.

The enzymes in yeast work on starchy materials to produce sugars on which the yeast can feed. As it does so fermentation starts and produces alcohol and carbon dioxide. This activity is used in bread-making to make the dough rise. The carbon dioxide is trapped in the mixture and forms minute holes. The alcohol evaporates in the heat of the oven. Both fresh and dried yeast can be used in bread-making. Some yeasts act more quickly than others. Yeast needs a warm place to make the bread rise well.

In beer-making and wine-making it is the carbon dioxide which is lost to the air and the alcohol that is retained. In wine-making some wild yeasts from the skins of the fruit are used to start off the fermentation and cultured yeasts are added later. Yeast is also used to make some cheeses. ■

Yemen

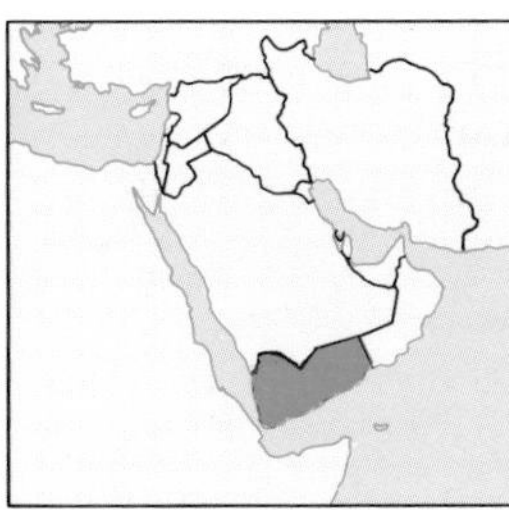

0 kilometres 500
(311 miles)
SAUDI ARABIA
OMAN
Red Sea
Saiwun
Arabian Sea
Hodeida
San'a
YEMEN
Mukalla
Ta'izz
Socotra
Aden
DJIBOUTI
Gulf of Aden
SOMALIA

Area 528,000 sq km (203,850 sq miles)
Capital San'a
Population 11,750,000
Language Arabic, English
Religion Muslim
Government Republic
Currency 1 Yemeni dinar = 1,000 fils

The Republic of Yemen is an Arab country on the southern tip of Arabia. It was formed in 1990 from two separate countries: the Yemen Arab Republic (YAR) which bordered the Red Sea and the People's Democratic Republic of Yemen (PDRY) on the southern tip of Arabia.

From a fertile plain adjacent to the Red Sea in the west the land rises sharply to reveal spectacular scenery. There are high volcanic plateaux and villages perched on the sides of mountains. Life in these villages has not changed for centuries. To the east beyond the mountains the land is mostly barren and rocky desert, although there are some fertile valleys, and temperatures remain high throughout the year. To the north lie the deserts of Saudi Arabia.

The PDRY was called the Protectorate of Aden when under British Rule.

The Yemen has only recently been opened up to modern development. It is very poor, but oil has been discovered, raising hopes for the future. The other main industries are agriculture and fishing. Yemen society is based on tribal loyalties and the people have a reputation for being fierce fighters.

It is hoped that Aden, the country's economic capital, will be redeveloped as a free port and regional centre for trade.

Its strategic position at the entrance to the Red Sea and its fine port of Aden made the former People's Democratic Republic of Yemen (PDRY) an important possession for Britain for 130 years. After heavy fighting, the country became independent in 1967 and was until 1990 allied to communist countries of Eastern Europe and to the USSR. An extremely poor country which relied heavily on foreign aid, the PDRY suffered civil war in 1986. The revolution in Eastern Europe in 1989/1990 removed the country's communist support. Union with the YAR took place in May 1990. ■

See also
Arabia
Arabs
Middle East
Muslims

Yoga

There are eight 'limbs' or stages of yoga practice:

1 Avoiding doing wrong (*yama*)
2 Acting rightly (*niyama*)
3 Physical exercises (*asana*)
4 Control of breathing (*pranayama*)
5 Control of the senses (*pratyahara*)
6 Concentration (*dharana*)
7 Meditation (*dhyana*)
8 Contemplation (*samadhi*)

What most people in Western countries mean when they say that they practise yoga is that they regularly perform special exercises, which are often easier for children than for adults, such as balancing on one leg, putting their limbs into unusual positions or standing on their heads. But there is more to yoga than this. The exercises are good not just for the muscles but also for the whole body, and you perform them slowly, holding the positions for some time. Also, you breathe very carefully. The exercises and the breathing together help you to relax, and for some people are the first stage of meditation.

Yoga is not a religion. It is practised by Hindus and Buddhists, but also by many other people. For those who take it seriously, it becomes a way of life. It keeps people fit and relaxed and helps them to cope with stress and develop their natural abilities. Yogis believe that control of the body will lead to a calm mind and to a better understanding of oneself and the world around.

Yoga comes from India, and is at least 5,000 years old. It used to be passed on by a *guru* (teacher) to chosen pupils, but now anyone can learn it provided they find a well-trained teacher. ■

See also
Meditation

Youth clubs

Youth clubs are almost always run by adults who want to help young people find something safe and worthwhile to do in their spare time. Many are attached to churches and religious groups, but in some countries, such as the USSR, they are provided by the government as a part of the education service.

These are clubs run by adults where young people gather in the evenings to play games or just to be together. There are many kinds of youth club, covering all age groups from about 8 to 25. Often there are weekend activities as well, including holidays, camps and play schemes. It is not easy to say how many young people go to youth clubs, but about one young person in every three belongs to something that you could call a youth club.

Youth leaders have to know when to stay in the background and how to help young people to run their own clubs. In some countries you can go to college and become a qualified youth leader in much the same way that other people become qualified teachers. It is not always an easy job and, naturally, not all youth clubs are as successful as others. Good ones, though, provide an important service in the areas where they exist. ■

The Young Men's Christian Association (YMCA) was founded in 1844 in London to provide activities for young men. It was followed in 1855 by the Young Women's Christian Association (YWCA). Both are now large international organizations with millions of members but they still provide youth clubs and activities for young people.

Yugoslavia

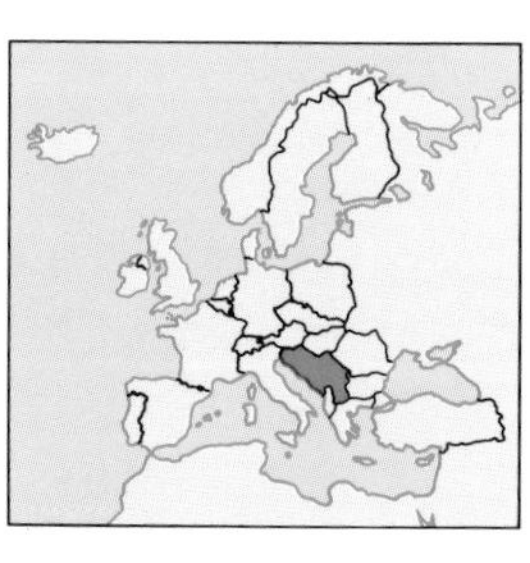

Area
255,804 sq km
(98,766 sq miles)
Capital
Belgrade
Population
23,000,000
Language
Serbo-Croat, Slovene, Macedonian, Albanian, others
Religion
Christian, Muslim
Government
Federal republic
Currency
1 Yugoslav dinar = 100 paras

Two alphabets are used: Roman in the north and Cyrillic in Serbia and the south.

Yugoslavia is a country in south-east Europe, made up of six smaller republics: Slovenia, Croatia, Serbia, Bosnia, Montenegro and Macedonia. Each has its own capital, languages and dialects, and traditions. Most of the people belong to one of these ancient nationalities, but there are other ethnic groups including Albanians, Hungarians and Turks. So there is a great variety of customs and culture. Northerners are mainly Catholic, while southerners belong to the Eastern Orthodox Church. There is also a large Muslim minority.

About half the population work on the land, growing maize, wheat, potatoes and sugar beet and plums and other fruit. Industry has grown especially in the north.

Generally, Yugoslavia is hot and humid in the summer and snowy in the winter. Near Lake Bled in the foothills of the Slovenian Alps there are excellent winter sports centres. On the coast of the Adriatic Sea the weather is sunny and mild for most of the year. The Roman ruins of Split and the medieval walls of Dubrovnik are popular with tourists.

Flashback

Yugoslavia has only existed as a single country since 1918. Before that the nationalities had been independent kingdoms or had been ruled as parts of big empires. The kingdom of Serbia was defeated in 1389 by a Turkish army and for over 400 years was part of the Muslim Ottoman empire. Later Slovenia and Croatia were part of the Austrian empire.

After World War I a new kingdom was created out of these different nationalities, with the King of the Serbs as monarch. During World War II, Yugoslavia was invaded by German, Italian and Bulgarian troops, but large groups of guerrillas, the partisans, continuously attacked the occupying forces. After the war their leader, Tito, declared Yugoslavia a federal republic. ■

During 1990 control by the Communist party weakened and the republics of Croatia, Slovenia, Montenegro and Macedonia voted for more freedom. In 1991 Slovenia and Croatia declared independence and parts of the country faced civil war.

See also
Alphabets
Christians
Europe
Muslims
Ottoman empire
Biography
Tito

Zaïre

Area
2,344,885 sq km
(905,364 sq miles)
Capital
Kinshasa
Population
33,940,000
Language
French, Lingala, Swahili, Luba, others
Religion
Christian, Traditional
Government
Republic
Currency
1 zaïre = 100 makuta

Zaïre, in central Africa, is Africa's third largest country after Sudan and Algeria. It has one of Africa's longest rivers, called the Zaïre (or Congo) River.

Zaïre consists mainly of high plains, divided by broad valleys. Mountains rise in the south and east. The climate is hot and rainy. The country contains thick forests and huge grasslands with scattered trees.

Zaïre has about 200 groups of people, each with its own language. The majority of people are farmers, who grow food crops, such as cassava, maize and rice. Some farmers grow coffee, which is sold abroad. Zaïre's chief export is copper.

Flashback

Zaïre was once ruled by powerful African kings, but the kingdoms lost their power in the 16th century. European traders took many people from the area and sold them as slaves in the Americas. In 1885, King Léopold II of Belgium declared the country to be his personal property. But the men who worked for Léopold treated the Africans so badly that Belgium's government took over in 1908. They ruled the country, which they called the Belgian Congo, until it became independent in 1960. It was renamed Zaïre in 1971. ■

See also
Africa

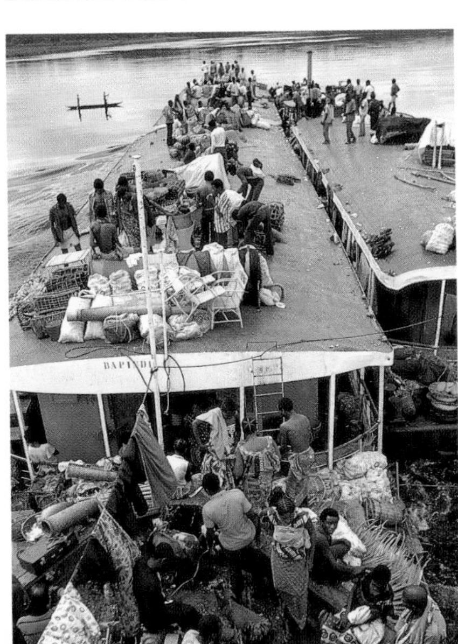

► **River boat leaving Kinshasa, carrying passengers and produce up the River Zaïre.**

Zambia

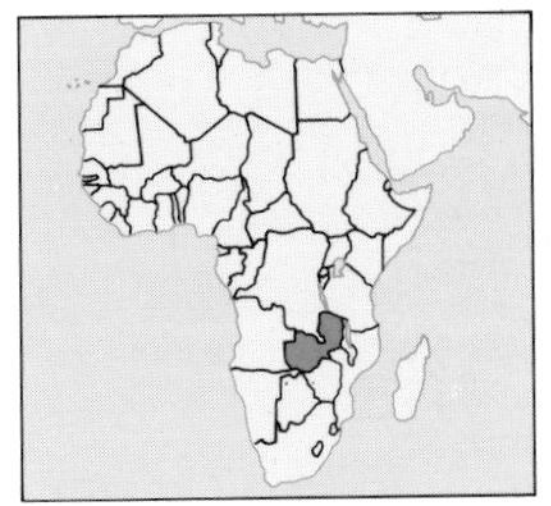

Area
752,620 sq km
(290,588 sq miles)
Capital
Lusaka
Population
6,990,000
Language
English, Bemba, Tonga, Nyanja, others
Religion
Christian, Traditional
Government
Republic
Currency
1 kwacha = 100 ngwee

Zambia, in south-central Africa, has high grassy plains, with some woodland and swamps. It is a warm country, with a rainy season between November and April. The River Zambezi flows through Zambia and in the south forms the border with Zimbabwe. On this border are the beautiful Victoria Falls and Lake Kariba, which has been created behind a large dam.

About 70 languages are spoken in Zambia, although English is used for official business. The majority of people are farmers and live in villages made up of groups of thatched houses similar to those found all over Africa. Zambians grow and eat a lot of maize which is ground into flour and cooked to make a thick porridge. Tobacco and cotton are also grown and sold as cash crops. Zambia's most valuable product, copper, is mined in the north in a region called the 'copperbelt'.

Flashback

In 1889, the British South Africa Company, which was searching for valuable metals, took over the area which is now Zambia. A railway was built, and soon many Britons arrived and began to farm the land near the railway. The area became a British colony named Northern Rhodesia in 1924. It was renamed the Republic of Zambia when it gained its independence in 1964. ■

Even though the population is growing fast there is no shortage of agricultural land. Indeed the government try to encourage people to remain in villages rather than drifting into towns.

See also
Africa

▼ **The women of a family are doing the washing in a village in the north-west province of Zambia.**

Zebras

Distribution
Savannah and dry scrub areas from Ethiopia to South Africa
Size
Head and body length 200–240 cm; shoulder height 120–140 cm
Weight
About 350 kg
Grevy's zebra is the largest species.
Number of young
1 suckled for about 7 months
Lifespan Up to 25 years

Subphylum Vertebrata
Class Mammalia
Order Perissodactyla
Family Equidae (horse family)
Number of species 3

► Large numbers of plains zebras still survive in some parts of Africa. A herd consists of many family groups and the adults in each group stay together for the rest of their lives.

Zebras have been called 'ponies in pyjamas', for these African wild horses are covered with black and white stripes. No two zebras have the same arrangement of stripes. A herd of plains zebras consists of many families and they recognize members of their own family and their neighbours by their different patterns.

As a family moves it keeps a strict order. A mare (adult female) leads. She is the dominant female and is followed by her foals. Behind her comes the next most dominant mare, and so on. In a big family, there may be as many as six mares. Right at the back comes the stallion, who is the father of all of the foals. If there is a weak or injured member of the family it will be protected by the whole group, who go slowly so that it is not left behind. The stallion fights off predators, such as lions, and sometimes loses his life so that his family can escape.

► Mountain zebras are thinner than plains zebras with narrower stripes and white bellies. Males greet each other by sniffing noses.

When a foal is being born the stallion stands near by to protect the mare. The foal is able to move around within an hour of birth. A female zebra will leave the group at around the age of two when a bachelor male steals her. She will join and leave several groups before she finally settles down in the group where she will spend the rest of her life. She will have her first foal at around four years old and after that may have a foal each year.

Young males leave their family and join a bachelor group when they are about four years old. They will take over a family of their own by the age of about six.

When they are not grazing, zebras spend a lot of time nibbling each other's fur. This not only keeps them clean, but is part of their social life.

The mountain zebra and Grevy's zebra are both much rarer and live in drier and more remote country. Mountain zebras also live in family groups but Grevy's zebras have a far less complex social life. ■

See also
Horses

Zimbabwe

Zimbabwe contains large areas of high grassland, called the high veld. On the River Zambezi, in the north, are the Victoria Falls and Lake Kariba, which Zimbabwe shares with Zambia. Most of Zimbabwe has a warm, moist climate. In the south is a hot region called the low veld.

The largest groups of people in Zimbabwe are the Shona and the Ndebele. Some whites (people of European origin), Asians and coloureds (people of mixed origin) also live in Zimbabwe. About 70 per cent of Zimbabweans work on farms. Other people work in towns, and some work in asbestos, chrome and gold mines. The chief food is maize. Farmers also grow tobacco as a cash crop. Most children go to primary schools, but Zimbabwe does not yet have enough secondary schools for all older children.

Flashback

About 1,000 years ago, the ancestors of the Shona people founded a prosperous civilization. They lived in towns made up of stone houses. The word Zimbabwe means 'house of stone'. These buildings are unusual, because most old houses in southern Africa had clay walls. The ruins of some of these towns still stand. The largest is called Great Zimbabwe. The people who lived there traded gold, copper and ivory on the coast for goods from China and India, and their land was later known as Mashonaland. To the west was Matabeleland, peopled by the Ndebele people.

British people began to settle in the area from 1888. In 1923 Mashonaland and Matabeleland became a single British colony called Southern Rhodesia. In the 1960s, the black Africans demanded independence from Britain. The country became fully independent in 1980 following fourteen years of unrest. It was renamed Zimbabwe. ■

◄ **The Zambezi River at the mile-wide Victoria Falls.**

◄ **Construction work in Harare, Zimbabwe's capital city.**

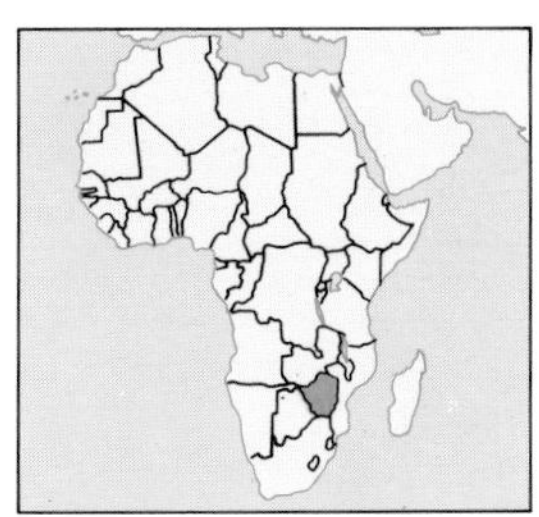

Area
390,580 sq km
(150,804 sq miles)
Capital
Harare
Population
9,000,000
Language
English, Shona, Ndebele
Religion
Christian, Traditional
Government
Parliamentary republic
Currency
1 Zimbabwe dollar = 100 cents

See also
Africa
African history

Biography
Mugabe
Rhodes

Zinc

Zinc is a bluish-white, brittle metal. Its main use is to protect iron and steel from rusting. Buckets, dustbins, wire netting, corrugated iron for roofing, and some parts of cars are dipped into molten zinc. This is left to harden. Then, even if the zinc is scratched, the iron or steel underneath does not rust. Coating iron with zinc in this way is called galvanizing.

Zinc also forms many useful alloys, including brass and solder. Like other animals, we need minute quantities of zinc salts in our food if we are to grow properly. Zinc is made from ores such as zinc blende, smithsonite and hemimorphite. Most of these come from the USA, Canada, Australia, Mexico and the USSR. ■

See also
Alloys
Metals

Zodiac

We cannot see the stars during the day because the Sun is too bright, but if we could we would notice the Sun slowly moving through the star patterns and making a trip right round the sky once a year. The band of constellations through which the Sun's path goes is called the zodiac.

The ancient Greeks divided the zodiac into twelve equal parts, called the signs of the zodiac. Each sign corresponds roughly to one of the zodiac constellations, though the official constellations astronomers use are not all equal in size.

Astrologers use the signs of the zodiac to make predictions about people's lives and characters. This depends upon a person's Sun sign – the sign that the Sun was in on the date of their birth. ■

▲ **This instrument is a brass Nocturnal made in 1543 in Germany, and engraved with the signs of the zodiac. Sailors could use this instrument to find out their position on the sea at night. It was made before the calendar was changed, when each month started about 10 days later in the year than it does now.**

Aries 21 March–19 April	**Leo** 23 July–22 August	**Sagittarius** 22 November–21 December
Taurus 20 April–20 May	**Virgo** 23 August–22 September	**Capricorn** 22 December–19 January
Gemini 21 May–21 June	**Libra** 23 September–23 October	**Aquarius** 20 January–18 February
Cancer 22 June–22 July	**Scorpio** 24 October–21 November	**Pisces** 19 February–20 March

See also
Celestial sphere
Constellations
Horoscopes

Zonation

Zonation can occur on a small scale. As you walk into a wood, look how the pattern of plant growth changes from the sunlit areas outside to the shaded places under the trees.

Most plants and small animals are very choosy about where they live. Often their choice depends on what looks to us like only slight changes in the environment.

If you were to climb a high mountain you would pass through different zones. At the lowest levels, you would find the slopes covered with forests. As you go up, the temperature drops and there is more wind. The big trees are replaced with shrubs. Higher still, there is a zone of grasses and low-growing plants. Above this only mosses and lichens cover the bare rocks. Highest of all there is nothing but snow and ice.

Zonation is also found on seashores because of the movement of the tides. ■

See also
Mountains
Seashore
Seaweeds

Zoologists

This comes from Greek words:
zoion meaning 'animal' and *logia* meaning 'study'.

Zoologists are scientists who study animals. Professional zoologists generally work in universities or large museums, or sometimes for industrial firms. They meet to discuss their work, and publish accounts of it in books and journals. Usually zoologists have a degree in zoology.

If you are interested in animals and want to become a zoologist, remember that the training is long and that jobs are few. You might consider instead becoming an amateur zoologist, studying animals just because you enjoy doing so. There is so much still to be discovered about most kinds of animals, that it is still possible for an amateur to become a world expert. ■

See also
Animal behaviour
Biologists
Ecology
Biography
Darwin
Goodall
Huxley
Lorenz

Zoos

◀ **The San Diego Animal Park in California, USA, is a vast area of land where animals are kept in conditions as close as possible to their natural habitat. Visitors can observe from a light railroad which circles the park and does not disturb the animals.**

Zoos are places where wild animals are kept in captivity.

In recent years many zoos have realized the importance of putting the interests of the animals first, so that they now have reasonable-sized enclosures, and are given adequate amounts of the correct food. In good zoos most animals live far longer than they could in the wild.

Today many zoos specialize in particular sorts of animals. Perhaps the most popular are the oceanaria which keep dolphins and other sea creatures. Another new type of zoo is the safari park, in which it is the visitors who are caged in their cars, and the animals have large areas in which to roam. There are still some bad zoos but fewer than there used to be.

Apart from keeping animals, modern zoos have three main functions: to study the animals and find out as much as possible about their habits; to educate visitors; and to breed from the captives. Often a zoo will send a single animal to another zoo where it may mate. As many wild animals stand on the brink of extinction, producing young in zoos may be the only way to save such species. This has already been done with Père David's deer, while nene (Hawaiian geese) and Arabian oryxes have been returned to their native lands where they had become extinct.

Flashback

The first zoos were collections of animals made by kings and noblemen in ancient Egypt and China. Wild animals were often taken as tribute from conquered countries. The emperor Nero is said to have had a tame tigress called Phoebe, while the favourite of Charlemagne, who kept many animals, was an elephant called Abul Aba.

In the past, as a rule, zoo animals had a short life, for the right food and conditions were seldom available. The first elephant brought to Britain in 1254 was housed in a special building 6 x 12 m (20 x 40 ft), which was certainly not big enough by modern standards. Over many centuries most zoos were miserable prisons for many animals, which were kept on their own. Such solitary confinement is the height of cruelty for social animals such as monkeys and apes. ■

Zoo is short for zoological gardens.

The earliest known animal collection was owned by Shulgi, a ruler in what is now Iraq, 2,000 years before Christ.

Keeping a zoo elephant for a year costs £5,000; a lion costs £1,500.

◀ **A panda in the Bronx zoo, New York City.**

See also
Conservation
Endangered species

Zoroastrians

Although Zoroaster was inspired by visions at the age of 30, it took him ten years to persuade anyone to follow his teachings.

Zoroastrians belong to one of the oldest religions in the world. They follow the teachings of the prophet Zoroaster (Zarathustra), who lived in Persia (modern Iran). Scholars argue about his dates, which may be about the 6th century BC or earlier. Some scholars think that Zoroaster may have lived as long ago as 1500 BC. Zoroastrian ideas were known over a wide area for a thousand years after Cyrus the Great established his empire in the 6th century BC. They probably influenced Jewish, Christian, Buddhist and Islamic ideas.

A small group of Zoroastrians moved from Persia to India in the 10th century and were called Parsis (Persians). Their descendants live mostly round Bombay and they are the largest surviving community. There are also small groups still in Iran, in Australia, Hong Kong, North America and Britain.

Beliefs

Zoroastrians call God *Ahura Mazda* (*Ohrmazd*), the Lord of Wisdom who created the world. He is constantly opposed by an evil force. God is symbolized by a sacred fire looked after by hereditary priests in a temple.

The evil force which opposes *Ahura Mazda* is called *Angra Mainyu*.

Men and women join equally in the struggle for good over evil in their lives through truth, compassion and active service for fellow human beings. After death, human souls will stay in heaven or hell until God finally triumphs over evil.

The sacred scriptures are called the *Avesta* and are in a language of their own called Avestan. They contain a variety of material, including seventeen hymns which were revealed to Zoroaster. Here is a prayer used daily by Zoroastrians.

The seventeen hymns are known as the *Gathas*.

'Blessed is he who leads the righteous life for its own sake and not in the hope of earthly gains or heavenly rewards.' ■

See also
Persians

Zulus

The Zulus are the largest of the ten main groups of black Africans in South Africa. Of the 5,680,000 Zulus, nearly two-thirds live in KwaZulu, which was once called Zululand, while the rest live in other parts of South Africa. KwaZulu is a 'Homeland' made up of a number of areas in Natal province which the South African government has set aside for the Zulus. Homelands are not independent nations, although they have elected governments to handle local matters.

When KwaZulu, the Zulu homeland, was set up in 1970, Chief Gatsha Buthelezi became Chief Executive Officer or Prime Minister. Buthelezi is the great-grandson of the Zulu chief Cetewayo who was defeated by the British in 1879.

In KwaZulu the men or boys herd cattle, while the women grow crops such as maize. The maize is ground into maize-meal and cooked to make a porridge, called *uputhu*. Porridge is the main food of the Zulus.

Many men cannot support their families in KwaZulu because there is not enough work. They work in the white areas of South Africa and send money home. Outside KwaZulu, the Zulus have even fewer rights and suffer more from racial discrimination.

◀ Like many black Africans, the Zulus have a tradition of being superb musicians and dancers. Here young girls are stamping out the rhythm of the drums with their feet.

Flashback

Between 1818 and 1828, a great warrior called Shaka created the Zulu nation from many black people in southern Africa. In the 1830s, the Zulu army clashed with white settlers. British troops defeated the Zulus in 1879. ■

See also
Africa
South Africa

Biography
Luthuli
Shaka